Communications
in Computer and Information Science 293

Rachid Benlamri (Ed.)

Networked Digital Technologies

4th International Conference, NDT 2012
Dubai, UAE, April 24-26, 2012
Proceedings, Part I

 Springer

Volume Editor

Rachid Benlamri
Lakehead University
Department of Software Engineering
Faculty of Engineering
955 Oliver Rd.
Thunder Bay, P7B 5E1, Ontario, Canada
E-mail: rbenlamr@lakeheadu.ca

ISSN 1865-0929   e-ISSN 1865-0937
ISBN 978-3-642-30506-1   e-ISBN 978-3-642-30507-8
DOI 10.1007/978-3-642-30507-8
Springer Heidelberg Dordrecht London New York

Library of Congress Control Number: Applied for

CR Subject Classification (1998): I.2, H.3, H.4, C.2, H.5, J.1

Typesetting: Camera-ready by author, data conversion by Scientific Publishing Services, Chennai, India

Printed on acid-free paper

Springer is part of Springer Science+Business Media (www.springer.com)

Preface

Networked digital technologies are reshaping the way we communicate, interact, collaborate, and share knowledge. Recent progress in telecommunications, networking, Semantic Web, mobile and ubiquitous computing has enabled new collaborative technology services for various disciplines in the sciences, humanities, and social sciences. The Fourth International Conference on Networked Digital Technologies (NDT 2012) aimed to provide support for concerted efforts in building federated digital technologies that will enable the formation of a network of digital technologies. We are honored to present in this volume the accepted papers of NDT 2012. The NDT conference has gained significance in the last three years and we hope to make it a prestigious conference in computer and information sciences. The NDT Program Committee included eminent researchers from 40 countries. Like the previous editions, NDT 2012 was co-sponsored (published) by Springer. NDT 2012 also attracted technical co-sponsorship from the IEEE – UAE Computer Section and the Middle-East Branch of the British Computer Society.

The Canadian University of Dubai, United Arab Emirates, was happy to organize this scholarly conference in April 2012. NDT 2012 consisted of paper presentations, tutorials, workshops, state-of-the-art lectures by keynote speakers, panel discussions, and student posters. We accepted 96 papers from 44 countries out of 228 submissions.

We are grateful to the Canadian University of Dubai for hosting this conference. Also, we would like to express our thanks to the Chairs, Program Committee, External Reviewers, and the Organizing Committee for their wonderful work. We are grateful to Springer for co-sponsoring the event. Finally, we would like to thank all the participants and sponsors.

April 2012   Rachid Benlamri

Table of Contents – Part I

Grid and Cloud Computing

Information and Data Management

Intelligent Agent-Based systems

Internet Modeling and Design

Mobile, Ad Hoc and Sensor Network Management

Table of Contents – Part II

Security and Access Control

Signal Processing and Computer Vision for Networked Systems

Social Networks

Web Services

Developing Casual Learning Games Using the Apache Pivot IIA Capabilities

Jinan Fiaidhi[1], Michael D. Rioux[1], Sabah Mohammed[1], and Tai hoon Kim[2]

[1] Lakehead University, Computer Science Department,
Thunder Bay, Ontatio, Canada
{jfiaidhi,mdrioux,mohammed}@lakeheadu.ca
[2] School of Information & Multimedia, Hannam University, Korea
taihoonn@hannam.ac.kr

Abstract. Game-based learning is becoming a popular academic necessity for the 21st century education. However, many challenges and obstacles are still facing facilitators to fully incorporate games into the educational processes and how to efficiently deliver the games to the students. This paper introduces the Apache Pivot as a simplified environment for developing casual learning games. Two steps have been taken to demonstrate the simplicity of using the Pivot environment for building educational games. The first involves the development of generic dashboard that can be used by the second step to generate specific educational games like the learning crossword.

Keywords: Educational Gaming, Pivot Installable Internet Application (IIA), Multimedia Learning Application (MLA), bXML.

1   Introduction

One of the fastest growing markets in the world is in "casual games". These are games that can be played for a few minutes at a time and are easily learned. They can be "ports" of real world analog games like Scrabble [1]. This model is important for the world of learning games, because it demonstrates the way that many nontraditional gamers like to play games. They play for short periods of time in games that are simple, fun and ubiquitously available [2,6]. The most important factor of good games always involves elements of play where such factor is rarely present at the traditional schooling courses. With play, learners are able to exercise different style of knowledge discovery including ([1], [3]):

1. freedom to fail;
2. freedom to experiment;
3. freedom to change identities;
4. freedom of effort; and
5. freedom of interpretation

Unfortunately, the success of educational games has been hindered by various barriers slowing or stopping their development and adoption. These barriers come from

R. Benlamri (Ed.): NDT 2012, Part I, CCIS 293, pp. 1–10, 2012.

various sectors, including industry, academia, the market, and the schools where such barriers include difficulty to satisfy curriculum requirements, attitudes towards gaming, logistics, high cost of development and rigid development process as well as limited resources of funding [2]. In this article we are presenting a methodology to design and develop educational casual games that is simple and ubiquitous based on the emerging technology of Apache Pivot IIA (Independent Internet Applications)[1] rich internet applications (RIA). Although there are other rich internet applications that can be used for developing casual games such as the Microsoft Silverlight[2] and Adobe Flash[3], these environments are more restrictive compared to the Apache Pivot IIA. Flash platform compared to Silverlight is more applicable to platforms like Linux or Solaris. Moreover, Silverlight even with Windows platforms require plugin to be downloaded and installed on their machines. Silverlight includes a "compact version of the .NET framework" which of course means that it can execute any of the .NET languages, including C# and VB.NET. The Flash Player 10 support streaming of the H.264 video codec but with lower efficiency compared to Silverlight. Apache Pivot is the platform we chose to use in developing casual educational games for reasons that gives you the ability to "easily construct visually engaging, cross platform, connected applications"[1]. Pivot 2.0 is a Java RIA replacement for Microsoft Silverlight and Adobe Flex that is not based on Swing; rather it provides an application framework featuring a robust set of UI components, Internet service integration and SVG graphics that can be used today with variety of devices and platforms. In addition, Pivot features the powerful BXML script which facilitates building the UI or other object graphs and very robust data binding by novice programmers. Several researchers, developers and novice programmers used Pivot for constructing sophisticated Web applications (e.g. iTune Search Client [4], Ubiquitous Learning Objects [5]).

2 Pivot Primitives for Developing Educational Game Applications

Pivot is an open-source platform for building rich internet applications in Java (or any JVM scripting language: Groovy, JavaScript, Scala, etc.). It provides developers tremendous ability to develop sophisticated applications including educational games. Pivot applications can be run as an applet or as stand-alone desktop application (installed or launched via Web Start) or even on mobile platform that supports JVM. Most of the Pivot primitives for developing RIA or educational games utilize the BXML language primitive. BXML is an XML compact format and allows containing binary data[4]. This is a great feature as it allows for adding different components to the Pivot Java Archive (JAR) files that make up the framework for the application UI. Pivot provides many design components that a programmer can use to create a UI to

---

[1] http://pivot.apache.org/index.html
[2] http://www.microsoft.com/silverlight/
[3] http://www.adobe.com/devnet/flash.html
[4] http://theprogrammersparadox.blogspot.com/2009/09/bxml.html

their exact specifications which is not only easy to use but has a familiar feel for the user. Pivots main primitives are called "Containers". There are two types of containers used, layout containers and navigation containers.

3   Developing a Pivot-Based Generic Gaming Dashboard

The goal for developing generic casual gaming dashboard is straightforward. It is to create a cross platform application in which a user can learn information of any topics the teacher may decide to use (see Figure 1).

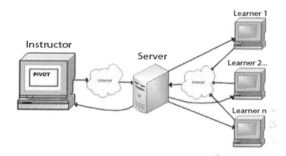

Fig. 1. Pivot IIA Educational Gaming Dashboard Architecture

The prototype dashboard has a few applications built in, with room for many more to be added. The first application added was a real time bXML renderer, where the user could test and retest their bXML code and see what the outcome is directly beside the code. The next two applications go hand in hand, a crossword builder, and a crossword solver. Both can be used as games or learning and testing tools, testing students on definitions and/or question and answers. In the Dashboard there are a few other secondary applications such as an RSS feed to a Java forum website, and a suggestion search engine. The RSS feed was made to be expanded. The student will eventually be able to subscribe to other users and when they publish a crossword the user will be notified and be able to download it. They will also be able to choose the subject that they subscribe to, so they will only get notified if a crossword was published in a certain subject area. However, before any of these applications, present or future, could be implemented the UI skeleton has to be made.

3.1   Creating the IIA Dashboard Skeleton

When creating the skeleton, we had the aforementioned bXML renderer in mind, so we wanted two main parts side by side, where the user could type in code on one side and the output would be produced in the other. We also wanted a top section for a title and to potentially put a file system in place keeping in mind that the people are used to the file system being in the top left hand corner. When creating the skeleton many of the Pivot primitives and their custom properties were used to fit the needed specifications. For the main two sections, sections 1 and 2 from Figure 4, the layout container SplitPane was used, which lets the user dynamically change the size of each side, so if he/she wanted to concentrate mainly on the code they could use the slider bar to make that side a desirable size. They can also change the orientation of the section by clicking either the horizontal or vertical radio button. We used the SplitPane a lot in the Dashboard because of how malleable you can make your environment for the user. They can choose to make it to their exact specification which is a great feature. For the left hand side portion, section 3 from Figure 4, the SplitPane from sections 1 and 2 was inside another SplitPane, which allows the user to change the size and orientation of all three sections. For section 3, the section that will hold all the current and future functionalities and applications of the dashboard, something that could hide and hold a lot of information and functionalities was required, and it also needed to display only the functionalities needed at any one time. For this the navigation container: Accordion was used. This was a perfect fit because each "fold" of the accordion has plenty of space to hold any sort of objects, and you can have many different "folds" that are easy to navigate through. The user/login portion of the dashboard was put in section 4 of Figure 2, and instead of wasting the extra space another SplitPane was used and a scroll bar was added to maximize the space that can still be useful. This coupled with a few other containers along with an added image in the top left corner made the basic skeleton and user interface for the IIA Dashboard.

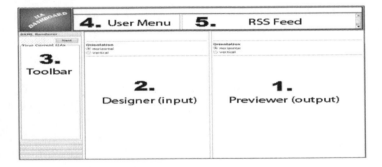

Fig. 2. Skelton of IIA dashboard

3.2   Creating the BXML Renderer

The bXML renderer portion of the dashboard is the easiest of all to make because of Pivot's built in class BXMLSerializer(). This is the class used to open the dashboard itself and what we used to take the bXML code the user types and render it into an application. All it takes is a typecast to a component from the code (byte array) and then adding it to a container (boxPane) in the following listing:

```
//rendering and setting preview to right side of splitPane stuff
private void renderIIA() throws IOException, SerializationException{

    BXMLSerializer bxmlSerializer = new BXMLSerializer();
    ByteArrayInputStream bais = new ByteArrayInputStream(
            dndTextArea.getText().getBytes());
    Component component = (Component)bxmlSerializer.readObject(
            bais);
    renderPane.removeAll();
    renderPane.add(component);

}
```

The bXML renderer works with a simple flow of commands in the main class. The user first clicks the "Render Code" button, which initiates the renderIIA function. This function takes code written in the text area from the leftPane, section 2 in Figure 4 and uses it with the BXMLSerializers method ReadObject. This method returns a component to the renderIIA function. If the component (which is a serialized version of the user's bXML code) is a valid serialized bXML application then renderIIA adds that component (the output) to the rightPane, section 1 in Figure 4, for the user to see and inspect. However, if the component is null, or in other words did not serialize properly renderIIA will throw an exception, informing the user that an error occurred somewhere in their code. If the user clicks on the "find error" button a stack trace will print out and help them track down the error in their bXML code. Figure 3 is a UML sequence diagram showing the steps taken to render a bXML application using the bXML renderer in the IIA Dashboard.

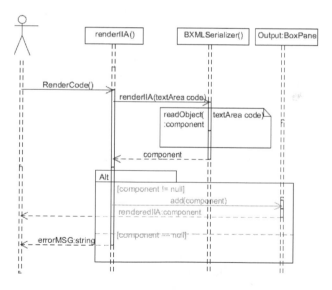

Fig. 3. bXML Renderer sequence diagram

4   Using the Generic Pivot IIA Dashboard to Create Crossword Game Builder

Crosswords provide opportunities for learners to practice and rehearse learning content in a fun way. Particularly useful for areas that have large specific vocabulary requirements, crosswords provide opportunities for learners to familiarize themselves with vocabulary and their definitions. Often this can act as a form of self-assessment, providing feedback and assisting in the construction of subject specific knowledge. The first task required to transform the generic dashboard into a dedicated game environment like the crossword is to create a dynamically changing grid where the instructor can create his/her educational crossword. The bXML tablePane was used to create the general layout of the crossword UI. However, the crossword builder eventually needed to be able to add/remove columns/rows, choose positions, enter words/clues and blackout spaces. A tablePane allows all of this with relative ease. To add a row all that is necessary is to call, CWBase.getRows().insert(row, rowCount), where CWBase is the tablePane, or crossword grid itself. A for loop is required to go through each cell to fill it with a blank panel, which is very easy. To add a column, the same is done replacing rows with columns in the above command; to remove either is the same but replace the .insert method with the .remove method. As for the positioning of the word placement and blacking out of squares, Pivots tablePane comes with a very useful built in mouse button listener called, mouseClick(Component component, Mouse.Button button, int x, int y, int count) which allows you to track the amount of times clicked within a second and to find which cell you are clicking by calling commands rowIndex = CWBase.getRowAt(y) and columnIndex = CWBase.getColumnAt(x). Once the cell is found it is simple to change its contents with either a letter and/or a colour. To put in a background colour:

CWBase.getCellComponent(firstClickR,i).getStyles().put("backgroundColor", colour) and for a letter: Label x = (Label) CWBase.getCellComponent(firstClickR, i); x.setText(character);

Finally for entering words and clues, simple text fields and buttons along with a few error checks were used to complete the crossword builder which is shown in figure 4. Using this builder, the user needs to press the 'generate CW' button to generate the required crossword based on a list of provided words that can be fetched from the dashboard repository of learning word lists. This is useful for an instructor wanting to make a crossword for their students quickly such as teaching them programming languages concepts.

The crossword builder is a simple enough application to use, with a small sequence of actions needed to place a word. A completed crossword consists of repeating this sequence of actions over and over again. Figure 5 provides a sequence diagram illustrating the activities required to create the crossword UI based on the generic dashboard primitives.

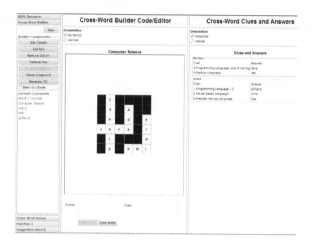

Fig. 4. Pivot IIA Crossword Builder Application for Teaching Programming Languages Concepts

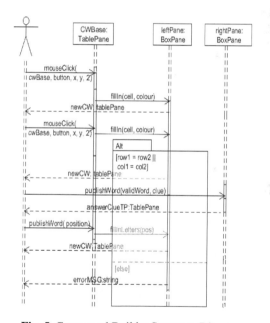

Fig. 5. Crossword Builder Sequence Diagram

The Pseudo code shown in Figure 6 illustrates the algorithm used in automatically creating the crossword UI from given list of words.

```
Pseudocode CWAutoGen
START
  DO 5 Times:
    read in list of words from file;
    for i = 0 to WordCount:
        sortWordbyLength into 4 groups;

    randomly select 2 words from each
        group to fill queue;
    place the first word in center;
    for i = 1 to 7:
        check for intersection between
            wordqueue[i] and placed words;
            if intersection
                place word;
            else
                i++;

    DO 3 Times :
      randomly select 2 words from each
          group to fill queue;
      for i = 1 to 8:
          check for intersection between
              wordqueue[i] and placed words;
              if intersection
                  place word;
              else
                  i++;
    END DO
  END DO
  for i = 1 to 5:
    rank crossword[i] based on size, number
        of words and proportions;
  return bestCrossword;
END
```

Fig. 6. Pseudo code of Auto Generation of a Crossword Puzzle

Moreover, if one has the option to create a crossword with the dashboard one should have the option to solve a crossword. Creating the crossword solver portion of the dashboard was very simple. All that it needed was to duplicate the builder application and remove a few sections such as: the answer section, the text area where the user enters the clue corresponding to their answer and the ability to click black boxes. The only thing that was necessary to add was a function to check if the crossword was completed properly. A few functions also needed a bit of reworking, but this task was minimal. Figure 7 illustrates the steps required to solve the generated crossword.

After the solver was complete, the idea of being able to publish crosswords to a server along with downloading crosswords to solve came to life. This was not a daunting task as Pivot allows you to remain in a pure Java language, which has many built in methods and classes that make client/server connections simple. However, since the coding was done in Java, with Java methods Pivot did not help in creating this portion of the Dashboard. When a user is in the solver and wants to download and solve a crossword from the server, they would press the "Get Crosswords" button. This will create a client, connect to the server and request to retrieve a crossword.

Once connected, the server takes the command, which in this case is retrieve crossword, and then chooses a crossword to send and sends it. The client prepares to receive it, and the receives the data and writes the crossword to the proper file using Java's BufferedWriter and FileWriter classes.

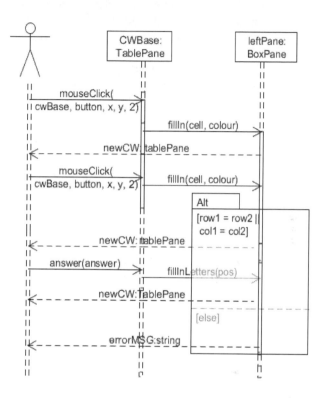

Fig. 7. Pivot IIA Crossword Game Solver Sequence Diagram

5 Conclusion

The needs to develop game-based learning environments and applications are ever growing. Researchers sees the skills students develop playing games as essential to a 21st century education, and conversely see little progress happening in schools still shackled to a 19th century factory model. Rich internet applications are seen to be good models to develop such ubiquitous learning games. Luckily there are many development environments and software packages that can help one create a successful application such as Microsoft Silverlight, Flash or Apache Pivot. Although all are qualified and useful our development experiment in this paper recommends the Apache Pivot for a few reasons. The first being that Pivot allows the programmer to design his or her application UI purely using very simple bXML primitives and implements all its required interaction activities using a purely Java environment.

Another selling point of Pivot is that it is the only open source IIA framework on the market which gives it a very good attitude and programming atmosphere. Pivot also comes with the best user forum one could hope for. In this paper, we used the Pivot environment to develop a generic casual gaming dashboard and use it later to generate an educational crossword game. Our research demonstrated that software technology like the Apache Pivot can enhance the instructor's abilities to develop educational games and prepares them to the 21 century education environment.

Acknowledgements. This work has been funded by Natural Sciences and Engineering Research Council of Canada (NSERC) and Dr. Jinan Fiaidhi of Lakehead University. This work was also supervised by Dr. Fiaidhi.

References

[1] Schleiner, A.: Does Lara Croft wear fake polygons? Gender and Gender-Role Subversion in Computer Adventure Games 34(3), 221–226 (2001)
[2] Klopfer, E., Osterweil, S., Salen, K.: Moving learning games forward. Technical Report, The Education Arcade, Massachusetts Institute of Technology (2009),
    http://education.mit.edu/papers/
    MovingLearningGamesForward_EdArcade.pdf
[3] Pink, D.H.: A Whole New Mind, p. 288. Publisher Riverhead Books, Media type Hardcover, (2006) ISBN 1-57322-308-5, OCLC Number 56755886
[4] Brown, G.: Using Apache Pivot to build an iTunes search client. IBM Developer Works Tutorial (October 13, 2009),
    http://www.ibm.com/developerworks/xml/
    tutorials/x-pivottut/x-pivottut-pdf.pdf
[5] Fiaidhi, J.: Towards Developing Installable e-Learning Objects utilizing the Emerging Technologies in Calm Computing and Ubiquitous Learning. International Journal of u- and e- Service, Science and Technology 4(1) (March 2011)
[6] Hammami, S., Aleid, H., Mathkour, H.: Game design in Game-Based Learning. International Journal of Information Studies 3(3), 128–134 (2011)

Remote Robotic Laboratory Experiment Platform Based on Tele-programming

Chadi Riman[1], Eric Monacelli[2], Imad Mougharbel[3], and Ali El-Hajj[4]

[1] Computer Engineering, Fahad Bin Sultan University, Tabuk, KSA
criman@fbsu.edu.sa
[2] LISV, Versailles University, Velizy, France
eric.monacelli@uvsq.fr
[3] Computer Engineering, Lebanese University, Beirut, Lebanon
imadmoug@lu.edu.lb
[4] Computer Engineering, American University of Beirut, Beirut, Lebanon
elhajj@aub.edu.lb

Abstract. Remote Laboratory Experimentation is a technique used in modern engineering laboratories to help academic researchers and students perform laboratory experiments remotely through the internet. Remote control of experiments is gaining more importance in training and education. However, remote real-time training on instruments programming still have some unresolved problems such as error management. In this paper, a platform for training students on remote robotic experiment control through tele-programming is presented. Programming sessions can be done by the trainee at many levels of control with built-in error management in order to avoid system freezing or malfunction. We also present a real experiment: programming navigation control of a mobile robot in the presence of obstacles using fuzzy control.

Keywords: Remote lab experimentation, HCI, Robotics, Computer Simulation.

1   Introduction

Remote Laboratory Experimentation is a distant control of an experimental setup accessed from different places and by different users (Figure 1). It is used in modern engineering laboratories to help academic researchers and students perform laboratory experiments remotely through the Internet. From the client side, a computer is connected to the internet with a Web browser from which the real experiment is to be conducted. On the server side, there are two important components: A lab server and a Web server. The lab server consists of a computer connected to the experiment's hardware and possibly to a webcam. The Web server, which is connected to the lab server, is responsible of managing the access by clients to the experimental setup.

The application carried out in Remote Experimentation can vary from a simple demonstration where interaction between the student and the experiment is on a simple level (view only), to a complex application where the student has more control

R. Benlamri (Ed.): NDT 2012, Part I, CCIS 293, pp. 11–22, 2012.

over the experiment. The first case is safe with limited teaching possibilities. The complex case has more teaching advantages but it also has malfunction risks due to a higher probability in committing errors by students. This type of training is sometimes accompanied with simulation software that can be used instead of the real experiment.

Tele-Programming is a remote laboratory platform in which control is done using program files exchange. These files are usually text files of small size which requires very low bandwidth. This type of remote experimentation is therefore suitable to low speed networks. This study evaluates some existing major platforms in tele-programming and suggests an improved low-cost platform with three programming levels based on student and course levels. For illustration purposes, this platform will be used for remote training on a mobile robot in a fuzzy logic environment.

The main problem in self programming is the need of a tutor either in the local place or in the remote lab, which can be replaced by a tele-tutorial system [2]. Our platform uses an error management module to identify errors, notify the student, and prevent system malfunction. Our idea is to support the training of the students by allowing failures in the experimentation. The system can manage different kind of failures and then send feedback to student. No software purchasing cost in involved because all processes are built using freeware.

In this paper, we will present an overview of literature survey for the domain in section 2. Our suggested platform architecture with the simulation module is described in section 3. Concluding remarks and future work are given in section 4.

2   Literature Survey

Many robotic laboratory platforms exist. Distance Learning platforms on robotics (DLR) are mainly concerned with learning, evaluation and security. In this section, the characteristics of some Existing DLR platforms [3-10] will be studied and used in the analysis of our suggested one.

The "Robotics & Automatic Control Telelab" discussed in [3] is a remote laboratory on robotics developed at University of Siena. It extends the field of application of the "Automatic Control Telelab" by adding experiments on a remote robot manipulator. This telelab is mainly intended for educational use, and its Matlab-based architecture allows students to easily put in practice their theoretical knowledge on robotics.

The work done in [4] presents new extensions to an existing remote laboratory. The remote lab serves as a means of a distant-programming environment, which provides users the possibility to use control systems, widely employed in industrial applications. The platform combined the access-control system of the laboratory infrastructure and virtual remote desktops to allow users to be absolutely independently of the place and time. Students can remotely control the physical experiments placed in the lab or use simulation software (such as a programmable logic controller simulator).

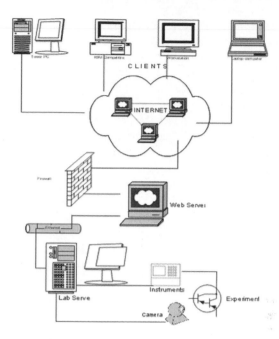

Fig. 1. Remote Lab Experimentation [1]

UJI Industrial Robotics Telelaboratory was presented in [5]. Students using this system are able to perform robotics and computer vision tele-experiments remotely via the Web, in order to combine the use of a field-programmable gate array (FPGA) to provide real-time vision processing, a conveyor belt, and a Motoman industrial manipulator. This work introduced the Simple Network Robot Protocol (SNRP), which permits the integration of network robots and sensors within an e-learning platform in a simple and reliable manner.

The development and experimental evaluation of an e-laboratory platform in the field of robotics was described in [6]. The system in its current configuration is designed to enable distance training of students in real scenarios of robot manipulator programming. The system has also a simulation option to perform virtual experiments. The concepts and techniques developed in the field of telerobotics and virtual reality, and their integration in the e-laboratory settings were explained. A preliminary study on a number of students was conducted to compare the pedagogical differences between real, virtual, and remote learning/training methodologies and experiences.

The Open Learning platform presented in [7] uses MS NetMeeting and Matlab real-time tools for control purposes. One of its characteristics is that the software development is simple, reducing expenses and minimizing faculty work. Another advantage is the use of existing off-the-shelves freeware software. It also has no need for Web-enabled Interfaces. This platform uses the Learning-by-Doing methodology but it doesn't present any solution related to safety problems.

The platform described in [8] uses the *Active-Learning* methodology. The design provides the remote user with the perception of reality which is due to the use of Learning Objects. Safety is provided by running a VRML (Virtual Reality Module Language) simulation before executing the control program, which may reduce any damage due to some manipulation errors. Control learning is limited to changing pre-defined controllers with their parameters.

In the Platform described in [9] uses the Learning by Tele presence, the *Learning-by-Doing* or *Active-Learning*. The remote user indicates obstacles to be avoided and the target to be reached. A simulation module based on a potential field algorithm draws the path and a control program runs in order to follow it. Infrared sensors are installed on the robot to provide security and increase autonomy. This system has some deficiencies due to the limited interaction with the user and limited experience of the student.

The platform developed in [10] is used for remote control of Lego mobile robots. The student uses Matlab/Simulink in order to design a controller to track a user defined trajectory. The control program is next transmitted to the server and executed. Three lights have been placed on the top of the robot in order to detect position and direction by means of a camera. A safety mechanism stops the experiment whenever the robot reaches a forbidden region. The control accuracy is based on a predefined model of the robot dynamics and needs to be changed with the physical environment.

The platform suggested in our work focuses on displacement control of a mobile robot. It benefits from useful techniques and methodologies developed in previous studies and adds improvements to them.

3   Suggested Remote Laboratory Platform

3.1   General Architecture

The suggested platform uses client-server architecture (Figure 2). The server provides training information such as description of programming methods, programming steps, and programmable devices. It is also responsible of communication with the remote client and with the robot.

Interoperability among users is achieved by using an Apache server and an HTTP browser. Apache server is very stable and widely available. The server software includes the modes of displacements, the reachable workspace of the robot, the response times of the actuators and the sensors as well as the sequence of procedures required for a given task. The Apache server communicates with the robot through a Common Gateway Interface (CGI) using C language. The user program is transmitted by the server to the CGI which transmits information to the robot according to the programming level. The robot is connected to the server through an RS232 HF serial port. Next, the CGI Program returns results to the client. A Webcam connected to the site returns feedback information on the framework environment.

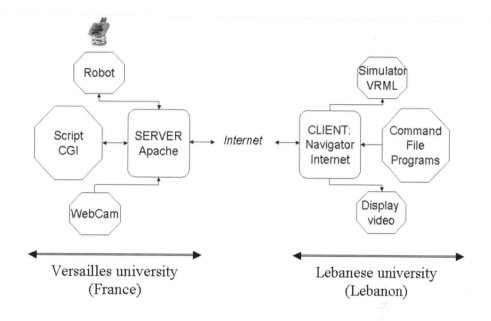

Fig. 2. The platform architecture

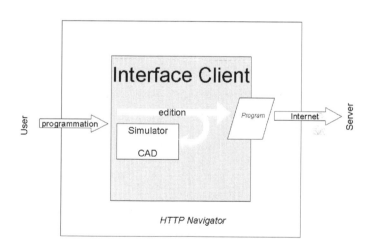

Fig. 3. Interface process

Interactions between the user interface and the platform is based on sending predefined instructions to the robot, and receiving status information (Figure 3). This interaction is performed in order to explore the robot parameters and to program its operation. Exploring parameters allows the understanding and the comparison between structures and sensitivity ranges of various controllers. Programming provides the ability of integrating the controller in a programming language. The program has to follow a predefined structure in order to be compatible with the error management module. In case of errors, the system sends an error report and reinitializes the platform for restarting the exercise.

3.2   Tele-programming Protocol

The suggested protocol for training on programming shows that there are three levels of tele-programming (Figure 4).

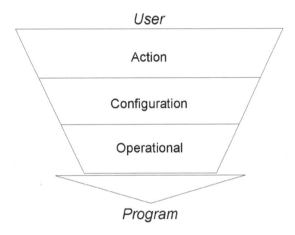

Fig. 4. The three programming levels

1. The direct action level is for introductory courses where a program corresponds to a sequence of instructions (advance, turn…). The first set of experiments is made at this level where the student will be learning the system specifications (functionalities and workspace) and the basic programming structures (loops, iterations…).
2. The configuration level is used for more specialized courses where programming integrates internal specifications. The student can modify internal parameters. This facilitates the understanding of control principles.
3. At the operational level the student learns how to control system using advanced programming. The program file is transmitted for execution on the server. The program can be directly executed either on the robot or its virtual simulated model. Virtual reality, for design engineer workshop, allows transmitting control instructions without syntax constraints. Contrarily, a textual way for transmission of control instructions needs more abstraction in the programming phase.

3.3   Used Robot and Its Control

The Khepera robot (Figure 5) has a diameter of 55 mm and a height of 30 mm. It is controlled by a Motorola processor 68331 with 256 KB of RAM and 18 KB of ROM. Its motion is due to two DC motors with encoders. It is also provided with 8 infra-red sensors. Because of its modularity and its important number of options, this product is widely used by researchers and teachers. It can be programmed in GNU C with LabView or Matlab.

Fig. 5. Khepera mobile robot

At the first level of programming, operations are based on actions available in the robot integrated libraries. These actions are simple: advance, turn, pause, avoid, measure sensors values... The user is therefore able to carry out a simple task in a complex environment.

At the configuration level, uploaded programs use fuzzy controllers that are structured with heuristic features close to human actions. Configuration is done on parameters relative to a classification of entries (data generated by sensors or robot status) and on fuzzy rules.

At the operational level, the transmitted source code implements the algorithmic structure and the robot control.

3.4   Error Management Module

An error management module (Figure 6) is included to deal with failures produced at any of the described levels. This module prevents deadlocks [11] and system freezing, and transmits feedback information which improves the student learning. It runs on the server in order to validate program syntax and semantics. It also supervises program execution using a watchdog concept. Furthermore, it controls the execution time and odometrical task limits. Therefore, students can test their programs without human tutor because of the feedback provided due to an abnormal response of the robot.

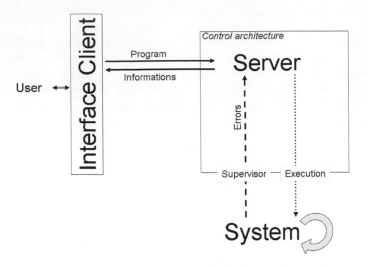

Fig. 6. Process of failure supervision

For a navigation task towards a goal in a complex space, two situations are considered as [11]:

1. Blocking situation (Figure 7): a bad choice of control parameters (control law or range of operation of proximity sensors) may cause a freezing in operation during obstacles crossing.
2. Vagrancy situation (Figure 8): the error causes divergence from the goal.

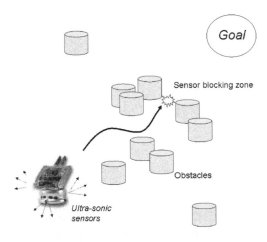

Fig. 7. Blocking situation

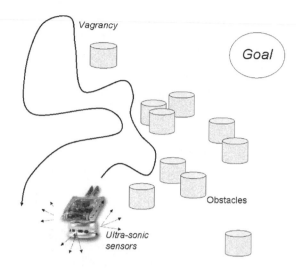

Fig. 8. Vagrancy situation

The first error type is due to a bad parameters configuration. The fuzzification parameters on inputs and selected rules of inference, lead to freezing during a simple navigation task in presence of obstacles. This allows students to understand the structural and logical definition of the configured fuzzy subsets. A simple modification of the number of subsets or the use of a symmetrical or asymmetrical triangular structure makes a navigation task successful or not.

The second error type occurs because of a programming problem (infinite loops, interruption, exception...). For example, infinite loops are suspected when blocking occurs without being associated with sensors configuration. Memory allocation problem is detected by the mechanism of integrated watchdog: the robot must periodically send execution status information. The training at this stage is concerned with the algorithm, its implementation, and its execution. Tools for coding and reliability analysis could be used during this learning stage [12].

3.5   Simulation Module

The aim of the simulation module is to perform a local test on the student program before being uploaded. The simulation phase has the following objectives:

1. Understanding the robot specifications and functions.
2. Testing programs without risks related to using the real robot.

Simulation is done in a VRML (Virtual Reality Modeling Language) environment, which is a 3-dimentional scene description language installed on the client station. First, the server transmits various documents to the client browser which interprets these documents with a possible help of plug-ins. In case this interpretation fails, these documents are transmitted to the VRML.

In a first step, the simulator visualizes the robot in order to present its functionalities (Figure 9): motion, perception and processing devices. Students, at this stage of training, can study these functions relative to mechanical, electronic and data processing concepts:

- Perception: Allows studying the principles, types, ranges, and positioning measurements of infra red sensors.
- Motion: Allows to study actuators specifications and types, as well as kinematics and power module devices.
- Processing: Allows studying processor characteristics (memory, temporal diagrams...).

In a second step, VRML simulator serves as a trial stage for programming. Students can study the behavior of the simulated robot in the action programming level.

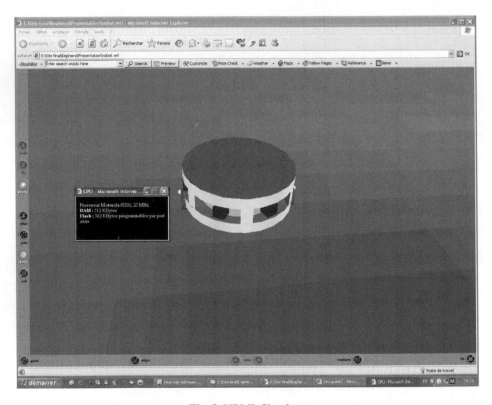

Fig. 9. VRML Simulator

Test experiments are to be set up between Saudi Arabia and France in the near future. The system will be installed on a computer server at the LISV lab (Versailles University). The server is to be connected by wireless link to the robot. A visual feedback will be used during the experiment in order to simplify operations and to improve learning process. The test task is a simple navigation with obstacle avoidance. The Khepera mobile robot will be installed in a limited enclosure for a safe displacement.

Server process is to be installed in computer server with real IP address in LISV lab (France). Client process is to be installed in a computer server with real IP address in Fahad Bin Sultan University (Saudi Arabia). Connection will be through the Internet via Socket Programming (using C++ or Java programming language).

4   Conclusion and Future Work

In this study, a platform for training on systems control by tele-programming was presented. According to the student academic profile, and in order to improve self-learning process, a protocol including various training levels and error management was validated.

In the near future, this approach will be evaluated based on experiments carried out through Internet connection between Saudi Arabia and France. The experiment for the student learning phase will a mobile robot programming using different levels: from predefined order to fuzzy logic programming. We will test the error management to improve knowledge feedback for students.

The platform will use free software and work with low bandwidth Internet connection. Our idea is to answer typical student constraints in term of flexibility and cost.

References

1. Mougharbel, I., El Hajj, A., Artail, H., Riman, C.: Remote Lab Experiments Models: A Comparative Study. International Journal of Engineering Education 22(4) (2006)
2. Böhn, A., Rütter, K., Wagner, B.: Evaluation of tele-tutorial in a remote programming laboratory. In: American Society for Engineering Education Annual Conference (2004)
3. Casini, M., et al.: RACT: a Remote Lab for Robotics Experiments. In: Proceedings of the 17th World Congress of The International Federation of Automatic Control, Seoul, Korea, July 6-11 (2008)
4. Burget, P., et al.: Remote Labs and Resource Sharing in Control Systems Education. In: Proceedings of the 17th World Congress of The International Federation of Automatic Control, Seoul, Korea, July 6-11 (2008)
5. Marin, R., et al.: Remote Programming of Network Robots Within the UJI Industrial Robotics Telelaboratory: FPGA Vision and SNRP Network Protocol. IEEE Transactions on Industrial Electronics 56(12) (December 2009)
6. Tzafestas, C.S., et al.: Virtual and Remote Robotic Laboratory: Comparative Experimental Evaluation. IEEE Transactions on Education 49(3) (August 2006)
7. Swamy, N., Kuljaca, O., Lewis, F.L.: Internet-Based Educational Control Systems Lab Using NetMeeting. IEEE Transactions on Education 45(2) (May 2002)
8. Fabri, D., Falsetti, C., Ramazzotti, S., Leo, T.: Robot Control Designer Education on the Web. In: Proceedings of the 2004 IEEE International Conference on Robotics and Automation, New Orleans (April 2004)

9. Von Borstel, F.D., Ponce, B.A., Gordillo, J.L.: Mobile Robotics Virtual Laboratory Over the Internet. In: Proceedings of the Fourth Mexican International Conference on Computer Science, ENC 2003 (2003)
10. Carusi, F., Casini, M., Hattichizzo, D., Vicino, A.: Distance Learning in Robotics and Automation by Remote Control of Lego Mobile Robots. In: Proceedings of the 2004 IEEE International Conference on Robotics and Automation, New Orleans (April 2004)
11. Smirnov, A., Monacelli, E., Delaplace, S.: Single adaptation mechanism for collaborating multi-robots. In: ICIN 2002 Conference, St. Petersburg, Russia (2002)
12. Klein, M.H., et al.: A Practitioners' Handbook for Real-Time Analysis: Guide for Real-Time Systems. Kluwer Academic Publishers, Boston (1993)
13. Abdessemed, F., Benmahammed, K., Monacelli, E.: A fuzzy based reactive controller for a non holonomic mobile robot. Robotic and Autonomous Systems Journal, 31–46 (2004)
14. Braitenberg, V.: Vehicles: Experiments in Synthetic Psychology. MIT Press (1984)
15. K-Team. User's Guide for Khepera mobile robot,
    http://www.k-team.com/download/khepera.html

Understanding Simple Stories through Concepts Extraction and Multimedia Elements

Masoud Udi Mwinyi, Sahar Ahmad Ismail, Jihad M. Alja'am, and Ali M. Jaoua

Qatar University, College of Engineering
Department of Computer Science and Engineering
Doha, Qatar P.O. Box 2713
{m.udi,200156689,jaam,Jaoua}@qu.edu.qa

Abstract. Teaching children with intellectual disabilities is a challenging task. Instructors use different methodologies and techniques to introduce the concepts of lessons to the children, motivate them and keep them engaged. These methodologies include reading texts, showing pictures and images, touching items, taking children to sites to see and understand, and even using the taste and smell senses (i.e., hot, cold). The objective of this work is to develop a system that can assist the children with special needs to improve their understanding of simple stories related to the animals and foods domain through multimedia technology. We use formal concepts analysis and a simple ontology to extract the keywords representing characters, actions, and objects from the story text and link them with the corresponding multimedia elements (i.e., images, sounds and clips). These elements are retrieved by querying Google database using Google APIs features. The instructors would have to validate the obtained results and select what is appropriate for the children in the classroom. The system allows the instructor to input the story text and get as output the multimedia story.

Keywords: Multimedia, Special Education, Keywords Extraction, Formal Concepts Analysis, Ontology.

1   Introduction

Children with mild and moderate intellectual challenges face a lot of problems in understanding simple text of stories. Special education instructors use different techniques and methodologies in order to explain the story to the children and keep them motivated and engaged. These techniques including reading the story text several times repeatedly, designing glossy images about the objects and characters of the story and show them to the children, generating sometimes the sounds of animals (i.e., birds, cats, dogs, camels, wolf) and objects (i.e., cars, motorbikes, bus, airplanes), and even using the taste and smell senses where there effects have been studied in our previous work [8]. Finding or developing these multimedia elements is problematic and hard to do [2]. The instructors ask generally their assistants to look for these elements from different resources like books, magazines, newspapers and

R. Benlamri (Ed.): NDT 2012, Part I, CCIS 293, pp. 23–32, 2012.

the Internet. They sometimes draw the characters of the story and record the corresponding sounds and present them to the children. Although these elements can be built with some efforts, they are however not suitable to all the children. In fact, the children in the same classroom can have always different understanding levels even though they have been classified as having the same intellectual challenges [3]. They need always additional elements in order to understand the concepts. Developing an intelligent system that can get as input the story text and generates the corresponding multimedia elements will be of great importance for both teachers and children as well as for their parents. In fact, children can understand better the story, teachers can improve the learning process as they have a collection of multimedia elements related to the stories; also the parents can use the system at home to help their children to review the story. They can also select different multimedia elements than those used in the classroom which may be found to be more suitable to their children. We propose in this work the first prototype of the system. We use formal concepts analysis FCA [1,12] with a simple animal ontology to extract from the story text the keywords belonging to the domain and we link them automatically with the corresponding multimedia elements (i.e., images, sounds, and short clips). We use Google APIs "Application Programmable Interface, Ilan.Google.API" [5] to query the Google image search database to retrieve and fetch the multimedia elements. Special education instructors can select the appropriate multimedia elements proposed by the system according to the levels of their children. They can input the story text to the system and build the corresponding multimedia story that can fit with the level of every child in the classroom.

2   Formal Concepts Analysis

The notion of formal concept analysis has been introduced by different scientific communities in the world under the name of maximal rectangle [4], and in graph theory as a maximal bipartite graph [6]. In addition it has been exploited in database concepts to introduce a new kind of dependencies called, iso-dependencies [4,7]. Independently we have introduced in [7] the difunctional dependencies as the most suitable name for iso-dependencies in database. Among the mathematical theories found recently with important applications in computer science, lattice theory has a specific place for data organization, information engineering, data mining and reasoning. It may be considered as the mathematical tool that unifies data and knowledge, as well as information retrieval and reasoning. In FCA terms, a space of information can be modeled as a formal context. A formal context is a triple (O,P,I) where O is the set of objects in that information space, P is the set of properties owned by some objects and I $\subseteq$ O x P; i.e. I is the binary relation that is a subset of the product of the set of objects and the set of properties in that information space.

Example 1. Let O be the following set of objects O = {Leech, Bream, Frog, Dog, Spike-weed, Reed, Bean, Maize}, and let P be the set of properties P = {a, b, c, d, e, f, g, h, i} where O is a set of some animals, and P is a set of the following properties: "a = needs water", "b = lives in water", "c = lives on land", "d = needs chlorophyll to produce food", "e = is two seed leaves", "f = one seed leaf", "g = can move around", "h = has limbs", "i = suckles its offspring". The binary context R is given in the following table 1 below.

Table 1. Binary context R relating objects and attributes

		a	b	c	d	e	f	g	h	i
1	Leech	1	1	0	0	0	0	1	0	0
2	Bream	1	1	0	0	0	0	1	1	0
3	Frog	1	1	1	0	0	0	1	1	0
4	Dog	1	0	1	0	0	0	1	1	1
5	Spike-Weed	1	1	0	1	0	1	0	0	0
6	Reed	1	1	1	1	0	1	0	0	0
7	Bean	1	0	1	1	1	0	0	0	0
8	Maize	1	0	1	1	0	1	0	0	0

A concept of a binary context is a binary relation that can be defined in terms of its objects (intents) and their shared attributes (extents) to be the collection of the maximum number of objects (set O) sharing the collection of the maximum number of attributes (set P). More formally, let f be a function from the powerset of the set of objects O (i.e., 2^O) to the powerset of the set of properties P (i.e., 2^P) in the binary context, such that:

$$f(A) = \{m \mid \forall\, g \in A \rightarrow (g, m) \in R\}$$

f(A) is the set of all properties shared by all objects of A (subset of O) with respect to the context R. Let g be a function from 2^P to 2^O, such that:

$$g(B) = \{g \mid \forall\, m \in B \rightarrow (g, m) \in R\}$$

g(B) is the set of objects sharing all the properties B (subset of P) with respect to the binary context R. The closure function is defined as follows:

$$closure(A) = g(f(A)) = A', \text{ and } closure(B) = f(g(B)) = B'$$

The meaning of A' is that a set of objects A is sharing the same set of properties f(A) with other objects (A'- A), relatively to the context R. A' is the maximal set of objects sharing the same properties as objects A. In example 1, if A = {Leech, Bream, Frog, Spike-weed}, then A' = {Leech, Bream, Frog, Spike-weed, Reed}. This means that the shared properties a, and b of the animals in A, are also shared by a "Reed", the only element in A'- A. The meaning of B' is that if an object x of the context R, verifies properties B, then x verifies also some number of additional properties (B'-B). B' is the maximal set of properties shared by all objects verifying properties B. In the previous example, if B = {a,h}, then B' = {a,h,g}. This means that any animal that needs water (a) and has lambs (h), can move around (g). For each subset B, we may create an association rule as follows: B → B'- B. The number of these rules depends on the binary context R. The formal concept is formally the pair (A, B), such that f(A) = B, and g(B) = A. We call A the extent and B the intent of the concept (A, B). If (A1, B1) and (A2, B2) are two concepts, (A1, B1) is called a sub-concept of (A2, B2), provided that A1 ⊆ A2, and B2 ⊆ B1. In this case, (A2, B2) is a super-concept (A1, B1) and it is written as follows: (A1, B1) < (A2, B2). The relation "<" is called the hierarchical order relation of the concepts. The set of all concepts of (G, M, I) ordered in this way is called the concept lattice of the context (G, M, I). A formal context can be represented as a hieratical concept lattice structure. Such structures have the tendency to grow exponentially in terms of the number of concepts they include. This problem is known to be NP complete [4,12] for which there have been a number of approximations algorithms to find the minimum number of concepts that can represent the maximum knowledge in a lattice with the minimal redundancy to save processing power and resource consumption. For that purpose, we have adopted in the proposed system a greedy approach for finding the minimal number of concepts entirely covering a binary relation based on a space optimization criterion described in details in [12]. In this method, the notion of optimal minimal contextual coverage refers to the decomposition of a binary relation R in a minimal set of optimal rectangles (or optimal concepts). FCA is used for deriving conceptual structures out of data. These structures can be graphically represented as conceptual hierarchies, allowing the analysis of complex structures and the discovery of dependencies within the data. FCA is based on the philosophical understanding that a concept is constituted by two parts: its extension which consists of all objects belonging to the concept, and its intension which comprises all attributes shared by those objects. One of the main objectives of this method is to visualize the data in form of concept lattices. Let K represent the formal context given in table 2. The following lattice is generated (fig. 1).

Table 2. Formal concepts linking objects and properties

		A	B	C	D
1	G1	1	1	0	0
2	G2	1	1	0	0
3	G3	0	1	1	0
4	G4	0	1	1	1
8	G5	0	0	1	1

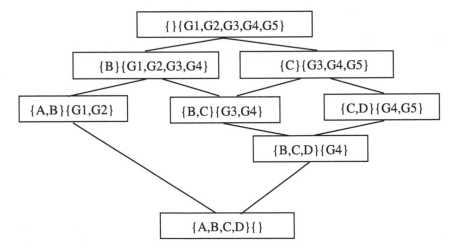

Fig. 1. Concept lattice of the context K

2.1   Galois Connection

Galois connection is a conceptual learning structure used to extract new knowledge from existing context (i.e., database, text), where a context is represented by a binary relation. We can decompose the context into a set of concepts and we can build a hierarchy of concepts known also as "Galois Lattice". A pair (f(A), h(B)) of maps is called a Galois connection if and only if we have the following equivalence:

$$A \subseteq h(B) \Leftrightarrow B \subseteq f(A)$$

It is also known that f(A) = fhf(A) and h(B) = hfh(B).

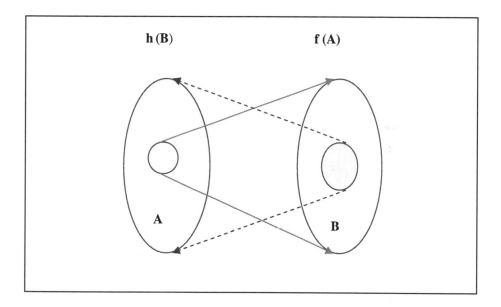

2.2   Optimal Concept or Rectangle

Let R be a binary relation defined from G to M. A rectangle of R is a pair of sets (A, B) such that $A \subseteq G$, $B \subseteq M$ and $A \times B \subseteq R$. A rectangle is called maximal or none enlargeable if and only if it is a concept. Since a binary relation can be represented by a relatively large number of concepts, optimization in space becomes an important scalability factor. A trade-off between storage saving and knowledge acquisition has to be made to address this optimization need. Thus, the gain function W(R) is defined as: W(R) = (r/dc)(r - (d + c)) where r is the cardinality or number of pairs in R, d is the cardinality of the domain (objects set) of R, and c is the cardinality of the range can be utilized to support the selection of a minimal significant set of concepts representing the relation. One key to optimizing information representation is to study the concepts pertaining to a pair in the binary relation and decide on the most optimally significant rectangle to include in a conceptual coverage. We can call a rectangle RE $\subseteq$ R containing an element (x, y) to be optimal if it produces a maximal gain W(RE (x, y)) with respect to other concepts containing (x, y).

3   The System Architecture

The proposed system consists of a number of components laid out into different modular layers. The core application components handle the processing of textual manuscripts of stories related to the animal and food domain and converts then the extracted entities into multimedia elements supporting the educational process. These components cover mainly four areas which are the following:

(1) the text processing used to eliminate stop-words and find the words stems or roots;
(2) the FCA extraction component;
(3) the learning component; and
(4) the multimedia mapping component.

The system architecture is based mainly on service oriented architecture which is an architectural paradigm that can be used to build infrastructures enabling those with some needs (i.e., consumers) and those with some capabilities (i.e., providers) to interact via services across disparate domains of technology and ownership. Services act as the core facilitator of electronic data interchanges yet require additional mechanisms in order to function properly. Using external component such as Google APIs services, our target is to utilize SOA to consume available multimedia search solution that will translate concepts and actions expressed in representative text segments into multimedia elements. Below screenshot shows some attempts of using Google APIs to find multimedia elements related to the sentence "dog eats meat".

Fig. 2. An example of a multimedia search service using Google APIs where we can retrieve simple images and short video clips corresponding to the sentence "dog eats meat". The last two images in this figure are short video clips tagged with their duration.

We can retrieve easily thousands of images and video clips that should be validated by the potential users of the system who are mainly the instructors and eventually the parents. The instructors can browse through these multimedia elements and store what is suitable into the data repository. We can also add a filtering algorithm to recognize some tagged images and clips and classify them automatically. The instructors can input the story text and the system will extract the keywords using FCA and the animal ontology and provide the list of multimedia elements. The instructors can browse through this list and build their multimedia-based stories with the suitable elements. Figure 3 below shows the components of the proposed system distributed into modular layers. This gives some flexibility when any modification is required. Modifying one layer doesn't affect necessarily the others layers.

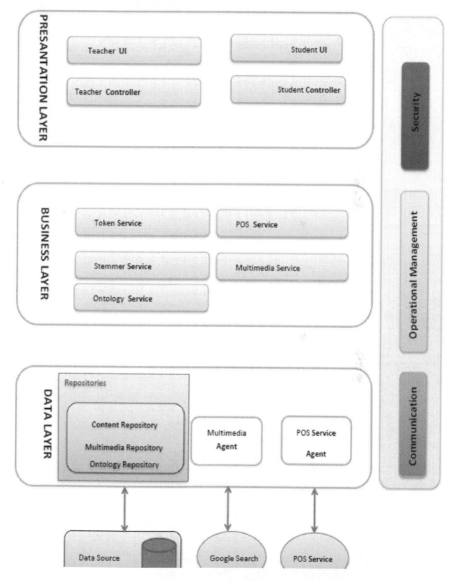

Fig. 3. The architecture of the proposed system is divided into layers. The instructors can use the system through its interface to browse through the sentences and the corresponding multimedia elements.

FCAs techniques help to build a graphical interface and associate the keywords with the sentences in which they appear as shown in figure 4 below. The instructors can browse easily through these keywords and sentences and see the linked multimedia elements. In fact, every sentence that contains some keywords will have a set of different multimedia elements where the instructors can select from.

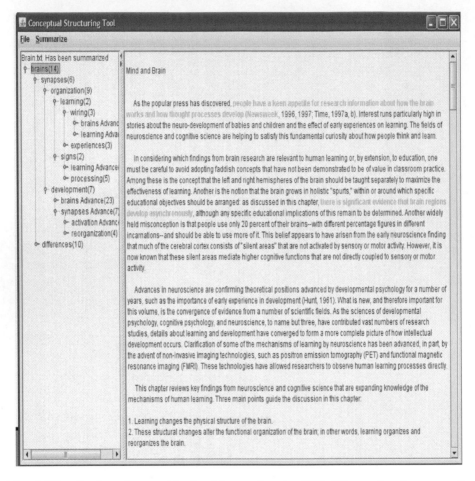

Fig. 4. Visualization of texts and related keywords using FCA. We can then browse easily through the keywords and the related sentences.

Example 2. "A lion attacked a Zebra and killed him then he ate him and got tired so he laid down on a tree branch".

For this text the system will extract first the named entities like the "lion" and "zebra" as they belong to the animal ontology. Then it will detect the action "attack" and the related objects understanding that the lion is acting on the zebra. In fact, the ontology helps to infer that based on lion's behavior. In the third step, the system understands the killing and feeling actions "killed", "gets tired", "laid down", and the object "tree branch" and display then the corresponding multimedia elements. These relations are also existing in the ontology. Some of these relations are: A lion can attack animals like Zebra and a rabbit. A rich ontology can improve the inference process and the outcome of the system. The instructors will have to validate the retrieved elements that should be presented to the children. These elements can includes images of the story characters (i.e., lion and Zebra) and objects (i.e., tree branch) and also their actions like "attack", "fill tired", and "kill". The following figure 4 can be a possible output of the original text which should be formed mainly by the instructor.

Fig. 5. The retrieved multimedia elements corresponding to the original text of the story. These elements consists of thousands of images and clips where the instructors can validate them and build his/her multimedia story.

4   Conclusion

We have proposed a new multimedia system to teach children with intellectual challenges in a very innovative way. We have used formal concepts analysis and a simple ontology for keywords extraction from the story text and we linked them with multimedia elements retrieved automatically from the Internet using Google APIs. The animal ontology helps to recognize the named entities, the relations between the objects, the animal's behaviors and the actions in the story. The system is being tested in the Shafallah center for children with special needs in Doha, Qatar.

Acknowledgments. This publication was made possible by a grant from the Qatar National Research Fund NPRP 09 - 052 - 5 - 003. Its contents are solely the responsibility of the authors and do not necessarily represent the official views of the QNRF.

References

1. Alja'am, J.M., Jaoua, A.M., Hasnah, A.M., Hassan, F., Mohamed, H., Mosaid, T., Saleh, H., Abdullah, F., Hassan, C.: Text Summarization based on Conceptual Data Classification. In: Alkhatib, G., Rine, D.D. (eds.) Agent Technologies and Web Engineering: Applications and Systems, pp. 195–209. IGI Global (2008)
2. Elsaddik, A.: Interactive Multimedia Learning. Springer (2001)
3. Evans, D.G., Bowick, L., Johnson, M., Blenkhorn, P.: Using Iconicity to Evaluate Symbol Use. In: Miesenberger, K., Klaus, J., Zagler, W.L., Karshmer, A.I. (eds.) ICCHP 2006. LNCS, vol. 4061, pp. 874–881. Springer, Heidelberg (2006)
4. Ganter, B., Wille, R.: Formal Concept Analysis. Springer (1999)
5. Google Ajax Language APIs, http://code.google.com/apis/ajaxlanguage/
6. Gunther, S., Ströhlein, T.: Relations and Graphs. Springer (1989)
7. Jaoua, A.: Pseudo-Conceptual Text and Web Structuring. In: The Third Conceptual Structures Tool Interoperability Workshop, CS-TIW 2008, pp. 22–32 (2008)
8. Miguel, A.G.R., El-Seoud, S.A., Edwards, A., Alja'am, J.M., Raul, A.S.: Integrating the Sense of Smell in an Educational Human-Computer Interface. In: International Conference on Interactive Collaborative Learning, ICL 2008, pp. 1–7 (2008)
9. Nickull, D., Reitman, L., Ward, J., Wilber, J.: Service Oriented Architecture (SOA) and Specialized Messaging Patterns. Technical White Paper, pp. 1–15, (2007), http://www.adobe.com/enterprise/pdfs/Services_Oriented_Architecture_from_Adobe.pdf

Extended UML for the Development of Context-Aware Applications

Mohamed Salah Benselim[1] and Hassina Seridi-Bouchelaghem[2]

[1] LabSTIC Laboratory, University of 08 Mai 45,
Guelma, Algeria
msbenselim@yahoo.fr
[2] LabGed Laboratory, University of Badji Mokhtar,
Annaba, Algeria
h_seridi@yahoo.com

Abstract. In a pervasive environment, systems and applications are influenced by several factors and features such as mobility, heterogeneity and distribution. So, new application will be able to adapt its services with the change of context of use and satisfy all users' preferences. In this work we present an UML extension for representing and modeling context because UML does not support all aspects of the context of use in an adequate manner. This extension is defined by some extensibility mechanisms and it is presented as a set of new tools for the unified modeling language. The proposed extension is based on UML notation and it permits obtaining a specific graphic representation of a contextual situation. Also, it facilitates the extraction and the modeling of all elements that can influence the current situation of the user. Our proposal consists on creating some stereotypes that are described by several tagged values and some constraints and that can be applied to the contextual model classes. Then we use a class diagram to describe the different types of context and their relationships. A case study is done in the medical domain in which we propose a new contextual model including all new stereotypes by using StarUML software modeling platform.

Keywords: Software engineering, context of use, modeling, UML, extensibility mechanisms.

1   Introduction

The development of context-aware software needs specific notations and concepts of modeling language to provide adapted applications and personalized information. Unified modeling language (UML) has been the standard object oriented modeling language used for modeling many aspects of software systems [1]. The main characteristic of UML is a set of extensibility mechanisms (stereotypes, tagged values and constraints) which are used for adding new modeling concepts and notations. So, UML is able to be extended in order to represent all aspects of a specific domain with appropriate notation. For this, we propose an extension of this language that can help us to model context-aware applications with specific notation. Using the new vision of concerns separation cited in [2] we isolate the contextual elements from the global

R. Benlamri (Ed.): NDT 2012, Part I, CCIS 293, pp. 33–43, 2012.

aspects of a system. Each of these elements has many features and constraints related to users, applications or environment. Then we propose some new UML components (stereotypes) to describe and to model all contextual elements. Also we attach some tagged values and constraints to the proposed stereotypes. Using these extensibility mechanisms we can build a complete UML profile for context modeling. We note that context is composed by different elements that have various properties and characteristics and that can be related through different relationships and each contextual element should be able to be represented by thus extension of UML.

2   Related Works

Several works have been led in the domain of context modeling by using the unified modeling language. But not many that used extension mechanisms to represent or to model the context of use. In [3] authors presented a model driven development framework for context awareness as an extension of UML. It consists of a domain specific modeling language called CAMEL (Context Awareness ModEling Language) which enables enriching independently defined UML models with the model of context aware behaviors. A visual language for context models in mobile distributed systems has been presented in [4] and the Context Modeling Profile (CMP) has been proposed. CMP is provided as a lightweight extension of UML without modifying the UML metamodel. In [5] a UML profile is proposed in order to model context-aware applications. This profile allows the context-aware applications designed by this profile to be integrated with existing UML-based software. Sheng and Benatallah proposed "Context UML" in order to develop the context-aware Web Services [6]. They modified some metaclasses of UML and so they built an extension of the UML metamodel. The proposed metamodel is then used for modeling context. Some works have introduced the UML extensibility mechanisms in different fields. In [7] authors presented an extension of UML for the representation of Web Service Description Language (WSDL). The proposed extension provides an UML notation which allows obtaining graphic representation of a Web service and facilitates the automatic generation of WSDL code from an UML diagram. In [8] a set of agents is presented and these agents are based on UML extension and are called AgentUML. There are other works that used UML extension like [9] where the UML modeling language is extended in order to model the structural and dynamic aspects of Multi-agent systems and [10] where authors proposed to extend and to customize the unified modeling language with web design concepts by using the Hypermedia Design Model. In the domain of ontology we have to note that many studies have been led by using the extending UML such as [11] and [12].

3   Context and UML

Future applications have to provide exact results and personalized information and they must be adequate with every variation of user's current situation. Ubiquitous information systems are characterized by many features like mobility, heterogeneity and distribution. These constraints represent the context of use of a situation. The concept of "context" has been defined in [13] as follows: "Context is any information that can be used to characterize the situation of an entity. An entity is a person, place, or object that is considered relevant to the interaction between a user and an application, including the user and applications themselves". From this definition, we can extract a few elements that constitute the main components of the context of use. These elements are: the user, location, time and environment. In the field of ubiquitous computing, these elements have a common feature such as change and variation. Also, any changes of the surrounding objects can directly affect the state of the current situation of a user. On the other hand, each user may have particular preferences related to content, presentation or information display. Ubiquitous computing offers many opportunities for access to information like random use, in time and space, of mobile devices by varying kinds of users including distant persons and nomad users. Because of user mobility, not only the time and location are constantly changing but also the surrounding objects (including nearby people) and environmental factors. Modification or change in one element of the context of use involves the transition of this context toward another state of the user's current situation. So, the user is facing a different situation that he is in a new context of use and with which he must be adapted. In previous works [14][15] we have presented a new development approach that can take into account all changes in context of use during the application development process and we proposed a new vision of MDA approach (Model Driven Architecture). Then we have demonstrated how it is possible to isolate the contextual aspects of a system and how to develop the contextual constraints independently from the business constraints of this system and from the technological constraints of the chosen platform [2]. This separation allows us to study all contextual information in a separate branch and without remaking the entire development process because of any changes in the context of use. As result we proposed a contextual model that is conform to a proposed metamodel by using the standard Unified Modeling Language (UML). But in spite of that we were not completely satisfied because the standard UML concepts do not support all aspects of the context of use in an adequate manner. Therefore we decided to find a better solution to represent the context by explicit and appropriate notation. UML is a standard object oriented modeling language offered by the Object Management Group (OMG) and it is used for modeling many aspects of software systems. UML has several features and characteristics, among these features we are interested here by extensibility mechanisms (stereotypes, tagged values and constraints) that are used to introduce new elements for modeling specific domains such as context awareness. So, UML can be extended for modeling contextual aspects that influence the current situation of the user. This extension can be considered as a profile and it is done by adding some new elements to the standard unified modeling language.

4   Extension of UML

As shown in the previous section, the context of use can be represented by specific UML notation. So we have to extend the unified modeling language by adding new elements that can represent the contextual aspects in appropriate form. But before modeling the context, we must identify and separate all elements that are able to influence the current situation of a user. We note that this situation may be influenced by several factors and constraints as follows [2]:

- Constraints related to the user himself (Identity, Profile, Behavior, Preferences, etc.).
- Constraints related to the application (Software, Hardware, Networks, interaction mode, etc.).
- Constraints related to the environment (Time, Location, Weather, Nearby persons, Surrounding objects, Available resources, etc.).

Each of these constraints must be represented by an adequate notation of UML language. For this we propose an extension of the standard UML that contains stereotypes, tagged values and constraints. A stereotype permits to define a new meaning of an existing UML metamodel element. Tagged values are always attached to a stereotype and their role is to indicate attributes of the created stereotype. Constraints define some restrictions of semantics for each added new element. Generally, all UML concepts (class, attribute, association, etc.) can be stereotyped.

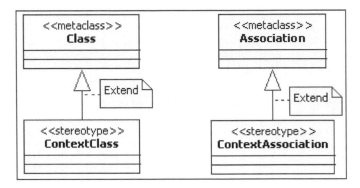

Fig. 1. Extension of the "Class" and "Association" UML metaclasses

Figure 1 presents a general view of the proposed extension. It shows how the UML metaclasses "Class" and "Association" are extended in order to create new UML elements that play a specific role in context modeling. The stereotype "ContextClass" is a new metaclass obtained by extending an existing UML metamodel element and it can be associated with other metaclasses. Its role is to represent the context of use of a system and it is defined by a set of elements "ContextElements" that represent all contextual aspects. Because of mobility of the user and because applications are distributed and distant, each of these contextual elements may have various features and constraints such are previously cited. To assure a better representation of the context in distributed applications development we propose to create specific stereotypes for taking into account all the components of this context and for providing an appropriate model. Figure 2 presents some stereotypes that are associated with the "ContextElement" stereotype and that define all specific constraints related to the context of a situation. "ContextRelevancy" indicates the relevance quantification of an element, it represents the level of importance that each contextual element may have. The type of a contextual element "ContextType" is provided by one of the following entities: the user, the application, the environment or the behavior. So each contextual element has one of the following stereotypes that are obtained by specialization of "ContextType" stereotype:

- "UserContext" : when information is directly related to the user,
- "ApplicationContext" : if information comes from application means,
- "EnvironmentContext" : if information is provided by the surrounding objects (other than user and application),
- "BehaviorContext" : it is provided by all behavioral interactions between the three entities (user, application, environment).

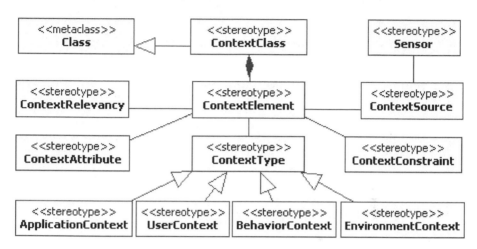

Fig. 2. The proposed "Class" stereotypes

"ContextAttribute" is a stereotype that permits to represent the properties of a contextual element class and to define all values that can be attached to instances of this class. The "ContextConstraint" constraints are defined by a restriction or a condition applied on an element class and they are used to model complex and important information such as domain, table, etc. The source of the contextual element "ContextSource" allows representing the specific hardware or software used for contextual information sensing. "ContextSource" assures the processing of all information captured by the "Sensor".

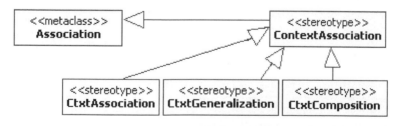

Fig. 3. The proposed "Association" stereotypes

Also, the UML metaclass "Association" is stereotyped in order to define new relationships that associate the created "Class" stereotypes (Figure 3). Each "ContextAssociation" can be specialized in order to have specific relationships such as (but not limited) "CtxtAssociation", "CtxtGeneralization" or "CtxtComposition".

These association stereotypes represent respectively a simple association, a generalization (or specialization) or a composition relationship between two "Class" stereotypes and a short description is presented in Table 1.

Table 1. Description of relationships

Relationship	Base class	Associated classes
IsProvidedFrom	CtxtAssociation	ContextElement, ContextSource
HasRelevancy	CtxtAssociation	ContextElement, ContextRelevancy
IsSpecializedTo	CtxtGeneralization	UserContext, ContextType
IsComposedBy	CtxtComposition	ContextClass, ContextElement

Constraints that are attached to the defined stereotypes are specified in order to extend the UML semantics. They permit to provide some conditions which are used as restrictions in modeling process. These constraints can be represented by using natural language or using OCL (Object Constraint Language). In Table 2 we present a short description of some constraints expressed with natural language.

Table 2. Description of constraints

Stereotype	Attached constraint
ContextElement	It must be related to the "ContextClass" class by composition
ContextRelevancy	It must be related to the "ContextElement" class by simple association
EnvironmentContext	It must be related to the "ContextType" class by generalization

Other exemple, if we need to limit the relevancy application field of a contextual element, we can define a specific constraint that will be attached to a "ContextElement" stereotype. This constraint can be written with OCL language as follows :

Context ContextClass inv:
Self.ContextElement->forAll(e : ContextElement | e.relevancy <= self.MaxValue and e.relevancy >= self.MinValue)

Tagged values are attached to stereotypes and they are considered as meta-attributes of metaclasses. They can be defined by a given attribute name and its value. They are used to represent and to specify attributes for the defined stereotypes. Table 3 presents an example of three proposed tagged values.

Table 3. Description of specific tagged values

Tagged value	Attached stereotype	Description
LevelOfRelevance= high|medium|low	ContextRelevancy	Degree of importance associated to each contextual element
TypeOfSensor= hardware|software	Sensor	Indicates the type of used tool for information sensing
StateOfUser= sitting|standing|...	UserContext	Indicates the state of the user in the current situation

5   Case Study

To implement our approach, an illustrative case study in the medical field (drugs) has been tested. The main goal of this project is to get a new contextual model that is conform to a proposed metamodel including all new stereotypes and by using StarUML software modeling platform. However, we can present a summary of this project. Our survey concerns several situations of using the pharmaceutical products (drugs). Drugs can be used by different users in various situations; that is to say that every situation has its own context of use including all factors and constraints cited in previous sections.

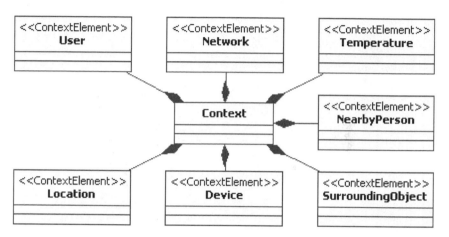

Fig. 4. The contextual elements of the system

Using the proposed UML extensibility mechanisms we can represent the context of use according to each situation. We consider that our system is influenced by the following contextual elements: user, location, device, temperature, network, nearby persons and surrounding objects. According to the "IsComposedBy" relationship (Table 1) and the attached constraint of "ContextElement" stereotype (Table 2), these elements compose the context of the system and they can be represented using the proposed stereotype "ContextElement" such as shown in figure 4.

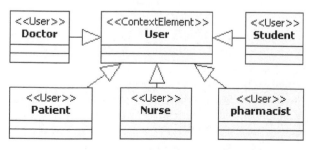

Fig. 5. Specialization of users

Each of the contextual elements can be specialized to represent specific entities. So we have to extract all possible occurrences of these entities that can be implied by the system in different situations. By specialization of "ContextElement" stereotypes we provide an appropriate representation of the specific entities and this will permit us to build a contextual model using an adequate notation. Figures 5 and 6 present some specialization examples of contextual elements respectively related to users and locations. Here we note that a person, like a Doctor, can be considered as a user when he uses drugs or he can be considered as a nearby person if he is present in the same location with another user (patient). Obviously contextual elements must have all required information that have been specified as stereotypes in figure 2 like attributes, constraints, type, relevancy and source.

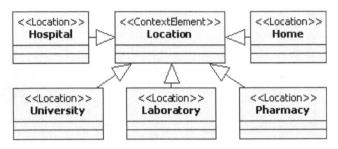

Fig. 6. Specialization of locations

Because of user's mobility in pervasive environment, the current situation of a user is variable and it changes constantly. So we have to model many various situations (contextual situations) of using the system.

Table 4. Comparison of three contextual situations

Contextual Elements	Contextual Situation 1	Contextual Situation 2	Contextual Situation 3
User	Patient	Patient	Patient
Location	Hospital	Home	pharmacy
Used Device	PDA, Mobile	PDA, PC	PC
Existing Network	LAN	Internet	Internet
Nearby persons	Doctor, nurse	parent	Pharmacist, friend
Surrounding objects	Medical tools	TV, Phone, Printer	Phone, Fax

In our project, a patient (as a user) can be in different situations when using drugs; for example, he can be at the hospital, at home or at the pharmacy. Here we have three contextual situations for the same user. Other example, a doctor (as a user) uses drugs at the hospital, at home, in the laboratory or at the university when teaching. In this case we have four different contextual situations. To illustrate the difference between three contextual situations related to the first example (patient) we collect corresponding information in Table 4. Having these elements and according to the proposed UML extension we can model the system by giving an appropriate class diagram. Needed relationships are summarized in Table 5.

Table 5. Description of needed relationships

Relationship	Related classes
IsLocatedIn	User, Location
Use	User, Device
HasTime	Device, Time
UseNetwork	Device, Network
IncludePersons	Location, NearbyPerson
ContainObjects	Location, SurroundingObject

Figure 7 presents a simplified class diagram for modeling the context of our system. In the proposed contextual model we presented all contextual elements that compose the context of use of the system and its relationships.

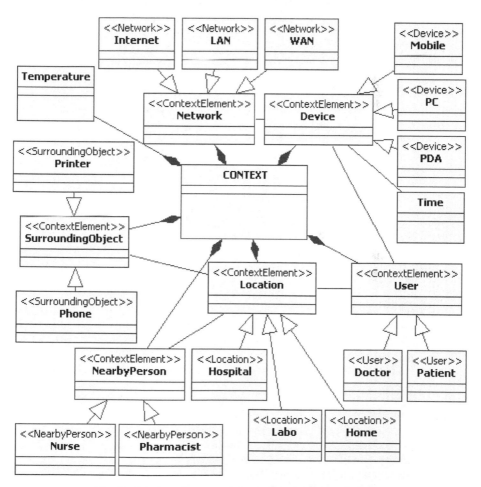

Fig. 7. The class diagram of the proposed contextual model

6   Conclusion

Context awareness is a particular domain that claims specific modeling concepts that are able to represent all contextual aspects of a system with appropriate tools. In this paper we proposed a new element notation for context defined by an extended version of the unified modeling language and by creating new UML concepts. We presented some stereotypes obtained by extending the UML metaclasses "Class" and "Association". Then we attached some tagged values and constraints to the proposed stereotypes. In the case study we presented a description of some contextual elements and we proposed a contextual model that can be used in context-aware applications development. As perspective we hope to continue this study while offering a more complete list of extensibility mechanisms. This will permit us to create a complete UML profile for context modeling. Also we hope to use the proposed extended UML in information systems adaptation and for information personalization.

References

1. OMG/UML, UML 2.1 Superstructure Specification, Document: ptc/06-04-02 (2006)
2. Benselim, M.S., Seridi-Bouchelaghem, H.: Development of context-aware applications in ubiquitous information systems. In: Proc. of the 13th International Conference on Enterprise Information Systems, ICEIS 2011, Beijing, China, June 8-11, vol. 3, pp. 223–228 (2011)
3. Sindico, A., Grassi, V.: Model driven development of context aware software systems. In: International Workshop on Context-Oriented Programming, COP 2009, Genova, Italy, July 7, pp. 1–5 (2009)
4. Simons, C.: CMP: A UML Context Modeling Profile for Mobile Distributed Systems. In: Proceedings of the 40th Annual Hawaii International Conference on System Sciences, HICSS 2007, Hawaii, USA, January 3-6 (2007)
5. Ayed, D., Delanote, D., Berbers, Y.: MDD Approach for the Development of Context-Aware Applications. In: Kokinov, B., Richardson, D.C., Roth-Berghofer, T.R., Vieu, L. (eds.) CONTEXT 2007. LNCS (LNAI), vol. 4635, pp. 15–28. Springer, Heidelberg (2007)
6. Sheng, Q.Z., Benatallah, B.: ContextUML: A UML-Based Modeling Language for Model-Driven Development of Context-Aware Web Services. In: 4th International Conference on Mobile Business. IEEE Computer Society, Sydney (2005)
7. de Castro, V., Marcos, E., Vela, B.: Representing WSDL with Extended UML. Revista Columbiana de Computation 5 (2004)
8. Odell, J., Parunak, H.V.D., Bauer, B.: Extending UML for Agents. In: Proceedings of AOIS Workshop at AAAI (2000)
9. da Silva, V.T., de Lucena, C.J. P.: Extending UML to Model Multi-Agent Systems. PUC-Rio Inf. MCC 08/04 (March 2004)
10. Baresi, L., Garzotto, F., Paolini, P.: Extending UML for modeling web applications. In: Proceedings of the 34th Annual Hawaii International Conference on System Sciences, HICSS 2001, Hawaii, USA, pp. 1285–1294 (2001)
11. Baclawski, K., Kokar, M.K., Kogut, P.A., Hart, L., Smith, J., Holmes, W.S., Letkowski, J.J., Aronson, M.L.: Extending UML to Support Ontology Engineering for the Semantic Web. In: Gogolla, M., Kobryn, C. (eds.) UML 2001. LNCS, vol. 2185, pp. 342–360. Springer, Heidelberg (2001)

12. Brockmans, S., Haase, P., Hitzler, P., Studer, R.: A Metamodel and UML Profile for Rule-Extended OWL DL Ontologies. In: Sure, Y., Domingue, J. (eds.) ESWC 2006. LNCS, vol. 4011, pp. 303–316. Springer, Heidelberg (2006)
13. Dey, A.K., Abowd, G.D., Salber, D.: A conceptual framework and a toolkit for supporting the rapid prototyping of context-aware applications. Human-Computer Interaction 16, 97–166 (2001)
14. Benselim, M.S., Seridi-Bouchelaghem, H.: Contextual adaptation of ubiquitous information systems. In: Proc. of the International Conference on Multimedia Computing and Systems, ICMCS 2009, Ouarzazate, Morocco, April 2-4, p. 135 (2009)
15. Benselim, M.S.: Une approche pour le développement d'applications sensibles au contexte. In: XXVIIe congress of INFORSID, Toulouse, France, May 26-29, pp. 479–480 (2009)

Semantic Aware Implication and Satisfiability for Conjunctive Queries in Semantic Caching

Muhammad Azeem Abbas, Muhammad Abdul Qadir, Munir Ahmad, and Tariq Ali

Center for Distributed and Semantic Computing,
Mohammad Ali Jinnah University Islamabad
azeem.abbas@uaar.edu.pk, aqadir@jinnah.edu.pk,
{munirahmad83,tariqali.1982}@gmail.com

Abstract. Finding satisfiability and implication results among queries is fundamental to several problems in databases especially in distributed databases. The known complexity of finding satisfiability of term S is $O(|S|^3)$. Similarly complexity of finding "Is S implies T (S→T)" is $O(S^3+K)$ Where $|S|$ is the number of distinct predicate attributes in S, and K is the number of predicate terms in T (S and T are conjunctive select-project-join(PSJ) queries). We show that with the induction of Cross Attribute Knowledge (C_{RA}) the above complexity is reduced to $O(|S - C_{RA}|^3)$ and $O(|S - C_{RA}|^3+K)$ for satisfiability and implication respectively.

1   Introduction

Satisfiability and implication results are fundamental to several problems in databases especially in distributed databases. It is widely used as a key to find equivalences among queries, query optimization, query rewriting and semantic cache query processing. When optimizing, an equivalent of the original query that is cheaper in execution is found through satisfiability and implication relation. Similarly a query is rewritten that either integrate multiple resources or used in dataware house design[1].

The process of computing available (probe query) and unavailable (remainder query) parts from prestored data fragments (cache) is highly effective in latency of data retrieval from distributed resources where communication cost is a major concern [2]. Since cached and incoming queries are formulas of conjunctive or disjunctive inequalities. So finding Probe (pq) and remainder (rq) queries is a problem of finding implication or satisfiability between cached query (QS) and user query (QU) formulas. The following definitions formally define the problems and notation to be used in the rest of this paper.

Definition 1. A select-project-join (PSJ) query Q is a tuple $< \pi_Q, \sigma_Q, \text{operand}_Q >$, where π_Q is Select Clause of query which contains projected attributes. operand$Q$ is the From Clause which contains relation of a database D, from which data is to be retrieved. σ_Q is Where Clause which contains conjunctive ($\wedge$) or disjunctive ($\vee$) compare predicates, a compare predicate is of

R. Benlamri (Ed.): NDT 2012, Part I, CCIS 293, pp. 44–54, 2012.
© Springer-Verlag Berlin Heidelberg 2012

the form P =(X op C) , P = (X op Y) or P=(X op Y +C), where X,Y $\in$ A {Attributes Set}, op $\in \{<, \leq, >, \geq, \neq\}$, C is a constant in a specific domain [1].

Definition 2. Implication is defined as "S implies T, denoted as S→T, if and only if every assignment that satisfies S also satisfies T".

Definition 3. Satisfiability is defined as "S is satisfiable if and only if there exists at least one assignment for S that satisfies T.".

Let us have a formula (Salary < 20K AND Salary > 8K AND Department = 'CS') is satisfiable, because the assignment 12K/Salary , CS/Department satisfies the formula. Similarly a formula (Salary>10K OR Salary<12K) is a tautology, because every assignment under this formula is satisfiable. We will use the following semantic cache application in our examples through the rest of the paper. A cached query with associated semantics stored in semantic cache along with resultant data is called a semantic region [3] or semantic segment [2]. If a user query (Q_U) posed over n semantic segments $(Q_{S1}, Q_{S2}, .., Q_{Sn})$ then this user query can either be totally answered (implies) or partially answered (satisfiable) or cannot be answered (unsatisfiable) from underlying segments.

So for above scenario, implication $(Q_U \rightarrow Q_S)$ means every tuple retrieved by evaluating Q_U can be obtained by evaluating Q_S i.e. the whole answer to Q_U is available locally in the cache. For satisfiability there are some tuples that can be retrieved by both Q_U and Q_S.

In case of implication user query (Q_U) shall be posed to the cache i.e. < $\pi_{QU}, \sigma_{QU}, operand_{QS}$ >.if satisfiability holds then user query (Q_U) is split into two parts i) pq = < $\pi_{QU \wedge QS}, \sigma_{QU}, operand_{Qs}$ > and ii) rq = < $\pi_{QU}, \sigma_{QU \wedge \neg QS}$, operand$_{QU}$ >. This splitting process is known as query trimming [4]. Query trimming is based on satisfiability and implication results. Let us assume that query trimming take O(QueryTrim) time. Then total (worst case) time taken by semantic cache query processing is $O(|Q_U|^3 + K) + O(|Q_U \wedge Q_S|^3) + O(QueryTrim)$ where K is number of terms in Q_S. In section III we show that with the induction of Cross Attribute Knowledge (CRA) [5] this complexity is reduced to $O(|Q_U - C_{RA}|^3 + K) + O(|Q_U \wedge Q_S - C_{RA}|^3) + O(QueryTrim)$.

Example 1: Consider an employee database with a relation name Emp (Empid, ,Department, Age, Salary,Exp). The domain of the Age, Salary, Department and Exp attributes of Emp are {20,...,100},{0.1K,...,1K,15K},{CS, EE, BI, BA},{1,..,50} respectively. Also suppose that the cache already has following cached segment.
$Q_S = < \pi_{Age,Salary,Exp}, \sigma_{Salary \leq 1K \wedge Salary \geq 40K}, Emp >$

2   Related Work

Satisfiability and implication results in databases [6],[7],[8],[9],[10] are relevant to the computation of probe and remainder query in semantic cache query processing for a class of queries that involve inequalities of integer and real domain. Previous work models the problem into graph structure. Hunt [9] provided an

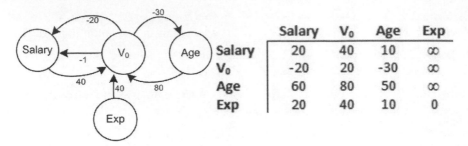

Fig. 1. (a) $[Q_{U1} \wedge Q_S]$ and $G_{QU1} \wedge Q_S$ (b) Shortest Path Table

algorithm of complexity $O(|Q|^3)$ for solving satisfiability problem; the expression S to be tested for satisfiability is the conjunction of terms of the form X op C, X op Y, and X op Y + C. Guo et al. [6] provided an efficient algorithm (GSW) for computing satisfiability with complexity $O(|Q|^3)$ involving complete operator set and predicate type X op C, X op Y and X op Y + C. Here we demonstrate GSW algorithm [6] for finding implication and satisfiability between two queries.

The GSW algorithm starts with transforming all inequalities into normalized form through given rules. It was proved by Ullman [7] that these transformations still holds equality. After these transformation remaining operator set become $\{\leq, \neq, \geq \}$.

- $(X \geq Y + C) \equiv (Y \leq X - C)$
- $(X < Y + C) \equiv (X \leq Y + C) \wedge (X \neq Y + C)$
- $(X > Y + C) \equiv (Y \leq X - C) \wedge (X \neq Y + C)$
- $(X = Y + C) \equiv (Y \leq X - C) \wedge (X \leq Y + C)$
- $(X < C) \equiv (X \leq C) \wedge (X \neq C)$
- $(X > C) \equiv (X \geq C) \wedge (X \neq C)$
- $(X = C) \equiv (X \leq C) \wedge (X \geq C)$

Satisfiability of a conjunctive query Q is computed by constructing a connected weighted-directed graph $GQ=(V_Q, E_Q)$ of Q after above transformation. Where V_Q are the nodes representing predicate attributes of an inequality and E_Q represent an edge between two nodes. An inequality of the form X op Y + C has X and Y nodes and an edge between them with C weight. The inequality X op C is transformed to X op V_0 + C by introducing a dummy node V_0.

According to GSW [6] algorithm, for any query Q if a negative-weighted cycle (a cycle whose sum of edges weight is negative) found in GQ then Q is unsatisfiable. Otherwise Q is satisfiable. Testing satisfiability among user query Q_U and cached segment Q_S require us to construct a graph ($G_{QU \wedge QS}$) of ($Q_U \wedge Q_S$) and check $G_{QU \wedge QS}$ for any negative weighted cycle. Negative weighted cycle is found through Floyd-Warshall algorithm [11]. Complexity of Floyd-Warshall algorithm is $O(|V|^3)$, so finding satisfiability become $O(|Q_U \wedge Q_S|^3)$.

An algorithm with $O(|S|^3 + K)$ complexity for solving the implication problem between two conjunctive inequalities S and T was presented by Ullman [7] and Sun [10]. Conjunctive queries of the form X op Y were studied by [8] and [9].

Implication between conjunctive queries of the form X op Y +C was addressed by GSW algorithm [6] with complexity $O(|Q_U|^2 + |Q_S|)$. GSW Implication [6] requires that Q_U is satisfiable. Satisfiability of Q_U can be checked by above mentioned steps. At first the implication algorithm constructs the closure of Q_U i.e., a universal set that contains all those inequalities that are implied by Q_U. Then, $Q_U \wedge Q_S$ if Q_S is a subset of the Q_U closure.

Example 2: Let us have a user query
$Q_{U1} = < \pi_{Age,Salary,Exp}, \sigma_{Salary \geq 20K \wedge Age \geq 30 \wedge Age \leq 80 \wedge Exp \leq 40}, Emp >$ over cached segment Q_S of Example 1. The directed weighted graph $G_{Q_{U1} \wedge QS}$ of $Q_{U1} \wedge Q_S$ is shown in Figure 1(a). Q_{U1} is satisfiable with respect to Q_S, as there is no negative weighted cycle in $G_{Q_U \wedge QS}$.

3   Cross Attribute Knowledge

In all previous work satisfiability and implication was only addressed for horizontal partitioned fragments. Where it was assumed that projected attributes of incoming user query and cached segment are same ($\pi_Q = \pi_S$). So implication and satisfiability was only applied to predicate part of the queries. Cross Attribute Knowledge (C_{RA}) consider both projected attributes of the queries and their predicates. The following definition formally defines the C_{RA}. Later we provide the effects of C_{RA} in satisfiability and implication problem.

Definition 4: Consider a cached query $Q_S = < \pi_{QS}, \sigma_{QS}, operand_{QS} >$, and a user posed query $Q_U = < \pi_{QU}, \sigma_{QU}, operand_{QU} >$ over the cached query (Q_S). Then a predicate attribute of user query (σ_U) is said to be cross attribute knowledge (C_{RA}) [5] if

- it is present in the cached query attribute (π_S) and
- it is not in cached query predicate (σ_S)

The C_{RA} is a predicate attribute and it behaves differently when appears in conjunction with other predicate attributes. So here we classify query predicate attributes into three categories: 1) The common predicate attributes (C_{PA}), 2) Cross Attribute Knowledge (C_{RA}) and 3) Non-Common predicate attributes (N-C_{PA}). This classification is formulated from conjunctive appearance of these categories. Every conjunctive appearance contributes to the answer differently. Their contribution can be shown with the examples given below (consider relation definition given in Example 1 for all examples given below):

Example 3: The data set of cached query (Q_S) is shown in Figure 2 (a,b,c,d) as white dotted line boxes. A user query ($Q_{U1} = < \pi_{Age,Salary,Exp}$, $\sigma_{Salary \geq 10K \wedge Salary \leq 30K \wedge Age \leq 70}$, Emp $>$) is shown as gray boxes over cached query (Q_S) in Figure 2 (b). According to C_{RA} definition, in this case the predicate attribute Age in user query (σ_{QU1}) is a C_{RA}. The C_{RA} is in conjunction with a predicate attribute (C_{PA}) Salary, which is common between cached querys predicate (σ_S) and user querys predicate (σ_{QU1}). This C_{PA} (Salary) implies cached query predicate i.e. ($\sigma_{QU1 \wedge CRA}$) S. So it can be concluded from the

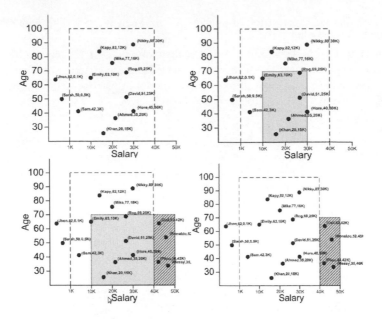

Fig. 2. (a top left),(b top right), (c bottom left), (d bottom right) Query Q over Cached Segment S

data set as shown in Figure 2 (b) that if C_{RA} appears in conjunction with C_{PA} and this C_{PA} implies cached query predicate attribute, then the whole answer of user query is present in semantic cache. This conclusion can be derived from lemma given below.

Lemma 1: Consider a cached query $Q_S =< \pi_S, \sigma_S, operand_S >$, and a user posed query with C_{RA} is $Q_U =< \pi_U, \sigma_U, operand_U >$. We define a new predicate attribute set $\sigma_{U'} = \{\sigma_U - C_{RA}\}$, (this can also be written as $\sigma_U = \{\sigma_{U'} \wedge C_{RA}\}$), Then we have a statement (which needs a proof) as:

– **If** (*operand*$_U$ = *operand*$_S$; and $\pi_U \subseteq \pi_S$; and user query without C_{RA}, $< \pi_U, \sigma_{U'}, operand_U >$, is fully answerable from the cache,) then $Q_U =< \pi_U, \sigma_U, operand_U >$ is fully answerable from Q_S.

Proof: Suppose we have a user query $Q_{U1} =< \pi_{U1}, \sigma_{U1}, operand_{U1} >$ that is fully answerable from $Q_S =< \pi_S, \sigma_S, operand_S >$ i.e. pq $= < \pi_{U1}, \sigma_{U1 \to S}, operand_S >$ and rq = null. Then let us consider another user query with new predicate set, $Q_{U2} =< \pi_{U2}, \sigma_{U2}, operand_{U2} >$ where the new predicate set is $\sigma_{U2} = \sigma_{U1 \wedge CRA}$. So Q_{U2} become

$$Q_{U2} =< \pi_{U2}, \sigma_{U1 \wedge CRA}, operand_{QU2} >$$

According to relational algebra splitting law [12],

$$Q_{U2} =< \pi_{U2}, \sigma_{CRA}(\sigma_{U1}), operand_{QU2} >$$

As per our assumption $\sigma_{U1 \to S}$, then

$$Q_{U2} = < \pi_{U2}, \sigma_{CRA}(\sigma_{U1 \to S}), operand_{QU2} >$$
$$Q_{U2} = < \pi_{U2}, \sigma_{CRA}(pq), operand_S >$$

Hence proved that any query that is answerable from semantic cache is also answerable while containing C_{RA} in conjunction.

Example 4: Figure 2 (c) shows an incoming user query ($Q_{U2} = < \pi_{Age,Salary,Exp}$, $\sigma_{Salary \geq 10K \wedge Age \leq 70}, Emp >$) over the cached query Q_S shown in Figure 2 (a). The gray color filled box shows the available part (probe query), where lined patterned area represents unavailable data or the remainder query. In this example the C_{PA} (Salary) satisfies the cached query predicate. So any conjunction of C_{PA} and C_{RA}, where C_{PA} satisfies cached query predicate will be partially answered from semantic cache. Lemma 1 can be easily extended for common predicate attribute satisfy case.

Example 5: A user query ($Q_{U3} = < \pi_{Age,Salary,Exp}, \sigma_{Salary > 40K \wedge Age \leq 70}, Emp >$) posed over the cached query Q_S is shown in Figure 2 (d). The C_{PA} (Salary) is unsatisfiable in this case. So the cached query Q_S does not contribute any answer to this query (Q_{U3}). C_{RA} behave according to C_{PA} when it appears in conjunction with it. That is; ($C_{PA} \wedge C_{RA}$) implies when C_{PA} implies, similarly ($C_{PA} \wedge C_{RA}$) satisfies when C_{PA} satisfies and ($C_{PA} \wedge C_{RA}$) does not contribute if C_{PA} does not satisfies. The other remaining predicate attribute i.e. non-common predicate attribute (N-C_{PA}) need special handling when it appears in conjunction with C_{PA} or C_{RA}. All previous semantic cache query processing techniques treats N-C_{PA} as non-satisfying condition. But our analysis and experimentation shows that N-C_{PA} can be treated as satisfying in many cases.

4   Satisfiability and Implication Based on Cross Attribute Knowledge

As proved in lemma 1 that if any conjunctive inequalities are satisfiable/implies then conjunction of these inequalities with CRA remain satisfiable/implies. So pruning C_{RA} from original conjunctive inequalities will also give correct results. This pruning of C_{RA} reduces complexity to $O(|Q_U - C_{RA}|^3 + K)$ for finding

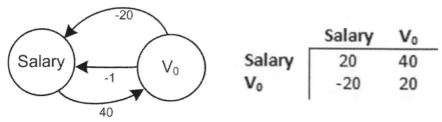

Fig. 3. (a) $[Q_{U1} \wedge Q_S]$ and $G_{(QU1 \wedge QS)-CRA}$ (b) Shortest Path Table

implication and $O(|Q_U \wedge Q_S - C_{RA}|^3)$ for computing satisfiability between user query Q_U and cached segment Q_S.

Example 6: The user query Q_{U1} in Example 2 over cached segment Q_S of Example 1 can be evaluated for satisfiability and implication with $\sigma_{QU1 \wedge CRA}$. The directed weighted graph $G_{(QU1 \wedge QS)-CRA}$ of $Q_{U1} \wedge Q_S$ is shown in Figure 3(a). Q_{U1} is satisfiable with respect to Q_S even with $Q_{U1} - C_{RA}$ as there is no negative weighted cycle. In previous section, we classified predicates of a user and cached query. There are two types of possible partitioning (horizontal and vertical) among user and cached queries. Our semantic cache query processing algorithm is based on all the combinations of predicates (C_{PA}, C_{RA}, N-C_{PA}), partitioning types (horizontal, vertical) and C_{PA} implication & Satisfiability results. In this way there are total thirty cases to be addressed.

Figure 4 below shows Semantic Cache Query Generator ($SCQG$) algorithm. An incoming user query QU and cached query Q_S posed over semantic cache is passed as input to $SCQG$ algorithm. These input queries are triplets, as discussed in definition 1. End results of $SCQG$ are an amending query, a probe query and a remainder query.

At the beginning of $SCQG$ algorithm, the parser function (line 4) separates all information available in semantics of the cached and user query. This information is then stored in global variables for further computation. The parser algorithm is shown in Figure 5.

As in above examples 3, 4 and 5, it is clear that answer to a user query is highly influenced by predicate classification. Our algorithm works accordingly to the appearance of respective predicate type. User posed incoming query and a cached query selected from semantic cache are given as input to $SCQG$. Selection of candidate cached segment is an open question. We select it in linear fashion. Our proposed algorithm generates available part (probe query) and unavailable part (remainder query). At line 4 parser function extract all semantic information present in both user and cached query.

First of all we find either incoming query and cached query are suitable for implication testing or not (line 5). This can be checked by finding a predicate term (N-$C_{PA(C)}$) that is in cached query but not in user query. If such term found then these queries are not suitable for implication testing. With this pre-decision we save implication evaluation time.

After that we still check whether these queries are suitable for satisfiability testing or not. If a common predicated attribute (C_{PA}) is present then we do satisfiability testing. But still complete user and cached query predicates are not evaluated for satisfiability rather pruned user and cached query predicates are evaluated. If satisfiability holds then incoming query is trimming into probe and remainder queries otherwise in case of unsatisfiability only remainder query is generated. If incoming and cached queries are not suitable for satisfiability testing then incoming query is trimming into probe and remainder query (line 9).

If user and incoming queries are suitable for implication testing, then we perform implication evaluation but with pruned predicates (line 12). After that if implication does not holds then we perform satisfiability testing.

SCQG () {
1 Input: Q_U (user query), Q_C (cached query)
2 Output: AmendQ (amending query), ProbeQ (probe
         query), RemQ$_1$ & RemQ$_2$ (remanider query).
3 Global Variable: K_A, A_1, A_2, C_{PA}, C_{RA}, N-$C_{PA(C)}$, N-
         $C_{PA(Q)}$, AmendQ, ProbeQ, RemQ$_1$, RemQ$_2$
4 **parser** (Q_U);
5 **ifExists**(N-$C_{PA(C)}$) {
6   **ifExists**(C_{PA}) {
7   **ifSatisfiable**($\overline{Q_U}$, Q_S) {

            pq = $<\pi_{Qu}, \sigma_{Qu} \wedge \sigma_{Qs},$ operand$_{Qs}>$
            rq = $<\pi_{Qu}, \sigma_{Qu} \wedge \neg \sigma_{Qs},$ operand$_{Qu}>$
            return pq, rq;
8   } **else** {

            rq = $<\pi_{Qu}, \sigma_{Qu} \wedge \neg \sigma_{Qs},$ operand$_{Qu}>$;
            return rq;
         }
9 } **else** {
         pq = $<\pi_{Qu}, \sigma_{Qu} \wedge \sigma_{Qs},$ operand$_{Qs}>$
         rq = $<\pi_{Qu}, \sigma_{Qu} \wedge \neg \sigma_{Qs},$ operand$_{Qu}>$
         return pq, rq;
      }
10} **else** {
11   **ifExists**(C_{PA}) {

12   **ifImplies**($\overline{Q_U}$, Q_S) {

            pq = $<\pi_{Qu}, \sigma_{Qu} \wedge \sigma_{Qs},$ operand$_{Qs}>$
            return pq;

12   **ifImplies**($\overline{Q_U}$, Q_S) {

            pq = $<\pi_{Qu}, \sigma_{Qu} \wedge \sigma_{Qs},$ operand$_{Qs}>$
            return pq;

13   } **else ifSatisfiable**($\overline{Q_U}$, Q_S) {

            pq = $<\pi_{Qu}, \sigma_{Qu} \wedge \sigma_{Qs},$ operand$_{Qs}>$
            rq = $<\pi_{Qu}, \sigma_{Qu} \wedge \neg \sigma_{Qs},$ operand$_{Qu}>$
            return pq, rq;
14   } **else** {
            rq = $<\pi_{Qu}, \sigma_{Qu} \wedge \neg \sigma_{Qs},$ operand$_{Qu}>$;
            return rq;
         }
15} **else** {
      pq = $<\pi_{Qu}, \sigma_{Qu} \wedge \sigma_{Qs},$ operand$_{Qs}>$
      rq = $<\pi_{Qu}, \sigma_{Qu} \wedge \neg \sigma_{Qs},$ operand$_{Qu}>$
      return pq, rq;
   }
}

Fig. 4. Semantic Cache Query Generator Algorithm

5   Implementation and Results

We implemented a prototype named Semantic Cache Query Generator ($SCQG$) to verify performance and correctness of our proposed algorithm. Experiments are designed to compare the performance of proposed algorithm and Ren et. al. [2] query processing technique. Our primary performance metric is response time while maximum data retrieval is an additional parameter which we observed is highly influential in semantic cache system. Our prototype is implemented in Java and local and remote data is stored in MySql database. Only precise data of cached queries is stored locally. Remote data server that is accessed through internet contains over 3.3 million rows [13]. Local data server contains approximately 30% of the whole data (either horizontally or vertically). Semantics of cached queries are kept in an extensible mark-up language (XML) file; in which each block represent clauses of a conjunctive SQL query. We experimented 1500 queries.The presented results are obtained by averaging the results of three runs of 500 queries over 50 stored queries. All 1500 queries are generated using random attributes and predicates. These random attributes and predicates are generated by strictly following the schema definition and domain values of the underlying database. All generated queries returns non-empty answer which shows their correctness. Ren et. al . [2] computes probe and remainder query by evaluating

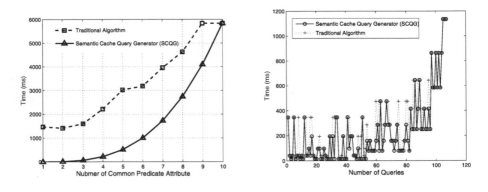

Fig. 5. Experimental Results

user and cached query for implication results at first. It then evaluates those queries for satisfiability if implication does not hold. This technique has higher time complexity as it adds up implication and satisfiability computational time.

Graph above shows time complexity comparison of traditional semantic cache query processing algorithm and $SCQG$. X-axis shows the percentage of similarity between incoming user query and cached segment predicates. Y-axis shows time complexity in milliseconds. Our algorithm compute probe and remainder query within constant time for cached and incoming queries that have similarity below 20%. For exactly equal queries both traditional and $SCQG$ takes equal time. But

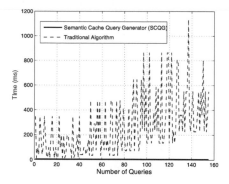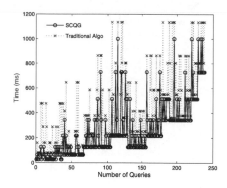

Fig. 6. Experimental Results

for all queries between 20 and 90 range are computed in polynomial fashion by *SCQG*. But traditional algorithm has high complexity for all queries despite of any similarity concern. Trend-lines clearly show the efficiency of our algorithm.

We grouped our experimented quires accordingly to the branches of our algorithm (*SCQG*). Figure [6] shows computational comparison of queries that does not fall in implication relationship. Our algorithm take pre-decision by evaluating predicate classification. The branch at line 10 of SCQG handle all such queries. Dotted line in graph above represent traditional algorithm. *SCQG* is shown in solid line. Efficiency of our algorithm is better in maximum situations.

The branch at line 9 of algorithm SCQG handles queries that does not have a common predicate attribute yet other predicate attributes exists. In this case it is known that both incoming and cached query satisfies each other, so our algorithm perform query trimming in constant time. Figure [7] shows time complexity of traditional algorithm (dotted line) and SCQG (solid line).

Figure [8] shows comparison of traditional (dotted line) and *SCQG* (solid line) algorithms for quires that fall under branch at line 5 of *SCQG* algorithm. Where incoming query have larger answer set than cached query and they both posses some common predicate attributes. Time complexity of *SCQG* remains low in all cases because traditional algorithm sums up implication and satisfiability complexity for satisfiable cases. Also for implication queries we prune incoming and cached query which reduces time complexity require to compute implication relationship.

6   Conclusion

Efficient and effective solutions for satisfiability and implication problem are needed as it is important and widely-encountered in database problems such as semantic cache. In this paper query predicates are classified based on their semantic meanings. An algorithm for semantic cache query processing based on satisfiability and implication relationship among cached and user query is proposed. The proposed algorithm computes the available and unavailable part from cache against the incoming user query. Our algorithm process query evaluation while keeping in view the semantic classification of the predicates of the underlying queries. This makes our algorithm time efficient over its predecessors.

References

1. Halevy, A.Y.: Answering queries using views. VLDB J. 10, 270–294 (2001)
2. Ren, Q., Dunham, M.H., Kumar, V.: Semantic Caching and Query Processing. IEEE Transactions on Knowledge and Data Engineering, 192–210 (2003)
3. Dar, S., Franklin, M.J., Jonson, B.T., Srivastava, D., Tan, M.: Semantic Data Caching and Replacement. In: Proceedings of 22nd VLDB Conference, Mumbai (1996)
4. Keller, A.M., Basu, J.: A Predicate-Based Caching Scheme for Client-Server Database Architectures. VLDB J. 5(2), 35–47 (1996)
5. Abbas, M.A., Qadir, M.A.: Cross Attribute Knowledge: A Missing Concept in Semantic Cache Query Processing. In: 13th IEEE International Multitopic Conference (INMIC 2009), Islamabad, Pakistan (2009)
6. Guo, S., Sun, W., Weiss, M.: On satisfiability, equivalence, and implication problems involving conjunctive queries in database systems. IEEE Trans. Knowl. Data Eng. 8(4), 604–616 (1996)
7. Ullman, J.D.: Principles of Database and Knowledge-Base Systems, vol. 11. Computer Science Press (1989)
8. Klug, A.: On Conjunctive Queries Containing Inequalities. ACM 35(1), 146–160 (1988)
9. Rosenkrantz, D.J., Hunt, H.B.: Processing Conjunctive Predicates and Queries. In: Proc. Conf. Very Large Databases, pp. 64–71 (1980)
10. Sun, X., Kamell, N.N., Ni, L.M.: Processing implication on queries. IEEE Trans. Softw. Eng. 5(10), 168–175 (1989)
11. Floyd, R.W.: Algorithm 97 Shortest Path. Comm. ACM 5(6), 345 (1962)
12. Garca-Molina, H., Ullman, J.D., Widom, J.: Database Systems: the Complete Book. GOAL Series (2001)
13. Sample database with test suite, Version 1.0.6 (February 2011), https://launchpad.net/test-db
14. Ali, T., Qadir, M.A., Ahmad, M.: Translation of relational queries into Description Logic for semantic cache query processing. In: 2010 International Conference on Information and Emerging Technologies (ICIET), June 14-16, pp. 1–6 (2010), doi:10.1109/ICIET.2010.5625709
15. Ali, T., Qadir, M.A.: DL based Subsumption Analysis for Relational Semantic Cache Query Processing and Management. In: 10th International Conference on Knowledge Management and Knowledge Technologies, Messe Congress Graz, Austria, September 13 (2010)
16. Ahmed, M., Asghar, S., Qadir, M.A., Ali, T.: Graph Based Query Trimming Algorithm for Relational Data Semantic Cache. In: The International Conference on Management of Emergent Digital EcoSystem, MEDES 2010 (2010)
17. Ahmad, M., Qadir, M.A., Ali, T., Abbas, M.A., Afzal, M.T.: Semantic Cache System, in the book Semantics; Afzal, M.T. (ed.), ISBN: 979-953-307-613-2

A Hierarchical Routing Protocols
for Self-organizing Networks

Hoon Kwon[1], Ho-young Kwak[1,*], Sang-Joon Lee[1], and Sung-Joon Lee[2]

[1] Faculty of Telecommunications and Computer Engineering,
Jeju National University, Jeju, Republic of Korea
{dreamerz,kwak,sjlee}@jejunu.ac.kr
[2] EZ Info Tech Inc,
Jeju Venture Maru #609, 1176-67, 2 do 2 dong, Jeju, Republic of Korea
ez@ez-tec.co.kr

Abstract. Recently studies and technological developments are being actively carried out on applying sensor networks using low-cost, low-power wireless sensors to USNs. Wireless sensor networks are changing from static network environments to active networks capable of generating various environments and rapid transformations, and in such environments the ability to collect and deliver data between sensor nodes is very important. Therefore, an autonomous, efficient network must be designed to link the sensor nodes together. It suggests strained routing protocols that can efficiently self-organized in the event of changes in sensor networks due to node obstruction and environmental factors, and proved their practicality and efficiency. The research also measured energy consumption per node and showed reduction of energy use of 68.1% for GTR, 65.6% for ComHRP, and 4.4% for CTR, and a comparison of average Hops by node according to route establishment between all nodes evidenced a 21.44% efficiency rate.

Keywords: Self-Organized, Hierarchical Routing Protocol, Sensor Networks.

1 Introduction

To realize USN is required different technologies such as signal processing, networks and protocols, embedded systems and distributed processing and Low-cost, low-power wireless sensor network based applications using sensors on the research and technology development is being accelerated[1][2][4].

These tiny sensors to provide sufficient reliability and accuracy is difficult, but Sensor miniaturization and low cost Consisting of hundreds of thousands in the Ad-Hoc Network Formation and Quality of Service over self-organizing sensor, providing high performance in terms of fault tolerant wireless sensor network can be built[1][2].

Wireless sensor networks rather than a static network environment, it is converted to a dynamic network environment, and between sensor nodes and autonomous

---

* Corresponding author.

R. Benlamri (Ed.): NDT 2012, Part I, CCIS 293, pp. 55–62, 2012.
© Springer-Verlag Berlin Heidelberg 2012

self-organizing network should be as efficient. It is an important factor to these wireless sensor networks to collect and transfer of information between nodes[5].

This paper is focused on self-organized hierarchical routing protocols to response to network problems and environmental change in a sensor network. Thus, it is proved that address allocation algorithm for self-organization and search between nodes are efficient. In the section 2, relevant studies and technologies are covered: the studies with related to wireless sensor network and routing protocol of ad-hoc network are investigated; in the section 3, address allocation methods for A-ComHRP and path setting methods are suggested; in the section 4,   conclusion and further study is described.

2   Related Works

Hierarchical routing protocol is a routing method to efficiently manage sensor network based on MAC and PHY of IEEE 802.15.4. Hierarchical routing protocol constitutes a tree type of network topology based on the address allocated while sensor node participates in the network. Therefore, each sensor node plays a role in sending collected data to other sensor node, using allocated address, like the relationship between parent and child. Thus, they are not necessary to have separate routing table to send data to definition node, which is appropriate protocol to sensor nodes whose hardware is small.

2.1   Hierarchical Routing Protocol

Path is determined by the number of hops from parent information and route node. To determine path, route node uses broadcast method and nodes around the route repeatedly performs broadcast and delivered to the node located in the final place of the network. Thus, when the path is determined, nodes desired to send data sends it to parent node. Then, parent nodes received the data in the same way. Again, they send the data to their parent nodes and finally to the route node.

It assumes the ideal topology that all nodes may have child node as parent node. As the depth of network gets deeper, the cost upon the worst search of path increases. Also, it has the limit that it is not responsive to the change of sensor network.

2.2   Hierarchical Routing Protocol That End Node Is Considered

Hierarchical routing algorithm is the routing protocol considered the case that routing is limited due to functional limitation of the existing Hierarchical routing protocol. Sensor node is divided into whether child node exists or not, that address is allocated to each node to handle routing. However, this method considers the part to allocate address and search path. Thus, it has the problem that it is not appropriate to address allocation and to set routing for network reconfiguration upon characteristics of sensor network that frequently changes.

2.3   Complement Hierarchical Routing Protocol

ComHRP[7] is the method to decrease overload of search traffic upon path setting in the existing hierarchical routing protocol. It suggests efficient address allocation method for sensor node. Thus, it shows efficiency in search between nodes through this. Address allocation method is to allocate temporary identification for node identification allocation on the terminal node, to decrease traffic upon search after terminal node, and to handle nodes that cannot have child nodes by environmental factor efficiently, and to cope with the dynamically environmental change more efficiently. However, when searching definition node under the condition that the network is stabilized, the method by [6] protocol and efficiency of path setting are not significantly different. For this reason, additional supplement is required for better method when setting path.

3   Suggested Protocol

3.1   Definition of Problem

Most of routing techniques in wireless sensor network provide node ID based on the static network environment, constitutes network based on the provided node ID and set up routing path. It is not appropriate to apply this method to USN environment which is dynamically changed since energy consumption increases due to the frequent reconfiguration of routing path.

On the contrary, among Ad-Hoc network routing techniques appropriate to the dynamic network environment, proactive routing method as a Table-Driven method requires frequent table renewal under USN environment, while reactive method increases the complication of periodic Synchronization and routing search and delay time, that causes decrease of efficiency.

Given various restrictions of USN environment, further studies on efficient wireless sensor network protocol are required to compensate the defect of existing wireless sensor network and apply merits of static and dynamic network environment.

Thus, this study designs hierarchical routing protocol that efficient reconfiguration is possible in the sensor network.

The routing protocol suggested in this study makes up for existing hierarchical routing protocol and is positively reflected to USN environment. Thus, the protocol is called as A-ComHRP(Adaptive Complement Hierarchical Routing).

3.2   Address Allocation Method

ComHRP suggested in the existing studies can improve the problems of the existing hierarchical routing protocol and indicates efficiency through address allocation algorithm.

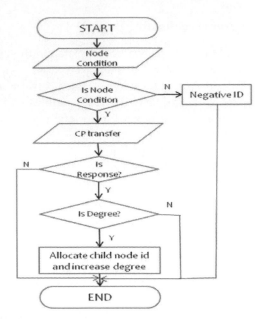

Fig. 1. Algorithm for address allocation of ComHRP

As shown in the Figure 1, algorithm for address allocation of ComHRP allocates imaginary ID using negative numbers for allocation or terminal node ID under unstable condition. Using this method, the existing hierarchical structure can be maintained as it is and traffic while searching can be decreased by omitting search stage toward the lower node using negative numbers. It has the merit of coping with the dynamic environment when disable node occurs or it is recovered.

Thus, the suggested A-ComHRP is designed to measure environmental change and problem of network while handling SYNC in the address allocation algorithm of ComHRP.

Through SYNC treatment, it can identify the condition of node: creation, insertion or deletion. It enables to check if it is device node or whether or not orphan condition.

In creation and insertion of nodes, address allocation method is used in the basic hierarchical routing, while coding absolute value method is used to change the node address with negative numbers in the device node. In this process, device node cannot have lower nodes, so that it reduces node traffic occurred during search between nodes and data transfer. For node deletion, address allocation method is decided upon the condition for node itself or lower nodes or for parent node. For the former case, "0" is multiplied to the address of lower node. If the node deleted when taking coding absolute value, it has "-0" value. When searching, if "-0" exists, search is stopped so that more search is not necessary.

For the latter case, it is considered to be the reconfiguration due to the problem. Thus, the relevant node indicates orphan condition.

In orphan condition, broadcasting occurs to reconfigure all nodes from the relevant sensor node and it is completed when the selected node becomes parent node in the existing studies. In this case, reallocation of node address frequently occurs upon traffic overload and reconfiguration to find the node.

However, A-ComHRP does not always search parent node by broadcasting same as the existing method. It estimates parent's neighbor node and casts the nodes first. Then, the selected nodes from parent's neighbor nodes are reconstituted as parent node. In this way, reallocation of node address is not necessary according to reconfiguration.

3.3   Path Search Method

To search from source node to definition node in the existing hierarchical routing, routing setting and data transfer passes through two stages: first, the highest sink node must be searched; second, path is set from sing node to definition node. Also in the previous study, to set path in ComHRP, process related to end node is added. This method may shorten search stage, but it is considerably longer than that in CTR method that has child node information as a subnet. To resolve this problem, this study applies new method of path setting as seen in Figure 2.

$$A_{PN} = \{ PN \,|SN \in TSN, (SN - 1)/SN_{mc}\}$$
$$A_{PN} = \{ PN \,|SN \in TSN, SN \bmod SN_{mc} , \text{if } n = 0 \ \rightarrow n = SN_{mc}$$

(1)

Here, to set path in A-ComHRP, SN_{de} and PN_{de} values are calculated by using the equation 1.

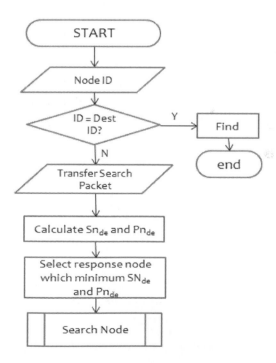

Fig. 2. Search Node Module

Using equation 1, parent node in node A are calculated: 1) take one from the value of its own node; 2) divide the result by the number of exponential order. To find how many nodes(n^{th} nodes) are there to the own node, divide own node by the number of order. Here, the remainder 'n' indicates the node location. That is, if the remainder is n, the value of node order means the node's location. If search is done by recursive method, the location of parent and own nodes can be found in each node. Also, the range of lower node to the own node can be calculated.

However, suggest protocol has bigger variance value of hop according to node and path setting in dynamic network. This occurs when the path is set by making a detour due to unexpected result during the process that following node is selected by searching a neighboring node within the range.

4   Performance Test

4.1   Path Setting Stage for Node Search

To evaluate path setting stages for node search, three cases are established. First, the difference of network depth is 1, indicating the structure is spread out with sink node as the center. Second, the difference is 2, indicating the structure is dispersed with sink node as the center. Third, the difference is 1 in the forest tree structure. In the general tree routing (GTR), path setting passes through stages in child node and upper node in order at the path setting for node search. Thus, path setting stage is shown longest.

In the tree routing that end node is considered(ETR), path setting packet is not sent to the lower stage if it is end node in the network configuration. Accordingly, path setting stage is shown shortened rather than the existing GTR method. Also in ComHRP, path setting stage is the same as ETR if tree routing path is established in the network.

For tree routing with child node information(CTR), path setting is rapidly performed by ID information of child node and information access via subnet. However, subnet tables on all child nodes are necessary for each node and table joint and mapping operation are required as well.

In each case, path setting stages considerably increases as the difference of depth gets larger. However, A-ComHRP proposed in this study reconstructs the shortest node path by using response packet of neighbor node existing within the radius according to broadcasting for node search. It demonstrates high efficiency in node search dispersed with sink node as the center.

4.2   Number of Average Search Hop in All Nodes

In Figure 3, average, Dispersion and Deviation of hop to node 20 is shown from the analysis results of hierarchical routing protocol and A-ComHRP according to simulation model mentioned above.

Existing hierarchical routing protocol indicates the number of hops created after finding optimized path, where change in path is not largely shown, maintained by the depth of network. However, the average number of hops according to search is 3.277 hops in 5×5 simulation model.

A-ComHRP suggested in this study does not search parent and child node in the created network at searching definition node from each node, but search neighbor node is searched through broadcasting within the radius and find the path that the difference between definition node and its parent node is the smallest to set the path. In this method, average number of hops shows 2.574 hops in 5×5 simulation model. This value proves efficiency of 21.44% in definition node search of A-ComHRP.

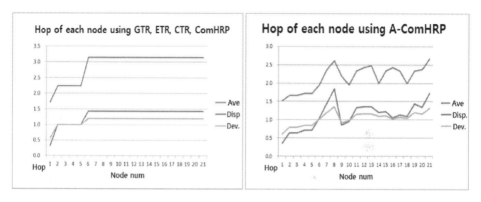

Fig. 3. Average, Deviation and Dispersion of Hop to nodes

4.3   Search Energy Consumption

The biggest energy consumption of sensor in the wireless sensor network indicates when sending and receiving of data packet. Therefore, this study measures energy consumption in each sensor nodes when performing path setting. Energy consumption model is designed by using first order radio model[3]. The suggested A-ComHRP in node setting shows that energy consumption is 68.1% compared to GTR and 65.6% compared to ComHRP. Energy saving indicates 0.4% compared to CTR. As a result, there is no big difference in energy consumption between CTR that optimized routing path is known and by node setting.

5   Conclusion

Hierarchical routing method, A-ComHRP is suggested and its effectiveness is proved through experiments to make up for the weakness of existing hierarchical routing method and ComHRP based on ComHRP and to cope with dynamic environment that frequently occurs in the sensor network.

A-ComHRP facilitates network reconfiguration responding to the frequent node change due to problems in dynamic environment as well as routing establishment and path setting in the static sensor network.

It does not set standard paths with the paths of the parent and child at path setting between nodes, but find the path that the value between definition node and its parent node is the smallest among neighbor node through broadcasting within the range. Therefore, path reset can minimize the path by search. Also, energy consumption by node for search is shown: 68.1% compared to GTR, the general hierarchical routing protocol and 65.6% compared to ComHRP and 4.4% of energy saving compared to CTR.

Average hop of search between all nodes indicates: 3.277 hops for 5×5 simulation in ComHRP; 2.574 hops for 5×5 simulation model in A-ComHRP. It shows efficiency of 21.44%.

Reconfiguration of terminal node in dynamic network is not different from ComHRP. However, reconfiguration by problem of middle node in child node does not search all nodes: original parent node becomes master parent node and brother nodes of master parent node are set as slave parent nodes. So network reconfiguration is done by these slave parent nodes. In this process, traffic by network reconfiguration can be reduced. To maintain the ideal network condition after problem solving process is completed in master parent node, A-ComHRP sends network sink message to master parent node first and reset path of master parent node if it is recovered. However, A-ComHRP has bigger variance value of hop according to node and path setting in dynamic network. This occurs when the path is set by making a detour due to unexpected result during the process that following node is selected by searching a neighboring node within the range. Processing delay time occurs to find the distance difference between definition node and its parent node when searching path. To improve these results, further studies are necessary.

Acknowledgments. This research was supported by the regional technology innovation program of the Ministry of Commerce, Industry and Energy, Republic of Korea.

References

1. Clare, Pottie, Agre: Self-Organizing Distributed Sensor Networks. In: SPIE Conference on Unattened Ground Sensor Technologies and Application, pp. 229–237 (1999)
2. Estrin, D., Govindan, R., Hedemann, J., Kumar, S.: Next Century Challenges: scalable Coordination in Sensor Netwroks. In: ACM MOBICOM 1999 (1999)
3. Heinzleman, W.R., Chandrakasan, A., Balakrishnan, H.: Energy-Efficient Communication Protocol for Wireless Microsensor Networks. In: HICSS 2000, pp. 1–10 (2000)
4. IAlkildiz, F., Su, W., Sankarasubramaniam, Y., Cayirci, E.: Wireless Sensor Network: A Survey. Computer Networks (2002)
5. Mirkovic, J., Venkataramani, G.P., Lu, S., Zhang, L.: A Self-Organizing Appoach to Data forwarding in Large-scale Sensor Networks. IEEE Personal Communication Magazine, 16–27 (2000)
6. Kim, D.Y., Cho, J., Jeong, B.S.: A Practical Algorithm for Clustering and Routing in Hierarchical Sensor Netowkrs. IEICE Trans. on Communications (2007)
7. Kwon, H., Kwak, H.Y., Park, G.R., Kim, J.H.: ComHRP: A Hierarchical Routing protocol in dynamic sensor networks. Computer and Information Sciences, 1–3 (2008)

A Practical Method for Evaluating the Reliability of Telecommunication Network

Mohamed-Larbi Rebaiaia[1], Daoud Ait-Kadi[1],
and Denis Page[2]

[1] Department of Mechanical Engineering, University of Laval,
Quebec (QC), Canada
Mohamed-larbi.rebaiaia@hotmail.com, daoud.aitkadi@gmc.ulaval.ca
[2] Direction générale des réseaux de télécommunications (DGRT)
1500, rue Cyrille-Duquet, Quebec, Canada
Denis.page@cspq.qc.ca

Abstract. The reliability of networks is defined as the probability that a system will perform its intended function without failure over a given period of time. Computing the reliability of networks is an NP-hard problem, which need efficient techniques to be evaluated. This paper presents a network reliability evaluation algorithm using Binary Decision Diagrams (BDD). The solution considers the 2-terminal reliability measure and proceeds first by enumerating the minimal paths set from which a BDD is generated. The algorithm has been implemented in Java and MatLab and experienced using a real radio telecommunication network. The results of such application have testified that the program didn't need large memory size and big time requirement.

Keywords: Minimal pathset, enumeration, two-reliability, networks, algorithm, graphs theory.

1 Introduction

A probabilistic graph $G = (V, E)$ is a finite set V of nodes and a finite set E of incidence relations on the nodes called edges. The edges are considered as transferring a commodity between nodes with a probability P called reliability. They may be directed or undirected and are weighted by their individual reliabilities (see figure 1). Such a graph models a physical network, which represents a linked set of components giving services. The reliability of networks is defined as the probability that systems (networks) will perform their intended functions without failure over a given period of time.

This paper presents an algorithm for determining the reliability of a given network G when one node is identified as the source user s and another as the terminal user t. The 2-terminal reliability $R(G)$, is defined as the probability that at least one path will exist from s to t.

R. Benlamri (Ed.): NDT 2012, Part I, CCIS 293, pp. 63–77, 2012.
© Springer-Verlag Berlin Heidelberg 2012

In the literature, practical techniques for determining the reliability of networks are classified as exact techniques, such as inclusion/exclusion SDP for sum of disjoints products and those based on the well-known network decomposition [1, 7, 9, 14, 20, 22]. Others techniques like simulation for example are considered as approximate methods [23]. In the former techniques, the problem consists of determining MPS for minimal paths set (respectively MCS for minimal cuts set) between s and t given the probability of success for each communication link (edge) in the network. By definition, a MPS (resp. MCS) is a path (respectively a cut) from which it is impossible to extract another path (respectively a Cut) [11, 13, 15, 18, 26].

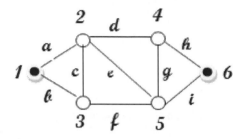

Fig. 1. A probabilistic weighted graph with six nodes (1, 2, 3, 4, 5 and 6) and nine undirected edges (a, b, ... , i)

The concept of MPS and MCS for determining the reliability of probabilistic graphs, appears to have been first explored by some authors in the beginning of the eightieth [1, 11, 18]. In such papers, different algorithms have been proposed to generate MPS/MCS for directed and undirected graphs. Some of them need special data preparation and require advanced mathematics [26]. Shier *et al.* proposed in [18], a simple method to generate MCS directly by inverting MPS. Such a solution has been soon discarded because it was impractical for generating MCS in the presence of large network. Hariri *et al.* give a simple and efficient algorithm. It was implemented and known as the SYREL tool [27]. The SYREL tool incorporates conditional probability, set theory, and Boolean algebra. In many practical cases, the evaluation of the reliability becomes problematic (NP-hard problem), so approximation becomes a possible way to obtain an efficient solution in a minimal running time. However, there are also other methods that find solutions in short time. One of the well-known methods uses BDDs (binary Decision Diagrams) [5, 6]. Because BDDs and reliability factoring representation [22] are formalized from the well-known Shannon decomposition theorem, they are more convenient to derive an algorithm to compute the reliability especially for networks with topologies that contains isomorphic subgraphs. The application of binary diagrams in the reliability analysis framework has been introduced by Coudert [16] and extended to fault trees by Rauzy [24]. Recently, a lot of papers published in reliability literature propose new algorithms based on Reduced ordered BDD (ROBDD). Hardy *et al.* [8] and Lin *et al.* [13] use ROBDD to derive interesting fast solutions for computing reliability of large systems such the 2×100 lattice network which has 2^{99} paths [13, 18]. More recently, an analytical method has been proposed to propagate uncertainties described by continuous probability density functions of a stochastic binary system means of Binary Decision Diagrams [28].

In this paper we propose an efficient algorithm evaluating the 2-terminal network reliability. The algorithm utilizes minimal paths set generated using one of the best and fast methods developed by us. The method uses a simple technique similar to the depth first search algorithm of Tarjan [19], which explores the graph by crossing nodes and edges from the top to the bottom and backtracks until all the nodes are marked. Each time a minimal path is found and a symbolic reliability function is generated by composing the last BDD with the actual one corresponding to the generated path. A new BDD is memorized for the next processing until no path is generated. At each composition, some operations are applied to reduce considerably the size of BDD by merging graphs and structure reductions.

The paper is organized as follows: Section 2 presents some preliminaries concepts such as network and s-t terminal reliability modeling and evaluation. Section 3, gives the description of minimal paths and minimal cuts sets and presents an illustrative example to enumerate them. In section 4, we present some procedures relative to binary decision diagrams representation and theirs extensions to cover network reliability class of problems. In section 5 we detail an experiment application of a real radio telecommunication network. Finally some concluding remarks are given in section 6.

2 Network Modeling

Consider a network $G = (V, E)$ as discussed below. For a specified set of nodes $K \subseteq V$ of G, we denote the K-terminal reliability of G by $R(G_K)$. When $|K| = 2$, $R(G_K)$ is called 2-terminal (or terminal-pair) reliability which defines the probability of connecting the source node with a target node. A success set, is a minimal set of the edges of G such that the vertices in K are connected; the set is minimal so that deletion of any edges causes the vertices in K to be disconnected and this will invalidate the evaluation of the reliability. Topologically, a success set is a minimal tree of G covering all vertices in K. The computation of the K-terminal reliability of a graph may require efficient algorithms. One such solution can be derived directly from the topology of the network by constructing a new parallel-series network using MPS of the original network such that each minimal path constitutes a branch of the parallel-series graph. Then, a characteristic expression $\Phi(X(t))$ is derived from the disjoint expressions of paths terms, and from which the reliability is evaluated after applying Boolean simplification processing. Figure 3, gives an example and the expression of its reliability. Note that $X(t)$ is Boolean state variables vector and each r_i is the value of the reliability of the component (edge) i which replaces the state variable x_i after the reductions.

3 Minimal Paths and Minimal Cuts Sets

Consider a system consisting of m components numbered from 1 to m. Each of these components may be in functioning or failed. Let x_i be the state component and x the state vector, they can be defined as follows:

- $x_i = \begin{cases} 1 & \text{if the component (node - link) is functioning} \\ 0 & \text{if the component (node - link) is failed} \end{cases}$
- $x = (x_1, x_2, \dots, x_m)$ state vector of the system S of order m such that $x \in \Omega_i = \{0,1\}^m$ the state space of the system;

The system is then represented by its structure function $\Phi: \Omega \to \{0,1\}$.

$$\Phi(x) = \begin{cases} 1 & \text{if the system is functioning when the state vector is } x \\ 0 & \text{if the system has failed when the state vector is } x \end{cases}$$

Systems for which $\Phi(x)$ is a non-decreasing function are called coherent systems [25].

Definition 1. If a system contains P MPS $P_1, P_2, \dots, P_p$ and C MCS $C_1, C_2, \dots, C_c$ its structure function can be represented by :

$$\Phi(x) = \max_{1 \le j \le P} \min_{i \in P_j} x_i = \min_{1 \le j \le C} \max_{i \in C_j} x_i \tag{1}$$

If we consider the mathematical expectation $E\{\Phi(X)\}$, and system components are s-independent, the reliability R of a system S can be computed using the following relation (2) :

$$R(S) = Pr\{\Phi(X) = 1\} = E\{\Phi(X)\} = \sum_{X \in \Omega_i} \Phi(X) Pr\{X = x\} \tag{2}$$

and

- $p_i = Pr\{X = 1\}$
- $q_i = Pr\{X = 0\} = 1 - p_i$

$$\tag{3}$$

Also, if MPS $= \{P_1, P_2, \dots, P_m\}$ and MCS $= \{C_1, C_2, \dots, C_m\}$ are mutually exclusive and suppose that $\bar{C}_j$ the inverse of a cut $\bar{C}_j$ represents the event "the components of the jth minimal cut are not functioning", the probability of the union of m events also represents the reliability of a system and can be written in the form of (4).

$$R(S) = \Pr(P_1 \cup P_2 \cup \dots \cup P_m) = \Pr(P_1) + \Pr(P_2) + \dots + P(P_m)$$
$$= 1 - (\Pr(\bar{C}_1) + \Pr(\bar{C}_2) + \dots + \Pr(\bar{C}_n)) \tag{4}$$

Note that, the last expression is easier to be evaluated since it involves a sum of products. Therefore the reliability evaluation become also is easier if we manage to express the MPS/MCS in a disjunctive form. Knowledge of MPS or MCS allows determining the structure function of any coherent system equivalent to that of the original system, such that the configuration is strictly series or parallel.

For the case of complex system $P_1, P_2, \dots, P_m$ are not necessary to be expressed in disjunctive form. They can be transformed using a simple probability theorem (Poincaré-formula) as it is showed in (5) [9, 14, 18].

$$R(S) = \Pr(\cup_i P_i) = \sum_{1 \le i \le m} Pr(P_i) - \sum_{1 \le i_1 < i_2 \le m} Pr(P_{i_1} \cdot P_{i_2}) + \dots + (-1)^{m+1} \cdot Pr(P_1 \cdot P_2 \cdot P_3 \cdots P_m) \tag{5}$$

The relationships for the probability of system failure using cuts set approach are,

$$R_f(S) = \Pr\left(\bigcup_i C_i\right) = \sum_{1 \le i \le n} Pr(\bar{C}_i) - \sum_{1 \le i_1 < i_2 \le n} Pr(\bar{C}_{i_1}.\bar{C}_{i_2}) + \cdots +$$
$$(-1)^{n-1}.Pr(\bar{C}_1.\bar{C}_2.\bar{C}_3 \cdots \bar{C}_n)$$

(6)

3.1 Illustrative Example

Consider a directed *bridge* network in figure 2 (a). MPS and MCS of the network are presented in (7) and (8):

$$\{P1 = \{x1, x4\}; \ P2 = \{x2, x5\} \ and \ P3 = \{x1, x3, x5\}\}. \tag{7}$$

$$\{C1 = \{x1, x2\}; \ and \ C2 = \{x2, x5\}; \ C3 = \{x1, x3, x4\}; \ C4 = \{x4, x5\}\} \tag{8}$$

If the equation (5) is applied using the graph structure of the bridge network (figure 2 (a)), the generated reliability expression is equal to,

$$R = \Pr(P_1 \cup P_2 \cup P_3)$$
$$= \Pr(P_1) + \Pr(P_2) + \Pr(P_3) - \Pr(P_1 \cap P_2) - \Pr(P_1 \cap P_3) - \Pr(P_2 \cap P_3) + \Pr(P_1 \cap P_2 \cap P_3)$$
$$= \Pr(\{x1, x4\}) + \Pr(\{x2, x5\}) + \Pr(\{x1, x3, x5\}) - \Pr(\{x1, x4\} \cap \{x2, x5\})$$
$$\quad - \Pr(\{x1, x4\} \cap \{x1, x3, x5\}) - \Pr(\{x2, x5\} \cap \{x1, x3, x5\})$$
$$\quad + \Pr(\{x1, x4\} \cap \{x2, x5\} \cap \{x1, x3, x5\})$$

$$= p_1 p_4 + p_2 p_5 + p_1 p_3 p_5 - p_1 p_2 p_4 p_5 - p_1 p_3 p_4 p_5 - p_1 p_2 p_3 p_5 + p_1 p_2 p_3 p_4 p_5$$

The reliability expression could also be generated if the structure function of the system is used. It can be written from figure 2 (b) as follows:

$$\Phi(X(t)) = 1 - (1 - x_1 x_4)(1 - x_2 x_5)(1 - x_1 x_3 x_5) = x_1 x_4 + x_2 x_5 + x_1 x_3 x_5 - x_1 x_2 x_4 x_5 - x_1 x_3 x_4 x_5 - x_1 x_2 x_3 x_5 + x_1 x_2 x_3 x_4 x_5$$

So the reliability is :

$$R(t) = \Pr(\Phi(X(t)) = 1)$$
$$= p_1 p_4 + p_2 p_5 + p_1 p_3 p_5 - p_1 p_2 p_4 p_5 - p_1 p_3 p_4 p_5 - p_1 p_2 p_3 p_5 + p_1 p_2 p_3 p_4 p_5$$

- Case MCS (first method : generation from MPS):

$$\Phi(X(t)) = (1 - \overline{x_1}\,\overline{x_4})(1 - \overline{x_2}\,\overline{x_5})(1 - \overline{x_1}\,\overline{x_3}\,\overline{x_5})$$
$$= (1 - \overline{x_1}\,\overline{x_4})(1 - \overline{x_1}\,\overline{x_3}\,\overline{x_5} - \overline{x_2}\,\overline{x_5} + \overline{x_1}\,\overline{x_2}\overline{x_3}\,\overline{x_5})$$
$$= (1 - [\overline{x_1}\,\overline{x_3}\,\overline{x_5} + \overline{x_2}\,\overline{x_5} - \overline{x_1}\,\overline{x_2}\overline{x_3}\,\overline{x_5} + \overline{x_1}\,\overline{x_4} - \overline{x_1}\,\overline{x_3}\overline{x_4}\,\overline{x_5} - \overline{x_1}\,\overline{x_2}\overline{x_4}\,\overline{x_5}$$
$$+ \overline{x_1}\,\overline{x_2}\,\overline{x_3}\,\overline{x_4}\,\overline{x_5}])$$

$R(t) = \Pr\big(\Phi(X(t)) = 1\big)$

$\quad = (1 - [\overline{p_1}\,\overline{p_3}\,\overline{p_5} + \overline{p_2}\,\overline{p_5} - \overline{p_1}\,\overline{p_2}\overline{p_3}\,\overline{p_5} + \overline{p_1}\,\overline{p_4} - \overline{p_1}\,\overline{p_3}p_4\,\overline{p_5} - \overline{p_1}\,\overline{p_2}p_4\,\overline{p_5}$

$\quad\quad + \overline{p_1}\,\overline{p_2}\,\overline{p_3}\,\overline{p_4}\,\overline{p_5}])$

- Case MCS (Second method series-parallel: by equivalence-figure 2(c)):

$\Phi(X(t)) = [(1 - (1 - x_1)(1 - x_2)][(1 - (1 - x_1)(1 - x_5)][(1 - (1 - x_4)(1 - x_5)][(1 - (1 - x_2)(1 - x_3)(1 - x_4)]$

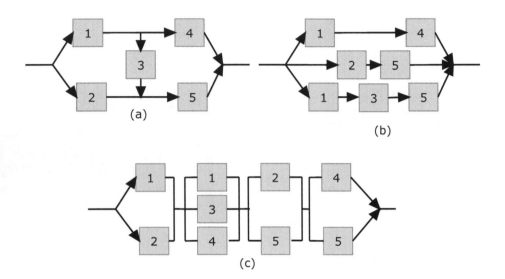

Fig. 2. .(a) System RBD structure, (b) Reliability structure of (a): case MPS. and (c) Reliability structure of (a): case MCS

4 Binary Decision Diagrams

Binary decision diagram (BDD) is a data structure for the symbolic representation of a given Boolean formula and an associated set of decomposition and reduction rules [12, 2, 5, 6]. Boolean formulas are represented using directed acyclic graphs. The mathematical form of a BDD can be written using the decomposition theorem of Shannon or the If-Then-Else function of Bryant [6]. The theorem of Shannon is as follows:

Theorem 1 (Shannon)

$$F(x_1, x_2, \cdots, x_i, \cdots, x_n) = \bar{x}.F(x_1, x_2, \cdots, 0, \cdots, x_n) + x.F(x_1, x_2, \cdots, 1, \cdots, x_n)$$

where x is one of the decision variables, and $F_{x=i}$ is the Boolean function evaluated at $x = i$. Based on theorem 1, Bryant obtains the ITE function as shown in the following:

4.1   ITE Function Manipulation

Suppose that A and B are Boolean functions. If x and y are two variables with an ordering operator ($<$) on variable, such as, $(x < y)$. Applying now the ITE function for the conjunction and the disjunction operators, we show it using the following procedure:

```
Function ite(f,g,h)
    if  f = 0
        Return h ;
    else if  f = 1  then
            Return g ;
        else if  (g = 1)∧ (h = 0) then
                Return f;
            else if g = h then
                    Return g;
            else if ∃ computed-table entry (f, g,h,H) then
                    Return H;
        end if
        xₖ ←top variable of f, g, h;
        H ← new non-terminal node with label xₖ;
                then H ← ite (f |xₖ=1, g |xₖ=1, h |xₖ=1);
                    else H ← ite (f | xₖ =0, g | xₖ =0, h
|xₖₖ=0);
        Reduce  H;
    Add entry (f, g, h,H) to computed-table;
        Return  H;
    end.
```

By choosing a total order over the variables, and applying recursively the Shannon decomposition, it is possible to replace the Boolean variable x by a Boolean function g as follows :

$$f_{x=g} = g \cdot f_{x=1} + g' \cdot f_{x=0}$$

Where f and g are Boolean functions and g' is the complement of g.

In addition to calculating the recursive function ite, we use identities relation to avoid the fact to calculate them again at each time when they occur in a term. These identities are defined as follows:

$$ite(f, 1,0) = f \; ; ite(1, g, h) = g; ite(0, g, h) = h; ite(f, g, g) = g; ite(f, 0,1) = f'$$

Suppose that A and B are Boolean functions. If x and y are two variables with an ordering operator ($<$) on variable, such as, $(x < y)$. Applying now the ITE function for the conjunction and the disjunction operators, we obtain:

$$ite(x, A_{x=1}, A_{x=0}) \wedge ite(x, B_{x=1}, B_{x=0})$$
$$= ite(x, (A_{x=1} \wedge B_{x=1}), (A_{x=0} \wedge B_{x=0}))$$
$$ite(x, A_{x=1}, A_{x=0}) \vee ite(x, B_{x=1}, B_{x=0})$$
$$= ite(x, (A_{x=1} \vee B_{x=1}), (A_{x=0} \vee B_{x=0}))$$
$$ite(x, A_{x=1}, A_{x=0}) \wedge ite(y, B_{y=1}, B_{y=0}) = ite(x, (A_{x=1} \wedge B), (A_{x=0} \wedge B))$$
$$ite(x, A_{x=1}, A_{x=0}) \vee ite(y, B_{y=1}, B_{y=0}) = ite(x, (A_{x=1} \vee B), (A_{x=0} \vee B))$$
$$\text{and} \quad B = ite(y, B_{y=1}, B_{y=0})$$

The following figure shows successive reductions which have been obtained by the application of the ITE procedure, where F is the function structure of a network, x_1, x_2, x_3 are the edge variables and $\overline{x_1}$ and $\overline{x_2}$ their complements.

$$F = x_1 x_2 + \overline{x_1} x_3 + x_1 \overline{x_2} x_3$$

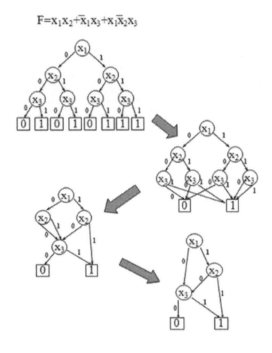

Fig. 3. Binary Decision Tree and its successive reduction graphs

4.2   From OBDD to ROBDD Transformation

Any OBDD can be reduced to a ROBDD by repeatedly eliminating in a bottom-up fashion, any instances of duplicate and redundant nodes. If two nodes are duplicates, one of them is removed and all of its incoming pointers are redirected to its duplicate. If a node is redundant, it is removed and all incoming pointers are redirected to its just one child. The procedure proceeds using information containing in the ROBDD data matrix (see figure 4).

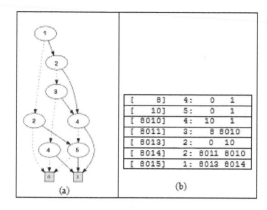

[8]	4:	0	1
[10]	5:	0	1
[8010]	4:	10	1
[8011]	3:	8	8010
[8013]	2:	0	10
[8014]	2:	8011	8010
[8015]	1:	8013	8014

(a) (b)

Fig. 4. A ROBDD and its memory representative (matrix in (b))

4.3 The APPLY Procedure

The APPLY procedure is an efficient tool to combine functions using binary operators like the conjunction and disjunction Boolean operators. It is the major core of our implementing algorithm. It can also be used to complement a function; it suffices in such case to complementing the values of the terminal vertices.

According to Bryant [6], the APPLY procedure takes graphs representing functions f_1 and f_2, a binary operator (say OP) and produces a reduced graph representing the function $f_1 [OP] f_2$. It proceeds as shown in the following figure (figure 5.) and according to the equation (9):

$$f_1 [OP] f_2 = \bar{x}_i \cdot \left(f_1|_{x_i=0} [OP] f_2|_{x_i=0} \right) + x_i \cdot \left(f_1|_{x_i=1} [OP] f_2|_{x_i=1} \right) \tag{9}$$

where $\bar{x}_i$ is the complement of the Boolean variable x_i.

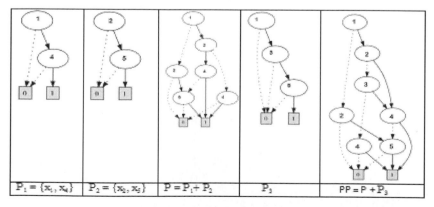

| $P_1 = \{x_1, x_4\}$ | $P_2 = \{x_2, x_5\}$ | $P = P_1 + P_2$ | P_3 | $PP = P + P_3$ |

Fig. 5. An example to show how APPLY algorithm proceeds to compose two Booleans expressions ($f_1 = ac$ and $f_2 = bc$)

4.4   Reliability Evaluation Using BDD

From the programming side, a BDDs simple procedure could be used to compute very easily the reliability of a network. The following algorithm do that job.

```
Algorithm Reliability_evaluation (G, v, z)
    Define the BDD relative to the Boolean 1, call the
    BDD_ONE ;
    Define the BDD relative to the Boolean 0, call the
    BDD_ZERO ;
    Initialise BDD_ALL = BDD_ZERO ;
    Apply the procedure ITE to get the BDD of TERM, say
    BDD_TERM ;
    Make BDD_AND = BDD_1 ;
      Do while .T.
         TERM = pathDFS(G, v, z)
         BDD_AND = BDD_AND .and. BDD_TERM  ;
       BDD_OR = BDD_OR .or. BDD_AND ;
            If last TERM has been encountered
                 Return .F.
            else  BDD_AND = BDD_1 ;
            endif
      enddo
 end.
```

4.5   Testing Example

Let a bridge network as shown in figure 8 from which it can generate 4 minimal paths. The Boolean combination of the minimal paths gives the expression $x_1x_4 + x_1x_3x_5 + x_2x_3x_4 + x_2x_5$ and from which the ROBDD of the figure 7 is designed giving the value of the reliability which is equal to 0.97848.

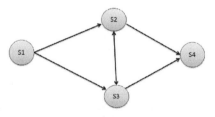

Fig. 6. A bridge network example

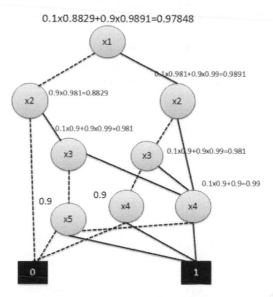

Fig. 7. The corresponding ROBDD and the process for computing the reliability of the network depicted in figure 6

5   CASE STUDY- A Radio Communication Network

To illustrate the algorithms presented in sections 3 and 4, we propose a practical application to a case study problem of undirected regional radio communication network showed in figure 8.

The radio system consists of equipment's scattered across a wide geographic area [25]. A radio equipment can be classified as either fixed, mobile, or portable and includes at least a transmitter, a receiver, and antenna system. Fixed equipment is located at a central site such as headquarter called Master site and usually consists (at least) of a base station, microphone, and antenna. The base station is used to transmit the signal generated through the microphone to portable and mobile equipment in a wide area deserved by the system. The range of the base station depends on its power, antenna system, terrain, carrier transporter (e.g. T1 or E1) and environmental conditions.

The basic components of the radio system are interconnected forming a network. Such network may contain the following necessary elements:

- Radios (portable and mobile).

- Sites (master sites, secondary Radio Frequency (UHF/VHF sites)).

- Zones (a zone or zones with one or more UHF/VHF sites).

- System (single zone or multiple zones with one or more UHF/VHF sites)

In the radio system, a zone is responsible for managing its own elements (sites, re-peaters, subscribers, UHF-VHF and microwave carriers) interconnected using a Local Area Network (LAN). The LANs are interconnected though a high-speed transport network to form a Wide Area Network (WAN). The WAN allows user configuration information, call processing information, and audio to be conveyed throughout the system.

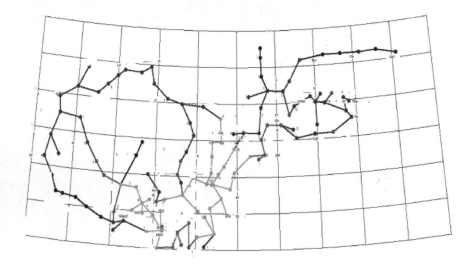

Fig. 8. A regional radio communication network

The graph in Figure 8, presents the radio communication network. Each node is a standard site or a master site. There are more than 160 sites and between them three master sites and one is used as standby and will be activated in case of an active mas-ter site falls. The link between sites is insured using microwave system. Table 1 and Table 2 give respectively the reliability of each site and the microwave link which is determined using the availability generated by the system. Because that the mean time to repair is negligible the reliability is taken as equal to the reliability. The application of the program gives the results depicted inTable 3.

Table 1. The reliability values on each node of the network(this matrix is uincomplete)

	A	B	C	D	E	F
A	0,99992175					
B		0,99987676				
C			0,99996686			
D				0,99987740		
E					0,99996722	
F						0,9999628

Table 2. The reliability of each microwave link between two nodes

	B	C	D	E	F	G
A	0,999987	0,999996	0,999998	0,999997	0,999992	0,999994
B	0,999992	0,999999	0,999996	0,999998	0,999999	0,999990
C	0,999986	0,999995	0,999989	0,999998	0,999998	0,999997
D	0,999999	0,999988	0,999985	0,999989	0,999993	0,999990
E	0,999996	0,999986	0,999988	0,999990	0,999982	0,999984
F	0,999970	0,999976	0,999997	0,999982	0,999997	0,999974
G	0,999999	0,999993	0,999998	0,999995	0,999997	0,999988
H	0,999995	0,999991	0,999998	0,999990	0,999999	0,999996
I	0,999999	0,999983	0,999987	0,999995	0,999996	0,999998
J	0,999987	0,999992	0,999990	0,999987	0,999998	0,999982
K	0,999985	0,999995	0,999986	0,999996	0,999997	1
L	0,999994	0,999994	0,999980	0,999993	0,999997	0,999991
M	0,999988	0,999991	0,999984	0,999998	0,999976	0,999998
N	0,999992	0,999992	0,999985	0,999985	0,999974	0,999999
O	0,999996	0,999982	0,999998	0,999999	0,999995	0,999999
P	0,999966	0,999997	0,999996	0,999988	0,999977	0,999979
Q	0,999994	0,999989	0,999999	0,999999	0,999990	0,999989
R	0,999996	0,999997	0,999985	0,999994	0,999997	0,999981
S	0,999998	0,999991	0,999996	0,999977	0,999992	0,999997
T	0,999999	0,999995	0,999999	0,999981	0,999998	0,999998
V	0,999999	0,999999	0,999993	0,999997	0,999987	0,999997

Table 2, presents the reliability corresponding to each node, where each node represents a station site. These values have been determined using other methods and how we have obtained them is not concerned in this paper, but the reader is invited to consult the project report in Ait-Kadi *et al.* (2009). The following table represents just a small part of the original result matrix.

Table 3. The reliability joining any two nodes (this is a part of a big table of dimension = 156 links x 156 links)

	B	C	D	E	F	G
A	0,99985	0,9997959	0,99992337	0,99984371	0,9998442920	0,99985826
B		0,9998054	0,99978802	0,99985322	0,9998538015	0,99986777
C			0,99993126	0,99971788	0,9997184606	0,99973243
D				0,99991406	0,9999146480	0,99992862
E				0,99969754	0,9996981246	0,99971209
F				0,99984189	0,9998424798	0,99985645
G					0,9998444940	0,99985846
H						0,99985904

6   Conclusion

A method for evaluating the 2-terminal reliability has been proposed in this paper. We have used depth first search (DFS) algorithm for minmal paths set discovering and

Binary Decision Diagrams (BDD) for reduction and evaluation of networks reliability. The program runs on some well-known benchmarks and gives good execution time. We remain convinced that the program will operate on more complex instances of hundreds of nodes and links and even more. We have applied the program to a regional radio communication network. Despite that the evaluation of the reliability is a big problem in our case, the program have computed the reliability of any path taken between any two nodes of the network and finally by composing all these reliabilities we compute the reliability of the network. We confirm that all the computing procedures were executed in a finite time not exceeding some seconds.

References

1. Abraham, J.A.: An Improved Algorithm for Network Reliability. IEEE Transaction on Reliability, 58–61 (1979)
2. Akers, S.B.: Binary Decision Diagrams. IEEE Transactions on Computers C-27, 509–516 (1978)
3. Andersen, H.R.: An Introduction to Binary Decision Diagrams, Lecture Notes. IT University of Copenhagen (1999)
4. Bollig, B., Ingo, W.: Improving the Variable Ordering of OBDDs Is NP-Complete. IEEE Transactions on Computers 45, 993–1002 (1996)
5. Bryant, R.E.: Graph-Based Algorithms for Boolean Function Manipulation. IEEE Transactions on Computers C-35, 677–691 (1986)
6. Bryant, R.E.: Symbolic Boolean Manipulation with Ordered Binary Decision Diagrams. ACM Computing Surveys 24, 293–318 (1992)
7. Dotson, W.P., Gobien, J.O.: A new analysis technique for probabilistic graphs. IEEE Trans. Circuits and Systems Cas-26(10), 855–865 (1979)
8. Hardy, G., Lucet, C., Limnios, N.: K-Terminal Network Reliability Measures With Binary Decision Diagrams. IEEE Trans. on Reliability 56(3), 506–515 (2007)
9. Heidtmann, K.D.: Smaller Sums of Disjoint Products by Subproduct Inversion. IEEE Transaction on Reliability 38, 305–311 (1991)
10. Institute of Electrical and Electronics Engineers, IEEE Standard Computer Dictionary: A Compilation of IEEE Standard Computer Glossaries, New York, NY (1990)
11. Jasmon, G.B., Kai, O.S.: A New Technique in Minimal Path and Cutset Evaluation. Reprinted from IEEE Transactions on Reliability R-34, 136–143 (1985)
12. Lee, C.Y.: Representation of Switching Circuits by Binary-Decision Programs. Bell Systems Technical Journal 38, 985–999 (1959)
13. Lin, H.Y., Kuo, S.Y., Yeh, F.M.: Minimal cutset enumeration and network reliability evaluation by recursive merge and BDD. In: Proceedings of the Eighth IEEE International Symposium on Computers and Communication, pp. 1341–1346 (2003)
14. Liu, H.H., Yang, W.T., Liu, C.C.: An improved minimizing algorithm for the summation of disjoint products by Shannon's expansion. Microelectronic Reliability 33, 599–613 (1993)
15. Locks, M.O., Wilson, J.M.: Note on disjoint products algorithms. IEEE Transactions on Reliability 41, 81–84 (1992)
16. Coudert, O., Madre, J.C.: Implicit and incremental computation of primes and essential primes of Boolean functions. In: Proc. of the 29th ACM/IEEE Design Automation Conference, pp. 36–39. IEEE Computer Society Press (1992)

17. Rudell, R.: Dynamic variable ordering for ordered binary decision diagrams. In: Proceedings of the IEEE/ACM Conference on Computer-Aided Design, pp. 42–47 (1993)
18. Shier, D.R., Whited, D.E.: Algorithms for generating minimal cutsets by inversion. IEEE Transaction on Reliability R-34, 314–319 (1985)
19. Tarjan, R.: Depth-first search and linear graph algorithms. SIAM Journal of Computing 1, 146–160 (1972)
20. Theolougou, R., Carlier, J.G.: Factoring & Reduction for networks with imperfect vertices. IEEE Transaction on Reliability 40, 210–217 (1991)
21. Valian, L.G.: The Complexity of enumerating and reliability problems. SIAM Journal of Computing 8, 410–421 (1979)
22. Wood, R.K.: Factoring algorithms for computing K-terminal network reliability. IEEE Transaction on Reliability R-35, 269–278 (1986)
23. Fishman, G.S.: A Comparison of four Monte Carlo methods for estimating the probability of s-t connectedness. IEEE Transaction on Reliability R-35, 145–154 (1986)
24. Rauzy, A.: New Algorithms for fault tree analysis. Reliability Eng. and Systems Safety 40, 203–210 (1993)
25. Ait-kadi, D., Rebaiaia, M.L., Merlano, A.: Modèle d'évaluation des performances du réseau national intégré de radiocommunications (RENIR). Laval University, RP, Canada (2009)
26. Yan, L., Taha, H., Landers, L.L.: A recursive Approach for Enumerating Minimal Cutsets in a Network. IEEE Transactions on Reliability 43, 383–388 (1994)
27. Hariri, S., Raghavendra: SYREL- A symbolic reliability algorithm based on path and cutest methods. IEEE Transactions on Reliability C-36, 1224–1232 (1987)
28. Ulmeanu, A.P.: Analytical Method to Determine Uncertainty Propagation in Fault Trees by Means of Binary Decision Diagrams. IEEE Transactions on Reliability 61(1), 84–94 (2012)

Combining Classifiers for Spam Detection

Fatiha Barigou, Naouel Barigou, and Baghdad Atmani

Computer Science Laboratory of Oran
Computer Science department, Faculty of Science,
University of Oran
BP 1524, El M'Naouer, Es Senia, 31000 Oran, Algeria
{fatbarigou,barigounaouel,atmani.baghdad}@gmail.com

Abstract. Nowadays e-mail has become a fast and economical way to exchange information. However, unsolicited or junk e-mail also known as spam quickly became a major problem on the Internet and keeping users away from them becomes one of the most important research area. Indeed, spam filtering is used to prevent access to undesirable e-mails. In this paper we propose a spam detection system called "*3CA&1NB*" which uses machine learning to detect spam. "*3CA&1NB*" has the characteristic of combining three cellular automata and one naïve Bayes algorithm. We discuss how the combination learning based methods can improve detection performances. Our preliminary results show that it can detect spam effectively.

Keywords: spam, cellular automaton, Naïve Bayes, classifier combination.

1   Introduction

Today, email has become very important in communication via the Internet. This is a quick and economical way to exchange information. However, users find themselves quickly overwhelmed with quantities of unsolicited or unwanted messages also known as spam. Indeed, some recent studies shows that about 95,6% of the e-mails sent daily are spam [30]. The major problem concerning spam is that it is the receiver who is paying in terms of its time, bandwidth and disk space.

This emergence involved the necessity of providing filtering systems designed to prevent access to spam. Many solutions have emerged. Some of them are based on the header of the email such as black list, white list and DNS checking. Other solutions are based on the text content of the e-mail such as filtering based on machine learning. Many techniques have been developed to classify e-mails –for good review the reader can look, e.g., [11].

In this paper, we propose a textual content-based analysis using two different machine learning algorithms for automatic spam filtering. We focus our attention on the combination of classifiers, and we demonstrate that it can be applied to improve the filtering performance of spam. The remainder of this paper is organized as follows. We overview related work according to spam detection in section 2. In section 3, we present our approach. The extraction of features vector is described, and

R. Benlamri (Ed.): NDT 2012, Part I, CCIS 293, pp. 78–89, 2012.
© Springer-Verlag Berlin Heidelberg 2012

the experimentation of each used algorithm is studied. We also show the efficiency of combining these algorithms to improve the filtering accuracy and we compare the results with other published works. Conclusions are finally drawn in section 4.

2   Related Work

A number of different approaches have been taken for spam filtering [20, 23]. Some of them are based on the header of the email such as black list [10], white list [12] and DNS checking [13]. However, these simplistic methods have several shortcomings. So researchers moved towards machine learning techniques for their success in text classification [21].

Upasana and chakraverty [25] presented a quantitative as well as qualitative comparative evaluation of existing text classification techniques with focus on email filtering and potential application to general email management. They presented the accuracy results of different text classifiers on different data sets for spam filtering.

Subramanian et al. [24] summarizes most common techniques used for anti-spam filtering by analyzing the e-mail content and also looks into machine learning algorithms such as Naïve Bayesian (NB) [17], support vector machine (SVM) [27] and neural network that have been adopted to detect and control spam [7].

The first scholarly publication on Bayesian spam filtering was by Sahami et al. in 1998 [17]. That work used bag of words representation and binary weighting. However, the training and the test data were not large enough in the experiment and the data was not publicly available.

Androutsopoulos et al. [2] compared a multinomial NB classifier with a KNN variant classifier named TIMBL; both methods achieved very high classification accuracy and clearly outperformed the keyword based filter of Outlook 2000.

Schneider [23] performed experiments with two statistical classifier models multivariate Bernoulli model and a multinomial model. To select the words within the vocabulary, different feature selection measures were used. Experiments obtained very high filtering rates higher than 95 %.

Vapnik et al. [27] are the first who propose SVM classification method to filter spam. They compared SVM with other classification techniques and find that SVM shows best performance with the binary feature vectors.

Zhang et al. [28] evaluate several learning algorithms on four corpora – Ling Spam, PU1, SpamAssassin, and ZH1. ZH1 is a private corpus of Chinese messages. Only the Total Cost ratio statistic is reported.

Cormack and Lynam [8] tested the real-world spam filtering tools SpamAssassin, Bogofilter, SpamProbe and CRM114 against the Ling Spam corpus. They found that real spam filters were in general unable to classify the Ling Spam messages correctly.

Recently, Santos et al. [19] explore the use of semantics in spam filtering by representing e-mails with the enhanced Topic-based Vector Space Model (eTVSM) which uses an ontology to represent the different relations between terms such as synonyms, homonyms and other linguistic phenomena [4]. Based upon this representation, they apply several well-known machine-learning models (NB, KNN, SVM and decision tree) and show that the proposed method provides high percentages of spam detection whilst keeping the number of misclassified legitimate messages low.

A number of ensemble classification methods have been also studied. Carreras and Marquez [6] improved results on the LingSpam corpus by using boosting decision trees with the AdaBoost algorithm. Compared with two learning algorithms, the induction decision trees (DT) and NB, the method clearly outperformed the above two learning algorithms.

Sakkis et al. [18] combined a Naïve Bayes (NB) and k-nearest neighbor (k-NN) classifiers by stacking method and found that the ensemble achieved better performance.

Lai and Tsai [15] compare four approaches, including NB, term frequency/inverse document frequency (TF-IDF), KNN and SVM in spam filtering. They used stemming technique and trimmed the stopping words in the preprocessing of emails and then combined with TF-IDF and NB methods. The results show the combination has the best performance than any single filters.

Rios and Zha [16] applied random forests (RF), an ensemble of decision trees, using a combination of text and meta data features. For low false positive spam rates, RF was shown to be overall comparable with support vector machines (SVM) in classification accuracy. Also, Koprincha et al. [14] studied the application of random forests to Spam filtering. The LingSpam and PU1 corpora with 10-fold cross-validation were used, selecting 256 features based on either information gain or the proposed term-frequency variance (TFV). Random forests produced the best overall results.

Shih et al. [22] proposed an architecture for collaborative agents, in which algorithms running in different clients can interact for the classification of messages. The individual methods considered include NB, Fisher's probability combination method, DT and neural networks. In the framework developed, the classification given by each method is linearly combined, with the weights of the classifiers that agree (disagree) with the overall result being increased (decreased). The authors argued that the proposed framework has important advantages, such as robustness to failure of single methods and easy implementation in a network.

For a complete review of these different machine learning algorithms used in spam detection we can refer to [11]. Although these studies have reported some encouraging results, more research efforts and better email filtering techniques are still in demand.

3   Our Approach to Spam Detection

The general principle of the approach of classification is the following: Let E be the set of e-mails to be classified. To each e-email e of E one can associate a particular attribute, namely, its class label C. C takes its value in the class of labels (0 for legitimate, 1 for spam). The attribution of e-mails to class label C is done by the function Ω called the classifier:

$$\Omega : E \rightarrow \{0, 1\}$$

Our study consists in building a system to predict the attribute class of each new e-mail. To do it three steps are considered:

- Pre-processing and selection step which consists of extracting the features from the training set and selecting those which best discriminate classes.
- Machine learning step which aims to construct a synthetic model by the use of algorithms.
- Evaluation and validation step which consists on assessing the quality of the learned model on the test data set.

3.1 Linguistic Preprocessing and Feature Selection

We used the publicly available LingSpam corpora [2]. It comprises 2893 different e-mails, of which 2412 are legitimate e-mails obtained by downloading digests from the list and 481 are spam e-mails retrieved from one of the authors of the corpus [1, 18].

The first step in the process of constructing a classifier is the transformation of the e-mails into a format appropriate for the classification algorithms. Using the indexing module that we have implemented, we can (a) establish an initial list of terms by performing a segmentation of text into words, (b) eliminate stop words using a pre-defined stop list and (c) we can also use a variant of the Porter algorithm to perform stemming of the different retained words. Prior experiments [5] have shown that stemming improves classification performance.

Since the number of terms after this preprocessing phase is still very high, and to reduce the computational cost and improves the classification performance, we must select those that best represent the emails and remove less informative and noisy ones. Based on a study of Yang and Pedersen [29] indicating the most used feature selectors in text categorization, we have implemented three feature selectors: Information gain (IG), mutual information (MI) and χ2-statistic (CHI). The system calculates the chosen measure for all the terms, and then takes the first k terms corresponding to larger scores.

After feature selection process, each e-mail is represented by a vector that contains a weighting for every selected attribute, which represents the importance of that term in that e-mail. We deal with a binary weighting. The j-th e-mail is represented by the characteristic vector $\overrightarrow{X_j} = (a_{1j}, a_{2j,...}, a_{kj})$ where $a_{ij} = 1$ if the term "i" is present in document "j", 0 otherwise.

3.2 Individual Classifiers

In our work, two algorithms including cellular automaton CASI [3] and Naïve bayes algorithms has been experimented.

Naïve Bayes Classifier

NB which is the most frequently used classifier in spam filtering [1] is a simple but highly effective Bayesian learner. It uses the training data to estimate the probability that an instance belongs to a particular class. In our experiments, each message is represented as a binary vector $\vec{x} = (x_1, \cdots, x_T)$ where $x_i = 1\,(i = 1 \cdots T)$ if a particular term t_i of the vocabulary is present, otherwise $x_i = 0$.

From Bayes' theorem, the probability that a message with vector $\vec{x} = (x_1, \cdots, x_T)$ belongs to category $C = \{spam, legitimate\}$ is: $P(c\,/\,\vec{x}) = \dfrac{P(c) \times P(\vec{x}\,/\,c)}{P(\vec{x})}$ since the denominator does not depend on the category, NB classifies each e-mail in the category that maximizes the product $P(c) \times P(\vec{x}\,/\,c)$ the a priori probabilities $P(c)$ are typically estimated by dividing the number of training e-mails of category c by the total number of training e-mails. And the probabilities $P(\vec{x}\,/\,c)$ are calculated as follows:

$$P(\vec{x}\,/\,c) = \prod_{i=1}^{i=T} P(x_i\,/\,c) \qquad \text{where} \quad P(x_i\,/\,c) \text{ is fraction of emails of class c that}$$

contain term t_i.

Cellular Automaton CASI [3]

Cellular automaton CASI (Cellular Automaton for Symbolic Induction) is a cellular method of generation, representation and optimization of induction graphs (Sipina method) generated from a set of learning examples. It produces conjunctive rules from a Boolean induction graph representation that can power a cellular inference engine. This Cellular-symbolic system is organized into cells where each cell is connected only with its neighbors (subset of cells). All cells obey in parallel to the same rule called local transition function, which results in an overall transformation of the system. CASI uses a knowledge base in the form of two layers of finite automata. The first layer, called *CelFact*, represents the facts base and the second layer, called *CelRule*, represents the rule base. In each layer, the content of a cell determines whether and how it participates in each inference step: at every step, a cell can be active or passive, can take part in the inference or not. The states of cells are composed of three parts: *EF*, *IF* and *SF*, and *ER*, *IR* and *SR* which are the input, internal state and output parts of the *CelFact* cells, and of the *CelRule* cells, respectively. The neighborhood of cells is defined by two incidence matrices called R_E, R_S respectively. They represent the input respectively output relation of the facts and are used in forward chaining.

- The input relation, noted iREj, is: if (fact i ∈ Premise of rule j) then iREj =1 else iREj = 0.
- The output relation, noted iRSj, is: if (fact i ∈ Conclusion of rule j) then iRSj =1 else iRSj =0.

The cellular automaton dynamics is implemented as a cycle of an inference engine made up of two local transitions functions $\delta fact$ and $\delta rule$.

- The transition function $\delta fact$, corresponding to the evaluation, selection and filtering phases is defined as:

$$(EF, IF, SF, ER, IR, SR) \xrightarrow{\delta_{fact}} (EF, IF, EF, ER + (R_E^T \times EF), IR, SR)$$

- The transition function $\delta rule$, corresponding to the execution phase, is defined as:

$$(EF, IF, SF, ER, IR, SR) \xrightarrow{\delta_{rule}} (EF + (R_S \times ER), IF, SF, ER, IR, \overline{ER})$$

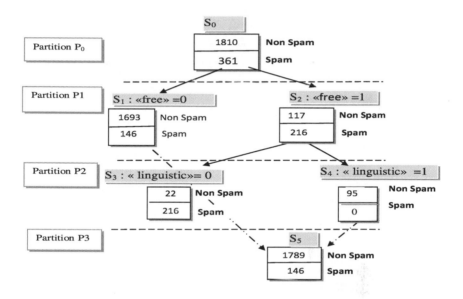

Fig. 1. Example of an induction graph

During the learning phase, the Sipina method produces a graph. From this graph, a set of rules is inferred. They are in the form of "if condition then conclusion". For example, in the graph of Figure 1, we have the rule "*if the term 'free' is absent (= 0) in the email then the email is legitimate*" (majority class of the node S1 in partition P1).

In the cellular automaton CASI, this set of rules is modeled as follows:

1. A Boolean facts base, *CelFact*, contains all the conditions and conclusions facts of such rules (e.g. "free" = 0; "free" = 1; class = legitimate; class = spam ...).
2. A Boolen Rule base, *CelRule*, contains all the generated rules.
3. An input matrix, R_E, memorizes premises of the rules.
4. An output matrix, R_S, memorizes conclusions of the rules.

Forward chaining will allow the model to move from initial configuration to the next configurations G(1), G(2) ... G(i). The inference stops after stabilization with a final configuration. At this step the construction of cellular model is complete.

Table 1 presents the final configuration corresponding to the example of Figure 1. Three rules, represented by CelRule layer are deduced from the graph. The premises and conclusions of these rules are stored in CelFact layer. The premises are the terms used in classification and the last two facts are the two classes. Note that no facts are established: EF = 0. In the input matrix R_E (respectively output matrix R_S) are stored the premises (respectively the conclusions) of each rule. The rule R1, for example, has as premise *"free = 0"*, and as a conclusion *"class = Legitimate"*. Interaction between these two layers is done by δfact and δrule.

Table 1. Cellular model: final configuration

Rules	ER	IR	SR
R1	0	1	0
R2	0	1	0
R3	0	1	0
CelRule			

Facts	EF	IF	SF
free=0	0	1	0
free=1	0	1	0
linguistic=0	0	1	0
linguistic=1	0	1	0
S3:class=spam	0	1	0
S5:class=legitimate	0	1	0
CelFact			

R_E	R1	R2	R3
free = 0	1	0	0
free =1	0	1	1
linguistic=0	0	1	0
linguistic=1	0	0	1
S_3:class=spam	0	0	0
S_5:class=legitimate	0	0	0

R_S	R1	R2	R3
free = 0	0	0	0
free =1	0	0	0
linguistic=0	0	0	0
linguistic=1	0	0	0
S_3: class=spam	0	1	0
S_5:class=legitimate	1	0	1

Experiments

To evaluate performance we calculated spam precision (SP), spam recall (SR), spam F1 measure (F1), accuracy (A) and the global error rate (E).

The experiments were performed with a k-fold cross validation with k = 10. In this way, our dataset was split 10 times into 10 different sets of learning sets (90% of the total dataset) and testing sets (10% of the total data). We conduct the training-test procedure ten times and use the average of the ten performances as final result. We have proceeded as follow:

- Stop word removal: stop words (from a list) were removed from each e-mail,
- Stemming: Porter's stemmer was applied.
- Term selection: Terms were selected based on IG, IM and Chi statistic.

Through these experiments, we found that the quality of prediction in CASI becomes increasingly better in terms of precision, recall and accuracy from 300 selected terms. We also found that the measure function IG leads to a better prediction (precision, recall and accuracy) than the other two ones. Finally, we found that the CASI approach is stabilizing from 500 selected terms when we use the IG function and leads to an interesting prediction quality: precision: 98.1% Recall: 84.2%, accuracy: 97.1%. This reduces the error rate to 2.9%.

NB reaches the maximum when the number of terms retained is equal to 200 then the performance degrades. With IG selection, we have precision=99.0%, recall=82,5%, accuracy=96,3.

When selecting with MI or Chi, the results are not satisfactory. We see that the recall is very low.

Table 2 presents the obtained results by the two algorithms on the LingSpam data set. It shows that the best algorithm is CASI with IG selector.

Table 2. Best configurations of NB, CASI and the corresponding performance

Classifier	*Feature Selector*	*Attribute size*	*SP (%)*	*SR (%)*	*F1 (%)*	*A (%)*
NB	IG	200	82,5	99,0	89,9	96,3
CASD-1	IG	500	98,1	84,2	90,62	97,1
CASD-2	χ2	200	75,0	4,20	7,95	84,1
CASD-3	MI	400	91,9	47,60	48,00	90,1

3.3   Classifier Combination

As shown in table 2, the CASI and Naïve Bayes algorithms displayed different performances on the metrics. Although CASI gives the best results when selecting with IG, combining algorithms may provide better results.

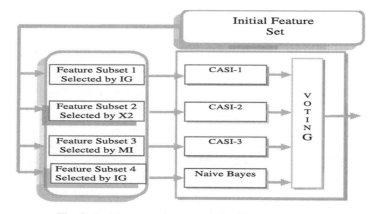

Fig. 2. Architecture of proposed classifiers combination

Previous theoretical research [9, 26] indicated that combining several classifiers is effective only if there is a substantial level disagreement among them. As a result, methods for creating ensembles focus on producing diversified base classifiers. Combination can be done by manipulating the training samples, manipulating the input features, using different learning techniques to the same data. In this paper, we have chosen to consider combination by manipulating both features and using two different classifiers (CASI and NB).

The proposed approach termed *3CA&1NB* (See figure 2) uses three cellular automata classifiers (CASI), where each one is trained with a feature subset. These subsets are selected with three different functions [29]: Information gain (IG), mutual information, and Chi-2 statistic respectively. These classifiers are combined with NB classifier trained with a feature subset selected by IG measure. In our work, we experiment a combining classifier method:

- Majority voting: e-mail is considered spam if the majority of classifiers (CASI-1, CASI-2, CASI-3, NB) or at least two classifiers considered it as spam.

Figure 3 presents a comparison between the three CASI predict models, the NB model and the majority voting model on the Ling Spam data set. The obtained results confirm the well interest to use the combining classifiers. Indeed, majority voting approach provides better results than CASI-1. One clearly sees the reduction in the global error rate of 0.29 for CASI-1 predict model to 0.20 by the majority voting.

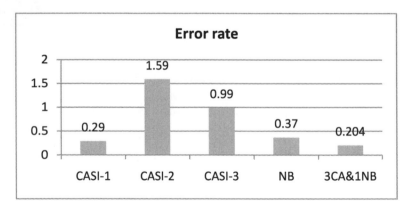

Fig. 3. Comparison of CASI model and NB model with combination approach

3.4   Comparison with Previous Work

To compare our classification method with other techniques, we include the results of experiments on the LingSpam corpus with two other classifiers proposed in the literature:

- NB: we include the best results reported by Androutsopoulos *et al.*[2] for the naive Bayesian approach. Using a version of the lemmatized LingSpam corpus and mutual information (MI) as a metric for attribute selection, they found that NB classifier works best with a term set equal to 100.
- K-NN: from the same paper [2], we include the best results reported for a variant of the nearest neighbor algorithm (TiMBL). As in the case of NB, they perform the selection of terms based on the MI metric, and obtain optimal results with a smaller number of terms (equal to 50) for $k = 1$ and $k = 2$.
- Ensemble approach (Stacking) developed by Sakkis *et al.*[18]. They combined a Naïve Bayes and k-nearest neighbor (k-NN) classifiers by stacking method.

Table 3 further highlights the performance of "3CA&1NB" compared to other published works. The results indicate improved performance when classifying with *3CA&1NB*. It is clear that the former outperforms NB, K-NN and stacking in accuracy and F1-measure

Table 3. Classification performance of 3CA&1NB compared to published works

	Spam P (%)	Spam R (%)	Spam F1 (%)	A (%)
NB	99,02	82,35	89,92	96,93
TiMBL(1)	95,92	85,27	90,28	96,89
TiMBL(2)	97,1	83,19	89,61	96,75
Stacking	90,8	91,9	91,3	97,1
3CA&1NB	98,2	89,36	93,54	97,96

4   Conclusion

In this paper, we studied and highlighted a combination of a cellular machine and NB classifiers based on content analysis for improving spam filtering. However, many future work directions can be considered.

As a future perspective, we will investigate the effect of combining more types of machine learning algorithms, which is expected to be positive, and also, exploring other combination techniques to further increase accuracy.

References

1. Androutsopoulos, I., Koutsias, J.: An Evaluation of Naive Bayesian Networks. In: Machine Learning in the New Information Age, Barcelona, Spain, pp. 9–17 (2000)
2. Androutsopoulos, I., Paliouras, G., Karkaletsis, V., Sakkis, G., Spyropoulos, C.D., Stamatopoulos, P.: Learning to filter spam e-mail: a comparison of a naïve Bayesian and a memory based approach. In: Proc. Workshop on Machine Learning and Textual Information Access, PKDD, Lyon, France, pp. 1–13 (2000)
3. Atmani, B., Beldjilali, B.: Knowledge Discovery in Database: Induction Graph and Cellular Automaton. Computing and Informatics Journal 26, 171–197 (2007)

4. Awad, A., Polyvyanyy, A., Weske, M.: Semantic querying of business process models. In: Proc. International Conference on Enterprise Distributed Object Computing Conference, EDOC, pp. 85–94 (2008)
5. Barigou, N., Barigou, F., Atmani, B.: A Boolean model for spam detection. In: Proceedings of the International Conference on Communication, Computing and Control Applications, Tunisia, pp. 450–455 (2011)
6. Carreras, X., Marquez, L.: Boosting trees for anti-spam email filtering. In: 4th International Conference on Recent Advances in Natural Language Processing, Bulgaria, pp. 58–64 (2001)
7. Clark, J., Koprinska, I., Poon, J.: A neural network based approach to automated e-mail classification. In: IEEE International Conference on Web Intelligence, Halifax, Canada, pp. 702–705 (2003)
8. Cormack, G., Lynam, T.: Online supervised spam filter evaluation. ACM Transactions On Information Systems 25(3) (2007)
9. Dietterich, T.G.: Ensemble Methods in Machine Learning. In: Kittler, J., Roli, F. (eds.) MCS 2000. LNCS, vol. 1857, pp. 1–15. Springer, Heidelberg (2000)
10. Green, T.: How URL Spam Filtering Beats Bayesian/Heuristics Hands Down (2005), http://www.greenviewdata.com/documents/white_papers/ssh_url_filtering_white_paper.pdf (last date accessed: January 8, 2012)
11. Guzella, T.S., Caminhas, W.M.: A review of machine learning approaches to spam filtering. Expert Systems with Applications 36(7), 10206–10222 (2009)
12. Heron, S.: Technologies for spam detection. Network Security, 11–15 (2009)
13. Jung, J., Sit, E.: An empirical study of spam traffic and the use of DNS black lists. In: 4th ACM Conference on Internet Measurement, New York, USA, pp. 370–375 (2004)
14. Koprinska, I., Poon, J., Clarck, J., Chan, J.: Learning to classify e-mail. Information Sciences 177, 2167–2187 (2007)
15. Lai, C., Tsai, M.: An empirical performance comparison of machine learning methods for spam e-mail categorization. In: 4th International Conference on Hybrid Intelligent Systems, pp. 44-48 (2004)
16. Rios, G., Zha, H.: Exploring support vector machines and random forests for spam detection. In: First International Conference on Email and Anti Spam (CEAS), California, USA (2004)
17. Sahami, M., Dumais, S., Heckerman, D., Horvitz, E.: A Bayesian Approach to Filtering Junk E-Mail. In: Learning for Text Categorization, AAAI Technical Report WS-98-05 (1998)
18. Sakkis, G., Androutsopoulos, I., Paliouras, G., Karkaletsis, V.: Stacking classifiers for anti-spam filtering of e-mail. In: 6th Proceedings of Empirical Methods in Natural Language Processing, Pittsburgh, PA, pp. 44–50 (2001)
19. Santos, I., Laorden, C., Sanz, B., Bringas, P.G.: Enhanced Topic-based Vector Space Model for Semantics-aware Spam Filtering. Expert Systems with Applications 39(1), 437–444 (2012)
20. Sanz, E.P., Hidalgo, J.M., Perez, J.C.: Email spam filtering. In: Zelkowitz, M. (ed.) Advances in Computers, vol. 74, pp. 45–114 (2008)
21. Sebastiani, F.: Machine learning in automated text categorization. ACM Computing Surveys 34(1), 1–47 (2002)
22. Shih, D.H., Chiang, S., Lin, I.B.: Collaborative spam filtering with heterogeneous agents. Expert Systems with Applications 34(4), 1555–1566 (2008)

23. Schneider, K.: A comparison of event models for Naive Bayes anti-spam e-mail filtering. In: 10th Conference of the European Chapter of the Association for Computational Linguistics, pp. 307–314 (2003)
24. Subramaniam, T., Jalab, H., Taqa, A.Y.: Overview of textual anti-spam filtering techniques. International Journal of the Physical Sciences 5(12), 1869–1882 (2010)
25. Upasana, P., Chakraverty, S.: A review of text classification approaches for e-mail management. International Journal of Engineering and Technology 3(2), 137–144 (2011)
26. Valentini, G., Masulli, F.: Ensembles of Learning Machines. In: Marinaro, M., Tagliaferri, R. (eds.) WIRN 2002. LNCS, vol. 2486, pp. 3–19. Springer, Heidelberg (2002)
27. Vapnik, V.N., Druck, H., Wu, D.: Support Vector Machines for Spam Categorization. IEEE Transactions on Neural Networks 10(5), 1048–1054 (1999)
28. Zhang, I., Zhu, J., Yao, T.: An evaluation of statistical spam filtering techniques. ACM Transactions on Asian Language Information Processing 3(4), 243–269 (2004)
29. Yang, Y., Pedersen, J.O.: A comparative study on feature selection in text categorization. In: Fisher, D.H. (ed.) Proceedings of ICML 1997, 14th International Conference on Machine Learning, Nashville, US, pp. 412–420. Morgan Kaufmann Publishers (1997)
30. http://www.enisa.europa.eu/act/res/other-areas/anti-spam-measures/studies/spam-slides (last date accessed January 16, 2012)

Exploring a New Small-World Network
for Real-World Applications

Hidefumi Sawai

Advanced ICT Research Institute,
National Institute of Information and Communications Technology,
Kobe 651-2492, Japan
sawai@nict.go.jp

Abstract. Emergent methods for self-organizing a new type of Small-World (SW) network with less average path-length than that obtained with conventional small-world networks are presented. One method is inspired by an Ant-Colony Optimization (ACO) algorithm, and the other is based on a weighted Monte-Carlo generation method for random graphs. The resultant network architecture common to these methods is a multi-star network, which yields a large clustering coefficient and the shortest average path-length among the conventional complex networks such as a Watts-Strogatz model and a Barabási-Albert model etc., from both a theoretical and an experimental analysis of the properties of those networks. Considering the advantageous properties of the multi-star network in real-world applications, it could be used to analyze human networks in SNS such as Twitter and Blog. Another possible application would be in the field of logistics. For example, the conventional airline network could become more efficient and convenient in the future than the current one because of fewer transits and a shorter cruising distance on average from any starting point to any destination on Earth. *abstract* environment.

Keywords: Small-World, Ant-Colony Optimization, Social Networking Service, Logistics.

1 Introduction

In the 1960's, S.Milgram performed a famous Small-world experiment using letter delivery in the US [1]. From this study, he coined the term "Six-degrees of separation", which means that people are separated from only six persons on average. Later, several researchers additionally performed similar experiments for various kinds of communities such as actors in Hollywood, co-authors of mathematical papers, etc. [2], which supported the claim made in Milgram's experiment. Recently, Yahoo began a similar experiment using Facebook to verify the "Six-degrees of separation" for the members in Facebook [5].

In this study, we will re-examine the characteristics of the Small-World using several network parameters, such as the number of nodes N, the average degree $\langle k \rangle$, the average path-length L, the clustering coefficient C, the link exchange probability ρ, etc., through experimental simulations using the $Dijkstra$ method[8], searching for the shortest path in several complex networks.

R. Benlamri (Ed.): NDT 2012, Part I, CCIS 293, pp. 90–101, 2012.
© Springer-Verlag Berlin Heidelberg 2012

Table 1. Comparing characteristics in typical complex networks [6]

Network	k (degree)	L (average path-length)	C (Clustering coefficient)
Real Network	power law $\propto k^{\gamma}$ etc.	small O(logN)	large O(1)
Complete graph	k=N-1	small 1	large 1
Lattice and cycle	uniform	large O(N^{1/D})	large O(1)
Tree	uniform	small O(logN)	small 0
Random graph	Poisson distribution	small O(logN)	small O(1/N)
Watts-Strogatz model	uniform	N/(2<k>) ; N <k> p/2<<1 Log(N<k>p)/(<k>²p); N <k> p/2 >> 1	(3<k>-6)(1-p)³/(4<k>-4)
Barabási-Albert model	power law $\propto k^{-3}$ etc.	small O(logN); m=1 O(logN/loglogN); m≧2	(m-1)(logN)²/8N

Generally speaking, it is said that the WS (Watts-Strogatz) [2] and BA (Barabási-Albert) [3] models yield comparatively shorter average path-lengths than those of the other complex networks. However, we will further try to have new Small-World networks emerge with a shorter average path-length (it might be the shortest one) in a self-organizing manner.

Next, we will analyze the resultant network architecture theoretically and experimentally. By defining a new network index R, we will show that the degree of the Small-World (we call it "Small-Worldness") can be evaluated for several complex networks. Finally, we will show that some novel applications can be considered using the network, such as an analysis of Twitter, the SNS (Social Networking Service) on the Internet, and logistics such as airline networks in real-world applications.

2   Features of Complex Networks

In Table 1, we summarize the features of conventional complex networks in terms of the Small-World using several network indexes. The followings are some network indexes used in this paper;

- Number of nodes: N,   Link probability: p
- Average degree: $\langle k \rangle$,   Average path length: L
- Clustering coefficient: C,   Link exchange probability: ρ

Comparing the average path-lengths among the complex networks in Table 1, the order of the average path-length L is $O(logN)$ for the Tree, random graphs and BA models as well as the real networks, which is comparatively shorter than for other kinds of networks. The clustering coefficient is large for real networks, lattices and cycles, but small for Trees and random graphs. For a WS model, starting from an extended cycle, as the link exchange probability ρ gradually increases from 0, it is well known that the average path length dramatically decreases in the range of small values of ρ. However, the WS model converges to a random graph as ρ reaches 1. The only graph that yields the smallest value of L (=1) and the largest value of C (=1) is the complete graph. From a Small-World viewpoint, it is necessary to know which network architecture has an absolutely small value of L, rather than the order of L (for example, $O(logN)$).

3   Emergence of the Small-World

Given a complex network with a number of nodes N and an average degree $\langle k \rangle$, one can obtain the average path length L using the $Dijkstra$ method [8] and the clustering coefficient C. Furthermore, we propose two self-organizing methods for generating a network architecture with a shorter path-length L than that obtained with conventional complex networks, without increasing the average degree $\langle k \rangle$.

3.1   A Method Inspired from ACO (Ant-Colony Optimization)

A self-organizing method for creating a Small-World inspired from ACO (Ant-Colony Optimization) [7] is described as follows:

(1) Generate a random graph with the number of nodes N and an average degree $\langle k \rangle$. In this case, the generation probability for each link is $p = \langle k \rangle/(N-1)$.

(2) Search for the shortest path from a start node V_s to a destination node V_d using the $Dijkstra$ method. Pheromones are spread by ants along the shortest path. The concentration of pheromones is zero independently of links in the initial stage.

(3) Each ant searches for the shortest path, and spreads some amount of pheromones while detecting the higher concentration paths in all combinations of node pairs V_s and V_d. As a result, a difference of pheromone concentration along each path will arise. Namely, the concentration of pheromones will be relatively higher for the paths on which more ants walked than for those on which less ants walked.

(4) Sort the links formed in step (3) on the order of high concentration of pheromones. Then, each vertex in two edges is randomly connected. As the average degree $\langle k \rangle$ increases when one or two edges are newly created, at the same time, cut the links with the order of less concentration of pheromones to keep the value of $\langle k \rangle$ as constant as possible.

(5) Calculate the average path-length L and clustering coefficient C for the newly created network in step (4).

(6) If the average path-length L is shorter than a pre-determined threshold value L_{th}, stop the operation. Otherwise, return to step (2) and repeat the steps from (2) to (5).

3.2   A Weighted Monte Carlo Method

Another method for creating a Small-World is to change the degree probability distribution in a multi-modal way, while maintaining the average degree $\langle k \rangle$ constant. In the following procedure, the bimodal Monte Carlo method for generating a network architecture is described. However, it is extendable to a multi-modal method.

(1) Assign the number of nodes N and an average degree $\langle k \rangle$ for a random graph.

(2) Assign two positive constants λ_1 and λ_2 so that $\lambda_1 + \lambda_2 = 1$, and $\lambda_2 > \lambda_1 > 0$.

(3) Express a distribution $Po^*(\lambda)$ as the superposition of two kinds of Poisson distribution $Po(\lambda_1)$ and $Po(\lambda_2)$ with averages λ_1 and λ_2 as follows:

$$Po^*(\lambda) = w_1 Po(\lambda_1) + w_2 Po(\lambda_2)$$

where,

$$w_1 = (\lambda_2 - \lambda)/(\lambda_2 - \lambda_1), \ w_2 = (\lambda - \lambda_1)/(\lambda_2 - \lambda_1), \ Po(\lambda) = e^{-\lambda}\lambda^k/k!$$

(4) Determine each component a_{ij} of the adjacency matrix $\mathbf{a}$ according to the probability distribution $Po^*(\lambda)$.

(5) For any two nodes i and j, the shortest path-length l_{ij} is calculated using the $Dijkstra$ method [8] or the equivalent following method [4]:

$$l_{ij} = arg\ min_l\ [\ (a^{l-1})_{ij} = 0 \ \ AND \ \ (a^l)_{ij} \neq 0\,], \quad 1 \leq i < j \leq N$$

(6) The average path-length L as the average of the shortest paths l_{ij} is calculated as follows:

$$L = \frac{1}{{}_nC_2} \sum_{i<j}^{N} l_{ij} = \frac{2}{N(N-1)} \sum_{i<j}^{N} l_{ij}$$

(7) If L is smaller than a pre-determined threshold L_{th}, stop the operation. Otherwise, go to step (8).

(8) To change the network topology, two constants λ_1 and λ_2 are adequately updated. Then go to step (2), and repeat steps (2) to (7).

4   Simulation Experiments

Simulation experiments were performed for five kinds of networks such as random graphs, BA models, WS models, Pseudo-Ant-SW models and Monte Carlo Bimodal models with N=50 and 100 nodes, respectively. (Owing to space limitations, we describe the results for N=100.) We obtain the average path-lengths L and clustering coefficients C for each network. When we generate a BA model, we start with a small complete network and add nodes with a number of edges n such as n=3, 4, 5, 6, etc. by "preferential attachment" to the initial network step by step. As a result, the average degree $\langle k \rangle$ becomes $\langle k \rangle = 5.88, 7.8, 9.7,$

11.58 etc.(e.g., with $N = 100$ nodes), deterministically. For an unbiased comparison of the indexes of several networks under the condition of N=constant and $\langle k \rangle$ = constant, the average degrees of the networks other than those of the BA model are set as close as possible to each value of the average degrees in the BA models. However, in some cases it is difficult to set the same values of $\langle k \rangle$ for random graphs because their edges are randomly generated with a probability of $p = \langle k \rangle / (N - 1)$. For the WS model, the average degrees have to be set deterministically as even numbers, such as $\langle k \rangle$ =6, 8, 10, 12, etc.. For the Pseudo-Ant-SW models and Monte Carlo Bimodal models, it is difficult to precisely control the values of the average degree $\langle k \rangle$.

For the clustering coefficients C, the values in BA model are largest among above three networks, and the values in the random graphs and WS models follow after it.

Next, when we compare the values of L and C obtained for the Pseudo-Ant-SW and Monte Carlo Bimodal models to those for the above three networks, the values of L are smaller, especially in the Monte Carlo Bimodal model which are small and less than 2.0. What we should notice is that $\langle k \rangle$ is reduced further, which indicates desirable characteristics to form a Small-World, while saving the resource of $\langle k \rangle$ as little as possible. Concerning the clustering coefficients C, both networks are larger than that of the random graph, and relatively large being almost equal to that of the BA model.

4.1   A Method Inspired from ACO

Figure 1 (left) shows the adjacency matrix reflecting pheromone concentration in the Pseudo-Ant-SW method. The thicker the color, the higher the pheromone concentration. Figure 1 (right) shows the multi-star network corresponding to the adjacency matrix in Figure 1 (left) from two different points of view. From these figures, we found that the network architecture consists of a few stars with many links and many peripheral nodes with a few links, and these peripheral nodes are mutually connected with a small probability. Furthermore, from the values of the adjacency matrix and the connection configuration around nodes number 40, 68 and 88, we can find a multi-star (in a sense, a "fractal") structure in the network. This is caused by the algorithm according to which the higher concentration nodes connect with each other in the Pseudo-Ant-SW method.

4.2   A Weighted Monte Carlo Method

Figure 2 (left) shows the adjacency matrix formed with the Monte Carlo Bimodal method. Only two star-nodes are connected with all the other nodes, and are randomly connected with each other with a small probability. Figure 2 (right) shows two different views of the multi-star network corresponding to the adjacency matrix shown in Figure 2 (left). (Note that the number of stars in this network is not one, but two, as shown in Figure 2.)

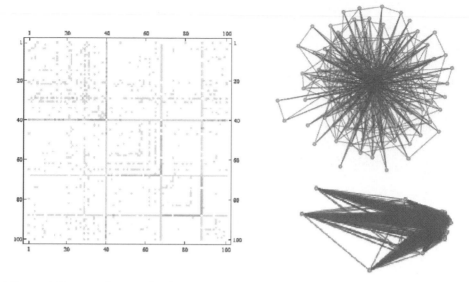

Fig. 1. Adjacency Matrix (left) and its corresponding network (right) generated by a method inspired from ACO (Pseudo-Ant-SW Method)

5   Theoretical and Experimental Analysis

We now present the results of a theoretical analysis of the multi-star network architecture common to Figures 1 and 2. When the number of stars in the multi-star network is n ($1 \leq n \leq N$), we can call it an "n-star network". Figure 3 shows n-star networks when $n=1$, 2, 3 and 4 stars are located at the center.

5.1   Theoretical Analysis of Multi-star Networks

For the n-star networks, the average degree $\langle k \rangle$, average path-length L and clustering coefficient C are calculated as follows;

$$\langle k \rangle = \frac{n(2N - n - 1)}{N}; \quad n = 1, 2, 3, ..., N \tag{1}$$

$$L = \frac{2N(N - n - 1) + n(n + 1)}{N(N - 1)}; \quad n = 1, 2, 3, ..., N \tag{2}$$

$$C = \frac{\frac{n\{_{n-1}C_2 + (n-1)(N-n)\}}{_{N-1}C_2} + (N - n)}{N}; \quad n = 2, 3, ..., N \tag{3}$$

$$C = 0; \quad n = 1$$

The relationships between $\langle k \rangle$ and n (Eq.(1)), L and n (Eq.(2)), and between C and n (Eq.(3)) are shown in Figure 4, at the upper left, upper right and bottom left of the figure, respectively. For $n=1$, the n-star network becomes a so-called

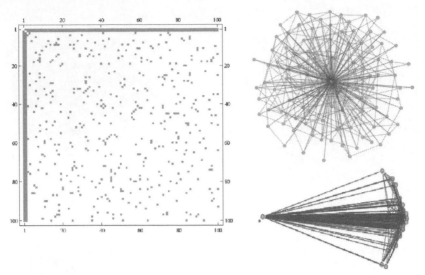

Fig. 2. Adjacency Matrix (left) and its corresponding network (right) generated by the weighted Monte Carlo method (Monte Carlo Bimodal model)

single star network, and the network becomes a complete graph for $n = N - 1$ and N. The average degree $\langle k \rangle$ monotonically increases from 0 to N. On the other hand, L monotonically decreases from 2 to 1 as n increases. The clustering coefficient C decreases once, reaching a minimum value around $\langle k \rangle = 33$, and then increases as n increases. If n is removed using Eqs.(1) and (2) to obtain the relationship between L and $\langle k \rangle$, we obtain Eq.(4) as follows:

$$L = \frac{2N - \langle k \rangle - 2}{N - 1} \tag{4}$$

The relationship between L and $\langle k \rangle$ for N =100 is shown in Figure 4 (bottom right). Although Eq.(4) is derived for $\langle k \rangle$ values, each value corresponding to $n = 1, 2, 3, .., N$, it can be shown that this equation is also valid for any intermediate values of $\langle k \rangle$ with arbitrary numbers of peripheral edges connected with each other, which are represented by dotted lines in Figure 3.

5.2   Comparison of SW Characteristics in Complex Networks

In this section, we analyze the characteristics of several types of complex networks using Lagrange multipliers. In the case of n-star networks, for a given value of $\langle k \rangle$, we define the R value as follows in order to obtain the minimum value of L;

$$R \equiv L + \lambda \langle k \rangle \tag{5}$$

By calculating the partial derivative of R with respect to n, we obtain $\lambda = 1/(N - 1)$. Substituting this formula into Eq.(5), we obtain the invariant $R \equiv 2$,

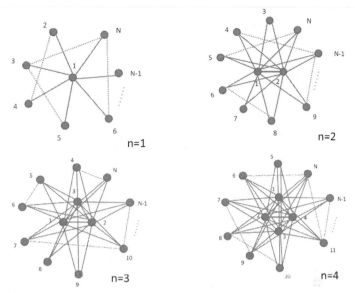

Fig. 3. Multi-star networks with star nodes at the center and their peripheral nodes. The star nodes fully connect with their peripheral nodes, and some peripheral nodes connect with some other peripheral nodes, as denoted by dotted lines.

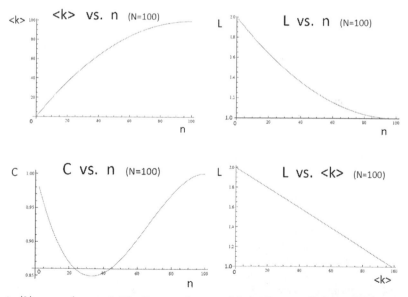

Fig. 4. $\langle k \rangle$ vs. n (upper left), L vs. n (upper right), C vs. n (bottom left), and L vs. $\langle k \rangle$ (bottom right) in multi-star networks with n-star nodes and their peripheral nodes

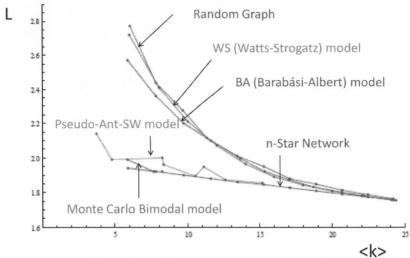

Fig. 5. L vs. $\langle k \rangle$ in several complex networks

independent of the values of L and $\langle k \rangle$. This means that the R value is invariant for n-star networks. Therefore, we can comparatively evaluate each network as the degree of Small-World (we may call it "Small-Worldness") based on this invariant R. The relationship between L, R and $\langle k \rangle$ can be determined and are shown in Figure 5 and Figure 6, respectively. The R values are always 2 for n-star networks, as mentioned before. On the other hand, other networks such as the random graph, the WS and BA models have relatively larger R values than 2. Although the BA model possesses a "scale-free" characteristic with the order of $L \propto O(logN)$, the R value is not small compared to that in the random graph and WS model. The proposed Pseudo-Ant-SW and Monte Carlo Bimodal models have remarkably small values of L and R. In particular, the R value in the Monte Carlo Bimodal model almost reaches 2 in n-star networks. This results indicate that these networks achieve the maximum "Small-Worldness" for a given average degree $\langle k \rangle$ (i.e., the minimum value of L with an appropriate average degree $\langle k \rangle$) .

6   Discussions: Towards Real-World Applications

6.1   Application to Internet Services

We discuss the scalability of the algorithms in forming the n-Star networks from a feasibility point of view in the real world. The n-Star networks always become less complex compared to an initial random network because two nodes with the edges of higher pheromone concentration are connected in the order of the pheromone concentration, which always caused a less complex network with a smaller average path length. This network architecture is scalable with

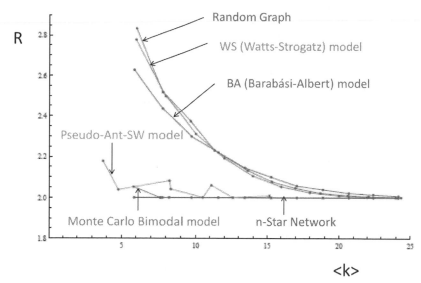

Fig. 6. R vs. $\langle k \rangle$ in several complex networks

a few n star nodes and their peripheral nodes with a total number of nodes N, whose average path length is always less than 2. This could also be applied to an analysis of a scalable social network in the real world, because only a few "star" persons often write interesting comments which can exert some influence, and their many followers (i.e., the peripheral nodes in an n-Star network whose number sometimes reaches millions of persons) only read their comments in a social network such as Twitter and Blog etc. This social network architecture could be similar to that of the n-Star network.

We now consider real-world applications using the n-star networks in the field of Internet services such as Twitter, Blog and the SNS (social networking service) etc. For example, one possible application would be a tool development using the *Dijkstra* method searching for the shortest path to acquaintances in an SNS such as Facebook. This tool will make it possible for us to search for the shortest path for any persons using a series of acquaintances step by step. If this rapid search function were realized on the Internet, the tool would be greatly beneficial for hobbies and businesses. Very recently, it seems that Yahoo just started a verification experiment on the SW using Facebook [5]. Even if the human network architecture is a random graph, it is well known that the relation between N, L and $\langle k \rangle$ is $logN = L \, log \, \langle k \rangle$ [6]. As the average degree $\langle k \rangle$ increases, the population which connected with each other under $L = 6$ also increases. When $\langle k \rangle$ reaches $\langle k \rangle$=43.7, the world population of 7.0 billion (at the present year of 2011) can be connected each other with L=6. Of course, the real human network is not random, but it shows a "scale-free" characteristics $P(k) \propto k^{-\gamma}$ and a relatively large clustering coefficient (Table 1). Therefore, each person could be connected with less than $\langle k \rangle = 43.7$, and on the contrary, L would be smaller if the same value of $\langle k \rangle$ is taken. Although the n-star network architecture might not fit the human network model at the world level because a few stars are fully connected with their peripheral people, this architecture might fit the relatively small human network community model in SNSs such as Twitter and Blog. because a few stars mainly send messages and their followers only receive the messages and read them, as mentioned above. In the near future, it can be expected to analyze the human network architecture using real-world data in Twitter and Blog.

6.2   Application to Logistics

Another possible application would be in the field of logistics, where each node can be assigned to each starting point, destination and depot of resources. In this transportation system, the network architecture (i.e., delivery routes) will be dynamically determined so that the total cost could be minimized. One of the important issues would be to determine the total solution of scheduling for dynamic routing in communications and the efficient transportation of resources, including data and utilities such as water, electricity etc., in relation to Smart-Grid [11][12] and Smart-City projects[13].

7   Conclusions

In this study, we re-examined the characteristics of the Small-World in several complex networks from the viewpoint of the "absolute" average path-length, because conventional complex networks known as Small-World are not necessarily SW in a rigorous sense. Two methods are proposed to create a new Small-World with the smallest average path-length L; one is a self-organizing method inspired from ACO (Ant-Colony Optimization), another is the Monte Carlo Bimodal method. where a network is generated by two kinds of superposed Poisson distributions with an average degree of $\langle k \rangle$. As a result, the two methods lead to a similar multi-star network architecture with an extremely short average path-length L. The former method is based on a bottom-up process, and the latter on a top-down process. It is very interesting that these two completely opposite directional approaches generated the same network structure, a *multi-star network*. Also, we compared several characteristics in conventional typical complex networks from some different viewpoints. Especially, we defined a new evaluation criterion, the R-value, in order to minimize the average path-length L when $\langle k \rangle$ is constant. We found that the R-value reaches a minimum value and is invariant for the n-star networks. Several kinds of complex networks can be evaluated based on the R-value in terms of the Small-World ("Small-Worldness"). These results are expected to be applied to the analysis of the SNS on the Internet, such as Twitter and Blog, etc. Especially, it is essential to speedup a tool searching for acquaintances using the *Dijkstra* method. Furthermore, as one of promising real-world applications in the field of logistics, the n-star network would be useful for implementing an efficient global airline network in the near future. [9][10]

Acknowledgements. The author would like to express his gratitude to Drs. H. Ohsaki, K. Leibnitz, H. Suzuki and F. Peper for fruitful discussions and their useful comments on this study, and to Dr.J-C. Terrillon for his proofreading this paper with some useful comments.

References

1. Milgram, S.: The Small-World Problem. Psychology Today, 61–67 (1967)
2. Watts, J.D.: Small Worlds, The Dynamics of Networks between Order and Randomness. Princeton University Press (1999)
3. Barabasi, A.-L., Albert, R.: Emergence of Scaling in Random Networks. Science, 509–512 (1999)
4. Dorogovtsev, S.N., Mendes, J.F.F.: Evolution of Networks, p. 221. Oxford University Press (2003)
5. Yahoo's SW experiment using Facebook,
   http://www.zdnet.com/blog/facebook/yahoo-facebook-test-8220six-degrees-of-separation-8221-idea/2678
6. Masuda, N., Konno, N.: Complex Networks, From Fundamentals to Applications, Kindai Kagaku-sha (2010) (in Japanese)
7. Bonabeau, E., Dorigo, M., Theraulaz, G.: Swarm Intelligence, From Natural to Artificial Systems. Oxford University Press (1999)
8. Dijkstra, E.W.: A Note on Two Problems in Connexion with Graphs. Numerishe Mathematik 1, 269–271 (1959)
9. Boeing 787 Dream Liner, http://www.newairplane.com/
10. Beaverstock, J.V., Smith, R.G., Taylor, P.J.: A Roster of World Cities. Cities 15(6), 445–458 (1999)
11. Sawai, H., Suzuki, H., Ohsaki, H.: Biologically Inspired Modeling of Smart Grid for Dynamic Power-Flow Control. In: Proceedings of CD-ROM, Bionetics 2010 (December 2010)
12. Sawai, H., Suzuki, H., Ohsaki, H.: Biologically Inspired Modeling of Smart Grid for Dynamic Power-Flow Control under Power Failure. IJAACS (Int. Journal of Adaptive and Autonomous Communication Systems) (in press, 2012)
13. Smart City Projects, e.g., www.smartcity-planning.co.jp/2011/news_jp/441/, www.city.yokohama.lg.jp/ondan/yscp/, www.amsterdamsmartcity.nl/#/en

Fast Algorithm for Deep Packet Inspection

Salam Barbary, Hikmat Farhat, and Khalil Challita

Notre Dame University-Louaize
Computer Science Department, Lebanon

Abstract. Efficient Matching multiple keywords against a stream of input is still an important task. This is essential for deep packet inspection where multi-keyword matching has to be done at wire-speed. While the Aho-Corasick algorithm is one of the best use algorithm, the efficiency of the algorithm depends on the implementation of the required data structures and the goto function. In this paper, an optimized implementation of the trie of the Aho-Corasick algorithm is presented. The key idea is to use a prime number signature to reduce the number of lookups. The performance of the suggested algorithm, in space and time, is compared with different implementations in use today.

Keywords: Aho-Corasick, Deep Packet Inspection, Finite State Automata.

1 Introduction

Deep packet inspection (DPI) is used for many applications such as performance reporting and service provisioning and other business intelligence services[2].The main idea is to search for patterns in the payload of packets. Moreover, this search has to be done at wire speed. Recently there has been a flurry of research in this area [7,5]. The Aho-Corasick algorithm[1] is widely used for the multi-string matching problem. Since etworks nowadays are capable of streaming several gigabits of data per second which is much more than what any regular computer can handle. In most cases DPI is applied only to time-insensitive content such as e-mail attachments. And in order to perform true DPI, the lack of speed is being cured by using more powerful computers to do the job, which costs a lot. Another issue is the speed of memory. In order for a router to perfom DI at wire-speed it needs to copy its content from the line card to the internal memory. DRAM, dynamic random access memory, is much slower that the speed of the processor. Thus, even if the processor is fast enough to do the scan, the memory will create a bottleneck. To solve that, a special kind of memory called Terneray Content Addressable Memory (TCAM), is used instead of DRAM [6]. On the down side, TCAM is usually very small, generates a lot of heat due to its speed and extra wiring, and is also expensive. In fact, lack of TCAM is considered to be a more serious problem than lack of speed in DPI. Thus, the answer to our original question is that we need to reduce resource consumption, time and memory, in order to cut down the cost of DPI. The Aho-Corasick algorithm implements multi-string matching in $O(n)$ which is very fast because it is linear

R. Benlamri (Ed.): NDT 2012, Part I, CCIS 293, pp. 102–111, 2012.

in the size of the input. However, the implementation of the algorithm requires making some decisions that can only be done quickly in theory. In practice , such decisions need $O(\Sigma)$ time, where Σ is the input alphabet, in order to be executed. Moreover, the environment or data structure that the algorithm implements is complicated and consumes a lot of memory. All in all, using this algorithm for DPI might not sound wise. However, as mentioned above, it is one of the best multi-string algorithms proposed.

This paper is organized as follows. In Section 2 the basic algorithm is presented. Different implementations of the algorithms is discussed in Section 3. Our main contribution is given in Section 4. We conclude in Section 5.

2   Basic Algorithm

The Aho-Corasick algorithm was introduced by A. Aho and M. Corasick in 1975[1]. The time complexity of the algorithm is $O(n)$ and it is used in many pattern matching software[3,4], most notably in the UNIX fgrep command. Although the algorithm holds smallest running time among its rivals; it requires some complicated steps in order to create its own data structure. These complicated steps consume some time that is considered valuable when dealing with small resources, similar to the case of fgrep.

The Aho-Corasick algorithm starts by constructing a special data structure called the Trie. A Trie is a tree-like data structure that obeys the rules of automata theory and, in particular, a deterministic finite automata (DFA):

1. Define Σ to be the set of symbols used.
2. Define Σ to be the language or the set of keywords recognized by the DFA.
3. A DFA is a set of nodes known as states. States are connected to each other through transitions, each of which represents a symbol in Σ.
4. Define a transition function σ where, given two states q and p; $\sigma(q,a) = p$. In other words, given that a transition exists, if the algorithm is at state q and reads a symbol a from the input it will go to state p.
5. Every state must know its next hop for every symbol in .
6. Define a start state s to be the entry point to the DFA.
7. Define one or more accepting states such that the program enters an accepting state if and only if one of the keywords in L is found in the text.

Given an alphabet Σ and a set of keywords L, also known as labels, the Aho-Corasick algorithm constructs its DFA according to the following steps:

1. Create the start state s, also known as root, and set all its transitions on Σ to point back to itself.
2. Read the set of keywords L and, for every keyword, add its valid symbols in sequence to the DFA as follows:
    (a) Set the current state to be root.
    (b) For every symbol read, check whether a transition exists from the current state on that symbol to another:

     i. If it exists, go to the state pointed at by the transition.

     ii. Else, create the state, set the transition on the symbol of Σ from the current state to point to the one created, set all transitions on Σ for the new state to point to NULL and go to the created state.

3. NULL transitions must be eliminated since all state transitions must point to valid states. To do that, set every NULL transition in every state to point to the state that represents the prefix of some other keyword that is equal to the largest suffix of the prefix represented by the current state. The reason behind this action and the method to do it will be described afterwards.

An example of such a DFA is illustrated in the figure below where $\Sigma = \{a, b, c\}$ and $L = \{cba, bac\}$. The continuous lines represent the valid transitions that were added during the addition of keywords; whereas the dashed lines represent the groups of the NULL transitions that were fixed later on. Moreover, states with labels in them are considered as accepting states.

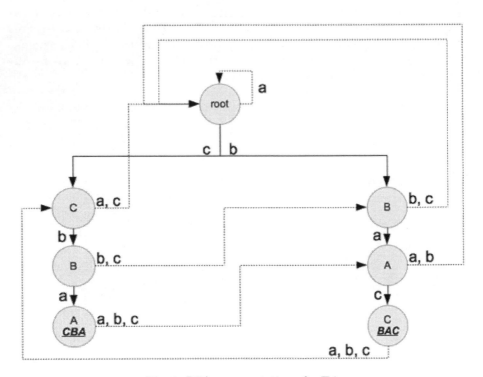

Fig. 1. DFA representation of a Trie

In order to simulate a DFA, the Trie data structure will construct a corresponding node for every state. The transitions between states in the DFA will be represented by pointers between nodes. And for the sake of distinguishing accepting nodes, every label will be added to its corresponding accepting node.

Algorithm 1. "Adding Keyword"

```
current=root
p=NEW_KEYWORD
for  i = 0 to n − 1 do
  u=current.next[p[i]]
  if u=null then
    u=createNode
    current.next[p[i]]=u
  end if
  current=u
end for
u.keyword=p
```

Thus, a node with its label set to NULL is not an accepting node. Moreover, in order to save memory and provide consistency, every node will create a list of its valid transitions only and will allocate a single variable for representing its NULL transitions. This is a good idea since all the NULL transitions of any given node will be replaced by the same value. Finally, to construct the Trie similar to the way the DFA was constructed above, the Aho-Corasick algorithm does the following:

1. Define the set of symbols or characters used in the input. For example, the English alphabet with some special characters.
2. Create the start node object, call it root.
3. Follow the mechanism described above to add the predefined set of keywords to the Trie.
4. Node transition:
   (a) If, on a certain node q on a certain input symbol a, there exists a valid transition to node p; go to p and consume a new symbol from the input. This type of transition, which is σ in the DFA, is known here as the goto function g().
   (b) If, on a certain node q on a certain input symbol a, no valid transition exists; use the NULL transitions representative variable to go to the state that holds the largest valid suffix of the current path or prefix and do not consume a new symbol from the input. This type of transition is known as the failure function f().
5. If the label of the current node is not NULL, recursively print it along with the label of the node pointed at by the failure function f(). The combination of the current node's label and the label its failure node is known as the output function out().

Given an input string *input* the algorithm below searches the Trie for a match.

Before going into further details, it is important to understand the reason behind the existence of the failure function; and the best way to achieve that is by an example.

Consider having the following language $L = price, certificate$. Now, if the string xpricertificatex was encountered in the input, the program must indicate

Algorithm 2. "Search Function"

```
q=root
T=input
for i = 0 to m do
  while  g(q,T[i]) = ∅ do
    q = f (q)
  end while
  q = g(q, T[i])
  if out(q) ≠ ∅ then
    print out(q)
  end if
end for
```

that both "price" and "certificate" were found. To do that, the algorithm will first read the first few symbols from the input until it matches "price". Upon matching, the program will call *out*() to report the result and will consume another symbol, which is r. Since there is no transition on r after e, the algorithm will try to find which label has a prefix that matches the largest suffix of "price". The result of this is the prefix "ce" of "certificate". Therefore, the algorithm will jump to node e of "ce" and try to find if there exists a transition on r and so on. The node e in "ce" that the algorithm jumped to, is the one pointed at by the failure function of the node 'e' in price. Thus, the failure function is important to instantaneously tell which node to jump to when no match exists on the symbol read from the input.

Finally, a sample of the Trie data structure is illustrated in the below figure. In this example: $\Sigma = [A - Z] \cup [a - z] \cup [0 - 9]$ and $L = \{"he", "her", "hero", "heroic", "heroin", "she", "shell", "ship", "shirt"\}$. And in order not to complicate the figure, only a single failure function is illustrated.

2.1 Searching

What this algorithm does, is that it calculates the failure value of nodes from the failure value of their parents. And since the failure values of parents are calculated prior to children, fetching their value when needed takes a single step. The chain of calculations starts by initializing the failure value of the root node's children to itself. In short, the algorithm does the following: For every node (parent) and for every symbol having a valid transition (child) If a transition exists from the failure of the parent on that particular symbol, set the failure value of the child equal to that transition Else, go to the failure of the parent and repeat the above action; until you reach the root This behavior can be illustrated by the figure below:

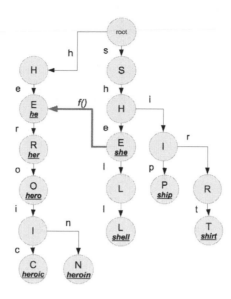

Fig. 2. An Example Trie

3   Implementation

The search function is merely a loop that consistently calls the goto function, which means that it is already optimized and runs in $O(n)$. However, it is the goto function itself that needs to be enhanced in order for the search to become faster. Theoretically the goto function has time complexity $O(1)$. However, practically this function is anything but trivial, and implementing it carelessly can severely affect the speed of the search function. The concept of the problem, however, is not due to the goto function's task but due to the properties of the Trie data structure. If the Trie was simply a BST, one can access any child from its parent in $O(1)$ time complexity. But the problem with the Trie is that every node can have 0 to $|\Sigma|$ children. Therefore, trying to access a child from the parent has to be done in $O(|\Sigma|)$. But what is required to achieve is access time in $O(1)$, which can easily be done theoretically. Encouragingly though, this behavior was required to be done on every node separately and not on the whole Trie. Below we discuss several ideas that can be used to implement the goto function in $O(1)$ time complexity. The main theme, in a nutshell, is to add some storing capabilities to each node such that it can know what are its children, and hopefully in $O(1)$. One important advantage to keep in mind is that we can neglect the overhead of constructing the data structure we use in terms of time and memory. Our only aim right now is to speed up the goto function.

There are a wide range of possible implementations of the goto function. Below we discuss some of the most popular implementations and later we compare them with our implementation.

Algorithm 3. "Failure Function"

Q=emptyeuque
for $a \in \Sigma$ **do**
  if q=g(0,a)$\neq \emptyset$ **then**
    f(q)=0
    addToQueue(q,Q)
  end if
end for
while not empty(Q) **do**
  r=removFromQueue(Q)
  for $a \in \Sigma$ **do**
    if ug(r,a)$\neq \emptyset$ **then**
      addToQueue(u,Q)
      v=f(r)
      while g(v,a)=$\emptyset$ **do**
        v=f(v)
      end while
      f(u)=g(v,a)
      out(u)=out(u)$\cup$ out(f(u))
    end if
  end for
end while

3.1   Using a Two-Dimensional Array

In this method, a two-dimensional array of size $|nodes| * |\Sigma|$ called the goto is created. Every node in the Trie will refer to a row in the array. And every symbol in the alphabet will refer to a column. The goto value of node ni on symbol sj is stored in $goto[ni][si]$. This method is, with no doubt, the fastest of all methods in this paper for retrieving the goto value. However, it consumes an enormous amount of memory. It is very inefficient to implement this method when the Trie is large; which is the case we are interested in. In terms of number of steps cn, c will be equal to 1. Thus the algorithm takes exactly n steps.

3.2   Using a Linked List

In order to reduce memory consumption, the authors suggest that every node implements a linked list of its children. The amount of memory consumed in this case is definitely minimal. However, the access time from parents to children is bounded by $O(|\Sigma|)$. This can be problematic because the goto function, as mentioned previously, is heavily used by the search function. Thus, the algorithm will take at most $|\Sigma| *n$.

3.3   Using an Indexed Table

Since the linked list method is not fast, or at least not fast enough; the authors introduce the idea of using an indexed (or hash) table. However, there are many questions that are associated with this decision. The first is how large should the table be? The second is what if there where more children than cells in the table? In order to be on the safe side, one must have number of cells equal to the maximum number of children a node can have. The amount of memory equal to $|nodes| * |\Sigma|$ two-dimensional array. The difference is simply that the columns will be distributed on the nodes rather than being stored in one place. There is really a good number of ways to deal with the issue of memory consumption of the indexed table. However, all of them vary between being memory inefficient or time inefficient. Therefore, the authors skip all of them and only describe the next two ideas.

3.4   Using a Combination of Index Tables and Linked Lists

Indexed tables are good when it comes to optimizing access time. And linked lists are good when it comes to memory consumption. Therefore, what the authors suggest is having a combination of both. In order to do this a hash table and a linked list will be implemented at each node. Some of the symbols will be indexed in the hash table, and the others will be added to the linked list if needed. In order to benefit most from this setting, the size of the hash table will be selected first; assume it is k. After that, the k highest frequency symbols are selected to be indexed. This method is a compromise between speed and memory consumption. And because it is a compromise; it does not win on any side. The indexed table will, in almost every node, waste memory because not all of its cells will be occupied. On the other hand, when a symbol is not indexed, the goto function will need $|\Sigma| - k$ steps to find it in the linked list.

3.5   Using a Binary Search Tree

Using a binary search tree is somehow, the best way of compromising between speed and memory consumption. A BST can find any item with a steady $O(\log(n))$ time complexity where n is the number of available transitions. On the down side, constructing a BST is not as fast as constructing other data structures; but this issue will be ignored since the goal here is optimizing the goto function. Another issue is that the nodes of a BST are twice as heavy as those of a linked list, since each node contains two pointers instead of one. To sum up then, in this case the goto function will need $\log(|\Sigma|)$ steps at most, and will consume twice the amount of memory of a linked list; which is not so bad.

4   Time Complexity Enhancement

4.1   The Prime Number Signature

This paper is the first to suggest the prime number signature method for property set encapsulation. The main idea is extracted from the fundamental theorem of arithmetic or the unique-prime-factorization theorem. The theorem states that

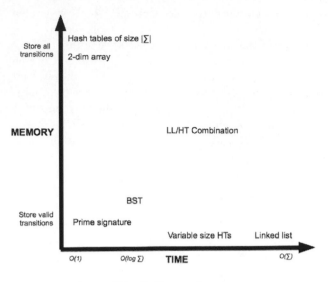

Fig. 3. Comparison

every natural number is either prime or can be uniquely factored as a product of primes in a unique way. The second property of this theorem, uniqueness, is the one behind proposing the prime number signature. Briefly, given a set of objects $P = O_1, O_2, ... O_n$ and another set Q, where Q is a proper subset of P, the prime number signature can determine if any object O_i of P is in Q in a single step. To do this, every object in P is assigned a prime ID number and Q is assigned an integer value called the signature, initialized to 1. To simulate the addition of object O_i to Q, the signature of Q will be updated by multiplying the ID number of O_i with it. At the end, the signature of Q will be equal to the result of multiplying all the ID numbers of the objects it hosts. The resulting signature of Q, according to the FTA, will only accept division on the prime numbers that participated in its formation. A pseudo code implementation of the idea is shown in the algorithm below.

4.2   Comparison of Methods

To assess the performance of our method we show in Figure 3 an easy comparison of all the strategies described above for implementing the goto function. The position of the item in the graph is determined according to four measures: time complexity when a transition exists, time complexity when a transition is missing, space complexity per node and node-independent space complexity. As can be seen from the figure our implementation provides optimization both in time and space.

Algorithm 4. "Turbo Search Function"

```
current=root_id
label_exists=RESERVED_PRIME
for each symbol Si in the input do
    SIDi = prime ID of Si
    while content[current] % SIDi ≠ 0 do
        current=content_failure[current]
    end while
    current=content_goto[g(current, SIDi)]
    if content[current] % label_exists = 0 then
        out();
    end if
end for
```

5   Conclusion

We have presented a fast and memory efficient version of the Aho-Corasick algorithm for multiple keyword matching. This type of algorithms is very important for deep packet inspection, among others. We have also compared our algorithm with previous implementations and shown that it has better overall performance. We are currently working on a parallel version of the discussed algorithm.

References

1. Aho, A.V., Corasick, M.J.: Efficient string matching: an aid to bibliographic search. Commun. ACM 18, 333–340 (1975)
2. Congdon, P., Farrens, M., Mohapatra, P.: Packet prediction for speculative cut-through switching. In: Proceedings of the 4th ACM/IEEE Symposium on Architectures for Networking and Communications Systems, ANCS 2008, pp. 99–108 (2008)
3. Dori, S., Landau, G.M.: Construction of aho corasick automaton in linear time for integer alphabets. Inf. Process. Lett. 98, 66–72 (2006)
4. Flouri, T., Melichar, B., Janoušek, J.: Aho-corasick like multiple subtree matching by pushdown automata. In: Proceedings of the 2010 ACM Symposium on Applied Computing, SAC 2010, pp. 2157–2158 (2010)
5. Kumar, S., Turner, J., Williams, J.: Advanced algorithms for fast and scalable deep packet inspection. In: Proceedings of the 2006 ACM/IEEE Symposium on Architecture for Networking and Communications Systems, ANCS 2006, pp. 81–92 (2006)
6. Peng, K., Tang, S., Chen, M., Dong, Q.: Chain-based dfa deflation for fast and scalable regular expression matching using tcam. In: Proceedings of the 2011 ACM/IEEE Seventh Symposium on Architectures for Networking and Communications Systems, ANCS 2011, pp. 24–35 (2011)
7. Smith, R., Estan, C., Jha, S., Kong, S.: Deflating the big bang: fast and scalable deep packet inspection with extended finite automata. In: Proceedings of the ACM SIGCOMM 2008 Conference on Data Communication, SIGCOMM 2008, pp. 207–218 (2008)

1+N Orthogonal Encoding with Multiple Failure Tolerance (1+N OEMFT)

José-Alejandro Niño-Mora and Yezid Donoso

Systems and Computing Engineering Department
Universidad de los Andes, Colombia
{ja.nino905,ydonoso}@uniandes.edu.co

Abstract. This paper proposes a mechanism for protecting data networks called 1 + N OEMFT, capable of protecting a connection set against a multiple failures scenario on the network links. The mechanism used guarantees the protection of a connection, provided the destination is not completely isolated from the network for failures occurred. The protection scheme uses the concept of 1 + N protection proposed in [16], [10] and [19], but unlike the codification of the data for each connection is made without the use of the XOR operation, instead used a matrix of orthogonal vectors, then a cluster in a single message. Additionally, it eliminates the convergence time imposed in [16], [10] and [19], allowing it recovered in the time that the target detects the fault.

Keywords: Terms—1+N, Protection, Restoration, P-Cycles, Multicast Shared Tree.

1   Introduction

Over the last two decades, we have shown great interest in research on techniques to protect transport networks against failures over its nodes and links, due to the impact of the loss of any of these physical components due to the large data capacities that are handled today. For this reason, a variety of techniques and mechanisms have been proposed as mentioned in [20], [21] that can be classified into two groups. Preventive mechanisms, which are set at the time of generating, the different connections and exist as a backup in case of an eventuality, and the reactive mechanisms that are executed when an event changes the state of the network.

Preventive mechanisms are known as protection mechanisms, while reactive mechanisms are known as restoration mechanisms. Each mechanism has its pros and cons, such as protection mechanisms provide a lower switching time than the Restoration, because the backup resources are pre-allocated since the beginning of the connection, making them immediately available when a failure is detected, while Restoration resources should be calculated and assigned once the fault has been detected. On the other hand, the protection mechanisms require greater use of resources as these are assigned to a connection, even without the existence of faults and the chance that are never used, while the resources in the mechanisms of Restoration are only

R. Benlamri (Ed.): NDT 2012, Part I, CCIS 293, pp. 112–125, 2012.

allocated when needed. For these reasons, although there are several proposals based on restoration mechanisms such as [3], [4], [7] and [17], most of the proposals found focus on the mechanisms of protection, to name a few [5], [8], [9], [10], [11], [12], [13], [14], [15] and [16], although it is normal to find proposals that are a hybrid between the two mechanisms as [1], [2], [6] and [18].

In [16] proposed a mechanism to save on the capacity to protect a set of connections by avoiding the use of protection 1 +1, 1:1, 1: N or N: M, instead this uses a single protection circuit capable of carry the encoded data of a set of connections by using XOR operations, which we call in the rest of the article as the protection frame. The protection scheme 1 + N offers substantial savings in the amount of resources allocated to a given number of connections, eliminating the need to provide backup links for every main link existing, on the contrary using a single logical link (physically is implemented as a shared multicast tree) regardless of the number of connections to protect, which pass through each of the destination nodes of the protected connections. Additionally, the protection scheme 1 + N eliminates the need of notify to a set of nodes, once the fault has been detected (depending on the scheme of protection or restoration is necessary to notify the origin, destination or nodes adjacent to the failures) for switching to the backup path, leaving this responsibility solely to the destination node.

The author of [16] proposed for the distribution of data protection, the use of a shared tree multicast and [10] proposes the use of a P-cycle. Both schemes are only able to recover from a single fault on a main path of some of the connections involved in the protection scheme. If there is more than one failure, it cannot recover the data from each connection affected, because the encoding mechanism is based on the property of the XOR operation, which when adds two times the same data, makes latter is canceled, so for one can be able to recover its own data from the protection circuit, it is necessary that the other N-1 connections have eliminated its share of the data in the protection frame through the XOR operation. In [19], the author extends the proposal of [10] to support multiple failures, with the restriction that each connection can support as many failures as P-Cycles are passing through the ends of the connection.

All proposals based on 1 + N encodings save bandwidth through the use of XOR-based coding where the size of data protection will be the size of the largest data encoded, on the other hand, all have the same disadvantage which each node that required to recover its own data from the data protection, only can do it once all the other nodes that are involved in the protection scheme that successfully received their data on the main working path, have been sent to the other nodes of the scheme (in [16] are propagate on another shared tree multicast, in [10] on the P-cycle and [19] through each of the P-cycles). This imposes a time of convergence between the nodes of the scheme, which imposes a waiting period enters the fault detection and the ability to recover from data protection. As you can guess, the schemes of [10] and [19] require a synchronization process for sending data on P-cycles, so the data sent at time t are distinguishable from those sent at time t+1.

This article proposes a new protection scheme based on the ideas of [16], where they use a protection scheme 1 + N on a single logical link to protect a number of connections by sending you encoded data, but unlike not used to XOR operation for encoding. The advantage of this approach is that data protection are encoded using orthogonal vectors, which allows each node in the time of detection of the fault, the ability to immediately extract the regarding information from the protection without the need for the convergence of the other nodes as in [16], [10] and [19]. Although the amount of data resulting from encoding outweigh the XOR-based schemes, has no problem because it uses compression on the data, thereby significantly reducing the size of the protection frame, also eliminates the need for propagate the data from each receiving node to all other nodes in the scheme once the destination has received the data by way of it working path, since the protection frame contains all the information necessary for the recovery process, thereby saving the bandwidth consumed. For these two reasons, although the amount of data generated for the protection frame is superior, the net amount of data transmitted over the network is lower than the scheme proposed in [16], [10] and [19] which generate fewer data for protection, but in [19] is directly proportional to the number of p-cycles used. The more p-cycles, the greater the size of data protection. Although these two schemes generate less data protection, are not as resilient to multiple failures as shown in the simulation section, since they fail to offer the same protection value as 1 + N OEMFT scheme.

The rest of the paper is organized as follows. Section 2 explains the algorithm of 1 + N OEMFT and the structure of the protection frame. Section 3 presents the mathematical model. Section 4 presents an example of how to generate the protection frame for a particular case and as is used to retrieve data from two connections that lost their main working path. Section 5 presents the simulation results between schemes 1+N OEMFT, [16], [10] and [19]. Finally, in Section 6 presents the conclusions.

2   Algorithm Description

In [16] is proposed a scheme based transport of data protection on a shared multicast tree, which distributes the data protection to each member of the multicast group. This offers the advantage that the routing process is left to the Network layer and multicast protocols, which guarantees us that since there is a route to the destination, the multicast tree can be created and modified to send the data protection to the destination. For this reason, the proposal of this article is based on the use of a shared multicast tree for the distribution of data protection, but the rest of the mechanism is different from that proposed in [16], by not using the XOR operation for coding but orthogonal vectors, which is encoded with each data set, which are then added together to produce what we call the protection frame. The protection frame is a set of encoded and compressed data that consists of a header and a payload. The header contains the information necessary for a node can decode the frame and extract your data in the recovery process. The data is encoded by a different orthogonal vector for each connection, ensuring that no cancellation problems as in the schemes [16], [10] and [19] when more than one connection sends the same data set.

The proposed algorithm consists of three phases that are conducted in different parts of the protection group, which are; Initialization, Propagation and Recuperation

Initialization

At this stage are selected which connections require protection and will be grouped within a protection group (a protection group is one involving a set of N connections where their data are encoded and propagated to all its members). Once you know how many connections are going to be protected in a group, we proceed to get the multicast tree root node (Rendezvous Node) chose by the multicast protocol, to whom is sent the data for each node that participates in the group. The root node will calculate the required protection parameters for the group and additionally calculate the shortest path to each node to build the tree that will be used for the propagation of data protection. The protection parameters to estimate are:

Matrix of Orthogonal Vectors: Orthogonal vectors used for coding the data for each connection are calculated by generating a square matrix with the number of rows equal to or greater than the number of connections to protect, so the size of the matrix will be a value of 2n. Each row of the matrix corresponds to an orthogonal vector, which will be assigned to a single connection. If the number of connections is not a multiple of the power of two, rows of the matrix remain unassigned. The matrix has the following pattern.

$$
\begin{array}{rr}
1 & 1 \\
1 & -1
\end{array}
$$

Hash from the IP of Each Destination Node: It is a unique code that identifies each node. Is generated from the 4 octets of the IP of the destination node of each connection and is used in conjunction with the module to know what row of the orthogonal matrix will be assigned to a particular connection.

Module: A numeric value that is used to perform the module operation on each Hash, which tells each receiver node what row of the matrix was used to encode your data. The purpose of this module is to provide a mechanism for each destination node, which requires using the protection frame, may know what orthogonal vector was used to encode your information. The modulus value is calculated so that each destination node who apply it on your hash gets a different value, with which it can seek on the protection frame and according to the position in which they appear from left to right, it will know what row of the matrix was used to encode the information. This mechanism avoids having to send the vector of each node in the frame, which is reflected in a significant saving in the size of the protection frame.

Payload: Are the protection data used in case of failures and are formed from the sum of the data for each connection already encoded. Before encoding, each connection data is appended with 8 additional bits, which correspond to sequence number, which identify each data segment if the previous was fragmented.

Propagation

At this stage, when the root node has armed protection frame from data sent by all or some members of the multicast group, is propagated to each of the members using the shared tree multicast previously assembled. This process is repeated each time new data require to be sending to every connections belonging to the protection group.

Recuperation

This stage is performed by the destination nodes of each connection protected by the scheme. When a node receives the protection frame, it will know is participating in the scheme of protection, and shall determine whether data in the protection frame exist for him. At this point the destination node can know for sure, in how many protected connections is involved and can determine whether it received data from the same number of connections, which can detect whether or not there is one or more faults. For this, the node must decompress and decode the frame and extract the value of the module from the header. Then calculate the hash of your IP address (as explained above) and divide it with the value of the module extracted from the header and take the value of the residue. The residue value will serve as the identifier in the header to see if there is a connection addressed to him. If at this point the node determines that is no data for him or that there has not been any failure, the process stops and discard the protection frame, otherwise it must determine which orthogonal vector was assigned for each connections, that was determined that failed. The protection frame indicates the total number of connections involved in the protection that the destination node can use to know the size of the orthogonal matrix used, and can be calculate it to choose the respective vectors. Once you have the orthogonal vectors for each connection, perform the decoding operation between each vector and the payload of the protection frame, thereby recovering the original data of each connection that lost it principal working path. If there is not data for this connection, the above result will be zero. In the event that a connection data have been divided into different protection frames, the destination node may keep track of which segments it has received by checking the value of the first 8 bits of the decoded message, which contains the sequence number. The latter is used to determine if all the connection data have been received.

Protection Frame Structure

The protection frame consists of a header and a payload section, both are encoded and compressed to reduce its size and thus require less bandwidth, which is reflected in a lower consumption of network resources. Figure 1 shows the fields of the protection frame of 1 + N OEMFT and the number of bits of each.

Delimitador	id Protección	Módulo	No Conexiones	No Destinos	Residuo(s)	Conexiones al mismo nodo	Carga Util
1 bit	32 bits	7 bits	7 bits	Variable	Variable	Variable	Variable

Fig. 1. Protection Frame of scheme 1+N OEMFT

The header is intended to provide all the information require to be used by the destination nodes of the network of protection, indicating which is the value of the chosen module, the number of connections involved in the protection scheme, which are the values of the residual of each connection (allowing to find out the row index of the orthogonal matrix used for the encoding of your data) and how many connections are established on each destination node (in this case, a destination node can be part of more of a connection, which receive more than one data set, each encoded with a different orthogonal vector). Moreover, the payload is the section that brings the result of the sum of the encoded data of each connection.

The header consists of a series of fields, of which only the first three (delimiter bit, module and number of connections) are always represented with the same number of bits, while the rest are represented by the number of bits needed only . The reason for not applying the exact binary encoding to the first three fields, is for the destination node can know in advance how many bits should be read in order to get these three values and from them to determine the number of bits used to encode binary the rest of the data, which is encoded with the exact bits to make a saving in the number of bits used and thus reduce the size of the protection frame. The header structure is defined below:

Delimiter bit (1 bit): It's a bit with value of one, which is used for the decoding process, to know where it begins the frame header. The information in the protection frame are grouped into sets of seven bits for the encoding process, if the total number of bits is not a multiple of seven, extra bits are added to complete the necessary bits for this reason at the time of decoding the protection frame may have more bits than the originals, so the delimiter bit will be useful to determine what bits are padding and should be discarded.

Protection ID (32 bits): It is used to identify the protection group. A destination node can participate simultaneously in several protection groups, which imposes the task of identify the correct protection frame for a respective set of connections, this is why is useful this ID.

Module (7 bits): Seven bits are used to represent the value of the module used for the allocation of orthogonal vectors to the connections involved in the protection scheme.

Number of Connections (7 bits): Contains the number of connections protected and encoded by the protection schema.

Number of Destinations (Variable): It indicates how many different destinations nodes participating in the scheme of protection. Their representation in bits equals the number of bits needed to represent the value of connections.

Residue (Variable): Contains the result of applying the operation module on the hash generated by the IP address of each destination node of each participant connections of the protection scheme. The number of bits used for representation is obtained from the number of bits needed to represent the value chosen for module protection scheme (Field number two in the header).

Number of Connections to the Same Destination Node (Variable): Indicates how many orthogonal vectors were assigned to each destination node. This is useful when a destination node participates in more than one connection in one protection scheme, so it should use a vector orthogonal to each connection.

3   Mathematical Model

Conventions

N = Number of connection to protect.
C = Set of connections to protect.
S = Set of source nodes of C.
D = Set of destination nodes of C.
W = Set of primary disjoint working paths from S to D
P = Data block of fixed-length to transmit.
R = Backup path associated to connections in C. It consists of a shared multicast tree from each S_i to D_i in C.

C_i = Connection belonging to C
S_i = Source of the communication
D_i = Destination of the communication
W_i = Primary working path of the connection C_i.
$Chip_i$ = Orthogonal code assigned to each connections C_i.
O_i = Octet i from IP address of each node S.
H_i = Hash of each IP address of each node S.
M_R = Data message sent by R.
M_{wi} = Data message sent on the primary working path.

----

* = Dot product between two vectors

Set of connections to protect   N

$$C = \sum_{i=1}^{N} C_i \tag{1}$$

Encoded message sent by R

$$M_R = \sum_{i=1}^{N} (P_i * chip_i) \tag{2}$$

Recovered message from path Ri by node Di

$$P_j = \sum_{i=1}^{\text{No bits } M_R \,/\, \text{No bits chip}_j} (M_R[i] * \text{chip}_j) \qquad (3)$$

ID from node D_i

$$H_i = \sum_{i=0}^{3} \text{Octeto}_{i+1} * 256^i \qquad (4)$$

4   Generation Example of 1+M OEMFT Protection Frame and Recovering from Two Connections Failed

Suppose we have 5 connections we want to protect.

C1 = 10.123.140.20 - 10.123.134.2, C2 = 10.123.140.10 - 10.123.134.150
C3 = 10.123.134.15 - 10.123.134.2, C4 = 10.123.140.84 - 10.123.140.120
C5 = 10.123.134.15 - 10.123.140.20

And the data transmitted by each connection are:

d1 = 1100001, d2 = 1100010, d3 = 1100011, d4 = 1100100, d5 = 1100101

The first thing the scheme does, is to calculate the size of the square orthogonal matrix required. In this case we have five connections which will require an 8x8 matrix. The reason for not using a 5x5 is because the scheme to produce the array works in powers of 2, so the smallest number that can be used to generate at least five rows is eight. The resulting matrix is:

```
1 -1  1 -1  1 -1  1 -1
1  1 -1 -1  1  1 -1 -1
1 -1 -1  1  1 -1 -1  1
1  1  1  1 -1 -1 -1 -1
1 -1  1 -1 -1  1 -1  1
1  1 -1 -1 -1 -1  1  1
1 -1 -1  1 -1  1  1 -1
```

After having the matrix, we proceed to find the value of the module that generates a unique number when operating on the hash of each IP address of the destination nodes. The smallest module that generates a different value for each destination IP in this example was 8. Once the module is the value that satisfies the condition, we proceed to store the different results of the residues from the module operation on the hash of each IP node destination and how many destination nodes are involved in more than one connection. The order of storage and the number of connections for each destination node determines which row of the matrix was used to encode their data. For this example we have the following data:

IP	Hash	Residue	N° Connections	Matrix Row
10.123.134.150	175867542	6	1	0
10.123.140.120	175869048	0	1	1
10.123.140.20	175868948	4	1	2
10.123.134.2	175867394	2	2	3 y 4

Now that each connection has been assigned an orthogonal vector your data is encoded with this vector as follows:

First are appended at the beginning, the 8 bits of the sequence number, then each bit of data is multiplied by 2 and subtracted by 1, to convert the zeros to -1, leaving the data represented by 1 and -1. Then each bit is multiplied by each of the bits in the orthogonal vector. This yields a new set of data about the size of the number of bits of the original data by the number of bits in the orthogonal vector. The encoded data of each connection are:

d1c = -1, 1, 1, -1, -1, 1, 1, -1, -1, 1, 1, -1, -1, 1, 1, -1, -1, 1, 1, -1, -1, 1, 1, -1, -1, 1, 1, -1, -1, 1, 1, -1, -1, 1, 1, -1, -1, 1, 1, -1, -1, 1, 1, -1, -1, 1, 1, -1, -1, 1, 1, -1, -1, 1, 1, -1, 1, 1, -1, -1, 1, 1, -1, 1, -1, -1, 1, 1, -1, -1, 1, 1, -1, -1, 1, 1, -1, -1, 1, -1, 1, 1, -1, -1, 1, 1, -1, -1, 1, 1, -1, -1, 1, 1, -1, -1, 1, 1, -1, -1, 1, 1, -1, -1, 1, 1, -1, -1, 1, 1, -1, -1, 1, 1, -1, 1, -1, 1, -1, -1, 1, 1, -1, -1, 1

d2c = -1, -1, -1, -1, -1, -1, -1, -1, -1, -1, -1, -1, -1, -1, -1, -1, -1, -1, -1, -1, -1, -1, -1, -1, -1, -1, -1, -1, -1, -1, -1, -1, -1, -1, -1, -1, -1, -1, -1, -1, -1, -1, -1, -1, -1, -1, -1, -1, -1, -1, -1, -1, -1, -1, -1, -1, -1, -1, -1, -1, -1, 1, 1, 1, 1, 1, 1, 1, 1, 1, 1, 1, 1, 1, 1, 1, -1, -1, -1, -1, -1, -1, -1, -1, -1, -1, -1, -1, -1, -1, -1, -1, -1, -1, -1, -1, -1, -1, -1, -1, 1, 1, 1, 1, 1, 1, 1, 1, -1, -1, -1, -1, -1, -1, -1, -1

d3c= -1, -1, -1, -1, 1, 1, 1, 1, 1, -1, -1, -1, -1, 1, 1, 1, 1, -1, -1, -1, -1, 1, 1, 1, 1, -1, -1, -1, -1, 1, 1, 1, 1, 1, -1, -1, -1, -1, 1, 1, 1, 1, 1, -1, -1, -1, -1, 1, 1, 1, 1, -1, -1, -1, -1, -1, -1, -1, -1, 1, 1, 1, 1, 1, 1, 1, 1, -1, -1, -1, -1, -1, -1, -1, -1, -1, 1, 1, 1, 1, 1, 1, -1, -1, -1, -1, 1, 1, 1, 1, -1, -1, -1, -1, 1, 1, 1, 1, 1, 1, 1, 1, -1, -1, -1, -1, 1, 1, 1, 1, -1, 1, -1, -1, -1

d4c = -1, -1, 1, -1, 1, -1, 1, -1, 1, -1, -1, 1, -1, 1, -1, 1, -1, 1, -1, -1, 1, -1, 1, -1, 1, -1, 1, -1, -1, 1, -1, 1, -1, 1, -1, 1, - 1, 1, -1, -1, 1, -1, 1, -1, 1, -1, 1, -1, -1, 1, -1, 1, -1, -1, 1, -1, 1, -1, -1, 1, -1, 1, -1, 1, -1, -1, 1, -1, 1, -1, 1, -1, -1, 1, -1, 1, -1, 1, -1, 1, -1, -1, 1, -1, 1, -1, 1, -1, 1, -1, 1, -1, 1, -1, 1, -1, -1, 1, -, 1, 1, -1, 1, -1, 1, -1, 1, -1, 1, -1, 1, -1, 1

d5c =-1, -1, 1, 1, -1, -1, 1, 1, -1, -1, 1, 1, -1, -1, 1, 1, -1, -1, 1, 1, -1, -1, 1, 1, -1, -1, 1, 1, -1, -1, 1, 1, -1, -1, 1, 1, -1, -1, 1, 1, -1, -1, 1, 1, -1, -1, 1, 1, -1, -1, 1, 1, -1, -1, 1, 1, -1, -1, 1, 1, -1, -1, -1, -1, 1, 1, -1, -1, 1, 1, -1, -1, -1, -1, 1, 1, -1, -1, 1, 1, -1, -1, -1, -1, 1, 1, -1, -1, 1, 1, -1, -1, 1, 1, -1, -1, 1, 1, -1, -1, -1, -1, 1, 1, -1, -1, 1, 1, 1, 1, -1, -1, 1, 1, -1, -1

When we have data on each connection encoded with their respective orthogonal vector, we proceed to add all encodings to obtain a single value. This sum is made bit by bit, but there is no carry, on the contrary each bit is a separate amount which is represented in decimal.

At this point, the scheme has all the information needed to assemble the protection frame.

The data of the protection frame are grouped by seven bits (which we call in this scheme, coding) and then are compressed. The end result is distributed by the multicast shared tree to each destination node that participates in the protection scheme. When the destination node receives the protection frame, it should determine whether the frame carries data for him, because the source node may have no data to send at the time that the frame was put together (The frame is assembled from time to time, taking the data that has received by the multicast tree root node, so there can be moments of time that one or more multicast group nodes have no data to transmit). To determine that the frame brings information to the destination node, is perform the following steps:

1. The frame is decompressed.
2. The frames are decoded, so in this step the grouping of seven bits is reversed.
3. Extract the first 15 bits of the frame, with which the destination node can know what the module value is assigned to that protection scheme and how many connections are involved. With the number of connections involved, you can calculate how many bits were needed to represent in binary the number of vectors allocated and how many different destinations are available for the number of connections involved.
4. Taking the number of participants connections and dividing on the number of different targets and bring it closer to the nearest integer above, the destination node can determine the number of bits used to represent in binary the number of connections that share the same value of residue. With the latter, the destination node can determine the total size of the frame header.
5. With the bit size of the residue and the number of connections on each destination node, destination node can get the different residues and number of connections on each destination node that is encoded in the protection frame.
6. At this point the destination node proceeds to calculate the result of the module on its own hash and search if this hash is on the protection frame header. If found it, will know there is data encoded for it. The position from left to right where the residue is found, will indicate to the destination node the index of the row of the orthogonal matrix to be used to decode the information. In case that there are more than one connection directed to the destination node, would take the number of vectors needed from the index indicated by the residue.

Recovery after detecting a fault

Once the destination node has determined if one or more faults have occurred and have obtained the respective orthogonal vectors, it can start the decoding process, which involves splitting the frame´s payload into sections of equal size as the vector and calculate the dot product between each section and the vector. The result of each section can be positive or negative, the positive values would be interpreted as ones and the negative values as zeros. At this point the node has the original information sent by the source node of the connection. If the result is zero, indicates that the connection at that point in time did not send data to the destination.

In this example, the working path for connections C1 and C3 failed, which both have the same node as the destination 10.123.134.2. The node 10.123.134.2 checks the protection frame, seeking for its residue (0010) and learns that there are two connections addressed to him. Counting from left to right, the position where its residue appeared at the protection frame header, the destination node knows that its data was encoded with rows 3 and 4 of the 8x8 orthogonal matrix. The recovery process is repeated for each vector as described above.

Vector of connection C1	Vector of connection C2
1, -1, -1, 1, 1, -1, -1, 1	1, 1, 1, 1, -1, -1, -1, -1

Splitting the payload into groups of equal size as the orthogonal vector (in this case in groups of 8) and calculating the dot product between each group and the vector, we get the original data vector, from which we remove the first 8 bits of the sequence number:

Recovered data of C1

Data = -8, -8, -8, -8, -8, -8, -8, -8, 7, 7, -7, -7, -7, -8, 7
     = 000000001100001 = 100001

Recovered data of C2

Data = -8, -8, -8, -8, -8, -8, -8, -8, 7, 7, -7, -7, -7, 8, 7
     = 000000001100011 = 1100011

5   Simulation Results

The proposal of this paper was compared against the proposals of [16], [10] and [19] using a simulator developed on Java technology. The purpose of the simulation was to compare the degree of protection offered by each scheme and how many additional bits were generated for each protection frame respectively. Not taken into account the time synchronization or convergence, because the proposed 1 + N OEMFT not have these parameters. The simulation tests were performed using the topology of NSFNET (National Science Foundation Network), which is a network of 16 nodes and 25 links.

The simulation comprised 50 iterations, each of which generates 5 random connections, which were provisioned with every protection schemes evaluated. In each iteration, the 5 connections were evaluated against 4, 8, 12 and 16 failed links randomly selected. The objective was to evaluate the simulation scheme who protect more connections and how many bits compose it protection frame. The simulator evaluation criteria are three:

Number of successful connections: Number of connections that have not had failures in its primary working path, plus the number of connections that were recovered after a failure by the scheme.

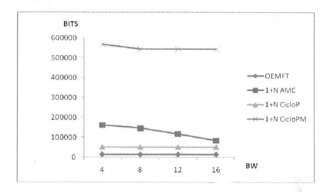

Fig. 2. Bandwidth Vs Protection bits

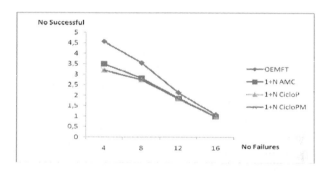

Fig. 3. Successful connections Vs Number of Failures

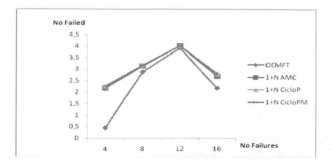

Fig. 4. Failed connections Vs Number of Failures

Number of failed connections: Number of connections that failed in its primary working path, and the scheme could not recover them.

Amount of protection bits generated: Measurement of bits generated for frame protection scheme.

Below you can see the average results of 50 iterations for the three evaluation criteria. Each graph contains the results of the four schemes.

From the results obtained from the simulation, we see that although the scheme 1 + N OEMFT has an exponential growth in data protection as more connections participating in the scheme, generated on average a less amount of data that the scheme protection in [19], which was due to the amount of p-cycles allocated to the scheme in [19] to make it tolerant of a M number of failures. The reason is that on each p-cycle, must be sent the protection data of all the nodes that make up the cycle and protection data are multiplied by a scalar of a linearly independent vector (which grows in proportion to the data size of the scale used) and then add all together by an XOR sum; this makes the total amount of data is proportional to the number of p-cycles.

In each iteration of the simulation scheme that protected more connections to the respective fault was that of 1 + N OEMFT, thanks to their distribution mechanism for the protection frame that reached all the destination node that at least has a healthy path. Although 1 + N OEMFT and [16] use the same distribution mechanism for the protection frame, [16] by relying on XOR sums could not recover when the number of failures was greater than one. Schemes [10] and [19] presented a recovery factor of zero because different faults of the simulation affected some links of the p-cycles, leaving multiple connections unprotected, that when they lose their primary working path, they did not have any backup path for recovering. Although the use of p-cycles is a very popular protection mechanism in mesh type network, in this simulation did not offer any protection because they shared several links with some of the primary working paths of some connections, which make them unsuitable at the time of failure. On the other hand, [19] could never offer the same degree of protection that 1 + N OEMFT, because the number of p-cycles passing through the connection pool was limited by the number of p-cycles in the network.

6   Conclusions

The proposal presented in this paper was compared against three schemes that use the same term of protection 1 + N [16] and [10] are schemes that only protect against a single failure, but [19] protects against as many failures as p-cycles could be assigned to protection. In all cases, 1 + N OEMFT offered a higher degree of protection because it protection frame was able to reach each destination node, as long as the node is not disconnected from the network (where all nodes links are down) and does not require the convergence process as in other schemes for the destination node to be able to use data protection, which makes its protection frame independent and each node only requires the frame for recovery, unlike [16], [10] and [19] that require protection data to pass each node in the scheme. Although the scheme 1 + N OEMFT has an exponential growth in protection data, as more connections are grouped under the same protection group, showed that on average generates less data protection than [16] and [19] thanks to the compression used. 1 + N OEMFT cannot compete against the amount of data generated by [10], but it compensate with the number of faults which can tolerate.

References

1. Zhang, J., Zhu, K., Mukherjee, B.: Comprehensive Study on Backup Reprovisioning to Remedy the Effect of Multiple-Link Failures in WDM Mesh Networks (2004)
2. Song, L., Zhang, J., Mukherjee, B.: A Comprehensive Study on Backup-Bandwidth Re-provisioning After Network-State Updates in Survivable Telecom Mesh Networks (2008)
3. Huang, Y.(G), Wen, W., Heritage, J.P., Mukherjee, B.: A Generalized Protection Framework Using a New Link-State Availability Model for Reliable Optical Networks (2004)
4. Huang, S., Xia, M., Martel, C., Mukherjee, B.: A Multistate Multipath Provisioning Scheme for Combating Node Failures in Telecom Mesh Networks (2009)
5. She, Q., Huang, X., Jue, J.P.: A Novel Graph Model for Maximum Survivability in Mesh Networks under Multiple Generic Risks (2007)
6. Prinz, R.G., Autenrieth, A., Schupke, D.A.: Dual Failure Protection in Multilayer Networks based on Overlay or Augmented Model (2005)
7. Bassiri, B., Heydari, S.S.: Network Survivability in Large-Scale Regional Failure Scenarios (2009)
8. Horie, T., Hasegaway, G., Murata, M.: Proactive recovery method against multiple network failures with overlay networking technique (2010)
9. Guo, L., Wang, X., Hou, W., Li, Y., Wang, C.: A New Differentiated Hamiltonian Cycle Protection Algorithm in Survivable WDM Mesh Networks (2009)
10. Kamal, A.E.: 1 + N Network Protection for Mesh Networks: Network Coding-Based Protection Using p-Cycles (2010)
11. Atkinson, G.W., Akyamac, A.A., Nagarajan, R.: Bandwidth-Efficient Protection Strategies for Multi-Protected Multi-Service Backbone Networks (2008)
12. Zhang, N., Bao, H.: Design of Protection Technology in WDM Optical Network (2009)
13. Askarian, A., Subramaniam, S., Brandt-Pearce, M.: Evaluation of Link Protection Schemes in Physically Impaired Optical Networks (2009)
14. Guo, L., Cao, J., Wang, X., Yang, T., Sun, Y., Zhang, J., Zhao, J.: Multi-Domain Wave-band Routing Protection Algorithms in WDM Networks (2010)
15. Guo, L., Wang, X., Zhang, X., Wang, H., Peng, Y.: Network Coding Protection Based on P-Cycles for Mesh Networks (2010)
16. Kamal, A.E.: A Generalized Strategy for 1+N Protection (2008)
17. Tang, Y., Cheng, G., Xu, Z., Al-Shaer, E.: Community-base Fault Diagnosis Using Incremental Belief Revision (2009)
18. Todd, B., Doucette, J.: Demand-Wise Shared Protection Network Design with Dual-Failure Restorability (2009)
19. Kamal, A.E.: 1+N Protection Against Multiple Link Failures in Mesh Network (2007)
20. Asthana, R., Singh, Y.N., Grover, W.D.: p-Cycles: An Overview (2010)
21. Haider, A., Harris, R.: Recovery techniques in next generation networks, Massey University (2007)
22. Zhang, J., Wang, X., Liu, H., Meng, J.: A Novel Access Control Strategy for Distributed Data Systems. Journal of Digital Information Management 8(5), 291–297 (2010)

The BASRAH System: A Method for Spoken Broadcast News Story Clustering

Zainab A. Khalaf Aleqili[1,2]

[1] School of Computer Sciences, Universiti Sains Malaysia (USM)
11800 Pinang, Malaysia
[2] Department of Computer Science, College of Science, University of Basrah
BASRAH, IRAQ
zainab_ali2004@yahoo.com

Abstract. In the current study, the BASRAH system was used to calculate confidence measures (CMs) and then use them to designate individual words provided by an automatic speech recognition system (ASR) as either accept or reject. This information about a recognized word can be used to reduce the impact of ASR transcription errors on retrieval performance. The system also can process multilingual broadcasts, which is more challenging than dealing with a single language. The BASRAH system is able to provide CMs for ASR output for large data sets based on a word acoustic score. In a case study, we successfully used the BASRAH system to first calculate CMs to clean up spoken multilingual (English and Malay) broadcast news transcription and then to identify the boundaries of the broadcast news stories.

Keywords: Spoken document retrieval, confidence measure, clustering, multilingual.

1 Introduction

Speech information retrieval systems are designed to retrieve and access spoken content. The process of speech retrieval uses two techniques: automatic speech recognition (ASR) and information retrieval (IR). ASR is used primarily in the digitization process to transcribe audio into text, and an IR system then is applied to access the desired information from the text [1-4]. However, ASR is an inaccurate process due to imperfect transcription of some spoken words, and this may cause a word mismatch in the retrieval step. Thus, one of the major challenges of SDR is the identification of word errors generated during the ASR step. Other obstacles to effective ASR include the lack of overt punctuation and formatting and problems detecting story boundaries (or story segments) [5, 6]. Processing stories that are broadcast in two or more languages (multilingual) poses another challenge. The BASRAH system described herein was designed to improve and enhance document retrieval performance by correctly detecting words and reducing the effect of incorrect words in ASR transcription of multilingual (English and Malay) broadcasts. It uses a confidence score and a clustering model to attain these goals.

R. Benlamri (Ed.): NDT 2012, Part I, CCIS 293, pp. 126–134, 2012.

2   Data Source

The data used to test the BASRAH system consisted of ~40 hours of news stories broadcast in the English language by Malay television stations. Although in English, these news reports used many Malay words, so the content was a mixture of Malay and English.

3   Proposed System

The system described in this paper, called BASRAH, was used to identify the story boundaries within multilingual (English and Malay) broadcast news recordings. After using recognition decoder output and computing confidence measures (CMs) to indicate the reliability of each word in the ASR transcription, the Euclidean algorithm is used to cluster the data. The goal of the clustering algorithm is to identify story boundaries and to prepare the data for other applications, such as classification, summarization, and title classification.

The BASRAH process proceeds in the stages described below:

Stage 1: This stage describes the ASR output. The text document is transformed into tokens separated by spaces. An IR system identifies and extracts these tokens, as some may be invalid words. In this study, we used CMs to remove the invalid words, as described below.

A recognition decoder typically generates data (i.e., words) in the form of an N-best list or word lattice. A CM then is computed to indicate the reliability that a speech segment was recognized correctly. This segment could be a sentence, a phrase, or a word. There are many different algorithms for estimating word-level CMs. They are based on word length, word acoustic score, or word density (i.e., the frequency of the word's occurrence in the N-best list) [3, 7-9].

In the BASRAH system, the CM is calculated based on word acoustic score, and the value of the CM then is checked against a threshold value to determine its acceptability. If the score is lower than the threshold, then the corresponding word is removed; otherwise the processing continues. The CM algorithm proceeds as follows:

```
Let D = [word₁, word₂, ..., wordₙ]
For each word in D
    Begin
            Compute Confidence Measure (CM)
            If (CM < threshold)
                    Remove word from D
    End.
```

Stage 2: Sentence boundary identification (SBI) refers to the problem of identifying the beginning and end of a sentence in natural language processing. This is an important step, as natural language processing tools require that the input text be divided into sentences. SBI can be challenging due to lack of punctuation marks in spoken documents, which leads to ambiguities in identifying sentence boundaries. In the present study, the Stanford Parser was used to identify sentence boundaries [10].

Stage 3: In this stage, an algorithm is used to assign a particular part of speech (POS) to each word in the document. POS tagging is the process of marking words in a text to correspond to a particular part of speech, and it is based on the definition and context relationship of a given word with related and adjacent words in a sentence. The POS tagger model contains a set of tags, including verb (V), noun (N), adverb (AV), adjective (AJ), to (TO), negation (NOT), conjunction (CJ), preposition (PP), determiner (DT), and other (OTH). Each word from the input sentence is matched with one of the tags in the tag set. The BASRAH system uses the Brill tagger algorithm to assign a POS tag to each word [11, 12].

The Brill tagger can be described as an "error-driven transformation-based tagger." It is an error-driven remedy in the sense that it oversees supervised learning and is transformation based [11-13]. In other words, a tag is set to every word and then is changed using a group of predetermined rules. Generally, WordNet captures only basic POS tags, such as noun, verb, adjective, and adverb. Therefore, the Brill tagger algorithm is used to assign appropriate tags to other words that do not fall into these categories. The Brill tagger algorithm for POS tagging proceeds as follows:

```
Let D = [word1, word2, ..., wordn]
For each word in D
    Begin
        If (probability (word) = 1)
            Tag = get tag from WordNet
        Else if (probability (word)   < 1)
            If (word = article)
                Tag = DT
            Else if (word = conjunction)
                Tag = CJ
            Else if unknown word
                Tag = OTH
    End
```

The output of this process is then stored in an XML document. Figure 1 shows an example of POS output [11, 13].

```
more/AV hiding/N behind/PP bushes/N with/PP traffic/V cops/V . government/N
protests/V gunned/V down/PP in/PP syria/N at/PP least/AV seventy/AJ five/N
killed/V . chief/N minister/N lim/OTH guan/N eng/OTH says/V it/N is/V highly/AV
unlikely/AJ that/CJ the/DT federal/AJ government/N would/MV build/V a/N
nuclear/AJ power/N plant/V in/PP the/DT state/N speaking/V to/TO reporters/N
he/N said/V the/DT assurance/N was/V given/V to/TO him/N by/PP energy/N green/V
technology/N and/CJ water/V minister/V datuk/OTH seri/OTH peter/N chin/N .
letter/V to/TO the/DT opposition/N led/V state/V government/N on/PP wednesday/N
datuk/OTH seri/OTH peter/N chin/N said/V if/CJ putrajaya/N was/V to/TO
construct/V the/DT plant/N it/N would/MV have/V to/TO abide/V by/PP the/DT
regulatory/AJ safety/N guidelines/N set/V by/PP the/DT international/AJ
atomic/AJ energy/N agency/N which/OTH include/V avoiding/V densely/AV
populated/V areas/N such/AV as/CJ in/PP penang/OTH . minister/V was/V replying/V
```

Fig. 1. POS output

Stage 4: Stopping words are removed at this stage. Stopping words are words that frequently occur in speech but have no real meaning themselves. As an example, the English articles "a," "an," and "the" have no real significance to the document's topic, yet they appear frequently in almost every document collection. To avoid the noise problem that arises from such generic terms and to reduce the size of the index, these words are deleted during the indexing stage. The removal of such words helps improve the quality of the search results by maintaining only the words that contribute specific information to each document [14].

Stage 5: In this stage, the stemming algorithm is used to improve the effectiveness of IR. During this process, variant forms of the same word with different endings are reduced to a common stem. Stems are useful in IR because they can be used to unify vocabularies. This process reduces both term variants and storage space and also increases the matching probability of the documents [15, 16]. The BASRAH system uses WordNet to stem each word in the document.

Stage 6: The result of the previous stage is a list of words that represents documents in the collection. To facilitate an efficient search through these words, an index that includes the frequency of each word is created.

Stage 7: Finally, news story boundaries are identified using the clustering algorithm.

There are varied types of fundamental modes of understanding and learning, and one of these is the organization of data into meaningful groupings. Specifically, cluster analysis is a formalized mode of examining into the methods and algorithms for grouping or clustering objects based on their measured or perceived intrinsic characteristics or the common properties they possess [17, 18].

The most common approach to grouping data involves calculating the Euclidean distance between objects; this distance is calculated as the square root of the total summation of squared differences between coordinates of a pair of objects [17]. If Cartesian coordinates, if $x = (x1, x2, ..., xn)$ and $y = (y1, y2, ..., yn)$ are two variables or points in Euclidean n-space, then the distance from x to y or from y to x is given by [19]:

$$d(x,y)=d(y,x)=\sqrt{\left(x_1-y_1\right)^2+\left(x_2-y_2\right)^2+\ldots+\left(x_n-y_n\right)^2}=\sqrt{\sum_{i=1}^{n}\left(x_i-y_i\right)^2}.$$

Multivariate data analysis then is applied to measure the distance between two samples or two variables. Figure 2 is a data flow diagram showing how the proposed BASRAH system proceeds, ultimately using Euclidean distance in the clustering step.

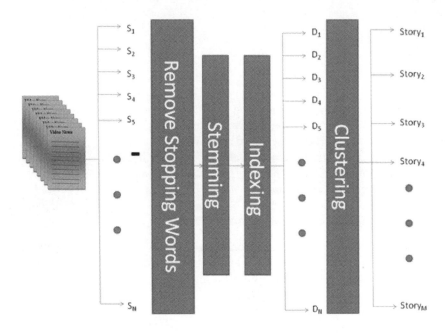

Fig. 2. Clustering model using Euclidean distance

4   Experimental Results

One of the major challenges of spoken document retrieval is identifying word errors generated by ASR. Another is dealing with spoken documents that include words in more than one language. The BASRAH system was designed to detect boundaries in multilingual (English and Malay) broadcast news stories. This system uses CMs of the ASR to minimize the word error rate in ASR transcription and a Euclidean distance algorithm for clustering.

In this experiment, we used broadcast news documents. We divided the documents into four experimental data sets. The first set contained more than 300 sentences containing 24 news stories; the second set contained 20 news stories consisting of 239 sentences; the third set contained 17 news stories with 164 sentences; and the fourth set contained more than 345 sentences containing 27 news stories. Figures 3 and 4 show the results of dataset 1 before and after undergoing the clustering process (i.e., stage 7), respectively.

Fig. 3. Dataset 1 before clustering

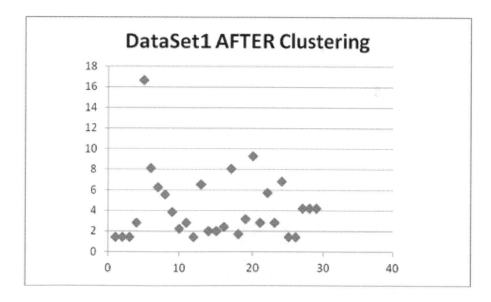

Fig. 4. Dataset 1 after clustering

5   Related Work

In addition to this study, a number of other attempts have been made to detect stories boundaries (i.e., to cluster stories) within spoken documents. For example, Hazen et al. [3] used two methods. In the first, they attempted to reduce recognition errors using an explicit model for identifying the presence of out-of-vocabulary (OOV) words. The second technique used a confidence scoring model to detect potentially misrecognized words from a group of confidence features extracted from the recognition process. The Akbacak system [19] uses language leveraging algorithms within a spoken information search system to process multilingual (English and Spanish) broadcast news for which training resources are limited. To process Turkish language documents, Parlak et al. [20] used subword units as recognition and indexing units to reduce the OOV rate and the index alternative recognition hypothesis to handle ASR errors. Lo et al. [4] described the application of a multiscale paradigm for Chinese spoken document retrieval in an attempt to improve retrieval performance. In a study of Indonesian spoken documents, Yonathan et al. [21] described four ASR result types: 1-best output, N-best output, N-best pronunciation output, and word posterior lattice. They used three types of query: phrase, single word, and sentence queries. Rosenberg et al. [22] presented results from a broadcast news story segmentation system developed for the SRI NIGHTINGALE system operating on English, Arabic, and Mandarin news shows to provide input to subsequent question-answering processes. Finally, the current system, BASRAH, was designed to detect story boundaries in multilingual (English and Malay) broadcast news stories. This system uses CMs of the ASR to minimize the word error rate in ASR transcription and a Euclidean distance algorithm for clustering.

6   Conclusions

The BASRAH system described herein was used to successfully identify story boundaries of multilingual broadcast news using the Euclidean algorithm after using recognition decoder output and computed CMs to indicate the reliability of each word in the ASR transcription. The important characteristic of the clustering method used in this system is that it can obtain the partitions automatically without knowing the number of news stories.

Acknowledgement. The auther would like to thank Basem H. A. (University of Sciences Malaysia, USM) and Maytham Alabbas (The University of Manchester, UK) for important suggestions and for helpful discussions. She also would like to extend thanks to the anonymous reviewers for their helpful comments. She owes her deepest gratitude to USM and TWAS for its support of her PhD research.

References

1. Arisoy, E., Can, D., Parlak, S., Sak, H., Saraclar, M.: Turkisk Broadcast News Transcription and Retrieval. IEEE Transactions on Audio, Speech and Language Processing 17, 874–883 (2009)
2. Chelba, C., Hazen, T.J., Salaclar, M.: Retrieval and Browsing of Spoken Content. IEEE Singal Processing Magazine 25, 39–49 (2008)
3. Jiang, H., Seneff, S., Polifroni, J.: Recognition confidence scoring and its use in speech understanding systems. Computer Speech and Language 16, 49–67 (2002)
4. Lo, W.-K., Meng, H.M., Ching, P.C.: Multi-Scale Spoken Document Retrieval for Cantonese Broadcast News. International Journal Of Speech Technology 7, 203–219 (2004)
5. Ostendorf, M., et al.: Speech Segmentation and its Impact on Spoken Document Processing (2007)
6. Lu, M.-M., Xie, L., Fu, Z.-H., Jiang, D.-M., Zhang, Y.-N.: Multi-Modal Feature Integration for Story Boundary Detection in Broadcast News. IEEE (2010) ISBN 978-1-4244-6245-2
7. Jiang, H.: Confidence measures for speech recognition: A survey. Speech Communication 45, 455–470 (2005)
8. Senay, G., Linarès, G., Lecouteux, B.: A Segment-Level Confidence Measure For Spoken Document Retrieval, vol. 11. IEEE (2011)
9. Skantze, G.: The use of speech recogition confidence scores in dialogue systems. Speech Technology (2003)
10. Stanford University, The Stanford Parser: A statistical parser,
    http://nlp.stanford.edu/software/lex-parser.shtml
11. Megyesi, B.: Brill's POS Tagger with Extended Lexical Templates for Hungarian. In: Proceedings of the Workshop (W01) on Machine Learning in Human Language Technology: ACAI 1999, pp. 22–28 (1999)
12. Sakti, S., et al.: In: Third International Workshop on Malay and Indonesian Language Engineering (MALINDO), Singapore (2009)
13. Megyesi, B.: Brill's Rule-Based Part of Speech Tagger for Hungarian. Stockholm University (1998)
14. Johnsont, S.E., Jourlint, P., Mooret, G.L., Jones, K.S., Woodlandt, P.C.: In: IEEE International Conference on Acoustics, Speech And Signal Processing (ICASSP), pp. 49–52 (1999)
15. Adriani, M., Asian, J., Nazief, B., Tahaghoghi, S.M.M., Williams, H.E.: Stemming Indonesian: A confix-stripping approach. ACM Transactions on Asian Language Information Processing (TALIP) 6 (2007)
16. Hartl, A.: Other Tips & Tricks: Word Stemming in Java with WordNet and JWNL (2010)
17. Cios, K.J., Pedrycz, W., Swiniarski, R.W., Kurgan, L.A.: Data Mining A knowledge Discovery Approach, pp. 289–306 (2007)
18. Jain, A.K.: Data Clustering: 50 Years Beyond K-Means1. Pattern Recognition Letters 31, 651–666 (2010)
19. Akbacak, M.: Rebust Spoken Document Retrieval in Multilingual and Nosiy Acoustic Envernments (2009)
20. Parlak, S., Saraclar, M.: Performance Analysis and Improvement of Turkish Broadcast News Retrieval. IEEE Transactions on Audio, Speech and Language Processing 20, 731–741 (2011)

21. Yonathan, A., Adriani, M.: Indonesian Spoken Document Retrieval Using Statistical Methods
22. Rosenberg, A., Hirschberg, J.: Story segmentation of broadcast news in English, Mandarin and Arabic. In: Proceedings of the Human Language Technology Conference of the NAACL, Companion Volume: Short Papers. Association for Computational Linguistics (2006)
23. Mousavipour, S.F., Seyedtabaii, S.: Dual Particle-Number RBPF for Speech Enhancement. Journal of E-Technology 2, 159–169 (2011)

Unsupervised Clustering Approach for Network Anomaly Detection

Iwan Syarif[1,2], Adam Prugel-Bennett[1], and Gary Wills[1]

[1] School of Electronics and Computer Science, University of Southampton, UK
{isle08,apb,gbw}@ecs.soton.ac.uk
[2] Eletronics Engineering Polytechnics Institute of Surabaya, Indonesia
iwanarif@eepis-its.edu

Abstract. This paper describes the advantages of using the anomaly detection approach over the misuse detection technique in detecting unknown network intrusions or attacks. It also investigates the performance of various clustering algorithms when applied to anomaly detection. Five different clustering algorithms: k-Means, improved k-Means, k-Medoids, EM clustering and distance-based outlier detection algorithms are used. Our experiment shows that misuse detection techniques, which implemented four different classifiers (naïve Bayes, rule induction, decision tree and nearest neighbour) failed to detect network traffic, which contained a large number of unknown intrusions; where the highest accuracy was only 63.97% and the lowest false positive rate was 17.90%. On the other hand, the anomaly detection module showed promising results where the distance-based outlier detection algorithm outperformed other algorithms with an accuracy of 80.15%. The accuracy for EM clustering was 78.06%, for k-Medoids it was 76.71%, for improved k-Means it was 65.40% and for k-Means it was 57.81%. Unfortunately, our anomaly detection module produces high false positive rate (more than 20%) for all four clustering algorithms. Therefore, our future work will be more focus in reducing the false positive rate and improving the accuracy using more advance machine learning techniques.

Keywords: K-Means, EM clustering, k-medoids, intrusion detection system, anomaly detection, outlier detection.

1 Introduction

Intrusion detection is a process of gathering intrusion-related knowledge occurring in the process of monitoring events and analyzing them for signs of intrusion [1][5]. There are two basic IDS approaches: misuse detection (signature-based) and anomaly detection. The misuse detection system uses patterns of well-known attacks to match and identify known intrusions. It performs pattern matching between the captured network traffic and attack signatures. If a match is detected, the system generates an alarm. The main advantage of the signature detection paradigm is that it can accurately detect instances of known attacks. The main disadvantage is that it lacks the ability to detect new intrusions or zero-day attacks [2][3].

R. Benlamri (Ed.): NDT 2012, Part I, CCIS 293, pp. 135–145, 2012.
© Springer-Verlag Berlin Heidelberg 2012

The anomaly detection model works by identifying an attack by looking for behaviour that is out of the normal. It establishes a baseline model of behaviour for users and components in a computer or network. Deviations from the baseline cause alerts that direct the attention of human operators to the anomalies [3][4][5]. This system searches for anomalies either in stored data or in the system activity. The main advantage of anomaly detection is that it does not require prior knowledge of an intrusion and thus can detect new intrusions. The main disadvantage is that it may not be able to describe what constitutes an attack and may have a high false positive rate [2][3][4].

2   Clustering Algorithms

Clustering is a technique for finding patterns in unlabelled data with many dimensions. Clustering has attracted interest from researchers in the field of intrusion detection [5,6]. The main advantage of clustering algorithm is the ability to learn from and detect intrusions in the audit data without explicit descriptions (intrusion signatures) which usually provided by security experts.

There are two different approaches to clustering-based anomaly detection. The first approach is called unsupervised clustering where the anomaly detection model is trained using unlabelled data that consists of both normal as well as attack traffics. The second approach is called semi-supervised clustering where the model is trained using normal data only to build a profile of normal activity. The idea behind the first approach is that anomalous or attack data forms a small percentage of the total data. Based on this assumption, anomalies and attacks can be detected based on cluster sizes, large clusters correspond to normal data and the rest of the data points, which are outliers, correspond to attacks [5,6,7].

Eskin et al.[7] and Portnoy et al.[8] introduced the use of clustering algorithms to detect network traffics anomalies. Their algorithm starts with an empty set of clusters and generates the clusters with a single pass through the dataset. First, the data set needs to be normalized (convert into Z form), it then computes the distance between each new instance and its centroid. The cluster with the shortest distance is selected, and if that distance is less than or equal W (the cluster width) then the instance is assigned to that cluster, otherwise it creates a new cluster with this instance as the centre.

Based on the previous assumption, the normal clusters (clusters which contain normal data) will have much larger number of instances compare to anomalous cluster. Eskin and Portnoy proposed an idea to model the normal traffic by selecting X percentage (where X is an input parameter) of clusters containing the largest number of instances and label them as normal and then they labeled the rest of the clusters as anomalous which might be considered as an intrusion/attack.

In this paper, we implement and compare the performance of five different clustering algorithms in our anomaly detection module which are k-Mean, improved k-Mean, k-Medoids, EM clustering and distance-based outlier detection algorithms.

2.1   k-Means

k-Means which is firstly proposed by James MacQueen, is a well-known and widely used clustering algorithm. k-Means is one of the simplest clustering algorithms in machine learning which can be used to automatically recognize groups of similar instances/items/objects/points in data training. The algorithm classifies instances to a pre-defined number of clusters specified by the user (e.g. assume *k* clusters). The first important step is to choose a set of k instances as centroids (centres of the clusters) randomly, usually choose one for each cluster as far as possible from each other. Next, the algorithm continues to read each instance from the data set and assigns it to the nearest cluster. There are some methods to measure the distance between instance and the centroid but the most popular one is Euclidian distance. The cluster centroids are always recalculated after every instance insertion. This process is iterated until no more changes are made. The k-Means algorithm is explained in this following pseudo code.

```
1. Select the total number of clusters (k)
2. Choose random k points and set as centroid
3. Calculate the distance from each instance to all
   centroids using Euclidean method
4. Assign each instance to the closest centroid
5. Recalculate the positions of the centroids
6. Repeat step 3-5 until the centroids do not change
```

2.2   k-Medoids

k-Medoids is a clustering algorithm similar to k-Means, which attempts to minimize the distance between points and its centre (centroid). A medoid is a data point which acts as an exemplar for all other data points in the cluster. The k-Means algorithm is very sensitive to outliers because if there is an object with a very large value, the data distribution may be biased or distorted [13]. In this case, k-Medoids is more robust to noise and outliers because in this algorithm the partitioning method is performed based on the principle of minimizing the sum of dissimilarities between each object in a cluster. The pseudo code of k-Medoids is explained below [13]:

```
1. Input a data set D consists of n objects
2. Input the number of clusters K
3. Select k objects randomly as the initial cluster
   centres or cluster medoids
4. Assign each object to the cluster with the nearest
   medoid
5. Calculate the total distance between the object and
   its cluster medoid
6. Swap the medoid with non-medoid object
7. Recalculate the positions of the k medoids
8. Repeat 4-7 until the medoids become fixed
```

2.3   EM Clustering

Expectation Maximization (EM) clustering is a variant of k-Means clustering and is widely used for density estimation of data points in an unsupervised clustering [14]. In the EM clustering, we use an EM algorithm to find the parameters which maximize the likelihood of the data, assuming that the data is generated from k normal distributions. The algorithm learns both the means and the covariance of the normal distributions. This method requires several inputs which are the data set, the total number of clusters, the maximum error tolerance and the maximum number of iteration.

The EM can be divided into two important steps which are Expectation (E-step) and Maximization (M-step). The goal of E-step is to calculate the expectation of the likelihood (the cluster probabilities) for each instance in the dataset and then re-label the instances based on their probability estimations. The M-step is used to re-estimate the parameters values from the E-step results. The outputs of M-step (the parameters values) are then used as inputs for the following E-step. These two processes are performed iteratively until the results convergence. The mathematical formulas of EM clustering are described in [14][15] and the pseudo codes can be found in [15].

2.4   Outlier Detection Algorithms

Outlier detection is a technique to find patterns in data that do not conform to expected behaviour [6]. Most of the clustering algorithms do not assign all points to clusters but account for noise objects, in other words clustering algorithms are optimized to find clusters rather than outliers. Outlier detection algorithms look for outliers by applying one of the clustering algorithms and retrieve the noise set, therefore the performance of outlier detection algorithms depends on how good the clustering algorithm captures the structure of clusters.

Outlier detection can be divided into two approaches: distance-based outlier detection and density-based outlier detection. The first method, distance-based outlier detection algorithms, works on the assumptions that the normal data objects have a dense neighbourhood and the outliers are far apart from their neighbours. The second method works on assumptions that the density around a normal data object is similar to the density around its neighbours while the density around an outlier is considerably different to the density around its neighbours. The density-based approach compares the density around a point with the density around its local neighbours by computing an outlier score. This paper focuses on distance-based outlier detection algorithm only.

The distance-based outlier detection approach,   which is based on the nearest neighbour algorithm was first introduced by Ng et al [16] and implements a well-defined distance metric to detect outliers, the greater the distance of the object to its neighbour, the more likely it is to be an outlier. This method calculates the distance between each pair of objects using a nested loop (NL) algorithm and then the objects which are far away from the majority are signed as outliers. The mathematical formulas of distance-based outlier detection methods and their pseudo codes are described in more details [16][17].

3   Experimental Setup

The following section describes the intrusion data sets used in the experiment, the performance metric used to evaluate the proposed system and the experimental settings and its results.

3.1   Intrusion Dataset

One of the most widely used data sets for evaluating IDS is the DARPA/Lincoln Laboratory off-line evaluation dataset or IDEVAL[9]. IDEVAL is the most comprehensive test set available today and it was used to develop the 1999 KDD Cup data mining competition [10]. In this experiment, we use the NSL-KDD intrusion data, which was provided to solve some problems in KDD'99, particularly that its training and test sets contained a huge number of redundant records with about 78% and 75% of the records being duplicated in the training and test sets, respectively. This may cause the classification algorithms to be biased towards these redundant records and thus prevent it from classifying other records [11].

Table 1. List of intrusions in training and testing data

Intrusions which exist in both training and testing data	Intrusions which only exist in testing data
back, buffer_overflow, ftp_write, guess_passwd, imap, ipsweep, land, loadmodule, multihop, neptune, nmap, phf, pod, portsweep, rootkit, satan, smurf, spy, teardrop, warezclient, warezmaster	apache2, httptunnel, mailbomb, mscan, named, perl, processtable, ps, saint, sendmail, snmpgetattack, snmpguess, sqlattack, udpstorm, worm, xlock, xsnoop, xterm

The intrusion data set consists of forty different intrusions classified into four main categories: DoS (Denial of Service), R2L (Remote to Local Attack), U2R (User to Root Attack) and Probing Attack. The training dataset consists of 25,191 instances and the testing dataset consists of 11,950 instances. The testing data set has many intrusions, which do not exist in the training data, as shown in Table 1.

3.2   Performance Metric

We use accuracy rate and false positive rate as the performance criteria based on the following metric shown in Table 2 below.

Table 2. Performance metric

		Actual Result	
		Intrusion	Normal
Predicted Result	Intrusion	True Positive (TP)	False Positive (FP)
	Normal	False Negative (FN)	True Negative (TN)

True Positive (TP) is a condition when an actual attack is successfully detected by the IDS. True Negative (TN) is a condition where normal traffic is detected as a normal, in other words there is no attack nor IDS alert is raised. False Positive (FP) is an alert that indicates that an attack is in progress when in fact there was no such attack. False Negative (FN) is a failure of IDS to detect an actual attack [12]. The accuracy rate and false positive rate are measured using the following formulae:

$$Accuracy\ rate = \frac{TP+FN}{TP+TN+FP+FN} \quad (1), False\ Positive = \frac{FP}{TP+FP} \quad (2)$$

3.3   Misuse Detection Module

Our proposed misuse detection module consists of five phases: feature extraction, dimensionality reduction, classification algorithms, apply model and performance measurement & analysis as explained in Figure 1 below.

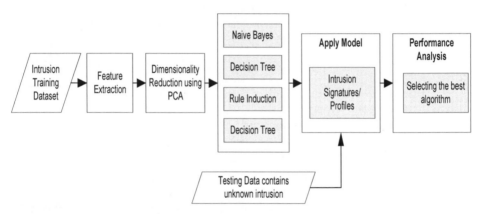

Fig. 1. Misuse Detection System Design

We use Principal Component Analysis (PCA) as a dimensionality reduction algorithm. Dimensionality reduction is the process of reducing the number of random variables under consideration, which is very useful to reduce the computational cost as well as to avoid over-fitting. After that, we apply four different classifiers (naïve Bayes, decision tree, rule induction and nearest neighbour) into the misuse detection module in order to find the best method in detecting intrusion based on accuracy, false positive and speed (computation time).

3.4   Anomaly Detection Module

We designed the anomaly detection module as shown in Figure 2 below. This module implements several unsupervised clustering algorithms which do not required labeled dataset. In the feature extraction module we select only numerical data and handle missing value, then we transform the data into normal form. Normalization is a popular method used to convert all attributes/variables to a common scale with an average of zero and standard deviation of one.

Intrusion data set consists of 41 attributes, which may have different scale and different distribution. Some attributes may have a wide range of values while other attributes are very narrowly distributed. These differences in distribution make it difficult to measure the similarities or significant differences between variables/ categories in the data sets. To solve this problem, we will convert the data set into normal form. Normalization (or standardization) is the most commonly used method to convert all attributes to a common scale with an average of zero and standard deviation of one.

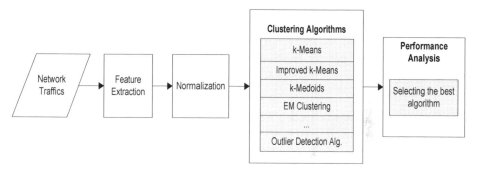

Fig. 2. Anomaly Detection System Design

Given a training dataset, the average and standard deviation feature vectors are calculated:

$$\text{avg\_vector}[j] = \frac{1}{N} \sum_{\substack{i=1 \\ k=0}}^{N} \text{instance}_i[j]$$

$$\text{std\_vector}[j] = \sqrt{\frac{1}{N-1} \sum_{i=1}^{N} (\text{instance}_i[j] - \text{avg\_vector}[j])^2}$$

where vector[j] is the jth element (feature) of the vector. Then each instance (feature vector) in the training set is converted as follows:

$$new\_instance[j] = \frac{instance[j] - avg\_vector[j]}{\text{std\_vector}[j]},$$

4   Experimental Results and Discussion

The following section discusses and analyses the results of both the misuse detection module and the anomaly detection module.

4.1   Misuse Detection Module

In the first experiment, we use only the training data which contains around 22 different types of intrusions and apply 10-fold cross validation in the misuse detection module. The results are shown in Table 3 below.

Table 3. Misuse Detection performance using 10 fold cross validation

Algorithm	Accuracy	False Positive
Naïve Bayes	89.59%	10.60%
Nearest Neighbour	99.44%	0.60%
Rule Induction	99.58%	0.40%
Decision Tree	99.56%	0.40%

Table 3 shows that misuse detection achieves very good results when detecting known intrusion. Three of the four algorithms (nearest neighbour, rule induction and decision tree) achieve more than 99% accuracy and the false positive rates are less than 1%.

In the second experiment, we use a testing data to evaluate the performance of intrusion model in the misuse detection module. The testing data contains 22 types of known intrusions and 18 types of unknown intrusions. The results of the second experiment are shown in Table 4 below.

Table 4. Misuse Detection performance using testing data

Algorithm	Accuracy	False Positive
Naïve Bayes	55.77%	34.80%
Nearest Neighbour	62.84%	20.90%
Rule Induction	63.69%	18.00%
Decision Tree	63.97%	17.90%

Table 4 shows that the misuse detection module does not perform well in detecting data which contains a large number of unknown intrusions where the highest accuracy is only 63.97% and the lowest false positive is 17.90%.

4.2   Anomaly Detection Module

We applied five unsupervised clustering algorithms which are k-Means, improved k-Means, k-Medoids, Expectation-Maximization (EM) clustering and distance-based outlier detection algorithm into the anomaly detection module and used an unlabelled dataset as an input and the results are shown in Table 5 below.

Compared to the misuse detection module which has an accuracy of only 63.97% (evaluated using testing data), the anomaly detection module has a better performance in detecting novel intrusion. These clustering algorithms are able to detect intrusions without prior knowledge. In this experiment, the distance-based outlier detection algorithm achieves the best accuracy with 80.15%, followed by EM clustering 78.06%, k-Medoids with 76.71%, improved k-Means 65.40% and k-Means 57.81%.

Table 5. Anomaly Detection accuracy using clustering algorithms

Algorithm	Accuracy	False Positive
k-Means	57.81%	22.95%
improved k-Means	65.40%	21.52%
k-Medoids	76.71%	21.83%
EM clustering	78.06%	20.74%
Distance-based outlier detection	80.15%	21.14%

Unfortunately, all of these algorithms have quite high positive rates with more than 20%. This means that there are around 20% of normal traffics predicted as intrusions. Because of the high positive rates, this anomaly detection module would not be viable in the real world. Therefore, our future work will be focused on how to reduce the false positive while still improving the accuracy.

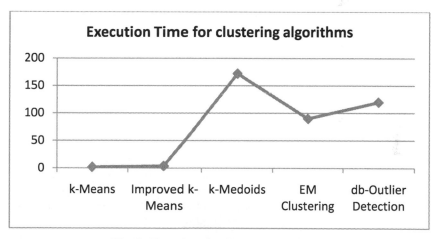

Fig. 3. Clustering algorithms execution time

Even though the distance-based outlier detection algorithm outperforms the other four algorithms in accuracy, unfortunately its computation time is relatively high. The k-Means algorithm is the fastest but its accuracy is the worst (57.81%), in contrast the k-Medoids algorithm is the slowest but its accuracy is relatively high (76.71%).

Since the distance-based outlier detection algorithm has achieved the highest accuracy, we continue our experiment by applying this algorithm in the anomaly detection module. Now we classify the intrusion dataset into four types of intrusion which are probing attacks, DoS attacks, R2L attacks and U2R attacks. The results are shown in Figure 4 below.

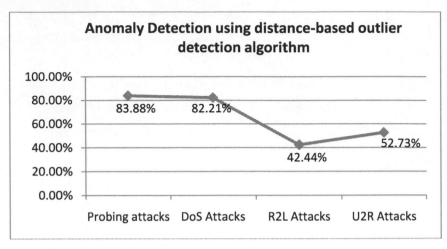

Fig. 4. Anomaly detection using distance-based outlier detection algorithm

This experiment shows that the distance-based outlier detection algorithm is able to detect probing attacks with 83.8% accuracy and DoS attacks with 82.21% accuracy. Unfortunately, this algorithm failed to accurately detect R2L attack (42.44%) and U2R attacks (52.73%). One reason is that the R2L attacks and U2R attacks have very similar behaviour with normal traffics which makes them very difficult to distinguish. Furthermore, the number of R2L and U2R attacks in intrusion dataset is very small compare to the whole data set. The number of R2L attacks is only 0.83% and U2R is only 0.04%.

5   Conclusions

Our experiment shows that the misuse detection technique achieves a very good performance with more than 99% accuracy when detecting known intrusion but it fails to accurately detect data set with a large number of unknown intrusions where the highest accuracy is only 63.97%. In contrast, the anomaly detection approach shows promising results where the distance-based outlier detection method outperforms the other three clustering algorithms with the accuracy of 80.15%, followed by EM clustering (78.06%), k-Medoids (76.71%), improved k-Means (65.40%) and k-Means (57.81%). Further experiment shows that the distance-based outlier detection performs very well in detecting probing attacks (83.88%) and DoS attacks (82.21%) but it fails to detect R2L attacks (42.44%) and U2R attacks (52.73%). Unfortunately, our anomaly detection module produces high positive rate (more than 20%) for all four clustering algorithms. Therefore, our future work will be focused in reducing the false positive rate and improving the accuracy using more advance machine learning techniques.

References

1. Gudadhe, M., Prasad, P., Wankhade, K.: A new data mining based network intrusion detection model. In: International Conference on Computer & Communication Technology (ICCCT 2010), pp. 731–735 (2010)
2. Panda, M., Patra, M.R.: Ensemble of Classifiers for Detecting Network Intrusion. In: International Conference on Advances in Computing, Communication and Control (ICAC3 2009), pp. 510–515 (2009)
3. Garcia-Teodoro, P., Diaz-Verdejo, J., Macia-Fernandez, G., Vazquez, E.: Anomaly-based network intrusion detection: Techniques, systems and challenges. Computer & Security 28(1-2), 18–28 (2009)
4. Davis, J.J., Clark, A.J.: Data preprocessing for anomaly based network intrusion detection: A review. Computer & Security 30(6-7), 353–375 (2011)
5. Patcha, A., Park, J.-M.: An Overview of Anomaly Detection Techniques: Existing Solutions and Latest Technological Trends. Computer Networks 51(12), 3448–3470 (2007)
6. Chandola, V., Banarjee, A., Kumar, V.: Anomaly Detection: A Survey. ACM Computing Survey Journal 41(3) (2009)
7. Eskin, E., Arnold, A., Prerau, M., Portnoy, L., Stolfo, S.: A Geometric Framework for Unsupervised Anomaly Detection: Detecting Intrusions in Unlabeled Data. In: Proceedings of the Seventeenth International Conference on Machine Learning, pp. 255–262. Morgan Kaufmann Publichsers Inc. (2000)
8. Portnoy, L., Eskin, E., Stolfo, S.: Intrusion detection with unlabeled data using clustering. In: Proceeding ACM Workshop on Data Mining Applied to Security (2001)
9. DARPA Intrusion Detection Data Sets,
   http://www.ll.mit.edu/mission/communications/
   ist/corpora/ideval/data/index.html
10. KDD Cup 1999 Intrusion Data Sets,
   http://kdd.ics.uci.edu/databases/kddcup99/kddcup99.html
11. Tavallaee, M., Bagheri, E., Lu, W., Ghorbani, A.: A Detailed Analysis of the KDD CUP 99 Data Set. In: Submitted to Second IEEE Symposium on Computational Intelligence for Security and Defense Applications, CISDA (2009)
12. Whitman, M.E., Mattord, H.J.: Principles of Information Security. Course Technology, 4th edn. (2011) ISBN: 1111138214
13. Vermurugan, T., Santhanam, T.: Computational Complexity between K-Means and K-Medoids Clustering Algorithms for Normal and Uniform Distributions of Data Points. Journal of Computer Science 6(3), 363–368 (2010)
14. Seetha, J., Varadharajan, R., Vaithiyananthan, V.: Unsupervised Learning Algorithm for Color Texture Segmentation Based Multiscale Image Fusion. European Journal of Scientific Research 67, 506–511 (2012) ISSN 1450-216X
15. Lu, W., Tong, H.: Detecting Network Anomalies Using CUSUM and EM Clustering. In: Cai, Z., Li, Z., Kang, Z., Liu, Y. (eds.) ISICA 2009. LNCS, vol. 5821, pp. 297–308. Springer, Heidelberg (2009)
16. Knorr, E.M., Ng, R.T.: Finding intensional knowledge of distance-based outliers. In: VLDB 1999: 25th Int. Conf. on Very Large Data Bases, San Francisco, pp. 211–222 (1999)
17. Orair, G.H., Teixeira, C.H.C., Meira Jr., W., Wang, Y., Parthasarathy, S.: Distance-based Outlier Detection: Consolidation and Renewed Bearing. In: The 36th Int. Conf. on Very Large Data Bases, Singapore (September 2010)

BNITE: Bayesian Networks-Based Intelligent Traffic Engineering for Energy-Aware NGN

Abul Bashar

College of Computer Engineering and Sciences
Prince Mohammad Bin Fahd University
Al-Khobar 31952, Kingdom of Saudi Arabia
abashar@pmu.edu.sa

Abstract. Network Management Systems (NMS) are used to monitor the network and maintain its performance with a prime focus on guaranteeing sustained QoS to the services. However, another aspect that must be given due importance is the energy consumption of the network elements, specially during the off-peak periods. This paper proposes and implements a novel idea of energy-aware network management that looks at a scenario where the NMS plays an important role in making the network energy efficient by predictively turning the network elements to sleep mode when they are underutilized. To this end, it designs and evaluates a Bayesian Networks (BN) based Intelligent Traffic Engineering (BNITE) solution, which provides intelligent decisions to the NMS for it to adaptively alter the operational modes of the network elements, with minimum compromise in the network performance and QoS guarantees. Energy-aware Traffic Engineering algorithms are developed for both stand-alone (single router) and centralised (multiple routers) scenarios to prove the concept. Simulated network experiments using NCTUns and Hugin Researcher have been used to demonstrate the feasibility and practicality of the proposed solution. Significant energy savings with minimal degradation in QoS metrics demonstrate the benefits of BNITE solution for real-world networks such as the NGN.

Keywords: Energy-awareness, Network Management Systems (NMS), Bayesian Networks (BN), Next Generation Networks (NGN).

1   Introduction

The Internet and the telecommunication network infrastructure is growing at a rapid pace and so is its energy consumption. It has been found that the telecommunication and computer network equipment consumes about 12.6 TW-h (TeraWatt-hour) per year, which is 13% of the total energy used by the Internet and telecoms sector [1]. This consumption translates to an annual cost of about $1 billion in the US alone, with proportional CO_2 emissions contributing to global warming [2]. As such, researchers from the Internet community have seriously started to work towards reducing energy consumption in network devices. However, with the global deployments of Next Generation Networks (NGN) and

R. Benlamri (Ed.): NDT 2012, Part I, CCIS 293, pp. 146–160, 2012.

the increasing demand from the consumers for multimedia rich applications, the energy expenditure is expected to increase further in the near future. It is observed that, the end-to-end QoS promised by the NGN is in direct conflict with the objective of saving energy in network equipment, since to provide the required QoS, the network should be up and running most of the time to provide for fault tolerance and resilience. This conflict is explored in this paper, along with a proposed solution based on an intelligent Network Management System (NMS), which is energy-aware.

One of the tasks of NMS is to monitor the performance of network elements under its purview on a regular basis [3]. It is quite possible that based on this observation, the NMS finds a part of the network to be underutilised under certain conditions or times of operation. If this situation is looked at from the energy utilisation point of view, then it can be said the network elements in that part of the network are inefficient, even though they are actively participating in forwarding the traffic which is sent to them. The question which has to be answered is: can the NMS be made intelligent enough to come up with a strategy to proactively put the under utilised network elements (or for that matter, certain ports of the network elements) in sleep mode to conserve energy and at the same time ensure optimised network performance without compromising on QoS guarantees such as maintenance of connected topology and fault-tolerance?

2   Related Work

Network Management Systems are used to maintain network infrastructure, assure smooth running of services, control the operational costs of the network and provide increased revenues to the service provider. Several standards related to NMS like the SNMP [4], CMIP and FCAPS are used to manage the information and communication technology (ICT) networks. Originally, NMSs were designed to manage networks with the prime focus on fault and performance issues. However, with the recent emphasis on making the network more energy efficient, the design of NMS needs to modify its functionalities to bring in the energy factor.

One of the earliest works which addresses the need to make the Internet energy-aware is from Gupta et al., where they suggest putting to sleep the underutilised network elements (either the complete router or some of its ports) [5]. They state the challenges of sleep mode decision-making and sleep time prediction. Christensen et al. have strongly supported the need for power management in computer networks, which if applied efficiently could be instrumental in saving significant energy [6]. Gunaratne et al. have proposed techniques like proxying, split TCP connections and link speed scaling to conserve energy in desktop PCs and LAN switches [7]. Gupta et al. have implemented the Dynamic Ethernet Link Shutdown (DELS) to show that the percentage of total time that a link can be shut down can be anywhere from 60% - 80% [8]. Chiaraviglio et al. have proposed some heuristic algorithms to implement power reduction in networks by switching off network elements and links and show that it is possible to save 10% - 25% energy [9]. Gunaratne et al. have shown that an Ethernet link with

Adaptive Link Rate (ALR) can operate at a lower data rate for over 80% of the time, yielding significant energy savings with a small increase in packet delay [10]. More recently, Mahadevan et al. have analysed the traffic data from real enterprise and data centre network to simulate and test their energy saving approaches and shown that they could save energy of the order of 16% [11].

The approach adopted in this paper differs from the above related research, by use of Machine Learning technique to accurately model the network behaviour (utilising the historic traffic data) and to adaptively control the operational modes (sleep/active) of the router ports. The motivation for using such an approach was to enable automated power management with real-time decision making capabilities. The next section describes in detail the general framework of such an approach.

3   Proposed BNITE Framework

The proposed BN-based Intelligent Traffic Engineering (BNITE) framework is shown in Fig. 1. It consists of three modules, namely, the Network Management System (NMS), the Decision Support System (DSS) and the Configuration Management System (CMS). The NMS is the central entity which interacts with the DSS and the CMS. The NMS is based on the SNMP protocol which collects network management data using the SNMP Management Information Base (MIB) of the network elements. In this study, two main data sets were focussed on, namely the energy consumption related data (denoted as the Energy Monitor in Fig. 1) and the data related to the QoS metrics (denoted as the QoS Monitor in Fig. 1).

The collected data is then fed from the NMS to DSS, where the latter builds a model of the network behaviour using the BN framework and provides the decision with regard to which network elements (or their ports) to put to sleep and for how long. The policy engine decides the high level policy which needs to be in place for effective decision making. Usually the network manager or the domain expert who has the domain knowledge can make appropriate policies for the required objectives. Once the decisions reach the NMS, it translates them for the CMS, which can actually affect configuration changes to the network elements.

The idea of BNITE can be effectively realised if there can be some way of predicting or estimating the future behaviour of the network elements. This prediction will form the basis for proactively putting a particular network element (or its ports) to sleep and intelligently re-routing the traffic through other network elements. The prediction task is performed by the DSS based on the observance of past management data, which is readily available to the NMS from the network elements. The huge amounts of network management data which needs to be analysed requires automated systems which can learn efficiently from past data. To this end, it is proposed to utilise the modelling power of BN and use the obtained model for prediction and decision making.

In preparation for the detailed description of the proposed approach (BNITE), a brief recap of BN theory is presented here. BN provides a graphical representa-

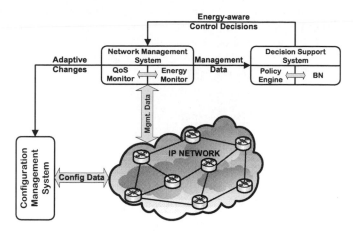

Fig. 1. The BNITE Framework

tion of relationships among the system variables of interest to the system modeller. Such a representation is depicted in Fig. 2, which is for a possible subset of network behaviour through variables namely, *Link Speed, Traffic Rate, Energy Consumed* and *Buffer Occupancy* (as four BN nodes) and three directed edges. A BN is composed of two key components, namely, the structure and the parameters which completely define the model.

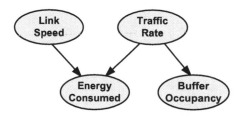

Fig. 2. BN in Energy Context

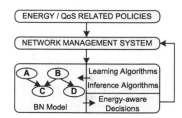

Fig. 3. BN in PBNM Context

The example enables a clear understanding of the BN modelling and its applicability to the desired objective of the proposed solution. From the modelling point of view, a given network is usually highly dynamic in terms of its topology and the supported services running over it. Further, it needs to perform under strict constraints of QoS and policies defined for improved resource utilisation. A large number of performance variables which need to be monitored on a regular basis by the NMS, calls for an intelligent and automated modelling system. It can be seen that the said requirements and the features provided by the BN, match with a fairly good degree. The conflicting goals of energy savings and QoS provisioning can be very well handled by the BN owing to its inherent modelling and prediction features. Fig. 3 portrays the application of BN in the context of policy-based network management (PBNM) aimed at reducing energy consumption, while respecting the QoS constraints.

4   Implementation of BNITE

This section describes the assumptions made for implementing BNITE and the policy level algorithm which forms the core of the solution. It is to be noted that the work presented here is an extension of our earlier preliminary work presented in [12].

4.1   Key Assumptions

For the purpose of proof of concept, a basic network topology and light traffic loads are considered, as will be described later. To demonstrate the practicality of the proposed approach, the initial implementation starts with a scenario in which single port sleep/wakeup decisions are made. Also, it is assumed that a dynamic routing protocol (e.g. RIP or OSPF) computes the updated routes whenever it is decided to change the port status (sleep or awake), without the framework explicitly passing messages to neighbouring routers. Finally, it is assumed that the framework has topology-awareness and restrictions are in place to make sure that critical links are not put to sleep.

4.2   BNITE Algorithms

To meet the objective of saving energy by putting the ports of network elements to sleep, a policy was designed which intelligently re-routes the traffic to other ports so as to maintain the required connectivity and QoS. It has been found from experience that, to keep the delay of each link under the threshold, the link utilisation should not exceed 70% [11]. Based on this prior information, the following mathematical model of the policy is designed.

The proposed architecture is distributed in nature. Hence, initially the focus is on a single router with n ports, each connected to links having a capacity of C_i bits/sec, where $i = 1, 2, ...n$. The power consumption of a port in active and sleep mode is assumed to be P_{active} and P_{sleep} respectively. Let the average incoming and outgoing traffic on each port be in_i and out_i bits/sec respectively. The link utilisation, which is defined as $U = (\frac{Throughput}{Link\ Capacity} * 100\%)$, for each link is monitored and discretised, as shown in Table 1. The minimum and maximum utilisation levels ($U_{min} = 40\%$ and $U_{max} = 70\%$) are selected based on the performance data given in [3]. Algorithm 1 implements the policy which makes the sleep and wakeup decisions for the ports of the router. This algorithm will be used in Experiment 1, which implements BNITE for single router scenario.

Table 1. Network Statistics for the BN Nodes

Node Name	States	Details
$Utilisation\_x\_y$ x = node number y = port number	{Low, Med, High}	Low (0 - 40%) Med (41 - 69%) High (70 - 100%)

Algorithm 1. BNITE Algorithm for Single Router

Initialise: N = Number of routers in the network

n = Number of ports of each router

CL = List of critical links which cannot be put to sleep

$Sleep_{threshold}$ = Threshold to put the port to sleep

$Wake_{threshold}$ = Threshold to wakeup the sleeping port

1: For each port $i = 1, 2, ...n$, monitor the link utilisation

$U_i = \frac{Total_i}{C_i} * 100\%$ where, $Total_i = in_i + out_i$

2: Build (update) the single router BN model

3: Find the port with the least utilisation i.e. the node in the BN

which has maximum value for the marginal probability $P(Low)$

4: Put the corresponding port to sleep if it crosses $Sleep_{threshold}$

and is not a critical link (assuming RIP updates the routes)

5: Update the BN model at regular intervals (1000 s) and keep

monitoring probability $P(High)$ of other BN nodes

6: If any other node's $P(High)$ exceeds $Wake_{threshold}$,

then wake up the sleeping port, **Else** leave it sleeping.

7: Go to **1**

In order to realise the objective of implementing the BNITE solution on multiple routers (Experiment 2), a centralised algorithm is presented as Algorithm 2. This algorithm works on centralised mechanism, which builds a single BN for all the routers present in the network.

5   Simulation Results

The domain under consideration for the proposed work is shown in Fig. 4. The network comprises of Customer Premises Equipment (CPE) (hosts which generate or receive traffic, e.g. 12, 14, 18), access network (switches, e.g. 6, 8, 9) and core network (routers, e.g. 1, 2, 3). It is assumed that all the network elements are SNMP-enabled and they have SNMP clients installed in them for sending MIB data to the NMS.

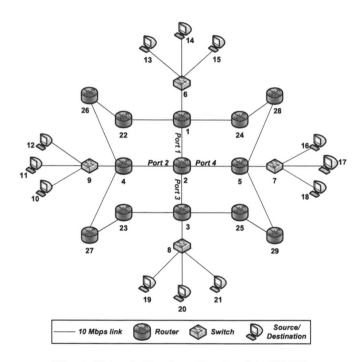

Fig. 4. Network Topology Simulated in NCTUns

5.1   The Simulation Setup

NCTUns (National Chiao Tung University network simulator) [13], was used to simulate the network topology as shown in Fig. 4. The choice of the topology was based on the criteria of redundant links across the hosts which guarantee connectivity even when some ports are put to sleep mode. The queue length

---

Algorithm 2. BNITE Algorithm for Multiple Routers

Initialise: N = Number of routers in the network

n = Number of ports of each router

CL = List of critical links which cannot be put to sleep

$Sleep_{threshold}$ = Threshold to put the port to sleep

$Wake_{threshold}$ = Threshold to wakeup the sleeping port

1: For each router $j = 1, 2, ..., N$

2: For each port $i = 1, 2, ..., n$, monitor the link utilisation

$U_{ji} = \frac{Total_{ji}}{C_{ji}} * 100\%$ where, $Total_{ji} = in_{ji} + out_{ji}$

3: Discretise U_{ji} into three levels $(Low, Med, High)$

4: Build (update) the centralised BN model having $j * i$ nodes

5: Cross check the BN dependency graph and the routing tables

for logical and physical consistencies

6: Find the under-utilised (highest $P(Low)$) and

over-utilised links (highest $P(High)$) from the BN model

7: Put to sleep the link(s) which are under-utilised

(i.e. $P(Low)$ crosses $Sleep_{threshold}$), except if it is critical link

8: Check if any link needs to be woken (when any other link's

$P(High)$ crosses $Wake_{threshold}$)

9: Update the BN model using *Sequential Learning* algorithm

every 1000s, go to **1**.

---

for all the routers was set to 50 packets and the ports were connected with bidirectional link with a capacity of 10 Mbps. Hugin Researcher [14], was used to generate the BN model from the network data. The learning and inference algorithms, which form the Hugin Decision Engine, were used in the BNITE solution through C++ APIs.

5.2   Traffic Characteristics

To simulate a hybrid traffic in NCTUns with maximum randomness, the source hosts were modelled as a Poisson process as shown in Table 2. Sources with node IDs 10, 11 and 12 were generating (unidirectional) traffic and sending it to destination hosts having IDs 20, 14, and 18 respectively. This setup was chosen so as to make sure that all links connected to *Router 2* (which is centrally located in the core network with marked port numbers, as shown in Fig. 4), were utilised for sending traffic.

Table 2. Characteristics of Traffic Sources (10, 11 and 12)

Parameter	Value
Packet Inter-arrival time	Exponential (0.001)
Packet Size (bytes)	Exponential (1024)
Traffic Start Time (s)	Constant (1.0)
Traffic ON state time (s)	Constant (60.0)
Traffic OFF state time (s)	Constant (30.0)

5.3   Experiment 1: BNITE for Single Router

This experiment was run for the simulated time of 10000 seconds and the statistics were collected to train the BN in the DSS. In the NCTUns simulator, the data was collected (as shown in Table 1), at regular intervals of 10 seconds. The DSS module then learned the BN model (both structure and parameters) using the observed data. To capture the real-time behaviour, re-training of the model was performed at an interval of 1000 seconds. Even though in a real network there are many MIB variables (literally in hundreds for each network element) which are monitored and collected, this experimental setup presents the general approach which can easily be extended to more variables.

Based on the collected data, the BN model for *Router 2* was obtained and is comprised of two components. The first component is the BN structure, which was learnt using the PC algorithm and is shown in Fig. 5. The marginal probabilities of the states of each node are also shown in the monitor windows beside the nodes. The second component is the CPTs which were learnt using the EM algorithm and are shown in Table 3. The CPTs give the probability relationships among the related nodes and are a way to quantify the strength of the

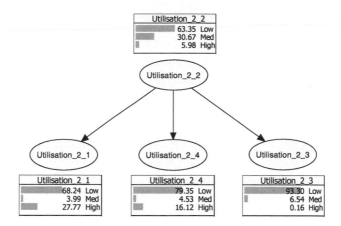

Fig. 5. BN Model for *Router* 2

dependencies among them. From Fig. 5 it is seen that *Port 3* has the lowest utilisation, *P(Low) = 0.933* (the highest probability of being in *Low* state). So it was decided to put *Port 3* to sleep mode at the simulation time of 2000 seconds.

Fig. 6 shows average throughput plot for all the ports of *Router 2*. Throughput of *Port 3* goes down and stays down, as the marginal probability *P(High)* of other ports are below the predefined threshold ($Wake_{threshold} = 0.7$) in this sample run. Updated routes cause a decrease in traffic at *Port 2* and *Port 4*.

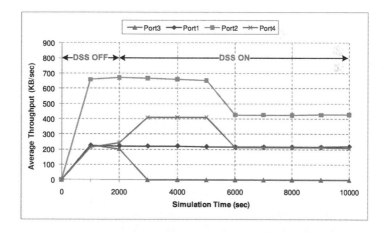

Fig. 6. Average Throughput at the Ports of *Router 2*

Fig. 7 shows the power consumption of *Router 2* in two scenarios (DSS is OFF and DSS is ON). For the purpose of depicting practical power consumption figures, the power ratings of an enterprise HP switch is considered [11].

Table 3. CPTs for the *Router 2* BN Model

Utilisation_2_2			
Low	0.634		
Med	0.307		
High	0.059		
Utilisation_2_1			
Utilisation_2_2	*Low*	*Med*	*High*
Low	0.995	0.022	0.763
Med	0.002	0.108	0.093
High	0.003	0.870	0.144
Utilisation_2_4			
Utilisation_2_2	*Low*	*Med*	*High*
Low	0.990	0.476	0.339
Med	0.005	0.112	0.135
High	0.005	0.412	0.526
Utilisation_2_3			
Utilisation_2_2	*Low*	*Med*	*High*
Low	0.990	0.856	0.717
Med	0.009	0.142	0.273
High	0.001	0.002	0.010

For a 10 Mbps link, the power consumption in active and sleep modes were used as $P_{active} = 0.42\ W$ and $P_{sleep} = 0\ W$. To see the cost at which the gain of power savings was achieved, the average round-trip time (RTT) was measured (for active (UP) and sleep (DOWN) modes), $RTT_{UP} = 126.567\ ms$ and $RTT_{DOWN} = 130.248\ ms$ for the link connected to *Port 3*. This meant an incremental delay of 2.9%, in comparison to a power saving of 25% per sleeping port for *Router 2*. This energy saving (by putting to sleep the router port) could be very small relative to the total power consumed by the router (the energy to power on the hardware). However, the saving is significant when compared to a small reduction in the QoS constraint of delay. It is argued here that, those applications and services which are delay insenstive, can benefit by the proposed approach. As such, it is concluded that the proposed approach is an effective intelligent Traffic Engineering solution which has an Energy-Awareness element to it.

5.4   Experiment 2: BNITE for Multiple Routers

This experiment extends the BNITE solution developed in the previous section to multiple routers in the network. For this purpose two real world network topologies are considered. Fig. 8 shows the ARPANet topology with 21 network nodes and 25 links to make the complete network. Similarly, the INDIANet topology is shown in Fig. 9, which consists of 20 nodes and 32 links. The links

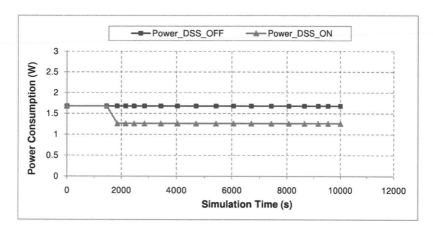

Fig. 7. Power Consumed by the Ports of *Router 2*

between nodes are bidirectional in nature and have 10 Mbps capacity. The reason for choosing these topologies is to provide a realistic way to perform the BNITE based simulation and also these topologies inherently have redundant links for re-routing the traffic when a particular link is put to sleep.

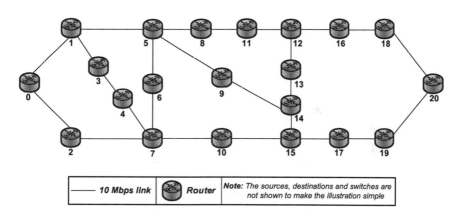

Fig. 8. ARPANet Topology for Experiment 2

The algorithm was implemented and the power savings were achieved by putting to sleep the underutilised ports. Fig. 10 shows the power consumption of the routers when the DSS was ON and OFF in the case of ARPANet topology. The DSS starts its operation after 2000s of the simulation time, as this time is used for training the centralised BN model. Similarly, Fig. 11 shows the power consumption for the INDIANet topology.

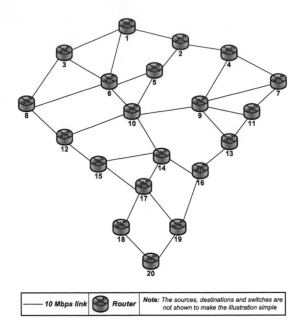

Fig. 9. INDIANet Topology for Experiment 2

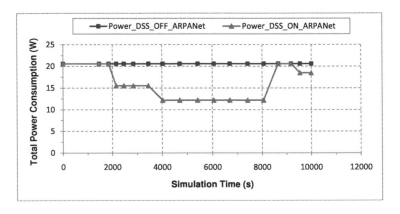

Fig. 10. Power Consumption in ARPANet Topology

The energy (Energy = Power × Time) calculations for each of the networks was calculated when DSS is OFF and DSS is ON. In the case of the ARPANet topology, the energy in the OFF state was 168 kJ (kilo Joules) and in the ON state was 118.86 kJ. This meant a energy savings of 49.14 kJ which was about 29.25%. Similarly in the case of the INDIANet topology, the DSS OFF energy was 221.76 kJ and DSS ON energy was 180.5 kJ. This resulted in a energy

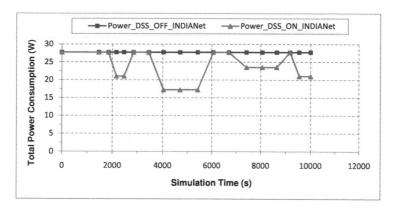

Fig. 11. Power Consumption in INDIANet Topology

savings of 41.26 kJ which was about 18.6%. However this energy savings was at the minimal cost of average delay metric, which was found to be about 5% in each case. This is a significant savings considering a lower degradation of QoS metric of *Delay*.

6 Conclusion

This paper presented the novel concept of using BN approach for providing an intelligent and energy-aware traffic engineering solution (called BNITE) in a core network. It presented the need for reduction of energy consumption in telecommunication networks. One of the issues which was primarily focussed on was, how to decide which router ports need to be put into the sleep mode with minimal degradation in QoS. To this end, an energy-aware algorithm was designed and developed, which formed the high level policy a network manager is interested in implementing. It described the details of modelling a network router based on its port utilisation data collected over an observation interval. It then presented the details of learning algorithms which were utilised to arrive at an accurate BN model. The simulated environment consisting of NCTUns and Hugin Researcher was designed and evaluated under various traffic scenarios. The results obtained from these experiments were promising and hence the BNITE solution was then extended to support sleep mode decision making for multiple routers, for which two real world network topologies were used, namely, ARPANet and INDIANet. Significant power savings were achieved in the multiple router scenario (of the order of 18.6% to 29.25%) at a cost of minimal delay increment of 5%. This was possible due to the presence of mutiple nodes and various redundant links available for rerouting the traffic to support QoS.

Acknowledgement. The author would like to acknowledge the support of Prince Mohammad Bin Fahd University for performing this research work.

References

1. Roth, K., Goldstein, F., Kleinman, J.: Energy consumption by office and telecommunications equipment in commercial buildings. In: Energy Consumption Baseline, Arthur D. Little, Reference No. 72895-00 (2002)
2. US Dept. of Energy and the Environmental Protection Agency: Carbon dioxide emissions from the generation of electric power in the United States (2000), http://www.eia.doe.gov/cneaf/electricity/page/co2_report/co2report.html
3. Comer, D.E.: Automated Network Management Systems. Prentice Hall Co., NJ (2006)
4. Harrington, D., Presuhn, R., Wijnen, B.: An architecture for describing SNMP management frameworks, RFC 3411, IETF (2002)
5. Gupta, M., Singh, S.: Greening of the Internet. In: ACM SIGCOMM 2003, pp. 19–26 (2003)
6. Christensen, K., Nordman, B., Brown, R.: Power management in networked devices. IEEE Computer 37(5), 91–93 (2004)
7. Gunaratne, C., Christensen, K., Nordman, B.: Managing energy consumption costs in desktop PCs and LAN switches with proxying, split TCP connections, and scaling of link speed. International Journal of Network Management 15(5), 297–310 (2005)
8. Gupta, M., Singh, S.: Dynamic ethernet link shutdown for energy conservation on ethernet links. In: IEEE ICC 2007, pp. 6156–6161 (2007)
9. Chiaraviglio, L., et al.: Energy-aware networks: Reducing power consumption by switching off network elements. In: GTTI 2008 (2008), http://www.gtti.it/GTTI08/papers/chiaraviglio.pdf
10. Gunaratne, C., Christensen, K., Nordman, B., Suen, S.: Reducing the energy consumption of ethernet with Adaptive Link Rate (ALR). IEEE Transactions on Computers 57, 448–461 (2008)
11. Mahadevan, P., et al.: Energy aware network operations. In: IEEE INFOCOM 2009, pp. 1–6 (2009)
12. Bashar, A., et al.: Employing Bayesian belief networks for energy efficient network management. In: IEEE National Conference on Communications (NCC 2010), pp. 1–5 (2010)
13. Wang, S.Y., Chou, C.L., Lin, C.C.: The design and implementation of the NCTUns network simulation engine. Elsevier Simulation Modelling Practice and Theory 15(1), 57–81 (2007)
14. Hugin Expert A/S: Hugin Researcher 7.3. (2011), http://www.hugin.com

Advance Planning and Reservation in a Grid System

Rusydi Umar[1,2], Arun Agarwal[1], and C.R. Rao[1]

[1] Dept. of Computer and Information Sciences, University of Hyderabad, Hyderabad, India
rusydi_umar@rocketmail.com, {aruncs,crrcs}@uohyd.ernet.in
[2] Dept. of Informatics Engineering, Ahmad Dahlan University, Yogyakarta, Indonesia

Abstract. Advance Planning and Reservation in a Grid System allows applications to request resources from multiple scheduling systems at a specific time in future and thus gain simultaneous access to sufficient resources for their execution. Existing advance reservation strategy will reject incoming reservation if requested resources are not available at that exact time. Therefore impact of advance reservations is decreasing resource utilization due to fragmentations. This paper proposes a novel advance planning and reservation strategy namely First Come First Serve Ejecting Based Dynamic Scheduling (FCFS-EDS) to increase resources utilization in a grid system. To achieve this we introduce a new notion that maps a user job to a virtual compute nodes (called logical view) which are subsequently mapped to actual compute nodes (called physical view) at the time of execution. A lemma ensures the success of such a mapping with increased resource utilization.

Keywords: Advance reservation, FCFS-EDS, resource utilization, planning.

1   Introduction

In most grid systems with traditional scheduler, submitted jobs will be placed in the wait queue if mandated resources are not available for them. Every grid system may use a different scheduling algorithm, for example First Come First Serve (FCFS), Shortest Job First (SJF), Earliest Deadline First (EDF), or EASY Backfilling [1] that executes jobs based on different parameters, such as number of resources, submission time, and duration of execution. With these scheduling algorithms, there is no guarantee about when these jobs will be executed [2].

To address the unwarranted waiting time issue and ensure that the specified resources are available for applications at a particular time in the future, we need an advance planning and reservation system [3]. Advance reservations [4] allow a user to request resources from multiple scheduling systems at a specific time in the future and thus gain simultaneous access to enough resources for their applications.

2   Literature Review

Many earlier literatures discuss about advance reservation strategy to increase resource utilization. We have attempted to broadly categorize these advance reservation strategies reported in the literature as follows:

R. Benlamri (Ed.): NDT 2012, Part I, CCIS 293, pp. 161–173, 2012.

2.1   Rigid Reservation

When users request for compute nodes, they must provide three parameters, start time, end time and number of compute nodes. The reservation system then searches for the availability of requested compute nodes in the specified time interval. If required nodes are unavailable, the request is rejected. This mechanism is known as rigid reservation and has been adopted into the Globus Architecture for Reservation and Allocation (GARA)[5],[6].

2.2   Elastic Advance Reservation

With rigid reservations, there is a shortcoming. If the users still want to reserve compute nodes then they must change the job parameters and again query for reservation until there is a match between the availability of compute nodes and the user's request. This mechanism brings an overhead due to communication traffic. Elastic reservation proposed by Sulistio et al. [7] takes the user request parameters as soft constrain. The reservation system instead of rejecting the request provides alternatives that can be selected by the user. Results show that their on-line strip packing (OSP) method performs better than first fit alternative (FF) and FF performs better than rigid reservation (RR). This strategy has been adopted in GridSim [8].

2.3   Overlapping/Relax Advance Reservation

In this strategy, user jobs are scheduled even if there are reservation violations in the deadlines because of overlapping of jobs. Peng Xiao et al. [9] used the overlapped time slot table, because they believed that applications tend to overestimate the reservation deadline to ensure their completion [10],[11]. They assumed that the real workload tends to overestimate the relative deadline with mean value by 35%. Experimental results show that this strategy can bring about remarkably higher resource utilization and lower rejection rate at the price of slight increase in reservation violation.

Peng Xiao et al. [12] added capacity issue in their relaxed model. They can limit the price of reservation violation as an impact of the relaxed reservation by adjusting parameter v^*.

Sabitha et al. [13] have introduced a relaxed resource advance reservation policy (RARP), which allows reservations to overlap each other under certain condition. But it is successful only in high reservation areas. So to cover both high and low reservation areas, trust is included in reservations. It can have better adaptation in the presence of both low and high reservation area when trust factor is considered.

2.4   Flexible Advance Reservation (Static)

In flexible advance reservation, user jobs are scheduled within given flexible constraints. Moaddeli et al. [14] has examined the impact of backfilling algorithm in a flexible advance reservation. In their examination they distinguished between aggressive backfilling and conservative backfilling. Aggressive backfilling has higher utilization than conservative one.

Kaushik et al. [15] proposed a flexible reservation window scheme. Window size is the difference between the earliest start time of the user request and latest possible start time of the request. By conducting extensive simulations, they conclude that, when the size of the reservation window is equal to the average waiting time in the on-demand queue, the reservation rejection rate can be minimized close to zero and increase resource utilization.

Castillo et al. [16] has proposed a scheduling algorithm to increase system utilization using a concept from computational geometry. Here deadline is equal or larger than the execution time. If the deadline is the same as the length of the job, it is called as immediate deadline, and if the deadline is longer than the execution time, it is known as general job deadline. To schedule the general job deadline, they use the following strategies: Min-LIP, which minimizes the leading idle period; Min-TIP, which minimizes the trailing idle period; First-fit, which returns the first (i.e., earliest) feasible idle period, regardless of the sizes of the leading and trailing idle periods; LACT (latest available completion time), where the scheduler assigns an arriving job to the server with the latest completion time that is earlier than the ready time of the new job. The result shows that Min-LIP gives the best system utilization compared to other strategies.

2.5   Flexible Advance Reservation (Dynamic, Physical View)

This strategy takes an advantage of shifting even earlier reservations made (subject to given flexible constraints) to make room for new incoming reservation. Chunming et al. [17] introduced time span when there is a time range for the starting time of the job. This time span is called slack-time. They proposed a novel mechanism called FIRST (FlexIble Reservation using Slack Time). The advantage of slack-time is that the starting time of the job can be shifted to improve resource utilization and to reduce rejection rate. If new reservation comes the reservation system reschedules all unexecuted reservation by taking one by one, according to the rule of FIFO, min slack, min-min, min-max, and suffrage policy to see whether there is a solution or not. If there is no solution then the new reservation request will be rejected. The result shows when compared to rigid reservation, FIRST gives better resource utilization and min-min based gives better result than the rest.

In FIRST as mentioned before, every time a new task comes, it reschedules the entire task. According to Netto et al. [18] rescheduling the task will have a better system utilization if the user can wait until 75% of waiting time has been passed, compared to 50% and 25%. They observe that the longer a user waits to fix their jobs the better the system utilization. They use five different sorting techniques: Shuffle, First in First out (FIFO), Biggest Job First (BJF), Least Flexible First (LFF), and Earliest Deadline First (EDF). They concluded that EDF technique has the best result in increasing resource utilization.

Behnam et al. [19] have introduced scheduling algorithm for advance reservation called GELSAR (Gravitational Emulation Local Search Advance Reservation) in grid system where the reservations can have a deadline (dj) which ca be equal or larger than a ready time (rj) + length of the reservation (lj). The Idea is to imagine that the search space is the universe and objects in this universe are the possible solutions. Every time the new reservation comes the GELSAR reschedule all reservation to find the best solution. If there is no solution the new incoming reservation is rejected. They compared their algorithm with other rescheduling algorithm (Genetic Algorithm, GA) and the found the result that their algorithm outperformed GA algorithm.

3   Proposed Advance Planning and Reservation Strategy

We propose a novel advance planning and reservation strategy namely First Come First Serve Ejecting Based Dynamic Scheduling (FCFS-EDS) to increase resources utilization in a grid system. To achieve this we introduce a new notion that maps a user job to a virtual compute nodes (called logical view) which are subsequently mapped to actual compute nodes (called physical view) at the time of execution. A lemma ensures the success of such a mapping with increased throughput. This approach can be categorized under Flexible Advance Reservation (Dynamic, Logical View).

3.1   Definition of Flexible Advance Reservation

Let us define "flexible advance reservation" as follows: "*Flexible advance reservations are reservations where the time between reservation request starting time (t_{es}) and reservation request end time (t_d) is longer than the execution time (t_e) of a job*" as shown in Fig 1.

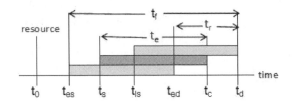

Fig. 1. Flexible Advance Reservation

t_0	:	current time
t_{es}	:	lower bound to start time of the job
t_d	:	upper bound to end time to execute the job
t_e	:	execution time of the job
t_r	:	relax time, define by $t_r = t_d - t_{es} - t_e$

t_{ls} : upper bound to start execution of the job, defined as $t_{ls} = t_d - t_e = t_{es} + t_r$

t_{ed} : lower bound to end time to execution of the job, defined as $t_{ed} = t_{es} + t_e$

t_s : start time to execute the job ($t_{es} \leq t_s \leq t_{ls}$)

t_c : completion time to execute the job ($t_{ed} \leq t_c \leq t_d$)

t_f : flexibility time, defined as $t_f = t_d - t_{es}$

f : the degree of flexibility, define as $f = \frac{t_f}{t_e}$, here $f \geq 1$, (if $f = \infty$, the job considered as non reservation job mode. If $t_s = t_0$ and $f = 1$ the job for reservation considered with top most priority leading to immediate reservation mode i.e., scheduling mode)

$userId$: identification of a user

$jobId$: identification of a job

$numJ$: number of jobs

$numCN$: number of compute nodes needed

$maxCN$: total number of compute nodes

3.2   FCFS-EDS Strategy

This strategy takes an advantage of shifting earlier reservations made (subject to given flexible constraints) to make room for new incoming reservation request. However the planning for reservation in our proposed model provides a logical view as against the physical view reported in the literature. Therefore we call our method as First Come First Serve-Ejecting Based Dynamic Scheduling (FCFS-EDS) strategy.

Let us assume that earlier "$n - 1$" reservation requests made to FCFS-EDS, specified by the following parameters: t_{es}, t_{ls}, t_e, $userId$, $jobId$, have been successfully scheduled. Definition of variables is explained in lines 4-9. Lines 10–14 initialize the variables.

Incoming "n^{th}" reservation request is scheduled based on first fit strategy (iteration of line 16-25). It tries to search for resources within the given constraints (t_{es} and t_{ls}) and without disturbing plan for previous "$n - 1$" reservation requests that were made. Let us call this as plan P_{old}. If within the given flexible constraints the search fails to allocate resources the algorithm tries to move around previous "$n - 1$" reservations to accommodate "n^{th}" reservation request (lines 31-44). If the resources are found then the search is declared successful and the algorithm outputs a new plan P_{new} that depicts "n" reservation requests as a logical view. If the search is a failure then the "$n - 1$" reservation request plan has to be restored to its previous state i.e. P_{old}.

The time complexity of FCFS-EDS algorithm is $O(n.m)$ where n is t_r and m is t_e.

```
Algorithm FCFS-EDS
1 Function searchAndAlloc(userId, jobId, tes, tls, te : integer) → boolean
2 //search and allocate job with given tes, tls, te
3 Dictionary :
4 start : integer /*start time of the job*/
5 finish : integer /*finish time of the job*/
6 min : integer  /*min free within interval  start - finish*/
7 t   : integer  /*timeslot of minimum available node between start to
finish*/
8 tr  : integer  /*relax time, length between of tes and tls*/
9  relax : integer /*different between start and tes time (start - tes +
1)*/
Algorithm :
10 tr ← tls - tes
11 succeed ← false
12 start ← tes
13 finish ← tes + te - 1
14 relax ← start - tes
15
16 while (!succeed and (relax≤tr)) do  /*searching by first fit strategy*/
17    /*searching minimum free node between start to finish*/
18    min,t ← minFreeNode(start, finish)
19      if(min > 0) then
20        allocate(userId, jobId, tes, start, tls, te)
21        succeed ← true
22      else
23        start ← t + 1
24        finish ← start + te - 1
25        relax ← start - tes
26 /*end while, the state is succeed=true or succeed=false (relax > tr)*/
27
28 start ← tes
29 finish ← tes + te - 1
30 relax ← start - tes
31 while (!succeed and (relax≤tr)) do
32    /*searching minimum free node between start to finish*/
33    min,t ← minFreeNode(start, finish);
34    if(min > 0) then
35      /*push or schedule the job to data structure using our lemma below
36      and update free node between start to finish*/
37      allocate(userId, jobId, tes, start, tls, te)
38      succeed ← true
39    else
40      /*try to shift a job that start at t time slot*/
41      if(!shiftNode(t)) then //can't be shifted, move start to index+1
42        start ← t + 1
43        finish ← start + te - 1
44        relax ← start - tes
45 /*end while, the state is succeed=true or succeed=false (relax > tr)*/
46 if (!succeed)
47   putBackAllShiftedJob()
48 return succeed
```

3.3   Illustration

To explain how FCFS-EDS works we introduce an example, If we have $maxCN$ compute node (physical view), let $maxCN$ is equal to 5 ($cn0 - cn4$) as physical nodes, then the number of virtual node (logical view) is also 5 ($v0 - v4$). Sequence of incoming reservation is depicted in Table 1, where $numCN \leq maxCN$ and $numJ$ are the number of jobs submitted by a $userId$. For example the given parameters for $userId = 3$ in the Table 1 implies the following: "*User 3 reserved 3 time slots at time slot 12 up to 14, needed 1 compute node for 1 independent job, and cannot be delayed/shifted.* ($t_{es} = t_{ls} = 12, t_e = 3, numCN = 1, numJ = 1$)".

Table 1. Parameters of reservation request

userId	t_{es}	t_{ls}	t_e	numCN	numJ
1	11	11	1	2	2
2	11	11	3	1	1
3	12	12	3	1	1
4	15	16	1	1	1
5	15	15	1	2	2
6	11	11	2	1	1
7	13	13	1	1	1
8	16	16	2	1	1
9	11	11	2	1	1
10	15	15	3	1	1

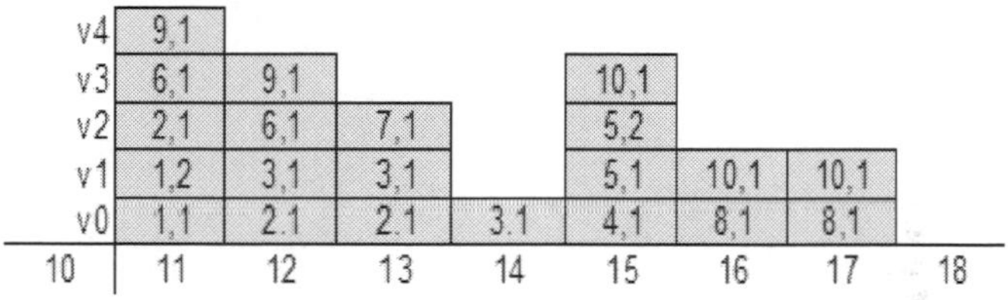

Fig. 2. Ten reservations have been allocated (Logical View)

The result of FCFS-EDS is a plan shown in Fig. 2, where x axis indicates time slot, and y axis indicates virtual compute node (**Logical View**). As there are 5 virtual compute nodes, they are shown along the y axis as $v0, v1, v2, v3$, and $v4$. The ten user reservations have been allocated during time slots 11 to 17. Consider $userId = 9$ from Table 1. The virtual computes nodes allotted to it are $v4$ at time slot $11(t_{es} = 11)$ and $v3$ at time slot 12 as only 1 job (requiring 2 execution time slots) has been submitted by this user.

Suppose User 11 wishing to reserve 3 time slots from 12 up to 14, needs 3 compute nodes for 3 independent jobs and each job can be delayed up to time slot 14 ($t_{es} = 12, t_{ls} = 14, t_e = 3, numCN = 3, numJ = 3$). See Fig.3.

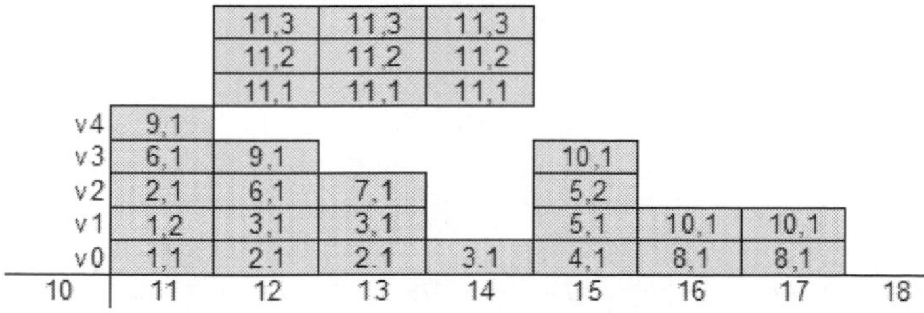

Fig. 3. User 11 makes a request for reservation

The result of FCFS-EDS is a plan for the new incoming reservation request from user 11 which is depicted in Fig. 4. Using conventional reservation or rigid reservation only one independent job from user 11 will be allocated and the other two will be rejected. From Fig. 4 it is seen that the same job on different time slot is allocated on different virtual compute nodes. On successful reservation a notification is sent to the user only once (in our approach as we are working at a logical view) whereas in other approaches it has to sent every time a revision is made in the plan (P_{new}) (physical view: reassignment of physical resources) [18,19].

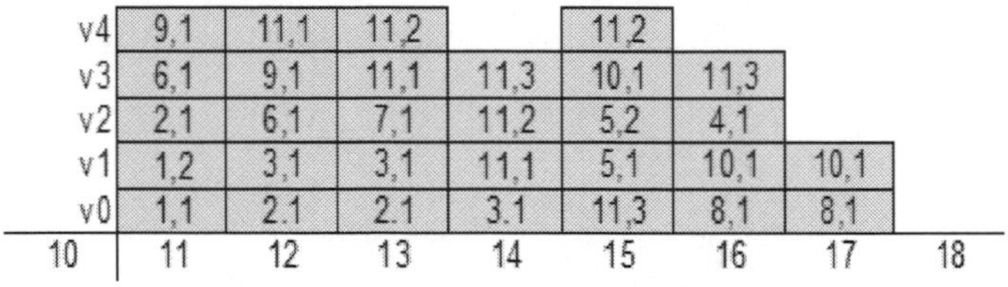

	11	12	13	14	15	16	17	18
v4	9,1	11,1	11,2		11,2			
v3	6,1	9,1	11,1	11,3	10,1	11,3		
v2	2,1	6,1	7,1	11,2	5,2	4,1		
v1	1,2	3,1	3,1	11,1	5,1	10,1	10,1	
v0	1,1	2,1	2,1	3,1	11,3	8,1	8,1	

Fig. 4. User 11 has been allocated using FCFS – EDF (Logical View)

3.4 Mapping of the Plan (Logical View) to Actual Compute Node (Physical View)

We introduce a Lemma to guarantee that the plan (logical view) can always be mapped into actual compute node (physical view), and once a job is started at certain compute node, then it will be executed on the same compute node for the entire time slot. Applying the lemma to the plan as depicted in Fig. 4, we guarantee that all the jobs will be executed as shown in Fig. 5 (Physical View).

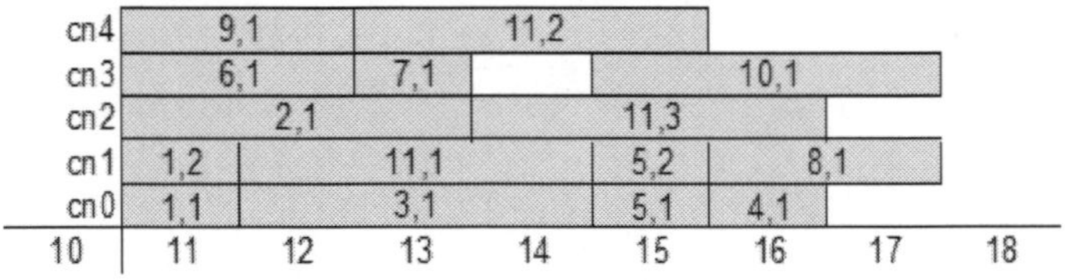

	11	12	13	14	15	16	17	18
cn4	9,1			11,2				
cn3	6,1		7,1		10,1			
cn2	2,1			11,3				
cn1	1,2		11,1		5,2		8,1	
cn0	1,1		3,1		5,1	4,1		

Fig. 5. Actual Compute Node Mapping (physical view) at $t_0 = 18$

The concept of proof of our advance planning and scheduling strategy is assured due to the following Lemma:

Lemma: *If one can plan for scheduling a job on the consecutive time slot on virtual compute nodes (which are selected freely) (Logical View) then it guarantees that the job will be executed on a dedicated physical node for the required execution time (Physical View).*

Proof:

Let $J(t)$ be is an array of size $maxCN$ (maximum number of compute node) scheduling plan at time slot t. i^{th} element of $J(t)$ is the job id that is assigned to i^{th} compute node at time slot t.

Let $JS(t)$ be the list (set) of jobs planed for time slot t associated to $J(t)$. Then

$JS(t) - JS(t + 1)$ indicates the list (set) of job finishes at time slot t

$JS(t + 1) - JS(t)$ indicates the list (set) of job start at time slot $t + 1$

$JS(t) \cap JS(t + 1)$ indicates list (set) of a job continuing from time slot t to $t + 1$

A_M is t to $t + 1$ assignment matrix of order $maxCN$ (of zeros and ones). $A_M(i, j) = 1$ indicates that job at time slot t is executed at compute node i and at time slot $t + 1$ is executed at compute node j.

A_M is a partial permutation matrix. One can construct complete permutation matrix, say C_M (which is a non singular matrix).

Let C be equal to $C_M{}^T$ then the multiplication between C_M and C is I

Thus the multiplication between A_M and C is PI

If the A_M is Partial Identity (PI) matrix,

Then the job at time t will be executed at the same compute node at time slot $t + 1$.

Else treat advance scheduling plan for $t + 1$ time slot as by multiply $J(t + 1)$ with C (one can easily verify that A_M for this will be PI).

4   Experiment

The comparison of our scheduling strategy FCFS-EDS is depicted in Table 2 and Table 3.

Table 2. presents the parameter that have been used by other researchers. The rows indicate possible parameter and column the scheduling strategies. The entries are notations/symbols, policy and name wherever provided by the authors otherwise dash has been used.

Table 3. records and compares the results obtained by applying the above example/illustration to other similar reported scheduling strategy. From Table 3. we can see that the scheduling strategy given by Netto et al. [18] and Behnam et al. [19] have the same result as reported by us, but it is important to note that their strategy reschedules all allocated reservation when a new reservation request arrives, and notifies the user once again with new set of physical resources where the job will be executed. In our approach once a plan (logical view) is created, the user is notified only once, as the lemma guarantees the availability of the physical resources for the job to be executed at runtime.

User requests, that are input for our FCFS-EDS, are generated randomly. The input specifications are:

a.   the rate of incoming reservation requests are assumed to follow poison distribution with mean 2.0,

b.   execution time (t_e) for reservation requests are between 5 to 48 timeslots distributed uniformly,

c.   earlier starting time (t_{es}) is between 0 to 48 timeslots distributed uniformly,

d.   percentage of user request that are for flexible advance reservation is assumed to at most 50% (selected randomly),

e.   relax time (t_r) is between 1 to 24 timeslots distributed uniformly and $t_{ls} = t_{es} + t_r$

f.   In the experiment it is assumed that a time slot is equal to 5 minutes (clock time).

Table 2. Comparison between other scheduling strategy

	Our work	Sulistio et al.	Castillo. et al.	Kaushik et al.	Xiao et al.	Chunming et al.	Netto et al.	Behnam et al.	Moadelli et al.
Current Time	t_0	-	-	-	t_0	-	-	$t = 0$	-
Time of the earliest start time of the job	t_{es}	t_{is}	r_j	-	t_{start}	t_{is}	t_r	r_j	t_{rt}
start time to execute the job	t_s	-	-	t_{start}	-	t_{start}	t_s	-	t_{st}
completion time to execute the job	t_c	-	-	t_{end}	-	-	t_c	-	t_{ct}
the end time to execute the job	t_d	t_{ie}	d_j	-	-	-	d	d_j	t_{dt}
execution time of the job	t_e	dur	lj	dur	d	dura-tion	t_e	Lj	t_{ad}
Relaxed time	t_r	-	-	W	-	slack	-	-	-
Degree of flexibility	f	-	-	-	-	-	-	-	-
Compute nodes needed	n	n	1	1	1	1	N		N
Name	flexible	elastic	general job deadline	unconstrained /flexible	relaxed	flexible	flexible	-	Flexible
Scheduling	FCFS - EDS	FCFS -OSP	FCFS Min-Lip	FCFS	FCFS	Min-min	EDF	GELSAR	FCFS

Table 3. Comparison of the results between FCFS_EDS and other similar scheduling strategy

	Name	Scheduling	Resources Needed	Result
Moadelli et al.	Flexible	FCFS	n	2 jobs from user 11 are accepted
Netto et al.	Flexible	EDF	n	3 jobs from user 11 are accepted
Behnam et al.	Flexible	GELSAR	n	3 jobs from user 11 are accepted
Our work.	Flexible	FCFS-EDS	n	3 jobs from user 11 are accepted

We compare the performance of the proposed method (FCFE-EDS with advance planning) and an existing approach (flexible advance reservation strategy without advance planning). With above inputs and total number of compute node is 30 ($maxCN = 30$), the utilization factors of both strategies are measured. The comparison of resource utilization of both strategies is shown in Fig 6. Percentage of utilization factor is calculated within sliding window of size 12 time slots (1 hour). Fig 6. shows that FCFS-EDS yields better utilization than the traditional strategy (without advance planning).

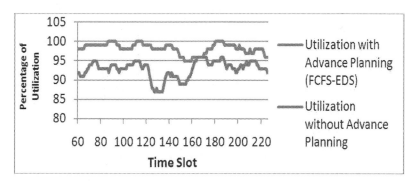

Fig. 6. Comparison of percentage of utilization factor between scheduling with Advance Planning (FCFS – EDF) and flexible advance reservation without Advance Planning

5   Conclusion

In this paper we proposed a novel advance planning and reservation strategy FCFS-EDS to increase resource utilization in a grid system. This strategy maps the job to a virtual node (logical view) and the Lemma guarantees that these jobs will be assigned to compute resources (physical view) for execution and will achieve higher resource utilization. We also experimentally compared the performance of the proposed method (FCFE-EDS with advance planning and reservation) which showed better performance than an existing approach (flexible advance reservation strategy without advance planning).

References

1. Mu'alem, A.W., Feitelson, D.G.: Utilization, Predictability, Workloads, and User Runtime Estimates in Scheduling the IBM SP2 with Backfilling. IEEE Transactions on Parallel and Distributed Systems 12, 529–543 (2001)
2. Sulistio, A., Buyya, R.: A Grid simulation infrastructure supporting advance reservation. In: 16th International Conference on Parallel and Distributed Computing and Systems, pp. 1–7. ACTA Press, Calgary (2004)
3. MacLaren, J.: Advance Reservations: State of the Art. In: Working Draft, Global Grid Forum (2003)
4. Smith, W., Foster, I., Taylor, V.: Scheduling with Advanced Reservations. In: 14th IEEE International Symposium on Parallel and Distributed Processing, pp. 127–132. IEEE Press, Cancun (2000)
5. Foster, I., Kesselman, C., Lee, C., Lindell, B., Nahrstedt, K., Roy, A.: A Distributed Resource Management Architecture that Supports Advance Reservation and Co-Allocation. In: 7th IEEE International Workshop on Quality of Service, pp. 27–36. IEEE Press, London (1999)
6. Czajkowski, K., Foster, I., Karonis, N., Kesselman, C., Martin, S., Smith, W., Tuecke, S.: A Resource Management Architecture for Metacomputing Systems. In: Feitelson, D.G., Rudolph, L. (eds.) IPPS-WS 1998, SPDP-WS 1998, and JSSPP 1998. LNCS, vol. 1459, pp. 62–82. Springer, Heidelberg (1998)
7. Sulistio, A., Kim, K.H., Buyya, R.: On Incorporating an On-line Strip Packing Algorithm into Elastic Grid Reservation-based Systems. In: 13th International Conference on Parallel and Distributed Systems (ICPADS 2007), pp. 1–8. IEEE Press, Hsinchu (2007)
8. Buyya, R., Murshed, M.: GridSim: A Toolkit for the Modeling and Simulation of Distributed Management and Scheduling for Grid Computing. Concurrency and Computation: Practice and Experience 14, 1175–1220 (2002)
9. Xiao, P., Zhigang, H., Xi, L., Liu, Y.: A Novel Statistic-based Relaxed Grid Resource Reservation Strategy. In: 9th International Conference for Young Computer Scientists, pp. 703–707. IEEE Press, Hunan (2008)
10. Lee, C.B., Snavely, A.: On the user-scheduler dialogue: Studies of user-provided runtime estimates and utility functions. International Journal of High Performance Computing Applications 20, 496–506 (2006)
11. Castillo, C., Rouskas, G., Harfoush, K.: Online algorithms for advance resource reservations. Journal of Parallel and Distributed Computing 71, 963–972 (2011)
12. Peng, X., Zhigang, H.U.: Relaxed resource advance reservation policy in grid computing. The Journal of China Universities of Posts and Telecommunications 16, 108–113 (2009)
13. Sabitha, R.B.S., Venkatesan, R., Ramalakshmi, R.: Resource Reservation In Grid Computing Environments: Design Issues. In: 3rd International Conference on Electronics Computer Technology, pp. 66–70. IEEE Press, Kanyakumari (2011)
14. Moaddeli, H.R., Dastghaibyfard, G., Moosavi, M.R.: Flexible Advance Reservation Impact on Backfilling Scheduling Strategies. In: 7th International Conference on Grid and Cooperative Computing, pp. 151–159. IEEE Press, Shenzhen (2008)
15. Kaushik, N.R., Figueira, S.M., Chiappari, S.A.: Flexible Time-Windows for Advance Reservation Scheduling. In: 14th IEEE International Symposium on Modeling, Analysis, and Simulation of Computer and Telecommunication Systems, pp. 218–225. IEEE Press, California (2006)

16. Castillo, C., Rouskas, G., Harfoush, K.: Online algorithms for advance resource reservations. Journal of Parallel and Distributed Computing 71, 963–972 (2011)
17. Chunming, H., Jinpeng, H., Tianyu, W.: Flexible Resource Reservation Using Slack Time for Service Grid. In: 12th International Conference on Parallel and Distributed Systems, pp. 327–334. IEEE Press, Washington (2006)
18. Netto, M.A.S., Bubendorfer, K., Buyya, R.: SLA-Based Advance Reservations with Flexible and Adaptive Time QoS Parameters. In: Krämer, B.J., Lin, K.-J., Narasimhan, P. (eds.) ICSOC 2007. LNCS, vol. 4749, pp. 119–131. Springer, Heidelberg (2007)
19. Behnam, B., Amir, M.R., Kamran, Z.F., Azedah, D.: Gravitational Emulation Local Search Algorithm for Advanced Reservation and Scheduling in Grid Computing Systems. In: 4th International Conference on Computer Science and Convergence Information Technology, pp. 1240–1245. IEEE Press, Seoul (2009)

A Memoryless Trust Computing Mechanism for Cloud Computing

Mohamed Firdhous*, Osman Ghazali, and Suhaidi Hassan

InterNetWorks Research Laboratory,
School of Computing,
Universiti Utara Malaysia,
Malaysia
mfirdhous@internetworks.my, {osman,suhaidi}@uum.edu.my
http://www.internetworks.my

Abstract. Trust management systems play an important role in identifying the quality of service in distributed systems. In cloud computing,
trust systems can be used to identify service providers who would meet
the requirements of customers. Several trust computing mechanisms have
been proposed in literature based on various trust metrics. Most of these
systems compute the trust scores incrementally from the previous values.
This is major vulnerability that can be exploited by adversaries to attack
the system forcing the trust scores towards extreme values. In this paper,
the authors present a memoryless trust computing mechanism which is
immune to such attacks. The proposed mechanism does not depend on
the previous trust scores hence it cannot be forced towards extreme values by repeated requests. The simulations experiments conducted show
that the trust scores computed using the proposed mechanism are more
representative and stable in the face of attacks compared to other systems.

Keywords: Cloud computing, trust management, memoryless trust
computing.

1 Introduction

Cloud computing has been accepted as the new paradigm in computing that
changes the way computing resources have been used and paid for. With the
advent of cloud computing, the marketing model of computing resources has
changed from purchase and own or lease to a utility one. Cloud computing makes
computing resources including hardware, development platform, software and
services available as utilities similar to electricity, water, gas and telephony over
the Internet [1]. There are several cloud service providers in the market selling
different services at different service qualities and prices. When customers would

---

* Mohamed Firdhous is with the Faculty of Information Technology, University of
Moratuwa, Sri Lanka. He is currently on study leave from the University of Moratuwa
pursuing his PhD in the School of Computing, Universiti Utara Malaysia, Malaysia.

R. Benlamri (Ed.): NDT 2012, Part I, CCIS 293, pp. 174–185, 2012.
© Springer-Verlag Berlin Heidelberg 2012

purchase cloud services from these service providers, they would like to have the best service for the price paid. Hence they would like to know the quality of the service providers before entering into a contract with them. So, a system that could quantify the Quality of Service (QoS) would be necessary which can be accessed by the clients. A trust management system that quantify the QoS of service providers can assist the clients to select the right service provider based on their requirements [2]. In this paper the authors propose an improved trust computing mechanism based on the response time of the service provider.

This paper consists of five sections as follows: Section 1 introduces the paper while sections 2 and 3 discuss cloud computing and trust and trust management respectively. Section 4 introduces the new trust computing mechanisms proposed in this paper along with the experiment conducted to verify it. Finally Section 5 concludes the paper with recommendation for future work.

2   Cloud Computing

Cloud computing has been considered to make computing the 5th utility in the line of electricity, water, gas and telephony [1]. Cloud computing helps organizations to fully outsource their resource requirements and concentrate only on their core activities. The main difference between cloud computing and traditional outsourcing is the total absence on a commitment with regard to the resource requirements at the beginning itself [3]. In the traditional outsourcing model where organizations lease their computing requirements from large data centres, they have to commitment on their usage at the beginning itself and they will be charged for the commitment irrespective of actual usage. But in the cloud computing model, no such commitment is necessary and the consumption of the resources can change along with the demand and they will be charged only for the consumption. Hence organizations can start small and grow big with time and along with this growth their computing resource requirement can also grow without any inhibitions. Also cloud computing can adapt to seasonal variations in the demand as well. This non commitment and string adaptation of resource utilization and the payment help organizations to invest their capital on their core business operations rather than on computing resources.

Resources hosted by the cloud computing systems can be made available and removed on the fly based on customer demand as they are hosted on virtualized platform [4]. The capability to bring and remove resources on the fly allows the service providers to sell the same physical hardware to multiple clients making the utilization of these resources higher which in turn helps them to reduce the cost of resources per user. Hence purchasing computing resources from a cloud provider help customers reduce the cost. Also, cloud computing help customers reduce their capital cost as the payment for cloud resources is based on utility. Since cloud resources can be added incrementally, the resources consumption closely follow the actual demand and the investment on these resources are fully rationalized.

Cloud computing services are currently marketed under three main categories. They are namely, Infrastructure as Service (IaaS), Platform as a Service (PaaS), and Software as a Service (SaaS) [5]. Under IaaS, computing resources such as processing power, hard drive space, memory, and database storage are made available on a virtualized platform. From a customer's point of view, he can treat the virtual resource made available as if it real and install the operating system and applications of his choice on it [6]. Hence a single physical computer may host multiple operating systems and several applications on them. The virtualization software installed on the computer provides the necessary isolation for these operating systems and application along with the required security [7]. The provisioning of software development platforms comprising operating system, development and testing tools and Application Programming Interface (API) is called the PaaS. PaaS helps application developers to reduce the cost and time of development as they need not be concerned about purchasing, installing and maintaining of hardware or software [8]. SaaS is the new paradigm in marketing software as a service rather than a commodity that to be purchased, installed and maintained in house [9]. Web based applications developed and hosted on the cloud system are marketed as services over the Internet. Users access these applications through a thin client usually a web browser. Clients who accesses the SaaS applications can customize them to suit their specific requirements [10]. This makes users feel the same as they are exclusively accessing a locally hosted application. Fig. 1 shows a cloud computing layered architecture comprising of physical hardware, virtualized hardware and cloud business layers.

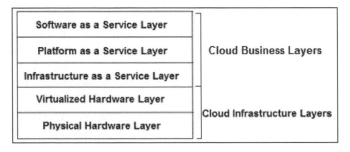

Fig. 1. Layers of Cloud Computing [11]

Apart from the three cloud computing services discussed above, new services have been introduced by developers under different names. Communication as a Service (CaaS), Data as a Service (DaaS), Network as a Service (NaaS) and Identity and Policy Management as a Service IPaaS are some of these services that are already available [12]. XaaS-Anything as a Service is commonly used by some researchers to combine all these services under a single name [13].

3   Trust and Trust Management

Trust helps users to select the right peer to interact with in distributed systems. Hence distributed systems like peer-to-peer systems, grid computing systems, cluster computing systems, sensor networks and cloud computing systems employ trust management systems to manage the interaction between their peers [6], [14], [15], [16], [17]. These trust systems base their decision on their prior experience in interacting with these peers in terms of their competence, benevolence, integrity and predictability. Firdhous et al., [6] have presented a trust computing system based on the response time of the server. The proposed system continuously monitors if the server meets the guaranteed response time with certain confidence levels. Depending on the response of the system, the trust values are continuously updated. The trust values are either improved or diminished depending on the actual performance of the server for a given confidence level. If the server response time is better than the required response time the trust value is improved while it is diminished when the server fails to meet the requirement. Also, multiple trust values are modified depending on the criteria met by the system on the assumption that if a more restrictive requirement is met, the system can meet all the less restrictive ones and on the other hand, if the system fails to meet any less restrictive requirement, it is assumed that the system would not meet more restrictive ones. The modification of the trust value has been carried out using a normalization parameter (δ), which is fractional difference between the required performance and actual performance.

The use of the previously computed trust scores and the required response time indirectly through the normalization parameter in this method can be exploited by the adversaries to attack the system in two ways. First, an adversary can report a large deviation of actual response time compared to the required response time. This would create a large normalization parameter resulting in a large modification to the trust score, which would then be used to compute the current trust score. Second, an adversary may continuously report the same response time making the system to modify the response time continuously towards an extreme value, that is either +1 or -1. Both these attacks can affect the performance of the trust computing system adversely. This is a major limitation of this mechanism. Hence it is necessary to make the system resilient to this kind of attack.

4   Computing Trust

Computation of trust involves three main stages [18]. they are namely;

1. Trust Formation
2. Trust Evolution
3. Trust Distribution

The computing involves two stages namely, trust formation and trust evolution. Trust forming is the computing of initial trust value for a system prior to its interaction with clients. The initial trust value can be either taken a neutral value (middle point) or computed using other information such as reported system capabilities including hardware, software and network. The trust evolution is the function of modifying the trust scores based on the performance of the system during serving the clients. Trust distribution is the sharing of trust scores of different systems with other cooperating trust management systems for building a larger system covering a wider region. In this paper only the trust computation is considered and trust distribution is left for future work.

4.1   Memoryless Trust Computing Mechanism

Fig. 2 shows the block diagram of a trust management system proposed in this paper. The monitor tracks the performance of the system and feeds the trust computing system with the most recent response time. The proposed model does not contain a trust forming unit as it is a memoryless mechanism which depends only on the recent performance of the system. The trust computing unit receives another input directly from the client. The client provides the required response time. Fig. 3 shows the trust computing unit in detail. The trust computing unit is made up of response time storage block, a summing point and a Sigmoid function unit. The response times are stored in a FIFO fashion maintaining a fixed number of most recent response times. The summer computes the difference between the median of response times stored in the data storage block and the required response and the results is then supplied to the sigmoid function unit. The Sigmoid function unit computes the trust value based on the input from the summer. The algorithm used for computing trust score is shown in Fig. 4.

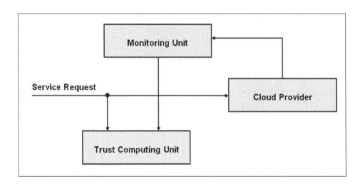

Fig. 2. Trust Management System

The trust computing algorithm presented in Fig. 4, calculates the trust score directly from the input using the Sigmoid function. Hence there is no necessity to track the previous trust values, it is only necessary to track the actual response times of the cloud provider in order to compute the normalization parameter (δ). The Sigmoid function is used in this algorithm due to its special properties

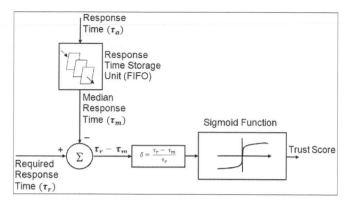

Fig. 3. Trust Computing Unit

required response time $= \tau_r$

actual response time $= \tau_a$

compute the median response time $= \tau_m$

compute the difference in response times $\bar{\tau} = \tau_r - \tau_m$

compute normalization parameter $\delta = \frac{\tau_r - \tau_m}{\tau_r}$

compute the trust score using sigmoid function $T = Sigm\ (\delta)$

Fig. 4. Trust Computing Algorithm

that are suitable for this kind of operation. The special properties that can be useful for trust management are:

- Shape of the curve (S-shape)
- Linear operation in the middle region
- Large input range (from $-\infty$ to $+\infty$)

Fig. 5 shows the shape of a Sigmoid curve. The non linear property of the Sigmoid function makes it very difficult to push the scores towards extreme values both positive and negative. The linear portion of the curve can be used to amplify the trust score differences in that region as most of the customers could be expected to operate there. The large input range makes the system robust as theoretically it would be impossible to break the system using extreme values.

In addition to the sigmoid function, the proposed system will perform better compared to other mechanisms as the proposed mechanism is essentially memoryless. The memoryless property results from non storage of previously computed trust values. The trust value computed for a given input is discarded immediately as it is not necessary to track the trust scores. The trust scores computed depend only on the actual performance of the system, which is tracked by the monitoring unit. Storing multiple response times and taking the median value

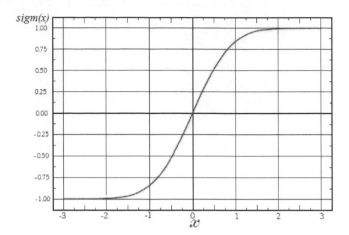

Fig. 5. Example Sigmoid Curve

make the system less error prone as temporary system fluctuations in performance will not affect the final results. Also, taking the median value helps to reduce the number of responses stored compared to other statistics like mean for consistent performance. Hence the proposed system is totally independent of user manipulation.

4.2   Experimental Setup

The proposed algorithm was tested using simulations and the results were compared against the original results. The simulation environment comprising individual units was created using GNU Octave software. The sigmoid function used in the experiment is shown in Eq. (1). The final trust score is computed using Eq. 2. The modification has been carried out in order to spread the trust scores between (-1, +1) without affecting the shape of the spread of scores. Thirty most recent response times were collected and stored in the Response Time Storage Unit for the purpose of computing the median response time. The number of samples were decided to be 30 as it is the smallest sample size required to represent normal distribution.

$$T_{temp} = \frac{1}{1 + e^{\delta}} \tag{1}$$

$$T_{final} = 2 * T_{temp} - 1 \tag{2}$$

In order to create a consistent environment during the experiment, the median response time of the system was maintained fixed while the required response times were generated using a random number generator. Fig. 6 show the modification of trust scores for services with random request times for both memoryless trust computing system and the multilevel threshold based trust computing system. From this figure, it can be seen that the trust scores computed by the proposed memoryless trust computing mechanism closely follows the request times while the trust scores computed by the multilevel threshold based mechanism is spread all over. The main reason for this is that the proposed mechanism bases its decision only on the difference between the requested time and the median access time, while the other method is influenced by the previous access times and it is continuous trust evolution mechanism.

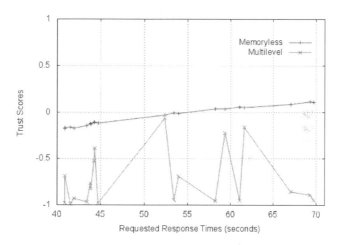

Fig. 6. Trust Scores for Random Request Times

Figs. 7 shows the computed trust scores by sending the same request time repeatedly. In both Sub Figures (a) and (b), it can be seen that the trust scores computed by the multilevel threshold based mechanism moves towards +1 while the trust scores computed by the memoryless trust computing mechanism remains unchanged. The main reason for this difference is that the memoryless mechanism carries out it computations independent of its trust scores while multilevel threshold based mechanism improves the trust scores from its previous value. The difference in trust scores computed by the multilevel threshold based mechanism in Figs. 7 (a) and (b) is due to the difference in request times. The trust scores shown in Fig. 7 (a) were computed using a larger time difference between the request and actual times is larger compared to that of Fig. 7 (b). Hence it is evident that by using a larger request time it is possible to drive the trust scores faster towards +1 in multilevel threshold based mechanism. Though the trust scores shown in 7 (b) approaches +1 slowly, it is definitely heading there. It must be noted that all these changes are happening while there is no improvement in the performance of the system (while the access time is kept unchanged). Hence it can be concluded that the memoryless trust computing mechanism performs better when large number of requests of the same types are coming or requests with apparently large request times are coming. Both these situations can be an indication of attacks.

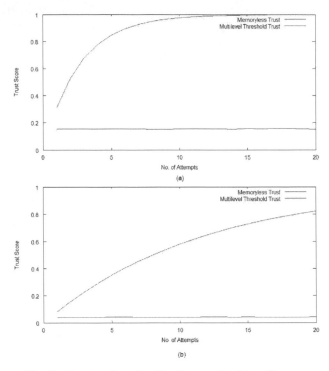

Fig. 7. Trust values for Continuous Positive Change

Similar to the result shown in Fig. 7, the result shown in Fig. 8 also is the outcome of repeated requests. Here also it can be seen that the trust scores computed using multilevel threshold based mechanism head towards the extreme trust score of -1, while the trust scores computed using the proposed memoryless mechanism stays stable.

Hence it can be concluded that the proposed mechanism is better and stable in the case of repeated requests and also the trust scores computed depends only on the most current performance of the system only. Since the performance of the system is represented by the median value of the recent response times, the computation is more stable and representative of the true status of the system as the median value is a more stable statistics and not affected by outliers.

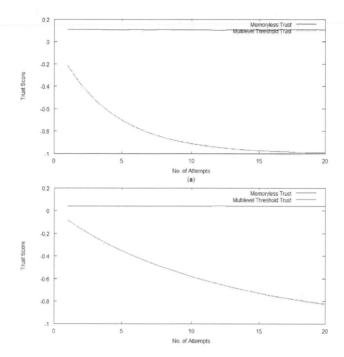

Fig. 8. Trust Computing Algorithm

5   Conclusions

In this paper, the authors have presented a memoryless trust computing mechanism that computes the trust scores for a cloud computing system based on the response time of the system. The proposed mechanism computes the trust scores using a non linear Sigmoid function. The sigmoid function has be selected for the computation of the trust scores due to their special properties, such as the shape and the large input range. The proposed system has been tested using simulations are the results were compared that of multilevel threshold based mechanism. The results proposed system were found to be better and more stable in the face of repeated requests. Also the trust scores computed using the proposed mechanism is more representative of the system performance.

References

1. Buyya, R., Yeo, C.S., Venugopal, S., Broberg, J., Brandic, I.: Cloud Computing and Emerging IT Platforms: Vision, Hype, and Reality for Delivering Computing as the 5th Utility. Future Generation Computer Systems 25(6), 599–616 (2009)

2. Firdhous, M., Ghazali, O., Hassan, S., Harun, N.Z., Abas, A.: Honey Bee based Trust Management System for Cloud Computing. In: 3rd International Conference on Computing and Informatics (ICOCI 2011), pp. 327–332. Universiti Utara Malaysia, Malaysia (2011)

3. An, B., Lesser, V., Irwin, D., Zink, M.: Automated Negotiation with Decommitment for Dynamic Resource Allocation in Cloud Computing. In: 9th International Conference on Autonomous Agents and Multiagent System (AAMAS 2010), pp. 981–988. ACM Press, New York (2010)

4. Zaman, S., Grosu, D.: Combinatorial Auction-based Allocation of Virtual Machine Iinstances in Clouds. In: 2nd IEEE International Conference on Cloud Computing Technology and Science (CloudCom 2010), pp. 127–134. IEEE Press, New York (2010)

5. Vecchiola, C., Pandey, S., Buyya, R.: High-Performance Cloud Computing: A View of Scientific Applications. In: 10th International Symposium on Pervasive Systems, Algorithms, and Networks (ISPAN), pp. 4–16. IEEE Press, New York (2009)

6. Firdhous, M., Ghazali, O., Hassan, S.: A Trust Computing Mechanism for Cloud Computing with Multilevel Thresholding. In: 6th International Conference on Industrial and Information Systems (ICIIS 2011), pp. 457–461. IEEE Press, New York (2011)

7. Zhao, F., Jiang, Y., Xiang, G., Jin, H., Jiang, W.: VRFPS: A Novel Virtual Machine-based Real-time File Protection System. In: 7th ACIS International Conference on Software Engineering Research, Management and Applications (SERA 2009), pp. 217–224. IEEE Press, New York (2009)

8. Rimal, B.P., Choi, E., Lumb, I.: A Taxonomy and Survey of Cloud Computing Systems. In: 5th Joint International Conference on INC, IMS and IDC, pp. 44–51. IEEE Press, New York (2009)

9. Prodan, R., Ostermann, S.: A Survey and Taxonomy of Infrastructure as a Service and Web Hosting Cloud Providers. In: 10th IEEE/ACM International Conference on Grid Computing, pp. 17–25. IEEE Press, New York (2009)

10. Kong, L., Li, Q., Zheng, X.: A Novel Model Supporting Customization Sharing in SaaS Applications. In: International Conference on Multimedia Information Networking and Security, pp. 225–229. IEEE Press, New York (2010)

11. Firdhous, M., Ghazali, O., Hassan, S.: A Trust Computing Mechanism for Cloud Computing. In: 4th ITU Kaleidoscope Academic Conference, pp. 199–205. IEEE Press, New York (2011)

12. Zhou, M., Zhang, R., Zeng, D., Qian, W.: Services in the Cloud Computing Era: A Survey. In: 4th International Universal Communication Symposium (IUCS), pp. 40–46. IEEE Press, New York (2010)

13. Mikkilineni, R., Sarath, V.: Cloud Computing and the Lessons from the Past. In: 18th IEEE International Workshops on Enabling Technologies: Infrastructures for Collaborative Enterprises (WETICE 2009), pp. 57–62. IEEE Press, New York (2009)

14. Cai, B., Li, Z., Cheng, Y., Fu, D., Cheng, L.: Trust Decision Making in Structured P2P Network. In: International Conference on Communication Software and Networks, pp. 679–683. IEEE Press, New York (2009)

15. Vijayakumar, V., Banu, R.S.D.W.: Security for Resource Selection in Grid Computing based on Trust and Reputation Responsiveness. Int. J. Computer Science and Network Security 8(11), 107–115 (2008)

16. Mishra, S., Kushwaha, D.S., Misra, A.K.: A Cooperative Trust Management Framework for Load Balancing in Cluster Based Distributed Systems. In: International Conference on Recent Trends in Information, Telecommunication and Computing, pp. 121–125. IEEE Press, New York (2010)
17. Tae, K.K., Hee, S.S.: A Trust Model using Fuzzy Logic in Wireless Sensor Network. World Academy of Science, Engineering and Technology 42(13), 63–66 (2008)
18. Carbone, M., Nielsen, M., Sassone, V.: A Formal Model for Trust in Dynamic Networks. In: 1st International Conference on Software Engineering and Formal Methods (SEFM 2003), pp. 54–61. IEEE Press, New York (2003)

Cost-Aware Performance Modeling
of Multi-tier Web Applications in the Cloud

Issam Al-Azzoni[1] and Derrick Kondo[2]

[1] King Saud University, Saudi Arabia
ialazzoni@ksu.edu.sa
[2] INRIA, France
derrick.kondo@inria.fr

Abstract. Typical web applications employ a multi-tier architecture. Traditionally, a pool of physical servers is used to host web applications. To handle the dynamic workloads which characterize today's web applications, several authors have proposed schemes for dynamic resource provisioning. Such schemes add more servers during peak loads and remove servers during other times. Advances in cloud computing technologies have created new perspectives for real-time dynamic provisioning. The elastic nature of cloud computing systems allows system administrators to quickly scale resources to respond to unexpected load changes. In such systems, dynamic provisioning is not only concerned with meeting Service Level agreements, but also must take into account monetary costs. In this paper, we exploit performance modeling in the context of cloud computing (Amazon EC2). Having such performance models enables understanding the trade-off between performance and cost, a cornerstone in developing dynamic provisioning performance management schemes.

Keywords: Amazon EC2, MVA, performance models, web applications, multi-tier.

1 Introduction

Typical web applications employ a multi-tier architecture. Each tier provides a certain functionality. We consider applications consisting of three tiers: web, application, and database tiers. The web tier manages presentation: it services static web requests, forwards dynamic content requests to the application tier, and sends the responses back from the application tier to the clients. The application tier manages the business logic. It services dynamic content requests by making queries and updates against the database. The database tier manages the storage of the web application's data.

A web application is deployed on a hosting platform consisting of one or more servers. To increase scalability and improve availability, each tier is deployed on its own set of servers with each set consisting of one or more servers. Web servers refer to the servers managing the web tier. Application servers and database servers are defined analogously. Example web servers include Apache

R. Benlamri (Ed.): NDT 2012, Part I, CCIS 293, pp. 186–196, 2012.
© Springer-Verlag Berlin Heidelberg 2012

and Microsoft Internet Information Server (IIS). Apache Tomcat, JBOSS, Sun Java System Application Server, and IBM WebSphere are some of the typical application servers. Example database servers include MySQL, Oracle, Microsoft SQL Server, and IBM DB2.

Traditionally, a pool of physical servers is used to host web applications. In such a framework, each physical server is dedicated to run a web server, an application server, or a database server. To handle peak loads, system administrators provision resources based on peak load predictions. However, the load can be seasonal. There can be significant high load during particular times of the day (e.g., mid-day) or the year (e.g., Christmas times for e-commerce applications) and relatively low load during most of the other times. Thus, provisioning based on peak loads can result in over-provisioning and thus increased costs and resource wastage.

To handle dynamic workload, several authors have proposed schemes for dynamic resource provisioning. Most of this work considers web applications that are hosted on a pool of physical servers [25,27]. However, given the changing dynamics of the workload and the costs of purchasing physical servers, hosting web applications on a pool of physical servers can be suboptimal.

Fortunately, advances in cloud computing technologies (such as virtual machines [3,4]) have created new perspectives for real-time dynamic provisioning. For example, Amazon EC2 [1] is a web service that provides resizable compute capacity in the cloud. The elastic nature of the service allows system administrators to quickly scale (up or down) to respond to unexpected load changes. Thus, system administrators have the ability to control how many servers are in use at any given point in time.

Using Amazon EC2 framework, it is possible to deploy each tier of a web application on an Amazon image and dynamically run (or terminate) instances of the image. Each Amazon instance provides a specific amount of compute capacity and is charged per instance-hour consumed. Depending on the provided compute capacity, Amazon charges different rates for each instance type. Different instance configurations can incur different monetary costs. With the emergence of frameworks such as Amazon EC2 framework, dynamic provisioning is not only concerned with meeting Service Level Agreements (SLAs), but also must take into account monetary costs. For example, a web application can be deployed using cheaper instance configurations that can also meet SLAs.

Performance models can play a big role in understanding the relation between provisioned resources, performance and costs. In this paper, we exploit performance modeling in the context of cloud computing (Amazon EC2). We want to validate the models given the new dimensions that such frameworks create. For example, EC2 instances are virtual machines potentially competing with other virtual machines which share disk and network resources. Furthermore, the use of virtual machines may impact the accuracy of resource utilization measurements needed to have good performance model results. Finally, the models need to take into account the heterogeneous nature of instances as well as the different costs.

Table 1. Amazon Standard Instance Types, Linux, US - N. Virginia, January 2011

Instance Type	CPU (#Virtual Cores)	RAM (GB)	Storage (GB)	Price ($/h)
Small	1	1.7	160	0.085
Large	4	7.5	850	0.34
Extra Large	8	15	1,690	0.68

This paper does not propose a new performance management scheme to meet SLAs. Rather, the paper validates a simple performance model for multi-tier web applications. This is the first step towards developing management schemes which constitute part of our future research.

The organization of the paper is as follows. In Section 2, we describe the Amazon EC2 cloud platform and the workload benchmark web application used in our experiments. Our modeling approach is described in Section 3. The experimental results are presented in Section 4. Section 5 gives an overview of the related work and Section 6 concludes the paper.

2   Experimental Environment and Workload Benchmark

Using Amazon EC2, We run multiple instances of different types in each tier. In this paper, we use the three standard Amazon instance types. Table 1 shows their compute capacities and prices. One EC2 virtual core provides the equivalent CPU capacity of a 1.0-1.2 GHz 2007 Opteron or 2007 Xeon processor [1].

An instance configuration specifies how many instances of each type are run to deploy the web application. For example, Figure 1 shows one sample configuration (SS, LS, E) in which two small instances deploy the web tier, one large and one small instances deploy the application tier, and one extra large instance deploys the database. We assume that each instance in the web tier employs a load balancer to distribute requests to instances in the application tier. The same is true for instances in the application tier to balance the load into the database tier. Note that we run one or more instances as workload generators which also distribute requests to the web tier instances. In practice, one can run an instance as a load balancer into the web tier instances using lightweight reverse proxies (*e.g.* nginx [9]) or transport-layer load balancing (*e.g.* IP Virtual Server [7]).

We use TPC-W [11] as the workload generator. TPC-W is a transactional web benchmark widely-used to evaluate e-commerce systems. It simulates the operation of an online bookstore which includes most functionalities that a typical e-commerce web site provides, including dynamic content generation, database transactions, authentication and multiple online browser sessions. The benchmark defines 14 request types requiring different compute capacity on each tier. Most request types include dynamic content generation which involves database

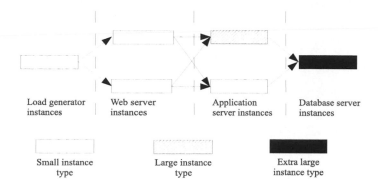

Fig. 1. Sample instance configuration (SS, LS, E)

queries ranging in complexity from simple select statements to more complicated ones. TPC-W defines three standard request mixes based on the weight of each type: the browsing, shopping, and ordering mixes. In the experiments, we choose a Java Servlet implementation of TPC-W from the PHARM group [12].

In TPC-W, there is a number of clients each generating workload by sending HTTP requests and receiving HTML (web) pages in response. When a client receives the web page, it waits for a certain amount of time (Think Time) before sending a new request. Although clients can have different session times, TPC-W specifies that the number of concurrent clients or emulated browsers (EBs) is kept constant throughout an experiment. Thus, when a client ends its session, the EB will terminate its connections and establish a new client session to maintain a constant number of clients. To generate different load intensities, we vary the two TPC-W parameters shown in Table 2.

Table 2. TPC-W Load Parameters

N	The number of EBs
Z	The client's average Think Time

3   Approach

We model a configuration as a single-class closed system with a network of queues. We use a closed system model since the the number of concurrent clients is kept constant throughout an experiment. Each queue represents a server (*i.e.* an instance in the configuration). The Think Time is modeled as an infinite server. Figure 2 shows a sample queueing network modeling the configuration (S, S, S).

The model is solved using Mean Value Analysis (MVA) [23]. MVA is a simple algorithm which assumes that when a new request enters the system, it sees

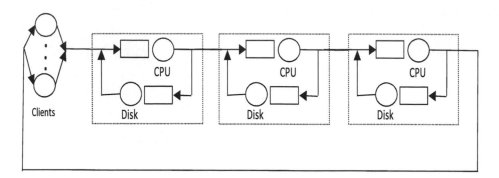

Fig. 2. Sample queueing network modeling the configuration (S, S, S)

the same average statistics as with the request removed from the system (see Algorithm 1). The MVA algorithm is used to compute the average response time R and throughput X of the application. The experiments in [22,29] show that MVA results in good throughput predictions for the shopping and ordering mixes of TPC-W. For the browsing mix, the bottleneck switching behaviour impacts the results [22]. We use the ordering mix throughout the experiments presented in Section 4.

MVA is an inexpensive iteration considering the systems in Section 4. The parameters to MVA are the service demands for each resource and the workload intensity parameters (N and Z). To obtain the service demands, we apply the Service Demand Law [21]:

$$\text{service demand} = \frac{\text{utilization}}{\text{throughput}}.$$

Thus, readily available operating system monitoring tools (such as sar of the sysstat package [10]) can be used to obtain the utilization of different resources. Also, Amazon EC2 provides monitoring tools that can be used in this context (*e.g.*, Amazon CloudWatch [2]). This enables measuring the service demands without the need for instrumenting the application or using costly monitoring tools. Other approaches model each instance as a $G/G/1$ system [27]. However, these approaches require parameters that may be expensive to obtain such as the variance of inter-arrival time and the variance of service time at each tier. For an instance, we only measure the CPU and disk service demands. The overall service demand D_i of a request at a server i is the sum of the CPU and disk service demands at that server.

Algorithm 1 assumes that each tier of a web application is deployed on a single instance. However, since we consider configurations that may have more than one instance per tier, *e.g.* (S, SS, L), we use an approximation by Seidmann [24]. In this approximation, if a tier consists of K identical instances (servers) each

Algorithm 1. MVA $(N, Z, L, D_1, \cdots, D_L)$

Inputs
N: Number of clients
Z: Think Time
L: Number of servers
D_i: Service Demand per request at server i
Outputs
X: System throughput
Q_i: Mean number of requests at the i-th server
R_i: Mean response time at the i-th server
R: Mean system response time (excluding Think Time)
for $i = 1$ to L **do**
$\quad Q_i = 0$
end for
for $n = 1$ to N **do**
$\quad$ **for** $i = 1$ to L **do**
$\quad\quad R_i = D_i(1 + Q_i)$
$\quad$ **end for**
$\quad R = \sum_{i=1}^{L} R_i$
$\quad X = \frac{n}{Z+R}$
$\quad$ **for** $i = 1$ to L **do**
$\quad\quad Q_i = X R_i$
$\quad$ **end for**
end for

having service demand D, then in the network model it is replaced by a single server i with $R_i = (D/K)(1 + Q_i) + (D/K)(K - 1)$.

In using MVA, the new contributions of our work are mainly as follows:

1. We show how to exploit the Service Demand Law to obtain the service demands using sar.
2. We construct good performance models using only the web server (Apache) logs and the resource utilization measurements provided by sar.

There are some limitations involving MVA when applied to model multi-tier web applications [21]. For example, web request arrivals may not be independent and can exhibit burstiness and heavy tails [20,22]. The transaction mix can also be nonstationary in the sense that the weights of the request types vary considerably over time [26]. Furthermore, MVA only provides the mean values of response times and thus it may not be straightforward to apply MVA in developing management schemes for SLAs specified in terms of a suitable high percentile of the response time distribution. Still, MVA is general enough to solve models for many commonly used multi-tier web applications.

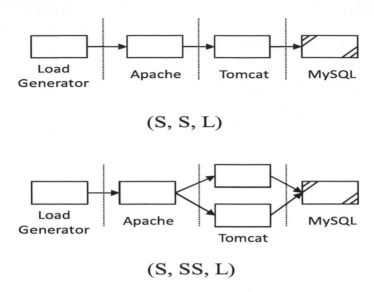

(S, S, L)

(S, SS, L)

Fig. 3. The configurations used in the experiments

4   Experimental Results

We use Amazon EC2 framework to test the performance of different configurations that deploy TPC-W. Apache [5], Tomcat [6], and MySQL [8] are used as the application, web, and database servers, respectively[1]. Each instance in a configuration runs a single server. Thus, a minimal configuration uses three instances: the first runs Apache, the second runs Tomcat, and the third runs MySQL.

We make the following design choices:

1. The performance of a web application depends on many factors, including parameters that set limits on the maximum number of connections that are served simultaneously. Since the focus of the study is on dynamic provisioning, we use the default parameters (Apache's MaxClient = 256 and Tomcat's MaxThreads = 200).
2. A fair load balancer is used to distribute requests from an Apache instance to the Tomcat instances. This is done using Jakarta Tomcat Connector.
3. We use a single large instance to run the MySQL server. Dynamic replication of databases is an open research problem and this is not the focus of this paper.

We modify the client in TPC-W so that image requests are disabled. Enabling image requests results in generating many automatically triggered requests which

---

[1] The Amazon images used in the experiments can be obtained by contacting the main author.

Table 3. Average CPU and Disk Utilizations and Demands

Instance	U (%CPU)	U (%Disk)	D^{CPU} (msec)	D^{Disk} (msec)	D (msec)
Apache	13.70	0.09	0.4535	0.00298	0.4565
Tomcat	96.48	0.11	3.1935	0.003641	3.1971
MySQL	22.34	4.66	0.7395	0.1542	0.8937

can impact the assumptions made by MVA-based models on the request arrival process. Furthermore, the use of caches to serve the images impacts performance and thus must be incorporated in the model. We also disable two TPC-W request types: the administration confirmation and request types. Administration requests generate extensive SQL queries and require service times that are several order of magnitude higher than the other request types.

We use instances placed in the same region. The goal of the experiments in this study is to compare the configurations (S, S, L) and (S, SS, L) in terms of average response times and monetary costs under a high load (both configurations are shown in Figure 3). Note that the first configuration is 8.5¢/h cheaper than the second configuration which translates into a saving of more than 725\$ a year.

The experiments are carried out as follows:

1. Obtain the resource demands when using the configuration (S, S, L) under the load $N = 300$ and $Z = 35$ milliseconds. The run lasts 1040 seconds. We collect the average CPU and disk utilizations using sar and measure the throughput and average response time using the Apache logs. We use the average utilization and throughput measurements to compute the CPU and disk demands.
2. Use MVA to calculate the mean response time, and compare with the measured average response time from Step 1.
3. Use the model to compute the mean response time when using the configuration (S, SS, L) under the same load.
4. To validate the results, we run TPC-W using the configuration (S, SS, L) under the same load to measure the average response time. The run lasts 1040 seconds.
5. Compare the model results (Step 3) with the measurement results (Step 4).

For Step 1, the average CPU and disk utilizations and the computed demands are shown in Table 3. These statistics are computed using all of the 314, 197 transactions in Apache log during the run. The resource demands are in milliseconds. For Steps 2 and 3, the average measured response times are shown in Table 4. The table also shows the mean response times calculated using MVA. As the table shows, using the MVA-based model results in an average response time prediction with relative error of less than ±5%.

Table 4. Predicted and Measured Average Response Times

Configuration	R (msec)	R (msec) (MVA)	Relative Error
(S, S, L)	933.76	923.06	-1.15%
(S, SS, L)	468.86	446.30	-4.81%

5   Related Work

Several previous studies have utilized performance models to guide resource provisioning. The authors in [27] propose a new dynamic provisioning technique for multi-tier web applications. The technique employs a $G/G/1$ system to model each tier. In their experiments, a cluster of 40 machines is used to host the web application. Their approach requires instrumenting the web and application servers to determine several parameters of the model.

In [19], the authors use a closed queueing network to model a three-tier web application with each tier hosted on a single server. With more emphasis on the multi-threaded (or multi-process) architecture of the web, application, and database servers, each tier is modeled as a single-queue having multiple servers with each server representing a worker thread. To apply MVA, the authors use an approximation proposed by Seidmann *et al.* [24] for multi-server queueing systems. The same model is used to guide capacity planning in [13]. The authors run each tier on virtual machines hosted on different servers. The goal is to provision the assignment of CPU to the virtual machines while ensuring SLAs are met. These approaches also require instrumenting the web and application servers to determine several parameters of the model.

In [14], the authors use a closed queueing network model to determine how many servers are required for each tier given an SLA stated in terms of the average response time. Each tier is modeled as a queue having multiple servers with each server corresponding to a web, application, or database server. To measure resource demands, they propose a profiling scheme that does not require instrumenting the application and is based on the Service Demand Law and regression. Their profiles capture the resource demand at per-request level and can be used to derive the resource demand for different request mixes. Our approach assumes a single mix and can be extended using similar profiling schemes. The authors assume that each tier has a homogeneous set of machines. In our work, the machines can be heterogeneous.

In [26], regression is used to calibrate the per-request type resource demands for nonstationary web application workloads. The data required for regression is obtained using access logs and a tool such as sar that monitors resource utilization. Their model uses an $M/M/1$ system for each resource. The empirical results show good response time predictions in real production applications. Our model can be extended to include different request types by using a similar regression technique.

Other policies apply concepts from control theory. These policies respond in a reactive way rather than the predictive, proactive approach of the other approaches. The authors of [15,17,28] propose a threshold-based policy, where lower and upper thresholds on performance measurements, *e.g.,* CPU utilization, are defined. When these thresholds are violated, the policy responds by allocating or deallocating resources. However, these thresholds need to be set based on performance targets as determined in the SLAs and this can be non-trivial. Another policy is suggested in [16] which uses reinforcement learning. This policy captures online the performance model of an application running on a cloud without any a priori knowledge. However, tuning reinforcement learning can be impractical. Another policy proposed by [18] implements an integral control technique called proportional thresholding. The policy focuses on elastic control of the storage tier in a multi-tier application running on a public cloud. The policy uses CPU utilization on the storage nodes as the sensor feedback metric. These policies assume homogeneous capacity and do not take economical costs into account.

6 Conclusion

This paper validates an MVA-based approach to predict the average response time for a web application hosted on a cloud computing platform. The approach does not require expensive instrumentation and results in good predictions. However, the approach, based on MVA, is not suitable for bursty or nonstationary dynamic workloads which characterize the general web applications. Yet, MVA-based models can always be used as a nice comparator. Such models can be exploited to better manage resource provisioning such that the SLAs are met while attempting to minimize the incurred costs. This constitutes the main part of our future work.

References

1. Amazon Elastic Compute Cloud (Amazon EC2), http://aws.amazon.com/ec2/
2. Amazon CloudWatch, http://aws.amazon.com/cloudwatch/
3. VMware, http://www.vmware.com/
4. Xen, http://www.xen.org/
5. The Apache Software Foundation, http://www.apache.org/
6. Apache Tomcat, http://tomcat.apache.org/
7. IPVS Software, Advanced Layer-4 Switching,
   http://www.linuxvirtualserver.org/software/ipvs.html
8. MySQL, http://www.mysql.com/
9. nginx, http://nginx.org/
10. sysstat, http://freshmeat.net/projects/sysstat
11. TPC-W, http://www.tpc.org/tpcw/
12. TPC-W Java Implementation, originated of PHARM at the University of Wisconsin - Madison, http://mitglied.multimania.de/jankiefer/tpcw/

13. Chen, Y., Iyer, S., Liu, X., Milojicic, D., Sahai, A.: Translating service level objectives to lower level policies for multi-tier services. Cluster Computing 11(3), 299–311 (2008)
14. Chen, Y., Iyer, S., Milojicic, D., Sahai, A.: A systematic and practical approach to generating policies from service level objectives. In: Proceedings of the Symposium on Integrated Network Management, pp. 89–96 (2009)
15. Chieu, T.C., Mohindra, A., Karve, A.A., Segal, A.: Dynamic scaling of web applications in a virtualized cloud computing environment. In: Proceedings of the Conference on e-Business Engineering, pp. 281–286 (2009)
16. Dutreilh, X., Rivierre, N., Moreau, A., Malenfant, J., Truck, I.: From data center resource allocation to control theory and back. In: Proceedings of the Conference on Cloud Computing, pp. 410–417 (2010)
17. Iqbal, W., Dailey, M.N., Carrera, D.: SLA-driven dynamic resource management for multi-tier web applications in a cloud. In: Proceedings of the Conference on Cluster, Cloud and Grid Computing, pp. 832–837 (2010)
18. Lim, H.C., Babu, S., Chase, J.S.: Automated control for elastic storage. In: Proceedings of the Conference on Autonomic Computing, pp. 1–10 (2010)
19. Liu, X., Heo, J., Sha, L.: Modeling 3-tiered web applications. In: Proceedings of the Symposium on Modeling, Analysis, and Simulation of Computer and Telecommunication Systems, pp. 307–310 (2005)
20. Menasce, D.A., Almeida, V.: Capacity Planning for Web Services: metrics, models, and methods. Prentice Hall, Upper Saddle River (2001)
21. Menascé, D.A., Almeida, V.A.F., Dowdy, L.W.: Performance by Design: Computer Capacity Planning By Example. Prentice-Hall, Upper Saddle River (2004)
22. Mi, N., Casale, G., Cherkasova, L., Smirni, E.: Burstiness in Multi-tier Applications: Symptoms, Causes, and New Models. In: Issarny, V., Schantz, R. (eds.) Middleware 2008. LNCS, vol. 5346, pp. 265–286. Springer, Heidelberg (2008)
23. Reiser, M., Lavenberg, S.S.: Mean-value analysis of closed multichain queuing networks. Journal of the ACM 27(2), 313–322 (1980)
24. Seidmann, A., Schweitzer, P., Shalev-Oren, S.: Computerized closed queueing network models of flexible manufacturing systems. Large Scale Systems 12(4), 91–107 (1987)
25. Singh, R., Sharma, U., Cecchet, E., Shenoy, P.: Autonomic mix-aware provisioning for non-stationary data center workloads. In: Proceeding of the Conference on Autonomic Computing, pp. 21–30 (2010)
26. Stewart, C., Kelly, T., Zhang, A.: Exploiting nonstationarity for performance prediction. In: Proceedings of the European Conference on Computer Systems, pp. 31–44 (2007)
27. Urgaonkar, B., Shenoy, P., Chandra, A., Goyal, P.: Dynamic provisioning of multi-tier Internet applications. In: Proceedings of the Conference on Automatic Computing, pp. 217–228 (2005)
28. Vaquero, L.M., Rodero-Merino, L., Buyya, R.: Dynamically scaling applications in the cloud. Computer Communication Review 41(1), 45–52 (2011)
29. Zhang, Q., Cherkasova, L., Smirni, E.: A regression-based analytic model for dynamic resource provisioning of multi-tier applications. In: Proceedings of the Conference on Autonomic Computing (2007)

Cyber Security: Vulnerabilities and Solutions for Telemedicine over Cloud Architectures

Shaftab Ahmed[1], Azween Abdullah[2], and M. Yasin Akhtar Raja[3]

[1] Department of Computer Science and Engineering, Bahria University, Islamabad, Pakistan
Shaftab_2010@yahoo.com
[2] Department of Computer and Information Sciences, Universiti Teknologi Petronas,
Bandar Seri Iskandar, 31750 Tronoh, Perak, Malaysia
azweenabdullah@petronas.com.my
[3] Physics and Optical Science, and Center for Optoelectronics & Optical Communications,
UNC Charlotte, NC, 28223-0001, USA
raja@uncc.edu
http://maxwell.uncc.edu/raja

Abstract. The acceptance of internet as a ubiquitous mechanism for ICT activities has revolutionized e-applications. Cloud computing is a new discipline to exploit the virtual environment over the internet for applications. Cloud service providers offer large infrastructure, computing power and software services configurable by the client at low upfront cost. But the vulnerability of cyber domain has led to serious security concerns of the clients regarding services and data management. Cyber security mechanisms have evolved in the past two decades to handle these problems at data transport and operation levels. To enhance user confidence in cloud computing, end to end security, data integrity, proof of retrievablity (POR), third party audit (TPA) along with forensic methods have been proposed. The security solutions offered by trusted platform group (TPG) can be used for cloud computing through integration with trusted platform modules (TPM) embedded in the client and server machines. The scheme addresses the physical security concerns posed by the portable data access units like mobiles, notebooks, iPADs and laptops. In this paper we proposed a cyber security solution for telemedicine over the cloud architectures based on available resources.

Keywords: Third Party Audit, Trusted Platform Module, Virtual Secure Machine, Proof of Compliance.

1   Introduction

Telemedicine is useful in bridging the gap between patients and doctors. The medical services may be provided in house as well as remotely through internet connectivity, which may be extended to remote / disaster struck area. Mobile adhoc Networks have been developed to provide information sharing over self-organizing temporary topology [1]. The cloud services provide ubiquitous cyber connectivity and resource

R. Benlamri (Ed.): NDT 2012, Part I, CCIS 293, pp. 197–207, 2012.
© Springer-Verlag Berlin Heidelberg 2012

sharing through data management and visualization tools. Medical doctors and researchers have access to large medical repositories for which role based security model is necessary.

Cloud computing applications for telemedic services have rapidly evolved in the recent past which provides a good cost performance tradeoff. The virtualization of resources and services over the internet domain exposes the users and service providers to a host of security problems and vulnerabilities. ICT companies and researchers are trying to develop acceptable security procedures for cloud computing to address security concerns of stakeholders.

Cloud computing offers vast range of opportunities to ICT companies who specialize in data archiving, sharing for scientific, engineering applications and e-commerce services. It provides a convenient model for on demand access to shared pool of configurable resources and services. The compose-ability of applications requires minimal user interaction for provision / release of resources. The broadband access allows a cloud service provider to offer SaaS (Software as a Service), IaaS (Infrastructure as a Service) and Paas (Platform as a Service). The controllability and flexibility are opposite to economy and efficiency. While the economies of scale demand abstraction, the security and access control over hardware / software and data sets reduce elasticity and increase service costs.

Threats to a cloud service model originate from web interface by cache interference, metadata corruption by malicious user or service provider. Hence the threats may be internal, external or by a rogue service provider. These issues are summarized in Table 1.

Cyber security is a term used to describe a set of practices, measures and / or actions to protect information and computers from attack. Mechanisms are being developed to balance vulnerabilities, threats and risks to provide acceptable service quality. A recent study of Cloud Security Alliance (CSA) [2-3] and IEEE shows that a large number of enterprises are interested to take advantage of cloud services, the Cloud Service Providers are offering very cheap services, and some of the notable are Google, Amazon, Salesforce, Microsoft etc.

Table 1. Security Threats in cyber domain

Security Threats	Functional Type	Tools / Activity
External	Spoofing, eavesdropping, Flooding, Man in the Middle, Denial of Service	Virus, Worm, Trojan Horse, Rootkits, Spyware
Internal	Side Channel, Cross scripting, SQL injection	Malicious illegal image software
Service Providers	Illegal use of client data Data Lock-In	Lack of control and audit obligations

Acceptability of cloud services for scientific and business solutions is hindered by the security concerns for which the ICT industry has to provide a universally acceptable framework. Subashini [4] has proposed development of a compliance framework globally accepted by the cloud service providers. Recent research to use Trusted Computing Platforms (TCP) and publication of its dynamics by Trusted Computing Group (TCG) has caught the eye of cyber security professionals for evolving a cloud security framework. The layered structure of TPM enabled software is shown in figure1. Embedded security through Trusted Computing Modules (TPM) are being used to handle the physical security threat posed by the use of PDAs and other mobile, wireless connectivity to the cyber domains [1].

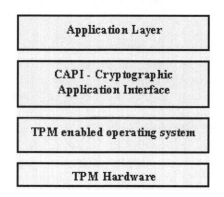

Fig. 1. Basic view of a TPM enabled software

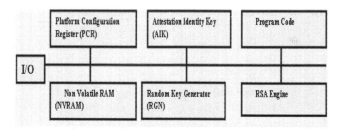

Fig. 2. Basic view of a TPM enabled software

The TPM consists of Random Number Generator (RNG), RSA engine, Non Volatile RAM (NVRAM), program code and execution integrity monitoring tools. It maintains a record of keys used to award certificates also. The software components of a typical TPM enabled environment are shown in figure 2.

2   Related Work

Large scale data storage systems mostly use non relational databases. Scalability, availability and security are some of the main requirements of such systems.

Enhancing security may reduce the scalability and openness. Jianying [5] has proposed a multi-tree database model using semantic clusters of relational database to address these issues.

Cyber security is the fundamental issue being addressed by experts considering launching applications over the cloud. Fujitsu has introduced end to end security concept for service oriented platform [6]. It is based on three principles, first one addresses network protection, terminal authentication and other procedures. Secondly the operating system establishes a clear difference between interconnection networks and application systems for sharing physical resources. Thirdly encrypted methods are used for physical storage of data on hard disks to enforce physical security against theft. High-Availability and Integrity Layer (HAIL) for cloud storage [7] enforces data integrity through distributed cryptography in the service layers for trust enhancement. The Proof of Retrievability (POR) [8-10] protocol is used to detect corruption or fault in data by challenge and response method periodically. The corrupt shares are updated by redistribution protocols. The data provenance tools help establish creation ownership and modification events on data objects through record of cyber domain activities by a Third Party Auditor (TPA) [11-13]. In cases of dispute the provenance methods provide digital evidence to forensic analysis.

The private clouds are managed through severs owned by the enterprise hence they present a trustworthy environment to the users. The public cloud services are exposed to problems of data transport, storage and resource sharing. Seam less extension of the computing architecture to community and global clouds is a challenging task.

Trusted Computing is the core requirement to address the concerns of stake holders to take advantage of virtual environments in the cloud. Chow [14] suggests additional contractual obligations for information centric security by self describing and self defending data objects over the virtual environments and hosts. Encrypted data transported to a machine in cyber domain creates a secure environment verified as trustworthy by high assurance remote server attestation before revealing itself. A trusted monitor or virtual machine [15-18] has a trusted monitoring component which provides proof of security compliance dynamically. The secure bootstrap of such monitors with TCP verification increases the depth of the Proof of Compliance (POC) [15].

2.1   TPM Client Initialization Protocol

The TPM provides root of trust by hardware and firmware support, which is used to build a chain of encryption keys and certificates issued. Trusted Computing Platform Alliance (TCPA) evolved a consensus on the specifications for TPA ensuring privacy and enhancing security [13]. It adds to the X.509 standard for digital certificates and other standards for Internet Protocol Security (IPSEC). Figure 3 shows TPM protocol used by Intel Corporation for platform authentication by Authentication Identity Keys (AIKs).

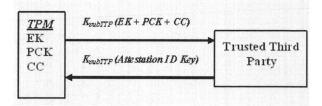

EK	Endorsement Key
	It is a Public Private key pair generated in the platform using the Root Key provided by the manufacturer. The private part of EK remains in the platform
PCK	Platform Certification Key
	Platform vender generates this key confirming the genuine status of TPM components
CC	Conformance Certificate
	It is generated by the vendor confirming the security properties of the platform through an accredited party.

Fig. 3. Platform Authentication by Attestation Identity Key (AIK)

The Endorsement Key (EK) may be provided by the manufacturer which is fixed; alternately EK may be locally generated by a Create_EK utility in the boot process using a root key provided by the manufacturer. The endorsement key is a public / private key pair generated within TPM; the private part of the key is never exposed outside. Attestation keys (AIKs) are used for platform authentication to the service provider. Endorsement Certificate contains public key of EK, Plat form Certificate provided by the vendor attesting that security components used are genuine and Conformance Certificate provided by an accredited third party. The certificates and public key of the platform are bundled and sent to Trusted Third Party (TTP) for registration. The TTP sends a signed ID called AIK, authenticating the trusted client. The TPM enabled system extracts and saves the AIK for future communications.

Microsoft Cryptographic Application Programmer Interface (CAPI) provides services to enable developers to add cryptography to Win 32 applications without knowledge of security hardware [13]. The cryptographic service providers develop modules bundled with operating system for root level certification. TCPA specifies integrity measurement of BIOS code at startup for enhanced integrity measurement. Such measures can be used for building confidence in virtual environments for program execution in the cloud.

3   Medical Services Architecture in Cloud (MSAC)

The cloud extends the medical services to virtual hospitals through internet connectivity allowing medical experts at geographically different locations to interactively discuss complicated medical issues to diagnose and plan medical therapy strategy, by sharing patient's medical record. To address the security of data services in virtual domain elaborate digital rights delegation and revocation mechanism is required based on trust relationship. Lifetime and workflow management of data must be bounded for availability and security purposes [17].

We propose to develop Medical Services Architecture in Cloud (MSAC) for ICT activities in trusted computing environment embedded in both hardware and software. The extended hospital over the cloud essentially requires client interface, data management and archiving system, multimedia services and network support for real time activity. We discuss the first three in the context of cyber security issues over the cloud.

3.1   Client Interface

The client interface provides access to data and applications for physicians, nurses, clinical investigators, researchers, administrators and managers, etc. as shown in figure 4. It enables implementation of secure infrastructure and simplifies the management of user and application environments. The main categories of activities handled by client interface are access to patient data, medical literature, case history browsing, use of clinical research tools and personal productivity tools. In the web enabled context the client interface may be hosted for limited accessibility offered to patients and other users. A client may be provided access on anytime anywhere basis including wired / wireless connectivity.

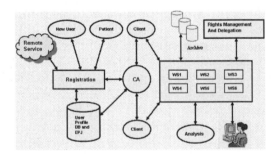

Fig. 4. Client interface and e hospital activities [17]

3.2   Database Management Archiving and Data Mining Model

The medical archiving system must record metadata to speedup location and interpretation of stored medical records and images. A catalogue is maintained for this purpose used by the search engine associated with the archive. The figure 5 below shows some features of medical database model.

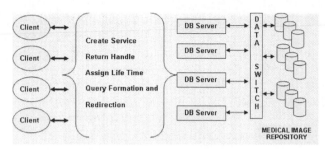

Fig. 5. Database model for MSAC [17]

The distributed database model of Apache Hadoop project is used to develop open-source software that can be used for clinical data processing involving large data archives. It provides reliable, scalable, software platform and infrastructure support over the cloud by using a framework for distributed processing of large data sets in clusters to enable parallel processing over the cloud. It uses Hadoop Database (HBase), Hadoop Distributed File System (HDFS), Hive, Pig and MapReduce.

The medical services data model of MSAC over the cloud will have embedded security mechanisms supported by Trusted Computing Protocols; figure 6 shows layers of the proposed model over the cloud architecture, where the SaaS, provides interface to Doctors, Patients, laboratory and nursing staff, the PaaS, supports Hospital Information system augmented by Trusted Computing Architecture and IaaS is the computing engine configured by the cloud service provider.

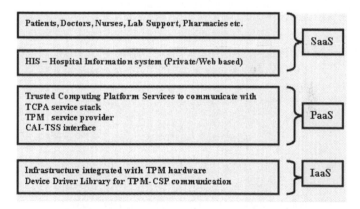

Fig. 6. Service layers of MSAC over the cloud

4   Cyber Security for Telemedicine in Cloud

E-Healthcare services over the cloud have to protect the Electronic Medical Records (EMR) through HIPPA compliant protocols. They require in-depth auditing capabilities for data management, back-up procedures and disaster recovery mechanisms. Telemedicine services in the cloud have to maintain audit trails of data access and management activities, for example; which user created, modified or copied the data objects etc. The architecture should allow security analysts to drill down into detailed activity logs or reports to establish access to data, the IP address used etc [18]. This data should be tracked, logged, and stored in a central location for extended periods of time for audit. Amazon has provided web services suit which can be used to create HIPPA compliant medical data management and applications in the cloud [19-20]. Amazon EC2 provides full root access and administrative control over its virtual servers. The Amazon Secure Storage Service (S3) can be accessed via Secure Socket Layer (SSL)-encrypted endpoints over the Internet.

5   Proposed Model for Cyber Security for Medical Services

We propose a medical community cloud to host services on a trusted computing environment of a cloud service provider like Amazon. The architecture and activities of MSAC over the cloud are shown in figure 7. To ensure dynamic security and integrity management, the CSP is bounded with Trusted Platform Control (TPC) procedures [11] and Service Level Agreement (SLA).

The security architecture in a medical community in MSAC will have embedded hardware level certification, periodic software attestation, key management and a Virtual Secure Machine (VSM) to monitor the activities of host infrastructure and services provided by the Cloud Service Provider, for intrusion detection or contract violations.

A qualified Trusted Node (TN) has to boot under a protocol exercised by embedded TPM [13]. It produces Platform Certification, Conformance Certification keys and Endorsement Certificate. Trusted Coordinator (TC) authenticates data and program activity in cyber domain through attestation of Trusted Nodes attested by a Trusted Third Party (TTP). It maintains a list of active Trusted Nodes (TN) along with their encryption keys. TC can inspect and verify the availability and integrity of these nodes through exchange of nonce periodically.

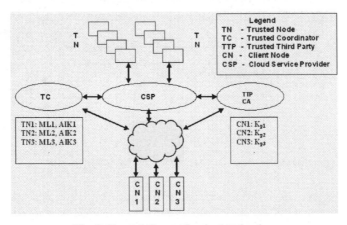

Fig. 7. Trusted Computing in the cloud

5.1   Trusted Computing Protocol

The proposed protocol for trusted computing in MSAC in the cloud domain is as under:

1. Client Node (CN), has the Public Key of Cloud Service Provider $K_{Pub\ CSP}$.
2. Trusted Nodes (TN) available to the CSP have integrated TPM module to compute a Measurement List (ML) at boot time used to bind the TPM with the processor under a protocol. It is basically a sequence of hashes generated which is stored for subsequent attestation.
3. A Trusted Coordinator (TC) maintains a pool of TN by issuing signed Attestation Identity Keys AIKs to Trusted Nodes (TN) by a protocol described in section II. TC maintains the MLs for Trusted Nodes available along with AIKs.
4. Client Node (CN) acquires a certificate of Secure Boot / Remote Attestation of TN from the TC by a protocol as under:

    - CN challenges TC by a nonce encrypted by public key of TC. $K_{Pub\ TC}(n_U)$
    - TC replies by its bootstrap measurements along with nonce encrypted by its private key $K_{Priv\ TC}(ML, n_U)$
    - CN attests TC's authenticity using public key $K_{Pub\ TC}(K_{Pub\ CN})$
    - TC attests CN through a similar protocol.
    - On successful exchange the public key of CN is saved in TC's database.

5. Client requests TC to assign required number of Trusted Nodes in the cloud
6. TC services client request by assigning Trusted Nodes TNs from a pool. TC provides their ML keys to the client for monitoring activities of the assigned TNs.
7. Periodic testing /validation may follow to monitor the TN activities

Note: The Amazon EC-2 machines offer root level access for this purpose.

5.2   Executing Client Application in Secure Environment

The Client level security monitoring can be enhanced by deploying a Virtual Secure Machine (VSM) on the TN under a mutually agreed protocol. The VSM proposed for Grid computing [15-17] ensures user level security by making a glass box environment or secure zone which uses intrusion detection system of its own.

The cloud architecture supported by CSP like Amazon provides Virtual Machine Instances (VMIs) to host the client applications. The VMI can be modified by integrating the proposed protocol of TPM; it may be called Trusted Virtual Machine Instance (TVMI). To enhance the security level a VSM can be transported to the TVMI which is self revealing and installing. After successful installation, VSM ensures that, even the system administrator at the service provider end will not be able to inspect or tamper with TN. The research and development of embedded design of TPM and dynamics of VSM is being pursued.

6   Conclusion

In this paper, we have discussed the vulnerabilities of the cloud computing applications and challenges for developers to provide an acceptable end to end security. The ICT industry has reached a consensus that security at the root level is necessary for acceptance of cloud computing by enterprises which may be targeted by the cyber crime perpetrator. Telemedical services over the cloud have been focused in our work. It is a multi-disciplinary activity involving the clients, enterprises and solution providers having a number of security concerns and solutions. The concept of TPM is the core which may satisfy the requirements of HIPPA. A model using TPM embedded in client, trusted nodes, and service providers with support of Trusted Third Party attestation procedures has been identified. The future scope of research will include development of a Virtual Secure Machine (VSM) for operational security in the cyber domain. The design of TPM modules using FPGAs will be used for integration. In the evolving standards of trusted cloud computing, it will be handy to provide off-the-shelves client configurable solutions.

References

1. Abu Bakar, A., Andul Rahman, R.I.: Secure Access Protocol using Group Based Access Control (GBAC) scheme. J. Info. Sec. Res. 1, 19–32 (2010)
2. Cloud Security Alliance : Security Guidance for Critical Areas of Focus in Cloud Computing V2.1 (2009), doi:
   https://cloudsecurityalliance.org/guidance/csaguide.pdf
3. ENISA - European Network and Information Security Agency report: Cloud Computing, risks and recommendations for information security (2009)
4. Subashini, S., Kavitha, V.: A survey on security issues in service delivery models of cloud computing. Journal of Network and Computer Applications (2010), doi:10.1016/j.jnca.2010.07.006
5. Zhang, J., Wang, X.: A Novel Access Control Strategy for Distributed Data Systems. J. Digital Info. Mgmt. 8, 291–297 (2010)
6. Hiroshi, C.S.: Cloud Computing Based on Service Oriented Platform. Fujitsu Sci. Tech. J. 45, 283–289 (2009)
7. Bowers, K.D., Juels, A., Oprea, A.: HAIL A High-Availability and Integrity Layer for Cloud Storage. RSA Laboratories, Cambridge
8. Wang, Q., Wang, C., Li, J., Ren, K., Lou, W.: Enabling Public Verifiability and Data Dynamics for Storage Security in Cloud Computing. In: European Symposium on Research in Computer Security - ESORICS, pp. 355–370 (2009), doi:10.1007/978-3-642-04444-1_22
9. Juels, A., Kaliski, B.: PORs: Proofs of Retrievability for Large Files. In: ACM CCS, pp. 584–597 (2007)
10. Harris, R.: Arriving at an antiforensic concensus. Examining how to define and control the anti-forensics problem. Digital Investigation 3, 44–49 (2006), doi:10.1016/j.diin.2006.06.005
11. Santos, N., Gummadi, K.P., Rodrigues, R.: Towards Trusted Cloud Computing. In: HotCloud 2009, Workshop on Topics in Cloud Computing (2009), doi:10.1.1.149.2162

12. TCG, https://www.trustedcomputinggroup.org
13. Bajikar, S.: Trusted Platform Module (TPM) based security on notebook PCs – White paper. Intel corporation, Mobile Platforms Group (2002)
14. Chow, R., Golle, P., Jakobsson, M., Masuoka, R., Molina, J.: Controlling Data in the Cloud: Outsourcing Computation without Outsourcing Control. In: CCSW 2009, Chicago, Illinois, USA (2009)
15. Ahmed, S., Qadir, A., Asad, R.: Security in large Scale Distributed Systems (Computational Grids: Critique and Solutions). In: HONET 2005, Int'l Symp., Islamabad, Pakistan (2005)
16. Ahmed, S., Mahmood, P.: Architecture for Grid Enhanced Operating System. In: HONET 2007, Int'l Symp., Dubai, UAE (2007)
17. Ahmed, S.: Grid Services Architecture for Archiving and Presentation of Medical Images. In: HONET 2007, Int'l Symp., Dubai, UAE (2007)
18. Ahmed, S., Raja, M.Y.A.: Tackling Cloud Security Issues and Forensics Model. In: HONET 2010, Int'l Symp., Proc. IEEE Xplore, Cairo, Egypt., pp. 190–195 (2011), doi:10.1109/HONET.2010.5715771
19. Protecting Personal Health Information in Research: Understanding the HIPPA Privacy Rule, Department of Health and Human Services, USA, NIH Publication Number 03-5388, http://www.hhs.gov/ocr/hippa
20. Creating HIPAA-Compliant Medical Data Applications with Amazon Web Services (2009), http://aws.amazon.com

High-Level Abstraction Layers for Development and Deployment of Cloud Services

Binh Minh Nguyen, Viet Tran, and Ladislav Hluchy

Institute of Informatics, Slovak Academy of Sciences,
Dubravska cesta 9, 845 07 Bratislava, Slovakia
{minh.ui,viet.ui,hluchy.ui}@savba.sk

Abstract. Cloud computing has emerged in recent years, while the illusion of the unlimited resources and feature-rich, is still considerably complex to use. Not only the migration between clouds is difficult - but also the development and deployment of a new, complex service from the beginning could be quite a challenge using today's cloud computing. In the paper, new high-level abstraction layers for cloud computing is presented. The abstraction layers will allow users to manage cloud resources form various clouds and simplify the process of developing and deploying services into those clouds. This approach will also solve absolutely the interoperability issue, thus improving the flexibility of cloud computing.

1   Introduction

The term of cloud computing may not be strange to scientific communities as well industry nowadays, as it grows very fast in the last five years with the support of infrastructures over network. Users' computer and companies have gradually changed their habit ways of using computational resources from own computer or server to centralized third party providers. In cloud environment, services are provided with higher availability and often lower cost than the traditional IT operations [1]. Therefore, cloud computing has become the main tendency of high-performance computing (HPC) technology today.

At the moment, it is difficult for users to develop and deploy applications on various clouds at the same time [2], [3], [4]. In principle, cloud applications could be built over PaaS (Platform as a Service) or IaaS (Infrastructure as a Service) types of cloud computing. PaaS clouds provide environments for hosting application services and API (Application Programming Interface) for implementing these services. The platforms will manage the execution of these services and offer some advanced features like automatic scaling. However, for existing (legacy) applications, PaaS may require complete rewritten applications using the dedicated API provided by the platforms what is not feasible for cloud developers. Furthermore, each platform can have different key features and API, what make moving applications from a platform to another is practically impossible.

R. Benlamri (Ed.): NDT 2012, Part I, CCIS 293, pp. 208–219, 2012.
© Springer-Verlag Berlin Heidelberg 2012

IaaS clouds provide resources (virtual machines, storage) as services where the users can have full access to the resources (often virtualized) and manipulate with them directly. For example, users can log into the virtual machines provided by IaaS providers and directly execute some commands or modify some files on the virtual machines. For existing applications, this approach requires many efforts for porting the applications to cloud computing.

In brief, the development, deployment and migration of cloud services are limited by several factors, including:

- PaaS are special purposed and limited to concrete platforms.
- IaaS are too low-level service. Users are forced to be administrators of their systems, they have to install and configure everything by themselves.
- The lack of suitable programming model for application development in IaaS.
- The lack of interoperability between clouds with each other.

Therefore, from the view of users, the need of an instrument which enables to simplify development and deployment of cloud services that plays an important role [5]. In this way, it is possible to achieve the highest work performance from diverse clouds. Users can write cloud services, pack them and deliver the code of the services for deployment on various clouds without any obstacles. In addition, users may choose these target cloud infrastructure to deploy the developed services and manage them in a unified user interface. The scientists are not IT experts who can use cloud computing to solve large or complex tasks.

This research primarily focuses on managing IaaS (like Amazon EC2 [6], Eucalyptus [7], OpenNebula [8] and others) to simplify the creation and use of virtual machines/clusters for developing and deploying services to various clouds at the same time. The abstraction layers could also make interoperability between providers from the view of users and enables opportunities for creating optimization (substituting, brokering) for users/consumers.

2   The Overview of the Abstraction Layers

In our concept, we change the relationships between the cloud providers, users and developers. The developers will have much more active role: they will define the interface, the list of actions what users can do, also the implementation how the actions will be realized in the cloud infrastructures. The users will interact with the cloud resources exclusively via the interface defined by the developers, not via the middleware functionalities. Implementation details of these actions, however, are not visible to users. Fig.1 show the relationships between participants in the cloud computing.

Technically, we implement high-level abstraction layers between developers/users and clouds with operating support for managing resources from the cloud systems. The new paradigm with abstraction layers in cloud environment is illustrated in Fig. 2. The abstraction layers will hide the implementation details of different cloud infrastructures, remove vendor lock-in. Users will manage the services via methods of the

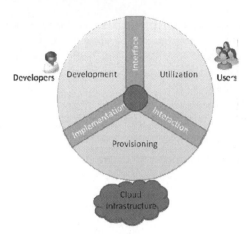

Fig. 1. Relationship between parties in cloud computing

reference objects so developers could control what users can do, and users will know what they should do via the methods without studying implementation details and technological backgrounds.

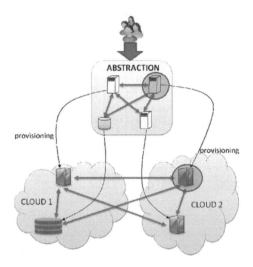

Fig. 2. Abstraction of cloud resources

The purposes of the abstraction layers are as follows:

- Abstraction between cloud resources and users: resources in the clouds (virtual machines, images, storages) are abstracted as objects and users can manipulate with them via the methods provided by the objects. The abstraction will allow changes in the backend without affecting functionalities and modification of developed applications in the abstraction layers;

- Abstraction of complex systems: via mechanisms like inheritance, composition and polymorphisms, developers can make abstraction of more complex systems with several components easily, and deploy them with a single click;
- Simplification of user interface: Users can manipulate resources as objects without dealing with implementation details;
- Interoperability: Applications and user' scripts developed in the abstraction layers will work for different cloud middleware from different providers;
- Optimization: The abstraction layers will allow optimization mechanisms like brokering, substitutions, load balancing and so on. For example, when the user creates a new virtual machine, the mechanism can choose which provider is best for the current instance.

3   Designing

3.1   Object-Oriented Approach

The abstraction layers rely on object-oriented approach to abstract computing resources. The resource is represented as an object where all information related to the resource is encapsulated as data members of the object. In this way, the manipulation with the resource will be done via member methods of the object. For example, assume that a virtual machine in the cloud is represented by an object vm, then starting the machine is done by $vm.start()$, uploading data/application code to the machine is done by $vm.upload(data)$, execution of a program on the machine is done by $vm.execute(command-line)$, and so on. More importantly, developers can concretize and add more details to resource description using derived class and inheritance. They also can define what users can do with cloud application via methods of abstract objects. Within commands, default values will be used whenever possible. Sometime, the users only want to create a virtual machine for running their applications; they do not care about concrete Linux flavor, or which key pair should be used. The interface should not force users to specify every parameter even if the users do not care about it. Abstraction layers also make space for resource optimization. The optimization can decide which options are best for users.

3.2   Abstraction Layers

The core of the abstraction layers is basic instance layer. It is a framework which consists of methods to manage and control virtual machines on different clouds (e.g. `start()`, `backup()`, `reboot()`, `terminate()` and others). The layer also provides other methods such as `upload()`, `download()` and `execute()` application packages or data on virtual machines. Besides its methods, the basic instance layer is linked to a repository containing virtual machine images of IaaS clouds which basic instance layer supports. In this way, assume that a user requires a virtual machine running on Amazon EC2 resource. The basic instance layer will use an available Amazon Machine Image (AMI) in the repository to create virtual machine at users' request. Some other time, user wants to create a virtual machine that runs on OpenNebula resource, the layer thus will use an available OpenNebula image in the repository. The number of IaaS clouds which the basic instance layer manages to be given, so the number of available images will be given. An image repository for the basic instance layer will bring many advantages, including respect for all of the features, functions and technologies from vendors, who are not required changing themselves for supporting the basic instance layer and conversely, the layer does not need any common standard among cloud systems. From the perspective of users, they can manipulate multiple clouds at the same time under a unified interface irrespective of how each cloud works. Through basic instance layer, the users also can easily upload, execute/install and download application packages on virtual machines from diverse clouds.

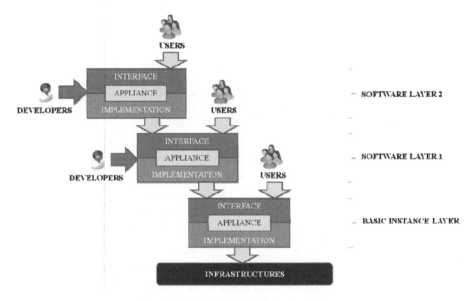

Fig. 3. Architecture of Abstraction Layers

Based on object-oriented approach, the basic instance layer allows inheritance in order to help developers create new abstraction layers upon it. Thus, the developer can define a software layer 1 with new methods for on demand from users. In other words, the software layer 1 will hide implementation details of the basic instance layer in its methods. Similarly, developers can also define methods for software layer 2 over software layer 1 according to user' needs without having to worry about how the preceding layer's methods operate.

A simple example, a user needs to store a database in cloud computing. Then, developer will use the basic instance layer to easily create a virtual machine and install MySQL package into this machine on any cloud. On this platform, the developers will define methods to interact with MySQL for users as `upload_database()`, `connect_database()`, `search_database()`, `import_item()` and so on which are call back basic instance layer's methods (e.g. `upload()`, `execute()`). In the principle, users do not have to care how their commands interact with basic instance layer. They only use the method that developer defined to use the database service. Moreover, after storing a number of different databases, the user wants to build wiki pages for easy database lookup. Developers can easily define a series of new methods for software layer 2 to create wiki pages with the connected available databases. For instance, `config_wiki()` method is defined by developer for software layer 2. It will automatically call back the `connect_database()` method of storage service (software layer 1) in order to link a wiki page with an available database. At the time, user only uses `config_wiki()` without knowing how the database is linked to his pages.

The compound object could be used for abstraction of systems with more than one virtual machine (e.g. cluster, PBScluster). Then, all virtual machines of the cluster will be placed in the same cloud, ensuring the network connection between virtual machines. More importantly, developers can deploy the whole system with a single command and customize monitoring service with user-defined actions on events.

3.3 Backup and Migration

Most of the cloud middlewares have supported backup or creating snapshot functions in order to store user data and program-specific configuration on virtual machine. As a result, users save the time in re-installing application as well as re-creating machine. Similarly, the abstraction layers also provide methods for developers to create a backup of systems or appliances. Thus, developers can define what will be stored during overwriting backup method, including whole virtual machine with operation system or only application data with their configurations. In the application backup case, backup data will be smaller, the backup process will be faster and the migration of appliances will be easier.

In our approach, the migration will be realized via backup-restore function. Then, developers only have to start a new virtual machine and restore application-specific configuration or data. This means that appliances can operate on different middlewares with different virtualization back-ends, removing vendor lock-in and allowing perfectly interoperability between clouds.

4 Example

4.1 Abstraction of a Virtual Machine

We started with a simple example how to create a virtual machine in the cloud and execute an application on the newly created machine. The following methods which are provided within basic instance layer:

```
Instance t = new Instance();
t.start();
t.upload("input.dat , myapp.exe");
```

```
t.excute("myapp.exe input.dat ouput.dat");
t.download("output.dat");
t.shutdown();
t.delete();
```

As Java language, users can choose if they will execute the commands one by one in interactive mode of Java shell, or create a script from the commands. The command in the first line will create an instance (a virtual machine) with default parameters (defined in configuration files or in the `defaultInstance` variable). The users can customize the instance by adding parameters e.g. `t = Instance (type=large)` or even more complex `t = Instance (type=medium, image=myImage, keypair=myKeypair)`. If the users want to create more instances with the similarity parameters, they can set common parameters to `defaultInstance`. Note that the instance is created without starting, so users can change parameters, e.g. `t.setKeypair(public, private)`.

The next commands in the example will start the virtual machine, upload the application and its data, execute the application on the virtual machine, download output data and terminate the machines. Users can get information about the virtual machines simply by command `print t`. The information given by the command is similar to the xxx-describe-instance in Amazon EC2 or Eucalyptus.

As it is shown in the example above, users do not have to deal with detailed information like IP address, SSH commands connection to the virtual machines and so on. They simply upload data, run application or download data with simple, intuitive command like `t.upload()`, `t.execute()`, `t.download()` and so on. Of course, if the users really need to run its own SSH connection, they can do it with informations (IP address, SSH key) from the `print t` command.

Now we can go further in abstraction by creating a function `execute()` from the commands. From this point, users can execute an application in the cloud only with a single command `execute()` with input/output data and command line as parameters.

Note that the abstraction (like `Instance` class or `execute()` command) does not only simplify the process of using cloud computing, but also allows experts (e.g. IT support staff of institutes/companies) to do optimization for users. The actual users of cloud computing do not have to be IT professionals but may be scientists, researchers, experts from other branches. For example, the IT staff can customize the virtual machines' creation by checking if there is free capacity in the private clouds first before going to public clouds.

4.2   Abstraction of MySQL Server

We continue with an example how to develop a database service within software layer 1. The service will inherit all functionalities from basic instance layer. In this way, developers can design quickly service commands for users what they are needed. The initialization of MySQL server which was configured by developers as follows:

```
public class MySQLServer {

    public void init(){
        Instance service = new Instance();
        service.install("mysql-server");
    }

    public void config() { //define method for users
        ...
    }

    public void upload_database(Data dat) {
        //define method
        service.upload(dat);
        service.execute(" ");
    }

    public void import_item(Item ite) {
        //define method
        service.execute(" ");
    }
    ...
}
```

After defining abstract objects for database service, users then can use simply the service:

```
MySQLServer m = new MySQLServer();
m.config();
m.upload_database("dat");
m.import_item("ite");
...
```

The developers also can go further in the use of abstraction layers to deploy appliances that are linked to the available database (e.g. web services, wiki pages, and forum). Meanwhile, users can use these appliances in simple and intuitive way.

4.3   Abstraction of Complex Systems

Besides simplifying the process of developing, deploying and using services, through abstraction layers, developers also are welcome to design complex systems such as cluster, HadoopCluster, PBSCluster etc. In this section, we will demonstrate how they create a cluster with compound object. In this example, N is the number of virtual machines running in parallel on the cluster. The commands look as follows:

```
public class Cluster {
   public void init() {
      for (int i = 1; i<= N; i++) {
         Instance head = new Instance();
         }
   }

   public void start() {
      // define method
      for (int i = 1; i<= N; i++) {
         head.start();
         }
   }

   public void config(){
      // define method
         ...
   }

   public void upload_cluster(Data dat){
      // define method
      for (int i = 1; i<= N; i++) {
         head.upload(dat);
         }
   }
      ...
}
```

Then users can easily create and use the cluster as follows:

```
Cluster c = new Cluster();
c.start();
c.config();
c.upload_cluster("dat");
   ...
```

Of course, developers can define derived classes from Cluster, e.g. PBSCluster, HadoopCluster, by modifying the configuration method in the Cluster class config(). More complex, they also can create an abstract object ElasticPBSCluster, a cluster with PBS where worker nodes are dynamically added and removed according to the actual loads of the PBS.

5   Related Work versus Our Contribution

Although some enterprises have provided standardizations and aim towards a scenario in which clouds could be interacted with each other without any trouble. However, each provider has built the standardizations which based on the features of their services. A typical example is Microsoft Azure [10], [11] that provides an open, standards-based, and interoperable environment with support for multiple Internet protocols, including HTTP, REST, SOAP, and XML, etc. Thus, if other providers want to apply the available Azure's standards, they must change their clouds in order to suit them. Therefore, in this way, most of the standardizations were defined that are not widely accepted.

Besides, Open Grid Forum (OGF) [12] also has the ambition to solve the problem of interoperability for IaaS. OGF defined OCCI (Open Cloud Computing Interface) [13] to provide an open standard API for existing IaaS cloud using RESTful (Representational State Transfer) protocol. Moreover, the main goal of OCCI is the creation of hybrid cloud operating environments independent from vendor and middlewares [14]. OCCI's documents separate OCCI core from OCCI interface, which has published. OCCI core model specifies base types, including: Entity, Resource, Link and Action. The Entity is an abstract type of the Resource and Link type; Resource describes concrete resources as the objects; while Link defines the relationship between Resources, the Action defines operation applicable to Entities. The OCCI model is developed in UML (Unified Modeling Language), but the types of the model are described by a graph structure which is similar to an OWL (Web Ontology Language) [15] ontology definition. This work has not been finished, it still under development in a preliminary state.

Distributed Management Task Force (DMTF) [16] has published Open Virtualization Format (OVF) [17]. The OVF is a virtual machine standard that provides a flexible, secure, portable and efficient way to distribute virtual machines between different clouds. Called virtual appliances [18], users can package a virtual machine in OVF and distribute it on a hypervisor. The OVF file is an XML file that describes a virtual machine and its configuration. Application-specific configuration can be packaged and optimized for cloud deployment, as multiple virtual machines, packaged and maintained as a single entity in OVF format.

Institute of Electrical and Electronics Engineers (IEEE) has two working groups (P2301 [17] and P2302 [18]) that have researched on standardization of cloud computing aspects. P2301 will serve as metastandard for cloud computing in critical areas such as applications, portability, management, interoperability interfaces, file formats and operation conventions. As the results, P2301 will provide a roadmap for all cloud providers building services under the standard. By the way, the project will enable interoperability, portability between clouds. Meanwhile, P2302 defines topology, protocols, functionalities and governance required for cloud interoperability and cloud federation. When completed, P2302 will ensure the ability of exchange data between clouds. However, cloud providers still may build their systems with distinct features to enable commercial competition.

Technically, the projects above force cloud providers to accept and support their products. Otherwise, they just have stopped at creating a common standard in order to solve interoperability issue. Some projects have not yet completed. Others have provided a product, but even then it is not considered comprehensive solution to the cloud problems (identified in Section 1). In comparison with the efforts, our approach has some advantages, including:

1. Providing the programming model for easy and controlled development and deployment of services over IaaS.
2. Providing a general-purpose solution for the application migration issue.
3. The abstraction layers are independently developed, not require support from underlying infrastructures.
4. Simplification of using cloud computing under the unified interface, lower barriers for new users.
5. Solving the interoperability among clouds, removing vendor lock-in.
6. Enabling the ability of automatic optimization in the background.

6   Conclusion and Future Work

In this paper, we have presented the novel high-level abstraction layers for development and deployment of cloud services. In our approach, we separate cloud developers and users with specific roles. Both only use functionalities of the abstraction layers without care about middleware implementation details. The core of the abstraction layers is the basic instance layer which provides implementation of basic instance for each known cloud middleware. Through the basic layer, the manipulation with the resource will be done via member methods of the object. The layer also allow developers to create cloud appliances easily via inheritance mechanisms whereas users can use simply these appliances. In addition, the abstraction layers also ensure interoperability between different cloud infrastructures which is one of the invaluable characteristic in cloud environment.

For the future, we plan to develop another abstraction layer of data management in clouds. The data abstraction layer will provide fully data storage and access in a secure way through different cloud providers. Like the abstraction layers of cloud resources and appliances, data abstraction layer also will be used to manipulate the data in order to decrease the access time and to increase flexibility with data. Data's mechanisms such as migration, replication and stripping will be exploited by the layer.

Acknowledgments. This work is supported by projects SMART ITMS: 2624012005, SMART II ITMS: 26240120029, VEGA No. 2/0211/09, VEGA 2/0184/10.

References

1. Buyya, R., Ranjan, R., Calheiros, R.N.: InterCloud: Utility-Oriented Federation of Cloud Computing Environments for Scaling of Application Services. In: Hsu, C.-H., Yang, L.T., Park, J.H., Yeo, S.-S. (eds.) ICA3PP 2010. LNCS, vol. 6081, pp. 13–31. Springer, Heidelberg (2010)

2. Ramakrishnan, L., Jackson, K.R., Canon, S., Cholia, S., Shalf, J.: Defining Future Platform Requirements for e-Science Clouds. In: Proceedings of the 1st ACM Symposium on Cloud Computing, pp. 101–106. ACM (2010)
3. Goscinski, A., Brock, M.: Toward dynamic and attribute based publication, discovery and selection for cloud computing. Future Generation Computer Systems, 947–970 (2010)
4. Kothari, C., Arumugam, A.K.: Cloud Application Migration (2010), http://soa.sys-con.com/node/1458739
5. Golden, B.: The Case Against Cloud Computing, http://www.cio.com/article/477473/
6. Amazon Elastic Compute Cloud (Amazon EC2), http://aws.amazon.com/ec2/
7. Eucalyptus community, http://open.eucalyptus.com/
8. OpenNebula: The Open Source Toolkit for Cloud Computing, http://opennebula.org/
9. Alex, H.: Hadoop in Practice. Manning Publications (2010)
10. Microsoft Windows Azure, http://www.microsoft.com/windowsazure/windowsazure/
11. Hay, C., Prince, B.H.: Azure in Action. Manning Publications (2010)
12. Open Grid Forum, http://www.gridforum.org/
13. Metsch, T., Edmonds, A., Nyrén, R.: Open Cloud Computing Interface – Core. In: Open Grid Forum, OCCI-WG, Specification Document (2011), http://forge.gridforum.org/sf/go/doc16161/
14. Moscato, F., Aversa, R., Di Martino, B., Fortis, T., Munteanu, V.: An Analysis of mOSAIC ontology for Cloud Resources annotation. In: Proceedings of the Federated Conference on Computer Science and Information Systems, pp. 973–980. IEEE Xplore
15. Baader, F., Horrocks, I., Sattler, U.: Description Logics as Ontology Languages for the Semantic Web. In: Hutter, W., Stephan (eds.) Mechanizing Mathematical Reasoning: Essays in Honor of Jörg H. Siekmann on the Occasion of His 60th Birthday. Springer, Heidelberg (2005) ISBN 978-3-540-25051-7
16. Distributed Management Task Force Inc., http://www.dmtf.org/
17. Open Virtualization Format, http://dmtf.org/sites/default/files/OVF%20Overview%20Document_2010.pdf
18. Virtual Appliances, http://www.vmware.com/appliances/getting-started/learn/
19. IEEE P2301 working group, http://grouper.ieee.org/groups/2301/
20. IEEE P2302 working group, http://grouper.ieee.org/groups/2302/

TPC-H Benchmark Analytics Scenarios and Performances on Hadoop Data Clouds

Rim Moussa[1,2]

[1] Lab. ITC&E Eng. –Univ. of Tunis
[2] CS Depart. ESTI –Univ. of Carthage
rim.moussa@esti.rnu.tn

Abstract. NoSQL systems rose alongside internet companies, which have different challenges in dealing with data that the traditional RDBMS solutions could not cope with. Indeed, in order to handle the continuous growth of data, NoSQL alternatives feature dynamic horizontal scaling rather than vertical scaling. To date few studies address OLAP benchmarking of NoSQL systems. This paper overviews NoSQL and adjacent technologies, and evaluates Hadoop/Pig using TPC-H benchmark, through two different scenarios of clouds. The first scenario assumes that data is saved on a data cloud and business questions are routed to the cloud for processing; while the second scenario assumes presummarized data calculus in a first step and multidimensional analysis in a second step. Finally, the paper reports thorough performance tests on Hadoop for various data volumes, workloads, and cluster' sizes.

Keywords: cloud, benchmark, TPC-H, Pig Latin, Hadoop, MapReduce.

1 Introduction

The Business Intelligence market continues growing and information analysts embrace well OLAP concepts and technologies. Indeed, according to Gartner's latest enterprise software forecast, the worldwide market for business intelligence (BI) software is forecast to grow 9.7 percent to reach US$10.8 billion in 2011. Gartner's view is that the market for BI platforms will remain one of the fastest growing soft- ware markets in most regions (refer to [1] for details). However, there are hurdles around dealing with the volume and variety of data, and there are also equally big challenges related to velocity, or how fast the data can be processed to deliver benefit to the business.

The relational database is the de facto the solution for data storage. However, it's well admitted that Relational Databases do not have linear scalability versus a pressing need for the analysis of large volumes of data. Big data can be difficult to handle using traditional databases, and multidimensional databases. Indeed, nice data presentation, demonstrated by OLAP servers through the great capability of navigation by intuitive spreadsheet like views and the data analysis from multiple perspectives offered by OLAP clients and servers, comes at performance cost, by an order of magnitude compared to SQL. Indeed ROLAP servers implement MultiDimensional

R. Benlamri (Ed.): NDT 2012, Part I, CCIS 293, pp. 220–234, 2012.
© Springer-Verlag Berlin Heidelberg 2012

eXpressions Language (MDX) as a wrapper over SQL (refer to TPC-H*d performances for details [2])

Most data storage systems are I/O bound; this is due to hard drives I/O performances which do not evolve as fast as storage and computing hardware (Moore Law) and communication devices (Gilder Law). Since the 80's with RAID systems, it's well known that the more we divide disk I/O across disk drives, the more storage systems outperform. In order to achieve high performance and large capacity, database systems and distributed file systems rely upon data partitioning, parallel processing and parallel I/Os. Besides high capacity and complex query performance requirements, these applications require scalability of both data and workload. It's well approved that the Shared-nothing architecture, which interconnect independent processors via high-speed networks, is most suited for requirements of scalability of both data and workload. Other architectures do not scale due to contention for the shared memory. Cloud Computing and in general distributed computing opens up several possibilities of advanced analytics and the associated massive scalability will help the enterprises. New analytical technologies related to NoSQL (Not only SQL) provide new avenues for enterprises to move Analytics to Cloud.

NoSQL systems rose alongside major internet companies, such as Google, Amazon, Twitter, and Facebook which have significantly different challenges in dealing with data that the traditional RDBMS solutions could not cope with. In order to handle the continuous growth of data, most NoSQL alternatives provide dynamic horizontal scaling. The latter is a way of growing a data cluster, without bringing the cluster down or forcing a complete re-partitioning through adding nodes. NoSQL systems advertise distributed programming framework using MapReduce. MapReduce (MR) framework is a patented software framework introduced by Google in 2004 [3]. It allows writing applications that rapidly process vast amounts of data in parallel on large clusters of compute nodes.

Apache Hadoop [4, 5], with roots in the open source community, is one of the most widely heralded new platforms for managing big data. Along with its core distributed file system (HDFS), Hadoop ushers in new technologies: the MapReduce framework for processing large data sets on computer clusters, the Cassandra scalable multi-master database, the Hive data warehouse, and the Pig Latin Language among other emerging projects. Apache Hadoop allows distributed processing of large data sets across clusters of computers using a simple programming model. It is designed to scale up from single servers to thousands of machines, each offering local computation and storage. Rather than rely on hardware to deliver high-availability, the library itself is designed to detect and handle failures at the application layer, so delivering a highly-available service on top of a cluster of computers, each of which may be prone to failures. Hadoop clusters grow very large, for instance, 1700 nodes at LinkedIn and 20,000 nodes at Yahoo.

A bench of NoSQL systems of data retrieval are existing to make computing on large data volumes, and new high-level languages by Microsoft Dryad (DryadLINK), Yahoo (Pig Latin), Google (Sawzal), Oracle (R language) have then emerged.

According to the InformationWeek e-magazine's survey, conducted in August 2010, from 755 IT professionals, 44% of Business IT never heard of NoSQL, 17% are not interested, and only 2% are using NoSQL (refer to [6] for details).

Enterprises such Yahoo!, Facebook, Last.fm, eBay, The New York Times, Twitter, Cloudera, etc. are using NoSQL. They report success stories after migration from relational database systems to NoSQL systems or to hybrid systems. However, we believe that these technologies must be used properly, and enterprises must be aware of the limitations of NoSQL, for providing real benefits. In this context, last two years a bench a papers were published on performance results of NoSQL systems.

This paper investigates usage of Hadoop distributed file system for saving data warehouses and Pig Latin language for data analytics and presents two On-Line Analytical Processing scenarios. The first scenario is a classical data analytics scenario, where each business question is translated into a pig script and run on a Hadoop cluster. The second scenario presents a more scalable and economical OLAP data analytics solution, where business questions are generalized and submitted once to a Hadoop cluster. The resulting summarized and aggregated data (a.k.a. aggregated tables in relational DB vocabulary) are then submitted to an OLAP server on-site for multidimensional analysis. We also report performance results of Pig Latin against the well known benchmark TPC-H –decision support system benchmark, for various data volumes, data schemas, and different cluster sizes.

The paper outline is the following: first, we discuss related work to highlight our contribution. In Section 3 we briefly present TPC-H benchmark. In Section 4, we overview Pig latin and scenarios devised for data analytics on a Hadoop cluster. Section 5, reports thorough performance tests on a Hadoop cluster running on French GRID5000 platform for various data volumes, data schemas and cluster sizes. Finally, we conclude the paper and present new work perspectives.

2   Related Work

There are few papers dealing with processing and evaluating by performance measurement analytics workloads for on NoSQL systems. Next, we briefly present related work and highlight our contribution.

Kim et al. [7] designed the benchmark: *MRBench* for evaluating MapReduce framework on Hadoop Distributed File System capabilities using TPC-H benchmark. They implemented all relational operations, namely, restriction, projection, product, join, grouping, sort, ...) and reported performance results of their algorithms for TPC-H with scale factor SF = 1, 3 -corresponding respectively to almost 1GB and 3GB of data, and for a fixed hadoop cluster size.

Other related work, investigated Pig/Hadoop for large large RDF datasets [8] and astrophysical data [9]. Pig Latin performances were investigated by Schätzle et al. [8] for processing of complex SPARQL queries on large RDF datasets. Similarly, Loebman et al. [9] develop a use case that comprises five representative queries for massive astrophysical simulations. They implement this use case in one distributed DBMS and in the Pig/Hadoop system. They compare the performance of the tools to each other. They find that certain representative analyses are easy to express in each engine's high level language and both systems provide competitive performance and improved scalability relative to current IDL-based methods.

Other research papers are focusing on translation of SQL into MapReduce. Iu and Zwaenepoel propose *HadoopToSQL* [10], which seeks to improve MapReduce performance for business-oriented workloads by transforming MapReduce queries to use the indexing, aggregation and grouping features provided by SQL databases. *Hadoop-ToSQL* statically analyzes the computation performed by the MapReduce queries. The static analysis uses symbolic execution to derive preconditions and postconditions for the map and reduce functions. It then uses this information either to generate input restrictions, which avoid scanning the entire dataset, or to generate equivalent SQL queries, which take advantage of SQL grouping and aggregation features. They demonstrate the performance of MapReduce queries, optimized by *HadoopToSQL*, by both single-node and cluster experiments. *HadoopToSQL* improves performance over MapReduce and approximates that of hand-written SQL. More recently, Lee et al [11] released *YSmart*. The latter is a correlation aware SQL-to-MapReduce translator, which is built on top of the Hadoop platform. For a given SQL query and related table schemas, *YSmart* can automatically translate the query into a series of Hadoop MapReduce programs written in Java. *YSmart* can detect and exploit the intra-query correlations to generate optimized Hadoop programs for very complex analytical queries. It is also developed for the purpose to create a teaching and learning tool for executing queries on top of Hadoop. Currently *YSmart* supports only subset features of SQL queries.

Other experimental papers are focusing on performances of NoSQL systems. Jia rewrited TPC-H workload into Hive QL and evaluated performance results of the Hive QL scripts [12] for a 1GB of TPC-H data (SF = 1) on a single hardware configuration, and Li et al. are investigating differences and resemblances, through comparison of Pig Latin and HiveQL for MapRedice processing of TPC-H benchmark workload [13]. Notice that our Pig scripts for TPC-H benchmark were released prior to their release [14].

This paper investigates the usage of Hadoop distributed file system for saving data warehouses and Pig Latin language for data analytics and presents two scenarios for data analytics in the cloud. The first scenario is a classical data analytics where each business question is translated into a pig script and run on a Hadoop cluster. The second scenario presents a scalable and economical OLAP data analytics solution, where business questions are generalized and submitted once to a Hadoop cluster. The resulting output, are then imported into an OLAP hypercube for multidimensional analysis. We report performance results of Pig Latin against the well known benchmark TPC-H –decision support system benchmark, for various data volumes, data schemas, and different cluster sizes.

3   TPC-H Benchmark

The TPC Benchmark™H (TPC-H) is a decision support benchmark [15]. It consists of a suite of business oriented ad-hoc queries and concurrent data modifications. The workload and the data populating the database have been chosen to have broad industry-wide relevance. This benchmark features decision support systems that examine large volumes of data. The workload is composed of 22 queries with a high degree of complexity. The workload answers real world business questions and includes multiple operators and selectivity constraints. It provides answers to the following classes of business analysis:

- Pricing and promotions,
- Supply and demand management,
- Profit and revenue management,
- Customer satisfaction study,
- Market share study,
- Shipping management.

Fig. 1 (source [7]) show TPC-H benchmark schema. Existing TPC-H implementation allow generation of raw data stored into 8 .tbl files ({*Region, Nation, Customer, Supplier, Part, PartSupp, Orders, LineItem*}.tbl files), using a specific scale factor. The latter indicates TPC-H data size. Indeed, a TPC-H scale factor 1 test means the TPC-H data volume is almost 1GB. Scale factors used for the test database must be chosen from the set of fixed scale factors defined as follows: 1, 10, …, 100000; resulting volumes are respectively 1GB, 10GB, …, 100TB.

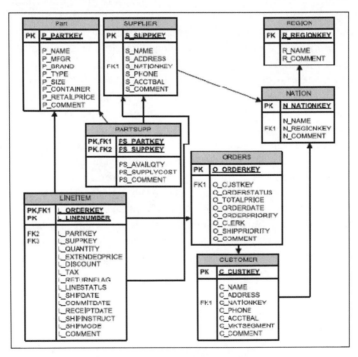

Fig. 1. TPC-H Benchmark Schema

Running TPC-H data warehouse benchmark requires both good scaling of parallel execution plans, and the ability to allocate resources between queries with parallel execution plans. At the system level, it requires a well balanced storage system.

We think it's a good benchmark for evaluating aggregation capabilities and scalability of Apache Pig/Hadoop.

4   Analytics' Scenarios for a Data Cloud

In this section, we will give a brief overview of Apache Pig, and a detailed description of devised On-Line Analytical Processing (OLAP) scenarios for a data cloud.

4.1   TPC-H Workload Translation into Pig Latin

Apache Pig is a platform for analyzing large data sets that consists of a high-level language for expressing data analysis programs, coupled with infrastructure for evaluating these programs [16, 17, 18]. The salient property of Pig programs is that their structure is amenable to substantial parallelization, which in turns enables them to handle very large data sets. At the present time, Pig's infrastructure layer consists of a compiler that produces sequences of Map-Reduce programs, for which large-scale parallel implementations already exist (e.g., the Hadoop subproject). Pig's language has the following key properties:

- Ease of programming. Indeed, it is trivial to achieve parallel execution of simple, data analysis tasks. Complex tasks comprised of multiple interrelated data transformations are explicitly encoded as data flow sequences, making them easy to write, understand, and maintain.
- Optimization opportunities. The way in which tasks are encoded allows the system to optimize their execution automatically, allowing the user to focus on semantics rather than efficiency.
- Extensibility. Users can create their own functions (User Defined Functions, UDF) to do special-purpose processing. These UDF are available in PiggyBank [19].

We worked with the raw data files generated by the TPC-H benchmark ({*region, nation, customer, supplier, part, partsupp, orders, lineitem*}.tbl files). Translation from SQL into Pig Latin requires expertise in devising query plans. Thus, we applied the following five hints in TPC-H SQL workload translation into Pig Scripts,

- *Hint 1: Load only required data in Pig storage and as soon as required.* This hint leads to better memory management. Indeed, the useless data are not loaded before their usage time.
- *Hint 2: Minimum Relation Scan.* Multiple predicates on a relation are performed once and thus only one scan of the relation is performed.
- *Hint 3: Unary operations prior to binary operations.* Unary operations have higher priority than binary operations. Consequently, restrictions and projections are performed prior to joins, cross products, unions, and intersections. This reduces intermediate results, and consequently I/O operations.
- *Hint 4: Enable Intra-task Parallelism.* We devise plans with multiple producer-consumer sub-plans, to increase intra-task parallelism features. This allows the execution of independent MapReduce tasks in parallel.

- *Hint 5: Right Join Algorithm Usage.* It's well approved that, Hash joins are used when joining large tables. Also, RDBMS optimizer uses Nested loop when joining tables, contain small number of rows with an efficient driving condition. The Sort-merge algorithm is used to join two independent data sources. Pig performs hash join by default, and allows explicitly Merge join.

Our Pig scripts of the translation of TPC-H workload into Pig Latin are available for download [14].

4.2   Classical TPC-H Analytics Scenario

The classical scenario is inspired by client/server architecture and conventional Decision Support Systems Architectures within enterprises. Most published papers in literature [7, 9, 10, 11, 12, 13] promote and evaluate this nominal scenario. Fig. 2 illustrates this scenario, where an analyst submits a business question (*hadoop job*) to the cloud (*hadoop cluster*), and waits for a response. The query here is for instance *Determine the total revenue between Europe and Russia in 1998.*

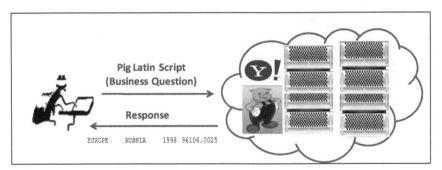

Fig. 2. Classical Analytic Scenario, with Pig latin/Hadoop on the backend for respectively data processing and data storage

The main disadvantages of this scenario are related to,

- Performance issues: the same query (with same or different parameters) may be executed several times, and for each run, the cloud devises an execution plan, re-loads data and re-executes mostly similar Map/Reduce tasks.
- Discontinuity of service: any network failure or congestion prevents the analyst from querying the cloud.
- High Cost: The enterprises using the cloud platform pays this service based on user-demand (bandwidth, CPU cycles, software, ...). This is advertised under the *measured service* characteristic (a.k.a. *pay as you go*). This scenario induces a high cost, due to the regular use of the cloud.

Next, we describe an alternative scenario overcoming most disadvantages of the conventional scenario.

4.3   OLAP Scenario on a Cloud

A cloud is a set of hardware, networks, storage (hardware), services, and interfaces (software) that enable the delivery of computing as a service based on user demand. As a consequence, the company is not in need of expert server administrators, and software licenses for PaaS and SaaS cloud service models. Most business cases for *cloud computing* is about, dynamic and up-to-date infrastructure, elasticity, measured service and other attributes that target reducing cost of computing by reduced operational expenditure.

Also, DSS based on Multidimensional databases (MDB) and OLAP technologies offer the following advantages (refer to seminal paper of Codd et al. [20]):

- Presentation: MDB enhance data presentation and navigation by intuitive spreadsheet like views that are difficult to generate in relational database, and which enable the analyst to navigate through the database and screen very fast for a particular subset of the data, because data is aggregated and summarized,
- Performance: MDB systems increase performance through OLAP operations (e.g. slice, dice, drill down, roll up, and pivot). Chaudhuri et al. [21] claimed that for complex queries, OLAP cubes can produce an answer in around 0.1% of the time required for the same query on relational data. Others [22-28] have also addressed this issue in different perspectives.

In database community, it's well admitted that Relational OLAP (ROLAP) is a technology that provides sophisticated multidimensional analysis, rather than Multidimensional OLAP (MOLAP). Indeed, ROLAP can scale to large data sets while MOLAP not.

The above overview of (*i*) cloud computing rationale: measured service and cost reduction, (*ii*) advantages of OLAP technologies, and (*iii*) ROLAP being the best architecture for dealing with large data sets, justify the sketch of a scenario aggregating data on the cloud and moving aggregated data for multidimensional analysis on the premises of the company.

Fig. 3 illustrates the NoSQL OLAP solution proposed, where an analyst submits a generalized business question (*hadoop job*) to the cloud (*hadoop cluster*), and waits for a response. The query here is for instance *Compute the total revenue for each region, each nation and every year*. The most important mechanism in OLAP which allows achieving such performance is the use of aggregations. Aggregations are built from the fact table by changing the granularity on specific dimensions and aggregating up data along these dimensions.   Hence, in the second scenario, we propose preaggregating data on the cloud platform, then importing data to an OLAP server on-site for high availability and performance concerns.   Data import and data presentation as a pivot table depends on data size and data dimensionality.

We conducted a numerical study over TPC-H benchmark workload, we were interested in computing the maximal number of rows returned and the OLAP hypercube size. We concluded that TPC-H business questions fall into three categories. Indeed,

- Half of the workload, namely business questions Q1, Q4, Q5, Q6, Q7, Q8, Q12, Q13, Q14, Q16, Q19 and Q22 return a fixed number of rows which do not scale with the TPC-H data set scale factor (SF). OLAP hypercubes sizes for these queries are relatively small (hundreds of rows). For instance, Q4 -*Order Priority Checking Query* determines how well the order priority system is working and gives an assessment of customer satisfaction. The generalized Q4 counts the number of orders ordered in a given quarter of a given year for each order priority. Q4 outputs at maximum 135 rows and the hypercube size is also 135 (*number of different order priorities* × *number of years* × *number of quarters/year*). For these queries, pre-summarized data might be imported in MS Excel (Pivot Tables) or Open office (Data Pilot) for multidimensional analysis.

- Other queries return really few rows compared to their hypercube size. These business questions have big dimensionality. For instance, Q15 hypercube size is: *line_ship_year* × *nbr_of_quarters* × *nbr_suppliers: SF×10,000*. Also, Q18 hypercube size is *nbr_of_orders: SF× 1,500,00*. Nevertheless, Q18 returns a dozen of rows for SF=1. For these queries, we do not recommend multidimensional analysis.
- The rest of TPC-H business questions, return a number of rows which varies with TPC-H scale factor. For these business questions, we do need robust OLAP servers. Also, storing aggregated data related to these business questions is high cost.

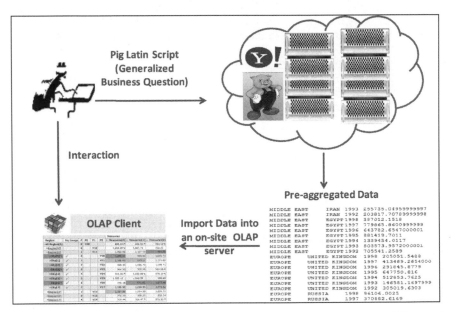

Fig. 3. NoSQL OLAP Solution, with Hadoop and Pig Latin for Data Storage and Processing, and an OLAP client on the frontend

5   Performance Results

The hardware system configuration used for performance measurements are Borderel, Bordereau and Borderline nodes located at Bordeaux site of GRID5000 platform. Each Borderel node has 24 GB of memory and its CPUs are AMD, 2.27 GHz, with 4

CPUs per node and 4 cores per CPU.   Each Borderline node has 32 GB of memory and its CPUs are Intel Xeon, 2.6 GHz, with 4 CPUs per node and 2 cores per CPU. All nodes are connected by 10Gbps Ethernet, and run Lenny Debian Operating System.   We deployed an available environment including Hadoop 0.20 [16] to evaluate Pig-0.8.0 on GRID5000 nodes.

5.1   Scalability Tests

We conduct experiments of evaluating Pig for various cluster size and various data sizes. Thus, the following figures show Pig performance results for N=3, 5, 8 nodes (i.e., 2, 4 and 7 *Hadoop Task Trackers/ data nodes* or *workers* and one *Hadoop master*). We generated TPC-H data files for SF=1, 10 resulting respectively in 1.1GB and 11GB.

Pig performances for 1.1 GB of TPC-H data (original tpch files).

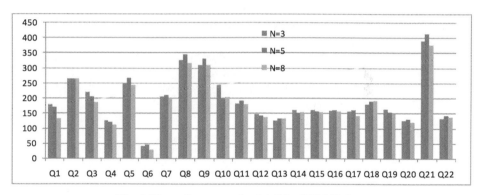

Fig. 4. Pig performances for 1.1 GB of TPC-H data

Notice that pig scripts execution times are not improved when the Hadoop cluster size doubles in size. Scripts which execution time decreases when cluster size increases correspond to business questions which do not perform any join operation, as Q1.

Pig performances for 11GB of TPC-H data (original tpch files).

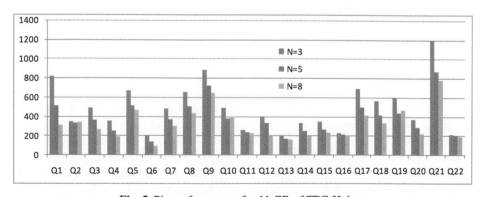

Fig. 5. Pig performances for 11 GB of TPC-H data

First of all, in comparison with results illustrated in Fig. 4 for 1.1GB of data, Pig presents good performance face to a 10 fold data size. Indeed, elapsed times for responding to all queries whether is the cluster size (N=3, 5, 8) for a 11GB TPC-H warehouse are at maximum 5 times and in average twice elapsed times for a 1.1 GB warehouse. We conclude that Pig/HDFS are suited for analytics over high volume of data.

5.2   TPC-H Schema Variation

In order to reduce communication and I/O and processing cycles due to join operations. We propose the merge of all TPC-H data files into one big file. Consequently, all joins are performed and all relations' files are combined into one big file. For that purpose, we combined TPC-H benchmark data files namely {*region, nation, customer, supplier, part, partsupp, orders, lineitem*}.tbl files into one big file using join operation.

We dropped all unused attributes to reduce the resulting file size. The latter is bigger than original files, since 3rd normal form is no more verified. We do think this physical data clustering, will improve map/reduce jobs. Thus, no more join operations are required. But, it leads to a high storage overhead. Indeed, data is redundant all over facts. For instance, *customer nation and customer region* are repeated for each *lineitem row*. The new data files corresponding to respectively SF=1 and SF=10 are respectively 4.5GB and 45GB, almost four times original data.

Pig performances for 4.5 GB of TPC-H data (single and big tpch file).

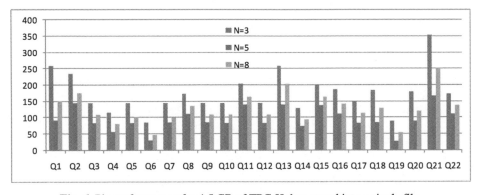

Fig. 6. Pig performances for 4.5 GB of TPC-H data stored into a single file

First of all, we notice that for all pig scripts, best performance results correspond to a cluster size equal to 5 with 4 *workers* and one *Hadoop Master*. This is a well admitted in practice for multithreaded servers and distributed systems. Indeed, when we measure pig scripts response times across cluster size, we watch a concave curve, with an optimum response time for a particular cluster size. Performance continues to degrade from this optimum onward. Also, in comparison with results illustrated improvements in Fig. 4, for 4 times data volumes, improvements vary from 10% to 80%. In general, distributed join execution is complex, and the MapReduce framework wasn't tuned for join processing. Pig Latin is proved cumbersome for joining relations.

Pig performances for 45GB of TPC-H data (single and big tpch file).

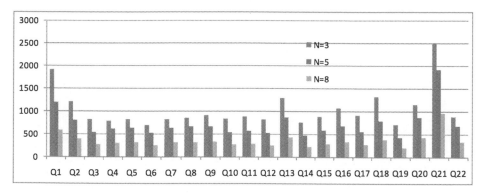

Fig. 7. Pig performances for 45 GB of TPC-H data stored into a single file

First of all, we notice that for all pig scripts, best performance results correspond to a cluster size equal to 8 with 7 workers. This explains that for large data sets, better performances are obtained with big clusters.

5.3   OLAP Scripts Tests

We recall that OLAP scripts pre-aggregate data for different dimensions. Hereafter, we report performance results pig scripts intended for OLAP, and we compare results to performances of running single queries for the Hadoop cluster composed of 5 nodes.

Pig performances for 4.5 GB of TPC-H data (olap vs single query).

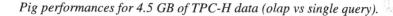

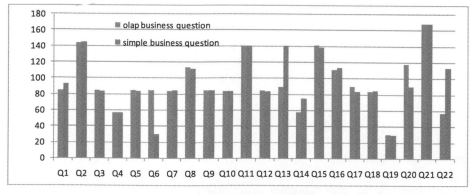

Fig. 8. OLAP business questions performances vs. simple parameterized business questions for 4.5 GB

For most business questions, elapsed times of OLAP business questions are almost equal to elapsed times for simple parameterized business question. The average overall degradation in performance is 5% for a data set of 4.5GB.

Pig performances for 45 GB of TPC-H data (olap vs. single query).

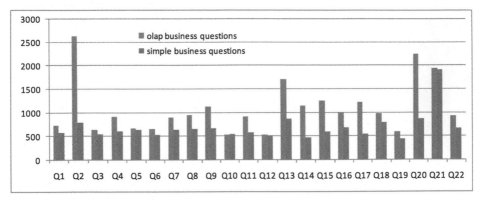

Fig. 9. OLAP business questions performances vs. simple parameterized business questions for 45 GB

Compared to degradations shown in Fig. 8, for a data set of 45 GB, the average overall degradation in performance is 60%. We think whether is the degradation related to running an OLAP business question vs. running a simple parameterized business question; The OLAP query is run once, while simple business questions run regularly.

6   Conclusion

This paper investigates analytics scenarios for data warehousing using cloud computing. The first scenario is a classical data analytics scenario where each business question is translated into a pig script and run on a Hadoop cluster. The second scenario presents a more scalable and economical OLAP data analytics solution, where business questions are generalized and submitted once to a Hadoop cluster. The resulting summarized and aggregated data, are then imported to an OLAP server on-site for multidimensional analysis. This scenario suits to half of TPC-H workload, which hypercube size and the size of pre-aggregated data is relatively small and does not vary with TPC-H scale factor. We also report performance results of Pig Latin/Hadoop against the well known benchmark TPC-H –decision support system benchmark, for various data volumes, data schemas, and different cluster sizes. Performance results proved that (*i*) Pig Latin is proved cumbersome for joining relations, (*ii*) for every large data set, it exists a particular cluster size featuring optimum response times (*iii*) pre-aggregating for OLAP analysis is proved efficient and economical, which meets cloud computing rationale.

In this paper, we investigated only the execution times. During experiments we also measured for business question, I/O costs of MapReduce tasks (namely *HDFS Bytes Read* and *HDFS Bytes Written*), as well as the cost of data transfer from mappers to reducers (namely *HDFS Reduce Shuffle Bytes*), and kept traces of Map/Reduce Phases details. These data will allow us to investigate particular results for TPC-H business questions. We also envision the implementation of OLAP servers for handling business questions with big dimensionality on cloud and approximate query processing in clouds for better performances.

References

1. Laskowski, N.: Gartner: Business intelligence software market continues to grow (2011), http://www.gartner.com/it/page.jsp?id=1553215
2. Moussa, R.: Revolving TPC-H benchmark into a Multidimensional Benchmark. Res. Rep. (2012)
3. Dean, J., Ghemawat, S.: MapReduce: Simplified Data Processing on Large Clusters. In: Proceedings of OSDI, pp. 137–150 (2004)
4. Hadoop Homepage, http://hadoop.apache.org/
5. Chuck, L.: Hadoop in Action. Manning (2010)
6. Information Week (September 20, 2010), http://www.informationweek.com/news/software/info_management/227500077?subSection=All+Stories
7. Kim, K., Jeon, K., Han, H., Kim, S.G., Jung, H., Yeom, H.Y.: MRBench: A Benchmark for MapReduce Framework. In: Proceedings of ICPADS, pp. 11–18 (2008)
8. Schätzle, A., Przyjaciel-Zablocki, M., Hornung, T., Lausen, G.: PigSPARQL: Ubersetzung von SPARQL nach Pig Latin. In: Proc. BTW, pp. 65–84 (2011)
9. Loebman, S., Nunley, D., Kwon, Y., Howe, B., Balazinska, M., Gardner, J.P.: Analyzing massive astrophysical datasets: Can Pig/Hadoop or a relational DBMS help? In: Proceedings of CLUSTER, pp. 1–10 (2009)
10. Iu, M., Zwaenepoel, W.: HadoopToSQL: a mapReduce query optimizer. In: Proceedings of EuroSys, pp. 251–264 (2010)
11. Lee, R., Luo, T., Huai, Y., Wang, F., He, Y., Zhang, X.: YSmart: Yet Another SQL-to-Map Reduce Translator. In: ICDCS, pp. 25–36 (2011)
12. Jia, Y.: Running the TPC-H Benchmark on Hive (2009), https://issues.apache.org/jira/secure/attachment/12416257/TPC-H_on_Hive_2009-08-11.pdf
13. Li, J., Koichi, I., Muzhi, Z., Diestelkaemper, R., Wang, X., Lin, Y.: Running Pig on TPC-H. Res. Rep. (December 2011), https://issues.apache.org/jira/browse/PIG-2397
14. Moussa, R.: TPC-H Benchmarking of Pig on a Hadoop Cluster. In: Proceedings of 2nd Intl. Conference on Communications & Information Technology (2012)
15. TPC-H Homepage, http://www.tpc.org/tpch/
16. Olston, C., Reed, B., Srivastava, U., Kumar, R., Tomkins, A.: Pig latin: a not-so-foreign language for data processing. In: Proceedings of SIGMOD Conference, pp. 1099–1110 (2008)
17. Apache Pig Homepage, http://pig.apache.org/
18. Gates, A.: Programming Pig. O'Reilly (2011)

234   R. Moussa

19. Piggy Bank Homepage, `http://wiki.apache.org/pig/PiggyBank`
20. Codd, E.F., Codd, S.B., Salley, C.T.: Providing OLAP to User-Analysis: an IT Mandate (white paper), `http://www.minet.uni-jena.de/dbis/lehre/ss2005/sem_dwh/lit/Cod93.pdf`
21. Chaudhuri, S., Dayal, U.: An Overview of Data Warehousing and OLAP Technology. SIGMOD Record, 65–74 (1997)
22. Usman, M., Asghar, S., Fong, S.: Hierarchical Clustering Model for Automatic OLAP Schema Generation. Journal of E-Technology 2(1), 9–20 (2011)
23. Bornaz, L., Victor, V.: Optimized OLAP Systems Integrated Data Indexing Algorithms. Journal of Information Technology Review 1(3), 145–150 (2010)
24. Hang, Y., Fong, S.: Algorithmic level stream mining for Business Intelligence System Architecture building. International Journal of Web Applications 3(1), 29–35 (2011)
25. Bourennani, F., Alsadi, J., Rizvi, G.M., Ross, D.: Manufacturing Processing Improvements Using Business Intelligence. Journal of Information Technology Review 2(3), 125–131 (2011)
26. Yousef, R., Odeh, M., Coward, D., Sharieh, A.: Translating RAD Business Process Models into BPMN Models: A Semi-Formal Approach. International Journal of Web Applications 3(4), 187–196 (2011)
27. Chaâbane, M.A., Bouzgu, L.: VerFlexFlow and Querying Language for Business Process Model. Journal of E-Technology 2, 69–78 (2011)
28. Zhang, J., Wang, X., Liu, H., Meng, J.: A Novel Access Control Strategy for Distributed Data Systems. Journal of Digital Information Management 8(5), 291–297 (2010)

An Incremental Correction Algorithm for XML Documents and Single Type Tree Grammars*

Martin Svoboda and Irena Mlýnková

XML and Web Engineering Research Group, Charles University in Prague
Malostranske namesti 25, 118 00 Prague 1, Czech Republic
{svoboda,mlynkova}@ksi.mff.cuni.cz

Abstract. XML documents represent an integral part of the contemporary Web. Unfortunately, a relatively high number of them is affected by well-formedness errors, structural invalidity or data inconsistencies. The purpose of this paper is to continue with our previous work on a correction model for invalid XML documents with respect to schemata in DTD and XML Schema languages. Contrary to other existing approaches, our model ensures that we are always able to find all minimal repairs. The contribution of this paper is the description and experimental evaluation of our new incremental algorithm, which is able to efficiently follow only perspective correction ways even to the depth of the recursion.

Keywords: XML, correction, validity, grammar, tree.

1 Introduction

XML documents [4] and related technologies represent a core part of the Word Wide Web. They are used for data interchange, sharing knowledge or storing semi-structured data. However, the XML usage explosion is followed also with a surprisingly high number of documents involving various forms of errors [7]. These errors can cause that documents are not well-formed, they do not conform to the required structure or have other data inconsistencies.

We focus on a problem of the structural invalidity of XML documents. In other words, we assume that inspected documents are well-formed, but they may not conform to a schema in DTD [4] or XML Schema [12]. Constructs of both these languages can formally be modeled by single type tree grammars [8]. Having a potentially invalid XML document, our goal is to finds its structural corrections with respect to a given grammar.

We start from the root node, continue towards leaves and propose minimal corrections of elements in order to obtain a valid document that is as close to the original one as possible. At each node of a tree, we attempt to statically investigate all allowed sequences of its child nodes and once we detect a local invalidity, we propose modifications based on operations capable to insert new minimal subtrees, delete existing ones or recursively repair them.

* This work was supported by the Czech Science Foundation grant P202/10/0573 and the Charles University Grant Agency grant SVV-2012-265312.

R. Benlamri (Ed.): NDT 2012, Part I, CCIS 293, pp. 235–249, 2012.

Related Work. Our correction framework is based mostly on approaches introduced by Bouchou et al. [3] and Staworko and Chomicky [9]. Though the authors of the former paper assume the same edit operations for transforming invalid trees into valid ones, they only work with local tree grammars (DTD) [8]. Moreover and contrary to our approach, the state space of a finite automaton for recognizing regular expressions is not inspected statically, but allowed sequences of child nodes are dynamically generated one by one. This traversal is not effective, requires a threshold pruning to cope with potentially infinite trees and repeatedly computes the same repairs. As a consequence, there may be situations, in which the algorithm is not able to find any repairs.

Authors of the second paper worked with the idea of graphs for representing all possible sequence repairs statically. However, their goal was to focus on querying incorrect data, not on their correction. Besides these two approaches, we can name also an approximate validation and correction approach by Boobna and Rougemont [2] based on testers and correctors from the theory of program verification. Repairs of data inconsistencies like functional dependencies, keys and multivalued dependencies are the subject of Flesca et al. [6] or Tan et al. [11].

Contributions. We have already introduced our correction model in [10]. Contrary to other existing approaches, it is suitable for corrections of entire XML documents, is always able to find all minimal repairs, does not need any threshold pruning, prevents repeated computations, and, finally, is able to represent all found repairs in a form of a compact structure based on nested multigraphs. However, the most important difference is that we consider a higher expressive class of regular tree grammars – in particular, single type tree grammars (XML Schema) and not only local tree grammars (DTD).

The purpose of this paper is to introduce our new correction algorithm. It is based on the same correction model, but is able to follow only perspective correction ways even to the depth of the recursive nesting. In other words, it preserves all features and advantages of our model, but computes repairs using a different strategy. We have also performed evaluation experiments and a prototype implementation of all our algorithms can be found at [5].

Outline. In Section 2, we present the essential theoretical background for our model of XML documents correction discussed in Section 3. A brief overview of all our correction algorithms together with an introduction of the new one is in Section 4, while Section 5 gives basic results of performed experiments. Finally, Section 6 concludes.

2   Preliminaries

The purpose of this section is to provide essential definitions from areas of regular expressions, finite automata and regular tree grammars. We need them in order to introduce our correction model, but since we want to focus on our new correction algorithm, we will not discuss the theoretical background in detail. The complete and accurate definitions can be found in our previous work [10].

2.1   XML Trees

Analogously to Bouchou [3], we model XML documents as data trees based on underlying trees with prefix numbering of nodes. We assume that $\mathbb{N}_0^*$ is a set of all finite words over the set of non-negative integers $\mathbb{N}_0$, ϵ is an empty word and . a symbol for the concatenation operation. A set $D \subset \mathbb{N}_0^*$ is an *underlying tree*, if the following conditions hold:

- D is closed under prefixes, i.e. having a binary *prefix relation* $\preceq$ (where $\forall u, v \in \mathbb{N}_0^*$ we define $u \preceq v$ if $u.w = v$ for some $w \in \mathbb{N}_0^*$) we require that $\forall u, v \in \mathbb{N}_0^*$, $u \preceq v$: $v \in D$ implies $u \in D$.
- $\forall u \in \mathbb{N}_0^*$, $\forall j \in \mathbb{N}_0$: if $u.j \in D$ then $\forall i \in \mathbb{N}_0$, $0 \le i \le j$, $u.i \in D$.

The first condition assures the expected hierarchical tree structure, the second ensures the expected order of sibling nodes. We say that D is an *empty tree*, if $D = \emptyset$. Items of D are called *nodes*, ϵ is a *root* node and a set of *leaf* nodes is defined as $LeafNodes(D) = \{u \mid u \in D$ and $\neg \exists i \in \mathbb{N}_0$ such that $u.i \in D\}$.

Although we have experimented also with attributes, we ignore them in the context of this paper and focus only on elements. Therefore, we are able to model XML documents using the following notion of data trees.

Definition 1 (Data Tree). *Let D be an underlying tree, $\mathbb{V}$ a domain for data values and $\mathbb{E}$ a domain of element labels (i.e. a set of distinct element names). Tuple $\mathcal{T} = (D, lab, val)$ is a* data tree, *if the following conditions are satisfied:*

- *lab is a labelling function $D \to \mathbb{E} \cup \{\text{data}\}$, where $\text{data} \notin \mathbb{E}$:*
    - *$DataNodes(\mathcal{T}) = \{p \in D \mid lab(p) = \text{data}\}$ is a set of data nodes.*
    - *If $p \in DataNodes(\mathcal{T})$, then necessarily $p \in LeafNodes(D)$.*
- *val is a function $DataNodes(\mathcal{T}) \to \mathbb{V} \cup \{\perp\}$ assigning values to data nodes, where $\perp \notin \mathbb{V}$ is a special symbol representing undefined values.*

In other words, data values and labels of elements are modeled using partial functions on underlying nodes. However, our algorithm proposes only structural corrections of elements, so the value function is not important for us.

Example 1. In Figure 1 we can find a sample data tree $\mathcal{T}$ for an XML fragment `<a><x><d/></x><d><d/><d/></d></a>`. The underlying tree equals to $D = \{\epsilon, 0, 0.0, 1, 1.0, 1.1\}$ and element names are depicted inside nodes.

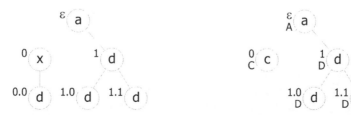

Fig. 1. Sample data tree   **Fig. 2.** Interpretation tree

2.2 Regular Expressions

Despite there are also other concepts of XML schema languages, the traditional ones provide constructs for restricting the allowed nesting of elements through definitions of permitted content models via regular expressions.

Having a finite nonempty alphabet Σ and a set $S = \{\varnothing, \epsilon, |, ., {}^{*}, (,)\}$ of special symbols, such that $\Sigma \cap S = \emptyset$, we can follow the widely accepted inductive definition of a *regular expression* r as a word over $\Sigma \cup S$. Trivial expressions are $\varnothing$, ϵ and x for $\forall x \in \Sigma$. If r_1 and r_2 are already defined regular expressions, $(r_1 | r_2)$ corresponds to a choice, $(r_1 . r_2)$ to a sequence and $r_1{}^{*}$ to an iteration.

The language of all words over Σ conforming to r is denoted as $L(r)$. Without loss of generality, we have chosen Glushkov automata [1] for recognizing such languages, because they are deterministic for *1-unambiguous* regular expressions required by DTD and XML Schema and without ϵ-transitions. Anyway, the *Glushkov automaton* for a regular expression r over an alphabet Σ corresponds to a deterministic finite automaton $\mathcal{A}_r = (Q, \Sigma, \delta, q_0, F)$, where Q is a *set of states*, Σ is an *input alphabet*, δ is a partial *transition function* $Q \times \Sigma \to Q$, $q_0 \in Q$ is an *initial state* and $F \subseteq Q$ is a set of *accepting states*.

2.3 Tree Grammars

Schemata in DTD and XML Schema languages, or at least their structural conditions on nesting of elements, can be formally modeled using *regular tree grammars* [8]. Their goal is to describe allowed generation of data trees, similarly as traditional grammars serve for generation of flat words.

Definition 2 (Regular Tree Grammar). *A regular tree grammar is a tuple* $\mathcal{G} = (N, T, S, P)$, *where:*

- *N is a set of* nonterminal symbols *and T a set of* terminal symbols,
- *S $\subseteq$ N is a set of* starting symbols,
- *P is a set of* production rules *of the form* $[a, r \to n]$, *where* $a \in T$, r *is a 1-unambiguous regular expression over N and* $n \in N$. *Without loss of generality, for each* $a \in T$ *and* $n \in N$ *there exists at most one* $[a, r \to n] \in P$.

Terminal symbols correspond to labels of elements in XML documents and nonterminal symbols represent types of these elements. But in the scope of DTD we do not distinguish between terminals and nonterminals, since there cannot be two different types for a particular element label. This observation is described by the problem of *competing nonterminals*. We say that two different nonterminal symbols n_1, n_2 are competing with each other, if there exist two production rules $[a, r_1 \to n_1]$, $[a, r_2 \to n_2] \in P$ sharing the same terminal a.

The presence of such symbols makes the processing more complicated, thus we define two grammar subclasses with less expressive power. We say that $\mathcal{G}$ is a *local tree grammar*, if it has no competing nonterminals, and that $\mathcal{G}$ is a *single type tree grammar*, if for each production rule $[a, r \to n]$ all nonterminals in r do not compete with each other and starting symbols in S do not compete with each other too. As a consequence, DTD schemata correspond to local tree grammars and XML Schema largely to single type tree grammars.

Now, we are ready to deal with the question of XML documents validity. We say that a data tree $\mathcal{T} = (D, lab, val)$ is *valid* against a grammar $\mathcal{G} = (N, T, S, P)$, if there exists at least one *interpretation tree* $\mathcal{N} = (D, int)$, where int is a function $D \rightarrow N$ such that $\forall p \in D$ there exists a rule $[a, r \rightarrow n]$ satisfying $int(p) = n$, $lab(p) = a$ and $int(p.0).int(p.1)\ldots int(p.k) \in L(r)$ for $k = fanOut(p) - 1$. If $p = \epsilon$ is the root node, then $int(p) \in S$. Since we only work with single type tree grammars, at most one required production rule may exist. Thus, we can correctly introduce a *grammar context* $\mathcal{C}_{t,n}$ for a given terminal t, assigned nonterminal n and found production rule.

Example 2. Suppose we have a grammar $\mathcal{G} = (N, T, S, P)$: $N = \{A, B, C, D\}$ are nonterminals, $T = \{a, b, c, d\}$ are terminals and $S = \{A, B\}$ are starting symbols. The set P contains transition rules: $\mathcal{F}_1 = [a, C.D^* \rightarrow A]$, $\mathcal{F}_2 = [b, D^* \rightarrow B]$, $\mathcal{F}_3 = [c, \varnothing \rightarrow C]$ and $\mathcal{F}_4 = [d, D^* \rightarrow D]$. Since there are no competing nonterminals, this grammar is a local tree grammar. It is clear that the data tree $\mathcal{T}$ from Example 1 is not valid against $\mathcal{G}$, since the element with label x is obviously not allowed. On the other hand, the data tree in Figure 2 is valid. The int function of the only possible interpretation tree is depicted there as well.

3   Corrections

In the previous section we have discussed the basic theoretical background of our correction model. Having an invalid data tree with respect to a given single type tree grammar, we would like to propose transformations leading to valid data trees. In this section, we present the main ideas of our model. Once again, details can be found in [10].

3.1   Edit Operations

The mentioned transformations are realized by edit operations. Via them we are able to add a new leaf node into a data tree ($addLeaf$), remove an existing one ($removeLeaf$), or change a label of an existing node ($renameLabel$).

Definition 3 (Edit Operations). *An edit operation e is a partial function transforming a data tree $\mathcal{T}_0 = (D_0, lab_0, val_0)$ into $\mathcal{T}_1 = (D_1, lab_1, val_1)$, denoted by $\mathcal{T}_0 \xrightarrow{e} \mathcal{T}_1$. Assuming that ϕ is equal to lab and val, we define these operations:*

- $e \equiv addLeaf(p, a)$ *for* $p \in D_0 \cup PosNodes(D_0)$, $p \neq \epsilon$, $p = u.i$, $u \in \mathbb{N}_0^*$, $i \in \mathbb{N}_0$, $u \notin DataNodes(D_0)$ *and* $a \in \mathbb{E}$:
    - $D_1 = [D_0 \setminus ExpNodes(D_0, p)] \cup IncNodes(D_0, p) \cup \{p\}$.
    - $\forall w \in D_0 \setminus ExpNodes(D_0, p)$: $\phi_1(w) = \phi_0(w)$.
    - $lab_1(p) = a$ *and if* $lab_1(p) = \mathtt{data}$, *then* $val_1(p) = \bot$.
    - $\forall (u.(k+1).v) \in IncNodes(D_0, p)$: $\phi_1(u.(k+1).v) = \phi_0(u.k.v)$.
- $e \equiv addLeaf(p, a)$ *for* $p = \epsilon$, $D_0 = \emptyset$ *and* $a \in \mathbb{E}$:

- $D_1 = \{p\}$, $lab_1(p) = a$ and if $a = \mathtt{data}$, then $val_1(p) = \perp$.
- $e \equiv removeLeaf(p)$ for $p \in LeafNodes(D_0)$, $p \neq \epsilon$, $p = u.i$, $u \in \mathbb{N}_0^*$, $i \in \mathbb{N}_0$:
  - $D_1 = [D_0 \setminus ExpNodes(D_0, p)] \cup DecNodes(D_0, p)$.
  - $\forall w \in D_0 \setminus ExpNodes(D_0, p)$: $\phi_1(w) = \phi_0(w)$.
  - $\forall (u.(k-1).v) \in DecNodes(D_0, p)$: $\phi_1(u.(k-1).v) = \phi_0(u.k.v)$.
- $e \equiv removeLeaf(p)$ for $p = \epsilon$, $D_0 = \{\epsilon\}$:
  - $D_1 = \emptyset$, lab_1 and val_1 are not defined anywhere.
- $e \equiv renameLabel(p, a)$ for $p \in D_0$, $a \in \mathbb{E}$ and $a \neq lab_0(p)$:
  - $D_1 = D_0$.
  - $\forall w \in [D_0 \setminus \{p\}]$: $\phi_1(w) = \phi_0(w)$.
  - $lab_1(p) = a$ and if $a = \mathtt{data}$, then $val_1(p) = \perp$.

We omit the definition of used auxiliary sets of nodes, but we can intuitively assume that *PosNodes* together with the underlying tree represent positions ready for insertions, whereas nodes in *ExpNodes* should be shifted by 1 to *IncNodes* or *DecNodes* after a performed node insertion or deletion respectively.

It is clear that individual edit operations can be combined into sequences, thus enabling more complex operations through which we can insert new subtrees, delete existing ones or recursively repair them. If we assign each edit operation e its $cost(e) \in \mathbb{N}_0$, the *cost* of the entire sequence $E = \langle e_1, \ldots, e_k \rangle$ can be introduced as $cost(E) = \sum_{i=1}^{k} cost(e_i)$. If not stated otherwise, we can assume $cost(e) = 1$ for all edit operations.

Example 3. Assume that we have edit sequences $\mathcal{X}_1 = \langle addLeaf(0, c), renameLabel(1, d) \rangle$, $\mathcal{X}_2 = \langle renameLabel(0, c), removeLeaf(0.0) \rangle$ and $\mathcal{X}_3 = \langle renameLabel(\epsilon, b), renameLabel(0, d) \rangle$. Applying these sequences separately to data tree $\mathcal{T}$ from Example 1, we obtain data trees depicted in Figures 3(a), 3(b) and 3(c) respectively. The cost of all these sequences is equal to 2.

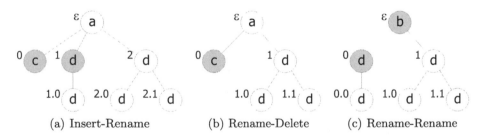

     (a) Insert-Rename   (b) Rename-Delete   (c) Rename-Rename

Fig. 3. Transforming sample data tree using edit operations

Our algorithm is always able to find all repairing sequences of edit operations with the minimal cost. This means that there cannot exist an edit sequence with a lower cost transforming the original data tree into a valid one. However, we do not directly generate these sequences – the output of the algorithm is a data structure describing all such sequences in a much compact way. For this purpose we need the notion of repairing instructions – they correspond to edit operations, but are not bound to particular nodes.

Definition 4 (Repairing Instructions). *For edit operations* $addLeaf(p, a)$, $removeLeaf(p)$ *and* $renameLabel(p, a)$ *with* $p \in \mathbb{N}_0^*$ *and* $a \in \mathbb{E}$ *we define associated* repairing instructions `addLeaf(a)`, `removeLeaf` *and* `renameLabel(a)` *respectively. Each repairing instruction is assigned with the corresponding* cost.

3.2 Correction Intents

The correction algorithm processes the provided data tree from its root node towards leaves. Being at a particular node, we need to correct a sequence of its child nodes. For this purpose we need to have resolved the grammar context for such parent node. This is not a problem, since we work with single type tree grammars. After we recursively process this sequence, i.e. find its minimal repairs, we can compose them into the repair structure and backtrack one level up.

The idea of finding minimal repairs for a sequence of sibling nodes is simple and is inspired by traditional techniques for correction of ordinary strings. The only problem is that we not only need to find allowed sequences at a given level, but we also need to consider nested subtrees and their recursive repairs. Anyway, if we want to repair a sequence of nodes, we can do it from left to right and simulate the work of the corresponding automaton. Contrary to Bouchou [3], we do not dynamically generate allowed sequences one by one, but according to Staworko [9] we investigate the automaton state space statically.

Having processed a sequence prefix and being in a particular automaton state, we can follow permitted transitions in order to consider all potential corrections. This idea is modeled by correction intents.

Definition 5 (Correction Intent). *Given* $\Omega = \{$`correct`, `insert`, `delete`, `repair`, `rename`$\}$ *as a set of all considered* intent types, *we define a* correction intent *to be a tuple* $\mathcal{I} = (type, A, L)$, *where:*

- *type* $\in \Omega$ *is an intent* type.
- $A = (p, e, v_I, v_E)$ *is an intent* action:
    - *p is a* base node *and e is a* repairing instruction,
    - $v_I = (s_I, q_I)$: $s_I \in \mathbb{N}_0$ *is an* initial stratum *and* q_I *is an* initial state,
    - $v_E = (s_E, q_E)$: $s_E \in \mathbb{N}_0$ *is an* ending stratum *and* q_E *is an* ending state.
- $L = (u, \mathcal{C}, Q_T, Y)$ *is an intent* assignment:
    - $u = \langle u_1, \ldots, u_k \rangle$ *for some* $k \in \mathbb{N}_0$ *is a sequence of nodes to be processed,*
    - $\mathcal{C}$ *is a* grammar context *and* Q_T *is a set of* target states,
    - $Y \subseteq \Omega$ *is a set of* allowed types *for nested correction intents.*

In other words, correction intents describe what actions are allowed at a given sequence position and automaton state and what demands do we have on the correction of nested subtrees. The processing of the entire data tree begins with a special intent (`correct`) with an undefined action. During the recursive processing we can insert new subtrees (`insert`), delete existing ones (`delete`) or recursively repair them with an option of preserving (`repair`) or modifying (`rename`) node labels.

Example 4. Suppose that within the starting intent $\mathcal{I}_{\bullet}$ for data tree $\mathcal{T}$ from Example 1 and grammar $\mathcal{G}$ from Example 2 we have invoked a nested `repair` intent $\mathcal{I}$ on base node ϵ. Thus we need to process sequence $u = \langle 0, 1 \rangle$ of nodes with labels $\langle x, d \rangle$ in context $\mathcal{C}_{a,A}$. Being at a position $(0,0)$, i.e. at stratum 0 (before the first node from u) and in the initial state $q_0 = 0$ of $\mathcal{A}_r$ for $r = C.D^*$, we can derive these nested intents:

$\mathcal{I}_1 = (\text{insert}, (\perp, \text{addLeaf}(c), (0,0), (0,1)), (\langle \rangle, \ldots, \{\text{insert}\}))$,
$\mathcal{I}_2 = (\text{rename}, (0, \text{renameLabel}(c), (0,0), (1,1)), (\langle 0.0 \rangle, \ldots, \Omega \setminus \{\text{correct}\}))$,
$\mathcal{I}_3 = (\text{delete}, (0, \text{removeLeaf}, (0,0), (1,0)), (\langle 0.0 \rangle, \ldots, \{\text{delete}\}))$.

3.3   Correction Multigraphs

Given a sequence of sibling nodes to be corrected, we can view correction intents also in a form of a multigraph inspired by Staworko [9]. Its edges correspond to nested intents and vertices to pairs of stratum numbers and automaton states.

Definition 6 (Repairing Multigraph). *Let $\mathcal{T}$ be a data tree, $\mathcal{G}$ a single type tree grammar and $\mathcal{I} = (type, A, L)$ an intent with $u = \langle u_1, \ldots, u_k \rangle$ and finite automaton $\mathcal{A}_r = (Q, N_R, \delta, q_0, F)$ for r from context $\mathcal{C}$ of $\mathcal{I}$. We define a repairing multigraph to be a tuple $\mathcal{M}_\mathcal{I} = (V, E, v_S, V_T, c)$, where:*

- *(V, E) is a directed multigraph:*
  - *$V \subseteq \{(s,q) \mid s \in \mathbb{N}_0, 0 \leq s \leq k, q \in Q\}$ is a set of vertices.*
  - *$E \subseteq \{(v_1, v_2, \mathcal{I}', \mathcal{R}_{\mathcal{I}'}) \mid \exists \mathcal{I}' \in NestedIntents(\mathcal{I}, v_1), \mathcal{I}' = (type', A',$ $L'), A' = (p', e', v'_I, v'_E)$ and $v_1 = v'_I, v_2 = v'_E\}$ is a set of edges.*
- *$v_S = (0, q_0)$ is a source vertex, $v_S \in V$.*
- *$V_T = \{v_T \mid v_T = (k, q_F), q_F \in F\}$ is a set of target vertices.*
- *c is the cost of the minimal repair for sequence u.*

The problem of finding minimal repairs for node sequences can now be easily converted to a problem of finding shortest paths in repairing multigraphs (considering path costs defined as a sum of intent repair costs associated to individual edges) – in particular, all shortest paths from the source vertex to any target vertex, since we want to simulate the recognition of the whole node sequence (i.e. from the zero to the last stratum) and simultaneously the automaton traversal (from the initial to any of the accepting states).

Contrary to exploration, correction and repairing multigraphs in [10], we work in this paper only with the simplified notion of the repairing multigraph and assume that it may be explored and evaluated only partially.

Example 5. Continuing with Example 4, we can represent all nested intents derived from $\mathcal{I}$ by a repairing multigraph $\mathcal{M}_\mathcal{I}$ with $v_S = (0,0)$ and $V_T = \{(2,1),$ $(2,2)\}$ in Figure 4. For simplicity, edges are described only by abbreviated intent types (I for `insert`, D for `delete`, R for `repair` and N for `rename`), supplemented by an optional parameter, and, finally, associated intent repair *cost*. Vertex names are concatenations of stratum numbers and automaton states. All shortest paths with the minimal cost equal to 2 are presented in Figure 5.

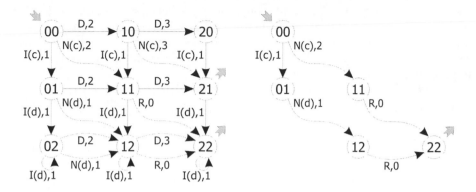

Fig. 4. Fully explored multigraph   **Fig. 5.** Pruned repairing multigraph

3.4 Intent Repairs

Finally, the repair structure for the entire correction intent is simply the repairing instruction together with the constructed repairing multigraph.

Definition 7 (Intent Repair). *Let $\mathcal{M_I} = (V, E, v_S, V_T, c)$ be a repairing multigraph for intent $\mathcal{I} = (type, A, L)$ with repairing instruction e. Then an intent repair for $\mathcal{I}$ is a tuple $\mathcal{R_I} = (e, \mathcal{M_I}, cost)$, where $cost = cost(e) + c$.*

Since the purpose of this paper is to present a new algorithm for exploring multigraphs, we will completely omit the translation process of repair structures to particular sequences of edit operations.

4 Algorithms

Once we have introduced the correction model with allowed edit operations for transformations of invalid data trees, we need to present the correction algorithm itself. It is obvious that its only purpose is to recursively evaluate correction intents, i.e. explore repairing multigraphs, compute nested repairs, find shortest paths and wrap them into repair structures.

The previous description in fact corresponds to the *naive algorithm*. For a particular intent, it always constructs the entire repairing multigraph with all its vertices and edges and recursively evaluates all its nested intents. The first optimization is represented by the *dynamic algorithm*. It does not construct the entire multigraph, but dynamically explores only those parts that are directly required by Dijkstra algorithm for finding shortest paths. Unfortunately, both these algorithms are useless in practice due to unacceptable ineffectivity.

The most apparent issue is caused by the top-down processing – we are repeatedly forced to compute the same intent repairs again and again. For example, if we want to delete a particular subtree from the original data tree, the resulting repair structure will always be identical, regardless in which branch of recursive nesting we invoke such deletion intent. In other words, we can evaluate the resulting repair only once and store it in some caching manager for further requests. For this purpose and for all intent types we have introduced *intent signatures*: though different intents, if they have the same signature, the resulting repair is the same. The *caching algorithm* described in our previous work [10] follows these principles.

However, we can still go further – towards another optimization strategy resulting into the *incremental algorithm*.

4.1   Tasks

The basic idea of the incremental algorithm is to evaluate correction intents incrementally in small steps in order to quickly leave not perspective ones. In other words, this algorithm attempts to follow promising correction ways even to the depth of the recursion. The goal of the multigraph exploration remains the same, but instead of requesting the complete evaluation of nested intents associated with inspected edges, we only request a small progress of their evaluation – step by step in order to refine their repair approximations.

The following notion of a correction task encapsulates this idea of partially and incrementally computed correction intents. Its working variables are used for storing the progress of computation, whereas its state serves for tasks scheduling. Symbol ° is used to mark structures that may be evaluated only partially.

Definition 8 (Correction Task). *Let* $\mathcal{I} = (type, A, L)$ *be a correction intent. We define a* task *for* $\mathcal{I}$ *to be a tuple* $\mathcal{K} = (\mathcal{I}, \mathcal{R}_{\mathcal{I}}^{\circ}, vars, state)$, *where:*

- $\mathcal{I}$ *is the associated correction intent.*
- $\mathcal{R}_{\mathcal{I}}^{\circ}$ *is an intent repair for* $\mathcal{I}$ *with multigraph* $\mathcal{M}^{\circ} = (V, E, v_S, V_T, c)$.
- $vars = (V_{reached}, E_{delayed}, c_{reached}, c_{fixed})$ *are working variables:*
    - $V_{reached} \subseteq V$ *is a set of* reached *vertices,*
    - $E_{delayed} \subseteq E$ *is a set of* delayed *edges,*
    - $c_{reached}$ *is a value of* reached *cost,*
    - c_{fixed} *is a value of* fixed *cost or* $\bot$.
- $state = (flag, s_{granted}, s_{unused}, T_{requesting}, T_{requested})$ *is a task state:*
    - $flag \in \{\text{suspended}, \text{requested}, \text{running}, \text{blocked}\}$,
    - $s_{granted} \in \mathbb{N}_0 \cup \{\infty\}$ *is a granted quota of processing steps,*
    - $s_{unused} \in \mathbb{N}_0 \cup \{\infty\}$ *is a number of remaining steps,*
    - $T_{requesting}$ *is a set of correction tasks waiting for* $\mathcal{K}$,
    - $T_{requested}$ *is a set of correction tasks for which* $\mathcal{K}$ *is waiting.*

A newly created task is assigned a **suspended** state. After we request processing of a selected task, it is turned to **requested** and using sets $T_{requesting}$ and $T_{requested}$ we store scheduling dependencies. Once a task is fetched for processing, it is turned to **running**. If it requests incremental computation of other nested tasks, it is turned to **blocked** and needs to wait until all requested tasks are processed. After this happens, unblocked tasks are requested automatically. If the whole repair is computed, the task is removed, otherwise changed to **suspended**.

Due to the lack of space, we cannot introduce all aspects of the incremental algorithm formally. Thus, only a description of the most important parts will be the subject of the following paragraphs.

4.2 Routines

The main routine is presented in Algorithm 1. The correction process is supported by a manager with caching structures for all existing tasks and computed repairs and a set of all requested tasks. After we initialize these structures (line 1), we create a task for the starting intent (line 2). While at least one requested task exists, we fetch it and perform one step of its incremental processing (lines 3 to 5). Finally, we only need to fetch the computed repair (line 6).

Algorithm 1. incrementalCorrectionRoutine

Input   : Data tree $\mathcal{T}$, single type tree grammar $\mathcal{G}$.
Output: Repair $\mathcal{R}_{\mathcal{I}_\bullet}$ for correction intent $\mathcal{I}_\bullet$.

1 TaskCache $\leftarrow \emptyset$; RepairCache $\leftarrow \emptyset$; $Scheduler \leftarrow \emptyset$;
2 requestTaskProcessing($undefined\ parent\ \bot,\ \mathcal{I}_\bullet,\ unlimited\ quota\ \infty$);

3 **while** $\exists \mathcal{K} \in Scheduler$ **do**
4 $\quad$ $Scheduler \leftarrow Scheduler \setminus \{\mathcal{K}\}$;
5 $\quad$ processCorrectionStep($\mathcal{T}$, $\mathcal{G}$, $\mathcal{K}$);

6 **return** RepairCache($signature(\mathcal{I}_\bullet)$);

The incremental step presented in Algorithm 2 directly follows the idea of Dijkstra algorithm. Until we have not processed all required vertices, we continue with the multigraph exploration (line 1). Once we are sure that the processed intent should be evaluated completely, we must process delayed edges (line 2). At the end of step processing, we change the task state and eventually request a parent task, if it is no longer blocked (line 3). Finally, if the repair is fully evaluated, we can publish it (lines 4 to 6).

Algorithm 2. processCorrectionStep

Input   : Data tree $\mathcal{T}$, grammar $\mathcal{G}$, correction task $\mathcal{K} = (\mathcal{I}, \mathcal{R}_{\mathcal{I}}^\circ, vars, state)$.

1 **if** $\mathcal{K}.vars.V_{reached} \neq \emptyset$ **then** processGraphExploration();
2 **if** $\mathcal{K}.vars.V_{reached} = \emptyset$ and $\mathcal{K}.vars.E_{delayed} \neq \emptyset$ **then** processDelayedEdges();

3 closeStepProcessing();

4 **if** $\mathcal{K}.vars.V_{reached} = \emptyset$ and $\mathcal{K}.vars.E_{delayed} = \emptyset$ **then**
5 $\quad$ RepairCache($signature(\mathcal{K}.\mathcal{I})$) $\leftarrow \mathcal{K}.\mathcal{R}_{\mathcal{I}}^\circ$;
6 $\quad$ TaskCache($signature(\mathcal{K}.\mathcal{I})$) $\leftarrow \bot$;

In Algorithm 3 we can see the multigraph exploration loop. First, we need to update path cost estimations to all reached vertices (line 1). In the loop (lines 2 to 8) we fetch the most promising reached vertex (line 3), set the current reached cost for the entire multigraph (line 4), resolve the termination condition (lines 5 to 6) and switch the selected vertex processing depending on its completeness (lines 7 to 8). A vertex is complete, if at least one its ingoing edge is fully evaluated and there are no open edges with lower cost estimations.

Algorithm 3. processGraphExploration

Global : Data tree $\mathcal{T}$, grammar $\mathcal{G}$, task $\mathcal{K} = (\mathcal{I}, \mathcal{R}^{\circ}_{\mathcal{I}}, vars, state)$, graph $\mathcal{M}^{\circ}$.

1 updateReachedVertices();
2 **while** $\mathcal{K}.vars.V_{reached} \neq \emptyset$ **do**
3     $v \leftarrow$ selectPerspectiveVertex();
4     $\mathcal{K}.vars.c_{reached} \leftarrow \mathcal{M}^{\circ}.getPathCost(v)$;
5   **if** $\mathcal{K}.vars.c_{fixed} \neq \bot$ *and* $\mathcal{K}.vars.c_{fixed} < \mathcal{K}.vars.c_{reached}$ **then**
6        $\mathcal{K}.vars.V_{reached} \leftarrow \emptyset$; **break**

7   **if** *vertex v is complete* **then** processCompleteVertex(v);
8   **else** processIncompleteVertex(v); **break**

The purpose of Algorithm 4 is to process a complete vertex. Since we need to find all shortest paths to any of all target vertices, we need to continue the exploration phase until the fixed cost is strictly greater than the reached one (lines 1 to 2). Next, we need to delay promising open edges (lines 3 to 5) and remove the currently processed vertex from reached ones (line 6). For each allowed outgoing edge (allowed nested correction intent), we accordingly extend the multigraph and reached vertices set (lines 7 to 12).

Algorithm 4. processCompleteVertex

Global : Data tree $\mathcal{T}$, grammar $\mathcal{G}$, task $\mathcal{K} = (\mathcal{I}, \mathcal{R}^{\circ}_{\mathcal{I}}, vars, state)$, graph $\mathcal{M}^{\circ}$.
Input   : Complete vertex v.

1 **if** $\mathcal{K}.vars.c_{fixed} = \bot$ *and* $v \in \mathcal{M}^{\circ}.V_T$ **then**
2     $\mathcal{K}.vars.c_{fixed} \leftarrow \mathcal{K}.vars.c_{reached}$; **break**

3 **foreach** $e = (v', v, \mathcal{I}', \mathcal{R}^{\circ}_{\mathcal{I}'})$ *ingoing edge to v* **do**
4   **if** *edge e is open and promising* **then**
5        $\mathcal{K}.vars.E_{delayed} \leftarrow \mathcal{K}.vars.E_{delayed} \cup \{e\}$;

6 $\mathcal{K}.vars.V_{reached} \leftarrow \mathcal{K}.vars.V_{reached} \setminus \{v\}$;
7 **foreach** $\mathcal{I}' = (type', A', L') \in NestedIntents(\mathcal{I}, v)$ **do**
8     $\mathcal{R}^{\circ}_{\mathcal{I}'} = (e', \mathcal{M}'^{\circ}, cost') \leftarrow$ getIntentRepair($\mathcal{I}'$);
9   **if** $v' = A'.v_E \notin \mathcal{M}^{\circ}.V$ **then** Add vertex v' into $\mathcal{M}^{\circ}.V$ and $\mathcal{K}.vars.V_{reached}$;
10   Add edge $e' = (v, v', \mathcal{I}', \mathcal{R}^{\circ}_{\mathcal{I}'})$ into $\mathcal{M}^{\circ}.E$;
11   **if** $v' \notin \mathcal{K}.vars.V_{reached}$ **then** $\mathcal{K}.vars.E_{delayed} \leftarrow \mathcal{K}.vars.E_{delayed} \cup \{e'\}$;
12   updateVertexRatings(v');

Finally, the only aim of Algorithm 5 for incomplete vertices is to request processing of nested intents associated with open and promising edges.

Algorithm 5. processIncompleteVertex

Global : Data tree $\mathcal{T}$, grammar $\mathcal{G}$, task $\mathcal{K} = (\mathcal{I}, \mathcal{R}_{\mathcal{I}}^{\circ}, vars, state)$, graph $\mathcal{M}^{\circ}$.
Input   : Incomplete vertex v.

1 **foreach** $e = (v', v, \mathcal{I}', \mathcal{R}_{\mathcal{I}'}^{\circ})$ *ingoing edge to* v **do**
2 | **if** *edge e is open and perspective* **then**
3 | | requestTaskProcessing(*requesting* $\mathcal{K}$, *requested* $\mathcal{I}'$, *assigned quota*);

---

5   Experiments

An experimental evaluation of correction algorithms suffers from several general problems. At least, we cannot compare existing algorithms to each other, if they do not provide exactly the same repairing constructs or work with different regular tree grammar classes. Therefore, the aim of this section is to present basic characteristics of the introduced incremental algorithm. Together with the caching one, they assume the same model and always find identical repairs, too.

Experiment results depend on characteristics of data trees to be repaired and associated grammars. We worked with a single type tree grammar $\mathcal{G} = (N, T, S, P)$ with a set of nonterminals $N = \{R, S, A, B, C, D, \mathsf{data}\}$, terminals $T = \{r, s, x, b, d, \mathsf{data}\}$, starting nonterminals $S = \{R, S\}$ and the following production rules in P: $\mathcal{F}_1 = [r, (B.C^*.D)^* \to R]$, $\mathcal{F}_2 = [s, (A.(B|D))^* \to S]$, $\mathcal{F}_3 = [x, R^*.S^* \to A]$, $\mathcal{F}_4 = [b, \varnothing \to B]$, $\mathcal{F}_5 = [x, (R|S)^* \to C]$, $\mathcal{F}_6 = [d, \mathsf{data} \to D]$, $\mathcal{F}_7 = [\mathsf{data}, \varnothing \to \mathsf{data}]$. This grammar involves either iteration and recursion, thus, we can consider it as non-trivial enough.

Data trees for experiments were generated by our simple generator and are available at [5]. Their size varied from 100 to 1000 nodes, maximal depth was equal to 5 and maximal fan-out to 8 nodes. In order to acquire accurate results, we generated 20 different data trees for each particular size and for each data tree we repeated 20 tests. We also removed results with execution times greater than detected median value increased by 20% to avoid scheduling anomalies.

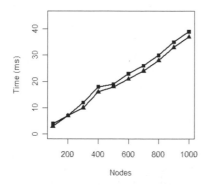
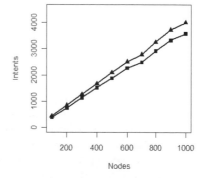

Fig. 6. Execution time dependency   **Fig. 7.** Intents count dependency

Average execution times can be found in Figure 6 – values for caching and incremental algorithms are marked by triangles and squares respectively. Although the incremental algorithm seems to be a bit worse in our sample conditions, the important aspect is that it needs to create and finish significantly less number of correction intents, as we can see in Figure 7. This disadvantage is caused only by overhead of our prototype implementation and, therefore, has potential to be improved. For example, we can use other strategies for assigning granted quota for nested tasks, or we can combine the caching and incremental algorithms together. Finally, this assumption is supported also by results in Table 1, where we can see relative numbers of created and finished tasks comparing to the caching algorithm (for data trees with 1000 nodes).

Table 1. Statistics of created and finished correction intents

Algorithm	Intents	All types	correct	insert	delete	repair	rename
Caching	Finished	4009	1	21	960	1058	1968
Incremental	Created	3584	1	14	960	1024	1583
		89%	100%	67%	100%	97%	80%
	Finished	2761	1	8	959	1018	774
		69%	100%	38%	100%	96%	39%

Not to omit technical details, all experiments were run on HP Pavilion dv7 laptop with Intel Core i7 Q720, 4 cores, 1.6 GHz and 4 GB memory under Microsoft Windows 7 operating system.

6   Conclusion

The purpose of this paper was to introduce a new algorithm for our correction model first presented in [10]. Having a potentially invalid XML document, we can find its corrections with respect to a given schema. These corrections are structural, i.e. we work only with transformations of elements. Composing elementary edit operations into sequences, we can modify data trees by inserting new subtrees, delete existing ones or recursively repair them in order to obtain new and valid data trees with the minimal distance to the original data tree.

The core of our model is the top-down recursive processing and the state space traversal of automata for recognizing regular expression languages with connection to regular tree grammars model of XML schemata. Contrary to other existing approaches, we have considered the class of single type tree grammars instead of only local tree grammars. Thus, we can work either with DTD and XML Schema languages. Moreover, we are always able to find all minimal repairs, we do not need to compute the same nested repairs repeatedly and we are also able to inspect only promising ways of corrections.

The new incremental algorithm directly follows our correction model. The only difference to the caching algorithm is that we encapsulate intent evaluation into tasks and perform their execution incrementally, i.e. only in small steps in order to continuously improve the approximation of the associated repair and its cost. Besides the description of this algorithm, we have also published its prototype implementation at [5] and performed a set of experiments.

Although the experiments presented in the previous section imply that the incremental algorithm is not faster than the caching one, we also worked with other grammars and documents and achieved the acceleration of even tens of percents. However, the most important is the confirmed assumption on which the incremental algorithm is built. We can process correction intents incrementally in steps and, thus, we do not need to finish all created tasks and we even do not need to create some of them. Since the number of correction intents is linear to size of data trees and grammar characteristics, both caching and incremental algorithms seem to be usable in practice. Additional improvements of execution times could be found in areas of granted quota assignment, methods of multigraph exploration or implementation optimizations as well.

References

1. Allauzen, C., Mohri, M.: A Unified Construction of the Glushkov, Follow, and Antimirov Automata. In: Královič, R., Urzyczyn, P. (eds.) MFCS 2006. LNCS, vol. 4162, pp. 110–121. Springer, Heidelberg (2006)
2. Boobna, U., de Rougemont, M.: Correctors for XML Data. In: Bellahsène, Z., Milo, T., Rys, M., Suciu, D., Unland, R. (eds.) XSym 2004. LNCS, vol. 3186, pp. 97–111. Springer, Heidelberg (2004)
3. Bouchou, B., Cheriat, A., Ferrari Alves, M.H., Savary, A.: Integrating Correction into Incremental Validation. In: BDA (2006)
4. Bray, T., Paoli, J., Sperberg-McQueen, C.M., Maler, E., Yergeau, F., Cowan, J.: Extensible Markup Language (XML) 1.1, 2nd edn. (2006), http://www.w3.org/XML/
5. Corrector Prototype Implementation, http://www.ksi.mff.cuni.cz/~svoboda/
6. Flesca, S., Furfaro, F., Greco, S., Zumpano, E.: Querying and Repairing Inconsistent XML Data. In: Ngu, A.H.H., Kitsuregawa, M., Neuhold, E.J., Chung, J.-Y., Sheng, Q.Z. (eds.) WISE 2005. LNCS, vol. 3806, pp. 175–188. Springer, Heidelberg (2005)
7. Mlynkova, I., Toman, K., Pokorny, J.: Statistical Analysis of Real XML Data Collections. In: Proceedings of the 13th Int. Conf. on Management of Data (2006)
8. Murata, M., Lee, D., Mani, M., Kawaguchi, K.: Taxonomy of XML Schema Languages using Formal Language Theory. ACM Trans. Internet Technol. 5(4), 660–704 (2005)
9. Staworko, S., Chomicki, J.: Validity-Sensitive Querying of XML Databases. In: Grust, T., Höpfner, H., Illarramendi, A., Jablonski, S., Fischer, F., Müller, S., Patranjan, P.-L., Sattler, K.-U., Spiliopoulou, M., Wijsen, J. (eds.) EDBT 2006. LNCS, vol. 4254, pp. 164–177. Springer, Heidelberg (2006)
10. Svoboda, M., Mlýnková, I.: Correction of Invalid XML Documents with Respect to Single Type Tree Grammars. In: Fong, S. (ed.) NDT 2011. CCIS, vol. 136, pp. 179–194. Springer, Heidelberg (2011)
11. Tan, Z., Zhang, Z., Wang, W., Shi, B.-L.: Computing Repairs for Inconsistent XML Document Using Chase. In: Dong, G., Lin, X., Wang, W., Yang, Y., Yu, J.X. (eds.) APWeb/WAIM 2007. LNCS, vol. 4505, pp. 293–304. Springer, Heidelberg (2007)
12. Thompson, H.S., Beech, D., Maloney, M., Mendelsohn, N.: XML Schema Part 1: Structures, 2nd edn. (2004), http://www.w3.org/TR/xmlschema-1/

Distributed RFID Shopping System

Amine Karmouche and Yassine Salih Alj

Al Akhawayn University in Ifrane, School of Science and Engineering,
PO BOX 2134, Ifrane, Morocco
{a.karmouche,y.salihalj}@aui.ma

Abstract. RFID technology has recently made significant advancements in the domain of retail sales. This paper presents a novel approach to the use of RFID technology in this field. Despite the current system architectures in RFID systems used in similar research projects, a distributed architecture and a suitable design are proposed. Users will be able to scan their purchased products by putting them in the shopping cart, view their current bill on the cart's touchscreen, and get directions in the shopping area. The motivation behind this different approach is to give customers more flexibility and control over their shopping cart. It will enable them to benefit from information about the products and aisles of the shopping space. Additionally, it will also enable the storage of customer transactions and location data to render it available for data mining purposes.

Keywords: RFID Shopping, RFID Tag, RFID Reader, Distributed Architecture, Indoor Positioning System.

1 Introduction

The Radio Frequency Identification (RFID) is a technology based on radio frequency communication between a number of tags and readers. It is increasingly used in many domains such as inventory management, supply chain management, retail sales and others.

A large body of work has been done on the application of the RFID technology in the enhancement of services in supermarkets and other shopping areas. The adopted approaches were mainly focused on the exit points in shopping areas. Those systems enable the customers to scan their shopping cart products by RFID readers at the exit of the supermarket and to generate the bill. Directions to specific aisles and areas, and discount information were also made possible. The waiting time in queues was significantly decreased, and the sales were smooth. However, the customer interaction with their bill was not tackled by those designs.

This paper's contribution to existing research is a distributed architecture for the RFID shopping system, where the scanning of products in a supermarket is performed at the level of each shopping cart. The customers can scan their purchased products by simply putting them in the shopping cart. They will also be able to see their current bill on the cart's touchscreen. The customers will have the choice to get directions in the shopping area, to be informed of their current location, and to set a threshold for the bill total.

R. Benlamri (Ed.): NDT 2012, Part I, CCIS 293, pp. 250–258, 2012.

The motivation behind this different approach is to lower the cost on implementation of such systems and increase the ease of integration in existing points of sale.

This paper first presents the system's distributed architecture, followed by the mechatronic system main components. Next, a cost estimation of the system is given, and a conclusion is presented as closing.

2   System Architecture

The architecture of the system is based on a distributed model as shown in figure 1. The scanning of the tags is not done at stationary points such as supermarket exits. Instead RFID readers are placed on each shopping cart to scan the RFID tags placed on each item. The shopping carts are also tracked by an Indoor Positioning System whose base point is located at the base. Composed of the transaction and the current location, the information is then sent to the base that serves in this case as an interface with a database where the data is stored permanently.

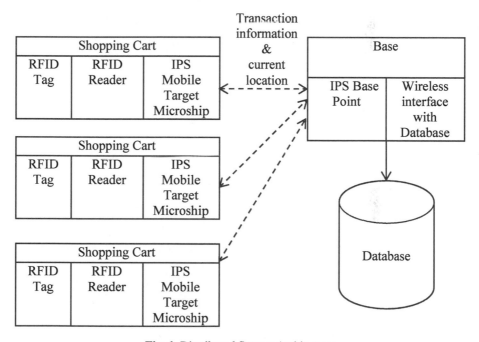

Fig. 1. Distributed System Architecture

3   Mechatronic System Design

The design of the mechatronic system encompasses many components such as actuators, sensors, signal conditioning and interfacing unit, digital control unit, and graphical displays as shown in figure 2.

Sensors such as RFID readers and IPS base point sense the radio and ultrasonic wave signals from the environment, and deliver them to the signal conditioning and interfacing unit, which converts the input signals to digital ones. These latter are then processed by the Peripheral Interface Controller (PIC). The results of the processed signal are then displayed to the user using graphical displays such as resistive touchscreens, and also given to actuators represented by the RFID tags and IPS mobile target microchip so that they can act on the environment by emitting radio and ultrasonic frequencies.

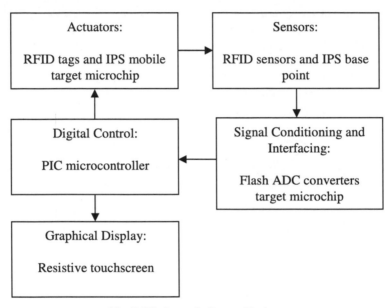

Fig. 2. Mechatronic System Design

3.1   Sensors and Actuators

RFID System Design. RFID systems are generally made of a reader and a suitable tag. Tags are classified as passive or active. Passive tags do not require a power supply; the power is instead supplied by the RFID reader as shown in figure 3.

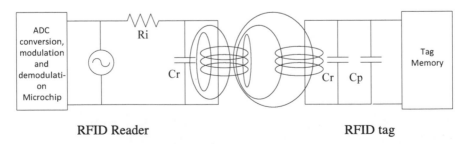

Fig. 3. RFID tag and reader internal design

The reader is composed of a coil antenna, a capacitor Cr, a resistor Ri, an alternative current source, and a microchip for analog to digital conversion, modulation and demodulation. As for the tag, it is made of an antenna, capacitors Cr and Cp along with a tag memory containing the information to be communicated to the reader.

When the passive tag encounters radio waves emitted by the reader, a magnetic field is formed by the tag antenna. Power is then drawn from the reader by induction of potential in the tag antenna, supplying energy to the tag circuit. The tag then sends the information encoded in its memory to the reader.

This specific application of the RFID technology requires the use of passive tags since they do not require a significant scanning range and have a small size compared to active ones.

This circuit, figure 3, resonates at 13.56MHz which represents the operating frequency of this RFID system. Therefore the tag chip can get a maximum input voltage through this parallel resonant circuit.

$$f = \frac{1}{2\pi\sqrt{LC}} \,. \tag{1}$$

$$L = \frac{1}{(2\pi f)^2 C} \,. \tag{2}$$

For the general case, according to equation (1), the resonant frequency of this parallel resonant circuit can be decided by the inductance of the tag coil antenna and the capacitance of capacitor Cr inside the tag. Then equation (1) can be transformed into equation (2) to find the corresponding inductance of the coil.

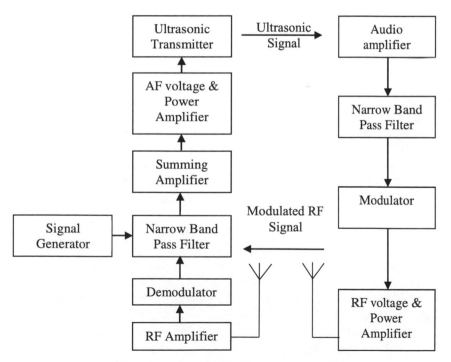

Fig. 4. Indoor positioning System Components

Indoor Positioning System (IPS). Indoor positioning systems aim at estimating the current location coordinates of a traceable object based on the availability of wireless signals used for communication.

Each shopping cart will be equipped by a wireless ultrasonic transmitter. The base point will be able to communicate with the Mobile target using ultrasonic signals and an antenna to receive the modulated radio frequency signal.

As figure 4 shows, the base point will send an ultrasonic signal to the mobile target receiver, which will be amplified, filtered, modulated, and amplified again using the RF and power amplifier to be ready to be sent by the antenna. The base point antenna will receive the RF signal sent by the mobile target, demodulate it, and filter it to render it available for processing. The process is then repeated at a constant rate, thus communicating with the mobile target continuously.

Based points will be deployed in a way to cover the entire area of the supermarket. The signals should be within reach at any location at the supermarket sales area. Concerning the location estimation, one of the methods used to realize it is triangulation.

This method uses geometric properties of triangles to estimate the target location. It has two derivations: lateration and angulation. Lateration estimates the position of an object by measuring its distances from multiple reference points. This latter is also called range measurement techniques. Instead of measuring the distance directly using received signal strengths (RSS), time of arrival (TOA) or time difference of arrival (TDOA) is usually measured, and the distance is derived by computing the attenuation of the emitted signal strength or by multiplying the radio signal velocity and the travel time. Besides, range estimation in some systems uses Roundtrip time of flight (RTOF).Angulation locates an object by computing angles relative to multiple reference points [1].

3.2 Signal Conditioning and Interfacing

Analog to Digital Converters. Analog-to-Digital converters or ADCs are considered as one of the most vital building blocks of an RFID system's operation. A wide range of ADCs exist and many are used according to the purpose and needs of their specific applications. For this application of RFID systems Flash ADCs are to be used. Flash ADCs are used in RFID tags and readers implementation thanks to their fast conversion [2].

As shown in figure 5, flash ADCs need many comparators. The comparator used in this circuit is mainly an amplifier without feedback. When the voltage has reached Vn1 , the comparator linked to it is automatically lead to a high voltage output, triggering the LED to light by representing it as a digital output (0001). The same process will be followed by the other comparators until it reaches the digital output (1111).

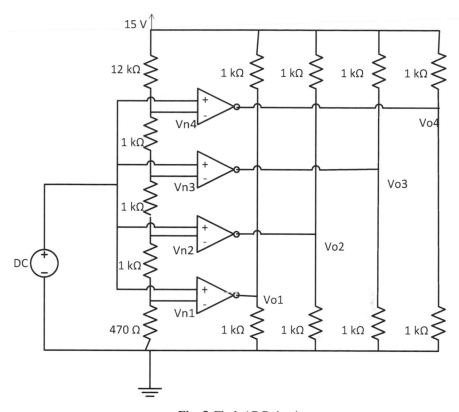

Fig. 5. Flash ADC circuit

This is a very effective way of converting analog to digital signals since all the comparators work together which makes this conversion productively fast; that is the reason behind calling it a flash ADC. The 1kΩ resistors are used to keep the comparators' output voltages high.

3.3   Digital Control Architecture

Microcontroller. A microcontroller is an embedded, special purpose computer that will be integrated in the system. Its main use is to perform all logic and arithmetic operations that are needed. In fact, the system's microcontroller is programmable and allows for the execution of all functionalities required such as setting the threshold as an input, addition and subtraction of prices, computing the total bill along with other functions that can be added and maintained as needed.

In general, the software that microcontrollers use is stored in a Read Only Memory that can have up to 1,000 bytes and 20 bytes of RAM for a typical low end microcontroller [3]. This memory space that these devices allow for will enable the system to store enough data entered by the user while shopping.

The system is to use a Peripheral Interface Controller (PIC) that provides many advantages. For instance, its speed is very distinguishable from other microcontrollers as it allows for the execution of 5 instructions per microsecond when operating at its maximum clock rate [4]. Furthermore, it has a simplified instruction set (only 35) [4]. It also allows for a robust protection system that ensures that the chip operates only when the voltage supplied meets the voltage specification and is reset if it is not functioning well [4]. Equally important, it is characterized by advanced programmable timer options that handle efficiently execution timing [4]. Furthermore, this device is equipped by a resilient output pin control that ensures driving output within a very small instruction execution time [4].

In addition to that, PIC is very easy to program through the use of a simple version of BASIC or flowcharts [5]. The PIC takes input from the touchscreen, which will be discussed in the upcoming section, and sends output signals to this latter in which results are to be displayed.

3.4   Graphical Displays

Graphical displays represent the system's interface with the user. The use of appropriate technology and the user friendliness on the graphical user interface are of great significance to the success of the system in case of deployment.

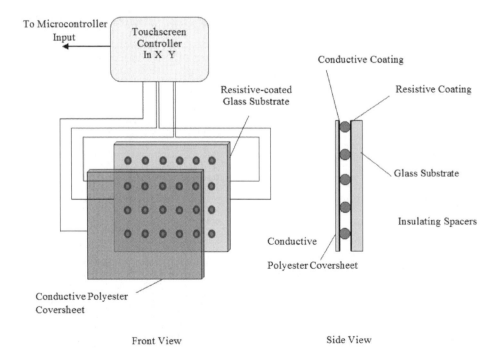

Front View   Side View

Fig. 6. Resistive Touchscreen

Resistive Touchscreen. This type of touchscreens uses two layers that are coated with a resistive and a conductive material. As shown in figure 6, these two layers are separated from each other by an air gap or spacers. On top of the whole mechanism will be a layer to provide resistance to scratches.

The monitor of the display is made operational in nature. Thus, when our finger touches the screen, a contact is made between the two layers and current flows through them. As the layers make contact at the same point, the correct location of the point is noted.

The location is calculated by the computer in the course of change in the electric field occurred by our touch. Thus when the position is known, it is passed on to a driver in the device which codes it and sends it to the OS of the device.

4   Cost Analysis

The cost of passive tags depends on the frequency of operation, the amount of copper used in the tag antenna, the packaging of the tag, and the memory size. UHF tags generally cost less than high frequency tags. Passive RFID tags generally cost from 20 US cents to 40 US cents. The cost of the passive tags used is lower than that of active tags currently used in many shopping places where the scanning is done at the level of the exit [6].

The readers for passive RFID tags are also of low cost due to their design. The lowest prices on the market can go up to 100 US $.

Concerning the IPS used in this system, its design is of very low cost due to the technology it uses, which was presented earlier. The cost of this type of IPS is 15 US $ [7].

As for the Peripheral Interface Controller, it comes in different versions which differ in prices based on their pin-out configurations and memory capacity. For instance, there are the PIC10F200, PIC10F202, PIC10F204 and PIC10F206which are offered in 6-pin SOT-23 packages [8]. The prices of all these devices range between 0.49$ and 0.65$ which are of low cost and can be afforded by any business entity [8]. The PIC10F200 costs $0.49, for the PIC10F202 and PIC10F204 both cost $0.57 each, and the PIC10F206 costs $0.65 [8].Other microcontrollers may cost a little more based on their peripherals and pin configurations such as the 8-pin PIC12F629 that is available under a cost of $1.29, or the 20-pin PIC16F628 that costs about $3.35 [9]. Any of the previous PICs can be used in the implementation of the system as they are feasible and affordable.

The deployment of such system has also a cost that depends on the scale of the project. The area to be covered by the IPS and the number of shopping carts moving in it, directly affect the overall cost of deployment.

5   Conclusion

This paper presented a new approach to shopping using the RFID technology. The distributed architecture has many advantages which renders it a good alternative to current approaches. One of the advantages is the improved customer service, by giving the customers control over their bills, directions and product suggestions. Another advantage is the low cost of RFID tags and readers since the scanning range is focused in the shopping cart space.

This approach presents an interesting opportunity to make use of the collected data for data mining purposes to have more insight on consumer behavior. Shopping spaces will be able to make adequate changes to fit the customers' expectations.

As future work, the prototyping of such mechatronic system is vital. Thus, error corrections and handling of special cases will be presented with simulations and experimental testing, the goal being a seamless shopping experience.

Acknowledgements. Many thanks go to students: Meryem El Khaddar, Meryem Ettouhami and Laila Khana for helping in the literature review process. Thanks also go to Al Akhawayn University in Ifrane for the international mobility grant.

References

1. Hui, L., Darabi, H., Banerjee, P., Liu, J.: Survey of wireless indoor positioning techniques and systems. IEEE Transactions on Systems, Man and Cybernetics, 1067–1080 (2007)
2. Pesonen, N., Jaakkola, K., Lamy, J., Nummila, K., Marjonen, J.: Smart RFID Tags. Development and Implementation of RFID Technology, 171 (2009)
3. How microcontrollers work. HowStuffWorks, Electronics (2011),
   http://electronics.howstuffworks.com/microcontroller1.html
4. PIC – Introduction. In: Electrofriends Microcontroller Projects, Circuit Diagrams (2011),
   http://electrofriends.com/articles/electronics/
   microcontroller-electronics-articles/pic/pic-introduction
5. Integrated circuits (Chips) In: Welcome to the Electronics Club (2011),
   http://www.kpsec.freeuk.com/components/ic.html
6. RFID system components and costs - RFID journal. In: RFID (Radio Frequency Identification) Technology News & Features, Web (2011),
   http://www.rfidjournal.com/article/view/1336
7. Randell, C., Muller, H.: Low cost indoor positioning system (unpublished)
8. Lawson, E.: New microchip PIC10 - The world's smallest microchip. In: Microcontroller.com (2004),
   http://www.microcontroller.com/news/Microchip_PIC10F.asp
9. PIC vs AVR smackdown. In: Limor (2011),
   http://www.ladyada.net/library/picvsavr.html

Efficient Detection of XML Integrity Constraints Violation*

Michal Švirec and Irena Mlýnková

Department of Software Engineering, Charles University in Prague, Czech Republic
svirooo@gmail.com, mlynkova@ksi.mff.cuni.cz

Abstract. Knowledge of integrity constraints (ICs) covered in XML data is an important aspect of efficient data processing. However, although ICs are defined, it is a common phenomenon that the respective data violate them. Therefore detection of these inconsistencies and consecutive repair has emerged. This paper extends and refines recent approaches to repairing XML documents violating defined set of ICs, specifically so-called functional dependencies. The work proposes a repair algorithm incorporating a weight model and a user interaction into the process of detection and subsequent application of appropriate repair of inconsistent XML documents. Experimental results are included.

1 Introduction

Nowadays, one of the most largely used standards for information representation on the Web is the eXtensible Markup Language (XML) [1]. The structure of an XML document is described with an *XML schema language*, usually DTD [1] or XSD [7]. Both also support some kind of semantic content (e.g. keys and foreign keys). But for improvement of semantic expressiveness, *integrity constraints* (ICs) for XML [2] have been defined. Similarly to the XML schemas, also ICs bring several problems. First, if ICs are not explicitly specified, they need to be detected from the given set of data. Second, if ICs are specified, XML document may not be consistent with respect to them, this needs to be detected and repaired.

In this paper we focus on the latter aspect of detection of ICs along with the repair of the inconsistent XML document. In particular, we deal with *functional dependencies* (FDs) [9] which are the most common semantic constraint used in relational databases. We propose an algorithm repairing violations for a given XML document and a set of FDs. Our two key contributions are as follows: First, we incorporate user interaction which is not used in any of the current works. Second, we optimize the detection process. For these purposes we incorporate a weight model to involve the user in the process of finding and applying the repair. We introduce the concept of repair candidates clusters called *repair groups* and a mechanism allowing to estimate the next selection on the basis of the previously selected candidates.

---

* Supported by the Czech Science Foundation, grant number P202/10/0573.

R. Benlamri (Ed.): NDT 2012, Part I, CCIS 293, pp. 259–273, 2012.

The paper is structured as follows: Section 2 provides basic definitions used in the text. Section 3 overviews the related works. Section 4 describes the proposed algorithm and Section 5 depicts its features using experiments. Section 6 concludes and outlines future work.

2   Basic Definitions

In this chapter basic definitions necessary in the following text are introduced. They are taken mainly from [3,5,6].

Definition 1. *Being given an alphabet of nodes $\mathbb{N}$ and an alphabet of node labels Σ, a tree T over $\mathbb{N}$ and Σ is a tuple $(r_T, N_T, E_T, \lambda_T)$, where $N_T \subseteq \mathbb{N}$ is the set of nodes, $\lambda_T : N_T \to \Sigma$ is a node labeling function, $r_T \in N_T$ is the distinguished root of T, and $E_T \subseteq N_T \times N_T$ is a set of edges s.t. starting from any node $n_i \in N_T$ it is possible to reach any other node $n_j \in N_T$, walking through a sequence of edges $e_1, \ldots, e_k$ which are connected and acyclic.*

Let us denote the set of leaf nodes as $Leaves(T)$ and the set of trees defined over an alphabet of node labels Σ as T_Σ.

Definition 2. *An XML tree is a pair $XT = \langle T, \delta \rangle$, where:*

i) *$T = (r, N, E, \lambda)$ is a tree from $T_{\tau \cup \alpha \cup \{S\}}$, where τ is a tag alphabet, α is an attribute name alphabet and S is a symbol not belonging to $\tau \cup \alpha$ (representing #PCDATA content of elements);*

ii) *given a node n of T, $\lambda(n) \in \alpha \cup \{S\} \Leftrightarrow n \in Leaves(T)$;*

iii) *$\delta : Leaves(T) \to Str$, where Str is a string alphabet, is a function associating a (string) value to every leaf of T.*

Example 1. Consider the XML document in Fig. 1. Its graphical representation as an XML tree is depicted in Fig. 2. The nodes have a label denoting the name of the element/attribute or a textual value and a unique identifier in brackets.

```
<bib>
 <book>
  <written_by>
   <author ano="A1">
    <name>John Writer</name>
   </author>
   <author ano="A1">
    <name>Eric Seller</name>
   </author>
  </written_by>
  <title>Some title</title>
 </book>
 <book>
  <written_by>
   <author ano="A2">
    <name>Adam Publisher</name>
   </author>
  </written_by>
  <title>Some title 2</title>
 </book>
</bib>
```

Fig. 1. An XML document

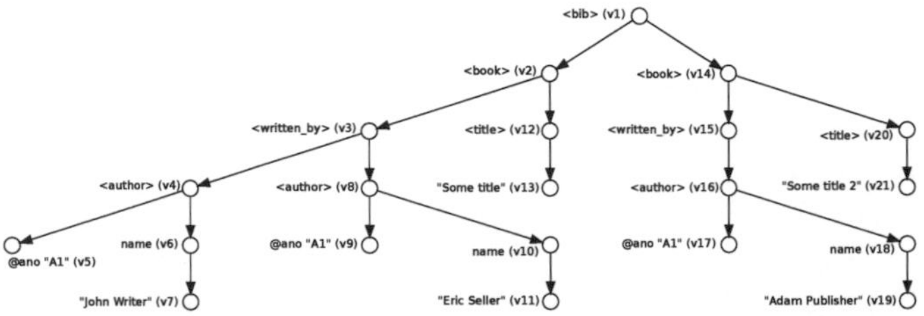

Fig. 2. An XML tree

Definition 3. *A DTD is a tuple* $D = (\tau, \alpha, P, R, rt)$, *where* τ *and* α *are of the same definition as in the* XML *tree,* P *is the set of* element type definitions, R *is the set of* attribute lists, $rt \in \tau$ *is the tag of the document root element.*

Definition 4. *A* path expression *is an expression of the form* $p = ('/'|'//')s_1$ $\ldots ('/'|'//')s_m$, *where* $s_1, \ldots, s_{m-1} \in \tau$, *and* $s_m \in \tau \cup \alpha \cup \{S\}$.

Definition 5. *Path* p *on a DTD* $D = (\tau, \alpha, P, R, rt)$ *is a sequence* $p = s_1, \ldots, s_m$ *of symbols in* $\tau \cup \alpha \cup \{S\}$ *s.t.:*

 i) $s_1 = rt$;
 ii) for each $i \in 2..m - 1$, $s_i \in \tau$ *and* s_i *appears in the element type definition of* s_{i-1};
 iii) $s_m \in \alpha \Rightarrow s_m$ *appears in the attribute list of* s_{m-1};
 iv) $s_m \in \tau \cup \{S\} \Rightarrow s_m$ *appears in the element type definition of* s_{m-1}.

Let us denote $paths(D)$ as the set of all paths which can be defined on a DTD D and $p(XT)$ (or $\{[\![p]\!]\}$) as the set of nodes from XML tree XT conforming to DTD D, which can be reached by the path $p \in paths(D)$, starting from the root of XT. The set of nodes reachable from a node v following path p is denoted as $\{v[\![p]\!]\}$. When there is only one node in $\{v[\![p]\!]\}$, we use $v[\![p]\!]$ to denote this node. Moreover, let $XT.p$ denote the *answer* of the path p applied on XT that is:

 - if $p \in EPath(D)$, where $EPath(D)$ denotes the set of the paths whose last symbol denotes an element, then $XT.p = p(XT)$;
 - if $p \in StrPath(D)$, where $StrPath(D)$ denotes the set of paths whose last symbol denotes either the textual content of an element or an attribute, then $XT.p = \{\delta_T(x) | x \in p(XT)\}$.

Example 2. Consider the XML tree XT from Ex. 1 conforming the DTD D defined below.

```
<!ELEMENT bib (book+)>
<!ELEMENT book (written_by, title)>
<!ELEMENT written_by (author+)>
<!ELEMENT author (name)>
<!ATTLIST author ano CDATA>
<!ELEMENT name PCDATA>
<!ELEMENT title PCDATA>
```

The set $paths(D)$ contains the following paths:

$$paths(D) = \{/bib, /bib/book, /bib/book/written\_by, /bib/book/written\_by/author,$$
$$/bib/book/written\_by/author/name, /bib/book/written\_by/author/name/S,$$
$$/bib/book/written\_by/author/@ano, /bib/book/title, /bib/book/title/S\}$$

Since different approaches use slightly different representation of an XML document, also the definition of a FD differs. In a relational database, a correspondence between values A and B in a tuple D models the FD denoted as $A \rightarrow B$. Since in XML there is no such standard tuple concept, the concept of XML tree tuples is introduced.

Definition 6. *Being given an XML tree XT conforming to DTD D, a* tree tuple *t of XT is a maximal sub-tree of XT, s.t. for every path $p \in paths(D)$, t.p contains at most one element.*

Example 3. Consider the XML tree *XT* in Fig. 2. The subtrees of *XT* shown in Fig. 3 are tree tuples, and the subtree in Fig. 4 is not, because the answer of the path */bib/book/written_by/author* contains two distinct nodes.

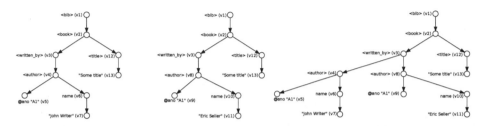

Fig. 3. Tree tuples of XML tree in Fig. 2   **Fig. 4.** Subtree of XML tree in Fig. 2 which is not tree tuple

Definition 7 (FD I.). *Given a DTD D, a* functional dependency *(FD) on D is an expression of the form $S \rightarrow p$, where S is a finite non empty subset of $paths(D)$ and $p \in paths(D)$.*

Example 4. Consider the XML tree in Fig 2. The following FD (I.) expresses that two distinct authors of the same book cannot have the same value of attribute ano:

$\{/bib/book, /bib/book/written\_by/author/@ano\} \rightarrow$
/bib/book/written_by/author

Definition 8 (FD II.). *Given a DTD D, a* functional dependency *is of the form $\sigma = (P, P', (P_1, \ldots, P_n \rightarrow P_{n+1}))$. Here P is a root path (path, where the first element is a root element of an XML document), or $P = \epsilon$ (empty path). Each $P_i(i \in [1, n])$ is a singleton leaf path, and there is a no non-empty common prefix for $P_1, \ldots, P_{n+1}$.*

Being given an XML document T conforming to D, we say that T satisfies σ if $\forall v \in \{[\![P]\!]\}, \forall v_1, v_2 \in \{v[\![P']\!]\}$, if $v_1[\![P_i]\!] \equiv v_2[\![P_i]\!]$ for all $i \in [1, n]$, then $v_1[\![P_{n+1}]\!] \equiv v_2[\![p_{n+1}]\!]$.

The main difference between the two definitions is that FD I. can use any path from $paths(D)$, whereas FD II. considers that each $P_i(i \in [1, n])$ is from $StrPaths(D)$, i.e. the constraint from Ex. 4 cannot be expressed by FD II., because of */bib/book/written_by/author*.

Example 5. The FD (II.) expressing that two distinct authors with different names of the same book cannot have the same value of attribute ano is defined as follows: $(bib/book, written\_by/author, (@ano \rightarrow name))$

3   Related Work

The current approaches dealing with the problem of finding optimal repair of violation of a FD can be divided according to the usage of elementary repair primitives.

Repairs and Consistent Answers. The authors of [3] are trying to find a minimal set of update operations, i.e. replacing a value and marking a particular node as unreliable, which makes XML data consistent. They introduce the concept of FD I. Since each inconsistency can have many possible strategies to repair it, the authors prefer those for which smaller changes are made to the original document.

The algorithm is based on reliability of elements in an XML tree:

Definition 9. *A R-XML tree is a triplet $RXT = \langle T, \delta, \varrho \rangle$, where $\langle T, \delta \rangle$ is an XML tree and ϱ is a reliability function from N_T to $\{true, false\}$, s.t. for each pair of nodes $n_1, n_2 \in N_T$ with n_2 descendant of n_1, it holds that $\varrho(n_1) = false \Rightarrow \varrho(n_2) = false$.*

To be able to create a repair, an R-XML tree must not satisfy FD according to definition of weak satisfiability:

Definition 10. *Being given an XML tree XT conforming a DTD D and a FD $F : S_1 \rightarrow S_2$, we say that XT satisfies F ($XT \models F$) if for each pair of tree tuples t_1, t_2 of XT*

$$t_1.S_1 = t_2.S_1 \wedge t_1.S_1 = \emptyset \Rightarrow t_1.S_2 = t_2.S_2$$

Being given a set of FDs $\mathcal{FD} = \{F_1, \ldots, F_n\}$ over D, we say that XT satisfies $\mathcal{FD}$ if it satisfies F_i for every $i \in 1..n$.

Definition 11. *Let $RXT = \langle T, \delta, \varrho \rangle$ be an R-XML tree conforming a DTD D, and $f : S \rightarrow p$ be a FD. We say that RXT weakly satisfies f ($RXT \models_w f$) if one of the following conditions holds:*

1. $\langle T, \delta \rangle \models f$;
2. *for each pair of tuples t_1, t_2 of RXT one of the following holds:*
   (a) *there exists a path $p_i \in S$ s.t.:*
   $$(\varrho(p_i(t_1)) = false) \vee (\varrho(p_i(t_2)) = false);$$
   (b) $(\varrho(p(t_1)) = false) \vee (\varrho(p(t_2)) = false).$

The repair of an R-XML tree which does not satisfy $\mathcal{FD}$ set of FDs is a pair of functions δ' and ϱ' s.t. RXT' tree composed of the original tree and the repair ($RXT' = \langle T, \delta' \cdot \delta, \varrho' \cdot \varrho \rangle$) weakly satisfies FD ($RXT' \models_w \mathcal{FD}$). The composition of the R-XML tree and the repair (i.e. composition of their δ and ϱ functions) is defined as follows:

Definition 12. *The* composition *of two functions δ_1 and δ_2 associating values to leaf nodes is*

$$\delta_1 \cdot \delta_2(n) = \begin{cases} \delta_1(n) & \text{if } \delta_1(n) \text{ is defined over } n, \\ \delta_2(n) & \text{otherwise} \end{cases}$$

Definition 13. *The* composition *of two reliability functions* ϱ_1 *and* ϱ_2 *associating a boolean value to nodes is*

$$\varrho_1 \cdot \varrho_2(n) = \varrho_1(n) \; AND \; \varrho_2(n).$$

With a repair $\langle \delta, \varrho \rangle$ of R-XML tree and a set of labeled nodes N of this tree, we denote $Updated_\delta(N)$ the set of nodes modified by δ. Analogously, we denote $True_\varrho(N) = \{n \in N | \varrho(n) = true\}$ and $False_\varrho(N) = \{n \in N | \varrho(n) = false\}$.

Definition 14. *Let* $RXT = \langle T, \delta, \varrho \rangle$ *be an R-XML tree conforming DTD D, $\mathcal{FD}$ a set of FDs and* $R_1 = \langle \delta_1, \varrho_1 \rangle$, $R_2 = \langle \delta_2, \varrho_2 \rangle$ *two repairs for RXT. We say that R_1 is* smaller *than R_2 ($R_1 \preceq R_2$) if $Updated_{\delta_1}(N_T) \cup False_{\delta_1}(N_T) \subseteq Updated_{\delta_2}(N_T) \cup False_{\delta_2}(N_T)$ and $False_{\delta_1}(N_T) \subseteq False_{\delta_2}(N_T)$. Repair R is* minimal *if there is no repair $R' \neq R$ s.t. $R' \preceq R$.*

An R-XML tree is used as an input for the main algorithm computing repaired R-XML tree described in Alg. 1. First, the algorithm computes all the possible repairs of tuples which do not satisfy a FD using the function `computeRepairs()` (lines 2-6). Next, all non-minimal repairs are removed from all possible repairs (line 7). In the last step, all the repairs are merged and a unique repaired R-XML tree is returned.

Function `computeRepairs()` (Alg. 2) gets an R-XML tree, a FD F and tuples t_1, t_2 of the R-XML tree as input and computes the repair as follows: If path p denotes a textual element, one of the two terminal values of $t_1.p$ or $t_2.p$ is changed, so that they become equal (line 3). Otherwise p denotes a node, so either the node $t_1.p$ or $t_2.p$ is marked as unreliable (line 5). For each path p_i on the left side of a FD F: If path p_i denotes a textual element, then one of the two terminal values $t_1.p_i$ or $t_2.p_i$ is changed to the newly generated value ($\perp$) (line 9). Otherwise p_i denotes a node, therefore one of the nodes $t_1.p_i$ or $t_2.p_i$ is marked as unreliable (line 11).

The main disadvantage of the approach is that the authors do not consider creation of new violations after repairing the initial violations. Also an unnecessary repair of some particular violation could be applied to an XML document because another repair could repair that violation before.

Algorithm 1. XML Repair

Require:
    $RXT = \langle T, \delta, \varrho \rangle$: R-XML tree conforming a DTD D
    $\mathcal{FD} = F_1, \ldots, F_m$: Set of FDs
Ensure: a unique repaired R-XML tree
  1: $S = \emptyset$ {set of repairs}
  2: **for all** $(F : S \to p) \in \mathcal{FD}$ s.t. $RXT \not\models_w F$ **do**
  3:     **for all** t_1, t_2 tuples of RXT s.t. t_1, t_2 do not weakly satisfy F **do**
  4:         $S = S \cup computeRepairs(F, t_1, t_2, RXT)$
  5:     **end for**
  6: **end for**
  7: $S = removeNonMinimal(S, RXT)$
  8: $\langle \delta', \varrho' \rangle = mergeRepairs(S)$
  9: **return** $\langle T, \delta' \cdot \delta, \varrho' \cdot \varrho \rangle$

Algorithm 2. *computeRepairs*(F, t_1, t_2, RXT)

Require:
    $RXT = \langle T, \delta\varrho \rangle$: R-XML tree conforming to DTD D
    $F : X \to p$ FD
    t_1, t_2 tuples of RXT
Ensure: S: Set of repairs
 1: $S = \emptyset$
 2: **if** $p \in StrPaths(D)$ **then**
 3:    $S = S \cup \{\langle \{\delta(p(t_1)) = t_2.p\}, \varrho \rangle\} \cup \{\langle \{\delta(p(t_2)) = t_1.p\}, \varrho \rangle\}$
 4: **else**
 5:    $S = S \cup \{\langle \emptyset, \varrho_{\{t_1.p\}} \cdot \varrho \rangle\} \cup \{\langle \emptyset, \varrho_{\{t_2.p\}} \cdot \varrho \rangle\}$
 6: **end if**
 7: **for all** $p_i \in X$ **do**
 8:    **if** $p_i \in StrPaths(D)$ **then**
 9:      $S = S \cup \{\langle \{\delta(p_i(t_1)) = \perp_1\}, \varrho \rangle\} \cup \{\langle \{\delta(p_i(t_2)) = \perp_2\}, \varrho \rangle\}$
10:    **else**
11:      $S = S \cup \{\langle \emptyset, \varrho_{\{t_1.p_i\}} \cdot \varrho \rangle\} \cup \{\langle \emptyset, \varrho_{\{t_2.p_i\}} \cdot \varrho \rangle\}$
12:    **end if**
13: **end for**
14: **return** S

Querying and Repairing Inconsistent Data. In [5] the authors also prefer minimal set of repair primitives applied to the XML document to form a repair and consider general ICs, not only FDs. The introduced repair primitives consist of *(general) repairs*, where both delete and insert operations are used, *cleaning repairs*, where for documents interpreted as "dirty" only delete operations are used to repair inconsistencies, and *completing repairs*, where for documents interpreted as incomplete, insert operations are used. Consequently, the structure of the XML document which conforms DTD D and violated FD can be updated.

The authors discover that the problem of deciding whether there exists a repair for a XML document in the presence of DTD with FDs is undecidable. Therefore they consider restricted forms of repairs, more specifically cleaning and completing repairs.

Improving XML Data Quality with FDs. The authors of [6] introduce a cost model which assigns a weight $W(v)$ $in[0, 1]$ to each leaf node v in the XML document. The weight may be automatically generated by statistical methods or it can be assigned by the user. An *optimal repair* is then the one with the lowest repair cost which is measured by the total weight of the modified nodes. The authors also found out that repairing one FD violation can violate another. Therefore, first, a *conflict hypergraph* capturing the initial FD violations is constructed and all the violations are fixed by modifying the values of all the nodes on a vertex cover of the hypergraph. Second, remaining violations are resolved by modifying the violating nodes and their *core determinants* to prevent of introducing new conflicts.

A repairing primitive is a node value modification, where for repairing algorithm a combination of two rules to resolve violation is used. Let us have an FD $\sigma = (P, P', (P_1, \ldots, P_n \to P_{n+1}))$ and consider two nodes v_1 and v_2 matching path P' in a subtree rooted at a node in $\{[\![p]\!]\}$. If the child nodes of v_1 and v_2 qualified by paths P_i have equal values for all $i \in [1, n]$ and their child nodes qualified by P_{n+1} have different values, then v_1 and v_2 violates σ. The first rule used to repair this violation is to change the value of the node qualified by P_{n+1} from v_1 to the value of v_2's child node that matches P_{n+1} (or reversely). The second rule is to choose an arbitrary $P_i(i \in [1,n])$ and introduce a new value to the node qualified by P_i from v_1 (or v_2).

To actually resolve the problem of repairing FD violations in an XML document, the authors convert this problem into then problem of *weighted vertex cover* for hypergraph [8]. Let us have hypergraph $g = (V, E)$, where each hyperedge $e \in E$ is a set of value nodes which violate some FD. In a repair of an inconsistent XML document, for each hyperedge at least one value node is modified, therefore it is essential to find a *vertex cover* (VC) for g, which is a set $S \subseteq V$, s.t. for all edges $e \in E$, $S \cap e \neq \emptyset$. Since the hypergraph is weighted, we can define weight of VC as the total weight of all vertices in S.

Finally, after repairing initial FD violations, there is a chance that new violations may be introduced, therefore the authors provided a method to do modifications on value nodes without incurring new conflicts.

4   Proposed Algorithm

The proposed algorithm is based on [3] due to simple representation of the XML data and operation of marking a particular node as unreliable, which can reveal forgotten inconsistencies in the data. It is split into three steps, where the second and the third step are repeated until all violations are repaired (see Alg. 3). First, an XML document and FDs are loaded and an XML tree with corresponding tree tuples is created. The next step computes repair groups containing repair candidates for FD violations. Third, the chosen repair candidate is applied to an XML tree.

Algorithm 3. Repair RW-XML tree

Require:
  $RXT = \langle RT, \omega \rangle$: RW-XML tree conforming to DTD D
  $\mathcal{FD} = F_1, \ldots, F_m$: Set of FDs
Ensure: a unique repaired RW-XML tree
1: $resultRXT = RXT$
2: **while** $resultRXT \not\models_w \mathcal{FD}$ **do**
3:     $S = \emptyset$ {Set of repair groups}
4:     **for all** $(F : S \to p) \in \mathcal{FD}$ s.t. $RXT \not\models_w F$ **do**
5:        **for all** t_1, t_2 tuples of RXT s.t. t_1, t_2 do not weakly satisfy F **do**
6:           $S = S \cup computeRepairGroup(F, t_1, t_2, RXT, S)$
7:        **end for**
8:     **end for**
9:     $R = getRepair(S, RXT)$
10:    $resultRXT = applyRepair(R, resultRXT)$
11: **end while**

4.1   Initial Data Model

To represent an XML document we use an extended R-XML tree called *RW-XML tree* with weights assigned to each node.

Definition 15. *A RW-XML tree is a pair $RWXT = \langle RXT, \omega \rangle$, where RXT is an R-XML tree and ω is a weight function from N_T to $[0, 1]$.*

The weight indicates correctness of the data the particular node holds. The higher the weight is, the more correct the node is. The weights are used to measure the cost of repair candidates, where candidate with the lowest cost is picked to be applied to the XML tree. This is also the first place, where user interaction can be implemented – the user can assign the weights to nodes manually or use some sort of statistical methods.

After creating the RW-XML tree from input XML data, a set of tree tuples is constructed. Since $paths(D)$ can be infinite (DTD can be recursive), the actual content of $paths(D)$ is modified to reflect the current structure of the RW-XML tree. Since the definition of a tree tuple says that answer to the path p contains at most one element, our modification has no effect on constructing tree tuples if a DTD defines some optional path which is not defined for the RW-XML tree $RWXT$ (the set $p(RWXT)$ is empty).

4.2   Computing Repair Groups

A *repair group* is a set of repair candidates, which repairs the same FD or modifies the same part of $RWXT$. Each *repair candidate* is a pair of functions $\langle \delta, \varrho \rangle$, which either modifies value of an RW-XML tree node (δ is defined) or marks a node as unreliable (ϱ is defined). The δ function of a repair candidate is defined the same way as in the XML tree and defines a new value of the RW-XML tree node. Similarly, the ϱ function defines the node which is marked as unreliable.

To be able to compute repair groups, we need to decide which FDs violate $RWXT$. This can be achieved by finding all tree tuple pairs that do not weakly satisfy particular FD. A repair group is then computed for each tuple pair (line 6 in Alg. 3). Function `computeRepairGroup()` (see Alg. 4) gets an RW-XML tree, a FD F, tuples t_1, t_2 and a set of repair groups RGS and computes the repair group containing repair candidates as follows: First, the repair candidates are created using function `computeRepairs()` from Alg. 2. Second, a check is performed whether the repair candidates intersect other candidates from existing repair groups (line 2): If the candidates intersect with some group, they are added to this group (line 3). Otherwise, a new repair group containing repair candidates is created (line 5).

Example 6. Consider XML data represented as XML tree XT in Fig 2. The XT violates FD
  $\{/bib/book, /bib/book/written\_by/author/@ano\} \rightarrow$
$/bib/book/written\_by/author$
because two authors of the same book have the same value of attribute @*ano*. One repair group with these repair candidates is created:

  - $R_1 = \langle \{\delta(v5) = \perp\}, \varrho_{\{\}}(v) \rangle$
  - $R_2 = \langle \{\delta(v9) = \perp\}, \varrho_{\{\}}(v) \rangle$

Algorithm 4. *computeRepairGroup*(F, t_1, t_2, RXT, RGS)

Require:
  $RXT = \langle T, \omega \rangle$: RW-XML tree conforming to DTD D
  $F : X \to p$ FD
  t_1, t_2 tuples of RXT
  RGS set of repair groups
Ensure: RG: repair group
  1: $S = computeRepairs(F, t_1, t_2, RXT)$
  2: **if** $candidatesIntersectRepairGroups(S, RGS)$ **then**
  3:     $RG = getIntersectingRepairGroup(S, RGS)$
  4: **else**
  5:     $RG = createNewRepairGroup(S)$
  6: **end if**
  7: **return** RG

- $R_3 = \langle \{\}, \varrho_{\{v4,v5,v6,v7\}}(v) \rangle$
- $R_4 = \langle \{\}, \varrho_{\{v8,v9,v10,v11\}}(v) \rangle$
- $R_5 = \langle \{\}, \varrho_{\{v2,v3,\ldots,v13\}}(v) \rangle$

First two repair candidates modify the value of an attribute @*ano* by assigning newly generated value ($\bot$). Next two mark each *author* node with its child nodes that have the same @*ano* attribute, respectively. The last candidate marks as unreliable a whole subtree with the *book* node holding *authors* with the same attribute as the root node.

Weight Model of a Repair Group. Being given a repair candidate R, $Modified_\delta(R)$ denotes the set of nodes modified by δ function from R. Analogously, we denote $Modified_\varrho(R)$ the set of nodes modified by ϱ function. The number of nodes modified by repair candidate R is denoted with $\lambda(R)$. Last, we denote $PS(R)$ a set of paths defining all nodes modified by R.

Example 7. Consider the XML tree from Fig. 2 and a repair candidate, which marks nodes $v12$ and $v13$ as unreliable. Then the set $PS(R)$ contains the following paths: /bib/book/title, /bib/book/title/text()

Since each repair candidate consists of a set of nodes which are modified, we can compute the cost of each candidate. Unlike in the original approach, we do not prefer repair candidates that modify the value of the nodes. Therefore, we added a coefficient k to the calculation of the repair candidate cost, so that the priority of repair candidate marking node as unreliable can be achieved.

Definition 16. *Being given an RW-XML tree RXT and a repair candidate R, we define the cost of R as: $cost(R) = \sum_{u \in Modified_\delta(R)} \omega(u) + \sum_{v \in Modified_\varrho(R)} \omega(v) \cdot k$, where k is the priority of repairing the candidate by modifying the node value in contrast to marking it unreliable.*

Definition 17. *Being given an RW-XML tree RXT and a repair group RG, we define the weight of RG as the sum of costs of all repair candidates in the RG.*

By default, k is set to such value that the cost of repair candidate marking as an unreliable node will be higher than the one that modifies node value. However, this is another place where user can intervene and change the priority of repair candidates.

4.3   Selection of Repair Candidate

From the repair candidates computed in the previous step, we must choose the one that is applied to the RW-XML tree. We introduce two distinct algorithms, without and with user interaction: The former algorithm simply selects the first repair group with the lowest weight, and from it the repair candidate with the lowest cost is selected. The latter allows the user to choose the repair candidate. Very important aspect of all user interactions in this kind of algorithm is that the user will not be willing to select more than, e.g., ten repairs. Therefore, we introduce a functionality to guess the next selection from selection done by the user before.

Function `selectRepairByUser()` responsible for selection of a repair candidate involving user interactivity is shown in Alg. 5. First, it decides whether the user is selecting repair candidates (*user selection mode*), or the user leaves decision making on the algorithm using his previous selections (*guess mode*) (line 2). In user selection mode, the user chooses from repair groups sorted by the weight the most convenient one, and from this group the repair candidate that will be applied on RW-XML tree (line 3). The last step of user selection mode is saving the information from selected repair candidate (line 4). This information consists of the FD which this candidate repairs, nodes the repair changes (their paths) and also whether the change was a value modification or marking a node as unreliable. In the guess mode (starting at line 5), the algorithm checks all repair groups whether one of them contains a repair candidate that is sufficiently similar to some previously selected repair candidate (line 6–12). This similarity is checked by function `canBeUsedUserSelection()` (see Alg. 6). If neither of the candidates is sufficiently similar, the algorithm chooses the repair candidate with the lowest cost from the repair group with the lowest weight (line 13–14).

Function `canBeUsedUserSelection()` determines whether current repair candidate RC is sufficiently similar to some repair candidate $S \in SR$. To be similar, RC must repair the same FD as S, it must use the same update operation as S and $\lambda(RC) \geq \lceil \lambda(S) \cdot t \rceil$ (line 2). Furthermore, if $\lambda(RC) = \lceil \lambda(S) \cdot t \rceil$, the set of paths $PS(RC)$ must be a subset of $PS(S)$ (line 3). Otherwise, there must exist a subset of $PS(S)$ with $\lceil \lambda(S) \cdot t \rceil$ elements that is a subset of $PS(RC)$. In other words, without taking into account threshold t, if a repair candidate R_1 modifies some nodes, the sufficiently similar repair candidate R_2 is the one that modifies at least the same nodes as R_1. t can reduce the number of modified nodes of some previously selected repair candidate R_1, which means that sufficiently similar repair candidate needs to modify fewer nodes that are similar with nodes modified by R_1.

Algorithm 5. $selectRepairByUser(RGS, SR, t)$

Require:
    RGS set of repair groups
    SR: set of repair candidates previously selected by the user
    t: threshold
Ensure: R: repair candidate
  1: $R = \emptyset$
  2: **if** $isUserSelection()$ **then** {the user selection mode}
  3:    $R = getRepairFromUser()$
  4:    $saveSelectedRepair(SR, R)$
  5: **else** {the guess mode}
  6:    **for all** RG in RGS **do**
  7:        **for all** RC in RG **do**
  8:            **if** $canBeUsedUserSelection(SR, t, RC)$ **then**
  9:                **return** RC
10:            **end if**
11:        **end for**
12:    **end for**
13:    $RG = getFirstRG(RGS)$ {RG with the smallest weight}
14:    $R = getFirstRepairCandidate(RG)$ {RC with the lowest cost}
15: **end if**
16: **return** R

Algorithm 6. $canBeUsedUserSelection(SR, t, RC)$

Require:
    SR: set of previously selected repair candidates by the user
    t: suitability threshold of previously selected repair candidates
    RC: the current repair candidate
Ensure: **true** if RC is similar to some previous repair candidate.
  1: **for all** S in SR **do**
  2:    **if** S repairs the same FD as RC and S use the same update operation as RC and $\lceil \lambda(SC) \times t \rceil \leq \lambda(RC)$ **then**
  3:        **if** $\lceil \lambda(SC) \times t \rceil = \lambda(RC)$ and $PS(RC) \subseteq PS(SC)$ **then**
  4:            **return** **true**
  5:        **end if**
  6:        **if** $\lceil \lambda(SC) \times t \rceil < \lambda(RC)$ and $\exists$ a subset s of $PS(SC)$ with $\lceil \lambda(SC) \times t \rceil$ elements, s.t. $s \subseteq PS(RC)$ **then**
  7:            **return** **true**
  8:        **end if**
  9:    **end if**
10: **end for**
11: **return** **false**

4.4 Application of the Repair Candidate

The selected repair candidate is finally applied to the RW-XML tree. If after this part the RW-XML tree does not violate any FDs, the whole repair algorithm ends at this point, otherwise repair groups are regenerated and the selection of the repair candidate part takes place again. To apply the selected repair candidate R to the RW-XML tree RXT means to compose δ and ϱ functions of R with the corresponding functions of R-XML tree contained in RXT. After application of the repair candidate, some of RW-XML tree nodes could become unreliable, which can lead to the situation that some of tree tuples are not anymore considered a tuple (it is no longer a maximal subtree). Therefore, before regeneration of repair groups we need to check all tree tuples to see whether they satisfy definition of tree tuple.

5   Experiments

Besides our approach, called **FDRepairer**, we have also implemented the algorithm proposed in [3] to be able to compare them using both real-world and synthetic data. Both were implemented as a part of a general schema inference framework for XML called *jInfer* [4].

The first real-world dataset originates from the XML data repository[1], specifically the Course data derived from university web sites. The consistency of data is evaluated against FD defined as: *Two courses starting at the same date and time are each situated in a different place.* The second dataset is a set of actors of IMDB database[2]. For this dataset, we defined FD as follows: *For each two authors, which played in the movie with the same name, the year of release of this movie must be the same.* Two synthetic datasets were constructed as well. The former one represents data introduced in Ex. 2 with FD presented in Ex. 4. The latter one is created according to Ex. 1 in [6].

For each dataset we perform the following: First, we run the original algorithm and collect information about how many nodes were modified with particular update operation. We split the value modification operation into two types – changing value to new one and copying the value from one node to another. Next, we use **FDRepairer** with minimal repair candidate selection mode, and we gather the information on how many repair groups were created before the first application of repair candidate and the total number of picked repair groups. We run our algorithm multiple times with different value of the coefficient k and assignment of node weights w.

The first real-world data are represented by **reed** and **wsu** documents. For each document we execute our algorithm with three different settings. First two use the default value of k ($k = 1.5$), for the last one, we set $k = 0.005$. For the last two executions we set for **reed** (**wsu**) the weight $w = 0.1$ for nodes in path `/root/course/time/start_time/text()` (or `/root/course/time/start/text()`). **actors** represents the second real-world dataset. Our algorithm is executed two times, where for both executions $k = 1.5$. Moreover, the second one has weight $w = 0.2$ for nodes in path `/W4F_DOC/Actor/Filmography/Movie/Year/ text()`.

Synthetic datasets represented by documents **bib** and **customers** were both used as an input for our algorithm two times, where the first execution was done with the default value of k. The second execution on **bib** uses $k = 0.1$ and on **customers** uses $k = 1.5$ and $w = 0.2$ is set to all nodes in path `/customers/country/c_list/customer/city/text()`.

All information gathered is shown in Tab. 1 and 2. The columns of are defined as follows: RG is the number of repair groups created before application of repair candidate, RGt is the total number of picked repair groups, U specifies the number of nodes marked as unreliable, NV defines the number of nodes changing value to a new one and ChV specifies the number of nodes with value copied from another node. FDR denotes **FDRepairer**.

---

[1] http://www.cs.washington.edu/research/xmldatasets/
[2] http://www.cs.wisc.edu/niagara/data.html

Table 1. Real-world datasets

data	rep.	k	w	RG	RGt	U	NV	ChV
	[3]	-	-	-	-	0	780	0
reed	FDR	1.5	-	218	195	0	195	0
	FDR	1.5	0.1	218	195	0	195	0
	FDR	0.005	0.1	218	195	5265	0	0
	[3]	-	-	-	-	0	2612	0
wsu	FDR	1.5	-	3520	653	0	653	0
	FDR	1.5	0.1	3520	653	0	653	0
	FDR	0.005	0.1	3520	653	20833	0	0
	[3]	-	-	-	-	0	62	62
actors	FDR	1.5	-	69	62	0	32	30
	FDR	1.5	0.2	69	79	0	0	79

Table 2. Synthetic datasets

data	rep.	k	w	RG	RGt	U	NV	ChV
	[3]	-	-	-	-	0	913	0
bib	FDR	1.5	-	1444	913	0	913	0
	FDR	0.1	-	1444	913	5478	0	0
	[3]	-	-	-	-	0	99	99
customers	FDR	1.5	-	232	136	0	72	64
	FDR	1.5	0.2	232	361	0	0	361

It is apparent that `FDRepairer` found for each dataset a repair that modifies less nodes than the original repair Alg. [3]. One exception where `FDRepairer` modifies more nodes is the case when we set value of k near 0, which marks nodes as unreliable. With this setting we want to demonstrate that with our approach it is possible to mark nodes as unreliable instead of modifying their values. This is not possible with the original repairer, since it prefers node value modification to marking node as unreliable.

Setting the weights of nodes affects the choice of strategies used to repair the violations. In datasets `actors` and `customers` setting the custom weight to nodes causes the node values to be changed to values of other nodes. It also causes modification of nodes defined by the path specifying the weights. In datasets `reed` and `wsu` setting the weights still changes the value of nodes to a newly generated one; however, for `reed` only values of nodes in path `/root/course/time/start_time/text()` are modified and for `wsu.xml` are modified values in path `/root/course/time/start/text()`.

6 Conclusion

The aim of this paper was to propose and implement an algorithm repairing XML FDs violations. We optimize the approach from [3], where we incorporate a weight model into the XML data representation, introduce a new concept of repair groups and exploit user interaction in the repair process. Besides the repair candidate selection we also introduced a mechanism allowing to guess the next selection based on the previous candidates selected by the user. Our experimental implementation based on the *jInfer* framework indicates clear that our approach found repairs with less modifications applied on the XML data. We have also shown that with the user interaction it is possible to change the usage of update operations used in repair and create more reasonable result.

The first main task in the further work is to extend paths defining FDs. With usage of more constructs that XPath provides, one can define more sophisticated FDs. Another part of the algorithm to be improved is clustering repair candidates into repair groups. The user can provide some additional criteria, that can change the resulting repair. Last but not least, the guessing part of the user selection algorithm can be improved by using more sophisticated heuristics to select proper repair candidate with regard to previous candidates selected.

References

1. Bray, T., Paoli, J., Maler, E., Yergeau, F., Sperberg-McQueen, C.M.: Extensible Markup Language (XML) 1.0, 5th edn., W3C (2008)
2. Buneman, P., Fan, W., Siméon, J., Weinstein, S.: Constraints for Semistructured Data and XML. SIGMOD Rec. 30, 47–54 (2001)
3. Flesca, S., Furfaro, F., Greco, S., Zumpano, E.: Repairs and Consistent Answers for XML Data with Functional Dependencies. In: Bellahsène, Z., Chaudhri, A.B., Rahm, E., Rys, M., Unland, R. (eds.) XSym 2003. LNCS, vol. 2824, pp. 238–253. Springer, Heidelberg (2003)
4. Klempa, M., Mikula, M., Smetana, R., Švirec, M., Vitásek, M.: jInfer XML Schema Inference Framework, http://jinfer.sourceforge.net/modules/paper.pdf, website of the project: http://jinfer.sourceforge.net
5. Flesca, S., Furfaro, F., Greco, S., Zumpano, E.: Querying and Repairing Inconsistent XML Data. In: Ngu, A.H.H., Kitsuregawa, M., Neuhold, E.J., Chung, J.-Y., Sheng, Q.Z. (eds.) WISE 2005. LNCS, vol. 3806, pp. 175–188. Springer, Heidelberg (2005)
6. Tan, Z., Zhang, L.: Improving XML Data Quality with Functional Dependencies. In: Yu, J.X., Kim, M.H., Unland, R. (eds.) DASFAA 2011, Part I. LNCS, vol. 6587, pp. 450–465. Springer, Heidelberg (2011)
7. Thompson, H.S., Maloney, M., Beech, D., Mendelsohn, N.: XML Schema Part 1: Structures, 2nd edn., W3C (2004)
8. Vazirani, V.V.: Approximation Algorithms. Springer (2001)
9. Vincent, M.W., Liu, J.: Functional Dependencies for XML. In: Zhou, X., Zhang, Y., Orlowska, M.E. (eds.) APWeb 2003. LNCS, vol. 2642, pp. 22–34. Springer, Heidelberg (2003)

Encoding Spectral Parameters Using Cache Codebook

Driss Guerchi and Siwar Rekik

Canadian University of Dubai,
Sheikh Zayed Road, Behind Shangrila Hotel,
P.O.BOX 117781, Dubai, UAE
{Driss,Siwar}@cud.ac.ae

Abstract. A new efficient approach to quantize the spectral line frequencies (LSF) in a coder is proposed. The use of the full search algorithm in the spectral parameters quantization causes high complexity and large hardware storage. Attempts to reduce the complexity have been performed by lowering the size of the LSF codebook. This option leads to a sub-optimal solution; the number of LSF vectors to be tested affects the performance of the speech coder. Cache codebook (CCB) technique enhances the search of the optimal quantized spectral information. In this technique the size of the main codebook is kept unchanged while the number of closest match searches is reduced. Unlike the classical quantizer design, the CCB method involves one main codebook embedding four disjoint sub-codebooks. The content of the CCB at any time is an exact reproduction of one of the four sub-codebooks. The search for the best match to an input vector is limited to the LSF vectors of the CCB. Some criteria are used to accept or reject this closest match. The CCB is updated whenever the decision is in favor of rejection. The cache codebook was successfully embedded in a CELP coder to enhance the quantization of the spectral information. The comparison simulation results show that the Codebook Caching approach yields to comparable objective and subjective performance to that of the optimal full-search technique when using the same training and testing database.

Keywords: LPC analysis, CELP coding, Cache codebook.

1   Introduction

Most conventional CELP (Code-Excited Linear Prediction) coders are limited in quality by the accurate spectral estimation required in the LPC analysis and quantization phases. The quantization of the spectral information in CELP coding suffers from high search complexity and large memory storage. For real-time applications, complexity and memory requirements represent the main coder specifications. Several sub-optimal algorithms have been proposed to reduce the search time, while sacrificing the speech coder Performance [1,2]. The tree search technique and the multistage vector quantization are widely used to encode the spectral parameters. These approaches speed up the search procedure while increasing the memory.

R. Benlamri (Ed.): NDT 2012, Part I, CCIS 293, pp. 274–280, 2012.

Our goal in the current work is to design a new low complexity LSF vector quantization technique while maintaining a constant bit rate and high speech quality [3]. To meet these requirements we propose a new efficient search method, called Codebook Caching (CCB). In this method the size of the main codebook is kept unchanged while the search computation load is reduced. The CCB approach involves one main codebook embedding four disjoint subcodebooks. At any search instance, the CCB is an exact reproduction of one of the four sub-codebooks. The search for the best match to an input vector is limited then to the LSF vectors of the current CCB. Some criteria are used to accept or reject this closest match. The CCB is updated whenever the decision is in favor of rejection [4].

In the CCB approach, LPC (Linear Predictive Coding) analysis is repeatedly performed, in the training and the testing phases, to collect the LPC vectors. These vectors are then converted to LSF domain for stability and efficient quantization requirements. The main codebook is sequentially designed in four phases. In each phase, only one sub-codebook is trained from the database of the collected LSF vectors. The four sub-codebooks are identified by different tags ranging from 1 to 4.

2   Conventional LSF Quantization

Most speech coders quantize the spectral parameters using Vector Quantization (VQ) codebooks [5]. While the VQ techniques reduce the coder bit rates, they increase drastically the search computation load. The performance of a VQ method is function of the size of the used codebook. A codebook with more codewords certainly excels in outputting the best match to the LSF parameters[6]. However, bigger size codebook means the need of more bits, an increase of the coder complexity, and more memory capacity to store the additional codewords [7]. Consequence, the search for the closest match consumes more time due to the increase of the number of comparisons between the input word and the codewords in the codebook

The need of more memory does not represent a big problem due to the advances in the chip technology. By contrast the delay, generated during the search for the closest match to an input LSF vector may prevent the speech coder from being adopted in some real tine applications. We face a tradeoff between the two most important attributes of speech coders: quality vs. delay. The Spectral information quantization in classical CELP coding is done as follows:

- LPC analysis to extract the spectral information;
- Conversion of the LPC coefficients to LSF vectors;
- Training the LSF codebook
- Full or sub-optimal codebook search for the closest match to an input LSF vector.

For efficient quantization, the two last steps must be done in a closer manner. The codebook search algorithm may exploit the design properties of the LSF codebook. It seems clear from this discussion that any attempt to improve the LSF quantization must involve one or more of the above steps. We propose in the following sections some techniques that optimize the search method while maintaining a fixed bit-rate and toll speech quality at the receiver.

3   Codebook Caching

In this section we propose a new technique called Codebook Cashing to reduce the complexity of the spectral information quantization. This technique consists of one main codebook incorporating four disjoint sub-codebooks. The training of the main codebook (MCB) is done in four phases. In each phase, only one sub-codebook is trained based on some criteria to be given in the subsequent sections. However, searching for the closest match to the input vector is restricted to only one of the four sub-codebooks. The selected sub-codebook for any search is called Cache Codebook (CCB). It contains, at any given time, a copy of one quarter of the main codebook. By this we limit the search of the best match to a set containing one quarter of the total reference vectors. No extra storage is needed to implement this technique since the content the CCB is always obtained from the MCB.

Caching technique is widely used in computing to increase the speed of memory access. Even though it has the same objective as Caching Codebook, conceptually they are based on two different approaches. Figure 1 illustrates the concept of Caching Codebook technique. The CCB is used to hold an exact reproduction of a corresponding subcodebook of code vectors from the MCB. In searching for the best match, the LSF vector at the output of the LPC analysis filter is first compared to all code vectors in the cache codebook. Once this process terminated, a decision has to be made on whether to accept or reject this codeword. The quantized LSF vector is to be used in the LPC synthesis filter if its spectral distortion with regard to the input LSF vector is smaller than a predefined threshold. Otherwise, the cache codebook has to be updated by a new LSF vectors groups.

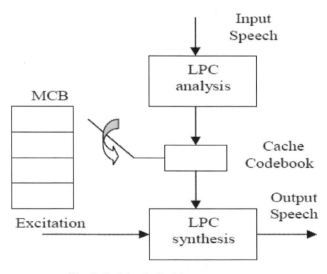

Fig. 1. Codebook Caching concept

4   Cache Codebook Design

In the CCB design, a large set S of LSF vectors is collected for the LSF codebook training phase. Four LSF vectors V_i are first selected randomly form the set S. These vectors will represent the centroids of the four subcodebooks $S_i (1 \leq i \leq 4)$. These subsets are reconstructed sequentially by clustering together the vectors of S with minimal spectral distortion,ε to their respective centroids. To ovoid any overlapping between the four sub-codebooks S_i, we select the four centroids such that the spectral distortion between any pair of centroids $V_i (1 \leq i \leq 4)$ greater than 2ε. The elements of each subset S_i are collected from the set S such that:

$$S_i = \left\{ V_{j \neq i} \in S : SD(V_i, V_j) \leq \varepsilon \right\}$$

Where ε is obtained statistically from some high performance speech coders, like the G.729 [8]. The threshold is the smallest possible spectral distortion between any input vector and its closest match reference in these coders. Hence, the four sub-codebooks form a partition of the MCB:

$$MCB = S_1 \cup S_2 \cup S_3 \cup S_4$$

And

$$S_1 \cap S_2 \cap S_3 \cap S_4 = \phi$$

At the end of the training process, each subset Si will be characterized by the centroid V_i (or a tag i) and the corresponding smallest spectral distortion ε_i with regard to all its elements:

$$\varepsilon_1 = \min_{V_{i \in S_i}} \left\{ SD(V_{i,} V_l) \right\}$$

5   Cache Codebook Search and Update

Search for the closest match to an input vector should be done first on the previous content S_i of the CCB. A comparator checks the spectral distortion, ε_{min} between the input vector and the centroid of to determine if it is smaller than the threshold ε. If this is the case, The CCB is used as if it were the MCB. The search of the closest match will be then limited to the vectors of the CCB. Satisfying a search for the best match in this way is called a hit. The advantage of this method is that for steady-state speech frames, the percentage of hits is very high (greater than 96 %). If it is a miss, the situation in which min ε_{min} is greater than ε, the content of the CCB need to be tested against the three other sub-codebooks to decide whether the CCB has to be updated or not. The miss number increases when the successive speech frames are non stationary or in the transition between different phonemes.

The performance of the Caching Codebook technique can be measured by the hit ratio, which is the ratio of hits to the total number of best match searches.

When the best match from the LSF cache codebook is rejected, the content of the cache codebook must be replaced by a new LSF vectors group from the MCB. Different algorithms can be implemented to perform this selection. Among them, we list the most recently used (MRU) and the most frequently used (MFU) algorithms. In these algorithms, the sub-codebook, to be copied to the cache codebook, is the one (among the remaining three sub-codebooks) that is the most recently used or the most frequently used, respectively. Here, we propose a new method that optimizes the search of the best vector match. The selected sub-codebook will be the one with the smallest spectral distortion (SSD), ε_i between the input vector and the centroids of each group. We believe that there exists among the vectors of the selected group some having smaller spectral distortions than that of the best match from the previous CCB with regard to the input vector. A simplified step-by-step illustration of the cache codebook design and updating is shown in Figure 2.

Table 1 presents the performance, in terms of the hit ratio, of the three algorithms cited above. It is clear that the SSD method outperforms the two other algorithms, in terms of the percentage of hitting the closest vector match.

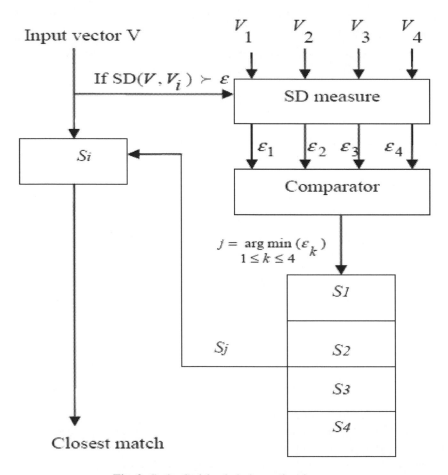

Fig. 2. Cache Codebook design and update

To code the best LSF match, we send to the decoder the code of the index chosen from the CCB, in addition to the tag number of the group to which it belongs. Two bits are required to code the tag number since there are four different groups.

Table 1. Performance of three CCB updating algorithms

Algorithm	Hit ratio after CCB updating (in %)
SSD	92
MRU	75
MFU	80

6   Evaluation and Conclusion

To separate the effects of the selection of the database on the codebook caching technique, we conducted our experiments on the same database used in full-search codebook. Two evaluations measures were adopted: one subjective based on an informal listening, and the second objective using the Segmental Signal-to-noise ratio (SegSNR) at the output of the decoder. The systems to be evaluated are three versions of a CELP coder. Everything is similar in these coders, except the LSF quantization. In the first coder, we use the most commonly known codebook in which a Full Codebook (FCB) search is to be performed for each input LSF vector.

In the second CELP coder, we implement the Codebook aching (CCB) technique discussed in this work. The third coder implements the Multistage (MSCB) approach to search the closest match. The database for training phase consists of 150 min of English and French speech from 8 speakers: four women and four men. Each speaker read the same short utterance 10 times. We used the weighted distortion measure of Paliwal and Atal [9] for training and testing. The same distortion measure is used to evaluate the LSF quantization in the three coders for six different input sentences uttered by other speakers. Table 2 shows the average spectral distortion between the input LSF vectors and their corresponding LSF best matches, while Table 3 presents the SegSNR for the three methods. As expected, the objective measure illustrates that the performance of the Codebook Caching technique are comparable to the full codebook search, however the complexity is drastically reduced in the CCB. The informal listening tests have revealed that the two techniques provide also comparable subjective quality.

The Codebook Caching technique reduces the execution time of the LSF parameters quantization process, while requiring the same bit rate as in the full search quantization. The overall complexity expense of the spectral parameters coding is reduced by at least 70%. However, this technique has the disadvantage of sacrificing little performance of the speech coder.

Table 2. SD performance of the Caching Codebook technique

LSF Quantization Technique	Avg SD (dB)	Outliers (in %)	
		2-4 db	>4dB
FCB	1.10	2.5	0.02
CCB	1.25	2.8	0.06
MSCB	1.30	3.0	0.07

Table 3. Objective performance of the Caching Codebook technique

LSF Quantization Technique	SegSNR (dB)
FCB	12.40
CCB	12.00
MSCB	11.95

Acknowledgement. We would like to express our sincere gratitude for the Research Centre of the Canadian University of Dubai for financial support.

References

[1] Qian, Y., Kabal, P.: Wideband speech recovery from narrowband speech using classified codebook mapping. In: Proc. Australian Int.

[2] Guerchi, D., Hmimia, A.: Pitch-synchronous linear analysis for automatic speech recognition systems. In: The 8th World Multi-Conference on Systemics, Cybernetics and Informatics, Orlando, Florida, USA (2004)

[3] Itakura, F.: Line spectrum representation of linear predictive coefficients of speech signals. Journal of the Acoustical Society of America 57(1), s35 (1975)

[4] Atal, B.S.: The History of Linear Prediction. IEEE Signal Processing Magazine 23(2), 154–161 (2006)

[5] Guerchi, D., Mermelstein, P.: Low-rate quantization of spectral information in a 4 kb/s pitch-synchronous CELP coder. In: IEEE Workshop on Speech Coding, Delavan, Wisconsin, USA (2000)

[6] Schneider, P., Hammer, B., Biehl, M.: Adaptive Relevance Matrices in Learning Vector Quantization. Neural Computation 21, 3532–3561 (2009)

[7] Salami, R.A., Laflamme, C., Adoul, J.-P., Massaloux, D.: A Toll quality 8 kb/s speech codec for the personal communications systems (PCS). IEEE Transactions on Vehicular Technology 43(3), 808–816 (1994)

[8] Guerchi, D., Mermelstein, P.: Low-rate quantization of spectral information in a 4 kb/s pitch-synchronous CELP coder. In: IEEE Workshop on Speech Coding, Delavan, Wisconsin, USA (2000)

[9] Chang, C.-C., Chou, Y.-C., Shen, J.-J.: A Discrete Wavelet Transform Based State-Codebook Search Algorithm for Vector Quantization. IEEE Transactions on Innovative Computing, Information and Control, ICICIC 2006, 197–200 (2006)

Incrementally Optimized Decision Tree for Mining Imperfect Data Streams

Hang Yang and Simon Fong

Department of Computer and Information Science, University of Macau,
Taipa, Macau SAR, China
{ya97404,ccfong}@umac.mo

Abstract. The Very Fast Decision Tree (VFDT) is one of the most important classification algorithms for real-time data stream mining. However, imperfections in data streams, such as noise and imbalanced class distribution, do exist in real world applications and they jeopardize the performance of VFDT. Traditional sampling techniques and post-pruning may be impractical for a non-stopping data stream. To deal with the adverse effects of imperfect data streams, we have invented an incremental optimization model that can be integrated into the decision tree model for data stream classification. It is called the Incrementally Optimized Very Fast Decision Tree (I-OVFDT) and it balances performance (in relation to prediction accuracy, tree size and learning time) and diminishes error and tree size dynamically. Furthermore, two new Functional Tree Leaf strategies are extended for I-OVFDT that result in superior performance compared to VFDT and its variant algorithms. Our new model works especially well for imperfect data streams. I-OVFDT is an anytime algorithm that can be integrated into those existing VFDT-extended algorithms based on Hoeffding bound in node splitting. The experimental results show that I-OVFDT has higher accuracy and more compact tree size than other existing data stream classification methods.

Keywords: Data stream mining, decision tree classification, optimized very fast decision tree, incremental optimization.

1   Introduction

Decision tree learning is one of the most significant classifying techniques in data mining and has been applied in many areas, including business intelligence, health-care and biomedicine. The traditional approach to building a decision tree, designed by Greedy Search, loads a complete batch of training data into memory and partitions the data into a hierarchy of nodes and leaves. The tree cannot be changed when new data are acquired, unless the whole model is rebuilt by reloading the complete set of historical data together with the new data. This approach may be unsuitable for unbounded input data, such as data streams in which new data continuously flow in at high speed [1].

R. Benlamri (Ed.): NDT 2012, Part I, CCIS 293, pp. 281–296, 2012.
© Springer-Verlag Berlin Heidelberg 2012

One challenge to decision tree induction is associated with the quality – noisy data and imbalanced class distribution – of the data streams, which generally render a data stream "imperfect" in this context. Noisy data that influence decision models and cause over-fitting problems exist in real world mass data mining. The term "imbalanced" data refers to irregular class distributions in a data set, i.e., a large percentage of training samples may be biased toward class A, leaving few samples that describe class B. Those imperfections significantly impair the accuracy of a decision tree classifier through the confusion and misclassification prompted by the inappropriate data. The size of a decision model will also grow excessively large under noisy data, an undesirable effect known as over-fitting.

In data stream mining, the decision tree learning algorithms construct a decision model incrementally over time. The implementation environment is non-stationary and computational resources are limited. VFML [2] is a C-based tool for mining time-changing, high-speed data streams. MOA [3] is Java-based software for massive data analysis. In both platforms, the parameters of VFDT must be pre-configured by users. For different tree induction tasks, the parameter setup is distinguished. We cannot know what the best configuration is until all possibilities have been tried. However, this is a barrier to using it in real-time applications because there is not enough time to implement "the best setup searching" under non-stopping data environments [4].

The objective of this study can be expressed in the following question: *how can incremental optimization help improve the performance of a data stream mining classifier under imperfect data stream inputs?* Following this primary research objective, the existing computational techniques used for incremental optimization are extended. An innovative and effective incremental optimization model called the Incrementally Optimized Very Fast Decision Tree (I-OVFDT) is presented here. Extensive experiments are conducted and the results are critically analyzed. For further experiments, the new incremental optimization model is infused with other similar data stream mining algorithms wherever technically possible and included in comparative tests vis-à-vis with I-OVFDT. It is anticipated that the new model will contribute valuable theoretical knowledge to the data mining community.

The contributions of I-OVFDT can be summarized briefly as follows. (1) It pioneers the combination of incremental optimization with decision tree models for high-speed data streams. (2) It proposes an optimization algorithm in which the parameters for tree growing are automatically computed instead of taken from fixed values. (3) It proposes an incremental model that balances the accuracy, tree size and learning time of tree models. (4) This optimization algorithm is also suitable for other tree inductions that inherit a similar node-splitting principle (using HB).

The remainder of this paper is structured as follows. We review the original decision tree algorithms and the mechanism of controlling tree growth in Section 2. Assumptions, metrics definitions and the optimization mechanism are given in Section 3. The tree building approach is presented in Section 4. An evaluation and experiment provide evidence that I-OVFDT delivers better performance than VFDT in Section 5. Conclusions are drawn in Section 6.

2   Decision Tree Learning For Data Streams

2.1   Decision Tree Using Hoeffding Bound

A decision-tree classification problem is defined as follows. S_i is a set of data stream with the form (X, y), where X is a vector of d attributes and y is the actual discrete class label. Attribute X_i is the ith attribute in X and is assigned a value of $X_{i1}, X_{i2} \ldots X_{ij}$, where $1 \leq i, j \leq d$. Suppose that HT is a tree induction using HB, such as VFDT. The classification goal is to produce a decision tree model from N examples that predicts the classes in future examples with a high accuracy. In data stream mining, the example size is unbounded that $N \rightarrow \infty$.

A VFDT algorithm [1] constructs a decision tree by using constant memory and constant time-per-sample. The tree is built by recursively replacing leaves with decision nodes. Sufficient statistics n_{ijk} of attribute X_{ij} values are stored in each leaf y_k. A heuristic evaluation function is used to determine split attributes for converting leaves to nodes. Nodes contain the split attributes and leaves contain only the class labels. The leaf represents a class according to the sample label. The main elements of VFDT include a tree-initializing process that initially contains only a single leaf and a tree-growing process that contains a splitting check that uses a heuristic evaluation function $G(.)$ and HB. VFDT uses information gain as $G(.)$.

$$\varepsilon = \sqrt{\frac{R^2 \ln \left(1/\delta\right)}{2n}} \tag{1}$$

The necessary number of samples (sample#) uses HB, shown in (1), to ensure control over errors in the attribute-splitting distribution selection. In the past decade, VFDT-extended variants have been developed by extending the original VFDT, which is based on the principles of using HB. Table 1 provides a comparison of these VFDT-extended studies and records their pros and cons.

Table 1. VFDT-extended Tree Models

Meth	Strength	Weakness
VFDT[1]	Pioneer that uses HB for infinite data streams	Not for imperfect data streams
CVFDT [6]	Uses sliding-window to deal with concept-drift	A fixed tie threshold Makes it hard to detect concept-drift quickly in cases of abrupt concept drift
VFDT$_C$ [7]	Provides Functional Tree Leaf	Not for real-world applications due to tree size explosion
UFFT [9]	One pass algorithm, forest of trees detects concept-drift	Builds a binary tree for each possible pair of classes, not a single tree induction approach
HOT [8]	Provides optional sub-trees And high accuracy post-pruning	Tree size explosion and slow computation speed
OcVFDT [10]	Combines one-class classifier with VFDT	Not for concept-drift
FlexDT [11]	Uses Sigmod function to handle imperfect streams	Slow computation speed

2.2   Node-Splitting Evaluation

Extended from the original desiderata in VFDT, Gama et al. [5] identify three performance dimensions that significantly influence the learning process:

- Space: the available memory is fixed;
- Learning time: the rate of incoming examples processing;
- Generalization power: how effective a model is at capturing the true underlying concept.

The focus is the generalized power of learning algorithm. Although they have recognized that the first two factors had a direct impact on the generalization power of the learning model, in this paper these three dimensions correspond to the tree size, the node-splitting time and the prediction accuracy.

The data stream problem is simulated using a large number of instances, as many as one million for both datasets. The mining approach is a one-pass process that differs from the traditional approach of loading the full set of historical data. The accuracy, tree size and time are recorded as the pre-defined values of τ and n_{min} change. From our previous experimental results [4], we found that:

- In general, bigger tree size brought higher accuracy and more learning time despite possibly causing an over-fitting problem.
- A bigger τ produced faster tree-size growth and longer computation time, but because of the limited memory, when τ reached a threshold the tree size did not increase (0.7 in LED24; 0.4 in Waveform21).
- n_{min} is proposed to control the learning time, and a bigger n_{min} brought a faster learning speed but a smaller tree size and lower accuracy.

The traditional approach to detecting the best parameter configurations for a certain task is to try all of the possibilities. This is impractical, however, for real-time applications. This paper proposes the novel concept of adaptively building an optimal tree model that combines with the incremental optimization mechanism, seeks a compact tree model and balances tree size, prediction accuracy and learning time on the fly. Consequently, the fixed installed parameters are replaced by an adaptive mechanism when new data arrive.

3   Incremental Optimization for Decision Tree Model

3.1   Assumption

Data arrive at the decision tree induction process with very little or no extra time available for refining the tree model. Intermittent pauses are assumed to be undesirable. Post-pruning mechanisms [12] eliminate the "noisy" tree-paths after the tree model has been established, making it unsuitable for use with data streams. Hence, this paper makes the following assumption: *the implementation of a post-pruning mechanism that stops the tree-building process to refine the model by pruning existing tree-paths is not allowed.*

3.2   Optimization Goal

Suppose that the optimization problem Π is defined as a tuple $(X, \mathcal{F}, \Phi)$. The set X is a collection of objects and the feasible solution $\mathcal{F}$ are subsets of X that collectively achieve a certain optimization goal. The set of all feasible solutions is $\mathcal{F} \subseteq 2^X$ and $\Phi: \mathcal{F} \to \mathbb{R}$ is a cost function of these solutions. A weight ω_x with every object x of X is defined as $\Phi(S) = \sum_{x \in S} \omega_x$. The optimal solution $\text{OPT}(X, \mathcal{F}, \Phi)$ exists if X and Φ are awareness, and the subset $S \subseteq X, S \in \mathcal{F}$ is optimizing $\Phi(S)$.

In decision tree form, the solution S is a decision tree model HT_x, whose algorithm is based on Hoeffding tree (HT) using HB in node-splitting control. Therefore, the incremental optimization functions can be expressed as a sum of several sub-objective cost functions:

$$\Phi(HT_x) = \bigcup_{D=1}^{M} \Phi_D(HT_x) \qquad (2)$$

where $\Phi_m : \mathcal{F} \to \mathbb{R}$ is a continuously differentiable function and M is the number of objects in the optimization problem. I-OVFDT is a new methodology for building a desirable tree model by combining with an incremental optimization mechanism and seeking a compact tree model that balances the tree size, prediction accuracy and learning time. Consequently, the fixed installed parameters are replaced by an adaptive mechanism when new data arrive. We consider the optimization as a minimizing cost function problem that:

$$minimize \ \Phi(HT_x) \ subject \ to \ HT_x \in X \qquad (3)$$

The proposed method will find a general optimization function $\Phi(HT_x)$ in (2) that simultaneously considers prediction accuracy, tree size and speed, where $M = 3$.

3.3   Metrics

When a new data stream arrives, it will be sorted from the root to a leaf in terms of the existing HT model. The data stream S_i contains information (X, y), where X is a vector of d attributes and y is the actual discrete class label in a supervised learning process. Attribute X_i is the ith attribute in X and is assigned a value of $X_{i1}, X_{i2} \ldots X_{ij}$, where $1 \leq i, j \leq d$. The decision tree algorithm uses $\widehat{y_k} = HT(X)$ to predict the class when a new data sample (X, y_k) arrives. The prediction accuracy $accu_n$ is dynamically changing with the example size n growing in an incremental learning process, defined as:

$$accu_n = \frac{\sum_{i=1}^{n} Predict(S_i)}{n} \qquad (4)$$

$$Predict(S_i) = \begin{cases} 1, if \ \widehat{y_k} = y_k \\ 0, if \ \widehat{y_k} \neq y_k \end{cases} \qquad (5)$$

To measure the utility of the three dimensions via the minimizing function in (3), the measure of prediction accuracy is reflected by the prediction error in (6):

$$\Phi_1 = erro_n = 1 - accu_n \qquad (6)$$

The classification's goal is to produce a decision tree model *HT* from *N* examples that predicts the class $\widehat{y_k}$ in future examples with accuracy *p*. In data stream mining, the example size is very large, even unlimited, so that $n \rightarrow \infty$.

A *tree path*, traveling from the root to a leaf, represents a regression pattern – the class $\hat{y}$ stated in the leaf. When an internal node splits to create a new leaf, the total number of leaves grows. A decision model is a tree-like structure that presents the patterns of non-linear relationship mapping between *X* and the class by the tree-paths. The number of leaves in the decision model represents the number of patterns/rules in this model. Therefore, *the definition of tree size is the number of leaves in the decision model*. When a leaf is being generated, the tree size grows. The data flow continuously with the decision model incrementally refreshing each time a new leaf is created. Therefore, the tree size function is:

$$\Phi_2 = size_n = \begin{cases} size_{n-1} + 1 & , if\ \Delta\bar{G} > HB \\ \\ size_{n-1} & , otherwise \end{cases} \tag{7}$$

Previously, Section 2.1 illustrated the conditions of VFDT node splitting, which inherits the use of HB in (1), where $\Delta\bar{G} = \bar{G}(x_a) - \bar{G}(x_b)$ is the difference between the two highest-quality attributes.

VFDT is a one-pass algorithm that builds a decision model using a single scan over the training data. The sufficient statistics that count the number of examples passed to an internal node, are the only updated elements in the one-pass algorithm. The calculation is a "plus one" incremental process that consumes little computational resources. Hence, the computation speed of this "plus one" operation for a new example passing is supposed as a constant value *R* in the learning process. The number of examples that have passed within an interval period of in node splitting control determines the learning time. In VFDT, n_{min} is a fixed value for controlling the interval time checking node splitting.

$$\Phi_3 = Time_n = R \times (n_{y_k} - n_{min}) \tag{8}$$

Suppose that n_{y_k} is the number of examples seen at a leaf y_k and the condition that checks node-splitting is $n_{y_k} mod\ n_{min} = 0$. The learning time of each node splitting is the interval period – the time defined in (8) – during which a certain number of examples have passed.

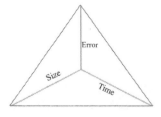

Fig. 1. A triangle of three-object utility models

Returning to the incremental optimization problem, the optimum tree model is the HT_x structure with the minimum $\phi(x)$. A triangle model is provided to illustrate the relationship amongst the three dimensions – the prediction accuracy, the tree size and the learning time. The three dimensions construct a triangle utility function shown in Figure 1. A utility function computes the area of this triangle, reflecting a balance amongst the 3 objectives in (9):

$$\Phi(HT_x) = \frac{\sqrt{3}}{4} \cdot (Erro_x \cdot Size_x + Erro_x \cdot Time_x + Size_x \cdot Time_x) \tag{9}$$

The area of this triangle $\Phi(HT_x)$ changes when node splitting happens and the HT updates. A min-max constraint of the optimization goal in (3) controls the node splitting, which ensures that the new tree model keeps a $\Phi(HT_x)$ within a considerable range. Suppose that $Max.\Phi(HT_x)$ is a HT model with the maximum utility so far and $Min.\Phi(HT_x)$ is a HT model with the minimum utility. The optimum model should be within this min-max range, near the $Mean.\Phi(HT_x)$:

$$Mean.\Phi(HT_x) = \frac{Max.\Phi(HT_x) - Min.\Phi(HT_x)}{2} \tag{10}$$

According to the Chernoff bound [15], we know:

$$|Opt.\Phi(HT_x^*) - Mean.\Phi(HT_x)| \leq \sqrt{\frac{\ln(1/\delta)}{2n}} \tag{11}$$

where the range of $\Phi_x(HT_x)$ is within the min-max model that $Min.\Phi(HT_x) < Opt.\Phi(HT_x^*) < Max.\Phi(HT_x)$. Therefore, if $\Phi(HT_x)$ goes beyond this constraint the existing HT is not suitable to embrace the new data input and the tree model should not be updated. The node-splitting condition is adaptively re-optimized in OVFDT such that: $\Delta\bar{G} > HB$, or $Opt.\Phi(HT_x^*) > Max.\Phi(HT_x)$, or $Opt.\Phi(HT_x^*) < Min.\Phi(HT_x)$, instead of a fixed tie-breaking threshold.

3.4   Embedded with Functional Tree Leaf

The Functional Tree Leaf [7], further enhancing the prediction accuracy via the embedded Naïve Bayes classifier, makes the prediction of HT. I-OVFDT is an incremental optimization that uses prediction accuracy, tree size and learning time. Embedding the Functional Tree Leaf is proposed to improve the performance of prediction by HT model. When these two extensions – an optimized tree growing process in the training phase and a refined prediction using the Functional Tree Leaf in the testing phase – are used together, the new decision tree model is able to achieve unprecedentedly good performance in terms of high prediction accuracy and compact tree size, although the data streams are perturbed by noise and imbalanced class distribution. The proposed model combines I-OVFDT and the Functional Tree Leaf to produce consistently good performance compared to VFDT and its variants.

For the actual classification, I-OVFDT uses $\hat{y}_k = HT_F(X)$ to predict the class label when a new sample (X, y) arrives. The predictions are made according to the observed class distribution (OCD) in the leaves, called Functional Tree Leaf F. Originally in VFDT the prediction used only the majority class Functional Tree Leaf

F^{MC}. The majority class only considers the counts of the class distribution, but not the decisions based on attribute combinations. The naïve Bayes Functional Tree Leaf F^{NB} was proposed to compute the conditional probabilities of the attribute-values given a class at the tree leaves by naïve Bayes. As a result, the prediction at the leaf is refined by the consideration of each attribute's probabilities. To handle the imbalanced class distribution in a data stream, a weighted naïve Bayes Functional Tree Leaf F^{WNB} and an adaptive Functional Tree Leaf $F^{Adaptive}$ are proposed in this paper.

Sufficient statistics n_{ijk} is an incremental count number stored in each node in the I-OVFDT. Suppose that a node $Node_{ij}$ in HT is an internal node labeled with attribute x_{ij}. Suppose that k is the number of classes distributed in the training data, where $k \geq 2$. A vector V_{ij} is constructed from the sufficient statistics n_{ijk} in $Node_{ij}$, such that $V_{ij} = \{n_{ij1}, n_{ij\,2}...n_{ij\,k}\}$. V_{ij} is the OCD vector of $Node_{ij}$. OCD stores the distributed class count at each tree node in I-OVFDT, helping to keep track of the occurrences of the instances of each attribute.

Majority Class Functional Tree Leaf. In the OCD vector, the majority class Functional Tree Leaf F^{MC} chooses the class with the maximum distribution as the predictive class in a leaf, where F^{MC}: arg max $f = \{n_{i,j,1}, n_{i,j,2}...\ n_{i,j,r}...\ n_{i,j,k}\}$, and where $0 < r < k$.

Naïve Bayes Functional Tree Leaf. In the OCD vector $V_{i,j} = \{n_{i,j,1}, n_{i,j,2}...\ n_{i,j,r}...\ n_{i,j,k}\}$, where r is the number of observed classes and $0 < r < k$, the naïve Bayes Functional Tree Leaf F^{NB} chooses the class with the maximum possibility, as computed by the Naïve Bayes, as the predictive class in a leaf. $n_{ij,r}$ is updated to $n'_{ij,r}$ by the naïve Bayes function such that $n'_{i,j,r} = P(X|C_f) \cdot P(C_f) / P(X)$, where X is the new arrival instance. Hence, the prediction class is F^{NB}: arg max $i = \{\ n'_{i,j,1}, n'_{i,j,2}...\ n'_{i,j,r}...\ n'_{i,j,k}\ \}$.

Weighted Naïve Bayes Functional Tree Leaf. In the OCD vector $V_{i,j} = \{n_{i,j,1}, n_{i,j,2}...\ n_{i,j,r}...\ n_{i,j,k}\}$, where k is the number of observed classes and $0 < r < k$, the weighted naïve Bayes Functional Tree Leaf F^{WNB} chooses the class with the maximum possibility, as computed by the weighted naïve Bayes, as the predictive class in a leaf. $n_{i,j,r}$ is updated to $n'_{i,j,r}$ by the weighted naïve Bayes function such that $n'_{i,j,r} = \omega_r \cdot P(X|C_f) \cdot P(C_f) / P(X)$, where X is the new arrival instance and the weight is the probability of class i distribution among all the observed samples, such that $\omega_r = \prod_{r=1}^{k} (v_r / \sum_{r=1}^{k} v_r)$, where $n_{i,j,r}$ is the count of class r. Hence, the prediction class is F^{WNB}: arg max $f = \{\ n'_{i,j,1}, n'_{i,j,2}...\ n'_{i,j,r}...\ n'_{i,j,k}\ \}$.

Adaptive Functional Tree Leaf. In a leaf, suppose that V_F^{MC} is the observed class distribution vector with the majority class Functional Tree Leaf F^{MC}; suppose V_F^{NB} is the observed class distribution vector with the naïve Bayes Functional Tree Leaf F^{NB} and suppose that V_F^{WNB} is the observed class distribution vector with the weighted naïve Bayes Functional Tree Leaf F^{WNB}. Suppose that y is the true class of a new instance X and E_F is the prediction error rate using a Functional Tree Leaf F. E_F is calculated by the average $E = error_i / n$, where n is the number of examples and $error_i$ is the number of examples mis-predicted using F. The adaptive Functional Tree Leaf chooses the class with the minimum error rate predicted by the other three strategies, where $F^{Adaptive}$: arg min $F = \{E_F^{MC}, E_F^{NB}, E_F^{WNB}\}$.

4   I-OVFDT Tree Building

The I-OVFDT tree-building approach is presented in the pseudo code in this section. On the base of the metrics, the input parameters are given in Figure 2. I-OVFDT is described in detail in Figure 3. For a new tree model, the tree should be initialized with a single root (Figure 4). When a new data stream arrives it traverses from the root to a predicted Functional Tree Leaf according to the existing tree model (Figure 5). If the node-splitting checks are met, the node-splitting estimation is implemented in Figure 6.

INPUT:
S :   A stream of sample
X :   A set of symbolic attributes
G(.) :   Heuristic function used for node-splitting
          estimation
δ :   One minus the desired probability of choosing a
          correct attribute at any given node
n_{min} :   The minimum number of samples between check
          node-splitting estimation
F :   A functional tree leaf strategy
OUTPUT:
HT :   A decision tree

Fig. 2. Pseudo code of I-OVFDT input variables

PROCEDURE: *OVFDT(S, X, G(.), δ, n_{min}, F)*
1. A data stream S arrives
2. IF *HT* is null, THEN *initializeHT(S, X, G(.), δ, n_{min}, F)*
    ELSE *traverseHT(S, HT, F)* and update *Error*
3. Label *l* as the predicted class among the samples seen so far at
    the leaf *l*.
4. Let n_{yk} be the number of samples seen at the leaf with class y_k.
5. IF the samples seen so far at leaf *l* do not all belong to the
    same class, and (n_{yk} mod n_{min}) is zero, THEN
6. Calculate *Size* by (7)
7. Calculate *Time* by (8)
8. *doNodeSplittingEstimation(S, X, G(.), δ, n_{min})*
9. Return *HT*

Fig. 3. Pseudo code of I-OVFDT overall approach

PROCEDURE: *initializeHT(S, X, G(.), δ, n_{min})*
1. Let HT be a tree with a single leaf l (the root). Let $X_l = X \cup \{X_\emptyset\}$
2. Let $G_l(X_\emptyset)$ be the G(.) obtained by predicting the class in S,
    according to F.
3. FOR each class y_k
4. // y_k is the class lable y with the kth label
5.   FOR each value x_{ij} of attribute $X_i \in X$
6.   Reset OCD: $n_{ijk}(l)=0$
7.   // $n_{ijk}(l)$ is the count of attribute with x_{ij} and y_k at leaf l
8.   END-FOR
9. END-FOR
10. Return *HT* with a single root

Fig. 4. Pseudo code of I-OVFDT tree initializing

One of our innovations is the optimized node-splitting condition, which combines with the incremental optimization model and the prediction of the Functional Tree Leaf. This innovation not only suits the original VFDT, but also some extensions, such as CVFDT and HOT, by proposing incremental optimization for incremental tree-building induction that settles the problems of mining high-speed data streams.

PROCEDURE: *traverseHT(S, HT, F)*
1. Sort S from the root to a leaf by HT. Update OCD in each node:
   $n_{ijk}(l)$ ++
2. Switch (F)
3.   Case F^{MC}: predict the class y'_k with max $n_{ijk}(l)$
4.   Case F^{NB}: predict the class y'_k with max NB prob.
5.   Case F^{WNB}: predict the class y'_k with max WNB prob.
6.   Case $F^{Adaptive}$: predict the class y'_k using F with Error$_{min}$
7. IF y'_k equals to the actual class label in S, THEN C_T ++
8. ELSE C_F ++
9. $Error = C_F/(C_T+C_F)$ in (4)
10. Return $Error$

Fig. 5. Pseudo code of I-OVFDT tree traversing

PROCEDURE *doNodeSplittingEstimation(S, X, G(.), δ)*
1. FOR each attribute $X_i \in X_l - \{X_\emptyset\}$ at the leaf l
2.   Compute $G_i(X_i)$
3.   Let X_a be the attribute with highest $G_i(.)$ and X_b with the
      2nd highest $G_i(.)$
4.   Compute HB with δ
5.   Let $\Delta G_i = G_i(X_a) - G_i(X_b)$
6. END-FOR
7. Calculate $\Phi_x(HT_x)$, according to *Error, Time and Size* in (9)
8. IF $(\Delta G_i > HB)$ or $(\Phi_x(HT_x) < \Phi_{min}(HT_x))$
      or $(\Phi_x(HT_x) > \Phi_{max}(HT_x))$
9.   Replace l by an internal node splits on X_a
10.   IF $(\Phi_x(HT_x) < \Phi_{min}(HT_x))$ $\Phi_{min}(HT_x) = \Phi_x(HT_x)$
11.   IF $(\Phi_x(HT_x) > \Phi_{max}(HT_x))$ $\Phi_{max}(HT_x) = \Phi_x(HT_x)$
12.   FOR each branch of splitting
13.   Add a new leaf l_m and let $X_m = X - \{X_a\}$
14.   Let $G(X_\emptyset)$ be $G(.)$ obtained by predicting the class in S,
         according to F at l_m
15.   FOR each class y_k and each value x_{ij} of each attribute
16. $X_i \in X_m - \{X_\emptyset\}$ and reset OCD: $n_{ijk}(l) = 0$
17.   END-FOR
18.   END-FOR
19. END-IF
20. Return updated HT

Fig. 6. Pseudo code of I-OVFDT tree growing

5   Experiment

5.1   Platform and Dataset

An I-OVFDT Java package integrated with a MOA toolkit was constructed as a simulation platform for experiments. The running environment was a Windows 7 PC with an Intel 2.8GHz CPU and 8Gb RAM. In all of the experiments, the parameters of the algorithms were $\delta = 10^{-6}$ and $n_{min} = 200$, the default values suggested by MOA, where δ is the allowable error in split decisions, with values closer to zero taking longer to decide (used in HB calculation), and n_{min} is the default number of instances a leaf should observe between split attempts. This section provides evidence of the improvement that I-OVFDT delivers compared to the original VFDT and others.

The experimental datasets, including pure nominal datasets, pure numeric datasets and mixed datasets, were either synthetics generated by the MOA generator or extracted from real-world applications that are publicly available for download from the UCI repository [9]. Each experimental dataset is described in Table 2. The generated datasets were also used in previous VFDT-related studies.

Table 2. Description of experimental datasets

Name	Nom#	Num#	Cls#	Type	Size
LED7	7	0	10	Synthetic	10^6
LED24	24	0	10	Synthetic	10^6
Waveform 21	0	21	3	Synthetic	10^6
Waveform 40	0	40	3	Synthetic	10^6
Random Tree Simple (RTS)	10	10	2	Synthetic	10^6
Random Tree Complex (RTC)	50	50	2	Synthetic	10^6
Cover Type (COVTYPE	42	12	7	UCI	581,012

Noise-Included Synthetic Data. *LED data* was generated by MOA. We added 10% noisy data to simulate imperfect data streams. The LED7 problem used 7 binary attributes to classify 10 different classes and the LED24 used 24 binary attributes. *Waveform* was generated by the MOA generator. The goal of this task was to differentiate between three different classes of Waveform. There were two types of waveform: Wave21 had 21 numeric attributes and Wave40 had 40 numeric attributes, all of which contained noise. *Random Tree (RTS and RTC)* was also generated by the MOA generator. The dataset was based on [12]. It built a decision tree by choosing attributes to split randomly and assigning a random class label to each leaf. As long as a tree was constructed, new samples were generated by assigning uniformly distributed random values to attributes. Those attributes determined the class label throughout the tree. **UCI Data** *Cover Type* was used to predict forest cover types from cartographic variables. It is a typical imbalanced class distribution data that all are real life samples.

5.2   Compared with VFDT

The first experiment compares I-OVFDT and VFDT with different tie-breaking thresholds, showing the performances of the three dimensions (prediction accuracy, tree size and learning time). In VFDT, the tie-breaking threshold is used to control tree-growth, which reflects tree size and learning time. This user-configured parameter also influences prediction accuracy in VFDT. We cannot know what the best setup is until all possibilities have been tried – an impractical scenario for online algorithms. I-OVFDT uses an incremental optimization model to balance the 3 factors.

Based on the previous experiment [4] we know that in I-OVFDT, the bigger tree size led to a higher accuracy even in cases of an over-fitting problem, but it took more learning time. In Table 3, similar instances of accuracy have been highlighted. For example, in the LED7 dataset, the similar accuracy of VFDT (τ=0.6) is selected as a benchmark for comparison to I-OVFDT, but the tree size has been reduced 27% in I-OVFDT. This phenomenon also appears in the other experimental data. Therefore, we find that I-OVFDT can obtain considerable accuracy, but for a smaller tree size than the original VFDT.

Table 3. I-OVFDT compared to VFDT (different τ)

Data	Dimension	I-OVFDT	VFDT τ=0.2	VFDT τ=0.4	VFDT τ=0.6	VFDT τ=0.8
LED7	Acc(%)	73.82	73.15	73.67	73.82	73.85
	Size(#)	2414 (-27%)	577	2189	3301	3326
	Time(s)	0.008	0.014	0.007	0.007	0.005
LED24	Acc(%)	73.81	73.10	73.57	73.77	73.80
	Size(#)	3074 (-20%)	510	1918	3738	3842
	Time(s)	0.007	0.032	0.010	0.006	0.006
WAVE21	Acc(%)	80.65	80.64	80.90	80.90	80.90
	Size(#)	2240 (-5%)	2364	3557	3557	3557
	Time(s)	0.015	0.015	0.010	0.010	0.010
WAVE40	Acc(%)	80.49	80.39	80.89	80.89	80.89
	Size(#)	2345 (-1%)	2369	3607	3607	3607
	Time(s)	0.026	0.026	0.018	0.018	0.018
RTS	Acc(%)	93.00	91.93	93.16	93.16	93.16
	Size(#)	2322 (-25%)	3081	2683	2683	2683
	Time(s)	0.012	0.009	0.010	0.010	0.010
RTC	Acc(%)	95.66	95.52	95.55	95.55	95.55
	Size(#)	975 (-35%)	1546	1492	1492	1492
	Time(s)	0.117	0.074	0.077	0.077	0.077

5.3   Compared with Functional Tee Leaf for VFDT

Majority class (MC) is the original function used in VFDT to predict class. A Naïve Bayes (NB) Functional Tree Leaf [7] is proposed to improve the prediction accuracy embedded in the leaf. This paper provides a new Functional Tree Leaf strategy called the Weight Naïve Bayes (WNB). In addition, the WNB has been integrated with a Hybrid Adaptive [3] functional leaf in MOA that uses the error rate as an adaptive scenario (ADP).

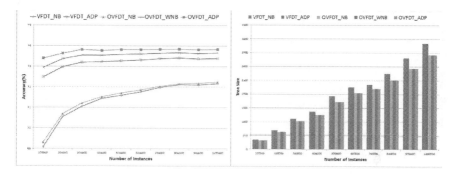

Fig. 7. Accuracy and tree size comparison of functional tree leaves for LED24 data

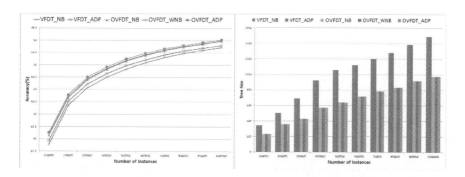

Fig. 8. Accuracy and tree size comparison of functional tree leaves for RTC data

In the second experiment, I-OVFDT is integrated with functional tree leaves, compared to VFDT. The experimental analysis (in Section 5.2) shows the best accuracy of VFDT (i.e., $\tau=0.8$ in LED24; $\tau=0.4$ in RTC). Figures 7 and 8 show that I-OVFDT has obviously better performance than VFDT when integrated with functional tree leaves, consequently producing higher accuracy and much smaller size.

5.4　Compared with VFDT-extended Tree Models

The third experiment shows the performance of I-OVFDT when integrated with existing VFDT-extended algorithms. The experimental data are Cover Type downloaded from UCI machine learning repository. These data are a typical sample of imbalance class distribution problems. As a benchmark analysis, we use the VFDT-extended algorithms in MOA as follows:

Ensemble HT. [13] is online bagging with 10 ensemble classifiers. **Adaptive-Size Hoeffding Tree (ASHT)** [14] is derived from the VFDT, but adds a maximum number of split nodes or size. **Hoeffding Option Tree (HOT)** [8] is derived from VFDT adding additional option nodes that allow several tests to be applied. The configuration is $maxOptionPaths=5$, $\delta=10^{-7}$ and $\delta'=0.999$. **AdaHOT** [14] is derived from HOT. Each leaf stores an estimation of current error. The weight of each node in the voting process is proportional to the square of the inverse of the error. The I-OVFDT incremental optimization is added to the abovementioned VFDT-extended algorithms. As the experimental results in Figure 9 show, I-OVFDT integration produces better accuracy than that of VFDT-extended algorithms.

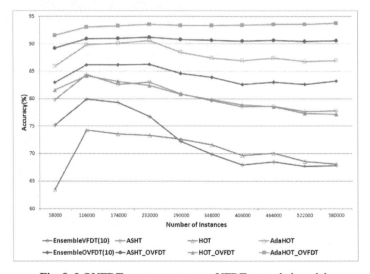

Fig. 9. I-OVFDT compares to some VFDT-extended models

6　Conclusion

Decision tree algorithms for mining data streams should be reliable and extendable. The original VFDT advocates a simple method of using Hoeffding Bound to control node splitting in tree construction. It succeeds as an anytime algorithm that only requires scanning data once and suits high-speed data environments. However, imperfect data causes problems such as over-fitting, tree size explosion and imbalanced class distribution that deteriorate classification accuracy. The original

VFDT uses a fixed tie-breaking threshold to handle tree size explosion. However, a pre-defined threshold cannot fit all applications at one time. We do not know what the best setup is until all possibilities have been tried, reducing the applicability of VFDT in real-time applications.

In this paper, we describe an incremental optimization model that combines with decision tree learning for mining data streams called the Incrementally Optimized Very Fast Decision Tree (I-OVFDT). A three-dimensional balance (prediction accuracy, tree size and learning time) is obtained that reduces the error and tree size. In addition, two new Functional Tree Leaf classification strategies are integrated into I-OVFDT, resulting in a better performance than the existing algorithms, especially for imbalanced class distribution data streams. Furthermore I-OVFDT is an anytime algorithm that can integrate with the existing VFDT-extended algorithms using HB. As the experimental results shown in Section 5, the advantages of I-OVFDT are significant.

References

1. Pedro, D., Geoff, H.: Mining high-speed data streams. In: Proc. of the Sixth ACMSIGKDD International Conference on Knowledge Discovery and Data Mining, pp. 71–80. ACM (2000)
2. Geoff, H., Pedro, D.: VFML-a toolkit for mining high-speed time-changing data streams (2003), http://www.cs.washington.edu/dm/vfml/
3. Bifet, A., Holmes, G., Kirkby, R., Pfahringer, B.: MOA: Massive online analysis. Journal of Machine Learning Research 11, 1601–1604 (2010)
4. Yang, H., Fong, S.: Moderated VFDT in Stream Mining Using Adaptive Tie Threshold and Incremental Pruning. In: Cuzzocrea, A., Dayal, U. (eds.) DaWaK 2011. LNCS, vol. 6862, pp. 471–483. Springer, Heidelberg (2011)
5. Gama, J., Sebastião, R., Rodrigues, P.P.: Issues in evaluation of stream learning algorithms. In: Proceedings of the 15th ACM SIGKDD International Conference on Knowledge Discovery and Data Mining (KDD 2009), pp. 329–338. ACM, New York (2009)
6. Hulten, G., Spencer, L., Domingos, P.: Mining time-changing data streams. In: Proc. of the Seventh ACM SIGKDD International Conference on Knowledge Discovery and Data Mining, San Francisco, California, pp. 97–106 (2001)
7. Gama, J., Ricardo, R.: Accurate decision trees for mining high-speed data streams. In: Proc. of the Ninth ACM SIGKDD International Conference on Knowledge Discovery and Data Mining, pp. 523–528. ACM (2003)
8. Pfahringer, B., Holmes, G., Kirkby, R.: New options for Hoeffding trees. In: Proc. of the 20th Australian Joint Conference on Advances in Artificial Intelligence, Gold Coast, Australia, pp. 90–99 (2007)
9. Gama, J., Medas, P., Rodrigues, P.: Learning decision trees from dynamic data streams. In: Proc. of the 2005 ACM Symposium on Applied Computing, Santa Fe, New Mexico, pp. 573–577 (2005)
10. Chen, L., Yang, Z., Xue, L.: OcVFDT: one-class very fast decision tree for one-class classification of data streams. In: Proc. of the Third International Workshop on Knowledge Discovery from Sensor Data, pp. 79–86. ACM (2009)

11. Sattar, H., Ying, Y.: Flexible decision tree for data stream classification in the presence of concept change, noise and missing values. Data Min. Knowl. Discov., 1384–5810 19(1), 95–131 (2009)
12. Bradford, J., Kunz, C., Kohavi, R., Brunk, C., Brodley, C.: Pruning Decision Trees with Misclassification Costs. In: Nédellec, C., Rouveirol, C. (eds.) ECML 1998. LNCS, vol. 1398, pp. 131–136. Springer, Heidelberg (1998)
13. Oza, N., Russell, S.: Online bagging and boosting. In: Artificial Intelligence and Statistics 2001, pp. 105–112. Morgan Kaufmann (2001)
14. Kirkby, R.: Improving Hoeffding Trees. PhD thesis, University of Waikato, New Zealand (2008)
15. Chernoff, H.: A measure of asymptotic efficiency for tests of a hypothesis based on the sums of observations. Annals of Mathematical Statistics 23, 493–507 (1952)

Knowledge Representation Using LSA and DRT Rules for Semantic Search of Documents

Sofiane Allioua[1,2] and Zizette Boufaida[2]

[1] Ecole Normale Supérieure, Constantine, Algeria
allioua.sofiane@gmail.com
[2] LIRE laboratory, Mentouri University, Constantine, Algeria
{allioua.sofiane,zboufaida}@gmail.com

Abstract. Search engines are supposed to return all relevant documents to users. The existing search engines read the text as a sequence of words without meaning. The search is then limited to find documents that contain the same words than the user's query that reduces the relevance in returned documents.

In this work, we propose a semantic search engine that represents user's information need by a pattern of relevance.

Our approach is characterized by the use of Latent Semantic Analysis (LSA) to find the words semantically correlated, semantic links are then created by using Discourse Representation Theory (DRT) that offers the possibility to translate a sentence from natural language to logical representation. The found links are saved in an ontology.

Information retrieval is executed by comparing the knowledge extracted from each document to the relevance pattern of user's request. This allows a better identification of information's needs, and restrict the set of documents returned.

Keywords: Web Semantic, Ontology, Information Retrieval, LSA, DRT.

1   Introduction

Sharing information has become today one of the most complex problems, due to the growth of the number of the documents in the web as well as diversity of information and their formats.

To make it easy for the user to obtain relevant document, current approaches [1] focus on documents representations and interrogation techniques. This latter deal with complex problems related to the ambiguity of natural language and words semantic representation [2].

In this paper, we propose the architecture of a semantic search engine support of latent semantic analysis [3] to generate a semantic space consisting of terms which correlate with the terms of the user's query. Then we use techniques of Discourse Representation Theory (DRT) to establish semantic links between these terms. The latter are stored in an ontology and used in research's step.

R. Benlamri (Ed.): NDT 2012, Part I, CCIS 293, pp. 297–306, 2012.

During the research, a multimodal dialogue is established with the user, allowing him to formulate his information needs formulated by pattern of relevance. Then we compare it with semantic structure of textual corpus.

This paper is organized as follows: Section 2 describes related work in the semantic research. In Section 3, we discuss the model of Latent Semantic Analysis. In Section 4, we suggest solutions to the problems of knowledge representation in information retrieval system. Section 5 deals with the advantages of multimodal user interaction with an information retrieval system, In Section 6, we describe the architecture of proposed system. Section 7 ends with conclusion and perspectives.

2   Related Work

The Information Retrieval Systems (IRS) is originally designed to find relevant documents dealing with a given subject. Actually, these systems describe information with a list of words and use a Boolean Searching to find documents that contain the same words as the query. This issue is obviously inadequate because the user doesn't know which terms are used in the documents collection, even if this kind of searching is relatively efficient. However the major results don't satisfy the user's needs and decrease the precision of the search.

Knowledge modeling approaches use ontologies presented by researchers as a solution to the problem of information representation in IRS

Corese [4] (Conceptual Resource Search Engine) is an RDF engine based on Conceptual Graphs (CG). It enables the processing of RDF Schema and RDF statements within the CG formalism. Research is based on semantic annotations that are instantiations of RDFS schemas.

SeseiOnto [5] is Semantic filtering tools for search engines. It provides the ability to match a conceptual structure extracted from a user's query with another conceptual structure. This last it extracted from a Web document found using a search engine such as Google.

Although these two research systems seem to be useful but they are not widely adopted, they have great disadvantage of being limited to a specific area rather than the Web.

Whatever the system used, a problem that the user confronts is to express its information need. Generally when a user knows what is in collection and how it is structured, it's simply for him to make the query. The system can help the user to define his queries by providing terms related to it. Ontology seems to be the appropriate solution to store these terms.

Based on studies of current search engines we noticed that:

- The user interaction with the system is an interesting source of information possibly for future search.
- The connections between different terms that are used in the document mostly give a semantic description of its contents.
- The query should not be limited to a list of words, but a semantic pattern of information needs have to be formed through dialogue with the user's system.

To clarify the user information needs, we have incorporated in our search engine, an additional step of reformulation of the query by adding significant terms to it. The idea is to recover from the initial query to return other terms that have a semantic link with it, these terms are returned to the user in order to reformulate his query (relevance feedback).

3   Latent Semantic Analysis

In this work, we represent the context of a document by a set of words connected by semantic links incorporated in an ontology. To make out the terms representing the information needs, we use the latent semantic analysis (LSA) [6] based on a multidimensional representation of words. The meaning of each word is characterized by a vector in a large space of dimensions. The proximity between two vectors makes the meaning of those words close.

In this analysis we make a matrix of occurrences of terms, and we use Singular Value Decomposition (SVD) to decompose this matrix into a product of three other matrices. The first one describes the original row entities as vectors of derived orthogonal factor values. The second one describes the original column entities in the same way. The third is a diagonal matrix containing scaling values. In order to get the semantic relationships between words, we reduce the rank of the third matrix before reconstructing the original matrix.

To reduce the number of terms in which we apply this analysis, we use TF * IDF measure [7], which permits us to evaluate how important a word in the collection of documents. The formula combines two criteria:

TF represents the importance of the term for a document (Term Frequency):

A term that appears several times in a document is more important than a term that appears only once.

- W_{ij} represents the number of terms occurrences in the document d_j.
- TF_{ij} represents the frequency of terms in document d_j.

$$TF_{ij} = \frac{W_{ij}}{|d_j|}$$ (1)

IDF is a measure of the general importance of the term (Inverse Document Frequency):

A term that appears in some documents is a better distinction than a term that appears in all documents.

- Df_i is the number of documents containing the term t.
- D is the number of documents in the corpus.

$$IDF_i(t) = \log\left(\frac{D}{Df_i}\right)$$ (2)

A term that has a high value of TF * IDF corresponds to an important distinction of a document.

After selecting the most significant words, we assign each term T_i a weight $W_{i, k}$ depending on the number of occurrences $C_{i,k}$ in the document D_k.

$$W_{i, k} = \frac{C_{i, k}}{\sum_{j=1}^{k} C_{j, k}} \tag{3}$$

To avoid the problem of the height values of terms occurrence in large documents (terms are considered important because occurrence is affected by length of document), we normalize the document length.

$$W_{i, k} = \frac{w_{i, k}}{\sqrt{\sum_{j=1}^{k} W_{j, k}^{2}}} \tag{4}$$

The semantic space is constructed from a singular value decomposition and decrease the rank of the matrix.

$$X_{m \times n} = U_{m \times r} \sum_{r \times r} V^{t}_{r \times n} \tag{5}$$

X: matrix terms/documents
U: is a matrix of terms (m x r)
$\sum$: is a diagonal matrix (r x r) containing the singular values of X
V: is a matrix of documents (r x n)

To determine semantic distance between two terms we calculate PEARSON's coefficient of correlation, represented by the formula:

$$R = \frac{\dfrac{\sum_{i=1}^{n}(x_i - \bar{x})(y_i - \bar{y})}{n-1}}{\sqrt{\dfrac{\sum_{i=1}^{n}(x_i - \bar{x})^2}{n-1}} \sqrt{\dfrac{\sum_{i=1}^{n}(y_i - \bar{y})^2}{n-1}}} \tag{6}$$

R: coefficient of correlation

R is +1 in the case of a perfect positive linear relationship, −1 in the case of a perfect decreasing negative linear relationship, and some value between −1 and 1 in all other cases, indicating the degree of linear dependence between the terms. The correlation becomes stronger between two terms if the coefficient is either −1 or 1. As it approaches zero terms are uncorrelated.

Indeed, two words can be considered if they are semantically close and used in similar contexts. The context is defined as the set of words that appear together. For example: the words (information, computer) are considered semantically close because they appear both in the same context (data, program, printer, etc.).

As a case of study, we have developed a tool to calculate the correlation matrix of term and document. We integrate TreeTagger [8] in our tool to perform lemmatization on English and finding a normalized form of a word. We use Java Matrix Package JAMA [9] which provides useful classes for constructing and manipulating dense matrix as well as fundamental operations like Singular Value Decomposition (SVD) used to decompose the matrix before decreasing its rank. The application result gives the following matrix:

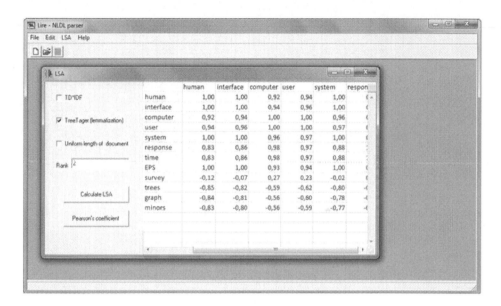

Fig. 1. Matrix of correlated terms

The semantic associations extracted by LSA are not limited to only synonym relations since they come from a treatment of co-occurrence of terms with their contexts.

The fact that the latent semantic analysis can be implemented makes possible its application in various fields.

The method is fully automatic and applicable to a large corpus.

LSA can be an answer to the question of the reusability of ontology. For example, it is possible to imagine an ontological base in the computer field, created by LSA from the analysis of large corpus. This database would contain all the terms represented in the semantic space.

For our system, the construction of ontology would then specify the relations between correlated terms returned by LSA.

4   Knowledge Representation in IRS

To establish semantic links between terms belonging to a semantic space, and after applying LSA on the textual corpus, we use the techniques of DRT (Discourse Representation Theory) [10].

The DRT is an approach that is used to represent logical form of linguistic utterances. Its principal is based on an intermediate level with rules that translate each linguistic expression in a logic model. The representation is built gradually when the interpretation is being progressed.

For each discourse, the DRT associates a representation called DRS (Discourse Representation Structure), which specifies the set of discourse referents.

A DRS is a partial information structure, the DRS of a complex sentence is built gradually, from the DRS K_0, representing the empty context. We step out through the treatment of the first part to get the DRS K_1. And It provides a context for the treatment of the second part to get the DRS K_2.

Example: Linux does not execute a DLL File.

Firstly we decompose the grammatical structure of the sentence (Fig. 2).

After applying the first rules of DRT on the sentence (Sentence→ Noun Phrase Verb Phrase, Noun Phrase→ Proper Name), we get the first structure with DRS K_1 and the word (Linux) as the first reference. To continue processing we decompose the rest of the sentence and we get a second DRS K_2 structure that adds to a second referent (DLL File) and a negative verbal relationship (doesn't execute) between these two referents (Fig. 3).

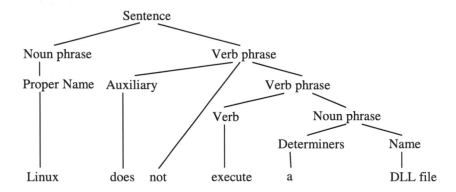

Fig. 2. The Structure of the sentence

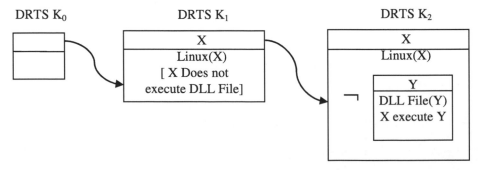

Fig. 3. DRS structures of a sentence

Subsumption Hierarchies:
Linux $\subseteq$ T
DLL File $\subseteq$ T
Rules Definitions:
execute (linux, T)
Concepts Definitions:
Linux:= $\neg(\forall$execute.DLL File)

Fig. 4. Knowledge representation in description Logics

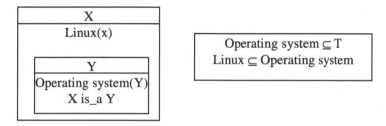

Fig. 5. Subsumption Hierarchies

The purpose behind this is to identify semantic relations between terms for onto-logical concepts in the text, so we can save the DRS interpretations in ontology, by adding rules to translate these interpretations to a description Logics (Fig. 4).

We can also make the concepts in subsumption hierarchies in ontology, by search-ing the sentences of the corpus with verbal relationship (is_a) or analyzing the restric-tions added to the concepts of the ontology.

Example: Linux is an operating system (Fig. 5).

In this example, we expressed a negative sentence in a logical form. With DRT, we can represent other aspects of natural language such as temporal aspects, the plural and semantic links between several sentences. This allows us to have a semantic de-scription and formal of a textual content, saved in ontology.

The knowledge stored in ontology provides the search engine a means of interpre-tation for user's queries and generates after several interactions with him, a diagram describing user's information needs.

5   Multimodal User Interaction

The search engine should be based on a driven-interaction dialogue adapted to exploit resources more efficiently. The problem is that the authors of documents and users use a variety of words to express the same concept.

Generally, the user specifies a query independently, and the system, perceived as a black box, returns a set of documents in response to this request. The risk that relevant terms for the research will be absent is significant. The diversion between the sense that the user wants to express and the sense interpreted by the system is inevitable.

The system should help the user to use the right terms. For this, we must provide a knowledge base, used to support the user through interaction with IRS in research information and help him to express his request, by leading him to make an appropriate reformulation of the query. In this case the task of IRS is to make a sense closer to the query for the user's needs

Research is expressed by a number of terms. These terms must be collected and used by the system. We find the terms given by the user to express request and further provided in return on the current response of the system.

Gradually, as the user interacts with the search engine a pattern of relevance is developed by analyzing the sentences entered by the user, compared with knowledge stored in the ontology.

To guide this interaction we have integrated into the search engine a dialogue manager (Fig. 6) so we can:

- Capture the conceptual representations of the subject from the query.
- Lead user's request by focusing on a topic.
- Reformulate or clarify the user's query.

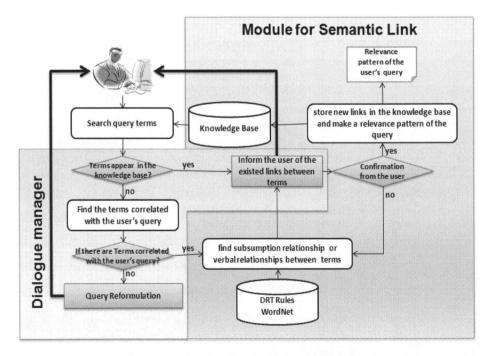

Fig. 6. User interaction with Dialogue Manager

6   Architecture of the Proposed Search Engine

The architecture of the semantic search engine proposed in this work (Fig. 7) consists of the following components:

Module for Semantic Link: with the LSA method described in Section 4, we select the most appropriate words in a document, then the words which are considered correlate by this analysis are linked and stored in the ontology.

Dialogue Manager: The words which hare considered near of the query are returned to the user. Therefore he could reformulate his request. All sentences of dialogue are converted to a new structure summarized in the form of semantic links between words.

Search Engine: Documents returned to the user are organized by comparing relevant pattern of the user's query with the semantic representations of document.

Knowledge Base: Contains ontologies generated by the system and other resources used in processing such as Wordnet and DRT Rules.

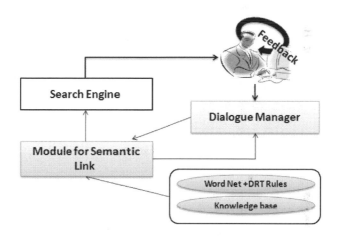

Fig. 7. Architecture of Semantic Search Engine

7   Conclusions and Perspectives

In this paper, we propose the architecture of a semantic search engine based on multimodal interaction to generate a relevant pattern which represents the information needs.

We note that the use of latent semantic analysis makes easy to situate the terms semantic space, and linking these terms by using DRT techniques. However, some DRT rules require more advanced methods in order to store these representations in ontology.

As a perspective we try to add more rules to represent sentences in ontology using DRT techniques. To realize this purpose, we specify representation in ontology for each grammatical word classes. Such representation must be able to express complex sentences in natural language, and don't generate errors when we perform reasoning.

References

1. Malingre, M., Serres, A.: Recherche d'information sur Internet: Approfondissement des moteurs de recherche. URFIST Bretagne-Pays de Loire (2007)
2. Allioua, S., Boufaida, Z.: Recherche sémantique d'images annotées, MCSEAI, Oran-Algeria, pp. 501–507 (2008)
3. Derwester, S., Dumais, S.T., Furnas, G.W., Landauer, T.K., Harshmann, R.: Indexing by Latent Semantic Analysis. Journal of the American Society for Informartion Science, 391–400 (1990)
4. Conceptuel Resource Search Engine,
   http://www.w3.org/2001/sw/wiki/Corese
5. Morneau, M.: SeseiOnto: Interfacing NLP and Ontology Extraction. In: IEEE/WIC/ACM International Conference on Web Intelligence (2006)
6. Landauer, K.T., Foltz, W.P., Laham, D.: An Introduction to Latent Semantic Analysis, pp. 12–19 (1998)
7. Salton, G.: Automatic Text Processing. Addison-Wesley (1989)
8. Schmid, H.: Probabilistic Part of speech Tagging Using Decision Trees (1991)
9. Efficient Java Matrix Library, http://code.google.com/p/efficient-java-matrix-library/wiki/EjmlManual
10. Kamp, H., Reyle, U.: From Discourse To Logic, Introduction to Model theoretic Semantics of Natural Language. In: Formal Logic and Discourse Representation Theory. Springer (1993)

Leaker Identification in Multicast Communication

Emad Eldin Mohamed and Driss Guerchi

School of Engineering, Applied Science and Technology
Canadian University of Dubai
Dubai, United Arab Emirates
{emad,driss}@cud.ac.ae

Abstract. Multicast is a communication mode in which data is exchanged among multiple end systems. An important concern in multicast communications is the protection of copyrights. While preventing copyright violations seems very difficult, tracing copyright violators (leaker identification) is more feasible and can be used as a deterrence alternative. In order to identify leakers in a multicast environment, every receiver should obtain a uniquely marked copy of the data. However, delivering unique copies from the sender to the receivers is inefficient. This paper investigates multicast leaker identification and introduces an efficient solution that is based on binary search tree. We introduce the notion of suspicious set that includes suspected end systems. When a leak is detected, all receivers are inserted in the suspicious set. Using a binary search, the suspicious set is refined successively until it includes only the leakers. An analytical study is conducted to evaluate the proposed solution.

Keywords: multicast communication, copyright protection, leaker identification, tracing traitor.

1   Introduction

Multicast communication concerns the transmission of data from a sender to multiple receivers. Many applications are based on multicast communication. Distance learning, teleconferencing, software distribution, and distributed databases are few examples of multicast based applications. Multicast communication can be implemented either at the network layer or at the application layer. An example of the network layer multicast is the IP multicast [8]. In IP multicast, the sender sends the message one time and the network routers (arranged in a delivery tree rooted at the sender with the receivers as its leaves) distribute the message to the appropriate receivers.

IP multicast has its advantages and disadvantages. Efficiency, flexibility, and scalability are the main strengths of IP multicast. Deployment of IP multicast, however, has been faced with many hurdles. Application layer multicast (also known as overlay multicast) [5] has been introduced as a more feasible solution. In overlay multicast, a delivery tree is built at the application layer such that receivers (rather than network routers) take on the responsibility of traffic delivery. Narada [6] and ALMI [13] are two examples of application layer multicast.

R. Benlamri (Ed.): NDT 2012, Part I, CCIS 293, pp. 307–315, 2012.
© Springer-Verlag Berlin Heidelberg 2012

An important concern in multicast communication is the protection of the copyrights of the multicast data [9]. Copyright protection is the protection granted to authors of original works against the illegal distribution or reproduction of their works. While the prevention of copyright violations seems very difficult to achieve, tracing copyright violators—also known as leaker identification or traitor tracing—is more feasible and can be used as a deterrence alternative. To identify a leaker in a multicast setting, every authorized recipient should receive a differently marked version of the data. Marking the data is a process known as fingerprinting [2, 7] and involves hiding a unique identifier (fingerprint) within the data. Whenever an illegal copy of the data is found, the fingerprint within the data is used to identify the receiver who leaked the data.

A typical leaker identification system consists of three main components: a fingerprint encoder, a monitoring system, and a control system. The fingerprint encoder embeds a fingerprint (as a function of the receiver identity) into the original data such that the fingerprint is invisible to the data recipient and at the same is detectable by the data owner. In addition, removing the fingerprint from the data by an opponent should render the data useless. The function of the monitoring system is to monitor the distribution of the copyrighted material and report any violation back to the control system. The control system compares the input from the monitoring system against the original data and fingerprint codes to identify the leaker.

In multicast settings, leaker identification requires that every receiver obtains a uniquely fingerprinted version of the data. However, this requirement if not satisfied in an efficient manner comes at a very high computation and communication costs. In this paper, we investigate leaker identification in application level multicast communication. We present an efficient solution that employs binary search trees and introduces the notion of suspicious sets. A suspicious set is a set that has as its elements some end systems from which one or more are the leakers. A set of cardinality 1 contains only one end system and exactly identifies the leaker. We use an analytical study to evaluate the performance of the proposed solution.

The rest of this paper is organized as follows. Section 2 discusses a simple solution for leaker identification. Section 3 introduces the new copyright protection technique along with the notion of the suspicious set. Performance evaluation is given in Section 4. Section 5 presents the related work in the field. Section 6 presents the conclusion of this paper.

2　Early Solution

A simple solution for multicast leaker identification is to provide each receiver with a copy of the data that is uniquely fingerprinted [11]. Fig. 1 demonstrates by example how this solution works. As the figure shows, there are 8 receivers in the system (R_1 through R_8). The sender S generates 8 differently fingerprinted versions of the data. It then encrypts each version using a unique key shared between the sender and the intended receiver. The sender forwards 5 versions of the data (P_1, P_2, P_3, P_4, and P_5) to end system R_1 (which acts as a receiver and as a router at the same time) and 3 versions of the data (P_6, P_7, and P_8) to R_6. End system R_1 decrypts its version (P_1) using its key and forwards the rest of the versions to the corresponding end systems. The procedure continues down to the leaf receivers. This way, each receiver ends up with its uniquely fingerprinted copy of the data. Thus, a leaked data copy can be traced back to its receiver.

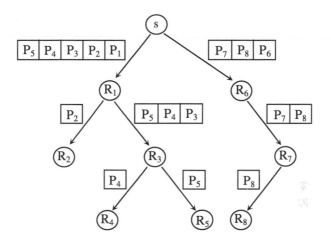

Fig. 1. Simple leaker identification in multicast communication

The above scheme suffers from two deficiencies. First, the communication overhead is high (for instance, the communication link between the sender S and the receiver R_1 delivers 5 copies of the same data). Second, and more important, for n receivers, the sender has to generate and encrypt n fingerprinted versions of the same data message.

3 New Solution

To overcome the deficiencies of the solution presented above, we use an efficient binary search tree technique and introduce the notion of suspicious set, which includes all end systems suspected as leakers. A suspicious set with a cardinality of 1 exactly identifies the leaker; whereas a suspicious set with cardinality greater than 1 need more refinement in order determine the exact leaker. An empty suspicious set means that there is no leak detected in the system.

The binary tree employed in our solution is used to organize the secret keys used in the system. All receivers are logically arranged in a binary tree as Fig. 2 demonstrates (the figure shows the tree for eight receivers, but it can be generalized to any number of receivers). The root of the tree is the sender. The leaf nodes of the tree designate the receivers. Each receiver R_i has a unique key KR_i shared between the receiver and the sender. The intermediate nodes provide group keys KG. Every receiver i knows its key KR_i as well as all group keys KG along the bath from this receiver upward to the sender. The sender knows all group keys and all receivers' keys. The proposed approach can be expressed as follows:

1. Let the number of receivers is n and let the universal set V is the set of all receivers:

$$V = \{R_1, R_2, ..., R_n\}. \tag{1}$$

2. The sender maintains a suspicious set A. Initially A is the empty set ϕ.

$$A = \phi. \tag{2}$$

3. The suspicious set A remains empty as long as no leakage is detected. As long as the suspicious set is empty, the sender fingerprints its multicast data and encrypts them using the root group key KG before sending to the multicast receivers. Doing so, we achieve a minimal overhead.

4. When a leakage is detected, the sender starts a procedure to identify the leaker. It first adds all multicast receivers to suspicious set (taking the union of A and V) resulting on a suspicious set that is equal the universal set V.

$$A = A \cup V. \tag{3}$$

5. The sender sends two versions of the data along the paths of the two branches of the key distribution tree. Each version is uniquely fingerprinted and encrypted using the group key of the branch KG_i. The multicast traffic is then monitored to detect leakage and identify which branch the leakage has started from. Only the receivers along the identified branch are included in the suspicious subset. Let the set G_i be a set with all receivers of branch i as its elements. The new suspicious set A can be determined as the intersection of A and G_i, Where G_i is the set from which a leak is detected.

$$A = A \cap G_i. \tag{4}$$

6. The procedure of step 5 is performed recursively until a specific receiver is identified as the leaker.

Using the suspicious set in the successive manner as explained above provides a significant saving on the sender computation cost as well as in the communication overhead (specially along the paths which do not include leakers) as Section 4 shows.

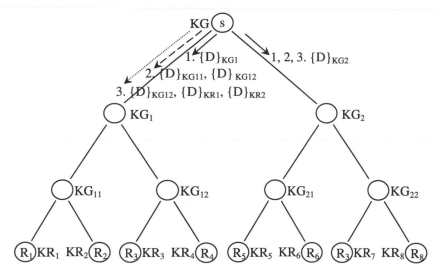

Fig. 2. Binary search tree leaker identification example

Fig. 2 demonstrates the operations of the leaker identification process. The figure assumes that the system includes 8 receivers and that receiver R_2 is the leaker. When a leak is detected, the sender starts the leaker identification process by sending two differently fingerprinted versions of the data copy (step 1 in the figure). The first copy is encrypted by KG_1 and the second by KG_2. The leak detection system monitors the system to detect from which branch the data is leaked. Since we assume that R_2 is the source of leak, the left branch is identified as the leak source. The sender in step 2 sends three differently fingerprinted versions of the data copy encrypted as follows: version 1 encrypted by KG_2 (to the right branch), the version 2 encrypted by KG_{11}, and version 3 encrypted by KG_{12}. The leak detection system monitors the system again to detect the leak source. In this case, it is the branch encrypted by KG_{11}. The sender in step 3 sends 4 differently fingerprinted versions of the data copy encrypted as follows: version 1 encrypted by KG_2, version 2 encrypted by KG_{12}, version 3 encrypted by KR_1, and version 4 encrypted KR_2. The leak detection system monitors the system for the last time to identify R_2 as the leaker.

4   Performance Evaluation

We evaluate the performance of the proposed solution against a base case of application level multicast where the delivery tree has the sender as its root and the receivers as the intermediate and leaf nodes. In this base setting, only one copy of the data is sent from the sender to the receivers (every receiver receives one copy) and every link in the delivery tree should not carry this copy more than one time.

The performance of the proposed solution can be measured along three dimensions: computation overhead at the sender, computation overhead at the receivers, and communication overhead. The computation overheads at the sender and receivers measure how many more copies the sender and receivers have to handle compared with the base case. Similarly, the communication overhead is a measure of how much extra traffic the network links have to carry compared with the base case.

Let the number of receivers in the multicast group be n. The depth d of the key distribution binary tree can be expressed as follows:

$$d = \lceil \log_2 n \rceil. \tag{5}$$

Where the function $\lceil x \rceil$ is the smallest integer larger than or equal to x.

4.1   Computation Overhead at the Sender

Let the processing effort to fingerprint and encrypt one data copy be P_f. The computation effort at the sender P_s, which constitutes the sender's computation overhead, can be expressed as follows:

$$P_s = \left(\sum_{i=1}^{d} (i+1) \right) P_f. \tag{6}$$

Equation (6) can be simplified as follows:

$$P_s = \frac{d^2 + 3d}{2} P_f. \tag{7}$$

Using the big-O notation, the sender's overhead is $O(\log_2 n)^2$, where n is the number of receivers.

4.2   Computation Overhead at the Receivers:

The computation overhead at the receiver P_r is simply the processing effort needed to decrypt the received version of the data. Let the processing effort to decrypt one data version is P_d. Then P_r can be given as follows:

$$P_r = P_d. \tag{8}$$

Using the big-O notation, the receiver's overhead is $O(1)$.

4.3   Communication Overhead

The number of extra sent data versions C can be expressed as follows:

$$C = \sum_{i=1}^{d} i. \tag{9}$$

Equation (9) can be simplified as follows:

$$C = \frac{d^2 + d}{2}. \tag{10}$$

Using the big-O notation, the communication overhead is $O(\log_2 n)^2$, where n is the number of receivers.

5   Related Work

Several researchers have investigated the problem of distributing copyright protected multicast data and proposed solutions for it. Examples of previous work include Chameleon [1], Watercasting [3], secure multicast protocol with copyright protection [4], WHIM [10], and trusted soft-engine based solution [12].

Chameleon [1] is an encryption-based fingerprinting that targets audio streams. The sender encrypts the multicast data and sends same version to receivers. Receivers, on the other hand, have different decryption keys. Decrypting the received data using different keys results in slightly different versions of the data. The scheme, however, is vulnerable to collusion attack.

Brown et al. [3] introduced Watercasting; a distributed watermarking scheme for multicast communication. The sender generates n differently watermarked copies of each packet, where $n \geq$ the tree depth d. The sender sends all copies to its router. When k copies of a packet are received by an intermediate router, the router ignores one of these copies and forwards the rest to its children based on the routers' position in the tree and their addresses. The last hop router forwards one copy to its receiver based on the identification key of the receiver. This approach, however, assumes network support at the routing level and requires senders to keep track of the multicast delivery tree. Moreover, the computation overhead at the sender is high.

WHIM is a scheme to watermark multicast video with a hierarchy of intermediaries (nodes) [10]. In this approach, an overlay network of nodes (each has a unique ID) is built to connect the sender to all receivers. Watermarks are generated and inserted by the overlay network nodes based on the location of the receivers in the overlay network. This approach is scalable. However, it assumes trusted nodes that are not sources of data leakage.

A watermarking technique suitable for multicasting video stream is proposed by Chu et al. [4]. In this technique, the sender generates two differently watermarked versions of the video frames and encrypts each version by a different key. The sender multicasts the two encrypted watermarked versions of the video frames to all receivers. On the receivers' sides, each receiver must have an identifying set of keys to decrypt the video frames such that only one version from each frame can be decrypted. The sequence of frames each receiver can decrypt results in a unique watermarked video stream for that receiver; enabling identification of leakers. This approach has the advantage of small communication overhead. However, key management is an issue. Moreover, the entire video stream frames should be used to identify the source of leak.

In the work presented by Pegueroles et al. [12], the authors proposed to use a trusted soft engine placed at the receivers. The sender sends one single encrypted version of the data to all receivers. For a receiver to access the multicast data, the receiver must use the soft engine to decrypt the data. This receiver side soft engine inserts a unique fingerprint in the data. The inserted fingerprint is then used to trace the receiver in case there is a detected leak. The communication as well as sender computation overheads are minimal in this approach. However, managing the receiver side trusted soft engines is a problematic.

6   Conclusion

In this paper, we have proposed a new efficient solution for leaker identification as a deterrence procedure to enforce copyright protection in application level multicast settings. The proposed solution assumes that the sender knows the identities of all receivers, which is feasible in application level multicast. In our proposed solution, receivers' secret keys as well as groups' keys are organized logically in a binary search tree. The paper introduces the notion of suspicious set that has as its elements all end systems that are suspected of leaking the information. A set with a cardinality of 1 includes only one end system and precisely identifies the leaker, whereas an empty set indicates that there is no leakage detection. When a leakage is detected, the suspicious set initially includes all end systems. The suspicious set is refined successively using the binary search tree to identify the exact leaker. The performance of the proposed solution is analytically evaluated. The analytical study shows that the receiver overhead is minimal and is $O(1)$. The sender's overhead and the communication overhead are $O(\log_2 n)^2$, where n is the number of receivers.

References

1. Anderson, R., Manifavas, C.: Chameleon – A New Kind of Stream Cipher. In: Biham, E. (ed.) FSE 1997. LNCS, vol. 1267, pp. 107–113. Springer, Heidelberg (1997)
2. Brassil, J., Low, S., Maxemchuk, N., O'Gorman, L.: Electronic Marking and Identification Techniques to Discourage Document Copying. In: Proceedings of IEEE Infocom 1994, vol. 3, pp. 1278–1287 (1994)
3. Brown, I., Perkins, C., Crowcroft, J.: Watercasting: Distributed Watermarking of Multicast Media. In: Proceedings of the First International Workshop on Networked Group Communication, pp. 286–300 (1999)
4. Chu, H., Qiao, L., Nahrstedt, K., Wang, H., Jain, R.: A Secure Multicast Protocol with Copyright Protection. ACM SIGCOMM Computer Communication Review 32(2), 42–60 (2002)
5. Chu, Y., Rao, S., Seshan, S., Zhang, H.: Enabling Conferencing Applications on the Internet Using an Overlay Multicast Architecture. In: Proceedings of ACM SIGCOMM 2001 (2001)
6. Chu, Y., Rao, S., Zhang, H.: A Case for End System Multicast. In: Proceedings of ACM SIGMETRICS, pp. 1–12 (2000)

7. Craver, S., Memon, N., Yeo, B., Yeung, M.: Can Invisible Watermarks Resolve Rightful Ownerships? In: Proceedings of the IS & T/SPIE Conference on Storage and Retrieval for Image and Video Databases, vol. 3022, pp. 310–321 (1997)
8. Deering, S.: Host Extensions for IP Multicast. Internet RFC 1112 (1989)
9. Judge, P., Ammar, M.: Security Issues and Solutions in Multicast Content Distribution: A Survey. IEEE Network 17(1), 30–36 (2003)
10. Judge, P., Ammar, M.: WHIM: Watermarking Multicast Video with a Hierarchy of Intermediaries. Computer Networks 39(6), 699–712 (2002)
11. Mohamed, E.: Copyright Protection in Overlay Multicast Communication. In: Fourth International Conference on Innovations in Information Technology (IIT 2007), Dubai, UAE, pp. 103–107 (2007)
12. Pegueroles, J., Fernández, M., Rico-Novella, F., Soriano, M.: A Practical Solution for Distribution Rights Protection in Multicast Environments. In: Gavrilova, M.L., Gervasi, O., Kumar, V., Tan, C.J.K., Taniar, D., Laganá, A., Mun, Y., Choo, H. (eds.) ICCSA 2006. LNCS, vol. 3982, pp. 527–536. Springer, Heidelberg (2006)
13. Pendarakis, D., Shi, S., Verma, D., Waldvogel, M.: ALMI: an Application Level Multicast Infrastructure. In: Proceedings of the Third Usenix Symposium on Internet Technologies and Systems (USITS), San Francisco, CA, USA, pp. 49–60 (2001)

Ratio-Based Gradual Aggregation of Data

Nadeem Iftikhar

Technology & Business, University College of Northern Denmark,
Sofiendalsvej 60, 9200 Aalborg SV, Denmark
iftikhar.nadeem@gmail.com

Abstract. Majority of databases contain large amounts of data, gathered over long intervals of time. In most cases, the data is aggregated so that it can be used for analysis and reporting purposes. The other reason of data aggregation is to reduce data volume in order to avoid over-sized databases that may cause data management and data storage issues. However, non-flexible and ineffective means of data aggregation not only reduce performance of database queries but also lead to erroneous reporting. This paper presents flexible and effective ratio-based methods for gradual data aggregation in databases. Gradual data aggregation is a process that reduces data volume by converting the detailed data into multiple levels of summarized data as the data gets older. This paper also describes implementation strategies of the proposed methods based on standard database technology.

Keywords: Data aggregation, ratio-based data aggregation, gradual data aggregation.

1 Introduction

In Europe, data about pesticide or fertilizer spray has to be logged in order to comply with environmental regulations. Initially, the data is kept in detailed format. As the data ages the detailed data may no longer be as useful as the new data. Also, the data may not be deleted due to governmental data retention policy. This excessive data volume may affect storage as well as query processing capacity of farming systems. Thus, one of the options is to reduce data by aggregating it. This data aggregation should not be a onetime process; rather it should be a continuous process, meaning that data should be aggregated gradually. In this way, newer data that is needed most should be coarse-grained. In addition, older data that may not be needed as frequently as the newer data; however, can be used for analysis purposes, should be fine-grained.

The main theme of this paper is to present ratio-based methods that are developed to perform gradual aggregation of data. The proposed methods are able to provide finely grained information, to aggregate data over any time span and to use tools already on the system with no modifications to existing application. The ratio-based aggregation leads up to two different scenarios: *variable aggregation* and *fixed aggregation*. In the first scenario, both time span and aggregation

R. Benlamri (Ed.): NDT 2012, Part I, CCIS 293, pp. 316–329, 2012.

ratio are variable. For example, user-defined time span and aggregation ratio could be used. The following rule, represents the variable aggregation scenario.

Rule: When data is *time_span* old; aggregate with a user-defined *ratio*.

In the second scenario, both time span and aggregation ratio are fixed. For instance, the data could be aggregated with a ratio of 1:2 when more than 3 months old, further with a ratio of 1:5 when more than 6 months old, furthermore with a ratio of 1:10 when more than 12 months old and so on. The following Backus Naur Form (BNF), represents the fixed aggregation ratio.

<aggregation> ::= *<time_span> <ratio>*
<time_span> ::= *"3 months"* | *"6 months"* | *"12 months"* |
        "18 months" | *"24 months"* | *"30 months"*
<ratio> ::= *"2"* | *"5"* | *"10"* | *"20"* | *"50"* | *"100"*

The BNF can be read as: an *aggregation* is based on a *time_span* followed by a *ratio*, a *time_span* is any one of the following strings *3 months* or *6 months* or *12 months* or *18 months* or *24 months* or *30 months* and a *ratio* is any one of the following numbers *2* or *5* or *10* or *20* or *50* or *100*.

In this paper, two alternate methods for ratio-based aggregation are proposed: *Interval-based* aggregation method and *row-based* aggregation method. The first method aggregates time intervals, whereas, the second method aggregates rows. The proposed methods are also capable of handling both of the above mentioned scenarios (variable as well as fixed aggregation). The main research questions presented in this paper are: i) aggregation could be based on variable ratio or fixed ratio and time span, ii) time span should be given as a period for which data should be aggregated, iii) aggregation could be initiated manually or automatically and iv) aggregation should be partial that means oldest data should be aggregated first.

To the best of our knowledge, this work is the first to provide implementation details and performance results of the ratio-based data aggregation methods, based on a real world case study. The rest of the paper is organized as follows: Section 2 discusses the related work. Section 3 gives details of a case study related to farming business. Section 4 provides the implementation details of the ratio-based aggregation methods. Section 5 provides evaluation of the proposed methods. Finally, Section 6 is devoted to conclusions and future work.

2   Related Work

Previously, other studies on data aggregation have been done. A comprehensive survey of most relevant techniques for the evaluation of aggregate queries on spatio-temporal data is presented by [1]. Efficient aggregation algorithms for compressed data warehouses are proposed by [2]. Techniques such as pattern identification, categorization, feature extraction, drift calculation and generalization for the aggregation of information are summarized in [3]. Multi-dimensional extension of the ER model to make use of aggregated data in complex analysis contexts is proposed by [4]. However, the main objective of these approaches is to perform one time aggregation rather than gradual aggregation, as presented in the current paper.

In the context of gradual data aggregation, work has also been reported. An efficient tree based indexing scheme for dynamically and gradually maintaining aggregates is presented in [5]. Aggregates are maintained using multiple levels of temporal granularities, older data is aggregated using coarser granularities while more recent data is aggregated with finer detail. The focal point of this work is on presenting effective indexing scheme for storing aggregated data; whereas, the motivation of the current paper is on presenting effective data aggregation methods. A data reduction system based on gradual data aggregation is also presented in [6]. The main aim of this work is to propose a language for specifying a strategy on archiving data and keeping time hierarchy based summaries of the archived data in data warehouses. On the other hand, the main attention of the current paper is on ratio-based aggregation. The semantic foundation for data reduction in dimensional data warehouses that permits the gradual aggregation of detailed data as the data gets older is provided by [7]. The work is highly theoretical and the main direction of this work is on querying multi-dimensional data that is being aggregated gradually. In contrast, the main emphasis of the current paper is to implement methods that allow the gradual data aggregation to take place in an effective and flexible manner. A time hierarchy based gradual data aggregation method with implementation strategy and real-life examples is proposed by [8]. The approach maintains summaries of the archived data in data bases at different levels of granularity. The main drawback of the time granularity-based approach is the fixed nature of time hierarchy.

The current paper is a continuation of the previous paper [9] that defines the ratio-based data aggregation methods for the first time in order to aggregate data gradually in databases/data warehousing; however, implementation details of these methods were left out. The present paper implements and evaluates the ratio-based data aggregation methods that are proposed in [9].

In addition, to the above mentioned single-model based techniques, multi-model based data aggregation techniques have also been proposed by [10], [11] and [12]. These techniques aggregate data according to multiple goals defined by multiple requirements rather than only one, such as storage space. These techniques are useful in order to aggregate data based on semantic similarities and can be incorporated in the proposed methods in future.

3   Case Study

This section presents a case study that is also used to explain the functionality of the ratio-based aggregation methods proposed in the remainder of this paper. This case study is about the management of chemical spray related activities carried out in fields by farming machinery, such as a tractor. These activities are expressed by tasks to distinguish all the work that is carried out by a contractor for a farmer in a particular field. One of the main requirements of this case study is to perform task based gradual data aggregation based on an aggregation ratio.

For this case study, a demo version of a system that controls and monitors the tractor and accompanying implements is considered. The system is composed of a number of sensors, actuators and processing electronics connected by a CAN-BUS (for controller area network) [13]. Applications written in C programming language collects information from the CAN-BUS, transforms it and stores it into SQLite database. The database consists of multiple tables; however the table that we are most interested in is Log_data table.

Table 1. Log_data table

Task	Parameter	Timestamp	Granularity	Value
8	1	1155208060	20	11.1
8	248	1155208070	30	2.46
8	247	1155208070	30	31.43
8	1	1155208080	20	11.2
8	41	1155208100	60	19
8	248	1155208100	30	2.96
8	247	1155208100	30	32.31
8	1	1155208100	20	11.2
8	1	1155208120	20	11.3
8	248	1155208130	30	3.12
8	247	1155208130	30	32.96
.	.	.	.	.

The Log_data table (Table 1) includes data that is being generated by the computer system installed on the tractor. It is used for logging, aggregating, reporting and analyzing of spray related data. The attributes of the Log_data table are: *Task, Parameter, Timestamp, Granularity* and *Value*. The Task represents a activity to distinguish all the work that is carried out in a particular field of a farm. The Task is a central element in data logging process (during any spray related activity) and may span for multiple periods of time. Data generated during spray process is logged against a particular Task. The Parameter represents a variable code for which a data value is recorded. Each Parameter has a different data logging frequency that is represented by the Granularity. For example, the logging frequency of Parameter 247 (amount of chemical sprayed in liters) is every 30 second, the logging frequency of Parameter 1 (tractor speed in km/h) is every 20 seconds and so on. The Granularity has dual purpose. First, it can represent the initial granularity of the captured value. Second, it can also represent the aggregated granularity of the stored value. The Timestamp represents an instance of time when a data value is recorded and it is in Coordinated Universal Time (UTC) format [14]. Lastly, the Value represents a numeric measure.

The rows in the Log_data table (Table 1) are interpreted as follow: at 11552080 60 UTC or 11:07:40 (hh:mm:ss) 1 value is stored, at 1155208070 UTC or 11:07:50

(hh:mm:ss) 2 values are stored, at 1155208080 UTC or 11:08:00 (hh:mm:ss) 1 value is stored, at 1155208100 UTC or 11:08:20 (hh:mm:ss) 4 value are stored, at 1155208120 UTC or 11:08:40 (hh:mm:ss) 1 value is stored and at 1155208130 UTC or 11:08:50 (hh:mm:ss) 2 value are stored and so on.

4   Ratio-Based Aggregation Methods

This section presents ratio-based aggregation methods. The methods aggregate Log_data values presented in Table 1, as per parameter per task level. Furthermore, the methods aggregate rows with a user defined ratio and time span. For example, the Log_data table (Table 1) initially contain rows with label 20, 30 and 60, which means the rows are recorded at every 20, 30 and 60 seconds. Suppose we like to aggregate these rows with a ratio 1:5 and a function MAX. As a result of this aggregation, the granularities of the aggregated rows are changed to 100, 150 and 300, as seen in Table 2, which means the rows contain (aggregated) values at every 100 seconds, 150 seconds and 300 seconds. Moreover, the proposed ratio-based aggregation methods can aggregate data with variable as well as fixed aggregation scenarios, as presented in Section 1.

Table 2. Aggregated Log_data table

Task	Parameter	Timestamp	Granularity	Value
8	1	1155208120	100	11.3
8	248	1155208130	150	3.12
8	247	1155208130	150	32.96
8	41	1155208100	300	19
.	.	.	.	.

The ratio-based methods presented in this paper are also considered with further two possible aggregation viewpoints: data "without holes" and data "with holes". Data "without holes" means that there are no missing values in the data and data "with holes" means that there are missing values. For instance, in the Log_data table (Table 3) with simplified information, we like to aggregate data with an aggregation factor of, say 1:5 and a function SUM. In the case of data "without holes" the first 5 rows will become 1 row where "0" denotes the start of the time period, as presented in Table 4.

On the other hand, if there are "holes" in the time points in that case what should be done. Suppose, we want to aggregate data presented in Table 5 with an aggregation ratio of 1:5 and a function SUM. The data "should" have a value every 2 seconds, however one row is "missing" for timestamp = 8. In this case, aggregation factor 5 could mean two things. First, since the current granularity is 2 seconds, aggregate to 10 second intervals. Thus, the first 4 rows will become 1 row where "0" denotes the start of the time period. The 5th row goes into the next 10 second period, as presented in Table 6 and further discussed in

Table 3. Detailed Log-data table (without holes)

Task	Parameter	Timestamp	Granularity	Value
4	1	0	2	3
4	1	2	2	3
4	1	4	2	2
4	1	6	2	2
4	1	8	2	3

Table 4. Aggregated Log-data table (without holes)

Task	Parameter	Timestamp	Granularity	Value
4	1	0	10	13

Table 5. Detailed Log-data table (with holes)

Task	Parameter	Timestamp	Granularity	Value
4	1	0	2	3
4	1	2	2	3
4	1	4	2	2
4	1	6	2	2
4	1	10	2	3

Section 4.1. Second, always aggregate 5 rows together. Then the 5 rows become 1 row where "12" is used to say that the time period is 12 seconds long, as presented in Table 7 and further discussed in Section 4.2.

4.1 Interval-Based Aggregation Method

This method aggregates time intervals rather than rows. It has further two possibilities. First, the source time period length is same for all data in the query and we know it. For example, in the case of (Table 3 and Table 5) it is 2 "Granularity". Second, the source time period may vary, which means it is unknown, as in the case study presented in Section 3. The Log-data table (Table 1) contains values at multiple time intervals such as, 20 seconds, 30 seconds and 60 seconds. The following program summarizes the working of the interval-based aggregation method for varying time period length for all data in the query. The gradual aggregation can be achieved by applying this program repeatedly with higher aggregation ratios.

Furthermore, the program in which source time period length is same for all data, consists of exactly same steps, except a slight change in the select query.

Table 6. Aggregated Log_data table I (with holes)

Task	Parameter	Timestamp	Granularity	Value
4	1	0	10	10

Table 7. Aggregated Log_data table II (with holes)

Task	Parameter	Timestamp	Granularity	Value
4	1	0	12	13

In the *group by* statement (lines 7-8), instead of variable time period, fixed time period is introduced (*group by round((L.timestamp)/(60*5),0)*(60*5);*).

Interval-based data aggregation program

Step 1: Aggregate data (SUM) which is more than six months old for parameter 41 (area sprayed in hectares) with an aggregation ratio of (1:5)

```
1   sql = "SELECT L.Task, L.Parameter, L.Timestamp,
2      L.Granularity, SUM(L.Value)
3   FROM Log_data L
4   WHERE L.Parameter = 41
5   AND L.Timestamp < strftime
6     ('%s', 'now', '-6month')
7   GROUP BY ROUND((L.Timestamp)/
8     (L.Granularity*5),0)*(L.Granularity*5);";
9   rc = sqlite3_prepare(db, sql, (int)strlen(sql), &stmt, &tail);
10  ...
```

The program consists of four steps. Steps 1), 2) and 3) relate to data aggregation; whereas, Step 4) correspond to gradual data aggregation. The first step (lines 1-10) aggregates data that is older than 6 months using SUM for parameter 41 with an aggregation ratio of 5 (1:5) and stores it in a record set. The most significant part of the statement is the GROUP BY clause (lines 7-8). The GROUP BY clause aggregates time intervals by using SUM function. The aggregation ratio is the user-defined ratio, such as, 2 (1:2), 5 (1:5) and so on. In the GROUP BY clause the Granularity represents the current level of granularity of the data to be aggregated. The Timestamp represents the beginning of each time span. The Timestamp field is first divided by (Granularity * aggregation_ratio) and then the ROUND() function is used to round the result to the nearest integer. Further, the rounded result is multiplied with the same denominator in order to get the time intervals based on the frequency and the aggregation ratio.

Furthermore, line 9 creates a prepare statement for fetching data from the database using *sqlite3_prepare* function call. The first parameter in the function call is the database handle itself which is a *sqlite3** pointer. The second parameter is the SQL statement which needs to be executed.

Step 2: Insert the aggregated data back into the Log_data table

```
11 qry1 = "insert into Log_data(Task, Parameter,
12    Timestamp, Granularity, Value)
13    values(?,?,?,?)";
14 while(rc == SQLITE_ROW) {
15    Task =  sqlite3_column_double(stmt, 0);
16    Parameter = sqlite3_column_int(stmt, 1);
17    Timestamp = sqlite3_column_double(stmt, 2);
18    Granularity = sqlite3_column_int(stmt, 3);
19    Value = sqlite3_column_int(stmt, 4);
20    rc1 = sqlite3_prepare(db, qry1,
21      (int)strlen(qry1), &stmt1, &tail1);
22    sqlite3_bind_double(stmt1, 1, Task);
23    sqlite3_bind_int(stmt1, 2, Parameter);
24    sqlite3_bind_double(stmt1, 3, Timestamp);
25    sqlite3_bind_double(stmt1, 4, Granularity);
26    sqlite3_bind_int(stmt1, 5, Value);
27 ...
```

Step 3: Delete the rows that have been aggregated

```
28 sql2 = "DELETE FROM Log_data
29 WHERE Log_data.Parameter = 41
30 AND Log_data.Timestamp < STRFTIME
31    ('%s', 'NOW', '-6MONTH')
32 AND Log_data.Granularity = ?;";
33 ...
```

Step 4: Go to Step 1 for higher level of aggregation

The second step (lines 11-27) retrieves the data from the record set and inserts the aggregated data back into the Log_data table. In line 13 "?" stand for parameter values, which filled in dynamically at the time of execution of the query. Lines 15-19, reads the values from the record set and lines 22-26 assign (or bind) the values to the parameters in the prepare statement (lines 20-21). A prepare SQL statement is a string containing SQL commands passed to *sqlite3_prepare()*.

The third step (lines 28-33) deletes the data from the Log_data table that just have been aggregated. In line 32 "?" stand for granularity of the data that is older than 6 months, which filled in dynamically at the time of execution of the query.

Finally, Step 4) represents gradual aggregation and it can be achieved by repeating the Step 1) to 3) with higher aggregation ratio. For example, if the data is initially aggregated with a ratio of 5 (1:5) in that case it can be aggregation with a ratio of 10 (1:10) and so on, as the data grows older.

4.2   Row-Based Aggregation Method

This method always aggregate rows based on the aggregation factor rather than time intervals. For instance, if we like to aggregate rows in Table 1 with an aggregation ratio 1:5 for parameter 41, this method will always aggregate five rows. Similarly, if the aggregation ratio is 1:10, in that case it will always aggregate ten rows and so on. One of the major differences in this method and the method presented in Section 4.1 is the *group by* statement. The row-based aggregation cannot be done using the *group by* statement instead it is done using a program (C, etc). Since the decision about what rows to put into a group depends on the previous rows, not on any values in the rows themselves. The following program summarizes the working of the row-based aggregation method. Similar to Section 4.1, the gradual aggregation can be achieved by applying this algorithm repeatedly with higher aggregation ratios.

Row-based data aggregation program

Step 1: Get the data that is more than six months old for parameter 41 in a single dimensional array for further processing

```
34 ret = sqlite3_get_table(db,
35 "SELECT L.Task, L.Parameter,
36   L.Timestamp, L.Granularity, L.Value
37 FROM Log_data L
38 WHERE L.Parameter = 41
39 AND L.Timestamp < strftime
40   ('%s', 'now', '-6month') ",&result, &rows, &cols, &errmsg);
41 ...
```

The program consists of five steps. Steps 1), 2), 3) and 4) relate to data aggregation; whereas, Step 5) correspond to gradual data aggregation. The first step (lines 34-41) fetches the data that is older than 6 months for parameter 41 and stores it in a single dimensional array.

The second step (lines 42-50) aggregates the data by executing a *loop*. In line 42, i starts with 9 as we need to start from the third row (first row contains the attribute names) of the single dimensional array, i must be less than the length of the result set and the value of i is incremented by 5 as there are 5 columns in the Log_data table (Table 1). For each increment in the *loop*, multiple *if else* statements are executed to check the aggregation ratio and level of granularity, while applying the aggregate SUM. In line 44, *If count* exceeds the aggregation_ratio the aggregated data is inserted into the Log_data table

(Table 1). Similarly, after the insertion of the first set of aggregated data, the
next set of aggregated data is calculated and process goes on until the end of for
loop.

*Step 2: Add the values (SUM) with an aggregation ratio of 1:5 by manipulat-
ing the array*

```
42 for(i = 9; i < cols * (rows + 1); i = i + 5)
43  {
44 if (count <= 5)
45    {
46      if (time == 0.0) { time = atof(result[i-3]);}
47      sum = sum + atio(result[i]);
48      count++;
49    }
50 ...
```

Step 3: Insert the aggregated data (SUM) into the Log_data table

```
51  sprintf(qry, "INSERT INTO Log_data \n"
52     "VALUES ('%d, %d, %.4f', '%d', '%d')", Task, Parameter
53     Timestamp, Granualrity, Value);
54  ret = sqlite_exec(db, qry, NULL, NULL, &errmsg);
```

Step 4: Delete the rows that have been aggregated

```
55 Step 4 is similar to step 3 of the interval-based program
```

Step 5: Go to Step 1 for higher level of aggregation

The third step (lines 51-54) inserts the aggregated data back into the Log_data
table. Furthermore, steps 4) and 5) of the row-based aggregation program are
similar to the steps 3) and 4) of the interval-based aggregation program
(Section 4.1).

5   Evaluation

An evaluation of the following aggregation methods has been done. Performance
tests have been carried out for single-level queries. The single-level queries aggregate data from a single level of granularity to a higher level of granularity. The
tests were designed to evaluate the effectiveness and efficiency of the following
methods.

Method I: Interval-based
Method II: Row-based
Method III: Time granularity-based

Table 8. Log_data table (with holes)

Rowid	Task	Parameter	Timestamp	Granularity	Value
1	8	41	1155208100	60	2000
2	8	41	1155208160	60	2000
3	8	41	1155208220	60	2000
4	8	41	1155208280	60	2000
5	8	41	1155208340	60	2000
6	8	41	1155208400	60	200
7	8	41	1155208460	60	200
8	8	41	1155208520	60	200
9	8	41	1155208580	60	200
10	8	41	1155208640	60	200
11	8	41	1155208700	60	500
12	8	41	1155208760	60	500
13	8	41	1155208820	60	500
14	**8**	**41**	**1155208880**	**60**	**500**
15	**8**	**41**	**1155209000**	**60**	**100**
16	8	41	1155209060	60	100
17	8	41	1155209120	60	100
18	8	41	1155209180	60	100
19	8	41	1155209240	60	100

In addition, to the ratio-based data aggregation methods (Methods I and II), time granularity-based data aggregation method (Method III) that is previously presented in [8], is also considered in the performance study. Method III aggregates data based on a user defined time hierarchy, such as second, minute, 2minute, 10minute, hour, day, month, quarter, year. When compared with the Methods I and II, Method III has a limitation. The limitation is due to the fixed nature of the time hierarchical structure. Once the hierarchical structure is defined and implemented, aggregation can only be performed based on predefined rules. For example, when data is 3 months old aggregate to a minute level from 20 seconds level or 30 seconds level. Similarly, when data is 6 months old aggregate to 2 minutes level from a minute level and so on. On the other hand, in the case of Methods I and II, there is quite a flexibility to select and apply various aggregation ratios.

In order to measure the effectiveness of the above mentioned methods, tests were performed on Log_data table (Table 8) having data at a single level of granularity with missing value. In Table 8, a row is missing between row number 14 and 15 (Timestamp = 1155208940 is missing). The results show Methods I and III produced the same output, shown in (Table 9) with an aggregation ratio of (1:5) and time granularity equal to 5 minutes, respectively. Both these methods use aggregate function SUM to produce aggregated rows (based on time intervals) with changed Granularity. On the other hand, Method II produced the results, shown in (Table 10) with an aggregation ratio of (1:5) and aggregate function SUM. As observed from the results (Table 10), Method II aggregate rows and in case of missing value it snatches the value from the next interval (Rowid 3, Table 10). Further aggregation with higher aggregation ratio and time granularity may be performed to further reduce the number of rows.

Table 9. Aggregated Log_data table (Method I and III)

Rowid	Task	Parameter	Timestamp	Granularity	Value
1	8	41	1155208340	300	10000
2	8	41	1155208640	300	1000
3	8	41	1155208880	300	2000
4	8	41	1155209240	300	500

Moreover, to measure the efficiency of the above mentioned methods, the methods were tested with 1,000,000 rows (20.5 MB). The tests were designed to measure the overall aggregation speed of each aggregation method in seconds. The overall aggregation process consists of: i) aggregating the existing rows based on single or different levels of granularity, ii) inserting the newly aggregated rows in the Log_data table and iii) deleting all the rows from the Log_data table that have just been aggregated. The tests were performed on a 2.0 GHz Intel Core Duo with 512 MB RAM, running Ubuntu 9.04, SQLite 3.6.18, and C GNU GCC. Every test is performed 5 times. The maximum and minimum values are discarded and an average is calculated using the middle three values.

Table 10. Aggregated Log_data table (Method II)

Rowid	Task	Parameter	Timestamp	Granularity	Value
1	8	41	1155208100	300	10000
2	8	41	1155208400	300	1000
3	**8**	**41**	**1155208700**	**360**	**2100**
4	8	41	1155209060	300	400

The results in Fig. 1 show that Methods I and III have demonstrated almost the same performance. The overall aggregation speed of both these methods is under 70 seconds, however, as mentioned earlier Method I is more flexible in terms of selecting and applying various aggregation ratios than Method III. This overall aggregation speed is quite satisfactory, given the fact that these two methods (Methods I and III) aggregate 1,000,000 rows, insert the aggregated rows back into the Log_data data and delete the rows from the Log_data table that have just been aggregated. In contrast, the overall aggregation speed of Method II is approximately 315 seconds, which is approximately 450% more than the previous two methods (Methods I and III). This difference in overall aggregation speed of Method II with Methods I and III is due to the fact that Method II performs the aggregation using a hand-coded *loop*, whereas, Methods I and III perform the aggregation using a SQL *group by* statement.

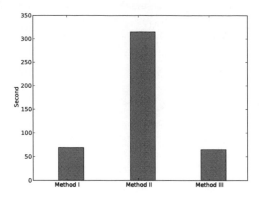

Fig. 1. Overall aggregation speed (note zoom on y-axis)

6   Conclusion

This paper proposed ratio-based methods for gradual aggregation of data. The methods are further classified into interval-based and row-based aggregation. Both, the interval-based and the row-based aggregation methods are very effective for aggregating data "without holes" and "with holes" by means of variable and fixed aggregation scenarios. The evaluation showed promising results by means of interval-based data aggregation technique and acceptable results using row-based data aggregation technique. In future research, the direction of interest is to implement a ratio-based data aggregation tool that is easy-to-use and easy-to-maintain. It is also interesting to investigate, how to deal with duplicate and missing data.

References

1. Lopez, I.F.V., Moon, B., Snodgrass, R.T.: Spatiotemporal Aggregate Computation: A Survey. IEEE Transactions on Knowledge and Data Engineering 17(2), 271–286 (2005)
2. Li, J., Srivastava, J.: Efficient Aggregation Algorithms for Compressed Data Warehouses. IEEE Transactions on Knowledge and Data Engineering 14(3), 515–529 (2002)
3. Rasheed, F., Lee, Y.K., Lee, S.: Towards using Data Aggregation Techniques in Ubiquitous Computing Environments. In: 4th IEEE International Conference on Pervasive Computing and Communication Workshops, pp. 369–392. IEEE Press, New York (2006)
4. Schulze, C., Spilke, J., Lehner, W.: Data Modeling for Precision Dairy Farming within the Competitive Field of Operational and Analytical Tasks. Computers and Electronics in Agriculture 59(1-2), 39–55 (2007)
5. Zhang, D., Gunopulos, D., Tsotras, V.J., Seeger, B.: Temporal and Spatio-temporal Aggregations over Data Streams using Multiple Time Granularities. Information System 28(1-2), 61–84 (2003)

6. Boly, A., Hebrail, G., Goutier, S.: Forgetting Data Intelligently in Data Ware-houses. In: IEEE International Conference on Research, Innovation and Vision for the Future, pp. 220–227. IEEE Press, New York (2007)
7. Skyt, J., Jensen, C.S., Pedersen, T.B.: Specification-based Data Reduction in Di-mensional Data Warehouses. Information System 33(1), 36–63 (2008)
8. Iftikhar, N., Pedersen, T.B.: Using a Time Granularity Table for Gradual Granular Data Aggregation. In: Catania, B., Ivanović, M., Thalheim, B. (eds.) ADBIS 2010. LNCS, vol. 6295, pp. 219–233. Springer, Heidelberg (2010)
9. Iftikhar, N., Pedersen, T.B.: Gradual Data Aggregation in Multi-granular Fact Ta-bles on Resource-Constrained Systems. In: Setchi, R., Jordanov, I., Howlett, R.J., Jain, L.C. (eds.) KES 2010. LNCS, vol. 6278, pp. 349–358. Springer, Heidelberg (2010)
10. Fan, J., Kambhampati, S.: Multi-Objective Query Processing for Data Aggrega-tion. Arizona State University, Computer Science & Engineering, Technical Report (2006)
11. Montagnuolo, M., Messina, A., Borgotallo, R.: Automatic Segmentation, Aggre-gation and Indexing of Multimodal News Information from Television and the Internet. Journal of Digital Information Management 8(6), 387–395 (2010)
12. Cuzzocrea, A.: Multiple-Objective Compression of Data Cubes in Cooperative OLAP Environments. In: Atzeni, P., Caplinskas, A., Jaakkola, H. (eds.) ADBIS 2008. LNCS, vol. 5207, pp. 62–80. Springer, Heidelberg (2008)
13. CAN-BUS, http://www.canbus.us
14. Coordinated Universal Time, http://en.wikipedia.org/wiki/Coordinated_Universal_Time

An Adaptive Arbitration Algorithm for Fair Bandwidth Allocation, Low Latency and Maximum CPU Utilization

M. Nishat Akhtar and Othman Sidek

Collaborative Microelectronic Design and Excellence Center,
Universiti Sains Malaysia, Nibong Tebal,
Penang,14300, Malaysia
nishat_akhtar2000@yahoo.com

Abstract. Utilization of adaptive algorithm for fair bandwidth allocation, low latency and maximum CPU utilization is proved to be a promising approach for designing system-on-chip for future applications. Adaptive arbitration is more advantageous then the other conventional arbitration algorithms for several reasons; these include fair bandwidth allocation among different masters, simple design and low cost over head. This article provides a comprehensive picture of research and developments in dynamic arbitration algorithm for masters according to the different traffic behavior. The papers published in standard journals are reviewed, classified according to their objectives and presented with a general conclusion.

Keywords: Adaptive arbiter, Fair bandwidth, Low latency, Real time system, System-on-chip.

1 Introduction

In today's world symmetric multiprocessing has become an operable option for computing in the world of embedded systems and technology is blended with complex chips that incorporate multiple processors dedicated for specific computational needs. In order to realize this complex multiple system-on-chip in the environment of intellectual property based methodologies, the communication architecture plays a major role. In any system-on-chip, in order to solve the bus contention, arbitration algorithm plays a major role. The fairness property plays a very crucial role among the various criteria of arbitration algorithms to solve the bus contention. The performance of multiprocessors systems depends more on the efficient communication among processors and on the balanced distribution of computation among them, rather than on pure speed of processor. Since arbiters are invoked for every transfer on the bus, they are considered to be in the critical path of bus based communication architecture and must be designed with a great care [1]. An efficient contention resolution scheme is required to provide fine-grained control of the communication bandwidth allocated to individual processor and avoid starvation of low priority transactions [2].

R. Benlamri (Ed.): NDT 2012, Part I, CCIS 293, pp. 330–343, 2012.
© Springer-Verlag Berlin Heidelberg 2012

Now a day's advanced super IC processors combined with high speed and performance which uses more and more heterogeneous cores have been integrated on a single chip [3]. The traditional bus based architecture cannot satisfy the communication requirement effectively between thousands of homogenous or heterogeneous IP's. Network-on-Chip (NOC) architecture can overcome the demerits of traditional bus based architecture. On the other hand, there are several disadvantage of NOC. First is regarding its physical size as it uses most of the space on the chip. It means, it deals with a heavy design size constraint on the nodes. The second disadvantage is its fixed framework layout of the network that means if a regular equidistant structure is chosen, the area can be lost because of some functional units. Third disadvantage is because of its fixed grid, the communication latency between two functional units becomes bigger due to non-linear data paths.

In symmetric multiprocessing the major architectural bottleneck is the internal bus which connects the processors and peripherals to the memory using an arbitrary network of shared channels [4]. In most cases, the bus bandwidth becomes a dominant barrier because of improper bandwidth allocation. To maintain the bus bandwidth in an efficient manner, the process of memory arbitration cannot be neglected as it is one of an essential factor for concurrent-computing. In an enhanced arbitration environment of SoC, the communication architecture should be fair enough to offer high performance to the wide range of masters according to their traffic behavior as the masters on a SoC bus may issue simultaneous requests. Thus, an arbiter is required to decide that which master should be granted for the bus access. Hence an arbiter should be designed in such a way that it suits the system by keeping high throughput and low starvation among the different masters.

2   Related Works

Many researchers focused on developing multi level arbitration scheme in order to achieve fair bandwidth allocation and to reduce the system latency. Laxmi Bhuyan [5] showed that if the priority to less frequent requests is given, then the probability of their acceptance is dramatically improved but at the same time there is a tremendous decrease in the bandwidth. V. Lakshmi et al. [6] proposed a novel arbitration scheme called time out arbitration, which ensures a degree of fairness for all the low priority requests in a given time slot but the amount of integrated circuits used in their design makes the cost of the device prohibitive for real time applications.

Enrico and Massimo [7] proposed a novel method of automatic synthesis of easily scalable bus arbiters with dynamic priority assignment strategies. They emphasized more on those arbitration mechanisms which can be implemented on silicon as a digital circuit, rather than getting concerned about how the selected arbitration policies can affect the performance of a multiprocessor system. The major disadvantage of common-bus multiprocessor system is the reduction of throughput caused by conflict between processors requiring access to the shared memory [8]. Ideally, throughput should increase directly with the number of processors but the bus contention diminishes this increase. There is a critical number above which the processors show no improvement and this critical number depends naturally, on the extent of bus used by the processors [9].

In order to design multiprocessor system according to their bandwidth requirement Yi Xu et al. [10] proposed an arbiter called an adaptive dynamic arbiter in which they designed a lottery bus algorithm approach where an arbiter can adjust the bandwidth proportion assigned to every processor automatically due to the situations of bus transactions aiming to reduce total task execution time. Compared with conventional architectures their architecture reduces the system latency but it does not allocate fair bandwidth to the processors.

In multithreaded environment efficient bandwidth allotment plays a major role because of the performance problem which may occur due to contention among application threads for the possession of the bus [4]. Alex Aravind [11] presented an algorithm which is a fully distributed software solution to the arbitration problem in multiport memory systems. His algorithm is purely based on First in First out (FIFO) and Least Recently Used (LRU) fairness criteria but the algorithm does not deal with fair bandwidth allotment to the different masters which may become a barrier to get a better performance.

Chien-Hua et al. [12] designed a real time and bandwidth guaranteed arbitration algorithm for system-on-chip bus communication in which RT_Lottery algorithm has been used to meet both hard real time and bandwidth requirements but in terms of fair bandwidth allocation it cannot compete with adaptive arbiter. Haishan Li et al. [13] proposed an algorithm called adaptive arbitration algorithm in which an arbiter can adjust priority automatically to provide the best bandwidth for different master according to their real time bus bandwidth needs. They showed that, it is possible to allocate fair bandwidth to a given set of processors with a very high degree of fairness.

An arbiter with fair bandwidth allocation and low latency seems to be of interest with many applications like real time computing system with critical requirements. Therefore, an attempt has been made to reduce the latency and to ensure high degree of fairness in terms of bandwidth among the processors designed according to their traffic behavior for real time computing system.

3   Classification of Masters on the Basis of Traffic Behavior

Chien-Hua et al. [12] designed a real time and bandwidth guaranteed arbitration algorithm for system-on-chip bus communication in which RT_Lottery algorithm has been used to meet both hard real time and bandwidth requirements. In their work following masters (processors) has been classified according to their traffic behaviors:

3.1   D_Type (D for Dependent)

D Type masters have no real time requirements and the next request is issued at the time depending on the finish time of the current request. In this case the interval time between two successive requests is the time from the issued time of the former to the finish time of the latter. Figure 1 shows an example. A 4 beat burst is generated by the traffic generator at cycle 2. The request is not granted until cycle 5 is finished at cycle 9. Suppose if the interval time is 10, then the next request will be issued only at cycle 19.

3.2   D_R Type (D for Dependent, R for Real-Time)

This is same as D Type master; the only difference is that they have extra real time requirements. Figure 2 shows an example. R_{cycle} is the real time requirement of the master which is set to 10 cycles. It is shown in the figure that the request issued at cycle 2 has to be finished before cycle 12 represented by dotted lines. A real time violation occurs if the request is not completed before cycle 12.

3.3   ND_R Type (ND for Not Dependent, R for Real-Time)

The issued time of a request from a ND_R Type of master is independent of the finish time of its previous request, and the interval time is the clock cycles between two successive requests. In figure 3, time interval assumed is 15. At cycle 17 second request is issued which directly depends on cycle 2 of the first request but not its finish time at cycle 9. In this case R_{cycle} is supposed to be smaller than the minimum possible interval time because the current request must be finished before the next request. It means that it is possible for the designers to assign tight real time requirements.

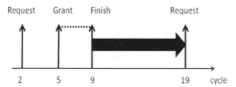

Fig. 1. D Type Master

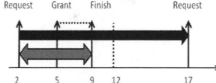

Fig. 2. D_R Type Master

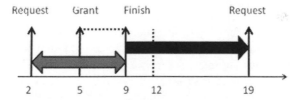

Fig. 3. ND_R Type Master

Chien-Hua et al. [12] conducted an experiment where masters designed according to their traffic behavior are put on a bus. For each type, design of a heavy traffic master and a light traffic master has been made. Here, both M1 and M2 are Dependent (D) type masters, M3 is a D_R type master, M4, M5 are ND_R type master and over here the requests issued by M1 have larger beat numbers and shorter average interval than those issued by M2. It is clear that M1 generate a heavier traffic load to the bus than M2. From table1 it is observed that the maximum bandwidth of each master is very different from each other because there are masters with heavy and light-traffic loads. The evaluated maximum bandwidth and the required bandwidth for each master are shown in the following table.

Table 1. Bandwidth Evaluation (Ref. Chien-Hua et al.)

	M1	M2	M3	M4	M5
Maximum Bandwidth (%)	63	18	63	19	17
Required Bandwidth (%)	20	5	40	10	17

It is observed that the total required bandwidth uses 94% of the total bandwidth.

4   Adaptive Arbitration Algorithm

Haishan Li et al. [13] proposed a novel arbitration algorithm which is known as Adaptive Arbitration (AA) algorithm. This algorithm is a dynamic priority algorithm. An arbiter adapting to this algorithm can adjust priority automatically to provide the best bandwidth allocation for different masters according to their real time bandwidth requirements. The experimental result shows that this novel algorithm meets both priority and equity in solving the bus bandwidth allocation. In a bus system the arbiter records the number of time each master has requested for the bus and the total time that all master have requested for the bus access. Using these two values the arbiter can calculate the bus access probability of the corresponding master by the division operation method. The priority weight of the master is decided by its probability of getting the bus access. A master who has the bigger weight owns the higher priority. It is unnecessary for an arbiter to recalculate all the probabilities and weights and to reorder the priority of masters when a new bus access request appears. The solution to this problem is to reduce the frequency of weight calculation and priority reordering [13]. The frequency here is defined as the adaptive cycle. The arbiter recalculates the weight and reorders the priority of the entire master when their total bus request arrives at the adaptive cycle. In adaptive arbiter with a two-level priority, the first level adopts adaptive arbitration algorithm and in the second level in order eliminate the starvation among all the masters, the static fixed priority algorithm has been adopted. The hardware in adaptive arbiter includes a public counter to record the total number of bus access requests. The value of public counter gets cleared all the time whenever it reaches the adaptive cycle. To record the number of bus access from each master there is a private counter dedicated to each master. Apart from all these there is a weight register and a left weight register which is assigned a weight value and is used to decide the priority of the corresponding master in the upcoming adaptive cycle. The higher priority is given to the master who has got a bigger weight. The left weight register records whether the weight of the master has been used in the adaptive cycle or not. If the value of the left weight register becomes zero then the master is put into the second level priority queue. At the end of every adaptive cycle all the registers are assigned new values.

5   Proposed Combination of Masters According to Their Traffic Behavior with Adaptive Adaptive Arbiter

It is very important for shared system-on-chip bus system to be designed in such a way that it meets both hard real time and bandwidth requirement. The difficulty to meet both real-time and bandwidth requirements generally depends on the total required bandwidth in a system [12]. In an unbalanced workload environment, different process requires different bandwidth. Due to the unbalanced bus requirements, the improvement due to parallelization of the code is not as high as compared to the sequential execution [14].

From section 3 it is clear that masters designed according to their traffic behavior uses 94% of the total bus bandwidth. Adaptive Arbiter (AA) used by Haishan Li et al. [13] is better than the conventional arbiters in terms of fair bandwidth allotment and latency. Since arbiter is an important functional module in multiprocessor, therefore it should be carefully designed in high performance systems [15]. In order to optimize the performance of the bus, the time required to handle the request should be minimized [16].   Adaptive arbiter can provide the best bus bandwidth allocation as it distributes different bus bandwidth according to the real-time needs of different masters. If masters designed according to their traffic behavior are put on to the adaptive arbiter architecture then not only bus bandwidth will be saved by 6% for the critical requirements but also it will help to get best possible bandwidth allocation for any real time system by utilizing the CPU cores to its maximum. In the following table the masters classified according to their traffic behavior are deployed to the adaptive arbitration architecture and a comparative analysis has been done in terms of fair bandwidth allotment.

Table 2. Comparative Analysis (Ref. Haishan Li et al. and Chien-Hua et al.)

Masters(processors)	Type	Fair Bandwidth allotted using AA
M1	D	27.3%
M2	D_R	26.5%
M3	ND_R	24.1%
M4	ND_R	22.1%

In the above table all masters requests for 25% of bus bandwidth where M1 is a heavy traffic master and generates a heavier traffic load to the bus. In the following figure architecture of the proposed system is shown.

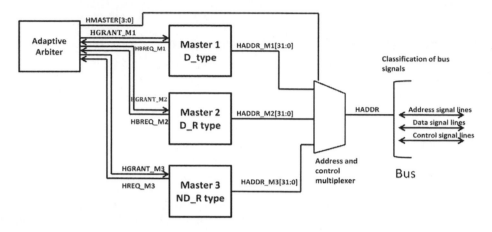

Fig. 4. Prototype of the proposed Architecture

6   Results and Discussion

An adaptive arbitration algorithm has been implemented in a tri-threaded environment which acts as a three separate events or masters clocked together. In order to analyze the impact of multi-threading on masters according to their different traffic behavior using adaptive arbitration architecture, we have conducted an experiment using SystemC whose libraries were ported in an integrated development environment composed of suitable profiler tools to measure the CPU usage. In our case, we used Visual Studio 2010 (EE) to implement SystemC using AMD Athlon ™ II X2 260 processor. Graph in figure 5 shows an average CPU utilization for the threads running in a non-preemptive environment.

In this case the race conditions occur because the programmer does not anticipates the fact that a thread can be preempted at any awkward position, which might allow another thread to read the block of code first. However the use of threads requires some precaution in communication libraries in order to avoid the race condition when the threads access the library concurrently [17]. This type of process does not utilize the CPU cores to the maximum and as the number of threads increases the bandwidth becomes the major barrier for the performance.

Graph in figure 6 shows an average CPU utilization for the threads running in a preemptive environment. Thread safety is one of the major criteria of multi-threading support. This means that communication in a multi-threaded application can be performed in multiple threads. Appropriate techniques should be used to utilize the multiple cores in order to make non-blocking communication primitives to progress in the background [17]. Various thread-scheduling policies try to achieve optimal utilization of the CPU as well as the bus bandwidth during each quantum [4]. Three major benchmarks have to be dealt over here which consists of CPU utilization, bus bandwidth consumption and system latency. If we compare figure 5 with figure 6, it

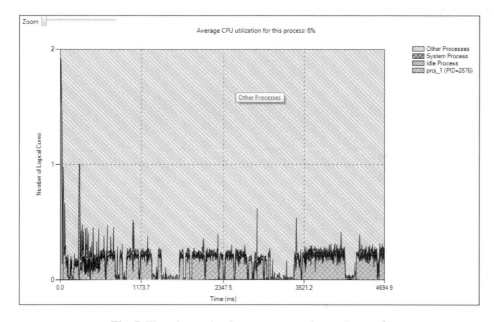

Fig. 5. Threads running in a non-preemptive environment

can be seen that, not only the CPU usage is utilized to its maximum using optimal bandwidth utilization as the threads are running in a preemptive environment but it also shows a decrement in the system latency.

Haishan Li et al. [13] presented an experimental study by taking two separate cases into consideration. The set of masters are M1, M2, M3 and M4. In their first case all the masters require the same amount of bus bandwidth. Graph in figure 7 shows the fluctuation in the bus bandwidth for the different arbitration algorithms when all the four masters requests for same amount of bus bandwidth. It is observed from the above graph that in case of adaptive arbitration algorithm the difference between the requested bandwidth and the allotted bandwidth is ± 2% where as in the case of static fixed priority algorithm its ± 8% and the minimum is in the case of round robin algorithm that is ± 0.15%.

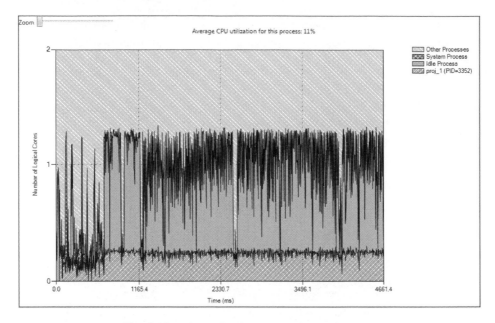

Fig. 6. Threads running in a preemptive environment

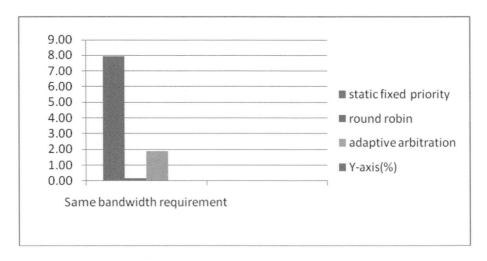

Fig. 7. Fluctuation in the bus bandwidth (Case I)

In the second case of Haishan Li et al. [13] all the four masters require different bandwidth and the proportion are 40%, 30%, 20% and 10% separately. The following graph shows the fluctuation in the bus bandwidth for the different arbitration algorithms when all the four masters requests for variable bus bandwidth.

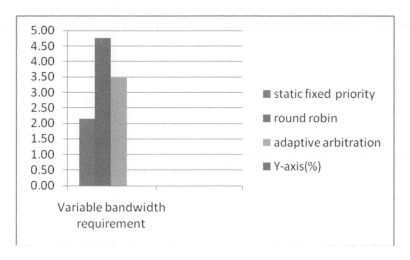

Fig. 8. Fluctuation in the bus bandwidth (Ref. Haishan Li et al.)

It is observed from the above graph that in case of adaptive arbitration algorithm the difference between the requested bandwidth and the allotted bandwidth is ± 3.5% where as in the case of round robin algorithm its ± 4.75% and the minimum is in the case of static fixed priority algorithm that is ± 2.15%. From the above two graphs it can be concluded that the static fixed priority algorithm or round robin algorithm can provide the best bandwidth allocation in one case but the worst bandwidth allocation in the other case. If compared with static fixed priority algorithm and round robin algorithm, the adaptive arbitration algorithm holds relatively good in both the cases.

Yi-Xu et al. [10] also conducted an experiment to evaluate the bus bandwidth utilization using lottery bus algorithm for four masters where each master requires variable amount of bus bandwidth. The following graph shows the fluctuation in the bus bandwidth for the adaptive arbitration algorithm and the lottery bus algorithm when all the four masters requests for variable bus bandwidth.

It is observed from the above graph that adaptive arbitration algorithm still holds better if compared with lottery bus algorithm by a margin of ± 0.20%.

It is observed from the table 2 that in terms of fair bandwidth allotment for the processors according to their traffic behavior the adaptive arbiter comes out to be superior if compared with other conventional arbiters. In a multi-microprocessor bus it was found that the point of saturation reached when five processors issued low level requests for the contention of the bus [18]. The following graph shows the comparison between the conventional arbiter and the proposed arbiter in terms of their bus bandwidth consumption.

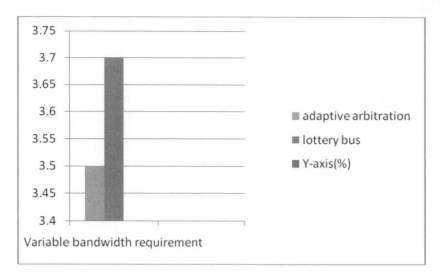

Fig. 9. Fluctuation in the bus bandwidth (Ref. Haishan Li et al. and Yi Xu et al.)

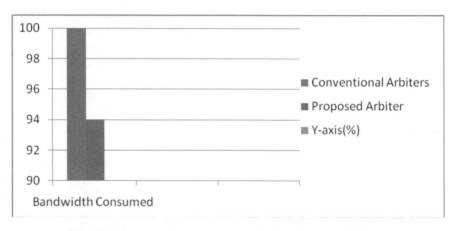

Fig. 10. Comparison between Conventional and Proposed Arbiter
(Ref. Haishan Li et al. and Chien-Hua et al.)

If compared with other conventional arbiter, the proposed arbiter reduces the consumption of bus bandwidth by 6%. During the process of adaptive arbitration if the time slot of any upcoming master is not to be utilized then immediately the second level of the arbiter comes into an action. If hardware overhead would not have been the major factor then the overall performance of the system could have been enhanced up to a large margin just by increasing the levels of arbitration and splitting the bus into multiple layer [19], [20]. Adaptive arbiter is a kind of dynamic arbiter, so as per the experiment conducted by Yi Xu et al. [10] where 4 ARM processors were tested along with Advanced Microcontroller Bus Architecture-AHB (AMBA-AHB) bus as the communication network. According to their experiment it is observed that the Dynamic Arbiter takes less time compared to Lottery Bus and Two-Level TDMA arbiter. Their execution time is shown in the following graph.

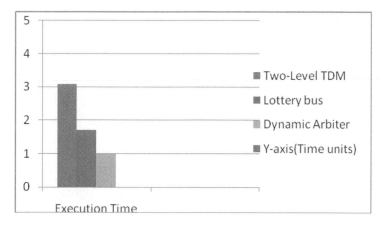

Fig. 11. Execution time of different arbiters (Experiment conducted by Yi Xu et al.)

After analyzing the above graphs it can be said that the proposed arbiter can solve the problem of maximum cpu utilization, fair bandwidth allotment and system latency for a real time computing system in a very efficient manner and with a very simple design if compared with conventional arbiters [21],[22].

7   Conclusion

An attempt on reducing the system latency and achieving a fair bandwidth allocation by utilizing the CPU cores to its maximum is being made. More investigation has to be done on reducing the system latency up to a large margin. The proposed arbiter architecture is purely a system level architecture and can be implanted on any real time systems such as biomedical devices which need a guaranteed fair bandwidth with negligible amount of latency. In a nutshell this arbitration technique helps in achieving a fair bandwidth allocation for the critical requirements by utilizing the CPU cores to its maximum and it also reduces the system latency up to an adequate margin. This article provides a comprehensive picture of the global scenario of an arbiter for real time computing system so as to enable researchers to decide the direction of further investigation.

Acknowledgement. This research is supported by Institute of Post Graduate Studies (IPS) unit of Universiti Sains Malaysia. I would like to thank both CEDEC and IPS for their support in this research.

References

1. Pasricha, S., Dutt, N.: On–Chip Communication Architectures: System-on-Chip Interconnect. Morgan Kaufmann, USA (2008)
2. Poletti, F., Bertozzi, D., Benini, L., Bogliolo, A.: Performance Analysis of Arbitration Policies for SoC Communication Architectures. Des. Autom. Embed. Syst. 8(2), 189–210 (2003)
3. Jian, W., Yubai, L., Qicong, P., Taiqiu, T.: A Dynamic Priority Arbiter for Network-on-Chip. In: IEEE International Symposium on Industrial Embedded Systems, pp. 253–256. IEEE Press (2009)
4. Antonopoulos, C., Dimitrios, S.N., Theodore, S.P.: Scheduling Algorithms with Bus Bandwidth Considerations for SMP's. In: IEEE International Conference on Parallel Processing, pp. 547–554. IEEE Press (2003)
5. Laxmi, N.B.: Analysis of Interconnection Networks with Different Arbiter Designs. J. Parallel Distrib. Comput. 4(4), 384–403 (1987)
6. Lakshmi, V., Wood, K., Downs, T.: A Four-Channel Communications Arbiter for Multiprocessor Arrays. Microprocess. Microsyst. 18(5), 253–260 (1994)
7. Macii, E., Poncino, M.: Automatic Synthesis of Easily Scalable Bus Arbiters with Dynamic Priority Assignment Strategies. Comput. Electr. Eng. 24(3), 223–228 (1998)
8. Nelson, J.C.C., Refai, M.K.: Design of a Hardware Arbiter for Multi Microprocessor Systems. Microprocess. Microsyst. 8(1), 21–24 (1984)
9. Bowen, B.A., Buhr, R.J.A.: The Logical Design of Multiprocessor Systems. Prentice Hall, Englewood Cliffs (1980)
10. Yi, X., Li, L., Ming-lun, G., Bing, Z., Zhao-yu, J., Gao-ming, D., Wei, Z.: An Adaptive Dynamic Arbiter for Multi-Processor SoC. In: 8th IEEE International Conference on Solid-State and Integrated Circuit Technology, pp. 1993–1996. IEEE Press (2006)
11. Aravind, A.A.: An Arbitration Algorithm for Multiport Memory Systems. ELEX 2(19), 488–494 (2005)
12. Chien-Hua, C., Geeng-Wei, L., Juinn-Dar, H., Jiang-Yang, J.: A Real Time Bandwidth Guaranteed Arbitration Algorithm for SoC Bus Communication. In: 11th Asia and South Pacific IEEE International Conference on Design Automation, pp. 24–27. IEEE Press (2006)
13. Haishan, L., Ming, Z., Wei, Z., Dongxiao, L.: An Adaptive Arbitration Algorithm for SoC Bus. In: IEEE International Conference on Networking, Architecture and Storages, pp. 245–246. IEEE Press (2007)
14. Bourgade, R., Rochange, C., De Michiel, M., Sainrat, P.: A Multi-Bandwidth Bus Arbiter for Hard Real Time. In: IEEE 5th International Conference on Embedded and Multimedia Computing, pp. 1–7. IEEE Press (2010)
15. Shanthi, D., Amutha, R.: Performance Analysis of On-Chip Communication Architecture in MPSoC. In: IEEE International Conference on Emerging Trends in Electrical and Computer Technology, pp. 811–815. IEEE Press (2011)
16. Shanthi, D., Amutha, R.: Design of Efficient On-Chip Communication Architecture in MPSoC. In: IEEE International Conference on Recent Trends in Information Technology, pp. 364–369. IEEE Press (2011)
17. Trahay, F., Brunet, E., Denis, A.: An Analysis of the Impact of Multi-Threading on Communication Performance. In: IEEE International Symposium on Parallel & Distributed Processing, pp. 1–7. IEEE Press (2009)
18. Scarabottolo, N., Bedina, A., Distante, F.: Implementation Guidelines of a Modular General Purpose Multi-Microcomputer. J. Syst. Architect. 9(5), 309–313 (1982)

19. Ruibing, L., Aiqun, C.: SAMBA Bus- A High Performance Bus Architectures for System-on-Chips. IEEE Trans. Very Large Scale Integr. (VLSI) Syst. 15(1), 69–79 (2007)
20. Lin, B.C., Lee, G.W., Huang, J.D., Jou, J.Y.: A Precise Bandwidth Controller Arbitration Algorithm for Hard Real-Time SoC Buses. In: Asia and South Pacific IEEE International Conference on Parallel & Design Automation, pp. 165–170. IEEE Press (2007)
21. Akhtar, M.N., Sidek, O.: An Arbiter with Fair Bandwidth Allocation and Low Latency for Real Time Computing System. In: International Conference on Computer Technology and Development, pp. 189–196 (2011)
22. Akhtar, M.N., Sidek, O.: An Intelligent Arbiter for Fair Bandwidth Allocation. In: IEEE Students Conference on Research and Development, pp. 322–327 (2011)

Aggressive and Intelligent Self-Defensive Network

Towards a New Generation of Semi-autonomous Networks

Ali Elouafiq[1,2], Ayoub Khobalatte[1,2], and Wassim Benhallam[2]

[1] Blue Sky Information Security
{ceo,cto}@blueskysec.com
[2] Al Akhawayn University in Ifrane (AUI)
School of Science and Engineering
Computer Science Departments
Ifrane, Morocco
{a.elouafiq,a.khobalatte,w.benhallam}@aui.ma

Abstract. Aggressive and Intelligent Self-defensive Network (AISEN) is an open-source distributed solution that aims at deploying a semi-autonomous network, which enables internal attack deception through misguidance and illusion. In fact, instead of simply preventing or stopping the attack as do traditional Intrusion Prevention Systems (IPS), AISEN drives attackers to attack decoy machines, which clone victim machines by mimicking their personalities (e.g. OS, services running). On top of that, AISEN uses rogue machines that clone idle production machines, which are able to detect human-aware zero-day attacks not seen by IPS. The solution uses real-time dynamic high-interaction honeypot generation, and a novel re-routing schema that is both router and network architecture independent, along with a robust troubleshooting algorithm for sophisticated attacks. Information captured and data gathered from these decoy machines will give CERTs/CISRTs and forensic experts critical data relevant to the sophistication of the attack, vulnerabilities targeted, and some means of preventing it in the future. This project reviewed former designs and similar studies addressing the same issues and emphasizes the added value of this open source solution in terms of flexibility, ease of use and upgrade, deployment, and customization.

Because AISEN seamlessly integrates with Security Information and Event Management (SIEM) software, it goes far beyond standard IPS/IDS alerts. It actually listens for suspicious activities and uncommon behavior (e.g. port scanning in a communication department network) to detect suspicious activities that a normal user would not do. AISEN is designed to enable potential integration with passive Strike-back modules that may be achieved in later work.

Keywords: Network, IDS, IPS, Firewall, Incident Response, Antivirus, zero-day, advanced persistent threats, internal attacks, honeypot, state-of-the-art, enterprise-class.

1 Introduction

Up to this day, many innovative and useful systems have been created offering functionalities that help securing networks. Examples of these would intrusion detection

R. Benlamri (Ed.): NDT 2012, Part I, CCIS 293, pp. 344–354, 2012.

systems (IDS), intrusion prevention systems (IPS), security information event managers (SIEMs), and honeypots. The goal of this project is to use these already existing technologies in accordance with each other and, as a result, provide an automatic self-defense mechanism that can be easily integrated in current networks.

Aggressive and Intelligent Self-Defensive network (AISEN) is an all-in-one solution that enables the different components in a given network to communicate with each other about the network's current state. In other words, it is a solution that intuitively reuses the already implemented security mechanisms available today in the market. The alarms generated by current SIEMs when an attack is detected are sent to a management server. These standardized alarm events should contain information about the type of the undergoing attack and the identities of the attacker and the victim, among other useful information. The management server then notifies the user agent installed at the level of the victim's machine, and asks it to redirect traffic to an appropriate centralized NAT Box. The choice of the NAT Box depends on the VLAN of the attacker and victim and on its availability. The NAT Box in turns forwards to the appropriate virtual honeypot for data capture and analysis. This insures the victim machine is not harmed, while keeping the attacker unaware of the rerouting mechanism and providing the security administrator with an overview of what is going on in the network.

In this paper, we will explain the most important features of AISEN, its components as well as it work flow.

2   System Architecture

2.1   System Overview

Aggressive and intelligent self-defensive network (AISEN) is a distributed security system that integrates different communicating components to ensure the network will benefit from live security monitoring, real time risk mitigation, and network obfuscation and deception. Essentially, AISEN relies on vendor neutral security information event management systems, third generation honeypot technology, and a distributed software architecture comprising intermediate network nodes, endpoint software agents, and a central management server. Following is a non-exhaustive list of features provided by AISEN:

Attack Detection and Prevention
AISEN relies heavily on vendor-independent SIEM technology available today. Most of these SIEMs are equipped with intrusion detection and prevention systems, which monitor the network, generate standardized events, and communicate them in real time to AISEN's management server (discussed later). Essentially, SIEMs represent a fundamental starting point for all features provided by AISEN.

Network Deception and Illusion
While securing the network and protecting the production environment, one critical feature is to prevent attacks. AISEN accomplishes this by providing obfuscation and

diversion by means of an open source software emulating different network stations: Honeyd.

Attack Rerouting
One of the fundamental features of AISEN is the ability to dynamically reroute attacks targeting our production environment to automatically generated honeypots in the Virtual Environment. This feature is truly a breakthrough in the field of network security, as it constitutes a paradigm shift from traditional approaches to static honeypot-based network security.

Automatic Honeypot Generation
This feature of AISEN entails the automatizing the process of launching, resuming, shutting down, or putting on hold all virtual machines in the Virtual Environment. This is possible because most of the virtual servers (i.e. machines that host honeypots) offer APIs to handle remote virtual machine handling. These honeypots can be either low or high interaction.

- *Real time discreet honeypot interaction upgrade.*

AISEN deals with attacks first using low interaction honeypots since they can be quickly set up and configured. However, an escalation towards high interaction honeypots in crucial to provide real system behavior, data capture, and, as a result, avoid compromising the rerouting process.

- *Virtual Environment Invisibility.*

Unlike traditional honeypot-powered security, AISEN does not allow any entity in the network to discover or communicate with honeypots directly. Instead, all incoming and outgoing traffic to/from the honeypots pass through a process called the NatBox. Furthermore, the Virtual Environment (the set of honeynets with honeywall) is put in a separate VLAN that only the NatBox can access. This ensures the Virtual Environment invisibility and therefore helps in the obfuscation of AISEN's internal structure.

Data Capture, Control, and Analysis
As aforementioned, AISEN relies on honeypots for data capture and analysis. However, implementing this functionality at the level of each single honeypot would be redundant and time consuming. This is the reason why all traffic to honeypots pass through a layer-2 machine named honeywall. This machine keeps track of all traffic for future data analysis.

Attackers profiling
Keeping track of attacks in the network insures attackers are identified and their behaviors kept track of for a predetermined period of time. This feature is called attackers profiling. However, AISEN only helps identifying these attackers; how to deal with these attackers is left to the network administrator.

Zero-day threat discovery

The system will allow us to discover zero-day threats such as new malwares, rootkits, locale exploits when the attacker will fall into the trap of the machine that mimics the real one. Moreover, if an attacker's behavior is suspicious, we have a chance to capture a zero day attack that will not be detected by the IPS/IDS or the SIEM technology involved [8].

Strike Back (Future Work)

The strike back is a still debated concept in the realm of information security. AISEN includes an optional module that can be used should the strike back be deployed in future networks. The Strike Back mechanisms are built upon the idea of putting fake sensitive information and vulnerabilities in the network to attract possible attackers. If such attacker is identified, the strike back module of AISEN refers to its built-in extensible knowledge base that contains different scripts to confuse the attacker or, in extreme cases, shut down their system.

Distributed Troubleshooting

Perhaps the most important feature of AISEN is the distribution of different modules in the network. This ensures the integrity of the network if one of these modules shuts down. Refer to rerouting workflow section.

The use of IDS and IPS in modern network is essential. Some SIEMs even include these in a package and, consequently, offer the administrator a total view of what's happening, live, in the network. AISEN is built on this fact as t assumes the existence of an entity which job is to monitor the network all the time.

2.2   System Components

SIEM with Intrusion Detection and Event Generation

The initial information gathering concerns both the attacker and the target. However, this only refers to basic characteristics such as collecting suspicious traffic and auxiliary information that describes the traffic, the events, and the incidents. Clearly, the information collected at this step is the result of a thorough analysis of the malicious activities detected by the IPS/IDS. Identifying and locating both the attacker and the victim is the intended outcome. In fact, the information collected about the victim host is tremendously important and will be used in the next step to create an environment that mimics its services and fingerprint [10].

Management Server

The Management server is the central brain of AISEN; it receives alerts from the related SIEM, processes the alert, and chooses the appropriate decision based on the degree of the alert and its master configuration. The Management Server logs all the alerts received along with the respective decisions taken, is responsible for managing the workflow, and detecting failures and errors in NatBoxes and User Agents. The management server should be customizable in the sense that the administrator can

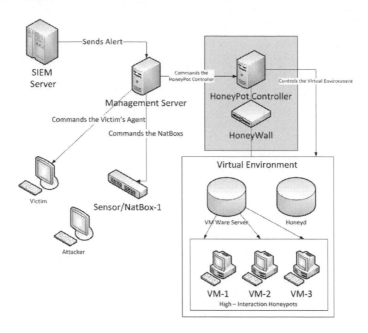

Fig. 1. AISEN's components

specify his or her own rules. The Management Server can be extended to manage multiple networks by receiving alerts from different SIEMs for different networks, then command and controls the appropriate NatBox, user agents and Virtual Environments.

Client Agent

The Client Agents (also called user agents) are programs that protect production machines on which they are deployed. The Client Agents are designed to forward traffic incoming from specific machines (i.e. attackers) to the appropriate NatBox or simply deny it, following orders sent by the Management Server. Client Agents are also responsible for reporting anomalies and malfunctions, which may occur, to the Management Server. The Client Agents have a dedicated protocol to communicate with AISEN as follows

NatBox

The NatBox is a pillar piece in the overall structure of the attack- rerouting process. Its primary objective is to perform both SNAT and DNAT[9] packets flying in both directions (Attacker to honeypot and honeypot to attacker). This provides greater security as it hides the honeypot identity from the attacker and adds another controllable hop in the interfacing between the attacker and the honeypot machine. The Management Server controls the NatBox and the Client Agents with which it communicates using specified messages for receiving instructions and sending states.

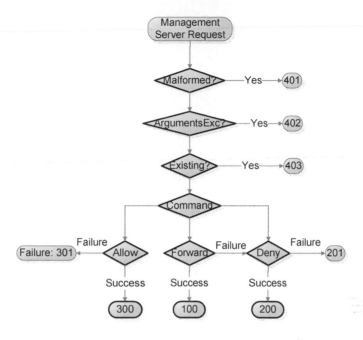

Fig. 2. Client Agent's workflow and protocol codes

The reason why NAT is not done at the level of victim machines is the lack of flexible and uniform NAT support across different windows operating systems [3][13]. Therefore, it has been decided that a number of intermediate devices (NatBoxes) would perform NAT; each of which spans across a user-specified portion of the network. In order to ensure that the solution is network independent, the NatBox should not be any of the sensitive network devices (e.g. routers or switches). It should, however, cover approximately the same area covered by a leaf router due to traffic constrains.

The interaction between the NatBox and Client Agents is show in the figure blow.

Virtual Environment (VE)
The Virtual Environment refers to the set of virtual hosts created by Honeyd (Low Interaction Honeypot, defined below) as well as the virtual machines created using VMware (high interaction honeypots). Access to the Virtual Environment must be through the HoneyGate, which acts as a gateway for all incoming and outgoing traffic of the VE.

Honeyd
Honeyd is an open source program that creates virtual hosts with customized personalities that mimic operating system and services of a real host. In our case, VEC will communicate to the Honeyd information regarding the host to mimic (OS, services). Installed on a single host, Honeyd can claim up to 65536 network addresses. This ability means that there is almost no chance of Honeyd not being able to create a virtual host upon request from the Management Server [12].

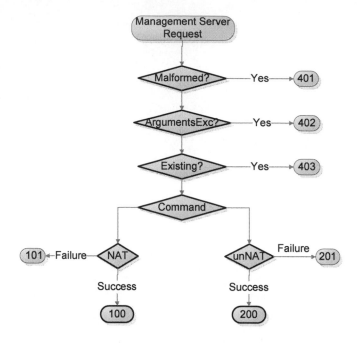

Fig. 3. NatBox's Workflow and protocol codes

VMware Server

VMware server will generate new virtual machines, shut down or suspend existing ones, and dynamically change their configurations upon requests from the VEC. Virtual machines, being high interaction honeypot, consume much more system resources. Consequently, VMware servers will have to follow default or administrator-based policies to optimize the use of these resources. For example, how to generate a new virtual machine in case the host running VMware server has consumed all of its resources? Possible solutions include shutting down the virtual machine that has been running the longest, idle the longest, or consuming the biggest chunk of system resources [5].

HoneyGate

The HoneyGate is a fundamental element in the chain of command initiated by the Management Server. Essentially, the HoneyGate consists of two interdependent modules that carry out logically different tasks. These are the HoneyWall and the Virtual Environment Controller (VEC).

HoneyWall

HoneyWall has been developed in the context of the honeynet project as a gateway device that separates high interaction honeypots from the rest of the network. This project makes similar use of honeyWall in the sense that it will act as a gateway device for both the low interaction honeypots (created using Honeyd) and the high interaction virtual machines (virtualized using VMware). In addition, HoneyWall will be responsible for capturing and logging the attacker's activities in the honeypots (data capture), containing these activities in order to minimize the risk of the attacker taking control of the honeypots (data control), and finally analyzing the captured data and converting it to useful information (data analysis) which is a major goal of this project[7].

Virtual Environment Controller (VEC)
The VEC is a module that listens to commands from the Management Server relevant to the Virtual Environment. In fact, the VEC is responsible for coordinating the two main actors involved in honeypot generation: Honeyd and VMware Server. Once an attack is detected by the Intrusion detection system, the Management Server is notified with information about attacker and victim. The Management Server then commands the VEC to prepare the floor for the creation of a honeypot that replicates the victim's system. As a first step, the VEC commands Honeyd to create a virtual host that emulates the same operating system and services running on the real victim. However, a virtual host emulated by Honeyd is considered a low interaction honeypot that can raise suspicions about its nature. Meanwhile, VEC initiates the creation of a high interaction honeypot by commanding VMware server with corresponding parameters; including th OS and services to run on the virtual machine. The time and processing overhead required to launch a new virtual machine is one of the reasons why attacks are not directly rerouted to the virtual machine (high interaction honeypot) but are rather rerouted first to a Honeyd-based virtual host. Consequently, the VEC is also responsible for evaluating if the interaction with the low interaction honeypot is advanced enough to require the generation of a high interaction virtual machine and shift the interaction to it. This makes the VEC responsible for managing the transition from the low to the high interaction honeypot as well as the optimization of the Virtual Environment's resources [14].

3   The Rerouting Process Architecture

3.1   Rerouting Overview

Rerouting refers to the redirection of attacks destined to victims' machines in the production environment to honeypots in the Virtual Environment. The rerouting process involves four main actors: the Client Agent, the NatBox agent, the VEC, and the Management Server. By using NatBoxes and Client Agents, the solution becomes vendor neutral. Alternatives such as modifying the routers configuration (e.g. adding entries in the routing table) are problematic as it is difficult to interface with different routers from different vendors. Moreover, changing routers configuration is difficult to troubleshoot and present higher chances of network Denial of Service when an error occurs. Moreover, attacks within a single subnet will be untreated.

NATing the traffic between the attacker and the honeypot at the level of the victim is also another alternative to AISEN's approach. However, this requires the Virtual Environment to be visible to the victims, and hence to attackers as well, which is clearly not feasible. Moreover, the victim based NATing is vendor/OS specific and lacks flexible and uniform support even across different versions of the same operating system.

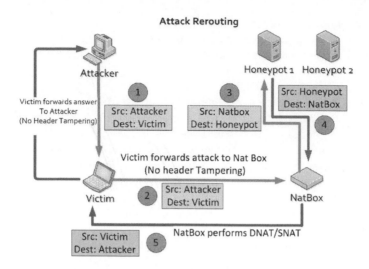

Fig. 4. AISEN's Rerouting Schema

The Client Agent/NatBox based rerouting is more easier to handle as the Client Agents, installed in all machines of the production environment, focus only on forwarding the suspicious traffic (with no packet header alteration) coming from the attacker to the NatBox. The ability to forward traffic is readily available in the majority of platforms. Work on optimizing the efficiency of the NatBox may be conducted later on.

As aforementioned, NatBox Agents are deployed in sensor devices (i.e. which role is to monitor network activity) that come with SIEM software. This location allows NatBoxes to be logically assigned to specific segments of the network. In a way, NatBoxes take advantage of the logical repartition of sensors in the network and will therefore receive requests only from Client Agents belonging to that network segment. Additionally, NatBoxes are the only machines able to interact with the Virtual Environment, making them hidden from the whole network. These features satisfy robust rerouting architecture as outlined below:

- *Deployment flexibility:* This rerouting scheme can be deployed in different network architectures.
- *Router Independence:* the rerouting process should not modify the router configurations. This constraint minimizes the risk of a denial-of-service (if an error occurs) and makes the process vendor independent.
- *One-to-one/Many-to-One Attacker-Victim mapping*: The rerouting process should map each attacker to a specific decoy, or all attackers targeting the same machine to the same decoy, as specified by the network administrator.
- *Troubleshooting:* The rerouting process should detect failures and errors at different levels of the process, and take appropriate decisions accordingly.
- *Encapsulation:* The Virtual Environment should be hidden from the actual network machines, and should be difficult to be detected by an attacker.

3.2   Workflow Overview

The Management Server receives Alerts mainly from the SIEM; the alert describes the Victim specifications, the attacker profile, and other important information. The Management Server then notifies the VEC to prepare a virtual host (i.e. low interaction honeypots) in the time it takes the high interaction honeypot to be ready. When the decoy is ready the Management Server notifies the NatBox to NAT the traffic coming from attacker to the victim according to the administrator preferences: One-to-One attacker-victim mapping or Many-to-One attacker-victim mapping.

When the NatBox is configured to reroute the traffic, the Management Server sends orders to the victim's Client Agent, so that it forwards all its traffic coming from the attacker to the NatBox.

The Agents in the client machines open a connection with the Management Server once it runs, and close it once it shuts down. This later one keeps track of both alive and idle machines in the Network. When an agent is Idle, the Management Server commands the VEC to create a temporary Honeyd virtual host and orders the appropriate NatBox to reroute the traffic destined to the Idle Victim to the Honeyd. When the Honeyd virtual host gets an important incoming traffic, it sends an alarm to the Management Server as a high alert. If there is no generated warning from the IPS/IDS, the data collected will have a high chance to be a zero-day attack. Henceforth, the Management Server commands the VEC to prepare a high-interaction honeypot to collect data.

4   Conclusion

Network security has always been considered one the most critical aspects of today's businesses. The time and effort put in place to provide information confidentiality, integrity, and availability is growing exponentially. However, as networks become bigger and more complex and attacks become more sophisticated, along with exponential growth of vulnerabilities found, traditional security measure are turning inefficient and, as a result, ineffective.

This paper explained how AISEN adds a layer of autonomy to already secured networks. This solution ensures integrity, scalability, and robustness, using a state-of-the-art rerouting architecture combined with a hybrid use of both low and high interaction honeypots. The need for human intervention has always been an issue as there are many factors that affect our performance such as unavailability, long response time, and human error. Network monitoring tools, automatic honeypot generation and malicious traffic rerouting along with AISEN's critical features will help make the security administrator's job easier by limiting them to the status of observer and decision maker, and helping the CERT/CSIRT teams gather evidences easily.

References

1. Jiang, X., Xinyuan, W.: Out-of-the-box Monitoring of VM-based High-Interaction Honeypots. Dissertation, George Mason University (2007)
2. Revolution Systems. Linux NAT in Four Steps Using Iptables (2010), http://www.revsys.com/writings/quicktips/nat.html (accessed October 11, 2011)

3. González, D.: Installing a Virtual HoneyWall Using VMware. In: Spanish Honeynet Project (2004), Available via Papers `http://honeynet.org.es/papers/vhwall` (accessed October 11, 2011)
4. The Honeynet Project. Configuring VMware and Installing Your Honeypots (2008), `http://www.honeynet.pk/honeywall/eeyore/page2.html` (accessed October 11, 2011)
5. Symantec. Open Source Honeypots, Part Two: Deploying Honeyd in the Wild (2010), `http://www.symantec.com/connect/articles/open-source-honeypots-part-two-deploying-honeyd-wild` (accessed October 11, 2011)
6. The Honeynet Project. The HoneyWall (2008), `http://www.honeynet.org` (accessed May 07, 2011)
7. Microsoft Technet. Defining Malware: FAQ (2003) `http://technet.microsoft.com/en-us/library/dd632948.aspx` (accessed on October 11, 2011)
8. The Internet Engineering Task Force. RFC 1631 - The IP Network Address Translator (NAT) (1994), `http://tools.ietf.org/html/rfc1631` (accessed on October 11, 2011)
9. Lane, A.: Understanding and Selecting SIEM/LM: Use Cases. In: Securosis Blog. Securosis (2010), `http://securosis.com/blog/understanding-and-selecting-siem-lm-use-cases-part-1` (accessed October 11, 2011)
10. Hudak, S.: Automatic Honeypot Generation and Network Deception. In: Scientific Literature Digital Library and Search (2008) (accessed on July 12, 2011)
11. Provos, N.: A Virtual Honeypot Framework. University of Michigan (2003) (accessed on September 4, 2011)
12. CyberCiti. Mac OS X: Set Port Forwarding Nat Router (Internet Sharing) (2010), `http://www.cyberciti.biz/faq/howto-configure-macosx-as-nat-router` (accessed on October 12, 2011)
13. Hecker, C., Kara, N., Brian, H.: Dynamic Honeypot Construction. University of Alaska Fairbanks (2006) (accessed October 11, 2011)

A 2-Dimensional Cellular Automata Pseudorandom Number Generator with Non-linear Neighborhood Relationship

Sang-Ho Shin[1], Dae-Soo Kim[2], and Kee-Young Yoo[3,*]

[1] Graduate School of Electrical Engineering and Computer Science, Kyungpook National University, 80 Daehak-ro, Buk-Gu, Daegu 702-701, South Korea
[2] Department of Information Security, Kyungpook National University
80 Daehak-ro, Buk-Gu, Daegu 702-701, South Korea
[3] School of Computer Science and Engineering, Kyungpook National University
80 Daehak-ro, Buk-Gu, Daegu 702-701, South Korea
{shshin80,stairways}@infosec.knu.ac.kr, yook@knu.ac.kr

Abstract. Until recently, two-dimensional (2-D) cellular automata (CA) pseudorandom number generator (PRNG) research areas have been done based on von Neumann with linear neighborhood relationship. Although the linear neighborhood relationship has an excellent random quality, its cycle length is less than the linear neighborhood relationship. The cycle length is an important w.r.t. cryptographically secure PRNG because of the property of non-prediction for next sequence.

This paper proposes 2-D CA PRNG based on von Neumann method with non-linear neighborhood relationship. In the proposed scheme, five elements (i.e. *self*, *top*, *bottom*, *left* and *right*) and two control elements (i.e. c_1 and c_2) with the combination of Boolean operator AND, XOR, or OR are used. The evolution function chooses one combination of XOR & AND and XOR & OR by two control elements. The number of rules in the proposed scheme is higher than previous schemes. To evaluate between the proposed scheme and previous schemes, the ENT and DIEHARD test suites are used in the experiments. In the experimental result, the randomness quality of the proposed PRNG was slightly less than or much the same previous schemes. However, the proposed scheme can generate various CA rule patterns and the number of rules is higher than previous schemes. The correlation coefficient between global state $G^{(t)}$ and $G^{(t+1)}$ of the proposed scheme is reduced because of using the non-linear neighborhood relationship.

Keywords: Cellular automata, Pseudorandom number generator(PRNG), Cryptography, Statistical tests.

1 Introduction

In the last 50 years, a generation of the secret key has been very important in cryptography because the secret key is a very important role in encryption and

---

* Corresponding author.

R. Benlamri (Ed.): NDT 2012, Part I, CCIS 293, pp. 355–368, 2012.

decryption processes. If a secret key (or private key) of OTP, DES, AES, RSA or ECC has been exposed to a malicious attacker, for example, the ciphertext can be decrypted by an attacker who knows the secret key.

Generally, the secret key must have two characteristics: high randomness quality and unpredictability. The generation of secret key and random number generation is considered to be the same in cryptography. If a randomness quality has been increased, secret key is secured. In pratice, the intentional generation of random number is difficult because it is generated from natural phenomenon such as thermal noise, air turbulence, sound from a microphone, the system clock, and so on [1]. Hence, a pseudorandom number that can be intentional generated and closes to property of random number has been studied in the past two decades [3,4,5,6,7]. The secret key of block cipher such as DES or AES generates the subsecret keys, and there should be no correlation between subsecret keys. After subsecret key was generated in t^{th} time step, that is, the subsecret key of $(t+1)^{th}$ time step should be no predict. In this sense, the secret key must have the high randomness quality and should be no predict.

The pseudorandom number generator (PRNG) based on cellular automata (CA) is a new prospective method designed to generate the pseudorandom numbers. It has been extensively studied over the past decades for its convenient implementation by means of self-reproduction and self-repair, respectively [2].

Von Neumann [8] was the first introduction to CA concept for modeling biological self-reproduction. By Wolfram later [9] on a mathematical model study for self-organizing statistical systems was conducted in Cellular Automata. A CA based pseudorandom number generator (PRNG) was first proposed by Hortensius et al. [10] in regards to a built-in self-test in three-neighborhood one-dimension (1-D) CA with two-state. By other researchers [11,12,13,14], since the 1-D CA PRNG has been proposed. In recent years, reaserch is turning into a two-dimensional (2-D) CA PRNGs [15,16,17]. In terms of trade-off between the design complexity and computation efficiency, one of them cannot be said to be better.

In this paper, a 2-D CA PRNG based on von Neumann with non-linear neighborhood relationship is proposed. In the proposed scheme, 5 elements and 2 control elements with the combination of Boolear operator AND, XOR, or OR are used. The number of rules of the proposed scheme is higer than previous schemes, and the pattern for cycle of a generated rule dose not circulate (i.e. cycle of "ρ" form). To estimate the randomness quality, ENT and DIEHARD test suites were used in the experiment. In the experimental results, the randomness quality of the proposed scheme is similar to or slightly less than prevous schemes.

This paper is organized as follows. Section 2 introduces cellular automata at one-dimension and two-dimension. The consideration and evolution process of the proposed scheme is discussed in Section 3. Section 4 presents the experimental results. Finally, Section 5 gives the conclusions.

2 Preliminaries

In this section, cellular automata (CA) in one-dimension (1-D) and two-dimension (2-D) are introduced.

2.1 Cellular Automata in 1-Dimension

CA are a dynamical system at discreted space and time. A CA consists of an array of cells, each of which can be in one of a finite number of possible states, updated synchronously in discrete time steps, according to a local, identical interaction rule. The next state of a cell is assumed to depend on itself and on its neighbors. The cells evolve in discrete time steps according to some deterministic rule that depends only on local neighbors. Each cell consists of a storage element (D flip-flop) and a combinational logic implementing the next state function. Table 1 describes notations of a characterized CA [2].

Table 1. Notations of a characterized CA

Notation	Description
i	The position of an individual CA cell
t	The time step
$s_i(t)$	The output state of the ith cell at the tth time step
$s_i(t+1)$	The output state of the ith cell at the $(t+1)^{th}$ time step

The next-state function with $(2k+1)$-neighborhood can be expressed by the following equation (1):

$$s_i(t+1) \;=\; f(\, s_{i-k}(t), \;\ldots, \; s_i(t), \;\ldots, \; s_{i+k}(t)\,), \qquad (1)$$

where k $(1 \leq k)$ and f indicate a radius of CA and a local function (known as a "*rule*") with a combinational logic, respectively.

Suppose that CA with n-state, $(2k+1)$-neighborhood, it can express a total of $n^{(2k+1)}$ distinct neighborhood configurations; that is, there can be a total of $n^{n^{(2k+1)}}$ distinct mappings from all these neighborhood configurations to the next state. Also, each mapping is called a rule of CA. If the next-state function of a cell is expressed in form of a truth table, then the decimal equivalent of the output is conventionally called the "*rule number*" for CA cells.

Consider CA with 2-state, 3-neighborhood, for example, the next-state function can be expressed by the following equation (2):

$$s_i(t+1) \;=\; f(\, s_{i-1}(t), \; s_i(t), \; s_{i+1}(t)\,), \qquad (2)$$

and the number of rules is $2^{2^3} (= 256)$. Table 2 shows the state transition for arbitrary rules in 2-state, 3-neighborhood CA. In Table 2, the top row gives all eight possible states of the three neighboring cells (the left, right neighbor of the ith cell, the ith cell itself) at the time t. The from second to fifth rows give the corresponding states of the ith cell at time $(t+1)$ for four CA rules. The corresponding combinational logic for the above rules can be specified as

$$\text{rule } 30 : s_i(t+1) = s_{i-1}(t) \oplus (s_i(t) \vee s_{i-1}(t)),$$
$$\text{rule } 90 : s_i(t+1) = s_{i-1}(t) \oplus s_{i+1}(t),$$
$$\text{rule } 150 : s_i(t+1) = s_{i-1}(t) \oplus s_i(t) \oplus s_{i+1}(t),$$
$$\text{rule } 202 : s_i(t+1) = (s_{i-1}(t) \wedge (s_i(t) \oplus s_{i+1}(t))) \oplus s_{i+1}(t),$$

where $\oplus$, $\vee$ and $\wedge$ are the Boolean operations XOR, OR and AND, respectively.

Table 2. The state transition for CA rules with 2-state, 3-neighborhood

Neighborhood state	111	110	101	100	011	010	001	000	rule number
Next state	0	1	0	1	1	0	1	0	(rule 90)
Next state	0	0	0	1	1	1	1	0	(rule 30)
Next state	1	0	0	1	0	1	1	0	(rule 150)
Next state	1	1	0	0	1	0	1	0	(rule 202)

2.2   Cellular Automata in 2-Dimension

A two-dimension (2-D) CA - the cells are arranged in a two-dimensional grid with connections among the neighboring cells - is a generalization of a 1-D. Consider a 2-D CA comprising mn cells organized as an $m \times n$ array with m rows and n columns. The state of CA at any time instant can be represented. The neighborhood function specifying the next state of a cell is assumed to depend on its neighbors and itself. For a 2-D CA, types of cellular neighborhoods are usually considered: five cells, consisting of one cell along with its four immediate non-diagonal neighbors (also known as von Neumann neighborhood); and nine cells, consisting of one cell along with its eight surrounding neighbors (also known as Moore neighborhood). Table 3 shows the notations of characterize a 2-D CA. Figure 1 shows the two types of 2-D CA geometric representation.

Table 3. The notations of characterize a CA at 2-D

Notation	Description
i, j	The position of an individual CA cell
t	The time step
$s_{i,j}(t)$	The output state of the i, j^{th} cell at the tth time step
$s_{i,j}(t+1)$	The output state of the i, j^{th} cell at the $(t+1)^{th}$ time step

In 2-D CA with von Neumann neighborhood, the next state $s_{i,j}(t+1)$ of the (i, j)-th cell of a 2-D CA is represented by the following equation (3):

$$s_{i,j}(t+1) = f(s_{i,j}(t),\ s_{i-1,j}(t),\ s_{i,j-1}(t),\ s_{i+1,j}(t),\ s_{i,j+1}(t)), \tag{3}$$

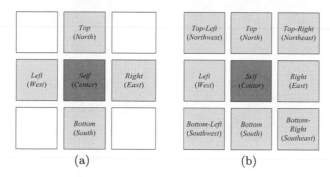

Fig. 1. The two types of 2-D CA geometric representation: (a) von Neumann neighborhood, (b) Moore neighborhood

where f is a Boolean function for five variables. There are $2^5 = 32$ distinct neighborhood configurations. Hence, to express a transition rule of 2-D CA in a manner similar to 1-D CA, 32 bits are required. In 2-D CA with Moore neighborhood, otherwise, the next state $s(t+1)$ of (i, j)-th cell of a 2-D CA is represented by the following equation (4):

$$s_{i,j}(t+1) = f(\bigcup_{k,\,l\,=-1}^{1} s_{i+k,j+l}(t)).$$ (4)

Since f is a Boolean function of five variables, there are $2^9 = 512$ distinct neighborhood configurations. Hence to express a transition rule of a 2-D CA in a manner similar to a 1-D CA, 512-bits are considered which is almost impossible to manage practically. Because their interesting properties and ease of the characterization, only CA with a linear neighborhood relationship (XOR) are considered [2].

In this paper, the proposed scheme based on von Neumann neighborhood is proposed, where considers five-neighborhoods that these consist of $self(= Center)$, $top(= North)$, $bottom(= South)$, $left(= West)$ and $right(= East)$. In CA with von Neumann neighborhood case, this dependency or rule can be expressed as a 5-bit number, where each bit signifies the presence of the corresponding dependency.

3 The Proposed Scheme

In this section, the main concept and evolution process of the proposed scheme is described.

General 2-D CA PRNGs have been proposed in linear neighborhood relationship (i.e. XOR) [15,16,17]. In this case, the number of rules is $2^6(= 64)$ which consists of 6 elements (that is, X (decide the linear or nonlilnear rule), C , N, S, W, E and a Boolean function XOR), and the next state $s_{i,j}(t+1)$ of the (i, j)-th cell of a 2-D CA is represented by the following equation (5):

$$s_{i,j}(t+1) = X \oplus (C \wedge s_{i,j}(t)) \oplus (N \wedge s_{i-1,j}(t)) \\ \oplus (S \wedge s_{i+1,j}(t)) \oplus (W \wedge s_{i,j-1}(t)) \oplus (E \wedge s_{i,j+1}(t)), \tag{5}$$

where $\oplus$ and $\wedge$ indicate Boolean function XOR and AND, respectively. In equation (5), a role of Boolean function AND is the only reference CA cells. Hence, it is completely linear neighborhood relationship which consists of the only Boolean function XOR. Also, 2-D CA with linear neighborhood relationship have the property that the randomness quality is the one of most CA configurations. A Boolean function XOR has the important property in terms of probability. It can be confirmed that the binomial distribution for the probability of XOR is $X \sim B(n, \frac{1}{2})$, where n is independent Bernoulli trials. That is, the expected value of the binomial distribution of the frequencies of occurrence of 0 for a XOR is decided by n [18].

However, this relationship has a problem which a cycle of generated CA cells can be circular (this problem is called the "O" problem). In terms of pseudorandom number generation, generated pseudorandom number should be a unique. If it looks like a circular form, it cannot be a unique pseudorandom number because one or more portions in generated pseudorandom number may be reuse in other portions. To solve the this problem, CA with a nonlinear neighborhood relationship should be used. A generated CA cell's sequences with nonlinear rules have a "ρ" form. In the "ρ" form, if non-circulation portion is used in order to generate the pseudorandom number, it can be a unique [19].

Therefore 2-D CA PRNG based on von Neumann neighborhood method with two control elements and a non-linear neighborhood relationship is used in the proposed scheme.

3.1   The Main Concept

The proposed scheme is based on non-linear neighborhhood relationship. It is the relationship of combinations of not only Boolean function XOR but AND, OR and NOT. If the relationship which consist of only AND, OR or combinations of AND and OR are made, the randomness quality is not good. However, generated CA cell's sequences with non-linear neiborhood relationship have a non-circulation portion. In terms of trade-off between the randomness quality and non-circulation, a proper method is used in this paper. The randomness quality of combinations of XOR & AND or XOR & OR are higher than combinations of only AND, OR or AND & OR. Also, the randomness quality of these combinations are less than or much the same combinations of only XOR. Hence, combinations of XOR & AND or XOR & OR are used in the proposed scheme. The detailed method is as follows.

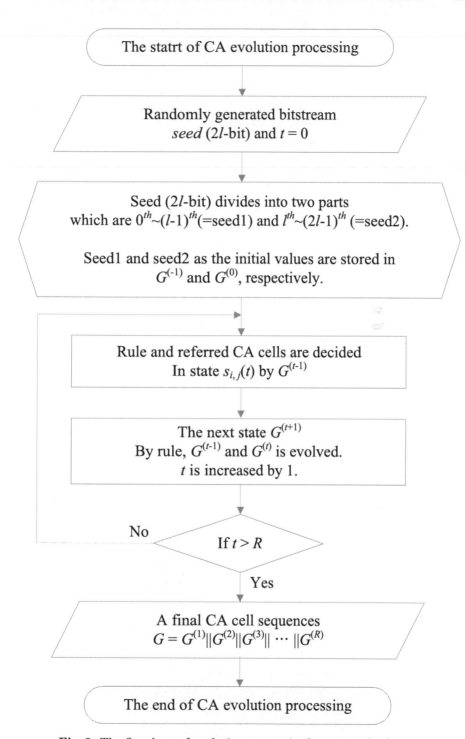

Fig. 2. The flowchart of evolution process in the proposed scheme

In the proposed scheme, two control elements (i.e. c_1, c_2) are used in order to select the neighborhood relationships. These can generate four cases, which are "00", "01", "10" and "11". In "00" or "01" cases, the evolution method is the same as von Neumann neighborhood method. In "10" and "11" cases, on the other hand, the combinations of XOR & AND and XOR & OR are used, respectively. Also, the number of XOR and AND is assumed to be the same. Hence, the next state $s_{i,j}(t+1)$ of the $(i,j)^{th}$ cell of a 2-D CA with non-linear neighborhood relationship is represented by the following equation (6):

$$s_{i,j}(t+1) = f_{c_1,c_2}(s_{i,j}(t), s_{i-1,j}(t), s_{i,j-1}(t), s_{i+1,j}(t), s_{i,j+1}(t)) \tag{6}$$

where f is an evolution function with c_1 and c_2.

For example, rules of 2-D CA with von Neumann neighborhood method are expressed as follows.

rule 31(0011111) : $s_{i,j}(t+1) = s_{i,j}(t) \oplus s_{i-1,j}(t) \oplus s_{i,j-1}(t) \oplus s_{i+1,j}(t) \oplus s_{i,j+1}(t)$
rule 59(0111011) : $s_{i,j}(t+1) = 1 \oplus s_{i,j}(t) \oplus s_{i-1,j}(t) \oplus s_{i+1,j}(t) \oplus s_{i,j+1}(t)$
rule 95(1011111) : $s_{i,j}(t+1) = 1 \oplus s_{i,j}(t) \wedge s_{i-1,j}(t) \oplus s_{i,j-1}(t) \wedge s_{i+1,j}(t) \oplus s_{i,j+1}(t)$
rule 95(1011111) : $s_{i,j}(t+1) = 1 \oplus s_{i,j}(t) \oplus s_{i-1,j}(t) \wedge s_{i,j-1}(t) \oplus s_{i+1,j}(t) \wedge s_{i,j+1}(t)$
rule 127(1111111) : $s_{i,j}(t+1) = 1 \oplus s_{i,j}(t) \vee s_{i-1,j}(t) \oplus s_{i,j-1}(t) \vee s_{i+1,j}(t) \oplus s_{i,j+1}(t)$
rule 127(1111111) : $s_{i,j}(t+1) = 1 \oplus s_{i,j}(t) \oplus s_{i-1,j}(t) \vee s_{i,j-1}(t) \oplus s_{i+1,j}(t) \vee s_{i,j+1}(t)$

where $\oplus$, $\wedge$ and $\vee$ indicate Boolean function XOR, AND and OR, respectively.

In example, even if rule 95 of third and fourth lines is the same for both, they have a different pattern by $s_{i,j}(t)$; that is, if $s_{i,j}(t)$ is 0, rule combination is expressed as $C \oplus N \wedge W \oplus S \wedge E$. Otherwise, rule combination is expressed as $C \wedge N \oplus W \wedge S \oplus E$. Although the number of rules in the proposed scheme is $2^7 (= 128)$, the number of rules is 64 (i.e. von Neumann neighborhood method) $+(2 \times 64)$ (i.e. non-linear neighborhood relationship) $= 192$ in practice becuase of a different pattern. Hence, the proposed scheme is better than previous methods can generate many CA rule patterns [15,16,17].

3.2   The Evolution Algorithm

Figure 2 shows the flowchart of evolution process in the proposed scheme. One round consists of two phases. The step-by-step process is explained as follows.

Initial Phase. The $4l$-bit initial seed is randomly generated. Then, the seed divides into four parts, 0th to $(l-1)^{th}$ ($= seed1$), l^{th} to $(2l-1)^{th}$ ($= seed2$), $2l^{th}$ to $(3l-1)^{th}$ ($= seed3$) and $3l^{th}$ to $(4l-1)^{th}$ ($= seed4$). The initial values $seed1$, $seed2$, $seed3$ and $seed4$ are stored in c_1, c_2, rule table and G^0 (Global states in 2-D CA), respectively. Each $seed$ consists of $s_{0,0}(t)$, $s_{0,1}(t)$, ..., $s_{m,m}(t)$ (where $m \times m = l$).

Evolution Phase. The rule and referred CA cells to evolve the next state $s_i(t+1)$ are decided in the present state $s_i(t)$. The detailed steps are as follows.

Input: $t = 1$, two control bits (c_1, c_2), a rule table and $G^{(0)}$
Output: $G^{(t)}$

Step 1: If i^{th} row and j^{th} cloumn in c_1 and C_2 is 00 or 01 to evolve the next state $s_i(t+1)$, then von Neumann neighborhood method is chosen. Else if i^{th} row and j^{th} cloumn in c_1 and C_2 is 10, the combination of XOR & AND is chosen. Otherwise, combination of XOR & OR is chosen

Step 2: If non-linear neighborhood method was chosen in Step 1, a combination pattern should be chosen by $s_{i,j}(t)$ in $G^{(t-1)}$. If $s_{i,j}(t)$ in $G^{(t-1)}$ is 1, N (North) and S (South) are chosen. Otherwise, W (West) and E (East) are chosen. And then, evole the next state with rule table and selected neighborhood method in Step 1 by Equation (6).

Step 3: c_1, c_2, rule table and $G^{(t-1)}$ are replaced by c_2, rule table, $G^{(t-1)}$ and $G^{(t)}$. t is increased by 1. If t is greater than R which is a repeating counter for producing sequence of a demanded pseudorandom number length, the round is finished. Otherwise, go back to the beginning of Step 1.

4 Experimental Results

In this Section, the randomness quality between the proposed scheme and previous schemes is analyzed.

4.1 The Statistical Evaluation Tools

In the experiment, ENT and DIEHARD test suites were utilized in order to evaluate the randomness quality.

In 1998, ENT test was first introduced by John Walker. This test is useful for evaluating pseudorandom number generators, statistical sampling applications, compression algorithms and the other applications where the information density of a file is interest. Originally, ENT test consists of six experiments which are entropy test, compression ratio test, chi-square test, arithmetic mean test, Monte Carlo value for π and Serial correlation coefficient (SCC). In this paper, however, the three tests which are the *Entropy test, Chi-square test*, and *SCC test* are chosen. Also, each test has a maximum score - *Entropy test*: 8.0, *Chi-square test*: 1.0 and *SCC test*: 0.0 - that the colser to the maximum score is high randomness quality [21]. Normally, it is first subjected to the ENT test before testing a better quality with DIEHARD test suite.

Georges Marsaglia from the Florida State University has devised a set of powerful statistical tests for testing randomness of sequences of numbers, called *DIEHARD battery of randomness tests*.

DIEHARD test suite is very important because it seems to be the most powerful general test of randomness. Many software and hardware generators that we have tested, and which claim "perfect randomness" actually fail one or more sections of DIEHARD. There are whole classes of frequently used software pseudorandom generators which are known to fail DIEHARD test suite, such as linear congruential and lagged Fibonacci generators.

DIEHARD test suite consists of 18 different and independent statistical tests. Results of tests are so called "p-values" that means are real, between 0 and 1.

For any given test, smaller p-value means better test result. An individual test is considered to be failed if p-value approached 1 closely, for example, if p-value is more than 0.9999 for any test, it is considered to be failed.

Most of the tests in DIEHARD return a p-value, which should be uniform on $0 \leq p < 1$ if the seed contains truly independent random bits. Those p-values are obtained by $p = f(X)$, where f is the assumed distribution of the sample random variable $X \sim N(\mu, \sigma^2)$ (That is, N, μ and σ^2 indicate the abbreviation of normal distribution, mean and variance, respectively). But that assumed f is just an asymptotic approximation, for which the fit will be worst in the tails. By all means, a $p < 0.025$ or $p > 0.975$ means that the RNG has "failed the test at the 0.05 level" [20].

4.2   The Experimental Results

The proposed scheme produces a l-bit output sequence in each round. DIEHARD test suite requires at least 10 MB regarding random number sequences. The proposed scheme needs the $(10^7 (MB) \times 8(bit)) \div l$ time rounds for DIEHARD test. On the other hand, ENT test suite requires fewer random number sequences, but the test is executed with the same 10 MB sequence for convenience and the next DIEHARD test. In the experiment, l and the number of rounds have been decided 1 MB (=8,000-bit). A total of 50 experiments were performed repeatedly.

Table 4 shows the result of the ENT test suite. In Table 5, the proposed scheme and three previous schemes [15,16,17] were compared. The results of Entropy and Chi-square test for previous schemes were supierior to the proposed scheme because they have been proposed based on linear neighborhood relationship. On the other hand, the rusult of SCC test for the proposed scheme is superior to privous schemes becuase of non-linear neighborhood relationship. The proposed scheme was focused on the elimination of O problem, while maintain the randomness quality such as previous schemes. SCC test has been performed that comparison between $G^{(t)}$ and $G^{(t+1)}$. Therefore, the correlation coefficient between $G^{(t)}$ and $G^{(t+1)}$ in the proposed scheme was reduced.

Table 4. Average values of ENT test

No.	Test Name	Average values			
		Tomassini	Guan^A	Guan^L	The proposed
1	Entropy	7.99871	7.99102	7.98995	**7.97655**
2	Chi-square	0.988972	0.991989	0.992792	**0.979254**
3	SCC	0.000257	0.000122	0.000207	**0.000151**

Guan^A: Asymmetric neighborhood PRNG of Guan et al.,
Guan^L: Lattice neighborhood PRNG of Guan et al..

Table 5. The result of DIEHARD test in p-value pass rate $\geq 75\%$

No.	Test Name	Average values			
		Tomassini	Guan^A	Guan^L	The proposed
1	Birthday Spacing	Pass	Pass	Pass	Pass
2	Overlapping 5-Permutation	Fail	Fail	Fail	Fail
3	Binary Rank 31 × 31	Pass	Pass	Pass	Pass
4	Binary Rank 32 × 32	Pass	Pass	Pass	Pass
5	Binary Rank 6 × 8	Pass	Pass	Pass	Pass
6	Bitsrteam	Pass	Pass	Fail	Pass
7	OPSO	Pass	Pass	Pass	Pass
8	OQSO	Pass	Pass	Pass	Pass
9	DNA	Pass	Pass	Pass	Fail
10	Count-The-1s 01	Pass	Pass	Pass	Pass
11	Count-The-1s 02	Pass	Pass	Pass	Pass
12	Parking Lot	Pass	Pass	Pass	Pass
13	Minimum Distance	Pass	Pass	Pass	Pass
14	3DS Spheres	Pass	Pass	Pass	Pass
15	Squeeze	Pass	Pass	Pass	Pass
16	Overlapping Sums	Pass	Pass	Pass	Pass
17	Runs	Pass	Pass	Pass	Pass
18	Craps	Pass	Pass	Pass	Pass
19	The number of pass	**17**	**17**	**16**	**16**

Guan^A: Asymmetric neighborhood PRNG of Guan et al.,
Guan^L: Lattice neighborhood PRNG of Guan et al..

Table 5 and 6 show the results of the DIEHARD test suite are shown and a mean of pass is considered when all p-values are exceeded by more than 75% and 85% at the significance level of 0.05, respectively. The randomness qualities of nonlinear neighborhood relationship were inferior to linear neighborhood relationship. In the Runs test, however, rules for the proposed scheme were passed. This result implies that the correlation coefficient between $G^{(t)}$ and $G^{(t+1)}$ in the proposed scheme was reduced. Because, the runs test analyzes the occurrence of similar events that are separated by events that are different. Hence, the proposed scheme reduces O problem from results of the ENT and DIEHARD test suites, while maintain the randomness quality such as previous schemes.

Table 6. The result of DIEHARD test in p-value pass rate $\geq 85\%$

No.	Test Name	Average values			
		Tomassini	Guan^A	Guan^L	The proposed
1	Birthday Spacing	Pass	Pass	Pass	Pass
2	Overlapping 5-Permutation	Fail	Fail	Fail	Fail
3	Binary Rank 31×31	Pass	Pass	Pass	Pass
4	Binary Rank 32×32	Pass	Pass	Pass	Pass
5	Binary Rank 6×8	Pass	Pass	Pass	Pass
6	Bitsrteam	Fail	Pass	Fail	Fail
7	OPSO	Fail	Fail	Fail	Fail
8	OQSO	Fail	Pass	Pass	Fail
9	DNA	Fail	Pass	Pass	Fail
10	Count-The-1s 01	Pass	Pass	Pass	Pass
11	Count-The-1s 02	Pass	Pass	Pass	Pass
12	Parking Lot	Pass	Pass	Pass	Pass
13	Minimum Distance	Pass	Pass	Pass	Pass
14	3DS Spheres	Pass	Pass	Pass	Pass
15	Squeeze	Pass	Pass	Pass	Pass
16	Overlapping Sums	Pass	Pass	Pass	Pass
17	Runs	Fail	Fail	Fail	Pass
18	Craps	Pass	Pass	Pass	Pass
19	The number of pass	**12**	**15**	**14**	**15**

Guan^A: Asymmetric neighborhood PRNG of Guan et al.,
Guan^L: Lattice neighborhood PRNG of Guan et al..

5   Conclusions

A 2-D CA with linear neighborhood relationship has some properties; an excellent randomness quality, nonprediction of next sequence, a simple hardware structure and regular design. However, its cycle length is less than linear neighborhood relationship (that is, "O" problem). Hence, the proper method which is a combination between linear and non-linear neighborhood relationships should be used.

This paper has been proposed a new 2-D CA PRNG based on von Neumann method with non-linear neighborhood relationship. To implement the evolution of 2-D CA with non-linear neighborhood relationship in the proposed scheme, two control bits (c_1, c_2) are used. Also, the porposed scheme has a simple hardware structure because of based on von Neumann neighborhood. The number of rules in the proposed scheme is higher than previous schemes. As the result, the correlation coefficient between $G^{(t)}$ and $G^{(t+1)}$ of the proposed scheme was superior to previous schemes, while maintained the randomness quality such as previous schemes.

Acknowledgments. This research was supported by Basic Science Research Program through the National Research Foundation of Korea(NRF) funded by the Ministry of Education, Science and Technology (No. 2010-0011968).

References

1. Menezes, A., van Oorschot, P.C., Vanstone, S.A.: Handbook of Applied Cryptography. CRC Press (1996)
2. Chaudhuri, P.P., Chowdhury, D.R., Nandi, S., Chattopadhyay, S.: Additive Cellular Automata Theory and Applications, vol. 1. IEEE Computer Society Press (1997)
3. ANSI X9.17: "American National Standard-Financial institution key management (wholsale)". ASX X9 Secretariat-American Bankers Association (1985)
4. FIPS 186: "Digital Signature Standard (DSS)". Federal Information Processing Standard Publication 186-3, NIST (2009)
5. PKCS #1: "Public-Key Cryptography Standards (PKCS) #1, RSA Cryptography Standard". RSA Lab
6. Blum, M., Micali, S.: How to Generate Cryptographically Strong Sequence of Pseudorandom Bits. SIAM Journal on Computing 13(4), 850–864 (1984)
7. Kaliski Jr., B.S.: A Pseudo-random Bit Generator Based on Elliptic Logarithms. In: Odlyzko, A.M. (ed.) CRYPTO 1986. LNCS, vol. 263, pp. 84–103. Springer, Heidelberg (1987)
8. von Neumann, J.: The Theory of Self-Reproducing Automata. In: Burks, A.W. (ed.). Univ. of Illinois Press, Urbana and London (1966)
9. Wolfram, S.: Statistical Mechanics of Cellular Automata. Rev. Mod. Phys. 55, 601–644 (1983)
10. Hortensius, P.D., Mcleod, R.D., Pries, W., Miller, D.M., Card, H.C.: Cellular automata-based pseudorandom number generators for built-in self-test. IEEE Transaction Computer-Aided Design 8, 842–859 (1989)
11. Guan, S.-U., Zhang, S.: An Evolutionary Approach to the Design of Controllable Cellular Automata Structure for Random Number Generation. IEEE Transctions on Evolutionary Computation 7(1), 23–36 (2003)
12. Guan, S.-U., Tan, S.K.: Pseudorandom Number Generation With Self-Programmable Cellular Automata. IEEE Transctions on Computer-Aided Design of Integrated Circuits and Systems 23(7), 1095–1101 (2004)
13. Tan, S.K., Guan, S.-U.: Evolving cellular automata to generate nonlinear sequences with desirable properties. Applied Soft Computing 7, 1131–1134 (2007)
14. Seredynski, F., et al.: Cellular automata computations and secret key cryptography. Parallel Computing 30, 753–766 (2004)
15. Tomassini, M., Sipper, M., Perrenoud, M.: On the generation of high quality random numbers by two-dimensional cellular automata. IEEE Transactions on Computers 49(10), 1146–1151 (2000)
16. Guan, S.-U., Zhang, S., Quieta, M.T.R.: 2-D Variation With Asymmetric Neighborship for Pseudorandom Number Generation. IEEE Transaction on Computers 23, 378–388 (2004)
17. Quieta, M.T.R., Guan, S.-U.: Optimization of 2-D Lattice Cellular Automata for Pseudorandom Number Generation. International Journal of Modern Physics 16(3), 479–500 (2005)

18. Shin, S.-H., Yoo, K.-Y.: Analysis of 2-State, 3-Neighborhood Cellular Automata Rules for Cryptographic Pseudorandom Number Generation. In: Proceedings on 12th IEEE International Conference on Computational Science and Engineering, pp. 399–404 (2009)
19. Shin, S.-H., Yoo, K.-Y.: An 1-Dimension Cellular Automata Evolution with 2-state and selective 4-neithborhood relationship. In: Proceedings of the IASTED International Conference, Modelling and Simulation (MS 2011), pp. 182–189 (2011)
20. Marsaglia, G.: DIEHARD Test suite (1998), http://www.stat.fsu.edu/pub/diehard/
21. Walker, J.: ENT Test suite (1998), http://www.fourmilab.ch/random/

FURG Smart Games: A Proposal for an Environment to Game Development with Software Reuse and Artificial Intelligence

Carlos Alberto B.C.W. Madsen, Giancarlo Lucca, Guilherme B. Daniel, and Diana F. Adamatti

Universidade Federal do Rio Grande - FURG, Centro de Ciências Computacionais, Rio Grande / RS, Brazil
{carlos.madsen,dianaadamatti,guilherme.daniel}@furg.br
{gico.lucca}@gmail.com
http://www.furg.br

Abstract. This paper presents a proposal for an environment to game development that uses software reuse and artificial intelligence. This environment is composed by a framework that implements the State project pattern, an edition tool and generation source code to object oriented basing to finite state machine. The main goal of this environment is to facilitate the implementation of the making-decision layer to NPC (Non-Player Characters) in the games.

Keywords: Framework, Finite State Machine, Design Patterns, Games, Non-Player Character.

1 Introduction

Since the begining of the games development, the industry uses the Finite State Machines (FSM) technique to develop the decision making layer to NPC (Non-Player Characters) [1].

However, the software complexity of the games is increasing. It demands a large quantity of working hours to have the product. In this context, the software reuse becomes fundamental and it must be widespread in this process, in order to decrease production time, rework and a good quality of the product. Despite the many qualities of the FSM and their massive use, their predictability in NPC behavior does not provide a satisfactory experience to the gamers. To have a more uncertality game, an alternative solution is to aggregate artificial intelligence algorithms, as artificial neural networks, fuzzy logic or genetic algorithms, into the FSM. However, the time to form a professional with these skills is large and expensive [3][2].

This paper proposes an environment to game development, focused on software reuse, where the NPC have a decision making layer implemented by FSM. This software consists of a framework that implements the State project pattern, a RAD (Rapid Application Development) edition of FSM and an edition tool and generation source code to object oriented based to finite state machine.

R. Benlamri (Ed.): NDT 2012, Part I, CCIS 293, pp. 369–381, 2012.

The paper is divided in five sections. Section 2 presents the finite state machines, their use in game development and how the FSM could be modeling through UML (Unified Modeling Language). Section 3 shows software reuse techniques focused on frameworks and design patterns. In Section 4, the proposed environment, called FURG Smart Games (FSG), is presented. Finally, Section 5 presents the conclusion and future work.

2   Finite State Machines (FSM)

The FSM have their origin in mathematics, specifically in the computability and complexity theory [2]. Its computational model had a great impact in the games industry, where normally it is an important piece in the implementation of NPC's decision making layer present in a game, being an important part in what is actually known as Game AI [1]. Through all this advantages, the FSM is widely used since its beginning until these days.

In this context, the FSM are a behavior model made of three fundamental elements: a S state finite set, I input events and $T(s,i)$ transition functions, where each of these S states represents a specific character behavior, considering that the machine actual state is unique. The I possible events set represents the stimulus that NPC can receive from the environment. Lastly, the transitional functions are responsible for defining which conditions must be pleased so the machine will move from its current state to another [11] [12].

Classically, the FSM is represented by a graph, where the vertices symbolize the states and the edges symbolize the transitions, as it is illustrated in the Figure 1 (adapted from [1]).

In the FSM presented on the Figure 1, we got the set of the possible states $S = \{Si,\ S1,\ S2,\ S3\}$, and its respective set of transitions $T = \{t1,t2,t3,t4,t5\}$. In this example, the machine starts at the state Si and remains in it until it receives an input event associated to the imput transition $t1$. If it has met its conditions, a transition will occur to the state $S1$, and so on.

There are two main ways of sorting this technique, known as Moore and Mearly machines. On the Mearly machine, the FSM output is due to transitions

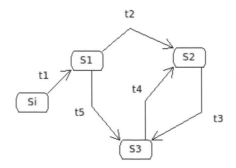

Fig. 1. Graphical representation of an FSM

between the states, whereas, on the Moore machine the output are generated as a product of the actual state. The FSM tipically used in games are the Moore ones, considering the sistem output. In this case, the character actions will be generated in their own states [13] [2].

The prolonged use and sucess of the FSM, on the games development is due to a large number of factors, as [11] [12] [14]:

- **Less developing time:** having in mind that they are conceptually simple, your project and implementation can be done relatively fast and is also easily extensible. There is also the possibility of using the project pattern State for its implementation.
- **Fast Learning curve:** the simplicity of this tool makes it easy to understand and use.
- **Predictability:** with a set of known inputs and an actual state known as well, the state transition is easily predictable, making the test and maintenance of the software easy.
- **Low Maintenance:** its implementation is performed by subdividing its source code. Typically, every state and its method, refering to the possible transitions, have their own separated code. Thus, if the implemented NPC acts somewhat unpredictably, it is easy to detect the source of the error.
- **Low computational cost:** just the code of the current state is accomplished every time, beyond a little logical code, that determine the actual state and when it will change.
- **Communication tool:** the FSM are simple enough to make it acessible to people who are not used to programming, such as designers and artists.

In order to demonstrate the use of FSM in games, it presents the Figure 2 (adapted of [2]), a complete example of an NPC model from this technique. In this case, the character is a soldier who must monitor and defend a territory. Initially, he is at his base (state "Homing"), and, his energy is high, he begins his patrolling (state "Patrolling"). Then, given his vital energy level and the appearance of enemies, he passes through the other states, molding, this way, his behavior.

Lastly, it can be observed that the FSM computational model has different definitions. However, the most used by the industry is the state transition diagram of UML (Figure 2), that is basically constituted by these components [15] [16]:

- **State:** describes the internal state of the NPC at a specific instant of time, besides being related to an activity and various actions.
- **Activity:** is a continuous execution and is not associated with an atomic state, represented by the label "do". It has been implemented with the NPC behavior, only by being interrupted in the transition to a next state.
- **Action:** is an atomic implementation, invoked in a state change. Usually, associated with a state, it has the action "entry", that is executed when the NPC enters the state, and "exit", that is invoked when the character leaves the state. For each transition there is the option to have a related action.

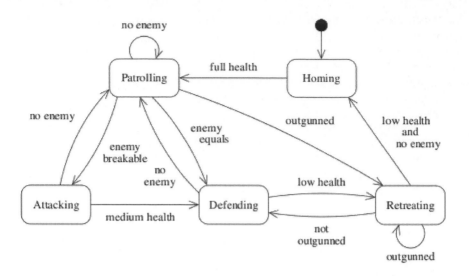

Fig. 2. FSM of a soldier (NPC)

- **Transition:** is a relation between two states indicating that an NPC can pass from a "State 1" to a "State 2" given the occurrence of an event. Optionally, each transition can have a guard condition and an action.
- **Event:** environment stimulus that can unleash a state transition.
- **Guard condition:** condition that must be true so a transition stimulated by an event can happen.
- **Start state:** state, represented by a filled black circle, that indicates where the FSM starts executing.
- **Final state:** state normally represented by a hollow empty circle that symbolize the end of the FSM execution.

With the objective of elucidating the functioning of the components presented above, in Figure 3 there is an explanation of how the transition occurs from the state "Patrolling" to state "Attacking" of FSM presented in Figure 2.

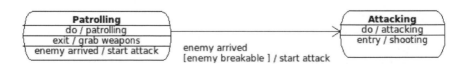

Fig. 3. Transition between the state Patrolling and Attacking

The transition presented in Figure 3 will happen by the follow steps:

1. The state "Patrolling" notices the occurrence of an event "enemy arrived", which has been associated with the transition to "Attacking", governed by the guard condition "breakable enemy" that has to be attended.
2. The "patrolling" activity that was being developed by "Patrolling" is interrupted.
3. It is performed the output action "grab weapons" from "Patrolling" state.
4. It is performed the action "start attack" associated with the transition.
5. It is performed the input action "shooting" from "Attacking" state.
6. Finally starts the execution of the "attacking" activity from "Attacking" state.

3   Software Reuse

The reuse is intrinsic to the process of solving problems used by the human race, since its beginnings, as the solutions for certain problems were found they were recorded and, if possible, adapted to other similar problems. This was possible due to the capacity of abstraction and adaptation the human beings have [6].

Nowadays the electronic games have their development process more and more intricate and in need of human resources, mainly because of the fact that the scope and complexity of such software have become bigger and bigger. Therefore, there is the need of reuse in software project, resulting in a systematic practice of development blocks, so that possible similarities and demands of different projects may be explored. In order to make the final product more reliable, flexible with an easy-to-do maintenance and evolution, with a better quality and with a less time consuming development [4].

Despite the reuse being a present practice in the software industry since the 1960s, with the advent of subroutines and macros, there was a technological jump in the end of the 1980s due to an intensive usage of the paradigm of programming objetct oriented. The orientation to objects provides an easy modularization, enabling the strong adoption of software reuse [5][4].

Nowadays we face several software reuse techniques, however among them we highlight the development based on frameworks and the design patterns.

3.1   Frameworks

A framework is a reusable and semi complete application which can be improved to produce customized applications, with specific characteristics as it gathers interrelated concrete and abstract classes, aiming at minimizing the effort of development and maintenance of certain software, making the reuse not only in the codification, but also in the analysis and project [7]. Besides the classes previously mentioned, this technique specifies as well how such instances should interact to each other [8][5][9].

For a framework to succeed, it must present the following basic characteristics: modularity, reusability, extensibility and control inversion [6]. Modularity is achieved by encapsuling the implementation of classes, providing access, for the developer, only to its interfaces. This characteristic facilitates the finding of possible problems besides simplifying the changes in the project, reducing, thus, the maintenance effort. Concerning the reusability we can highlight the considerable advantage this technique offers. The programming through generic and preformatted components is notoriously more productive. The extensibility happens due to a bigger extension capacity of its components, enabling, through the heritage mechanism, the customization according to the problem domain faced. And, finally, the control inversion is important as it involves the capacity to respond to external events, keeping the application execution control [8][7].

Finally, there are two distinct forms to implement such tool, one known as the "white box" and the other as the "black box"[8]. In the White Box ones, the reuse is done exclusively by heritage of abstract classes which are available in the framework. Therefore, the developer must necessarily create subclasses to customize and implement the necessary resources for its application. On the other hand, it is necessary to have a deep knowledge of how the groups of classes works internally, causing problems for the modularity. Differently, the Black Box ones act predominantly through the composition, so the developer is only concerned about matching the instantiated objects, from the existing concrete classes, the best way possible, taking into consideration what is to be implemented. As the name suggests, the internal functioning of the classes is fully abstracted from the user, then benefiting the modularity.

3.2   Design Patterns

This reuse technique describes a certain problem and the essence of its solution, therefore it can be adapted for several applications, due to its abstract nature it does not emphasizes implementation details. It can be seen as a description of knowledge and accumulated experiences of a certain proved solution for a common problem.

As a result, a design pattern names abstracts and identifies key aspects of a structure of common design, in order to make it useful to create object oriented software. This close connection to object oriented programming happens due to the fact the patterns have characteristics of objects, such as the heritage and polymorphism. They are defined as: *"descriptions of communicating objects and classes which should be customized to solve a general design problem in a specific context"* [10].

Finally, according to Gamma et. al [10] and Sommerville [6] there are four essential elements of a design pattern:

- **Pattern name:** reference which may be used to describe a pattern problem, its solutions and consequences in one or two words.
- **Problem:** describes in which situation the pattern must be used, explaining the problem and its context. It may include a list of conditions which should be fulfilled so the usage of the pattern makes sense.

- **Solution:** describes the elements which compose the design pattern, its relationships, its responsibilities and collaborations. In this item specific implementations are not described, as the pattern works more as a template, so it provides an abstract description of a problem and how a group of classes and objects may solve the problem.
- **Consequences:** they are results of advantage and disadvantage analysis of pattern application. They include its impact on the flexibility, extensibility or portability of a system.

3.3   Design Pattern State

State is a behavioral pattern, which means it has as objective to control the manner in which the objects. In this NPCs context, interact among them, encapsulating interchangeable behaviors and using delegation in order to decide which behavior should be used [17]. Thus, allowing that a certain object change its behavior according to its internal state, giving the impression that this object changed its class [10] [15]. Real time applications, as games, tend to be benefited specially from this architecture because they frequently work with a perspective of event and changes of state.

An example of use of this pattern can be seen on Figure 4, related to the FSM presented on Figure 2, in which it can be observed that the game can launch events to be served by NPC, which delegates the task to its current state.

4   FSG Environment

The development environment of the decision making process, from the FSM, proposed in this paper, is divided into a framework and a RAD tool for automating source code. A previous work of the authors is presented in [18].

4.1   Framework FSG

The proposed framework aims at facilitating the incorporation techniques of AI in the development of games, assuming that the process of decision making of the NPC is implemented by a FSM, highly used technique by the industry. In the FSG each transition present in the machine may be related as an AI technique, such as artificial neural networks, genetic algorithms and fuzzy logic, through its guard condition. As a result, the character's behavior is not strictly deterministic, making the game more realistic.

To achieve this purpose, the developer that uses the tool will face two very distinct ways of working. Firstly, concerning the Finite State Machine (FSM), topic of this paper, he/she should make use of the heritage in order to implement the current methods in the super abstract classes, as well as know in which order and moment the FSG will make use of them. In this case, its usage is seen as in the White Box type. On the other hand, the present AI techniques are

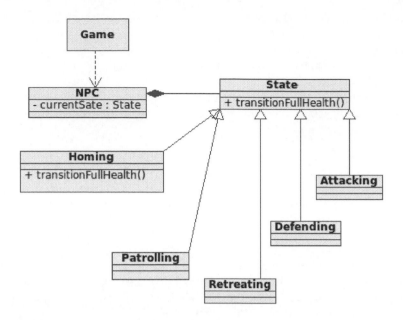

Fig. 4. Example of class model of Stare Project pattern

fully abstracted, provided by concrete classes. Thus the developer is limited to associate and gather its instances, characterizing a Black Box framework.

It is believed that with this work methodology, the FSG understanding is facilitated as it is necessary to have a deeper knowledge concerning the FSM, which is mentioned in section 2 as conceptually simple and with low learning curve. On the other hand, concerning the AI techniques, which usually demand a bigger learning period for its implementation, the framework already performs such task, then the developer only needs to know in which moments a technique must be used over another.

Still, due to the fact the games are implemented in several languages and are executed in distinct platforms, the choice for the proposal and implementation of the FSG was made in an XML based language, similar to Java (the formal description of this language will not be presented here, as this is not the focus of the paper). By using a RAD tool, this XML and later translation for a programming language will be created, as long as there is support for object orientation.

In the Figure 5 we show the FSG classes diagram, in which we call attention for three abstract classes: FSGCharacter, FSGState and FSGAITechnique. From the FSGCharacter class there is the NPC implementation, where we see the presence of the attribute "currentState" which shows in which condition the machine is, the "transition" method, responsible for the transtition between the states and finally the "activity" method, which sets the character's behavior responsibility to the method of the same object name "currentSate". In the FSGState class, all the states found in the FSM must be implemented. We call attention for the

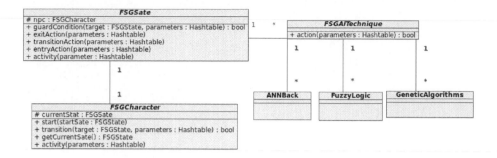

Fig. 5. Class diagram of the FSG

fact that all actions, activities and guard conditions proposed in the UML study diagram, are expected in its method. Finally the FSGAITechnique class, works as an interface for the AI techniques, present in the framework, and the FSM state transitions, normally their objects are instantiated within the "guardCondition" method of a certain class inheriting FSGState.

Finally, considering what has been exposed above and presented in section 3, it is clear that the tool, besides conforming to the UML states model, presents a consistent implementation of the State design pattern.

4.2   RAD (FSG: Finite-State Machine)

The second part of development environment is a RAD. It is a tool responsible for the graphic edition of FSM and source code in standard FSG. The edition is done through UML simplified state diagram, where issues such as actions, activity and guard conditions are not presented, taking into consideration that are already available in framework class FSGState as Figure 6 shows. Still in this figure we can note in the left that the software allows, in case of a state, the class name specification which will inherit FSGstate, and in a transition case, the method definition shoot the same, as well as name of the method responsible for implementing its guard condition.

As shown in subsection 4.1 there is the possibility of relating the guard condition to a specific AI technique, shown in Figure 7. In it the developing defines the class name which will inherit FSGAITTechnique, choose the technique and lastly load an XML file with its configuration.

In the example of Figure 7 the file must contain the artificial neural network definition as well as the values of its weights previously trained. The RAD allows other algorithms, beyond the presented, to be cataloged.

Then, the developer can request the generation of the NPC source code in the programming language of his/her preference, as presented in Figure 8. It can be observed that the tool identifies the use of an AI technique related to "enemy breakable" transition, this way it informs that the codes that refer to the implementation of this technique will also be generated.

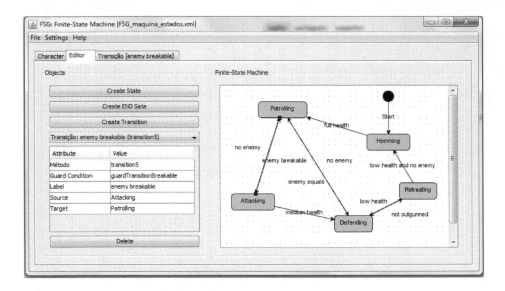

Fig. 6. FSM Edition in RAD tool

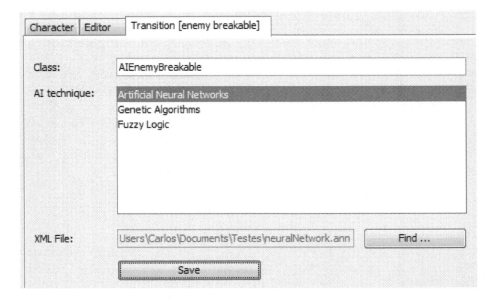

Fig. 7. Relating one transition with an AI technique

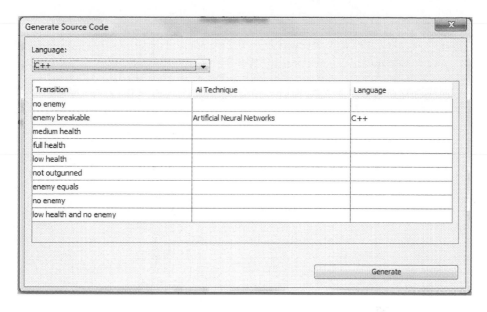

Fig. 8. Generating the NPC source code

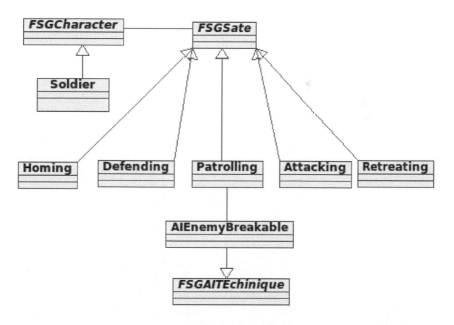

Fig. 9. Class diagram of the source code generate to the FSM from Figure 6

The generation of this source happens in two steps. Firstly RAD generates all the NPC and AI algorithms classes connected to its XML specified based language. After that, it invokes a translator, previously cataloged in the software, corresponding to the selected programming language. The programmer translates this XML in source code. Nowadays, it is possible to translate to the programming languages: C++, Java, PHP and Python.

Lastly, to the NPC "soldier" presented in Figure 6, we have a source code generated according to the diagram of classes in Figure 9.

5   Conclusion and Further Work

The FSM is a consolidated technique in the game industry to implement decision making in NPC. However, this technique is deterministic and it needs to be used together with AI algorithms. Nowadays, the AI use and the wide complexity of new games, makes the software reuse become a crucial task. In this context, we believe that the proposed environment is relevant, because it incorporates the State project pattern to implement the FSM as well as a tool to UML state diagram of the UML. Related to AI techniques, the environment makes an abstraction of them and generate source code to several languages (multiplatform).

As further work, we will expand the quantity of programming languages in the RAD and implement specific RAD for each AI algorithm. To validate the environment, a complete game will be implemented.

References

1. Bourg, D.M., Seeman, G.: AI for Game Developers, p. 400. O'Reilly (2004) ISBN: 0596005555
2. Smed, J., Hakonen, H.: Algorithms and Networking for Computer Games, p. 286. John Wiley & Sons Ltd., University of Turku, Finland (2006)
3. Bittencourt, G.: Inteligência Artificial - Ferramentas e Teorias, 3rd edn., p. 371. Universidade Federal de Santa Catarina, Florianópolis (2006) ISBN 8532801382
4. Oliveira, K.S., Mattos, H.D.: Abordagens de Reuso de Software no Desenvolvimento de Aplicações Orientadas a Objetos. XII Escola Regional de Informática. Faculdades Luiz Meneghel (FFALM), Curitiba, Brazil (2006)
5. Weschter, E.O.: Arquitetura do Gerador de Aplicaes Web Baseado no Framework TITAN, p. 93. Universidade Federal do Mato Grosso do Sul, Campo Grande (2008)
6. Sommerville, I.: Software Engineering, 8th edn., p. 549. Addison-Wesley (2007)
7. Bittencourt, J.R., Osório, F.: ANNEF - Artificial Neural Networks Framework: Uma Solução Software Livre para o Desenvolvimento, Ensino e Pesquisa de Aplicações de Inteligência Artificial Multiplataforma. In: Free Software WorkShop, Porto Alegre, Brazil, vol. (2), pp. 13–16 (2001)
8. Medeiros, F.N., Medeiros, F.M., Domnguez, A.H.: FA PorT: Um Framework para Sistemas Portfólio-Tutor utilizando Agentes. In: Symposium on Computers in Education, vol. (18), pp. 08–10 (2006)

9. Ferreira, F.M.G.: Desenvolvimento e Aplicações de um Framework Orientado a Objetos para Análise Dinâmica de Linhas de Ancoragem de Risers, p. 109. Universidade Federal de Alagoas, Alagoas (2005)

10. Gamma, E., Helm, R., Johnson, R.: Design Patterns - Elements of Reusable Object Oriented Software, p. 416. Bookman (2005) ISBN: 9780201633610

11. Rabin, S.: AI Game Programming Wisdom, 1st edn., p. 672. Charles River Media (2002) ISBN: 9781584500773

12. Alberto, A.D.B.: Uma estratégia para a minimização de máquinas de estados finitos parciais, p. 99. Universidade de São Paulo, São Paulo (2009)

13. Dinízio, C.S., Simões, M.A.C.: Inteligência Artificial em Jogos de Tiro em Primeira Pessoa. Universidade de Tiradentes. Revista de Iniciação Científica, Minas Gerais, Brazil (2003) ISSN: 15198219

14. Malfatti, S.M., Fraga, L.M.: Utilizando Behaviors Para o Gerenciamento da Máquina de Estados em Jogos Desenvolvidos com Java 3D. In: Brazilian Symposium Games (2006)

15. Larman, G.: Applying UML and Patterns: An Introduction to Object Oriented Analysis and Design and Iterative Development, p. 507. Bookman (2004) ISBN: 9780137488803

16. Booch, G., Rumbaugh, J., Jacobson, I.: The Unified Modeling Language User Guide, p. 576. Addison-Wesley Professional (2000) ISBN-13: 9780201309980

17. Freeman, E., Robson, E., Bates, B., Sierra, K.: Head First Design Patterns, p. 688. O'Reilly Media (2004) ISBN: 9780596007126

18. Madsen, C.A.B.C.W., Adamatti, D.F.: Using Artificial Intelligence in Computational Games. Journal of Information & System Management 1(2), 60–67 (2011)

Scalable Content-Based Classification and Retrieval Framework for Dynamic Commercial Image Databases

Serkan Kiranyaz[1], Turker Ince[2], and Moncef Gabbouj[1,*]

[1] Tampere University of Technology, Tampere, Finland
{serkan.kiranyaz,moncef.gabbouj}@tut.fi
[2] Izmir University of Economics, Izmir, Turkey
turker.ince@ieu.edu.tr

Abstract. Large-scale commercial image databases are getting increasingly common and popular, and nowadays several services over them are being offered via Internet. They are truly dynamic in nature where new image(s), categories and visual descriptors can be introduced in any time. In order to address this need, in this paper, we propose a scalable content- based classification and retrieval framework using a novel collective network of (evolutionary) binary classifier (CNBC) system to achieve high classification and content-based retrieval performances over commercial image repositories. The proposed CNBC framework is designed to cope up with incomplete training (ground truth) data and/or low-level features extracted in a dynamically varying image database and thus the system can be evolved incrementally to adapt the change immediately. Such a self-adaptation is achieved by basically adopting a "Divide and Conquer" type approach by allocating an individual network of binary classifiers (NBCs) to discriminate each image category and performing *evolutionary* search to find the optimal binary classifier (BC) in each NBC. Furthermore, by means of this approach, a large set of low-level visual features can be effectively used within CNBC, which in turn selects and combines them so as to achieve highest discrimination among each individual class. Experiments demonstrate a high classification accuracy and efficiency of the proposed framework over a large and dynamic commercial database using only low-level visual features.

Keywords: content-based image classification, content-based image retrieval, evolutionary neural networks, Particle Swarm Optimization, Multilayer Perceptron.

1 Introduction

Proper management of large-scale commercial image databases that are getting i common and popular nowadays, is a challenging task since they are usually dynamic in nature in terms of content and visual descriptors (features). The content-based image retrieval (CBIR) has been an active research field for which several feature extraction, classification and retrieval techniques have been proposed up to date. However, when the database

* This work was supported by the Academy of Finland, project No. 213462 (Finnish Centre of Excellence Program (2006 - 2011).

R. Benlamri (Ed.): NDT 2012, Part I, CCIS 293, pp. 382–398, 2012.

size dynamically varies and usually grows larger, it is a common fact that the overall classification and retrieval performance significantly deteriorates. Particularly the key questions, e.g. 1) how to select certain features so as to achieve highest discrimination over certain classes, 2) how to combine them in the most effective way, 3) which distance metric to apply, 4) how to find the optimal classifier configuration for the classification problem in hand, 5) how to scale/adapt the classifier when large number of classes/features are (incrementally) introduced and finally, 6) how to train the classifier efficiently to maximize the classification accuracy, still remain unanswered. The current state-of-the-art classifiers such as Support Vector Machines (SVMs) [1], [2], Bayesian Classifiers, Random Forests (RFs) [3], and Artificial Neural Networks (ANNs) cannot cope with such requirements since a single classifier, no matter how powerful and well-trained it may be, cannot discriminate efficiently a vast amount of classes, over an indefinitely large set of features. Furthermore, since both image categories (classes) and features are not static, rather dynamically varying as a natural consequence of such image repositories, static and fixed-structured classifiers cannot scale such changes without proper configuration updates and a full-scale re-training.

Another major question that still remains in CBIR is the how to narrow the so-called "Semantic Gap" between the low-level visual features that are automatically extracted from images and the high-level semantics and content-description by the humans. Among a wide variety of features proposed in the literature, none can really address this problem alone. So the focus has been drawn in the fusing several features in a most effective way since whenever the classifiers involved, the increased feature space may eventually cause the so-called "Curse of Dimensionality" phenomenon that significantly degrades the classification accuracy. In [11], three MPEG-7 visual features, Color Layout Descriptor (CLD), Scalable Color Descriptor (SCD) and Edge Histogram Descriptor (EHD) are fused to train several classifiers (SVMs, KNN and Falcon-ART) for a small database only with two-classes and 767 images. This work has clearly demonstrated that the highest classification accuracy has been obtained with the proper feature fusion. This is indeed an expected outcome since each feature may have a certain level of discrimination for a particular class. In another recent work [12], this fact has been, once again, confirmed where authors fused three MPEG-7 features: SCD, Homogenous Texture Descriptor and EHD and trained SVM over the same database. Basic color (12 dominant colors) and texture (DWT using quadrature mirror filters) features were used in [13] to annotate image databases using ensemble of classifiers (SVMs and Bayes Point Machines). Although the classification is performed over a large image database with 25K images and 116 classes from Corel repository, the authors used above 80% of the database for training and another database to evaluate and manually optimize various kernel and classifier parameters. In [14] SVMs together with 2-D Hidden Markov Model (HMM) are used to discriminate image class in an integrated model. Two features, 50-D SIFT (with a dimension reduction by PCA) and 9-D color moments (CM) are used individually in two datasets using 80% of the images for training, and the classification accuracies are compared. In all these image classification works and many alike, besides the aforementioned key problems there are other drawbacks and limitations, e.g., they can work with only a limited feature set to avoid Curse of Dimensionality and used the major part of the database, some as high as 80% or even higher for training to sustain a certain level of classification accuracy. They are all image classification methods for static databases assuming a fixed GTD and fixed set of features where feature and class scalability and dynamic adaptability are beyond their scope.

In order to address these problems and hence to maximize the classification accuracy which will in turn boost the CBIR performance, in this paper, we shall focus on a global framework design that embodies a collective networks of evolutionary classifiers. Specifically in this approach, the following objectives will be targeted:

- *Evolutionary Search*: Seeking for the optimum network architecture among a collection of configurations (the so-called Architecture Space, AS) as in [4].
- *Evolutionary Update in the AS*: Keeping only "the best" individual configuration in the AS among indefinite number of evolution runs.
- *Feature Scalability*: Support for. Any feature can be dynamically integrated into the framework without requiring a full-scale initialization and re-evolution.
- *Class/Feature Scalability*: Support for large and varying number of features and classes. Any class can dynamically be inserted into the framework without requiring a re-evolution.
- *High efficiency* for the evolution (or training) process: Using as compact and simple classifiers as possible in the AS.
- *Online (incremental) Evolution*: Continuous online/incremental training (or evolution) sessions can be performed to improve the classification accuracy.
- *Parallel processing*: Classifiers can be evolved using several processors working in parallel.

In this way, we shall achieve as compact classifiers as possible, which can be evolved and trained in a much more efficient way than a single but complex classifier, and the optimum classifier for the classification problem in hand can be *searched* among a proper collection of classifiers. At a given time, this allows designation of a dedicated classifier for discriminating a certain class type from the others based on a single feature. The CNBC can support varying and large set of visual features among which it optimally selects, weights and fuses the most discriminative ones for a particular class. Each NBC is devoted to a unique class and further encapsulates a set of *evolutionary Binary Classifiers* (BCs), each of which is optimally chosen within the architecture space (AS), discriminating the class of the NBC with a unique feature. For instance for an NBC evolved for the *sunset* class will most likely select and use mostly the color features (rather than texture, and edge) and the most descriptive color feature elements (i.e. color bins in histogram) for discriminating this particular class (i.e. red, yellow and black), are weighted higher than the others. In a dynamic image database each incremental evolution session will "learn" from the current best classifier configurations and can improve them further, possibly as a result of an (incremental) optimization, which may find another configuration in the AS as the "optimal". The optimality *therein* can be set with a user-defined criterion. Moreover, with each incremental evolution, new GTD for some set of images and/or new classes/features can also be introduced which signals the CNBC to create new (or to update) the corresponding NBCs and BCs within to adapt dynamically to the change. In this way the CNBC will be able to dynamically *scale* itself to the indexing requirements of the image database whilst striving for maximizing the classification and retrieval accuracies. The exhaustive search with the numerous runs of the Back-Propagation method, is used as the primary evolution technique. In [15], a basic and static CNBC topology has initially been applied for macro invertebrate classification. In the current work, we shall focus on a CNBC framework where evolutionary feed-forwards ANNs (MLPs) and SVMs are used as the BCs; however, any other classifier type can also be used within CNBC framework as long as they can be incrementally evolved (or trained).

The rest of the paper is organized as follows. Section 2 briefly presents the evolutionary classifiers. The proposed image classification framework is explained in detail in Section 3, and the classification results and performance evaluation over large and dynamic image databases are given in Section 4. Finally, Section 5 concludes the paper and discusses future research directions.

2   Evolutionary Classifiers

In this section we shall discuss the methodology for achieving the first objective that is the search for the optimal classifier configuration. For MLPs the Back Propagation (BP) [10], which can be used exhaustively to search for the optimal classifier in an AS, is used. BP is the most commonly used training technique for feed-forward ANNs. It is a supervised training technique which has been used in pattern recognition and classification problems in many application areas. BP has the advantage of applying directed search and has a local search ability. However, BP is just a gradient descent algorithm in the error space, which can be complex and may contain many deceiving local minima (multi-modal). Therefore, BP gets most likely trapped into a local minimum, making it entirely dependent on the initial (weight) settings. Yet due to its simplicity and relatively lower computational cost, BP can be applied exhaustively over the network architectures of AS with random initializations to find out the optimal architecture for the problem in hand. Since AS is composed of only compact networks, with such an exhaustive application, the probability of finding (converging) to a (near-) optimum solution in the error space is significantly increased.

The BP algorithm can be summarized as follows:

1. Initialize the weights w_{jk}^l and biases θ_k^l randomly.

2. Feed pattern p to the network and compute the output $y_k^{p,l}$ of each neuron.

3. Calculate the error between the computed output $y_k^{p,o}$ of each output neuron and the desired output t_k^p as $e_k^{p,o} = t_k^p - y_k^{p,o}$.

4. For each neuron k, calculate the partial derivatives $\dfrac{\partial E^p}{\partial h_k^l}$, where E^p is the total error energy defined as $E^p = \dfrac{1}{2}\sum_{k\in o}(e_k^{p,o})^2$ and h_k^l is a uniform symbol for each parameter w_{jk}^l, θ_k^l, μ_k and σ_k.

5. Update the parameters as follows:

$$h_k^l(t+1) = h_k^k(t) - \eta\frac{\partial E^p}{\partial h_k^k} \tag{1}$$

where η is the learning rate parameter.

6. Repeat steps 2-5 until some stopping criteria is reached.

One complete run over the training dataset is called an *epoch*. Usually many *epochs* are required to obtain the best training results, but, on the other hand, too many training *epochs* can lead to over-fitting. In the above realization of the BP algorithm the network parameters are updated after every training sample. This is called the *online* or *sequential* mode. The other possibility is the *batch* mode, where all the training samples are first presented to the network and then the parameters are adjusted so that the total training error is minimized. The *sequential* mode is often favored over the *batch* mode as it requires less storage space. Moreover, the *sequential* mode is less likely to get trapped in a local minimum as updates at every training sample make the search stochastic in nature. Hence *sequential* BP mode is used for MLP training/evolution. Further details about BP can be found in [10].

For SVMs, a similar sequential search has been performed to find out the best classifier type. For this, all standard kernel types such as *linear, polynomial*, radial basis function *(RBF)* and *sigmoid,* are individually used whilst searching for the best internal SVM parameters, e.g., the respectable penalty parameter, $C=2^n$; for $n=0,..,3$ and parameter $\gamma=2^{-n}$; for $n=0,..,3$, whenever applicable to the kernel type. The incremental training of both MLPs and SVMs are skipped due to space limitations.

3   Image Classification Framework

This section describes in detail the proposed classification framework; the Collective Network of (Evolutionary) Binary Classifiers (CNBC), which uses user-defined ground truth data (GTD) as the training dataset to configure its internal structure and to evolve its binary classifiers (BCs) individually. Before going into details of CNBC, a general overview for the proposed classification system will be introduced in the next sub-section.

3.1 The Overview of the Framework

The proposed image classification system is designed to dynamically adapt (or scale) to any change and update in an image database. As shown in **Fig. 1**, new image(s) can be inserted into the database for which the user may introduce new class(es) via relevance feedbacks, and/or new feature(s) can be extracted, at any time convenient. As long as the user provides new ground-truth data (GTD) for the new classes, the existing classifier body, CNBC, can incrementally be evolved if the need arises, i.e. if the existing CNBC (or some NBCs in it) fails to classify these new classes accurately enough. We used MUVIS system [5] to extract a large set of low-level visual features that are properly indexed in the database along with the images. Unit normalized FVs formed from those features are fed into the input layer of the CNBC where the user provided GTD is converted to target class vectors (CVs) to perform an incremental evolution operation. The user can also set the number of evolutionary runs or the level of classification accuracy desired. Any CNBC instance can directly be used to classify a new image and/or to perform content-based image queries, the result of which can be evaluated by the user to introduce new class(es), yielding another incremental

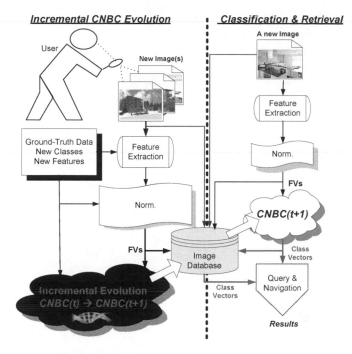

Fig. 1. The overview of the proposed framework

evolution operation and so on. This is an ongoing cycle of human-classifier interaction, which gradually adapts CNBC to the user's class definitions. New low-level features can also be extracted to improve the discrimination among classes, which signals CNBC to adapt to the change simultaneously. In short, dynamic class/feature adaptability and scalability are the key-objectives aimed within the CNBC design. Before going into the details of the CNBC framework, next sub-section will first introduce the evolutionary update mechanism that keeps the best BC networks in the AS during numerous incremental evolutionary runs.

3.2 Evolutionary Update in the Architecture Space

In order to improve the probability of convergence to the global optimum, several evolutionary runs can be performed. Let N_R be the number of runs and N_C be the number of configurations in the AS. For each run the objective is to find the optimal (the best) classifier within the AS with respect to a pre-defined criterion. Note that along with the best classifier, all other configurations in the AS are also subject to evolution and therefore, they are continuously (re-) trained with each run. So during this ongoing process, between any two consecutive runs, any network configuration can replace the current best one in the AS if it surpasses it. **Fig. 2** demonstrates an evolutionary update operation over a sample AS containing 5 MLP configurations. The table shows the training MSE which is the criterion used to select the optimal configuration at each run. The best runs for each configuration are highlighted and the best configuration in each run is tagged with '*'. Note that at the end of the three runs, the overall best network with MSE = 0.10 has the configuration: 15x2x2 and thus used as the classifier for any classification task until any other configuration surpasses it in a next run during an evolutionary update. In this way, each BC configuration in the AS can only evolve to a better state, which is the main purpose of the proposed evolutionary update mechanism.

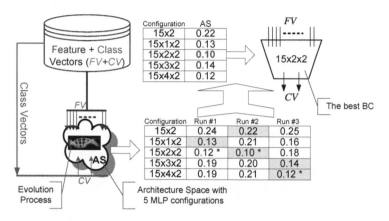

Fig. 2. Evolutionary update in a sample AS for MLP configuration arrays $R_{min} = \{15, 1, 2\}$ and $R_{max} = \{15, 4, 2\}$ where $N_R = 3$ and $N_C = 5$. The best runs for each configurations are highlighted and the best configuration in each run is tagged with '*'.

3.3   Collective Network of Binary Classifiers

The Topology

To achieve the third and fourth objectives mentioned earlier, i.e. the scalability with respect to a varying number of classes and features, a dedicated framework encapsulating a network of binary classifiers (NBCs) is developed, where NBCs can evolve continuously with the ongoing evolution sessions i.e. cumulating the user supplied ground truth data (GTD) for images and thus forming the training dataset. Each NBC corresponds to a unique image class whilst striving to discriminate only that class from the rest of the classes in the database. Moreover, each NBC shall contain varying number of evolutionary binary classifiers (BCs) in the input layer where each BC performs binary classification using a single feature. Each FV of a particular feature is only fed to its corresponding BC in each NBC. Therefore, whenever a new feature is extracted, its corresponding BC will be created, evolved (using the available GTD logs so far), and inserted into each NBC, yet keeping each of the other BCs "as is". On the other hand, whenever an existing feature is removed, the corresponding BC is simply removed from each NBC in the CNBC. In this way scalability with respect to varying number of features is achieved and the overall system can adapt to the change without requiring re-forming and re-evolving from scratch.

Each NBC has a "fuser" BC in the output layer, which collects and fuses the binary outputs of all BCs in the input layer and generates a single binary output, indicating the relevancy of each FV of the KFs belonging to the training dataset clips, to the NBC's corresponding class. Furthermore, CNBC is also scalable to any number of classes since whenever a new class is defined by the user, a new corresponding NBC can simply be created (and evolved) only for this class without requiring any need for change on the other NBCs as long as they can accurately discriminate the new class from their corresponding classes. This allows the overall system to adapt dynamically to the varying number of classes. As shown in **Fig. 3**, the main idea in this approach is to use as many classifiers as necessary, so as to divide a large-scale learning problem into many NBC units along with the BCs within, and thus prevent the need of using complex classifiers as the performance of both training and evolution processes degrades significantly as the complexity rises due to the well-known curse of dimensionality phenomenon.

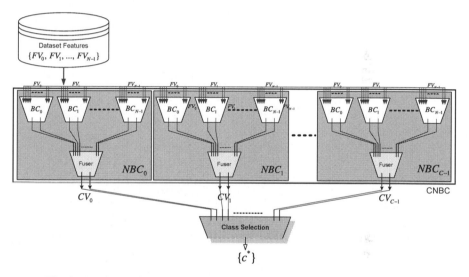

Fig. 3. Topology of the proposed CNBC framework with C classes and N FVs

A major benefit of this approach with respect to efficient evolution process is that the configurations in the AS can be kept as compact as possible avoiding unfeasibly large storage and training time requirements. This is a significant advantage especially for the training methods performing local search, such as BP since the amount of deceiving local minima is significantly lower in the error space for such simple and compact ANNs. Especially, when BP is applied exhaustively, the probability of finding the optimum solution is significantly increased. Also note that evolving the CNBC may reduce the computation time significantly since it contains simple and compact classifier networks, each of which can be individually evolved by a separate CPU (recall the objective □– Parallel Processing) and hence the overall computation time can be reduced as much as desired, which in practice leads to a significantly lower computation time compared to training a single but complex ANN classifier.

In order to maximize the classification accuracy, we applied a dedicated class selection technique for CNBC. We used 1-of-n encoding scheme in all BCs, therefore, the output layer size of all BCs is always two. Let $CV_{c,1}$ and $CV_{c,2}$ be the first and second output of the cth BC's class vector (CV). The class selection in 1-of-n encoding scheme can simply be performed by comparing the individual outputs, e.g. say a positive output if $CV_{c,2} > CV_{c,1}$, and vice versa for negative. This is also true for the fuser BC, the output of which makes the output of its NBC. FVs of each dataset item are fed to each NBC in the CNBC. Each FV drives through (via forward propagation) its corresponding BC in the input layer of the NBC. The outputs of these BCs are then fed to the fuser BC of each NBC to produce all CVs. The class selection block shown in **Fig. 3** collects them and selects the positive class(es) of the CNBC as the final outcome. This selection scheme, first of all, differs with respect to the dataset class type, i.e. the dataset can be called as "uni-class", if an item in the dataset can belong to only one class, otherwise called as "multi-class". Therefore, in a uni-class dataset there must be only one class, the c^*, selected as the positive outcome whereas in a multi-class dataset, there can be one or more NBCs, $\{c^*\}$, with a positive outcome. In the class selection scheme the winner-takes-all strategy is utilized. Assume without loss of generality that a CV of $\{0, 1\}$ or $\{-1, 1\}$ corresponds to a positive outcome where $CV_{c,2} - CV_{c,1}$ is maximum. Therefore, for uni-class datasets, the positive class index, c^*, ("the winner") is determined as follows:

$$c^* = \arg \max_{c \in [0,C-1]} (CV_{c,2} - CV_{c,1}) \tag{2}$$

In this way the erroneous cases (false negative and false positives) where no or more than one NBC exists with a positive outcome can be properly handled. However, for multi-class datasets the winner-takes-all strategy can only be applied when no NBC yields a positive outcome, i.e. $CV_{c,2} \leq CV_{c,1} \ \forall c \in [0, C-1]$, otherwise for an input set of FVs belonging to a dataset item, multiple NBCs with positive outcome may indicate the multiple true-positives and hence cannot be further pruned. As a result, for a multi-class dataset the (set of) positive class indices, $\{c^*\}$, is selected as follows:

$$\{c^*\} = \left(\begin{array}{ll} \arg \max_{c \in [0,C-1]} (CV_{c,2} - CV_{c,1}) & \text{if } CV_{c,2} \leq CV_{c,1} \ \forall c \in [0, C-1] \\ \{ \arg_{c \in [0,C-1]} (CV_{c,2} > CV_{c,1}) \} & \text{else} \end{array} \right) \tag{3}$$

Evolution of the CNBC

The evolution of a subset of the NBCs or the entire CNBC is performed for each NBC individually with a two-phase operation, as illustrated in **Fig. 4**. As explained earlier, using the feature vectors (FVs) and the target class vectors (CVs) of the training dataset, the evolution process of each BC in a NBC is performed within the current AS in order to find the best (optimal) BC configuration with respect to a given criterion (e.g. training/validation MSE or classification error, CE). During the evolution, only NBCs associated with those classes represented in the training dataset are evolved. If the training dataset contains new classes, which do not yet have a corresponding NBC, a new NBC is created for each, and evolved using the training dataset.

In Phase 1, see top of **Fig. 4**, the BCs of each NBC are first evolved given an input set of FVs and a target CV. Recall that each CV is associated with a unique NBC and the fuser BCs are not used in this phase. Once an evolution session is over, the AS of each BC is then recorded so as to be used for potential (incremental) evolution sessions in the future.

Recall further that each evolution process may contain several runs and according to the aforementioned evolutionary update rule, the best configuration achieved will be used as the classifier. Hence once the evolution process is completed for all BCs in the input layer (Phase 1), the best BC configurations are used to forward propagate all FVs of the items in the training dataset to compose the FV for the fuser BC from their output CVs, so as to evolve the fuser BC in the second phase. Apart from the difference in the generation of the FVs, the evolutionary method (and update) of the fuser BC is same as any other BC has in the input layer. In this phase, the fuser BC learns the significance of each individual BC (and its feature) for the discrimination of that particular class. This can be viewed as the adaptation of the entire feature space to discriminate a specific class in a large dataset, or in other words, a crucial way of applying an efficient feature selection scheme as some FVs may be quite discriminative for some classes whereas others may not and the fuser, if properly evolved and trained, can "weight" each BC (with its FV), accordingly. In this way the usage of each feature (and its BC) shall optimally be "fused" according to their discrimination power of each class. Similarly, each BC in the first layer shall in time learn the significance of individual feature components of the corresponding FV for the discrimination of its class. In short the CNBC, if properly evolved, shall learn the significance (or the discrimination power) of each FV and its individual components.

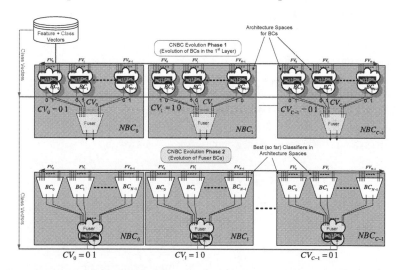

Fig. 4. Illustration of the two-phase evolution session over BCs' architecture spaces in each NBC

Incremental Evolution of the CNBC

To accomplish another major objective (IV: Incremental Evolution), the CNBC framework is designed for continuous "incremental" evolution sessions where each session may further improve the classification performance of each BC using the advantage of the "evolutionary updates". The main difference between the initial and the subsequent (incremental) evolution sessions is the initialization of the evolution process: the former uses *random* initialization whereas the latter starts from the last AS parameters of each classifier in each BC. Note that the training dataset used for the incremental evolution sessions may be different from the previous ones, and each session may contain several runs. Thus the evolutionary update rule compares the performance of the last recorded and the *current* (after the run) network over the *current* training dataset.

During each incremental evolution phase, existing NBCs are *incrementally* evolved *only if* they cannot accurately classify (or discriminate) the training (positive) samples of the new (emerging) classes. In that, an empirical threshold level (e.g. 95%) is used to determine the level of classification accuracy required for the *new* GTD encountered. The NBCs for the new classes are directly evolved *without* such verification and they use the available (or *log*) GTD of the existing NBCs (their positive samples) during their evolution process as negative samples. Therefore, for each evolution session new and log GTD are individually fused to evolve both new (initially) and existing NBCs (incrementally).

The exhaustive search via repetitive BP training of each network in the AS, the first step of an incremental training will simply be the initialization of the weights w_{jk}^l and biases θ_k^l with the parameters retrieved from the last record of the AS of that BC. Starting from this as the initial point, and using the *current* training dataset with the target CVs, the BP algorithm can then perform its gradient descent in the error space.

4   Experimental Results

In this section, we first detail the commercial database used and the feature extraction techniques performed for the extensive set of classification and content-based image retrieval experiments. We then investigate the classification performance of the proposed CNBC framework by performing comparative evaluations against a state-of-the-art classifier. Finally, we shall demonstrate the performance gain in terms of improved retrieval accuracy that can be achieved using the proposed CNBC framework as compared to the traditional similarity based retrievals.

4.1 Database Creation and Feature Extraction

We used MUVIS framework [5], to create and to index the following two databases by extracting 10 features for each as presented in Table 1, and images are downloaded from a commercial Real Estate website, [16].

- *Real_30K* Image Database: There are 30000 images obtained in various resolutions covering 20 diverse classes: *1) Bathroom, 2)   Bedroom, 3) Corridor, 4) Dining room, 5) Empty room, 6) Façade, 7) Floorplan, 8) Gym, 9) Inner entrance, 10) Kitchen, 11) Laundry room, 12) Living room, 13) Office, 14) Outdoor, 15) Sauna, 16) Scenery, 17) Basement, 18) Storage, 19) Terrace, and 20) Toilet.*
- *Real_60K* Image Database: This database is obtained by adding 30000 images over *Real_30K* database with the common 20 diverse classes as presented above.

Table 1. 10 Features extracted per Real Estate database

FV	Feature	Parameters	Dim.
1	HSV Color Histogram	H=6, S=2, V=2	24
2		H=8, S=4, V=4	128
3	Dominant Color	$N_{DC}^{\max} = 6, T_A = 2\%, T_S = 15$	27
4	Descriptor	$N_{DC}^{\max} = 8, T_A = 2\%, T_S = 15$	35
5	Color Structure Descriptor	32 bins	32
6		64 bins	64
7	Local Binary Pattern		16
8	Gabor	scale=4, orient.=6	48
9	Ordinal Co-occurence	d=3, o=4	36
10	Edge Histogram Dir.		5

As detailed in Table 1, some of the basic color (e.g. MPEG-7 Dominant Color Descriptor, HSV color histogram and Color Structure Descriptor [6]), texture (e.g. Gabor [7], Local Binary Pattern [8], and Ordinal Co-occurrence Matrix [9]) and edge (e.g. Edge Histogram Direction [6]) features, are extracted. Some of them are created with different parameters to extract several features and the total feature dimension is obtained as 415. Such a high feature space dimension can thus give us opportunity to test the performance of the proposed CNBC framework against the "curse of dimensionality" with the large number of features.

4.2 Classification Results

We partitioned the *Real_30K* database where 35% of the items are spared for testing and the rest (65%) was used for evolving the CNBC, which is then used "as is" for the classification of the *Real_60K*. In this way we can test the scalability capability of the proposed classifier topology. For exhaustive BP, the learning parameter is set as $\lambda = 0.01$ and iteration number is 1000. We use the typical activation function: hyperbolic tangent ($\tanh(x) = \dfrac{e^x - e^{-x}}{e^x + e^{-x}}$). For the AS, we used simple configurations with the following range arrays: $R_{\min} = \{N_i, 8, 2\}$ and $R_{\max} = \{N_i, 16, 2\}$, which indicate that besides the single layer perceptron (SLP), all MLPs have only a single hidden layer, i.e. $L_{\max} = 2$, with no more than 16 hidden neurons. Besides the SLP, the hash function enumerates all MLP configurations in the AS, as shown in Table 2. Finally, for the exhaustive BP, $N_R = 10$ independent runs are performed for each configuration in the AS.

As for the competing classifier, we used Random Forest (RF) despite the fact that it is a static classifier that cannot adapt dynamically to the variations in features, classes and/or any update in training dataset (e.g. when new GTD present). Therefore, the two classifiers will only be compared in terms of their batch (static) learning and generalization capabilities over two static databases. Since in the proposed CNBC framework, the optimal BC (in this work the best MLP or SVM) configuration within each NBC is searched by a sequential search, in order to provide a fair comparison, for the RF, the best number of trees within the forest is also searched from 10 to 50 in steps of 10 and then the best one found is used for classification. Table 3 presents the classification performances, Precision (P) and Recall (R) over the test set (35%) of the *Alma_30K* database and over the entire *Alma_60K* database. The best precision performance has been obtained with RF whereas the best recall performance has been achieved with CNBC in both databases. However, being a static (fixed) classifier, RF has to undergo a new search for the best parameters and re-training each time whenever a change occurs whereas CNBC has the ability to adapt to the change incrementally while keeping its internal structure intact.

Table 2. The architecture space used for MLPs

Dim.	Conf.	Dim.	Conf.	Dim.	Conf.
0	$N_i \times 2$	6	$N_i \times 6 \times 2$	12	$N_i \times 12 \times 2$
1	$N_i \times 1 \times 2$	7	$N_i \times 7 \times 2$	13	$N_i \times 13 \times 2$
2	$N_i \times 2 \times 2$	8	$N_i \times 8 \times 2$	14	$N_i \times 14 \times 2$
3	$N_i \times 3 \times 2$	9	$N_i \times 9 \times 2$	15	$N_i \times 15 \times 2$
4	$N_i \times 4 \times 2$	10	$N_i \times 10 \times 2$	16	$N_i \times 16 \times 2$
5	$N_i \times 5 \times 2$	11	$N_i \times 11 \times 2$		

Table 3. Classification performances of the CNBC (with both BC types) and RF over the test set of Alma_30K and the entire Alma_60K databases

	Alma_30K		Alma_60K	
Classifier	P (%)	R (%)	P (%)	R (%)
CNBC (BC=MLP)	53.33	56.15	53.8	60.7
CNBC (BC=SVM)	48.5	58.72	58.35	66.05
RF	59.2	54.6	69.76	64.83

Due to space limitations, we had to skip an extensive set of classification experiments for demonstrating class and feature scalabilities of the proposed CNBC framework.

4.3 Retrieval Results

The traditional retrieval process in MUVIS is based on the query by example (QBE) operation. The features of the query item are used for (dis-) similarity measurement among all the features of the visual items in the database. Ranking the database items according to their similarity distances yields the retrieval result. The traditional (dis-) similarity measurement in MUVIS is accomplished by applying a distance metric such as L2 (*Euclidean*) between the feature vectors (FVs) of the query and each database item. When a CNBC is used for the purpose of retrieval, the same (L2) distance metric is now applied to the class vectors (CVs) at the output layer of the CNBC (20x2=40-D for *both* databases). In order to evaluate the retrieval performances with and without CNBC, we use average precision (*AP*) and an unbiased and a limited formulation of the *Normalized Modified Retrieval Rank (NMRR(q))*, which is defined in MPEG-7 as the retrieval performance criteria per query (q). It combines both of the traditional hit-miss counters; *Precision – Recall,* and further takes the ranking information into account as given in the following expression:

$$AVR\,(q) = \frac{\sum_{k=1}^{N(q)} R(k)}{N(q)} \quad and \quad W = 2N(q)$$

$$NMRR\,(q) = \frac{2\,AVR\,(q) - N(q) - 1}{2W - N(q) + 1} \leq 1 \tag{4}$$

$$ANMRR = \frac{\sum_{q=1}^{Q} NMRR\,(q)}{Q} \leq 1$$

where $N(q)$ is the number of relevant (via *ground-truth*) images in a set of Q retrieval experiments, $R(k)$ is the rank of the kth relevant retrieval within a window of W retrievals, which are taken into consideration during per query, q. If there are less than $N(q)$ relevant retrievals among W then a rank of $W+1$ is assigned for the remaining (missing) ones. $AVR(q)$ is the average rank obtained from the query, q. Hence the first relevant retrieval $(R(1))$ is ranked by counting the number of irrelevant images *a priori* and note that if all $N(q)$ retrievals are relevant, then $NMRR(q)=0$, the best retrieval performance is thus achieved. On the other hand, if none of relevant items can be retrieved among W then $NMRR(q)=1$, as the worst case. Therefore, the lower $NMRR(q)$ is the better (more relevant) the retrieval is, for the query, q. Both performance criteria are computed by querying *all* images in the database (i.e. batch query) and within three retrieval windows: 100, 200 and total number of ground truth images, $N(q)$ for each query q. The latter choice henceforth makes the *AP* identical to average recall and average F1 measures, too. The reason we also computed the performance measures for practical window sizes such as 100 and 200 is that a common user will unlikely be interested all the $N(q)$ retrievals particularly in such large databases. As presented in Table 4, it is evident that the CNBC can significantly enhance the retrieval performance regardless of the window and the database sizes. There is, however, a performance drop between the CNBC retrieval performances due to the fact that CNBC was not yet "incrementally evolved" for the *Alma_60K* database but average precision levels higher than 52% can still be achieved.

Table 4. Retrieval performances (%) of the four batch queries in each Real Estate databases

Retrieval Method	Window Size	Real_30K		Real_60K	
		ANMRR	AP	ANMRR	AP
CNBC	100	30.7	69.13	47.18	52.61
	200	31.13	68.72	47.64	52.21
	N(q)	32.62	66.9	50.33	49.04
Traditional	100	61.27	38.09	60.49	38.9
	200	63.42	36.03	62.55	36.93
	N(q)	68.06	31.28	69.4	29.95

Over each database, four batch queries are performed to compute the average retrieval performances, two with and two without (the traditional query) using the
CNBC. Whenever used, the CNBC is evolved with the BC type MLPs. For visual
evaluation, **Fig. 5** presents four typical retrieval results with and without using the
proposed CNBC framework. All query images are selected among the test set and the
query is processed within the entire database.

Fig. 5. Four sample queries within *Real_30K* (top) and *Real_60K* (bottom) databases where
the first 24 retrievals are shown. The top-left image is the query and irrelevant retrievals are
pointed with a red 'X' at the right-bottom corner of the image.

5   Summary and Conclusions

In this paper, a novel CNBC framework is introduced to address the problem of accurate and scalable content-based image classification within large and dynamic commercial image databases. CNBC is a *Divide and Conquer* type of approach, which reduces both feature and class vector dimensions for individual classifiers significantly, thus enabling the use of as compact classifiers as possible. The optimum classifier for each classification problem at hand and per feature can be searched individually and at a given time, this allows to create a new dedicated classifier for discriminating a certain class type from the others with the use of a single feature. Each (incremental) evolution session "learns" from the current best classifier and can improve it further using the new GTD, possibly finding another configuration in the AS as the new "optimal" classifier. Such an evolutionary update mechanism ensures that the AS containing the best configurations, is always kept intact and that only the best configuration at any given time is used for classification and retrieval. Experimental results demonstrated that the proposed evolutionary classifier framework provide an efficient solution for the problems of *scalability* and *dynamic adaptability* by allowing both feature space dimensions and the number of classes in a database dynamically varying. Whenever the CNBC is evolved in "batch" mode, it can compete and even surpass other state-of-the-art classifiers such as RF.

Although the results indicate that all the aforementioned objectives have been successfully fulfilled, even higher accuracy levels can still be expected from the CNBC framework with the addition of new powerful features with superior discrimination and content description capabilities.

References

[1] Kressel, U.: Pairwise classification and support vector machines. Advances in Kernel Methods - Support Vector Learning (1999)

[2] Chang, C.C., Lin, C.J.: LIBSVM: a library for support vector machines (2001), http://www.csie.ntu.edu.tw/~cjlin/libsvm

[3] Zou, T., Yang, W., Dai, D., Sun, H.: Polarimetric SAR Image Classification Using Multi-features Combination and Extremely Randomized Clustering Forests. EURASIP Journal on Advances in Signal Processing 2010, Article ID 465612, 9 pages (2010)

[4] Kiranyaz, S., Ince, T., Yildirim, A., Gabbouj, M.: Evolutionary Artificial Neural Networks by Multi-Dimensional Particle Swarm Optimization. Neural Networks 22, 1448–1462 (2009)

[5] MUVIS, http://muvis.cs.tut.fi/

[6] Manjunath, B.S., Ohm, J.-R., Vasudevan, V.V., Yamada, A.: Color and Texture Descriptors. IEEE Trans. On Circuits and Systems for Video Technology 11, 703–715 (2001)

[7] Manjunath, B., Wu, P., Newsam, S., Shin, H.: A texture descriptor for browsing and similarity retrieval. Journal of Signal Processing: Image Communication 16, 33–43 (2000)

[8] Ojala, T., Pietikainen, M., Harwood, D.: A comparative study of texture measures with classification based on feature distributions. Pattern Recognition 29, 51–59 (1996)

[9] Partio, M., Cramariuc, B., Gabbouj, M.: An Ordinal Co-occurrence Matrix Framework for Texture Retrieval. EURASIP Journal on Image and Video Processing 2007, Article ID 17358 (2007)

[10] Chauvin, Y., Rumelhart, D.E.: Back Propagation: Theory, Architectures, and Applications. Lawrence Erlbaum Associates Publishers, UK (1995)

[11] Spyrou, E., Le Borgne, H., Mailis, T., Cooke, E., Avrithis, Y., O'Connor, N.E.: Fusing MPEG-7 Visual Descriptors for Image Classification. In: Duch, W., Kacprzyk, J., Oja, E., Zadrożny, S. (eds.) ICANN 2005. LNCS, vol. 3697, pp. 847–852. Springer, Heidelberg (2005)

[12] Chen, H., Gao, Z., Lu, G., Li, S.: A Novel Support Vector Machine Fuzzy Network for Image Classification Using MPEG-7 Visual Descriptors. In: International Conference on MultiMedia and Information Technology, MMIT 2008, December 30-31, pp. 365–368 (2008), doi:10.1109/MMIT.2008.199

[13] Chang, E., Goh, K., Sychay, G., Gang, W.: CBSA: content-based soft annotation for multimodal image retrieval using Bayes point machines. IEEE Transactions on Circuits and Systems for Video Technology 13(1), 26–38 (2003), doi:10.1109/TCSVT.2002.808079

[14] Qi, G.-J., Hua, X.-S., Rui, Y., Tang, J., Zhang, H.-J.: Image Classification With Kernelized Spatial-Context. IEEE Trans. on Multimedia 12(4), 278–287 (2010), doi:10.1109/TMM.2010.2046270

[15] Kiranyaz, S., Gabbouj, M., Pulkkinen, J., Ince, T., Meissner, K.: Network of Evolutionary Binary Classifiers for Classification and Retrieval in Macroinvertebrate Databases. In: Proc. of IEEE Int. Conf. on Image Processing, ICIP 2010, Hong Kong, September 26-29, pp. 2257–2260 (2010)

[16] Finnish Realstate site, http://www.etuovi.com/

A Requirement Aware Method to Reduce Complexity in Selecting and Composing Functional-Block-Based Protocol Graphs

Daniel Günther, Nathan Kerr, and Paul Müller

Integrated Communication Systems (ICSY)
University of Kaiserslautern
Kaiserslautern, Germany
{guenther,kerr,pmueller}@informatik.uni-kl.de

Abstract. Future Internet research activities try to increase the flexibility of the Internet. A well known approach is to build protocol graphs by connecting functional blocks together. The protocol graph that should be used is the one most suitable to the application's requirements. To find the most suitable graph, all possible protocol graphs must be evaluated. However, the number of possible protocol graphs increases exponentially as the number of functional blocks increases. This paper presents a method of representing the protocol graph search space as a set of search trees and then uses forward pruning to reduce the number of protocol graphs evaluated. We evaluate our proposed method by simulation.

Keywords: future network, composition, complexity, protocol graph.

1 Introduction

In the current ISO/OSI stack model of the Internet, protocols dictate the availability and composition of network functionality. A flexible architecture, as often discussed in the Future Internet research area, will be able to support the desire to dynamically choose certain mechanisms based on the requirements of a particular application. In the 90s many approaches dealt with flexible configurations or functional modules. This idea was the vision for projects like Adaptive [3], DaCaPo [8], and FCSS [6]. More recent projects with similar goals are 4WARD [9,11], NENA [10] and SONATE [2]. This research has grown into a big scientific area. The research seeks to provide domain specific network compositions, more flexibility through functional composition and application aware compositions. In general, the basis for providing this functionality consists of functional blocks, which represent network functionality and are combined into protocol graphs.

These approaches generally work in the way shown in Figure 1. An application provides its requirements which are combined with network offers and any addition criteria from the system. A selection and composition system draws from a pool of functional blocks to create a protocol graph which fulfills the application's requirements.

R. Benlamri (Ed.): NDT 2012, Part I, CCIS 293, pp. 399–407, 2012.

This paper assumes that functional blocks take packets as input and produce packets as output. Functional blocks are connected together to form protocol graphs, which are directed acyclical graphs consisting of nodes with two connections at most. One connection is for the entry port, the other for the exit port. Both the sender and receiver use the same graph with the input/output flow reversed.

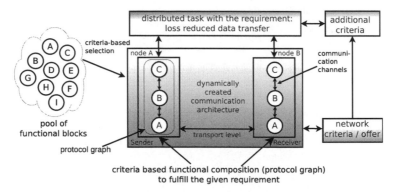

Fig. 1. General Model for Functional-Block-Based Future-Internet Approaches

2   Motivation

The number of possible protocol graphs depends on the number of functional blocks in the pool. The growth of possible protocol graphs is exponential.

To find the most appropriate protocol graph from the set of possible protocol graphs, all possible protocol graphs need to be considered. Protocol graphs that do not fulfill the requirements and constraints can be dropped, while those that can be used need to be compared.

This paper presents a method of representing the protocol graph search space as a set of search trees and defines three heuristics for selecting which protocol graphs will be extracted from the search space for later comparison.

Section 3 presents related work. Section 4 presents our method of representing protocol graphs as a set of search trees and presents the complexity-reduction heuristic methods which we propose to use. Section 5 evaluates our method. Sections 6 and 7 present our conclusions and future work.

3   Related Work

Several different approaches exist to reduce or explore the protocol graph search space. NENA [10] provides a set of human composed protocol graphs. This reduces the runtime selection process to a smaller set of precomposed graphs.

Template-based approaches use experts to build outlines or skeletons of protocol graphs that have slots for functional blocks that fulfill a specific class of functionality. For example, a template may have a slot for encryption, but does not specify which encryption mechanism is used. While templates reduce the protocol graph search space, they have the same problem as fully designed network stacks in that they may not do just what an application needs. This problem can be mitigated by introducing a set of situational templates (e.g., one for file transfers, one for video conferencing). This is one step better than the fully manual process, but it is still limited to the available templates.

Genetic algorithm approaches [4] fully embrace time constraints. These approaches can return the best graph found in a set amount of time. There are no guarantees about the quality of the protocol graph, or even that an appropriate graph will be found, assuming that one exists.

Both of these approaches assume that the base problem of searching the entire set of possible protocol graphs is too time consuming. This paper looks at ways of efficiently searching the entire set of possible protocol graphs. Only by searching the whole space can the most appropriate solution be guaranteed to be found.

One way of efficiently searching an entire space is with search trees. This is the approach applied here.

4   The RACR-SP Approach

The Requirement Aware Complexity Reduction – Selection Process (RACR-SP) consists of two parts. First, the protocol graph search space is represented as a set of search trees. Second, the tree is searched using a set of requirement aware heuristics to reduce the complexity.

The result of RACR-SP is a set of protocol graphs which fulfill the requirements. All graphs which do not fulfill the requirements are excluded from further evaluation. This reduces the number of protocol graphs that need to be directly compared to determine which one best fulfills the requirements.

4.1   Graph Representation

To fully explore a protocol graph search space, we represent protocol graphs as a set of search trees. This representation assumes that each node in a protocol graph can only have one entry edge and one exit edge. This means that protocol graphs look like network stacks, but without defined layers like the ISO/OSI layer model. Each functional block receives packets as input and produces packets as output.

Furthermore, a functional block can only appear once, if at all, in a protocol graph. All possible protocol graphs are encoded into a set of trees. The root of each tree is a network offer. Each branch begins with one functional block and then spreads out with the other functional blocks. Figure 2 shows the tree generated for three functional blocks: A, B, and C. N is a network offer.

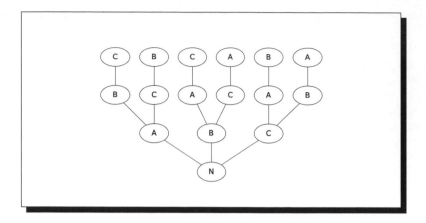

Fig. 2. The Tree Model to Present the Search Space

4.2   Complexity Reduction

The search tree is processed using depth-first iterative-deeping search [1] with forward pruning [5]. Each processed protocol graph is evaluated to see if it can fulfill the requirements or not. The maximum depth searched in the tree can be set. This also sets the maximum length of the the returned protocol graphs, which can be no more than the number of available functional blocks.

The following heuristic methods are provided to influence the search process.

4.2.1   Heuristic Method 1: All Graphs Found (AGF)

All Graphs Found (AGF) searches the entire space. This presents the worst case for all three heuristics presented in this paper. The other methods will stop searching or prune branches when a suitable graph is found. This heuristic does not. As a result, it will find all the protocol graphs which fulfill the application requirements.

If there is a suitable graph, at least one graph will be returned. As more than one graph may be returned, the most suitable of these graphs must be selected. This selection process will be covered in our future work.

4.2.2   Heuristic Method 2: First Suitable Graph (FSG)

First Suitable Graph (FSG) returns the first suitable protocol graph that is found. This is the fastest method, and requires no further work to select the best available graph, as it only returns one graph. There is no guarantee that the best graph will be found, only that a suitable graph – if one exists – will be found.

The worst case for this heuristic is that all possible protocol graphs will be searched and evaluated. This is no worse than AGF.

4.2.3   Heuristic Method 3: Prune If Fits (PIF)

Prune If Fits (PIF) works by not continuing to follow a branch when a suitable graph has already been found on that branch. The unsearched portion of the branch is pruned from the search space. This method is adapted from the idea of forward pruning.

Doing this should produce fewer suitable graphs than AGF. By pruning branches, the total number of protocol graphs considered is reduced at the cost of not guaranteeing that the most suitable graph is found (if one exists). This tradeoff should reduce the time required to select a graph while not overly reducing the possibility that the most suitable graph is not found.

While finding the most suitable graph is not guaranteed, the graphs not considered use more functional blocks than the ones considered. The use of more functional blocks will generally consume more resources and increase the impact of the protocol graph (e.g., increased computation, data rate, delay).

4.3   Example Search Process

Figure 3 shows how an example computation could look. This example uses three functional blocks: A, B, and C. N represents the network offer. The maximum depth searched is three.

At first the algorithm checks to see if the network offer (N) can fulfill the application requirements. In this example it does not. Now all the protocol graphs with a length (k) of one are checked: NA, NB, and NC. This example assumes that some combination of the provided functional blocks will fulfill the requirements.

NB and NC are found to fulfill the application requirements. The PIF heuristic method would then prune the branches extending from NB and NC. FSG would stop evaluating graphs at NB (NC would not be evaluated), and return the protocol graph NB.

After k is incremented by one, the AGF and PIF methods will continue by evaluating NAB and NAC, which are found to not fulfill the requirements. The next graphs to be evaluated would be NBA and NBC. However, the PIF heuristic dropped those branches because NB and NC already fulfill the application requirements. AGF will evaluate these nodes now and then continue with NCA and NCB, which also would have been dropped by PIF.

After k is incremented by one, NABC and NACB are evaluated by both AGF and PIF. Neither of these graphs fulfill the application requirements.

If the PIF heuristic is used, evaluation stops here and the graphs NB and NC are returned.

AGF would continue evaluation with NBCA, NBAC, NCAB, and NCBA; none of which fulfill the requirements. As there are no more graphs to evaluate, AGF returns the graphs NB and NC.

As shown in this example, RACR-SP can reduce the number of protocol graphs evaluated. In the next section, we use simulation to evaluate our approach.

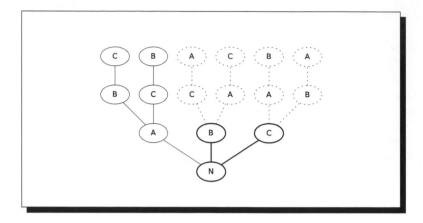

Fig. 3. Example Search Process

5 Evaluation

To evaluate our approach we first implemented the defined heuristics (AFG, FSG, and PIF) in the OMNeT++ [7] simulation environment. This implementation allows us to execute each heuristic method given a set of application requirements, a network offer, and a set of functional blocks. The specific details for each of these items are not specified here, as we are interested in how the heuristics perform, not how well the returned protocol graphs fulfill the requirements.

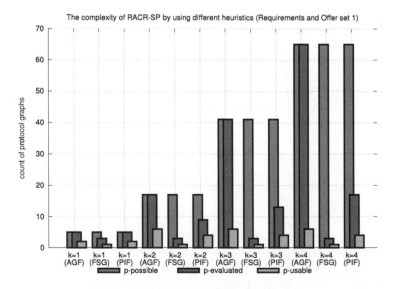

Fig. 4. The Influence of Used Heuristics

Our simulation specified application requirements, a network offer, and a set of four (4) functional blocks with their associated impact functions. Impact functions are used to calculate the effect of a functional block on the network offer. We used the simulation to measure how many protocol graphs there could be with the given maximum protocol graph depth (k_{max}), how many protocol graphs were actually evaluated, and finally how many protocol graphs were usable (i.e., fulfilled the application requirements). Figure 4 shows all the data we gained from our simulated scenarios.

Figure 5 shows how many protocol graphs are evaluated by each heuristic method. AGF always evaluates every protocol graph; this line is the worst case for all three heuristics.

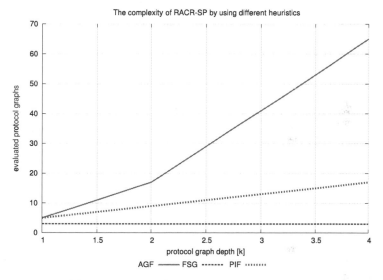

Fig. 5. Number of Evaluated Protocol Graphs

FSG stops evaluation as soon as it finds a graph which fulfills the application requirements. PIF prunes branches when an requirements fulfilling graph is found. Except in the worst case, PIF evaluates fewer graphs than AGF, but more than FSG. This empirical evaluation only shows the type of results that could be expected in a situation similar to that which was simulated. A theoretical evaluation would be needed to show anything more. As we needed an implementation to continue our direction of research, we think this evaluation is sufficient.

6   Conclusion

This paper presents RACR-SP, a method of representing the protocol graph search space as a set of search trees and the requirement aware heuristics used to control the search of those trees.

Three heuristic methods are presented. All Graphs Found (AGF) evaluates all possible graphs. This method will find every protocol graph that fulfills the application's requirements. First Suitable Graph (FSG) will evaluate as many graphs as needed to find a suitable graph. This may be as few as one, or as many as every possible graph.

Prune If Fits (PIF) searches down every branch of the search tree; pruning the unsearched part of the branch once a suitable graph on that branch has been found. Except in the worst case, this process evaluates fewer graphs than AGF. While PIF will not find every suitable graph, the excluded graphs are deeper (have a greater k) than the already suitable graph on that branch. We assume that a deeper graph has greater impact and will therefore be less suitable. This simple method reduces the number of graphs that will have to be compared later in a way that will probably not remove the best graph from consideration.

Our empirical evaluation indicates that the heuristics function in the manner we envisioned.

7   Future Work

Now that the total number of graphs that need to be compared is reduced by using the method described in this paper, our future work will focus on how exactly to compare the graphs to find the best one. This work is made easier by assuming that the presented graphs fulfill the application requirements, leaving us with the problem of determining which graph is best.

Acknowledgment. This work has been created as part of the G-Lab project, funded by the German Federal Ministry of Education and Research (BMBF).

References

1. Korf, R.E.: Depth-first iterative-deepening: An optimal admissible tree search. In: Artificial Intelligence, pp. 97–109. Elsevier Science Publishers B.V. (1985)
2. Müller, P., Reuther, B.: Future internet architecture - a service oriented approach. IT - Information Technology 50(6), 383–389 (2008)
3. Schmidt, D.C., Box, D.F., Suda, T.: Adaptive: A dynamically assembled protocol transformation, integration and evaluation environment. Concurrency - Practice and Experience (1993)
4. Schwerdel, D., Reuther, B., Müller, P.: On using evolutionary algorithms for solving the functional composition problem. In: 10th Würzburg Workshop on IP: Joint ITG, ITC, and Euro-NF Workshop "Visions of Future Generation Networks" (2010)
5. Smith, S.J.J., Nau, D.S.: An analysis of forward pruning. In: Proceedings of the AAAI 1994 (1994)
6. Stiller, B.: Fukss: Ein funktionsbasiertes kommunikationssubsystem zur flexiblen konfiguration von kommunikationsprotokollen. GI/ITG-Fachgruppe Kommunikation und Verteilte Systeme (1994)

7. Varga, A., Hornig, R.: An overview of the omnet++ simulation environment. In: SimuTools, p. 60 (2008)
8. Vogt, M., Plagemann, T., Plattner, B., Walter, T.: A run-time environment for da capo. In: Proceedings of INET 1993 International Networking Conference of the Internet Society (1993)
9. Völker, L., Martin, D., Khayat, I.E., Werle, C., Zitterbart, M.: An architecture for concurrent future networks. In: 2nd GI/ITG KuVS Workshop on the Future Internet (2008)
10. Völker, L., Martin, D., Werle, C., Zitterbart, M., Khayat, I.E.: A node architecture for 1000 future networks. In: Proceedings of the International Workshop on the Network of the Future 2009. IEEE (2009)
11. Völker, L., Martin, D., Werle, C., Zitterbart, M., Khayat, I.E.: Selecting concurrent network architectures at runtime. In: Proceedings of the IEEE International Conference on Communications, ICC (2009)

Modeling and Analyzing MAC Frame Aggregation Techniques in 802.11n Using Bi-dimensional Markovian Model

Nazeeruddin Mohammad* and Shahabuddin Muhammad

College of Computer Engineering and Science,
Prince Mohammad Bin Fahd University (PMU), Al Khobar,
Kingdom of Saudi Arabia
{nmohammad,smuhammad}@pmu.edu.sa

Abstract. Increased expectations and demand for higher rates led to the development of new physical layer technologies in Wireless LANs. However, the current medium access control (MAC) needs to be improved to fully utilize higher physical-layer transmission rates. Several aggregation mechanisms have been recently proposed to improve the MAC layer performance of 802.11n. In this paper, we analyze some of the key aggregation mechanisms proposed. For analysis we adapted widely used Bianchi's analytical model and applied it for various aggregation techniques. We also compare the analytical details of various strategies and provide a unified analytical framework for continued research in this direction.

Keywords: 802.11n, Aggregation, CSMA/CA, MAC, WLANs.

1   Introduction

Wireless LANs (WLAN) are becoming increasing ubiquitous because of the flexibility and the freedom they offer to the users. Their popularity has led to several improvements in the physical layer technologies for wireless networks. The latest IEEE 802.11n [1] standard has utilized MIMO (multiple-input and multiple-output) and OFDM (orthogonal frequency division multiplexing) techniques to achieve transmission rates upto 600 Mbps [2,3]. However, several studies have shown that the improvements in the physical layer data rates will not be sufficient to improve the overall throughput [4]. The primary reason behind this is the overheads related to physical layer headers and contention time. These overheads do not decrease proportionally with the increase in physical data rates and dominate frame transmission time at higher physical data rates.

The throughput at MAC layer can be improved by mitigating frame overheads & contention time. One way of achieving this is by aggregating several frames in a single large frame, thereby minimizing channel idle time (fewer SIFS and backoffs) and frame overheads (fewer PHY headers). Few schemes [5,6] tried

---

* Corresponding author.

R. Benlamri (Ed.): NDT 2012, Part I, CCIS 293, pp. 408–419, 2012.

to improve MAC efficiency by sending a train (burst) of frames after winning DCF contention window, and hence sharing contention overhead across multiple frames. In BlockAck strategy [7] a train of frames are transmitted without waiting for individual acknowledgments (ACK), and then the whole block is acknowledged (BACK) with single acknowledgment frame, thereby reducing the overhead due to ACKs and SIFS.

IEEE 802.11n Task Group (TGn) has adopted frame aggregation to improve the MAC layer efficiency and throughput. Frame aggregation schemes attempt to improve MAC efficiency by reducing waiting time during CSMA/CA back-off period for successive frame transmissions, and minimizing the transmission time for preamble and frame headers [8]. IEEE 802.11n TGn has defined two frame aggregation schemes, namely aggregate MAC Service Data Unit (A-MSDU) and aggregate MAC Protocol Data Unit (A-MPDU). A-MSDU mechanism joins several MAC Service Data Units (MSDUs) to form a single big MAC Protocol Data Unit (MPDU). along with the Frame Check Sequence (FCS) are added to form PSDU. On the other hand, A-MPDU concatenates several MSDUs (each with their own MAC header and FCS) to form Physical-layer Service Data Unit (PSDU). However, transmitting large frames is not encouraged in error-prone channels because single bit-error causes all frames to be retransmitted. Aggregation with Fragment Retransmission (AFR) [4] scheme tries to address this issue by providing mechanisms for partial retransmission of affected frames.

In addition to aggregation, 802.11n standard specifies bidirectional data transfer method over a single transmission opportunity (TXOP)[9,10]. When a sender is allocated a TXOP, it informs surrounding stations (STAs) the time that the channel will remain busy. However, many times the transmission finishes before the reserved time and channel remains idle. In bidirectional method, the receiver STA is allowed to send packets to the sender STA in the reverse direction for the remaining TXOP time. This feature is useful in sending small feedback packets to the sender during the actual data transmission period.

802.11 has been extensively analyzed and various models have been proposed in order to better understand the performance of 802.11 DCF throughput. DCF is a carrier sense multiple access with collision avoidance (CSMA/CA) scheme with binary slotted exponential backoff. Bianchi's analytical model [11] is one of the widely used schemes that is not only simple but it can also predict accurately system throughput for a number of wireless stations in ideal channel conditions. Bianchi's model treats the backoff window size in the protocol as bi-dimensional Markovian chain. Using this chain, Bianchi attempts to compute the probability that a station transmits in a randomly chosen slot time and ultimately derives normalized system throughput as the fraction of time the channel is used to successfully transmit payload bits.

We have used Bianchi's analytical model to analyze various schemes proposed to enhance the saturation throughput in 802.11n. Our contribution is the comprehensive analytical treatment of 802.11n by exploring several enhancement schemes proposed for the latest protocol. Our analysis encompasses the following important scenarios:

Fig. 1. DCF two-way handshake transmission sequence

1. DCF two-way handshake
2. DCF four-way handshake
3. Aggregation with fragment retransmission (AFR)
4. Aggregated-MPDU (A-MPDU)
5. Aggregated-MSDU (A-MSDU)
6. A-MPDU and A-MSDU with bidirectional data transfer

In each of the above scenarios, we investigate the key parameters involved in the equation for saturation throughput and highlight the changes in those parameters for the case of ideal as well as error-prone channels.

2   Throughput Analysis

For the throughput analysis of 802.11n, we adopt Bianchi's model [11] which models the bi-dimensional process $\{s(t), b(t)\}$ with discrete-time Markov chain. If $W_i = 2^i CW_{min}$ and the maximum contention window $CW_{max} = 2^m CW_{min}$ then $s(t)$ represents the stochastic process for backoff stage $(0 \dots m)$ and $b(t)$ represents the stochastic process for the backoff time counter. Using this model, we analyze the probability of successful transmission and the MAC throughput in the various proposals suggested for 802.11n. In the entire analysis, we will assume that there are fixed number of stations in the WLAN and each transmitting station has saturated traffic, that is, each station is working in full load and has attained stable condition. In other words, each transmitting station has always data to send. Also, we assume that regardless of the number of retransmissions the conditional collision probability for each frame is constant and independent.

The mathematical notation used in this paper is summarized in Table 1. We tried to maintain consistency in the symbols instead of a wide variety of notations used in the literature.

If τ represents the stationary probability that a station (STA) transmits in a randomly chosen slot time, then it can be computed as [11]

$$\tau = \frac{2(1 - 2p)}{(1 - 2p)(W + 1) + pW(1 - (2p)^m)} \tag{1}$$

Here, p is the unsuccessful transmission probability.

2.1   DCF with Two-Way Handshake

First we consider basic Distributed Coordinated Function (DCF) which consists of two-way handshake protocol where a station sends a frame and waits for

Table 1. Mathematical Notation

Symbol	Meaning
τ	Stationary probability that a station transmits in randomly chosen time
W	Minimum congestion window size
m	Maximum backoff stage, $i \in (0, m)$ where $W_i = 2^i W$
n	Total number of stations
f	Number of fragments or sub frames in an aggregated frame
$E[P]$	Expected payload
T_e	Virtual time slot length for error transmission sequence
T_s	Average time the channel is sensed busy because of successful transmission
T_c	Average time the channel is sensed busy by non-colliding stations because of a collision
T_{sifs}	Time duration for transmitting a SIFS
T_{difs}	Time duration for transmitting a DIFS
T_{eifs}	Time duration for transmitting an EIFS
T_{ack}	Time duration for transmitting an ACK
T_{hdr}^{phy}	Time duration for transmitting a physical header
T_{hdr}^{mac}	Time duration for transmitting a MAC header
T_f	Time duration for transmitting one AFR frame payload
L_{frag}	Fragment length in bytes
L_{fcs}	FCS length in bytes
L	Total MAC frame length in bytes
L_{hdr}	Total length of MAC header in bytes
$L_{hdr+fcs}$	Total length of MAC header and FCS in bytes
L_{data}	Full payload of MAC frame in bytes
p	Probability of unsuccessful transmission
p_b	Probability of single bit error
p_e	Error probability for non-ideal channel
p_c	Collision probability

its acknowledgment in a unidirectional channel. The possible time sequence for basic DCF is shown Fig. 1. The normalized throughput (S) for ideal channel and error-prone channel are calculated as follows.

Ideal Channel. For an ideal channel, the successful transmission means only one STA transmits out of n STAs at any given time. The probability that a STA does not transmit in randomly chosen slot time is $1 - \tau$. The probability that $n - 1$ STAs do not transmit will be $(1 - \tau)^{n-1}$. For an ideal channel, the unsuccessful transmission is because of collision and hence the probability that a transmitted packet encounters a collision (p) is given by

$$p = p_c = 1 - (1 - \tau)^{n-1} \tag{2}$$

Since the probability that no STA transmits is $(1-\tau)^n$, the probability P_{tr} that at least one station transmits will be

$$P_{tr} = 1 - (1-\tau)^n \tag{3}$$

The probability of exactly one transmission is $\binom{n}{1}\tau(1-\tau)^{n-1}$. Therefore, the probability P_s that a transmission is successful is given by the probability that exactly one station transmits, condition on at least one station transmits [11]

$$P_s = \frac{n\tau(1-\tau)^{n-1}}{1-(1-\tau)^n} \tag{4}$$

The normalized throughput S is the ratio of expected payload transmitted in a slot time to the expected length of a slot time. If $E[P]$ is average packet payload size, then

$$S = \frac{P_{tr}P_sE[P]}{P_1\sigma + P_2T_s + P_3T_c} \tag{5}$$

Where P_1, P_2 and P_3 are the probabilities that a slot is empty, it contains a successful transmission, and it contains a collision respectively and σ is the duration of an empty slot time. Thus, $P_1 = (1-P_{tr})$, $P_2 = P_{tr}P_s$, $P_3 = P_{tr}(1-P_s)$. Ignoring the transmission delay, T_s and T_c can be written as (see Fig. 1):

$$T_s = T_{data} + T_{sifs} + T_{ack} + T_{difs} \tag{6}$$

$$T_c = T_{data} + T_{eifs} \tag{7}$$

The expected payload for DCF two-way handshake under ideal channel conditions is given by:

$$E[P] = (L - L_{hdr+fcs}) \tag{8}$$

Channel with Error. Since the channel is error prone, the unsuccessful transmission could be due to frame collision or channel error. Hence, the unsuccessful transmission probability (p) in Eq. 1 needs to be adjusted for both collisions and transmission errors. Thus, p can be expressed as

$$p = 1 - (1-p_c)(1-p_e) \tag{9}$$

where $p_c = 1-(1-\tau)^{n-1}$ is the collision probability and p_e is the error probability on the condition that there is a successful transmission in the time slot. The throughput Eq. 5 can now be written for error prone channel as

$$S = \frac{P_{tr}P_sE[P]}{P_1\sigma + P_2T_s + P_3T_c + p_eT_e} \tag{10}$$

where T_e is the virtual time slot length for error transmission sequence. It can be given as

$$T_e = T_{data} + T_{eifs} \tag{11}$$

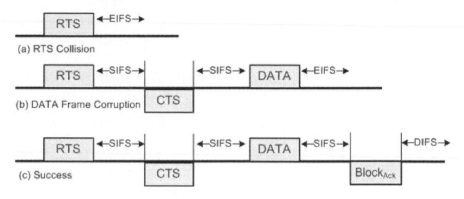

Fig. 2. RTS/CTS unidirectional access

T_c and T_s remain the same. Also note that in Eq. 10, P_2 is now equal to $P_s P_{tr}(1 - p_e)$.

The only unknowns left out in Eq. 10 are p_e and $E[P]$. As we are aware that any single bit error would corrupt the entire frame, thus

$$p_e = 1 - (1 - p_b)^L \tag{12}$$

$$E[P] = (L - L_{hdr+fcs})(1 - p_e) \tag{13}$$

2.2 DCF with Four-Way Handshake

DCF with four-way handshake uses RTS/CTS (Ready to Send/Clear to Send) control packets. A station that wishes to send a data frame exchanges RTS/CTS frames with the intended recipient before sending the actual data frame. This mode fixes the "hidden node" problem. The possible time sequence for DCF with four-way handshake in unidirectional data transfer is shown in Fig. 2. DCF four-way throughput analysis is similar to DCF two-way analysis of Section 2.1. The normalized throughput is given by Eq. 5 and Eq. 10 for ideal and error-prone channel conditions respectively. The only difference is in the duration of T_s, T_c and T_e, which are given by:

$$T_s = T_{rts} + 3T_{sifs} + T_{cts} + T_{data} + T_{ack} + T_{difs} \tag{14}$$

$$T_c = T_{rts} + T_{eifs} \tag{15}$$

$$T_e = T_{rts} + T_{cts} + T_{data} + T_{eifs} + 2T_{sifs} \tag{16}$$

2.3 Aggregation with Fragment Retransmission (AFR)

AFR [4] scheme works by combining several packets into one large frame and dividing this frame into multiple fragments. Fragmentation is done to avoid retransmission of the whole frame in case of any packet corruption during the

Fig. 3. Aggregation with fragment retransmission

transmission. Only the fragment containing the corrupted packet is retransmitted, thus increasing the overall performance. AFR also employs zero-waiting policy in which frames don't wait for all the fragments from upper layer to arrive. Instead, frames are transmitted as soon as a station wins transmission opportunity. Thus, AFR offers improved throughput through aggregation, fragmentation for selective retransmission and zero-waiting scheme.

AFR can also be modeled using Bianchi's model and the throughput Eq. 5 can be directly applied for ideal as well as error-prone channels as follows:

$$S_{afr} = \frac{P_2 E[L]}{P_1 \sigma + P_2 T_s + P_3 T_c} \tag{17}$$

It should be noted that AFR considers partially corrupted frames due to channel noise as successful transmission. Since $E[L]$ is the expected number of successfully transmitted bits instead of frame payload size, it can be calculated as:

$$E[L] = \sum_{i=0}^{f} \binom{f}{i} \cdot (p_e^{frag})^i \cdot (1 - p_e^{frag})^{f-i} \cdot (L - i \cdot L_{frag})$$

where fragment error rate p_e^{frag} is given as

$$p_e^{frag} = 1 - (1 - p_b)^{L_{frag} + L_{fcs}} \tag{18}$$

L_{fcs} is added in Eq. 18 as each fragment in AFR data frame has FCS (see Fig. 3). Substituting the value of p_e^{frag} in Eq. 17 and simplifying to get

$$S_{afr} = \frac{P_2 \cdot L \cdot (1 - p_e^{frag})}{P_1 \sigma + P_2 T_s + P_3 T_c} \tag{19}$$

The other unknown values T_s and T_c in Eq. 17 are different for DCF two-way handshake and DCF four-way handshake.

In case of DCF two-way handshake, T_s and T_c are given as:

$$T_s = T_{data}^{afr} + T_{sifs} + T_{ack} + T_{difs} \tag{20}$$

$$T_c = T_{data}^{afr} + T_{eifs} \tag{21}$$

where $T_{data}^{afr} = T_{hdr}^{phy} + T_f$.

For DCF four-way handshake, T_s and T_c are given as:

$$T_s = T_{rts} + T_{cts} + T_{data}^{afr} + 3T_{sifs} + T_{ack} + T_{difs} \tag{22}$$

$$T_c = T_{rts} + T_{eifs} \tag{23}$$

2.4   A-MPDU/A-MSDU Frame Aggregation

In this section, we will model A-MPDU and A-MSDU schemes using Bianchi's model [11]. Aggregated A-MPDU and A-MSDU frames can be transmitted using either DCF two-way handshake or DCF four-way handshake, and hence the analysis of A-MPDU and A-MSDU for DCF two-way hand shake and four-way hand shake will be similar to the standard analysis of Sections 2.1 and 2.2 respectively. The normalized throughput for A-MPDU and A-MSDU is given by Eqs. 5 and 10 respectively for ideal and error-prone channel conditions. However, the expected payload values ($E[P]$) in these equations depend upon the aggregation method and channel condition, and can be estimated as follows.

Ideal Channel. A-MSDU and A-MPDU frame structure is shown in Fig. 4. Assume that there are f subframes in the each aggregated A-MSDU and A-MPDU frame.

In A-MSDU, for each subframe there is an additional overhead of subframe header (14 bytes) and padding (0-3 bytes). Hence, the expected payload size for A-MSDU is

$$E[P] = L - L^{oh}_{a-msdu} \tag{24}$$

where $L^{oh}_{a-msdu} = L_{hdr+fcs} + \sum_{i=1}^{f}(L_{subhdr} + L_{pad})$.

On the other hand, each subframe in A-MPDU has a separate MAC header, a delimiter (4 bytes), variable size padding (0-3 bytes) and FCS. Hence the expected payload for A-MPDU is given by:

$$E[P] = L - \sum_{i=1}^{f}(L_{hdr+fcs} + L_{dlim} + L_{pad}) \tag{25}$$

The above equation can be rewritten as

$$E[P] = \sum_{i=1}^{f}(L_i - L^{oh}_{a-mpdu}) \tag{26}$$

where L_i is i_{th} subframe of the aggregated A-MPDU frame and $L^{oh}_{a-mpdu} = L_{hdr+fcs} + L_{dlim} + L_{pad}$.

It should be noted that T_s is slightly different for A-MPDU/A-MSDU as single block ACK will be sent instead of individual ACKs.

$$T_s = T_{rts} + T_{cts} + T_{data} + T_{back} + 3T_{sifs} + T_{difs} \tag{27}$$

Error Prone Channel. In order to calculate the values for p_e and $E[P]$ in Eq. 10, we first consider the case for A-MSDU where any single bit error would corrupt the entire frame, thus

$$p_e = 1 - (1 - p_b)^L \tag{28}$$

$$E[P] = (L - L^{oh}_{a-msdu})(1 - p_e) \tag{29}$$

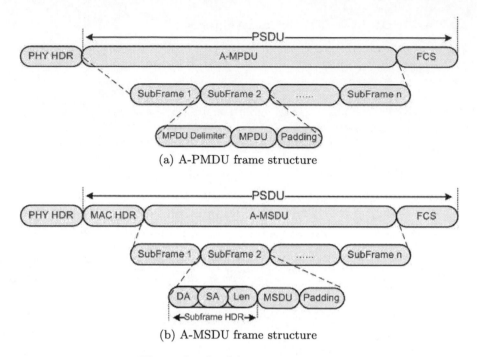

(a) A-PMDU frame structure

(b) A-MSDU frame structure

Fig. 4. One-level frame aggregation

In the case of A-MPDU, error occurs when all the sub-frames are corrupted. Therefore, we can write

$$p_e = \prod_{i=1}^{f}(1 - (1 - p_b)^{L_i}) \tag{30}$$

$$E[P] = \sum_{i=1}^{f}(L_i - L_{a-mpdu}^{oh})(1 - p_b)^{L_i} \tag{31}$$

where i ranges from 1 to the total number of aggregated sub-MPDUs frames (f).

2.5   Bidirectional Data Transfer

A key enhancement in 802.11n specifications is bidirectional data transfer. In this section, we will extend the A-MSDU/A-MPDU analysis of Section 2.4 for bidirectional data transfer. The possible time timing sequence for DCF four-way handshake with bidirectional data transfer is shown in Fig. 5. The DATA frames in this figure represent A-MPDU/A-MSDU aggregated frames.

The normalized throughput equations for bidirectional data transfer remain the same and are given by Eqs. 5 and 10 respectively for ideal and error-prone

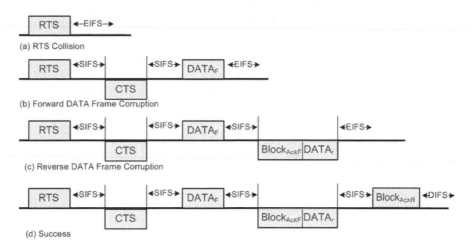

Fig. 5. RTS/CTS bidirectional data transfer

channel conditions. However, the expected payload value ($E[P]$) should accommodate both forward and reverse payloads. In the ideal channel case, $E[P]$ is the sum of forward and reverse payloads. If we assume that the data in the reverse direction is also aggregated and it contains b subframes then $E[P]$ for A-MSDU and A-MPDU is given by the following equations respectively.

$$E[P] = L_f + L_b - 2 * L^{oh}_{a-msdu} \tag{32}$$

$$E[P] = \sum_{i=1}^{f}(L_i - L^{oh}_{a-mpdu}) + \sum_{i=1}^{b}(L_i - L^{oh}_{a-mpdu}) \tag{33}$$

Also T_s should be modified to accommodate the reverse payloads, and it is given by:

$$T_s = T_{rts} + 4T_{sifs} + T_{cts} + T^{f}_{data} + T^{f}_{back} + T^{r}_{data} + T^{r}_{back} + T_{difs} \tag{34}$$

Error Prone Channel. In this case, an error can occur during the forward or reverse transmission. Hence the error probability has two components ($p_{e,f}$, $p_{e,r}$) corresponding to figure 5(b) & 5(c). The virtual time slots corresponding to error transmission in the forward and reverse directions are given by:

$$T_{e,f} = T_{rts} + 2T_{sifs} + T_{cts} + T^{f}_{data} + T_{eifs} \tag{35}$$

$$T_{e,b} = T_{rts} + 3T_{sifs} + T_{cts} + T^{f}_{data} + T^{f}_{back} + T^{r}_{data} + T_{eifs} \tag{36}$$

The error probabilities in the forward and reverse directions are dependent on aggregation method.

For A-MSDU, the error probabilities in the forward sequence and reverse sequence are given by

$$p_{e,f} = 1 - (1 - P_b)^{L_{for}} \tag{37}$$

$$p_{e,r} = (1 - P_b)^{L_{for}}(1 - (1 - P_b)^{L_{rev}}) \tag{38}$$

The expected payload for A-MSDU in the bidirectional mode is:

$$E[P] = (E_p^f + E_p^r)(1 - p_{e,f} - p_{e,r}) + E_p^f p_{e,r} \tag{39}$$

where E_p^f and E_p^r are the expected payloads given by Eq. 24.

In case of A-MPDU, the error probability in the forward direction can be calculated as:

$$p_{e,f} = \prod_i (1 - (1 - p_b)^{L_{i,f}}) \tag{40}$$

The error probability in the reverse direction ($p_{e,r}$) is dependent upon the success of the forward transmission. Assuming the reverse data is also aggregated:

$$p_{e,r} = (1 - p_{e,f})[\prod_i (1 - (1 - p_b)^{L_{i,r}})] \tag{41}$$

The expected payload for A-MPDU in bidirectional transmission is given by Eq. 39, where E_p^f and E_p^r are the expected payloads in the forward and reverse directions. These can be calculated by using Eq. 26.

2.6   Conclusion and Future Work

In this paper we analyzed and compared the normalized MAC throughput for various aggregation schemes in 802.11n using Bianchi's analytical model. The following are some conclusions that can be drawn from the analysis.

In ideal channel conditions A-MSDU performs very well since there is no overhead of MAC headers & FCSs. Conversely, when BER increases A-MPDU outperforms A-MSDU where single bit error corrupts the whole A-MSDU aggregated frame. A-MPDU obviates the need to resend the entire aggregated frame since the receiver can delineate a received A-MPDU frame and sends a BlockAck allowing individual data frames to be acknowledged or retransmitted.

Bidirectional data transfer provide significant improvement over unidirectional data transfer when receiver has always data to send in the reverse direction (for example, applications like voice chatting). On the other hand, it won't add any advantage over unidirectional data transfer in terms of MAC throughput if the data is predominantly unidirectional, except that higher layer protocol can benefit from reverse data in terms of timely acknowledgments.

Larger frame size increases the probability of collision (P_3) thereby decreasing the throughput.Since aggregation schemes employ larger frame size, they can benefit from four way handshake(RTS/CTS) to reduce the probability of collision because of smaller RTS/CTS control frames. AFR scheme reduces the probability of error (P_e^{frag}) by fragmenting the frame and selectively retransmitting the erroneous fragment thus improving the overall throughput.

In future, we would like to simulate aggregation schemes and compare the simulation results with our analysis. We would also like to analyze and simulate multi-level aggregation schemes and compare them with the existing schemes.

References

1. IEEE Computer Society: Wireless LAN Medium Access Control (MAC) and Physical Layer (PHY) specifications: Enhancements for Higher Throughput, IEEE P802.11n-D2.0 (2007)
2. Feng, K., Huang, Y., Lin, J.: Design of MAC-defined aggregated ARQ schemes for IEEE 802.11n networks. Wireless Networks 17(3), 685–699 (2011)
3. Xiao, Y.: IEEE 802.11n: Enhancements for higher throughput in wireless LANs. IEEE Trans. Wireless Communication 12(6), 82–91 (2005)
4. Li, T., Ni, Q., Malone, D., Leith, D., Xia, Y., Turletti, T.: Aggregation with fragment retransmission for very high-speed WLANs. IEEE/ACM Transactions on Networking 17(2), 591–604 (2009)
5. Tourrilhes, J.: Packet frame grouping: Improving IP multimedia performance over CSMA/CA. In: Proc. ICUPC, pp. 1345–1349 (1998)
6. Vitsas, V., Chatzimisios, P., Boucouvalas, A.C., Raptis, P., Paparrizos, K., Kleftouris, D.: Enhancing performance of the IEEE 802.11 distributed coordination function via packet bursting. In: IEEE GLOBECOM (2004)
7. Xiao, Y., Rosdahl, J.: Performance analysis and enhancement for the current and future IEEE 802.11 MAC protocols. ACM SIGMOBILE Mobile Computing and Communications Review 7(2), 6–19 (2003)
8. Lin, Y., Wong, V.W.S.: Frame Aggregation and Optimal Frame Size Adaptation for IEEE 802.11n WLANs. In: IEEE GLOBECOM (2006)
9. Liu, C., Stephens, A.P.: An analytic model for infrastructure WLAN capacity with bidirectional frame aggregation. In: Proc. of IEEE WCNC, pp. 113–119 (2005)
10. Skordoulis, D., Ni, Q., Chen, H., Stephens, A., Liu, C., Jamalipour, A.: IEEE 802.11n MAC frame aggregation mechanisms for next-generation high-throughput WLANs. IEEE Wireless Communications, 40–47 (2008)
11. Bianchi, G.: Performance analysis of the IEEE 802.11 distributed coordination function. IEEE Journal of Select. Areas Communication 18(3), 535–547 (2000)

Towards a Successful Mobile Map Service: An Empirical Examination of Technology Acceptance Model

Eunil Park[1], Ki Joon Kim[1], Dallae Jin[1,2],
and Angel P. del Pobil[1,3]

[1] Department of Interaction Science, Sungkyunkwan University,
Seoul, South Korea
{pa1324,veritate}@skku.edu
[2] Department of English Language and Literature, Seoul National University,
Seoul, South Korea
skydaia7@snu.ac.kr
[3] Department of Computer Science and Engineering, University Jaume-I,
Castellon, Spain
pobil@icc.uji.es

Abstract. The present study conducted structural equation modeling (SEM) analyses on data collected from 1,011 participants in order to examine the role of Technology Acceptance Model (TAM) in predicting mobile map service users' attitudes toward the service. Results from the analyses indicated that perceived mobility and perceived locational accuracy significantly influenced user acceptance and intention to use mobile map services via portable computing devices. In particular, increase in perceived mobility positively affected perceived usefulness while perceived locational accuracy also positively affected perceived usefulness and ease of use of using mobile map services. In addition, the present study revealed stronger effects of attitude on the behavioral intention to use than perceived usefulness, while the effects of perceived usefulness was stronger on attitude than perceived ease of use. Implications of notable findings and limitations are discussed.

Keywords: Mobile map service, Portable computing device, Technology Acceptance Model.

1 Introduction

Mobile map service is one of the most frequently used geographic information system (GIS) services offered on mobile devices, which provides users with satellite views of specific areas and directions to designated locations [1]. In 2012, more than 40 million users access to mobile map services in their mobile phones on a daily basis [2]. This increasing popularity of mobile map service is a result of the recent developments in wireless technologies (e.g., wireless communications and localization methods) and portable computing devices that have made it possible to deliver accurate, convenient access to mobile map services [3-4].

R. Benlamri (Ed.): NDT 2012, Part I, CCIS 293, pp. 420–428, 2012.

However, few studies have assessed the attitudes and intentions of mobile map service users although these two factors are considered keys to successful implementations of a new technology [5-9]. The present study, therefore, aims to examine mobile map service users' attitudes toward the technology and their future intentions to use the service by using the Technology Acceptance Model (TAM).

2   Literature Review

2.1   Mobile Map Services

Google Inc. offers two types of mobile map services: Google Maps and Google Earth [10-11]. After its first debut in February 2005 for the Internet users and later in November 2007 for mobile users [12-13], more than 150 million users are now using Google's map service [10], [14]. A key characteristic of Google Maps is that it provides mobile map services using localization via 3G or WIFI connections rather than GPS.

Google Earth is a geographical information service offering numerous view-points [13]. To provide users with various overview images, Google Earth gathers images taken from satellites, planes, and GIS 3D systems. Google Earth was first released by Central Intelligence Agency and Google in 2004, and its mobile version was later released in 2008 (downloaded over a billion times by 2011) [17]. In the mobile version, users are able to see images retrieved from both Google Maps and Google Earth [15-16].

In South Korea, NHN Corporation released an Internet map service called Naver Map [18-20]. Similar to Google Maps, Naver Map offers an online map service in South Korea, and provides real street view images taken in 2010 [20] (Fig. 1, 2). Since its debut in 2007, Naver Map has gained much popularity and now more than a half million people use the service on their mobile devices [18], [20].

2.2   Technology Acceptance Model (TAM)

Developed by Fred David [5-7], TAM is a well-known information systems model that explains how users' attitudes toward and acceptance of new technologies are shaped. In TAM, perceived usefulness (i.e., perceived degree to which users believe that their task performance may be enhanced by using a technology) and perceived ease of use (i.e., perceived degree to which users believe that using a technology is effortless) determine users' attitudes toward new technologies, intention to use, and real usage [5-9].

As summarized in Fig. 3, representative characteristics (i.e., external variables) of a technology have significant effects on perceived usefulness and perceived ease of use. Previous studies have shown that external factors only had indirect effects on users' attitudes and intentions [21-22].

Fig. 1. Mobile map services on smartphones
(left and center: Naver Map, right: Google Maps

Fig. 2. Naver Map's street views

3 Research Framework

3.1 Hypotheses Based on TAM

Findings from previous studies demonstrated the critical role of TAM in evaluating relationships between a specific technology and users' perceptions of the technology. A number of previous studies indicated that perceived ease of use and usefulness are key determinants of users' attitude towards a technology, and this attitude and perceived usefulness significantly affect intention to use the technology in future. Previous studies also indicated that mobile technology can be studied in terms of TAM [5-9], [21-22]. The present study, therefore, employs TAM as the fundamental basis for understanding mobile map users' acceptance and intention, and hypothesizes:

- H1. Perceived ease of use is positively related to perceived usefulness.
- H2. Perceived ease of use is positively related to attitude.
- H3. Perceived usefulness is positively related to attitude.
- H4. Perceived usefulness is positively related to behavioral intention to use.
- H5. Attitude is positively related to behavioral intention to use.

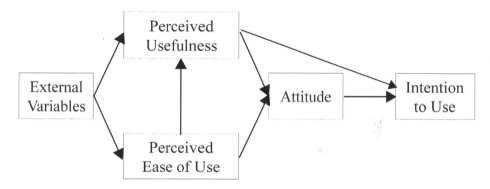

Fig. 3. The original technology acceptance model

3.2   The Influence of Perceived Mobility and Perceived Accuracy (Reliability)

Perceived mobility is defined as the level of user awareness of the mobility value of mobile systems or devices [23]. Users experience mobility when they access to mobile map services through portable computing devices. Perceived mobility is one of the most important factors for mobile services [24], and it plays a critical role in determining perceived usefulness [23] and perceived ease of use.

Perceived locational accuracy refers to the degree to which users are being aware of their correct locations. Most mobile map applications (Fig. 1) are able to pinpoint users' physical location and display it on the screen [4], [10-11], [20]. Since they are interactive real-time systems, users can easily find their current location and directions to destination. Therefore, users are more likely to be satisfied and perceive the mobile map services more useful when the services accurately show users' current, physical locations.

The present study, therefore, hypothesizes:

- H6. Perceived mobility is positively related to perceived ease of use.
- H7. Perceived mobility is positively related to perceived usefulness.
- H8. Perceived locational accuracy is positively related to perceived usefulness.

3.3   Conceptual Model

Based on our hypotheses, we propose the following conceptual model (Fig. 4).

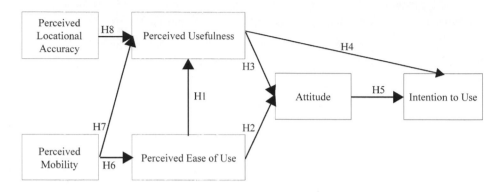

Fig. 4. The proposed conceptual model

4   Method

4.1   Participants

1,011 mobile map service users (45% male, 55% female) participated in our experiment. Participants' age ranged 19 to 40, with a mean of 28.1 years (SD = 4.4). All participants owned electronic devices (91% smartphones, 9% tablet PCs) with access to the mobile map service.

4.2   Apparatus and Procedure

Participants were asked to meet the experimenter in front of Seoul City Hall, and provided with a small note with an address written on it. Participants were instructed not to use any kinds of transportation such as bus, subway or etc. Average distance from the starting point to the destination was about 2.5 km straight-line and 3.7 km on foot (Fig. 5). After the experiment, participants completed a survey questionnaire measuring their perceptions and evaluations of the mobile map service. They were then debriefed and paid $10 for their participation.

4.3   Measurements

Validated questionnaire items from previous studies were adopted. Participants responded to each item by marking on a 7-point Likert-type scale ranged from 1 (strongly disagree) to 7 (strongly agree). Perceived mobility was an index composed of six items adapted from a study by Huang et al. [23]. Perceived accuracy (reliability) of location was an index composed of four items adapted from studies by Park et al. and Loomis et al. [4], [25]. Items for the four TAM constructs, including perceived ease of use (four items), perceived usefulness (four items), attitude towards smartphone use (three items), and intention to use a smartphone (three items) were adapted from the original TAM studies by Davis [5-9].

Fig. 5. Interactive maps of portable computing devices (from Naver Map)

5   Results

Results from descriptive statistics are reported in Table 1.

5.1   Analysis Method

Structural equation modeling (SEM) was used to examine the proposed conceptual model. Confirmatory factor analysis (CFA) was also used to evaluate the measurement model with LISREL 8.70 software. Reliability and validity were tested by the maximum likelihood method. Given that more than 200 samples are typically recommended for a SEM analysis [26], the present study used 1,011 samples to satisfy this recommendation.

5.2   The Measurement Model

CFA was used to test the measurement model. The measurement model showed a good fit between the data and the measurement model. The fit indices were $\chi^2/d.f.=2.99$, $GFI=0.961$, $NNFI=0.952$, $CFI=0.955$, $SRMR=0.049$, $RMSEA=0.048$.

In addition, the values of Cronbach's alpha (Table 1) and composite reliability indicated strong reliability. The factor loadings of all items exceeded 0.7, meaning that all items' factor loadings were significant. For satisfying discriminant validity, Fornell and Lacker [27] recommended that the square root of the average variance extracted (AVE) of each construct exceeded the correlation between two constructs, and all constructs in the present study did meet this recommendation.

5.3   Hypothesis Testing

All hypotheses were supported, as reported in Table 2 and Fig. 6. The SEM and the maximum likelihood method were used to test the proposed model. The test indicated a good fit between the data and the proposed model: $\chi^2/d.f.$=2.96, *GFI*=.956, *NNFI*=.965, *CFI*=.973, *SRMR*=.044, *RMSEA*=.042.

Hypotheses based on the TAM (H1, H2, H3, H4, and H5) were supported. Consistent with previous TAM studies, perceived ease of use significantly affected perceived usefulness (H1, β=0.45, *p*<0.001) and attitude (H2, β=0.09, *p*<0.01). Perceived usefulness significantly affected attitude (H3, β=0.51, *p*<0.001) and behavioral intention to use (H4, β=0.29, *p*<0.001). Attitude had significant effects on behavioral intention to use (H5, β=0.58, *p*<0.001). Attitude and perceived usefulness explained 60.9 % of the variance of behavioral intention to use. 31.8 % of the variance of attitude was explained by perceived ease of use and usefulness.

H6, H7, and H8 explained the relationships between the two external factors and two beliefs of the TAM. Perceived mobility affected perceived ease of use (H6, β=0.62, *p*<0.001) and perceived usefulness (H7, β=0.25, *p*<0.001). Perceived locational accuracy significantly influenced perceived usefulness (H9, β=0.20, *p*<0.001). Furthermore, perceived mobility explained 38.2% of the variance of perceived ease of use. Perceived mobility and perceived locational accuracy explained 44.4% of the variance of perceived usefulness.

Table 1. Descriptive analysis and Cronbach's α of all constructs

	Mean	Standard deviation	Cronbach's α
Perceived Mobility	5.00	1.18	0.81
Perceived Locaional Accuracy	4.98	1.21	0.84
Perceived Ease of Use	5.47	0.97	0.91
Perceived Usefulness	5.20	1.02	0.88
Attitude	5.21	0.94	0.83
Behavioral Intention to Use	5.21	1.01	0.87

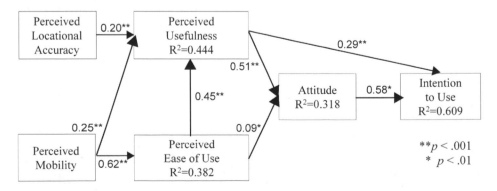

Fig. 6. Path analysis

Table 2. Summary of hypothesis testings; *p <. 01, **p<.001 (PE: Perceived Ease of Use, PU: Perceived Usefulness, AT: Attitude, IU: behavioral Intention to Use, PM: Perceived Mobility, PLA: Perceived Locational Accuracy)

Hypotheses	Path			Standardized coefficient	SE	CR	Results
H1	PE	→	PU	0.45**	.029	15.09	Supported
H2	PE	→	AT	0.09*	.031	2.62	Supported
H3	PU	→	AT	0.51**	.032	15.56	Supported
H4	PU	→	IU	0.29**	.020	12.26	Supported
H5	AT	→	IU	0.58**	.025	24.36	Supported
H6	PM	→	PE	0.62**	.020	25.01	Supported
H7	PM	→	PU	0.25**	.024	8.41	Supported
H8	PLA	→	PU	0.20**	.018	8.37	Supported

6 Discussion

By examining the four TAM constructs and two external factors, the present study successfully demonstrated that perceived mobility and locational accuracy were indeed distinctive characteristics of mobile map services. Consistent with findings in previous TAM studies, our results from the SEM indicated that perceived mobility and perceived locational accuracy significantly influenced user acceptance and intention to use mobile map services via portable computing devices. In particular, increase in perceived mobility positively affected perceived usefulness while perceived locational accuracy also positively affected perceived usefulness and ease of use of using mobile map services. In addition, the present study revealed stronger effects of attitude on the behavioral intention to use than perceived usefulness (H5 and H4), while the effects of perceived usefulness was stronger on attitude than perceived ease of use.

Although all eight hypotheses of the present study were statistically supported, there are several issues that should be taken into consideration in future research. First, the present study did not fully consider participants' characteristics as potential covariates. That is, participants' individual differences such as gender and age might have affected their perceptions. Future studies should address these covariates and consider additional cognitive factors other than perceived mobility and locational accuracy.

Acknowledgment. This research was supported by World Class University program through the National Research Foundation of Korea funded by the Ministry of Education, Science and Technology (R31-2008-000-10062-0).

References

1. Oulasvirta, A., Estlander, S., Nurminen, A.: Embodied interaction with a 3D versus 2D mobile map. Personal and Ubiquitous Computing 13(4), 303–320 (2009)
2. Berg Insight AB, Mobile aps and navigation (2007),
   http://www.berginsight.com
3. Weiser, M.: The computer of the 21st century. Scientific American 265(3), 94–100 (1991)

4. Park, E., Kim, S., del Pobil, A.P.: Can I go there?: The Effects of Digital Signage on Psychology of Wayfinding Users. Journal of Next Generation Information Technology 2(4), 47–58 (2011)
5. Davis, F.D.: Perceived usefulness, perceived ease of use, and user acceptance of information technology. MIS Quarterly 13, 319–340 (1989)
6. Davis, F.D., Bagozzi, R.P., Warshaw, P.R.: User acceptance of computer technology a comparison of two theoretical models. Management Science 35, 928–1003 (1989)
7. Davis, F.D.: User acceptance of information technology: system characteristics, user perceptions and behavioral impacts. International Journal of Man-machine Studies 38, 475–487 (1993)
8. Venkatesh, V.: Determinants of perceived ease of use: Integrating control, intrinsic motivation, and emotion into the technology acceptance model. Information Systems Research 11, 342–365 (2000)
9. Venkatesh, V., Morris, M., Davis, G., Davis, F.D.: User acceptance of information technology: Toward a unified view. MIS Quarterly 27(3), 425–478 (2003)
10. Google Inc., Google Maps, http://maps.google.com
11. Google Inc., Google Earth, http://google.com/earth
12. Miller, C.C.: A beast in the field: The Google Maps mashup as GIS/2. Cartographica: The International Journal for Geographic Information and Geovisualization 41(3), 187–199 (2006)
13. Vandenburg, M.: Using Google Maps as an interface for the library catalogue. Library Hi Tech 26(1), 33–40 (2008)
14. Wikipedia, Google Maps, http://en.wikipedia.org/wiki/Google_Maps
15. Lisle, R.J.: Google Earth: a new geological resource. Geology Today 22(1), 29–32 (2006)
16. Patterson, T.C.: Google Earth as a (not just) geography education tool. Journal of Geography 106(4), 145–152 (2007)
17. The Official Blog of Google Inc., Google Earth downloaded more than one billion times, http://googleblog.blogspot.com/2011/10/google-earth-downloaded-more-than-one.html
18. Lee, J.K.: Web 2.0 and OpenAPI. In: The 14th Korea Internet Conference. Korea Internet Security Agency, Seoul (2006)
19. Lee, C., Yang, J., Kim, D., An, B., Kim, N.: Ubiquitous Service Model for Information Convergence of Jeju Island Culture, Tourism, Sport and Traffic. The Journal of The Institute of Webcasting, Internet and Telecommunication 8(4), 97–104 (2008)
20. NHN corporation, Naver Map, http://map.naver.com
21. Pagani, M.: Determinants of adoption of third generation mobile multimedia services. Journal of Interactive Marketing 18, 46–59 (2004)
22. Moon, J.W., Kim, Y.G.: Extending the TAM for a World-Wide-Web context. Information & Management 38, 217–230 (2001)
23. Huang, J.H., Lin, Y.R., Chuang, S.T.: Elucidating user behavior of mobile learning: A perspective of the extended technology acceptance model. The Electronic Library 25, 585–598 (2007)
24. Siau, K., Shen, Z.: Mobile communications and mobile services. International Journal of Mobile Communications 1, 3–14 (2003)
25. Loomis, J.M., Silva, J.A., Philbeck, J.W., Fukusima, S.S.: Visual perception of location and distance. Current Directions in Psychological Science 5(3), 72–77 (1996)
26. Anderson, J.C., Gerbing, D.W.: Structural equation modeling in practice: A review and recommended two-step approach. Psychological Bulletin 103, 411–423 (1998)
27. Fornell, C., Larcker, D.F.: Evaluating structural equation models with unobservable variables and measurement error. Journal of Marketing Research 8, 39–50 (1981)

VND-CS: A Variable Neighborhood Descent Algorithm for Core Selection Problem in Multicast Routing Protocol

Youssef Baddi and Mohamed Dafir Ech-Cherif El Kettani

Information Security Research Team – ISeRT
ENSIAS - Mohammed V-Souissi University
Rabat, Morocco
{baddi,dafir}@ensias.ma

Abstract. Core Selection CS problem consists in choosing an optimal multicast router in the network as the root of the shared path multicast tree (SPT). The choice of this designated router (refer to as the "Rendezvous Point RP" in PIM-SM protocol and the "core" in CBT protocol) is the main problem concerning multicast tree construction; this choice influences multicast routing tree structure, and therefore influences performances of both multicast session and routing scheme. The determination of a best position of the Rendezvous Point is an NP complete problem: it needs to be solved with a heuristic algorithm. In this paper we propose a new Core Selection CS algorithm based on Variable Neighborhood Descent algorithm, based on a systematic neighborhood changing. VND-CS algorithm selects the core router by considering both cost and delay functions. Simulation results show that good performance is achieved in terms of multicast cost, end-to-end delay and tree construction delay.

Keywords: Core, VND-CS, PIM-SM, SPT, Multicast routing.

1 Introduction

Traditional applications using the Internet require a unicast communications. However, some important new emerging applications (videoconferencing) require simultaneous communication between groups of computers. Therefore, Deering [1] proposed a new technique called IP multicast routing, which entrusts the task of data duplication to the network: applications can send one copy of each packet and address it to the group of involved computers; the network takes care of message duplication to the receivers of the group. Multicast IP is a bandwidth conserving technology that reduces traffic in the network, and by the many, the bandwidth consumption also.

Multicast communication is based on a multicast tree for data routing; multicast routing protocols are built using two kinds of multicast trees: source based trees and shared trees. With source based trees, a separate tree is built for each source. With a shared tree, one tree is built for the entire group and shared among all senders; core based trees have a significant advantage in terms of routing resources more than source-based trees in that only one routing table entry is needed for the group[2].

R. Benlamri (Ed.): NDT 2012, Part I, CCIS 293, pp. 429–443, 2012.

Shared trees can be constructed using a core based tree: in this paper, we will focus on core based tree construction. It requires the selection of a central router called "Rendezvous point" RP in PIM-SM protocol [3] and "core" in CBT protocol [4]. Finding out an optimal position of this router is a very well knew problem called core selection problem. Core selection directly impacts on the structure of the tree and the performance of multicast routing scheme. Current implementations of PIM-SM [3] and CBT [4] protocols decide on the core router selection administratively [5], based only on priority and IP address of each candidate core. This leads to high cost, high delay, and high congestion. Core selection problem first proposed by Wall [6], is an NP complete problem [2] [7] [8], which needs to be solved with a heuristic algorithm.

This paper is organized as follows. In the next section, we describe the core selection problem. Section 3 presents the state of research of the core selection problem in the literature. Section 4 is devoted to the description of a mathematical modeling of core selection problem. Section 5 describes the proposed VND-CS algorithm for the core selection problem. Simulation results are reported in Section 6. Finally, Section 7 provides concluding remarks.

2   Background

The main role of a multicast routing protocol consists in managing multicast groups and routing multicast messages through an optimal multicast tree in order to reach all group nodes, which facilitates the operation of multicast packet duplication. Constructing a unique multicast tree covering all multicast groups members (receivers and sources) at the same time is known by the minimum Steiner tree problem (MST) [9]; this problem is NP complete [2][7][8], and seeks to find a low-cost tree by minimizing cost and transmission delay. Because of the difficulties in obtaining SMT, especially in larger graphs, it is often deemed acceptable to use other optimal trees to replace SMTs through a heuristic algorithm. Multicast routing protocols are classified in two categories, as mentioned earlier (SBT and ST) [10].

Source based tree SBT or Shortest Path Tree SPT is composed of the shortest paths between the source as root and each receivers of multicast group. The main motivations behind using a source based tree SBT are the simplicity of building in a distributed manner using only the unicast routing information, and optimization of transmission delay between source and each receiver [7]. The main drawbacks of SBT are: additional costs for maintaining SPT trees, and the number of statements to be stored in the nodes complexity is $O(S * G)$ (S is the number of sources and G is the number of groups) [7]. The shortest path tree SPT is used by several multicast routing protocols such as DVMRP [11], MOSPF [12], and PIM-DM [13].

Source-based trees in general are mostly suitable for small-scale, local-area applications. The main motivation for their use is delay optimization during multicast forwarding. They are not adapted to sparse mode situation because of the additional overhead of tree maintenance; also the scalability of source-based protocols tends to degradation in terms of network resource consumption [7].

Core based trees are more appropriate when there are multiple sources in the multicast group. Under this approach, Core-based trees separate the concept of source from that of the tree root. One node in the network is chosen as the center, and the sources forward messages to the center. Like SBT tree, a shortest path multicast tree is constructed rooted at the selected core, offering better flexibility and extensibility. And only routers on the tree need to maintain information related to group members. It gives good performance in terms of the quantity of state information to be stored in the routers and the entire cost of routing tree [12] [13] [14].

Joining and leaving a group member is achieves explicitly in a hop-to-hop way along the shortest path from the local router to core router resulting in less control overhead, efficient management of multicast path in changing group memberships, scalability and performance [1][15].

Several multicast routing protocols in the literature use core-based tree: Protocol Independent Multicasting-Sparse mode PIM-SM [3] and Core-Based Tree (CBT) [4]. Current implementation of PIM-SM [3] and CBT [4] protocols divide the tree construction problem into two sub-problems, the first is center selection problem and the second is routing problem. PIM-SM [3] and CBT [4] uses for center selection a special router called Bootstrap router (BSR) [16], which notifies a set of candidate cores. Every node uses a Hash function to map to one core according to the address of the group; this hash function is based on router priority and his IP address. Both of these parameters do not guarantee the selection of an optimal core. This leads to high cost, high delay, and high congestion. This problem first proposed by Wall [6], is an NP complete problem [2] [7] [8], which needs to be solved through a heuristic algorithm.

In this paper, we propose a new Core Selection Algorithm VND-CS based on a "Variable Neighborhood Descent". VND algorithm has already been applied successfully to resolve a wide variety of NP-hard problems [11] [17] [18] [19] [20] to select a global optimal solution using several neighborhoods structures systematically, but not yet in core selection problem. VND-CS can simultaneously minimize the delay and cost of the multicast tree. It attempts to find the best core using a fitness function.

3   Literature Review

There are several proposals, algorithms and mechanisms for core selection problem in the literature. A variety of these algorithms are compared in [7]. Among proposed selection algorithms, we find the Random Source-Specific Tree (RSST) heuristic, in which, the center is chosen randomly among the sources. It is comparable to selecting the first source or the initiator of the multicast group, as proposed in PIM [3] and CBT [4] protocols.

Shields and Garcia-Luna-Aceves [21] have proposed OCBT to avoid looping problem, present in the initial design of CBT [4]. Theoretically, Optimal Center-Based Tree OCBT selection algorithm is the best. It considers all nodes as a list of candidates' cores: From this list, the best node is selected. But practically, this process requires more processing time because it is required to calculate the actual cost of the tree rooted at each node in the network each time, and pick the one which gives the lowest cost. Several other algorithms which operate on all nodes in the network, as OCBT with change of the loss function; was proposed by Wall [6], especially Maximum-Centered Tree (MCT), Average-Centered Tree (ACT) and Diameter-Centered Tree (DCT). To reduce the area of research and the execution time, Minimum Shortest Path Tree (MSPT) is suggested. This approach requires calculating the actual costs for the trees rooted at each group member, and chooses the member with the lowest cost.

Topology-Based Algorithm [8] uses the domain topology and sub-graph constructed from the multicast group to select a single core closest to topology center. This selection method requires knowledge of more information than random selection method; this information should quickly include characteristics that was not altered.. All selected cores by this algorithm for all multicast groups are supposed to be in the proximity of the center of network. Therefore, the multicast traffic will converge at this region and the increase of multicast groups will cause overload at cores. Topology-Based Algorithm will use an excessive number of nodes to calculate optimal core: the execution time becomes important, especially in a large topology internet such as. Time complexity is equal to $O(|N|)$.

To reduce the search area used by the Topology-Based Algorithm, and select a distributed cores for all multicast groups in the network domain, [8] proposed group-based algorithm: it takes as parameter location information of all group multicast members (recipients and sources) in addition to information about the network topology, which makes it more complex and requires more information. Unlike the topology-based algorithm which selects a core for the entire network, group-based algorithm selects a core for each group; the core selected is close to the group members, thus avoiding convergence of traffic, this selection process need a list of all multicast group members and its time complexity is equal to $O(|D|)$. Group-based algorithm is more efficient when the multicast group is located in the same topological area, the practical implementation of this algorithm depends not only on the availability of information about the multicast group members and their locations, but also requires an effective and reliable mechanism for the core migration to other cores during a change of the multicast group members distribution.

Tournament-based algorithm proposed by Shukla, Boyer, and Klinke [15] executes a Distributed tournament between nodes to determine a center. For this tournament-based algorithm needs a list of all sources and members at each source and receivers group. Algorithm execution starts with matching sources with group members in declining order of hop-count metric. If the number of sources and members is odd, the remaining nodes are matched randomly. The winner of each pair is determined by finding the node in the proximity to the middle of the shortest path connecting the pair. Algorithm execution finishes when one winner remains. Tournament-based algorithm involves cooperation between nodes, and requires knowledge of the network topology. Finding middle of path between each pair requires an exchange of route tracing messages and takes $O(|D|^2)$ as complexity time.

Tabu Search algorithm for RP selection (TRPSA) [22] is a distributed core selection algorithm based on dynamic meta-heuristic Tabu Search TS algorithms proposed first by Glover [23] to solve combinatorial optimization problems in PIM-SM protocol [3]. TRPSA [22] tries to find a local solution after a certain finite number of iterations by using memory structures that describe the visited solutions. The basic idea of the TRPSA [22] algorithm is to mark the best local solution obtained in order to prevent the research process to return back to the same solution in subsequent iterations using a data structure to store the solutions already visited, this structure is called tabu list. However, the method requires a better definition of stopping criterion and effective management of the tabu list, since the choice of stopping criterion and tabu list size is critical and influences the performance of the algorithm. According to [22], TRPSA has $O(|E| + (|S| + |D|) * |N|^2)$ complexity.

Many others algorithms select RP on the basis of QoS constraints. This kind of RP selection can provide every member of the group with multiple QoS criteria guarantee, such as end-to-end delay, delay variation, bandwidth and so on. But, these algorithms set are highly complex and QoS is hard to be guaranteed for the new group members, and needs a large quantity of information such as network topology, group member, and link bandwidth and so on. Such information is not always available in a large topology such as Internet. A new DDVCA (delay and delay variation constraint algorithm) proposed in [24] is a typical RP selection algorithm considering QoS constraints.

Table 1 present a comparative study of existing core selection algorithms.

Table 1. Comparative study of Single-core selection algorithms

Algorithms	Search Area	Cost function	Complexity
Topology-Based [8]	List of group members and sources	Node-count	$O(|N|)$
Group-Based [8]	list of group members and sources	Node-count	$O(|D|)$
Tournament [15]	All network nodes	weight function	$O(|D|^2)$
TRPSA [22]	All network nodes	weight function	$O(|E| + (|S| + |D|) * |N|^2)$

4   Mathematical Modeling

A computer network is modeled as a simple directed and connected graph $G = (N, E)$, where N is a finite set of nodes and E is the set of edges (or links) connecting the nodes. Let $|N|$ be the number of network nodes and $|E|$ the number of network links. An edge $e \in E$ connecting two adjacent nodes $u \in N$ and $v \in N$ will be denoted by

$e_{(u,v)}$, the fact that the graph is directional, implies the existence of a link $e(v,u)$ between v and u. Each edge is associated with two positive real value: a cost function $C(e) = C(e(u,v))$ represents link utilization (may be either monetary cost or any measure of resource utilization), and a delay function $D(e) = D(e(u,v))$ represents the delay that the packet experiences through passing that link including switching, queuing, transmission and propagation delays. We associate for each path $P(v_0, v_n) = (e(v_0, v_1), e(v_1, v_2), \ldots, e(v_{n-1}, v_n))$ in the network two metrics:

$$C(P(v_0, v_n)) = \sum_{0}^{n-1} C(e(v_i, v_{i+1}))$$ (1)

And

$$D(P(v_0, v_n)) = \sum_{0}^{n-1} D(e(v_i, v_{i+1}))$$ (2)

A multicast tree $T_M(S, C, D)$ is a sub-graph of G spanning the set of sources node S $\subset$ N and the set of destination nodes D $\subset$ N with a selected core C. Let |S| be the number of multicast destination nodes and |D| is the number of multicast destination nodes.

In Protocols using Core-based tree, all sources node needs to transmit the multicast information to selected core via unicast routing, then its well be forwarded to all receptors in the shared tree, to model the existence of these two parts separated by core, we use both cost function and delay following:

$$C(T_M(S, C, D)) = \sum_{s \in S} C(P(s, C)) + \sum_{d \in D} C(P(C, d))$$ (3)

$$D(T_M(S, C, D)) = \sum_{s \in S} D(P(s, C)) + \sum_{d \in D} D(P(C, d))$$ (4)

Core selection problem tries to find an optimal node C in the network with an optimal function Opt_F by minimizing as possible both $C(T_M(S, C, D))$ and $D(T_M(S, C, D))$.

$$Opt\_F(C, T_M) = C(T_M(S, C, D)) + D(T_M(S, C, D))$$ (5)

In general it's impossible to optimize the cost function and the transmission delay at the same time, we will use two positives weights values w_c and w_d associated respectively to the cost function and transmission delay as follows:

$$Opt_{F(C, T_M)} = w_c C(T_M(S, C, D)) + w_d D(T_M(S, C, D)) \text{ with } w_c + w_d = 1$$ (6)

5   A Variable Neighborhood Descent for Core Selection VND-CS

5.1   Basic Variable Neighborhood Descent Search Algorithm

Many combinatorial optimization algorithms have been widely exploited for solving research problems (Hill climbing and tabu search algorithms). These algorithms allow selecting a local optimal point by trajectory following with a single neighborhood.

Contrary to all others kind of meta-heuristics based on local search methods, Mladenović and Hansen [25] proposed a recent meta-heuristics Variable Neighborhood Decent VND Algorithm based on the simple idea of a systematic neighborhood changing arbitrarily. VND has been applied successfully to a wide variety of NP-hard problems to select a global optimal solution such as the travelling salesman problem [17], Job Shop Scheduling Problems [18], the clustering problem [20], Arc routing problems [11], and nurse rostering [19].

The use of more than one neighborhood provides a very effective method that allows escaping from a local optimum. In fact, it is often the case that the current solution, which is a local optimum in one neighborhood, is no longer a local optimum in a different neighborhood; therefore, it can be further improved using a simple descent approach.

As defined by Mladenović and Hansen [25], in the VND paradigm, a finite set of neighborhoods structures N_k (k =1; . . . ; k_{max}) and an initial solution S are generated, starting from this initial solution, a so-called shaking step is performed by randomly selecting a solution S' from the first neighborhood. If this solution (S') improve the weight function used one starts with the first neighborhood of this new solution (S←S'); otherwise one proceeds with the next neighborhood. This procedure is repeated as long as a neighborhood structure allows such iteration.

5.2   A Variable Neighborhood Descent for Core Selection Problem

The main motivation behind the use of the VND search algorithm to solve core selection problem is the use of several neighborhoods to explore different neighborhood structures systematically. Our goal is to break away from a local minima, this use is based on three facts:

1.   If node N_1 is a local minimum for one neighborhood structure N_k is not necessary so with another one $N_{k'}$.
2.   A global minimum solution S is a local minimum for all possible neighborhood structures.
3.   For the core selection problem local minima for all neighborhood structures is relatively close and localized in the same place.

In this section we provide a detailed description of the Variable Neighborhood Descent algorithm for core selection Problem VNS-CS, and his three process phases: the initialization process, Stopping conditions phase and the shaking step. After, the source code will be discussed according to the features of core selection problem; we consider the solution object such as node and neighborhood like the set of neighboring nodes.

5.3   Initial Solution

The first step of variable neighborhood descent search is to define an initial solution. Many methods can be used to generate this solution; the simplest is to select randomly one node in the network as initial solution. There are other methods that try to reduce the selection area and generate an initial solution from an ordered set of multicast group members.

5.4   Neighborhood Structures

VNS-CS uses neighbor nodes concept to generate neighborhood structures: a node u is neighbor of another node v if an edge e(u, v) between u and v exists. We propose to compute a neighborhood structure N_j throught the following formula (with neighbor(S) a set of neighbor nodes of S):

$$N_j(S) = \begin{cases} \text{neighbor}(S) & \text{if } j = 1 \\ \bigcup_{x \in N_{k-1}(S)} N(x) & else \end{cases}$$

5.5   Shaking

In the shaking step we explore the kth neighborhood of an initial solution S to generate a local minimum solution S related to this neighborhood structure $N_k(S)$.

After a random selection of a one local solution S in k^{th} neighborhood structure, S' is compared to S. If S' is better than S, it replaces S (S ← S') and the algorithm starts all over again with k ← 1. Otherwise, k is incremented and algorithm continues the shaking step with next neighborhood structure.

5.6   Stopping Conditions Phase

From an initial solution, the shaking and movement steps continues until a stopping condition is met.

In case of small problem instances, where the best solution is usually found very quickly, the stopping conditions with a limit on the maximum number of iterations is sufficient. This stopping condition is not enough when large-scale problem is treated. Hence, many stopping conditions have been added for large-scale topology. These conditions are the maximum CPU time allowed and the maximum number of non-improving iterations.

5.7   VNS-CS Algorithm and Pseudo Code

In this section as presented in Algorithm 1, a step by step VND-CS algorithm for core selection problem is presented, containing seven steps:

step 1. Set maximum iteration number, maximum number of iteration Without Improvement;

step 2. Select initial solution S;

step 3. Choose the k_{max} scalar, select the set $_{of}$ neighborhood structures N_k, for k = 1, . . . , k_{max}, that will be used in $_{the}$ search; choose a stopping condition;

step 4. Check the stopping criterion. If it is satisfied go to step 7; otherwise, go to nest step;

step 5. Take at random a solution S' from N_k (S);

step 6. Check if objective function value of solution S' is less than objective function value of solution S, then move to S' solution and continue the search with N_1 (k ← 1) from step 4; otherwise, set k ← k + 1 and also continue the search from step 4;

step 7. Output the best solution core selected.

Algorithm 1. VNS-CS Pseudo code

```
Input: i = 0; totalIt = 0; currentit = 0;
Input: maxItWithoutImprovement, initialSolution, maxit,
SolutionChk, BestSolution
   1. BestSolution ← initialSolution ;
   2. while i<maxItWithoutImprovement && totalIt<maxit do
   3.      lastSCost←OptF( BestSolution ); k←0;
   4.      while currentit < maxit && k < kmax do
   5.           if totalIt > maxit then
   6.               break ;
   7.           end
   8.           getNK(s) ;
   9.           SolutionChk ← getRandomNk(s) ;
   10.          if optF(SolutionChk)> OptF(BestSolution) then
   11.              k←k+1 ;
   12.          else
   13.              BestSolution ← SolutionChk;
   14.              k←0;
   15.          end
   16.          totalIt ← totalIt + 1 ;
   17.          currentit ← currentit + 1 ;
   18.      end
   19.      if lastSCost > optF(BestSolution)) then
   20.          i←0;
   21.      else
   22.          i←i+1 ;
   23.      end
   24. end
   25. return BestSolution ;
```

5.8   Complexity Analysis

The complexity of VND-CS algorithm is explained line by line in the following. Line 1 is initialization statement. Their complexity is $O(1)$. Line 2 and 4 are a judgment statements of the while loop, and its complexity is $O(1)$. Line 3 is initialization statement. Their complexity is $O(1)$. Lines 5-7 are judgment statements and their complexity is $O(1)$. Line 8 generate the kth neighborhood structures, the complexity is $O(|\text{neighborhood structures}|^k)$, the average value of $|\text{neighborhood structures}|$ is $(2|E|/|N|)$, then the total complexity is $O((2|E|/|N|)^k) < O(|E|)$. Line 9 select randomly one solution from N_k (S), their complexity is $O(1)$. Line 10 computes and compare weight function and their complexity is $O(|S| + |D|)$. Lines 11-17 correspond to assignment, their complexity is $O(1)$. Lines 22-23 form a while loop. Generally it take less time than $|N|$, then the complexity is $O(|N| * (O(1) + O(|E|) + O(1) + O(|S| + |D|) + O(1))) = O(3|N| + |N||E| + |N|(|S| + |D|))$. Line 24 is a return statement, and its complexity is $O(1)$. Therefore, the complexity of the algorithm is $O(1) + O(1) + O(3|N| + |N||E| + |N|(|S| + |D|))$, that is, $O(3|N| + |N||E| + |N|(|S| + |D|))$.

6   Simulation Results

In this section, we use simulation results to demonstrate the effectiveness of the proposed algorithm described above. To study the performance of our selection algorithm VNS-CS, we implement it in a simulation environment, we use the network simulator NS2 and the random graph generator GT-ITM, and we adopt Waxman [26] as the graph model. Our simulation studies were performed on a set of 100 random networks. The values of $\alpha = 0.2$ and $\beta = 0.2$ were used to generate networks with an average degree between 3 and 4 in the mathematical model of Waxman.

To demonstrate the performance of this algorithm (VNS-CS), we compare it with the following algorithms, including random (R), group-based (GB) [8], and Tabu RP selection (TRPS) [22].

Based on the cost function in the formula (6), Fig. 1 presents a comparison study of multicast tree Cost generated by each algorithm, the performance of Random selection is the worst, followed by GB and TRPS, VND-CS shows better performances, and it has the minimal cost.

End-to-end delay refers to total time taken for a packet to be transmitted across a network from source to all destinations as presented in formula (4). Fig. 2 shows that VND-CS is the best among all the algorithms on End-to-end delay, with TRPS and GB following it, and Random is the worst.

Bandwidth or throughput refers to how much data is transferred through the multicast tree. Fig.1 gives the average number of successful multicast data packet transfer through a multicast tree produced by each algorithm. Fig. 3 indicates that all algorithms give similar performance in small topology with few nodes, but bandwidth consumption by VND-CS algorithm becomes rapidly better with the increase of network scale.

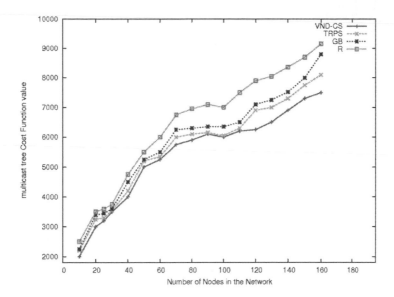

Fig. 1. Comparison of multicast tree Cost

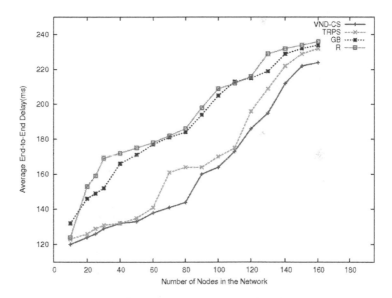

Fig. 2. Comparison of end-to-end delay

Construction tree delay designates the required time to build all multicast tree branches after receiving all membership requests explicitly sent by all receivers. Simulation results presented in Fig 4 shows that VND-CS outperforms all others algorithms in Construction tree delay constraints when multicast group are widely localized. However GB presented the same performances as VND-CS when the receivers of a multicast group are geographically located in same area.

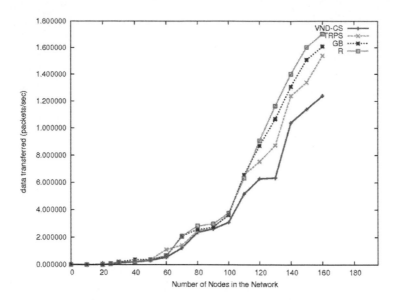

Fig. 3. Comparison of Bandwidth consumption

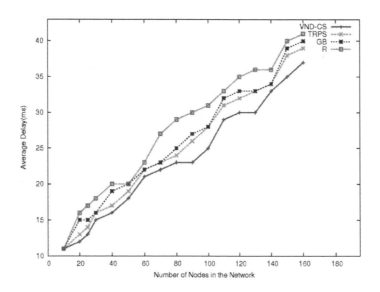

Fig. 4. Comparison of construction tree delay

It can be seen from Fig 7, that GB algorithm requires more iterations, this number increases with the number of multicast group member. Followed by TSRP algorithm that requires less iteration, the algorithm VND-CS converges to an optimal core in a minimum number of iterations because of the use of variable neighborhood which avoids small cores.

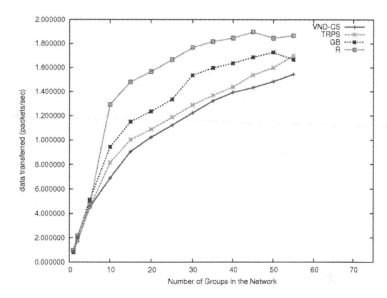

Fig. 5. Comparison of supported groups

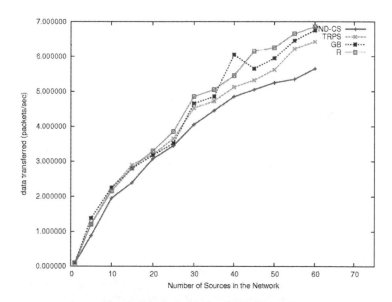

Fig. 6. Comparison of supported source

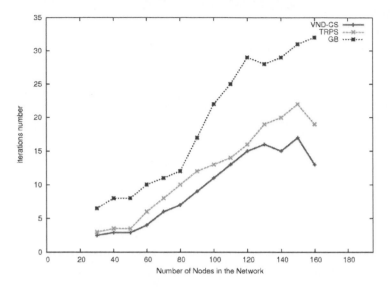

Fig. 7. Comparison of iterations when the algorithm finished

7   Conclusion

In this paper we have investigated the problem of finding a good core router in a distributed manner. Core Selection CD problem affects directly the structure of the tree and the performance of the routing scheme of multicast consequently. Current algorithms decide on core router administratively, which leads to high cost, high delay, and high congestion. To solve these problems, VNS-CS is proposed based on VND heuristic algorithm. To present our proposition we started with a brief overview of multicast routing protocols and two types of multicast trees SBT and CBT. We reviewed and analyzed the cost and delay function. We reviewed the Rendezvous Point selection algorithms studied in literature for their algorithmic structures. Simulation results show that our algorithm presents good performances in multicast cost, End-To-End delay and other aspects. Our future work is focused on extending this algorithm to support multiple QOS criteria imposed by receivers across the network.

References

1. Deering, S.E., Cheriton, D.R.: Multicast routing in datagram internetworks and extended lans. ACM Transactions on Computer Systems 8, 85–110 (1990)
2. Zappala, D., Fabbri, A., Lo, V.M.: An evaluation of shared multicast trees with multiple cores. Telecommunication Systems 19(3-4), 461–479 (2002)
3. Fenner, B., Handley, M., Holbrook, H., Kouvelas, I.: Protocol Independent Multicast-Sparse Mode (PIM-SM): Protocol Specification (Revised). RFC 4601 (2006)
4. Ballardie, A.: Core based trees (CBT version 2) multicast routing – protocol specification. RFC 2189 (1997)

5. Ramalho, M.: Intra- and inter-domain multicast routing protocols: A survey and taxonomy. IEEE Communications Surveys and Tutorials 3(1), 2–25 (2000)
6. Wall, D.W.: Mechanisms for Broadcast and Selective Broadcast. Ph.D. thesis, Stanford, CA, USA (1980)
7. Karaman, A., Hassanein, H.: Core-selection algorithms in multicast routing - comparative and complexity analysis. Comput. Commun. 29(8), 998–1014 (2006)
8. Calvert, K.L., Zegura, E.W., Donahoo, M.J.: Core selection methods for multicast routing, pp. 638–642 (1995)
9. Mehlhorn, K.: A faster approximation algorithm for the steiner problem in graphs. Inf. Process. Lett. 27, 125–128 (1988)
10. Wei, L., Estrin, D.: The trade-offs of multicast trees and algorithms (1994)
11. Tagmouti, M., Gendreau, M., Potvin, J.Y.: A variable neighborhood descent heuristic for arc routing problems with time-dependent service costs. Comput. Ind. Eng. 59 (2010)
12. Moy, J.: MOSPF: Analysis and Experience. RFC 1585 (Informational), Internet Engineering Task Force IETF (1994), http://www.ietf.org/rfc/rfc1585.txt
13. Farinacci, D., Li, T., Hanks, S., Meyer, D., Traina, P.: Protocol independent multicast - dense mode (pim-dm): Protocol specification (revised). RFC 3973 (2005)
14. Waitzman, D., Partridge, C., Deering, S.E.: RFC 1075: Distance vector multicast routing protocol (1988)
15. Shukla, S.B., Boyer, E.B., Klinker, J.E.: Multicast Tree Construction in Network Topologies with Asymmetric Link Loads. Ph.D. thesis (1994)
16. Bhaskar, N., Gall, A., Lingard, J., Venaas, S.: Bootstrap Router (BSR) Mechanism for Protocol Independent Multicast (PIM). RFC 5059 (Proposed Standard) (2008)
17. Carrabs, F., Laporte, G., Cordeau, J.: Variable neighborhood search for the pickup and delivery traveling salesman problem with LIFO loading. Centre for Research on Transportation, Montréal, Québec (2005)
18. Sevkli, M., Aydin, M.E.: Variable neighbourhood search for job shop scheduling problems. JSW 1(2), 34–39 (2006)
19. Burke, E., De Causmaecker, P., Petrovic, S., Berghe, G.V.: Variable neighborhood search for nurse rostering problems, pp. 153–172. Kluwer Academic Publishers, MA (2004)
20. Hansen, P., Mladenovic, N.: Variable neighborhood search: Principles and applications. European Journal of Operational Research 130(3), 449–467 (2001)
21. Shields, C., Garcia-Luna-Aceves, J.J.: The ordered core based tree protocol. In: Proceedings of the INFOCOM 1997. Sixteenth Annual Joint Conference of the IEEE Computer and Communications Societies. Driving the Information Revolution, p. 884. IEEE Computer Society, Washington, DC (1997)
22. Hua, W., Xiangxu, M., Min, Z., Yanlong, L., et al.: Tabu search algorithm for RP selection in pim-sm multicast routing. Comput. Commun. 33(1), 35–42 (2010)
23. Glover, F.: Tabu Search - Part II. INFORMS Journal on Computing 2(1), 4–32 (1990)
24. Kim, M., Bang, Y.-C., Choo, H.: On Core Selection Algorithm for Reducing Delay Variation of Many-to-Many Multicasts with Delay-Bounds. In: Mitrou, N.M., Kontovasilis, K., Rouskas, G.N., Iliadis, I., Merakos, L. (eds.) NETWORKING 2004. LNCS, vol. 3042, pp. 200–210. Springer, Heidelberg (2004)
25. Hansen, P., Mladenovi, N.: Variable neighborhood search: Methods and recent applications. In: Proceedings of MIC 1999. pp. 275–280 (1999)
26. Waxman, B.M.: Routing of multipoint connections. IEEE Journal on Selected Areas in Communications 6(9), 1617–1622 (2002), http://dx.doi.org/10.1109/49.12889

An Efficient Algorithm for Enumerating Minimal PathSets in Communication Networks

Mohamed-Larbi Rebaiaia and Daoud Ait-Kadi

Department of Mechanical Engineering, University of Laval,
Quebec (QC), Canada
Mohamed-larbi.rebaiaia@hotmail.com,
daoud.aitkadi@gmc.ulaval.ca

Abstract. The reliability of complex networks is a very sensitive issue which requires implementing powerful methods for its evaluation. Many algorithms have been proposed to solve networks reliability problem as those based on minimal pathsets and cutsets approximation. The enumeration of minimal pathsets can be obtained very easily, it just needs to use an ordinary algorithm to determine the paths/cuts, but in case the network size is large, more efficient algorithms are needed. This paper presents an intuitive algorithm to find all minimal paths. The algorithm proceeds recursively using an efficient procedure traversing cleverly the structure of a graph. Its complexity has been checked to be better than those developed until now. The program is simple, compact, modular and easy to be embedded to any software which evaluates the reliability as those based on sum-of-disjoint product approach. During our experiment tests, we have enumerated several networks of varied complexities and the comparison with demonstrated literature approaches is systematic.

Keywords: Minimal paths set, enumeration, two-reliability, networks, algorithm, graphs theory.

1   Introduction

The concept of MPS/MCS (minimal pathsets, minimal cutsets) is a very effective tool to determine the reliability of a system from the disjoint form of its terms. A path P is defined as a set of adjacent nodes connected using edges (network components) so that if all the components are failure-free, the path is considered as up and leads the network to be considered up. A path P is minimal if it has no proper sub-paths. Conversely, a cut C is a set of edges such that their removal leads the network to fail. A cuts set is minimal if no proper cut exists. Technically, this means that the failure of the cutset components ensures that the entire system fails and the failure of a minimal path component discard the expression path from computing network reliability. Enumerating all the MCS may be a feasible way to evaluate the reliability if the number of MPS is too huge to be enumerated practically. One example of this kind of networks is the complete network (10 × 10) which contains 45 edges and 109601 MPS and the 2 × 100 lattice network contains 299 MPS and 10000 MCS. Several

R. Benlamri (Ed.): NDT 2012, Part I, CCIS 293, pp. 444–458, 2012.

algorithms have been developed to enumerate MPS/MCS, most of them require advanced mathematics or can only be applied either directed or undirected graphs and alternative solutions have been proposed by different authors [13, 14, 22]. Some are specific to the determination of MCS [9, 10, 16] and others to MPS [7]. Some MCS methods are highly related to the MPS so that they are derived from them. Shier [9], has proposed a technique for generating the minimal cuts from the minimal paths, or vice versa, for coherent systems [1]. The algorithm is a recursive 2-stage expansion based upon De Morgan's theorems and Quine-type minimization. Jasmon [14] uses an algorithm which proceeds in two steps. The first step concerns the deduction of link cutsets from node cutsets and the second deduce the basic minimal paths using network decomposition. So, in addition to the enumeration of cutsets directly, it is possible to obtain them from the inversion of minimal paths [3, 6]. In [24], Kantarci and Mouftah, introduced a heuristic that performs a faster search for the nearly optimal locations of Optical Network Units (ONUs). Al-Ghanim [5] presents a heuristic programming algorithm to generate all MPS. The algorithm proceeds by creating a path, then iterates back from an explored node in the current path using unexplored nodes until to reach the source node. The procedure uses each discovered path to generate new MPS from sub-paths. The above procedure is repeated until all MP are found. The problem with Al-Ghanim's algorithm is that, it produces redundant MPS, which needs a tool to avoid them using extensive comparison. Recently, Yeh et al. [8] presented (initial and terminal nodes) a simple algorithm for finding all MPS between the source and the sink nodes. It is based on the universal generating function. Before that, Yeh in [7] proposes a simple heuristic algorithm for generating all minimal paths. The algorithm proceeds by adding a path, or an edge into a network repeatedly until the network is equal to the original network. Also, Liu et al. in [17] and Shier in [9] have used two different algorithms showing that a 2×100 lattice network has 299 paths but contains 10,000 minimal cutsets.

2   Notation and Acronym

MPS/MCS   Minimal pathsets/cusets.
DFS   Depth first search algorithm.

$G(X, E)$ Network with node set X and the edge set E,
             where t and s are respectively the source node and
             the sink node. G may be directed or undirected.
$n = |X|$,   Number of nodes of the network.
$m = |E|$ Number of nodes of the network.
variable   a variable represents   an edge or a node.
e_{ij} $e_{ij} \in E$ is a directed edge from node i to node j.
p_{e_i} Functioning probability of e_i
p_{ij} Functioning probability of the edge taken between
             node i and node j

3   Networks Reliability Modeling

Let $G(X,E)$ be an arbitrary graph in term of direction and let P be an arbitrary family of (source-sink) pairs of nodes of $G : P = \{(s_i,t_i) \in E \times E \mid i \in [k] = \{1,...,k\}\}$. It is assumed that $s_i \neq t_i$ for all $i \in [k]$. Consider that each edge and each node could be subjected to random s-independent failure occurrences and are weighted with a probability p_i. For a specified set $K \subseteq X$ of G, we denote the K-terminal reliability of G by $R(G_K)$. When the cardinality of K is 2 $(|K| = 2)$, it is called 2-terminal (or terminal-pair) reliability which defines the probability of connecting the source node with a target node. In the most cases, it suffices to have a 2-terminal relation to evaluate the reliability of networks. The generalisation of the problem is called the K-terminal reliability, and considers the subset K $(|K| > 2)$ differently from the 2-terminal reliability. A success set, is a minimal set of the edges of G such that the nodes in K are connected; the set is minimal so that deletion of any edges causes the nodes in K to be disconnected. Topologically, a success set is a minimal tree of G covering all nodes in K. In the same way, by using the conjunction of all of minimal paths we can evaluate the reliability of the network. There is another way to compute the reliability by considering minimal cuts. They can be derived by inverting the terms of minimal paths or by determining them using algorithms or heuristics [3, 6].

Some definitions are necessary to introduce the problem of MPS/MCS. By hypothesise, let that:

- Each node and each edge have two states: working or failed. The states of edges are s-independents.
- The graph is connected and free-loops.
- In case of parallel edges, they are systematically replaced by one edge whose reliability is obtained using parallel relation $p_{i,j} = p_i + p_j - p_i p_j$.
- If two edges are in series, the second is deleted and the reliability of the first one is replaced by the product of the two edges reliabilities ($p_{i,j} = p_i p_j$).

To introduce our algorithm, we need first to give some preliminary definitions, lemmas and theorems. They are presented as follows:

Definitions

1- A path of length q is a chain $\mu = (x_1,...,x_q)$ in which the terminal endpoint of arc μ_i is the initial endpoint of arc μ_{i+1} for all $i < q$. Hence, we often write $\mu = (x_1, x_{k+1})$, where k is the number of edges.

2- The dimension of a path $P = (x_1, -, x_{k+1})$ (we note $dim(P)$) is equal to the number of edges which is k. Node x_1 is called the initial endpoint and node x_{k+1} is called the terminal endpoint.

3- A graph G is said to be *connected* if between any two nodes $x, y \in X$ there exists a chain $\mu(x,y)$.

4- A graph G is said to be *quasi-strongly connected*, if for all $, y \in X$, there exists a path $\mu(x, y)$ or a path $\mu(y, x)$.

5- A path P in a graph G is said to be a *1-path* if any two nodes $x, y \in X$ of the path, they are linked by only one edge.

6- Any path in a graph G which is a *1*-path is said to be a branch.

7- A 1-path P is said to be maximal, if and only, if it connects the n nodes of the graph. Thus, the dimension is $\dim(P) = |X| - 1 = n - 1$.

8- An arborescence is defined as a tree that has a root. In other words see *Corollary 1*.

9- Node x_i is a brother of node $x_i \neq x_j$ if node x_i and node x_j have the same parent.

10- A partial graph of $G(X, E)$ is the graph $G(X, V)$ whose node set is X and edge set is V such that the graph G without the edges $E - V$.

11- Let $e_r = (x, y) \in E$, a co-edge is another edge $e_m = (x, y) \in E$. In other words, $e_r \| e_m$, they are parallel and form a cycle.

12- PathSet (PS): PS is the set of 1-paths in a graph G connecting the source s and the sink t.

The following Lemma explains how to evolve in a branch.

Lemma 1. At any node in the generation tree T, if T, a) contains a vertex v that is marked (has been visited), and b) does not have an edge to any children node in X that it is not marked, then the branch need not be expanded further and it is needed to backtrack to proceed the research from another brother node if it exist.

The proof of this Lemma is trivial because the above paragraph explains the procedure.

Corollary 1. ([12] page 35). A graph G has a partial graph that is arborescence if, and only if, G is quasi-strongly connected.

Property 1. A graph G with at least two nodes and an edge, the deletion of the edge separates s from t, and thus discard this link from computing the reliability.

Theorem 2. (Let H be a graph of order $n > 1$.) The following properties are equivalent (and each characterizes the arborescence):

(1) H is a quasi-strongly connected graph and this property is destroyed if we add to H, an arc of G not included in H, thus we create a cycle.

(2) If each arc of G not included in H can be added to H and creates a cycle, this arc is a cocycle and the set of such arcs constitutes a basis of independent cocycles of dimension $n - 1$. Thus we can create $m - n + 1$ cycles.

(3) H is quasi-strongly connected and if we can create $m - n + 1$ cycles, thus we generate $m - n + 1$ different minimal paths.

Let us demonstrate just a part of this theorem so that (1) => (2) and (2) => (3).

Proof:

(1) => (2), is simple to be demonstrated, it follows theorem 13 (Berge [12] (page 30)) and the above definition 4. From property (1), H is quasi-strongly connected graph and thus it is connected and without cycles. Thus H is a tree. Therefore H has m-n+1   arcs.

(2) => (3). If we can create one cycle by connecting any two node of H using an edge of X not included in H, then we can travel through H using such edge belonging to a new path. Thus if the set of possible created cycles is equal to $m - n + 1$ then we create $m - n + 1$ different paths.

Theorem 3. In a (directed or undirected) graph with n nodes, if there is a 1-path from node x_i to node x_j $(i \neq j)$, then the dimension of such path is maximal and equal to $n - 1$, thus the path is also minimal and the graph contains only one MPS.

Proof: if we suppose that the 1-path uses all the nodes of the graph, such that no node occurs more than once, it is normal that two nodes are used as terminal ends of an edge and for linking three nodes it is needed a sequence of two edges. Recursively we deduce that $n - 1$ edges are necessary for linking n nodes. Thus the path is maximal. Also, suppose that the path is of dimension $n-1$ and it is not minimal then if we add another edge to the path, then necessary such edge will link two nodes of the path which are already linked by an edge. Thus we create a cycle and the path loses its properties. We conclude that the path is minimal.

Theorem 4. In a (directed or undirected) graph with n nodes, if there is at least one minimal path (MPS) from node s to node t $(s \neq t)$, then the dimension of such path is maximal and equal to $\dim(MPS) = q$ where $q \leq$ n-1 edges. In other words, the maximal length of an MPS is equal to n-1.

Proof : The demonstration of theorem 4 is a consequence of theorem 3, and thus it can be deduced easily because if we suppose that the path is of $\dim(MPS) = q$ then it uses $q - 1$ edges and if we add another edge to such path, either we create a cycle and thus the MPS forget its properties or we get another path of dimension $q + 1$, which is not minimal because we have linked the terminal node with another node of the graph.

Theorem 5. Given a graph $G(X, E)$. Suppose that G contains a path such that $|X| = n$. The following properties are equivalents:

(1) Path MPS is a branch of G of dimension q, and by adding a new edge $e_r \in E$ to the branch we create a new cycle. Necessary the edge e_r is a co-edge of the existing one.

(2) If such cycle exist and is of *dimension* 2, the deletion of the corresponding co-edge of e_r creates a new MPS,

(3) The set of all the MPS constitutes an arborescence whose node root is s and the leaves are all t.

Proof:

(1) =>(2). Path MPS is a 1-path and thus it is a branch by definition 7. Its dimension is equal to q by theorem 4, so by adding any edge $e_r \in E$ in $E - (edges\ of\ MPS)$ so that to link any two successive nodes we create a co-edge and thus a cycle (not a circuit in case of directed graph). So, if we delete the edge e_r from the cycle we create a new MPS exactly the same of the first one but with a new edge replacing e_r. Thus we have created a new MPS from s to t.

(2) =>(3). If the deletion of each co-edge create an MPS and thus a branch, thus all the branches constitutes the ramifications of a graph tree and thus an arborescence with s as root and the occurrence of t are the terminal nodes of the branches which are the leaves.

(3) =>(1). As each branch from root s to t constitute a path, and by the property of arborescence, each path is a minimal path and thus a branch.

The following theorems assure that MPSs are unique and the set of MPSs is complete.

Theorem 6: The algorithm generates the MPSs without repetition.

Theorem 7: The algorithm does not miss any MPS.

Theorem 8: All the generated MPSs form a basis of independent paths, so that each element of the vector corresponds to an edge. If the graph is undirected the sign of the vector element is not represented and if the graph is directed, the sign must be positive.

Thus, the demonstration of theorem 6 and theorem 7 is simple due to the theorems 1 to 5 and lemmas 1 and 2. This is explained by the fact that the algorithm constructs the 1-path step by step without missing any edge not marked. For Theorem 8, the MPSs are independent because each MPS is different from the immediate past-generated one by at least one edge component, and this is recursively unrolled on the successive MPSs, which constitutes a basis of independent vectors.

4   A Procedure for Enumerating Minimal Pathset

To enumerate MPSs it is important to look over nodes and edges composing a path from the source until reaching the sink nodes. There are different ways of doing that. Several algorithms, heuristics and metaheuristics have been proposed to determine MPS. One of the recent works is due to Yeh [8]. It is based on a simple Universal Generating Function method to search for all MPS in a Network. The algorithm involves simple recursive procedure combined with simplification. Another best algorithm is presented by Colbourn [4]. The problem of evaluation the network reliability is an NP-hard problem and enumerating MPS is also NP-hard [24].

In the following we present a fast procedure to deduce minimal pathsets. The kernel of the procedure uses a recursive function based on the depth first search algorithm [19].

Note 1. *The complexity of the depth first search algorithm is* $O(|V| + |E|)$.

For more precision to get just a minimal path we have to traversing the graph using depth first search algorithm. For that we use dynamic data structures: a stack S which will contain the edges of the path. The following algorithm will be executed to find paths. Each execution cycle corresponds to a minimal path. This procedure will be called recursively as many times as there is a possibility to reach the terminal node by a new branch.

Suppose that G is the graph model and s and t are respectively initial and terminal nodes. S is a stack data structure used to memorize successive edges forming a minimal path. Note that stack S works dependently of two others stacks (they are not appeared in the following algorithm). A stack $S1$ is used to mark the explored nodes during the research in each branch of the graph. The marking of $S1$ is a function to avoid the redundancy and assures the condition so that each path is minimal. Stack $S2$, contains the MPS and another stack called $S3$, is used to memorize the position of an edge in the successive list of edges. This helps to trace the minimal path. For looking for the MPSs in graph branches, the algorithm unrolls a tree which has its root in the first edge of the MPS. .

The algorithm proceeds recursively and the choice is always the initial node. The procedure explores one of the adjacent edges and continues until the terminal node is found so that one MPS has been created. Then by backtracking action the last node is used to get onto another branch.

The following pseudo-algorithm gives an overview of the procedure.

It is clear that a recursive call is present in the body of the main program and inside the procedure PathDFS. The calls assure the fact to find a minimal path and then to go back to try to find another one. The algorithm stops when the operation of backtracking and forwarding didn't find any edge not marked.

4.1   Algorithm to Enumerate Minimal Pathset

The algorithm has been programmed in the last versions of MatLab and Java. Note that each state is illustrated using the well-known Bridge Network. Table 1, details the execution steps of the algorithm and figure 2, shows the minimal pathsets generated by the algorithm.

Note that, the stack S is a generic data structure which replaces the stack S1, S2 and S3.

The following pseudo-Algorithm formally presents the MPS generator and illustrates it with two examples. The first one with precision and the second gives all-MPS. The program generates each MPS exactly once, without missing any MPS, and without duplication.

```
algorithm stack S = pathDFS(G, v, z)
  setLabel(v, VISITED);
  S.push(v);

  begin
    if v = z
        return  S.elements();
      for all e in G.incidentEdges()
        if getLabel(e) = UNVISITED
            w = opposite(v, e);
        if getLabel(w) = UNVISITED
            S.push(e);
            pathDFS(G, w, z)
            S.pop(e);
        else
            S.pop(v);

end.

program  Main(input { a connected graph with nodes set,
              edges  set,  a  source  node  and  a  source
              node})
  {declaring dynamics vectors and stacks (put in them
  zeros)};
  {declaring dynamics and stacks (put in them zeros)};
  Do while .true.
      pathDFS(G, v, z)
      if {the last minimal path have been encountered}
          return .false.
  enddo
Output: All MPS found in the graph;

end.
```

Theorem 9.   The above algorithm generates all the minimal paths of a network so that they are minimal, independent and not redundant.

The demonstration of theorem 9 follows naturally the results of theorems 5, 6, 7 and 8.

4.2   Detailed Description of the Algorithm

Based on the discussions presented in section 2 and the present section in accordance of the above pseudo-algorithm and theorem 8 which insures the construction of the MPSs, such that no duplicate MPS is generated and all the MPSs are minimals, we propose the following heuristic algorithm. The heuristic gives more details than those presented in the above pseudo-algorithm.

1. Assign node numbers sequentially from 1 (source node) to N the sink node (e.g. bridge network: node 1: 1, node 2: 2, node 3: 3 and node 4: 4).
2. Create automatically the adjacency matrix representation of the network (fig 1 (b)), and a dynamic empty pathsets matrix so that its dimension is null.
3. Start from the initial node 1 (mark it using stack $S1$)- and generate the next order nodes call them Next (Next = children(node 1)). Note that Next is a dynamic vector and its size is the number of children. At the beginning it is a null vector.
4. Check if the encountered node is different from the sink node. If so check if all the elements of $S1$ have been marked. If so go to 8, otherwise go to 5.
5. For each element of the vector check if the node has been marked, if it is so, go to 6, otherwise mark it and put the edge (node parent-node children) in the stack $S2$ and mark the position of the relative edge in the stack $S3$ and go to 7.
6. If the element has been marked, backtrack to return to another brother node. If it exists go to 5, otherwise go to 4.
7. Go forwarding until the sink node has been encountered. If so, copy $S2$ in the pathsets matrix, backtrack and go to 5.
8. Print the pathsets matrix and Stop.

Note that the application of the algorithm using Bridge network (Fig 1.) is illustrated in Table 1 as explained in the following illustration.

4.3   Illustration Step-by-Step Example

Consider a 4-node, 5-edges bridge network with its adjacent matrix enumerated by the order of edges taken from 1 to 5 (Fig (b)) (step 2). Note that we have numbered 1 the source node and 4 the sink node (step 1).

- Step 3. Mark the node 1, so the $S1(1) = 1$, go to   step 4.
- Step 4. Node 1 ≠ Node 4 go to step 5.
- Step 5. Determine children(node 1): children(1) = {2,3}. Node 2 is the first node and it is not marked because $S1(2) ≠ 1$. Then, we mark Node 2, and $S2(1) = 1$ (edge between node 1 and node 2) and the position of edge 1 in the stack S3 is marked ($S3(1) = 1$). Go to step 7.
- Step 6 and Step 7. We determine the children of node 2 etc. We continue alternating steps 4, 5 and 6 until the sink node is encountered. If so backtrack (see fig (a), then (b) and (c)).
- Step 8. Print MPS matrix and STOP.

The results of the above illustration are detailed in Table 1. We can see that at the beginning, the stacks are empty and theirs dimensions is null. They receive at each step of the algorithm certain value numbered by 1 if a new node is added to the path. A position in stack $S2$ corresponds to the encountered edge where all the edges of a path are represented.   Stack $S3$ is an indicator of the edge position. When a MPS is built and the terminal node is compared, the algorithm decrements the last position of the stack and continues to do so until a non-marked edge is found. Then a new MPS is generated and followed by a third one.

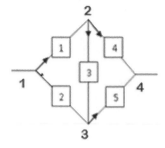

Table 1. And its relative adjacency matrix

Nodes	1	2	3	4
1	0	1	2	0
2	0	0	3	4
3	0	0	0	5
4	0	0	0	0

Fig. 1. Bridge network

Table 2. Minimal paths set enumeration of the bridge network

Operations	Stack S1/ Nodes i				Stack S2/ Edges j					Stack S3/ Edge position				
	s_1	s_2	s_3	s_4	x_1	x_2	x_3	x_4	x_5	P_1	P_2	P_3	P_4	P_5
Top(push(i,s)) = i	1				x_1					0				
Top(push(i,s)) = i	1	1			x_1		x_3			1	-	1	-	-
Top(push(i,s)) = i	1	1	1		x_1		x_3		x_5	1	-	1	-	1
Remove(i, s) = s	1	1			x_1		x_3		-	1	-	1	-	-
Remove(i, s) = s	1				x_1		-			1	-	-	-	-
Top(push(i,s)) = i	1	1			x_1			x_4		1	-	-	1	-
Remove(i, s) = s	1				x_1			-		1	-	-	-	-
Remove(i, s) = s	-				-					-	-	-	-	-
Top(push(i,s)) = i	1					x_2				-	1	-	-	-
Top(push(i,s)) = i	1	-	1			x_2				-	1	-	-	-
Remove(i, s) = s						x_2			x_5	-	1	-	-	1
Remove(i, s) = s	1	-	1			x_2			-	-	1	-	-	-
Isempty(s) = true					-					-	-	-	-	-
Stop.														

The minimal pathsets are :   MPS = { {x_1, x_3, x_5}; {x_1, x_4 }; {x_2 x_5 }}.
The structure function of the network is: $\varphi(x) = 1 - (1 - x_1 x_4)(1 - x_2 x_5)(1 - x_1 x_3 x_5)$, which, corresponds to a new representation of the network where the MPSs are considered in parallel. Thus, the reliability of the network is equal to the mathematical expectation of the structure function $E(\varphi(x))$. It is computed after using Boolean simplification rules:

$$R(G) = E(\varphi(x)) = r_1 r_4 + r_2 r_5 + r_1 r_3 r_5 - r_1 r_2 r_3 r_5 - r_1 r_2 r_4 r_5 - r_1 r_3 r_4 r_5 + r_1 r_2 r_3 r_4 r_5.$$

and if any $r_i = 0.9$ (the individual reliabilities corresponding to each edge), then the network reliability is equal to $R(G) = 0.9756$

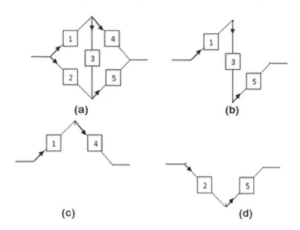

(a)   (b)

(c)   (d)

Fig. 2. (a) The bridge network. (b) the 1st first MPS. (c) the 2nd MPS and (d) the 3rd MPS

Example 2.

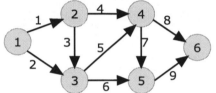

Fig. 3. A 6-node, 9-link example network (directed)

Fig. 4. A 6-node, 9-link example network (undirected)

Table 3. All the minimal paths of the network in figure 3

#	Minimal Pathset
1	1, 3, 5, 7, 9
2	1, 3, 5, 8
3	1, 3, 6, 9
4	1, 4, 7, 9
5	1, 4, 8
6	2, 5, 7, 9
7	2, 5, 8
8	2, 6, 9

Table 4. All the minimal paths of the network in figure 4

#	Minimal Pathset
1	1, 4, 8, 12, 16
2	1, 4, 8, 13
3	1, 4, 9, 15, 13
4	1, 4, 9, 16
5	1, 5, 11, 9, 16
6	1, 5, 12, 16
7	1, 5, 13
8	2, 7, 5, 12, 16
9	2, 7, 5, 13
10	2, 8, 12, 16
11	2, 8, 13
12	2, 9, 15,13
13	2, 9, 16

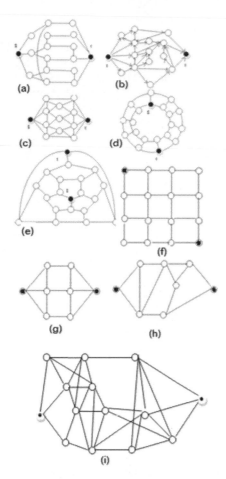

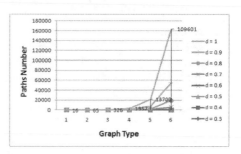

Fig. 6. Exponential growth nature of MPS enumeration

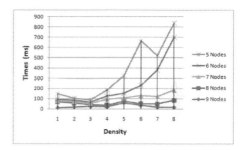

Fig. 7. Exponential growth nature of MPS enumeration

Fig. 5. Benchmark Networks

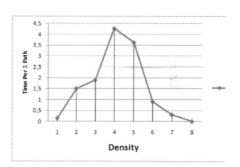

Fig. 9. Time per one path for the graph of fig 8

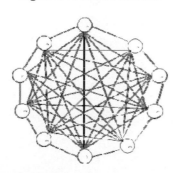

Fig. 8. A complete network with number of nodes equal to 10

4.4   Experimental Examples

The examples are all taken from the literature. We have compiled examples which have been used as benchmarks for demonstrating the implementation of our algorithm. The run times shown in the examples are determined by the execution of the algorithm. For our results the host computer was a simple laptop personal microcomputer and the implementation was compiled by Java 1.6.1 and MatLab 2009. The times required for the execution of the algorithm using the benchmark of the figure 5 are presented in table 3. This table gives the number of MPS and the corresponding execution time. We can remark that the time is in seconds and at my thought it is the smallest amount by comparison with those found in the literature. For example it is 1/1000 less than the results of Yeh et al. [8]. We have used some others networks with density variants. The results are shown in figure 6 and figure 7. Figure 9 represents the execution time per one path for a complete graph of dimension 10 nodes with a variation of density equal to [0.3, 0.4, 0.5, 0.6, 0.7, 0.8, 0.9. 1]. We can remark that despite the number of MPS which grows exponentially, the time per one path falls to a small value. Note that all the times values are in seconds/1000 and are the effective execution times and do not include the time required to perform I/O operations. Our program solves the 2-terminal minimal pathset enumeration problem and thus it can be used as input procedure for evaluating networks reliability. The program can also be extended to be used for the case of K-terminal networks. So the implementation uses dynamic data structures such that each effective representation is performed by dynamic lists and queues structures. So at each time of the execution processing, the system keeps only one cell to represent physically any element used to memorize or to compute a part of the calculus. However, it is preferable to use a computer system with a processor and a memory manager that runs under 64-bit.

Table 5. Detailed experimental results relative to the figure 5 networks

Networks	Number of Nodes	Number of Edges/Arcs	Number of MPS	Time (sec)
A	17	23/46	136	0.106287
B	16	30	36	0.043412
C	13	30/60	3972	1.577472
D	20	29/58	432	0.274192
E	20	29/58	516	0,265083
F	16	24/48	184	0.209079
G	8	13/26	29	0,033207
H	8	12/24	24	0.021653
I	14	36/72	42036	248.21824

5   Conclusion

In this paper, we have proposed a depth first search-based algorithm to enumerate all minimal pathsets of a network. The program can be used as an input to some tools provided for network reliability measures. The research considers the source-sink problem and can be extended to solve all-reliability and K-reliability cases. The algorithm is finite and the execution time for enumerating MPS of all the networks is very small comparing to some implementations published in the literature. The testing networks are not elementary because the edges are replaced by double arcs which generate a large number of paths. According to the properties of the depth first search we can demonstrate that all the MPSs are independents and didn't contain redundant subsections so that to ensure that the MPS are minimal. The comparison with others techniques and others benchmarks gives us an advantage due to the time and space consuming computer capacities.

References

1. Barlow, R.E., Proschan, F.: Mathematical Theory of Reliability. J. Wiley & Sons (1965) (reprinted 1996)
2. Aggarwal, K.K., Misra, K.B., Gupta, J.S.: A fast algorithm for reliability evaluation. IEEE Trans. Reliability R-24, 83–85 (1975)
3. Abraham, J.A.: An Improved Algorithm for Network Reliability. IEEE Transactions on Reliability R-28, 58–61 (1979)
4. Colbourn, C.J.: The combinatorics of network reliability. Oxford University Press, New York (1987)
5. Al-Ghanim, A.M.: A heuristic technique for generating path and cutsets of a general network. Computers & Industrial Engineering 36, 45–55 (1999)
6. Heidtmann, K.D.: Smaller sums of disjoint products by subproduct inversion. IEEE Trans. Reliability 38(3), 305–311 (1989)
7. Yeh, W.-C.: A simple Heuristic Algorithm for Generating All Minimal Paths. IEEE Transactions on Reliability 56(3), 488–494 (2007)
8. Yeh, W.-C.: A simple Universal Generating Function Method to Search for all Minimal Paths in Networks. IEEE Transactions on Reliability 39(6), 1246–1254 (2009)
9. Shier, D.R., Whited, A.E.: Algorithms for generating Minimal Cutsets by Inversion. IEEE Transactions on Reliability R-34(4), 314–319 (1985)
10. Patvardhan, C., Prasad, V.C.: Vertex Cutsets of Undirected Graphs. IEEE Transactions on Reliability 44(2), 347–353 (1995)
11. Rebaiaia, M.L., Ait-Kadi, D., Merlano, A.: A Practical Algorithm for Network Reliability Evaluation Based on the Factoring Theorem-A Case Study of a Generic Radiocommunication System. Journal of Quality 16(5), 323–336 (2009)
12. Berge, C.: Graphs and Hypergraphs. North Holland Publishing Company (1973)
13. Soh, S., Rai, S.: Experimental results on preprocessing of path/cut terms in sum of dis-joint products technique. IEEE Trans. Reliability 42(1), 24–33 (1993)
14. Jasmon, G.B., Kai, O.S.: A New Technique in Minimal Path and Cutset Evaluation. Reprinted from IEEE Transactions on Reliability R-34(2), 136–143 (1985)
15. Lee, C.Y.: Representation of Switching Circuits by Binary-Decision Programs. Bell Systems Technical Journal 38, 985–999 (1959)
16. Lin, H.Y., Kuo, S.Y., Yeh, F.M.: Minimal cutset enumeration and network reliability evaluation by recursive merge and BDD. In: Proceedings of the Eighth IEEE International Symposium on Computers and Communication, vol. 2, pp. 1341–1346 (2003)
17. Liu, H.H., Yang, W.T., Liu, C.C.: An improved minimizing algorithm for the summation of disjoint products by Shannon's expansion. Microelectronic Reliability 33(4), 599–613 (1993)

18. Locks, M.O., Wilson, J.M.: Note on disjoint products algorithms. IEEE Transactions on Reliability 41(1), 81–84 (1992)
19. Tarjan, R.: Depth-first search and linear graph algorithms. SIAM Journal of Computing 1(2), 146–160 (1972)
20. Ait-kadi, D., Rebaiaia, M.L., Merlano, A.: Modèle d'évaluation des performances du réseau national intégré de radiocommunications (RENIR). Rapport de recherche (2009)
21. Yan, L., Taha, H., Landers, L.L.: A recursive Approach for Enumerating Minimal Cutsets in a Network. IEEE Transactions on Reliability 43(3), 383–388 (1994)
22. Hariri, S., Raghavendra: Syrel A symbolic reliability algorithm based on path and cut-set methods. IEEE Transactions on Reliability C-36(10), 1224–1232 (1987)
23. Valian, L.G.: The Complexity of enumerating and reliability problem. SIAM Journal of Computing 8, 410–421 (1979)
24. Kantarci, B., Mouftah, H.T.: Availability and Cost-Constrained Long-Reach Passive Optical Network Planning. IEEE Transactions on Reliability 61(1), 113–124 (2012)

An Efficient Emergency Message Dissemination Protocol in a Vehicular Ad Hoc Network

Zouina Doukha, Samira Moussaoui, Noureddine Haouari,
and Mohamed E.A. Delhoum

Computer Science Department, Faculty Of Electronic and Computer Science,
USTHB, El Alia BP n°32, Bab Ezzouar, Algiers, Algeria
{zdoukha,smoussaoui}@usthb.dz,
haouarin@gmail.com,
amine-del@hotmail.fr

Abstract. Dissemination of emergency messages is a critical research area which aims to avoid traffic fatalities. Due to inherent characteristics of vehicular ad hoc networks and the emergency of the messages, most of developed applications are based on the broadcasting messages. The most basic strategy is called flooding. This strategy is well studied in the context of mobile ad hoc networks and has been shown it causes contentions, collisions and redundancy, well known as the 'broadcast storm problem'. The majority of existing solutions focuses on decreasing the number of relay nodes and discards the use of unicast messages. In this paper we study a new strategy that combines the use of unicast and broadcast modes at the same time. Simulation results show that the proposed protocol achieves low latency in delivering emergency warnings in spite of the use of unicast messages and these results can be enhanced by modifying the MAC layer protocol parameters.

Keywords: Dissemination, Vehicular ad hoc networks, Vehicle to Vehicle communication, unicast mode, broadcast mode, multi-hop.

1 Introduction

Advances in wireless technologies are opening up exciting possibilities for the future of vehicular ad hoc networks that will have a positive impact on the quality of the driving: more security and more comfort thanks to the various services offered.

Vehicular ad hoc networks (VANETS) are emerging as a particular type of mobile ad hoc networks (MANETS) formed by moving vehicles equipped with wireless interfaces which allow them to communicate during their travel. Both of MANETS and VANETS use the same wireless technology. But VANETS are different because of many features. The most important, the topology and the node movement are constrained by roads, signposts and obstacles like buildings. This must be taken into account in dissemination protocols design, especially the dissemination of emergency messages. The existing solutions [4,9,10,11,12,13] use multi-hop broadcast strategy to

R. Benlamri (Ed.): NDT 2012, Part I, CCIS 293, pp. 459–469, 2012.

access to a great number of vehicles in dangerous area with acceptable delivery delays. Many ideas are proposed to overcome the broadcast storm problem [5] by decreasing the number of vehicles relayed to rebroadcast the emergency message: One relay vehicle would make the best strategy. We think that this strategy maintain the redundancy problem because the broadcast transmission is performed every one hop so that the area between two relay nodes is covered at least twice.

Our approach uses the unicat mode to disseminate the emergency message as far as possible on the road in a multi-hop way. Each hop is at most equal to the nodes transmission range. Broadcasts are performed every two hops to make all vehicles informed.

The rest of the paper is organized as follow. In section 2, we present the related works. In section 3, we describe the 'UUB' protocol strategy and the integration of the prioritization mechanism. In section 4, we present simulation results, and, we conclude the paper in section 5.

2   Related Work

Recently, several dissemination protocols emerged. The methods are differentiated according to the type of the applications. The comfort applications are varied, for example, a request about the availability of a product or about a place in a car park. In these applications, the peer to peer communication mode is the most used. One of the approaches adopted is the epidemic approach [2] inspired from the epidemiology domain. It is based on a simple principle. Any vehicle carrying information sends it to any vehicle that enters its communication range. In [1], the proposed solution differs by taking into account the VANETS characteristics and the road parameters like speed limits and traffic density.

On the other hand, emergency applications aim to reduce the probability and severity of accidents on the roads by providing alert messages to vehicles located in dangerous region. An emergency message is characterized by its location, its zone of relevance and its validity duration. So, emergency message dissemination protocol must ensure these spatial and temporal constraints. Indeed, all vehicles close to the incident location have to be advised in time, so that they have the possibility to act consequently.

In emergency applications, the multi hop broadcast mode is the most used. The simplest way to perform the dissemination is by simple flooding: When a node receives a broadcast message for the first time, it rebroadcasts it immediately. This strategy causes collision, contention and redundancy problems well known as "Broadcast storm problem" [5]. In [5], the broadcast storm problem was studied and analyzed in mobile ad hoc networks. There are five proposed schemes to face this problem: The probabilistic scheme, the Counter-based scheme, the distance-based scheme, the location-based scheme, and, the cluster-based scheme. All these schemes converge on the idea to prevent certain vehicles having received the message to rebroadcast it.

In vehicular ad hoc networks several protocols [6,7,8,14] proposed solutions at the MAC layer. Other solutions [4,9,10,11,12,13] adapted an approach inspired from [5] to the VANETs environment. In [9], when a node receives a broadcast message, it waits a waiting time (WT) that is conversely proportional to the distance separating it from the sender and rebroadcasts the received message. So, the nodes which are in the limit of the sender transmission range rebroadcast the message more quickly. Duplicated messages are ignored. This solution decreases contentions and collisions but the redundancy problem still remains. In [4], the proposed strategy reduces the number of vehicles which have to rebroadcast the received message. A vehicle rebroadcasts a received message with probability   that is calculated dynamically using the information about the vehicles density in its neighborhood. This information is obtained through the periodic HELLO messages. In [10], when a node receives a broadcast message, it waits a time called "defertime" (which is conversely proportional to the distance between the sender and the receiver), before making a decision to rebroadcast it. If the message is received only once during the "defertime", the node is considered as a relay and decides to rebroadcast the message; otherwise, the node does not rebroadcast it. So, the farthest node in the transmission range of the sender is always the relay node. This method decreases the nodes that have to rebroadcast the message to only one node. This solution is supposed to be in traffic with a single way and does not take advantage from vehicles moving in the opposite direction [11,12,13]. In [13], authors identify three regimes for the vehicular traffic: dense traffic regime, sparse traffic regime and regular traffic regime. Their solution allows a vehicle to transit between three behaviors according to the traffic density which is known by using periodic beacon messages.

All the above presented solutions use the broadcast mode at every one hop. So all vehicles located between the sender and the receiver, receive the message at least twice causing redundancy. In [16], the proposed solution uses the broadcast and the unicast modes at the same time. A unicast message is forwarded from a relay vehicle to the next relay in the opposite of the vehicles direction. The distance between two relay nodes is at most equal to vehicles transmission range. When a node receives a unicast message, it first forwards it to the next relay and decides whether it has to broadcast it. This protocol suffers from collisions which occur between messages and beacons. Our approach is based on the use of the EDCA (Enhanced Distributed Channel Access) mechanism which is specified to provide differentiation service and prioritization mechanism at IEEE 802.11e MAC layer [15,19]. We differentiate messages by their priority so that the data messages are assigned to a high priority class and the beacon messages are assigned to a low priority class.

3   Assumptions and Protocol Description

In this section, we give the assumptions and we present our protocol strategy:

3.1   Assumptions

We assume that the vehicles use wireless communication through omni directional radio antennas of transmission range R. Each vehicle is equipped with a device enabling it to obtain its geographical location in a current time, like GPS device, and, a preloaded digital map, which provides general information about roads. The vehicles periodically exchange their own physical location, moving velocity and direction information enclosed in their periodic beacon messages. This information are maintained and updated locally to be used to calculate the distance between vehicles. Emergency messages are sent in the opposite of vehicles direction. We use EDCA (Enhanced Distributed Channel Access) mechanism at the IEEE 802.11e MAC layer to provide prioritization between messages.

3.2   Dissemination Strategy

An emergency message can be generated by a vehicle (called initiator) in a dangerous situation. For example, in case of an accident, a vehicle can recognize it is in a dangerous situation through sensors that are able to detect internal events like airbag ignition. Omni antennas used in wireless transmission allow a mobile node to transmit its signal all around it within a transmission range R.

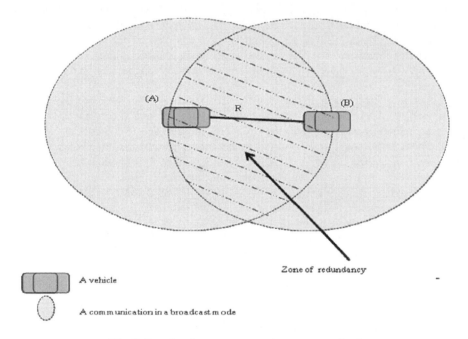

Fig. 1. Broadcasting at every one hop causes redundancy

Actually, dissemination protocols have improved their performances by decreasing the effects of storm problem. However, the fact that the message is broadcasted at every one hop causes unavoidable redundancy in the zone between two relay vehicles. Figure 1 shows a zone of redundancy represented by the intersection between two areas covered by the broadcast messages respectively performed by nodes A and B.

To the best of our knowledge, existing protocols discarded the use of the unicast mode because it needs more time than the broadcast mode. However, it is more reliable [19, 20] and we can show using simulation that the latency is not affected.

In our approach, we use the unicast mode between relay nodes to propagate the information as far as necessary while the broadcast mode is used every two hops to inform nodes that there is an emergency situation. So, the redundancy zone will be eliminated as it is shown in figure 2.

In this section we present the UUB protocol design [16] to perform the dissemination of an emergency message according to our approach.

3.2.1 The 'UUB' Protocol

The initiator vehicle selects among its neighbors behind it, the farthest one, and, sends it a unicast packet data that contains the emergency message. The farthest node is considered as a relay. It first transmits a unicast message to the farthest neighbor behind it within its transmission range to ask it to act like an initiator and then broadcasts the message. So, there are two unicast messages followed by one broadcast message to reach two hops.

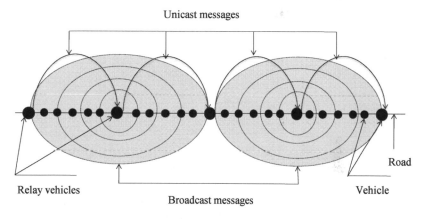

Fig. 2. General scheme of the disseminat

In figure 3, when vehicle B receives the vehicle A packet, it first sends a packet which contains the emergency message to vehicle C in a unicast mode, and then broadcasts it. Vehicle C sends immediately its unicast message to the farthest vehicle from it in its vicinity (vehicle D) which acts like vehicle B.

Considering figure 3, supposing that the broadcast performed by vehicle B failed, In this case vehicle A resends its packet to vehicle B which is asked to perform only the broadcast. At the same time, vehicle C has already sent its packet to vehicle D which acts like vehicle B. Consequently, the propagation time of emergency message is not delayed.

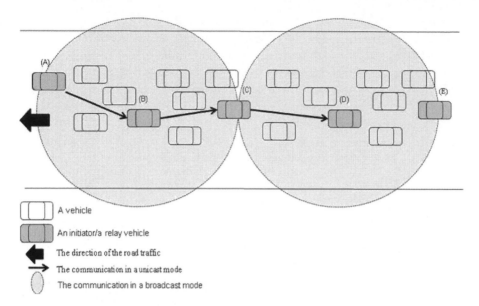

Fig. 3. The dissemination scheme on a section of road

So, the proposed protocol has two characteristics:

- On one hand, we can see that there are two processes in progress at the same time: the unicat and the broadcast transmissions,

- On the other hand, the fail of a broadcast performed by one relay node does not affect the following ones anymore. So, the dissemination process continues its track while the problem can be treated locally by resending the message.

3.2.2 Network Fragmentation

The proposed protocol distinguishes two types of relay nodes. The first one has only to forward the received message to its farthest neighbor. The second type has furthermore to broadcast the message. When a relay node has no contact behind it (this situation is commonly known as fragmentation), it waits until a new contact enters its transmission range and sends a unicast message to it to inform it that it must act as an initiator node. If the relay belongs to the second type, it first sends the message in a broadcast mode to inform all vehicles above, and then waits a new contact.

3.2.3 Messages Prioritization

The activation of beacon messages at the MAC layer can cause dramatically a large number of collisions between data and beacon messages. Due to the emergency of our application, we adopt the EDCA (Enhanced Distributed Channel Access) protocol which is specified to provide differentiation service and prioritization mechanism at IEEE 802.11e MAC layer [19]. We differentiate messages by their priority so that the data messages are assigned to a high priority class and the beacon messages are assigned to a low priority class.

4   Simulation

In this simulation, we study the effect of prioritization on the UUB protocol. The parameters of our simulation are listed in table 1.

Performance evaluation of the protocols was conducted using the widely adopted Network Simulator NS2 [18]. We used various mobility scenarios generated with the MOVE generator [17] by varying the vehicles densities. Vehicles move in the same direction on a road of 10 km composed of 4 lanes. The maximum vehicles speed is equal 30 m/s.

Table 1. Simulation Setup

Parameter	Value
Mac Layer	IEEE 802.11 / IEEE 802.11e with EDCA mechanism
Transmission range	250m
Beacon interval	1sec
Road length	10 km
Number of lanes	4
Traffic density	2, 4, 6 and 8 vehicles/km/lane
Maximum vehicle velocity	30 m/s

On the following, we denote UUB respectively (UUB+) the protocol UUB without (resp. with) prioritization mechanism.

The simulation results show that the delivery rate of the two protocols reach **100%** for all mobility scenarios with none or partial fragmentation. Indeed, all vehicles generated in the simulation have received the emergency message. So, the simulation shows that the UUB and the UUB+ protocols are reliable.

On the other hand, the coexistence of beacon messages and the data dissemination messages in the same stack of protocols can dramatically cause collisions as it is shown figure 4 with the UUB graph. In the simulation file traces we can see that the collisions occur between messages and beacons; and between beacons themselves.

Other simulations are performed with the UUB+ protocol with the same scenarios and we can see that surprisingly, prioritization allows no collisions to (UUB+).

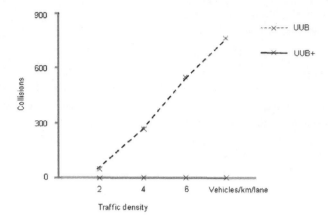

Fig. 4. Mean number of collisions

The mean number of generated messages is higher in UUB as it is shown in figure 5. This is due to the drops caused by collisions. So, dropped messages are regenerated which makes more messages.

Figure 6 shows mean number of redundant messages. A message is redundant when it is received more than once. Few redundant messages are generated in both UUB and UUB+. They are generally due to the acknowledgment reception which is functional.

Small delays are reached in the simulations of the two protocols. The dissemination delay is the interval of time between the first generated message and the first message received by the last informed vehicle in the network.

It is shown in figure 7 that UUB+ gives the best delays. This is due to the prioritization mechanism which eliminated collisions. If a fragmentation occurs, the delay depends on the fragmentation duration.

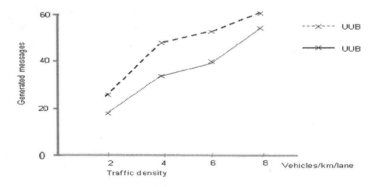

Fig. 5. Mean number of generated messages

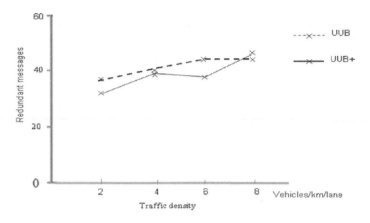

Fig. 6. Mean number of redundant message

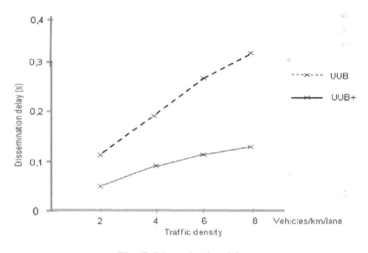

Fig. 7. Dissemination delay

5   Conclusion

In this paper we showed that the use of the unicast mode in an emergency dissemination can give good performances in term of delay and efficiency. In the proposed strategy two processes get in progress at the same time. The first makes progress the dissemination process toward the rest of the vehicles while the second treats the broadcasting at each two hops. The unicat mode is used as a means of improving the broadcast mode, so that the broadcasted message can reach two hops simultaneously without redundancy. The EDCA prioritization mechanism used at the MAC layer permits to UUB protocol to overcome collisions.

We can say firstly, that the unicast mode can be suitable for the dissemination service. Secondly, discarding the use of beacons for the reason that they cause collisions is not a good choice because on one hand most of the existing protocols especially routing protocols are beacon-based, on the other hand beacon messages provide crucial information about the topology which can be used in several applications.

Our future work consists on proposing solutions at the MAC layer of the IEEE 802.11p protocol to enhance the existing dissemination protocols performances.

References

1. Zhao, J., Cao, G.: VADD: Vehicle Assisted Data Delivery in Vehicular Ad Hoc Networks. IEEE Transactions on Vehicular Technology 57(3), 1910–1922 (2008)
2. Xu, B., Ouksel, A., Wolfson, O.: Opportunistic Resource Exchange in Inter vehicle Ad-hoc Networks. In: IEEE International Conference on Mobile Data Management, MDM (2004)
3. The Institute of Electrical and Electronics Engineers, IEEE: Wireless LAN Medium Access Control (MAC) and Physical Layer (PHY) Specifications. ANSI/IEEE Std.802.11 (1999), http://standards.ieee.org
4. ALshaer, H., Horlait, E.: An Optimized Adaptive Broadcast Scheme for Inter-vehicle Communication. In: Proceedings of the 61st IEEE Vehicular Technology Conference, VTC, Stockholm, Sweden (2005)
5. Ni, S.Y., Tseng, Y.C., Chen, Y.S., Sheu, J.: The Broadcast Storm Problem in a Mobile Ad Hoc Network. In: Proceedings of the 5th Annual ACM/IEEE International Conference on Mobile Computing and Networking, Seattle, Washington (1999)
6. Borgonovo, F., Capone, A., Cesana, M., Fratta, L.: ADHOC MAC: A New MAC Architecture for Ad hoc Networks Providing Efficient and Reliable Point-to-point and Broadcast Services. Wireless Networks WINET 10(4), 359–366 (2004)
7. Korkmaz, G., Ekici, E., Ozguner, F.: Black-Burst-Based Multi-hop Broadcast Protocols for Vehicular Networks. IEEE Transaction on Vehicular Tech. 56(5), 3159–3167 (2007)
8. Zanella, A., Pierobon, G., Merlin, S.: On the Limiting Performance of Broadcast Algorithms over Unidimensional Ad-hoc Radio Networks. In: WPMC 2004, Abano Terme Padova, Italy (2004)
9. Briesemeister, L., Schafers, L., Hommel, G.: Dissemination Messages among Highly Mobile Hosts Based on Inter Vehicle Communication. In: Proceedings of IEEE Intelligent Vehicles Symposium, USA, pp. 522–527 (2000)
10. Benslimane, A.: Optimized Dissemination of Alarm Messages in Vehicular Ad-Hoc Networks (VANET). In: Mammeri, Z., Lorenz, P. (eds.) HSNMC 2004. LNCS, vol. 3079, pp. 655–666. Springer, Heidelberg (2004)
11. Yu, Q., Heijenk, G.: Abiding Geocast for Warning Message Dissemination in Vehicular Ad Hoc Networks. In: Proceedings of the IEEE Vehicular Networks and Applications Workshop Vehi-Mobi (2008)
12. Schwartz, R.S., Barbosa, R.R.R., Meratnia, N., Heinjek, G., Scholten, H.: A Simple and Robust Dissemination Protocol for VANETs. In: 16th European Wireless Conference, Italy, pp. 214–222. IEEE Computer Society Press (2010) ISBN 978-1-4244-5999-5

13. Tonguz, O., Wisipongphan, N., Bai, F., Mudalige, P., Sadekar, V.: Broadcasting in VANET. In: Proceedings of Mobile Networking for Vehicular Environments, pp. 7–12 (2007)
14. Li, M., Lou, W., Zeng, K.: OppCast: Opportunistic Broadcast of Warning Messages in VANETs with Unreliable Links. In: Proceedings of 6th International Conference on Mobile Ad-hoc and Sensor Systems, pp. 534–543 (2009)
15. Booysen, M.J., Zeedally, S., Van Rooyen, G.J.: Survey of Media Access Control Protocols for Vehicular Ad Hoc Networks. IET Communications 5, 1619–1631 (2011)
16. Doukha, Z., Moussaoui, S.: Dissemination of an Emergency Message in a Vehicular Ad Hoc Network. In: International Conference on Communication, Computing and Control Applications (CCCA), Tunisia (2011) ISBN 978-1-4244-9795-9
17. Karnadi, F.K., Mo, Z.H., Lan, K.C.: Rapid Generation of Realistic Mobility Models for VANET. In: IEEE Wireless Communication and Networking Conference, WCNC, pp. 2506–2511 (2007)
18. The Network Simulator, http://www.isi.edu/nsnam/ns/
19. IEEE 802.11e/D13.0: Part 11, Wireless LAN Medium Access Control (MAC) and Physical Layer (PHY) specifications: Medium Access Control (MAC) Enhancements for Quality of Service (QoS). Draft supp. to IEEE 802.11 std. (2005)

An Energy Saving Data Dissemination Protocol for Wireless Sensor Networks

Dalila Iabbassen[1,2] and Samira Moussaoui[1]

[1] Faculty of Electronic and Computing Department,
University of Sciences and Technology HOUARI BOUMEDIENE (USTHB),
BP 32 EL ALIA 16111 BAB EZZOUAR Algiers Algeria
[2] Faculty of Economic, Commercial and Management Sciences
University of Algiers 3. Algeria
iabdalila@gmail.com,
moussaoui_samira@yahoo.fr

Abstract. Recently, Mobile Agents have been used for efficient data dissemination in wireless sensor networks. In the traditional Client/Server architectures, data sources are transferred to a destination while in Mobile Agents architectures, a specific executable code passes through relevant sources to collect data. Mobile Agents can be used to significantly reduce the cost of communication, especially through low bandwidth, by moving the processing function to the data, rather that bringing the data to a central processor. This work proposes to use a Client/Server approach using Mobile Agents to aggregate data in a planar architecture of wireless sensor network.

Keywords: Wireless Sensor Networks, Energy Saving, Data Dissemination, Data Aggregation, Mobile Agents.

1 Introduction

Due to their realism and concrete contribution, WSNs (Wireless Sensor Networks) has attracted a growing number of manufacturers. Indeed, the need for continuous monitoring of a given environment is quite common in various activities of society. Industrial processes, military tracking applications, habitat monitoring, and precision farming are just some examples of a wide and varied range of possible applications of continuous monitoring offered by WSNs. Unfortunately, WSNs are not perfect! Because of their low cost and their deployment in areas sometimes hostile, the motes are quite fragile and vulnerable to various forms of failure: breaking, low energy ... and so on. These problems make WSNs systems with innate fragility, which should be considered as a normal property of the network. This limitation of resources necessitates some form of cooperation on a large scale where interactions between sensors can be extremely complex. This requires the establishment of a protocol at the middleware layer for the dissemination and retrieval of data in an efficient manner.

The purpose of the data dissemination is to send any type of information (data or applications) to all nodes affected by this information, while minimizing the number of transmission nodes and the energy cost [1]. Data dissemination is considered as a main phase of energy consumption in the communication of WSNs [2]. Hence the way

R. Benlamri (Ed.): NDT 2012, Part I, CCIS 293, pp. 470–482, 2012.
© Springer-Verlag Berlin Heidelberg 2012

to eliminate redundant data traffic and reduce communication costs are the main challenges of the data dissemination. On applications of WSNs such as environmental monitoring, data dissemination is very important. Indeed, it is known that the ineffectiveness of the data dissemination causes broadcast storms and blocks all data ommunications in the network [3].

In most WSNs, sensors are deployed in an area to extract environmental data. Once the data collected by multiple sources (multiple sensors in the vicinity of the captured event), they will be transmitted via multiple hops to a single destination (sink). This, coupled with the fact that the information collected by sensors neighbors is often redundant and correlated, and that energy is the most precious resource, requires the use of data fusion. Instead of transmitting all data to a central node for processing, the data is processed locally and only aggregate information is returned to the sink. Data fusion reduces the number of packets to be transmitted via the sensors, and therefore energy consumption and bandwidth. Its advantages are evident, especially in a large-scale network.

Depending on how to collect data and process them, we can distinguish two approaches of data dissemination in WSNs:

Client/Server based data dissemination: The sink sends queries to sensor nodes, each sensor node will then process the request and send the desired data individually to the sink which will process and aggregate it.

Mobile agent based data dissemination: The sink dispatches one or more mobile agents to sensor nodes. This agent will carry the code for data processing. In this way, the data will be aggregated and processed locally at the sensor nodes, then the agent will collect the data already processed to send it to the sink.

In the collaborative process, the client/server model is the most widely used, where the individual sensors (clients) send the raw or pre-treated data to a treatment center (server) and data integration is performed in the center (usually at the sinks or super nodes). As mentioned above, there are some drawbacks with this model that should be considered especially for WSNs. Indeed, despite the unreliability and the limited bandwidth of wireless links used in sensor networks, in addition to the constraint of energy that is critical in WSNs, the protocols using the client / server paradigm in this type of networks are numerous (DD [4], TTDD [5], LBDD [6]).

DD (Directed Diffusion) [4] is one of the most used approaches in many works on sensor networks. DD is a protocol for data dissemination using multiple paths for routing information. The sink broadcasts an interest in the form of a query in order to interrogate the network on a particular data, and then it determines the best path to use for receiving data.

In TTDD (Two Tier Data Dissemination) [5] each source node creates a virtual grid on the network. This grid is then used by the routing protocol to route queries and data between the source and the mobile sink.

2 Line Based Data Dissemination Protocol

LBDD (*Line-Based Data Dissemination protocol*) [6] defines a virtual structure formed as a band in the middle of the interest area. Nodes positioned inside of the band are called inline-nodes. This band represents an area of appointments for queries and data storage.

This protocol assumes that each node knows its geographical position and the coordinates of the interest area. LBDD uses then a geographic routing.

The operation of LBDD consists of two main steps:

- Dissemination: when a node detects a stimulus, the data is generated and sent to the nearest inline-node;
- Collection: to collect different data, the sink sends a perpendicular query to the band. The first inline-node which receives the query will propagate it in both directions of the band to attain the nodes with the required data. The data will be then sent directly to the sink.

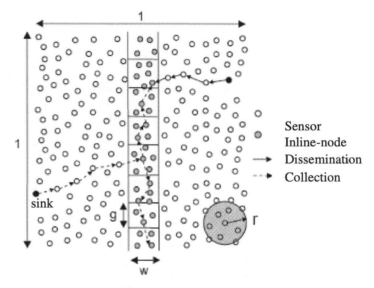

Fig. 1. LBDD architecture

Due to its simplicity and ease of deployment, the Client/Server paradigm is the most used in distributed environments especially in WSNs. However, this solution has been criticized for consuming high bandwidth and energy, and even big latency. For this, there was the appearance of a new paradigm using Mobile Agents.

A MA consists of a process code and a state (variable values, the next instruction ... etc.).. Initially a MA resides on the machine that created it. It is then dispatched to run on a remote host called generally a server. When an MA is dispatched, the entire code of the MA and its execution state is transferred to the host.

The host provides a suitable execution environment for the MA. The MA will use the host resources (CPU, memory ... etc..) to perform its task. After completing his work at the host, the MA will migrate to another machine. Since the execution state is transferred to the host, the MA can resume execution at the point where it stopped at the old host. In this way, the MA will continue its round until the last machine on its route, to finally return to the machine that created it.

The use of MAs in computer networks has advantages but also disadvantages, such as code caching and security in certain scenarios. Nevertheless, they are successfully used in various applications such as parallel programming, data collection, e-commerce and mobile computing. As described in [9], many inherent advantages (such as scalability and awareness of energy) of the MA architecture makes it more suitable for WSNs that the client / server architecture [11]. In fact, mobile agents can be used to significantly reduce the cost of communication, especially through low bandwidth, by moving the processing function to the data rather than bring the data to a central processor [7] [8] [10].

3   Mobile Agent Based Wireless Sensor Networks

Based on the principle that the communication cost to send an information using a long message is usually less than sending the same information using several short messages, the MAWSN protocol (Mobile Agent based Wireless Sensor Networks) [7] will perform several concurrent tasks associated with small amounts of data by a single packet carrying multiple queries, and concatenate the results in a single package to reduce the communication cost.

The context of application and design of MAWSN highlights some assumptions:

- The sink knows all sources nodes to be visited by the MA.
- The itinerary of a AM is already designed before dispatching the MA.

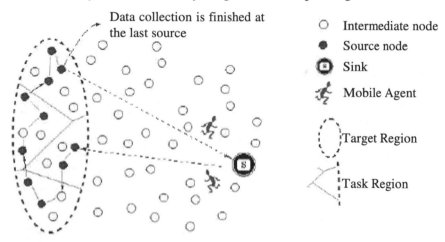

Fig. 2. MAWSN architecture

As In this approach, the sink sends queries to multiple targets simultaneously via a mobile agent. The data in the target region are collected by the mobile agent one by one, and all combined tasks are executed one after the other, so that the entire process will take longer. If the quality of service requirements (eg, latency) is not violated, especially if the target area is far from the sink, the energy gain from this execution combination could be important.

The MAWSN author offered another mobile agent architecture combined with Directed Diffusion, MADD (Mobile Agent based Directed Diffusion) [8] trying to eliminate the maximum of assumptions (choice of target nodes and establishment of the MA visiting sequence) of MAWSN via the combination of Directed Diffusion approach to the mobile agent approach.

By moving the processing code to the data, a MA can avoid the transmission of intermediate data in the network, continue working even in the presence of disconnections in the network, and then complete the entire task faster than the Client/Server traditional solutions.

However, a MA is not always better than a Client/Server solution. For example, if the code of the agent is greater than all the intermediate data, the MA will be less efficient in this case, since it will transfer more bytes over the network than the Client/Server solution.

In addition, if the network is fast, the agent will be less efficient even if the code is smaller. With a fast and reliable network, the interpretation of the agent at the sensors is slower than the transmission of intermediate data to the sink. However, if the network speed and reliability go down, or the data size increases, the case changes considerably.

Decide for a better approach (Client/Server or Mobile Agent) for wireless sensor networks is not a fixed choice, but it depends strongly on the network characteristics and topology and its application.

4   Mobile Line Based Data Dissemination

In order to optimize the data dissemination, we have opted for a mobile agent solution [7] based on an appointment area inspired from the LBDD approach [6].

The advantage in the appointment area is to avoid the blind search of the data and the sink in the interest area. For this, we will assign some nodes located in the appointment area , the role of data storage generated by all the sensors in the network. Thus, each source node that detects an event in the interest area, will generate the corresponding data and send it directly to the appointment area, where it is stored. Subsequently, when a sink node wishes to collect some information, it will generate a query that will also be directed directly to the appointment area, where all data reside. In this way, we avoid the problem of network congestion by eliminating the messages broadcasted to find the data across the network.

In order to collect efficiently the data stored in the appointments area, we will use a mobile agent whose mission is to aggregate the data collected in order to reduce the size of the packet transmitted to the sink and reduce the energy consumption and the bandwidth which are critical resources in wireless sensor networks.

Our approach is used for continuous applications where nodes periodically generate data, and also for event-driven applications where nodes generate data when an event arises in the field of capture. The proposed solution will perform multiple simultaneous tasks associated with small amounts of data carried by a single pack. The result will be concatenated into a single package to give a better aggregation in order to reduce the communication cost [7].

In order to build the appointment area, we will use a structure in the form of a rectangular band placed in the interest area. We assume that the network has a localization system, such as a GPS (Global Positioning System). In this way, each node is supposed to know its location and the coordinates of the interest area, which means that each node can know at any moment if it belongs to the appointment area.

In addition, the nodes must be synchronized in order to make the periodic change of the appointment area.

4.1   Mobility of the Appointment Area

In our approach, the interest area is divided into N rectangular bands that do not interfere with each other. At a given time, only one band i (i $\in$ [1, N]) will represent the appointment area for the data collected by the sensor nodes and sink queries. After the lapse of a period T, the band i+1 will be activated as a current appointment area instead of the band i, and so on. This process is executed periodically to balance the charge among all network nodes and therefore increase the lifetime of the network.

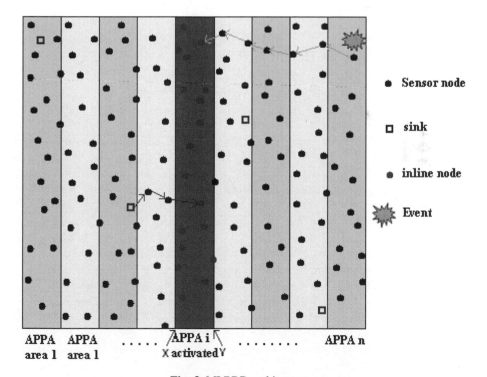

Fig. 3. MLBDD architecture

By using the localization system and the synchronization of nodes, changing the appointment area does not generate any additional messages. Indeed, as the nodes are synchronized, each of them at any time, is autonomously informed on the appointment area to be used for sending data and queries.

4.2   Dissemination of Captured Data

When an event arises in the interest area, source nodes having captured it will generate the relevant data and send it directly to the actual appointment area. Since the nodes are equipped with a localization system, data packets will be routed to the appointment area using a greedy geographic routing [12]. Each node will route the packet perpendicularly to the rectangular band. This will balance the charge between nodes and avoid congestion.

Data storage. To balance the charge between all the inline-nodes (nodes that belong to the current appointment area), data storage in the appointment area should not focus on specific inline-nodes.

The use of clusters for data storage creates an overhead in the construction of the clusters. In addition, data storage in clusterheads concentrates the charge on those in addition to the overhead caused by the periodic election of the clusterhead.

MLBDD tries to minimize the overhead while ensuring that all inline-nodes are involved in the task of data storage. To do this, when the captured data arrives at the first inline-node, it will be stored in its memory or that of its direct neighbors in turn.

Data collection - The Mobile Agent itinerary. When a sink have to collect certain information from the network, it will create a mobile agent and send it directly to the activated appointment area, using the same geographic routing used to disseminate data to the rectangular band. The mobile agent contains the query of the sink and the processing code of the data to be collected (aggregation code). The MA will carry a package containing several queries [7], where each query corresponds to a different application.

When the MA arrives at the first inline-node (node belonging to the actual appointment area), it will choose another inline-node among its immediate neighbors to host the MA. The choice of the MA host will be in turn as it did for the choice of inline-node when storing data collected by sensors.

In order to minimize congestion and collisions, we differentiate between the inline-node that hosts the MA and the one that distributes the interest of the sink in the appointment area. Indeed, the first inline-node that receives the MA from the sink will broadcast the interest throughout the appointment area by using a multihop geographic routing. Then, each inline-node receiving this message and possessing the data referred to in the interest, will send a reply containing its location to the node hosting the MA.

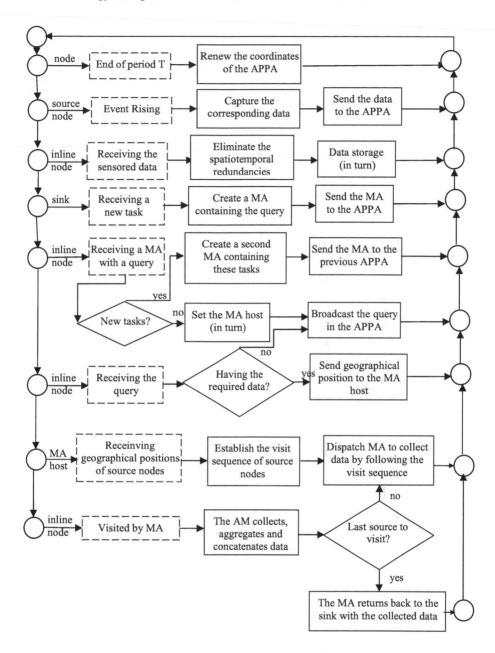

Fig. 4. Flowchart of the MLBDD protocol

After receiving the responses of inline-nodes, the MA will establish a logical sequence of visiting these nodes, based on their geographical position as follows (fig.5):

-Divide the rectangular band into two equal bands.

-For each sub-band, classify inline-nodes to be visited based on their geographical position, in order to draw a straight line from one end to another.

-Concatenate the two sub-sequences established for making the full sequence of the inline-nodes route. For routing from one node to another, we will also use the greedy geographic routing.

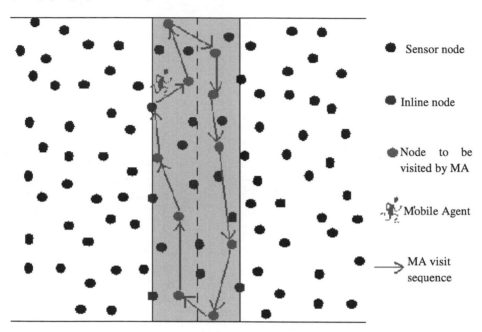

Fig. 5. Mobile Agent visit sequence

Data Aggregation. Having established the visits sequence of inline-nodes, the MA will browse the nodes by aggregating data as it collects them [7]:

- Elimination of the application redundancy: With the development of WSNs, "a deployment, multiple applications" is a trend due to the nature of the specific applications of sensor networks. In general, given the constraints of storage capacity, it is impossible to store every application in the local memory on-board sensors. The sink attributes to the MA the processing code (behavior) based on the need of a specific application. The code carried by the MA requires local processing of raw data in the inline-nodes as requested by the application. This behavior allows a reduction of the amount of transmitted data by allowing only relevant information to be extracted and transmitted.

- Elimination of spatial redundancy: The degree of correlation of data collected between sensors is closely related to the distance between the sensors, so it is very probable that the sensors close to each other generate redundancies of collected data. So, the MA aggregates the individual data when it visits each inline-node. Although this aggregation technique is commonly used in protocols for data dissemination based on the clustering or aggregation tree, the aggregation assisted by MA requires no additional cost to build these special structures.

- Data concatenation: Based on the principle that the communication cost for sending a long message is usually less than sending the same amount of data using several short messages, we use a unification technique of packets, which concatenates the data from several small packets into a larger package to reduce communication costs. Due to the concatenation of the data, the communication cost of intermediate sensors can be reduced to increase the lifetime of the network. However, these energy savings can usually be obtained at the expense of a prolonged latency.

4.3   Performance Evaluation

To evaluate the performance of the MLBDD solution and compare it with other similar works, we performed simulations. To do this, we used the Glomosim simulator (Global Mobile Information System Simulator).

Table 1. Simulation parameters

Area dimensions	200m x 200m
Nodes	400
Simulation period	15 minutes
Communication range for each node	37.67 meters
Nodes position	random
Period for the appointment area switching	3 minutes
Period of creating data	1 second
Period of creating sink requests	1 minute
MA eliminating redundancy rate	10%
MA fusion factor	1

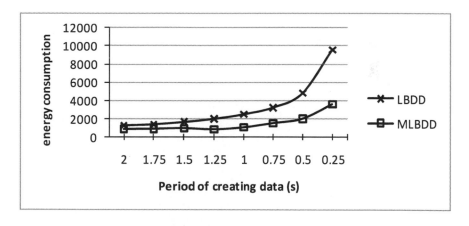

Fig. 6. Energy / Data charge

According to the graph above, we find that the energy consumption increases when we increase the frequency of data creation. This is due to the increased traffic generated by the dissemination and storage of data. However, the consumption of energy in LBDD is always higher than MLBDD; this is because LBDD disseminates data in the whole group in the area of appointments while MLBDD stores each data in a single node belonging to the appointment area.

We can also see in fig.7 that the energy consumption in the two approaches LBDD and MLBDD increases as the number of nodes in the network increases. Because, as more nodes there are as traffic increases between these nodes. However, LBDD energy consumption increased by 154,311 between 200 and 600 nodes, whereas it increased by only 87,371 in MLBDD. This is because LBDD uses data diffusion for storage while MLBDD uses diffuses queries and MA for the collection. And since data packets are usually larger than the controls messages and queries, the total LBDD energy is higher than MLBDD.

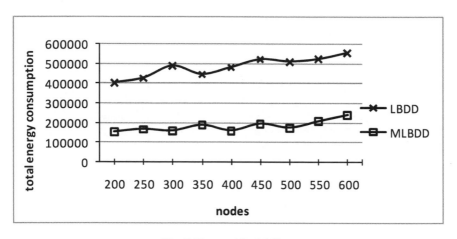

Fig. 7. Energy / Scalability

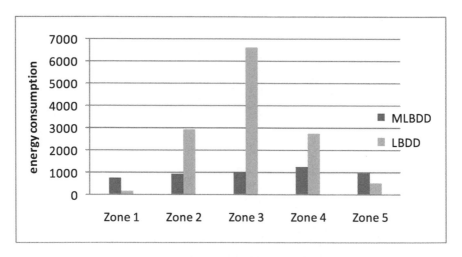

Fig. 8. Energy /Zone structure

The histogram above shows the energy consumption in each band of the interest area. Indeed, LBDD concentrates the charge in the middle area (since it uses a static oppointment area) while MLBDD spread the charge across all areas. This will directly affect the network lifetime. Indeed, the lifetime of the network in LBDD depends directly on the lifetime of the inline-nodes while in MLBDD lifetime does not depend on some special network nodes.

5   Conclusion

As the energy factor is one of the most important constraints that guide the design of protocols in wireless sensor networks, they must incorporate mechanisms that allow users to extend the lifetime of the entire network. For this reason, we developed the MLBDD approach (Mobile Line Based Data Dissemination) whose main objective is to extend the network lifetime, by using an equitable energy dissemination approach which limits the energy cost and communication while maintaining a balance of energy consumption between all nodes. MLBDD uses also a mobile agent [7] to collect data in the appointment area by using aggregate functions to reduce the amount of data transmitted and reduce the communication energy and bandwidth.

The simulation results showed that MLBDD improves greatly the energy consumption and balance the charge among all nodes in the network. Thus, MLBDD is suitable for applications requiring long lifetime where the field deployment is inaccessible as in the environmental monitoring applications ... etc.

References

1. Cartigny, J., Ingelrest, F., Simplot-Ryl, D.: Localized LMST and RNG based minimum energy broadcast protocols in ad hoc networks. Ad Hoc Networks, 1–16 (2005)
2. Lu, J., Valois, F.: On the Data Dissemination in WSNs. In: The Third IEEE International Conference on Wireless and Mobile Computing, Networking and Communications, WiMob 2007 (2007) 0-7695-2889-9/07
3. Ni, S., Tseng, Y., Chen, Y., Sheu, J.: The broadcast storm problem in a mobile ad hoc network. In: Proc. of the International Conference on Mobile Computing and Networking (MobiCom), Seattle, USA, pp. 151–162 (1999)
4. Intanagonwiwat, C., Govindan, R., Estrin, D.: Directed diffusion: a scalable and robust communication paradigm for sensor networks. In: Proceedings of the 6th Annual ACM/IEEE (MOBICOM 2000), USA, pp. 56–67 (2000)
5. Ye, F., Luo, H., Cheng, J., Lu, S., Zhang, L.: A two-tier data dissemination model for large-scale wireless sensor networks. In: MobiCom 2002: Proceedings of the 8th Annual International Conference on Mobile Computing and Networking, pp. 148–159. ACM Press, New York (2002)
6. Ben Hamida, E., Ziviani, A., Dias de Amorim, M.: Dissémination dans les réseaux de capteurs avec puits mobiles. In: 9th International Symposium on Telecommunications Algorithmic, pp. 85–88 (2007) (INRIA-00176965, version 1)
7. Chen, M., Kwon, T., Yuan, Y., Leung, V.C.M.: Mobile Agent Based Wireless Sensor Networks. Journal of Computers 1(1) (2006)

8. Chen, M., Kwon, T., Yuan, Y., Choi, Y., Leung, V.C.M.: Mobile agent-based directed diffusion in wireless sensor networks. EURASIP Journal on Advances in Signal Processing, Article ID 36871 (2007)
9. Hairong, Q., Yingyue, X., Xiaoling, W.: Mobile-Agent Based Collaborative Signal and Information Processing in Sensor Networks. Proceeding of the IEEE 91(8), 1172–1183 (2003)
10. Shakshuki, E., Malik, H., Denko, M.K.: Software agent-based directed diffusion in wireless sensor network. Telecommunication Systems 38(3-4), 161–174 (2008)
11. Aiello, E.F., Fortino, G., Guerrieri, A.: Using Mobile Agents as Enabling Technology for Wireless Sensor Networks. In: The Second International Conference on Sensor Technologies and Applications (2008)
12. Medjiah, S., Ahmed, T., Krief, F., Gélard, P.: AGEM: Un Protocole de Routage Géographique Angulaire Adaptatif. In: French Conference on the Protocols Engineering, CFIP, Strasbourg, France (2009)

An Ω-Based Leader Election Algorithm for Mobile Ad Hoc Networks

Leila Melit[1] and Nadjib Badache[2]

[1] Department of Computer Science, Jijel University, Algeria
melitleila@univ-jijel.dz
[2] Laboratory of Computer Systems, USTHB, Algiers, Algeria
badache@mail.cerist.dz

Abstract. Leader election is a fundamental control problem in both wired and wireless systems. The classical statement of the leader election problem in distributed systems is to eventually elect a unique leader from a fixed set of nodes. However, in MANETS, many complications may arise due to frequent and unpredictable topological changes. This paper presents a leader election algorithm based on the omega failures detector, where inter-node communication is allowed only among the neighboring nodes along with proofs of correctness. This algorithm ensures that every connected component of the mobile ad hoc network will eventually elect a unique leader, which is the node of the highest priority value from among all nodes within that connected component. The algorithm can tolerate intermittent failures, such as link failures, network partitions, and merging of connected network components.

Keywords: Leader election, mobile ad hoc networks, omega failures detector, priority index.

1 Introduction

A mobile ad hoc network or MANET [1] (Mobile Ad hoc NETwork) is a collection of mobile nodes that can communicate via message passing over wireless links. The nodes are free to move around in a geographical area and are loosely bounded by the transmission range of the wireless channels. Since a node is completely free to move around, there is no fixed final topology. Nodes that are in transmission range of each other can communicate directly otherwise, they communicate via message relay. Characteristics that distinguish ad hoc networks from existing distributed networks include concurrent and unpredictable topology changes due to arbitrary mobility pattern of nodes, dynamic wireless link formation and removal, network partitioning and disconnections, limited bandwidth and energy, and highly variable message delay. These characteristics signify mobile ad hoc network as a challenging domain for implementing distributed algorithms [2].

Leader election is a fundamental control problem in both wired and wireless systems. In the context of wireless networks, leader election has a variety of applications such as key distribution, routing coordination and general control. The classical statement of the leader election problem is to *eventually elect a unique leader* from a

R. Benlamri (Ed.): NDT 2012, Part I, CCIS 293, pp. 483–490, 2012.

fixed set of nodes. Indeed, several algorithms have been proposed to solve this problem. However, in the context of mobile ad hoc networks, though, link changes are common and may cause the network to split into multiple connected components or cause some components to become separated from the leader. Additionally, two connected components, each with its own leader, may merge. It is important to realize that it is impossible to guarantee a unique leader at all times. For example, when a network partition occurs or when two components merge, it will take some time for a new leader to be elected. Thus, the definition of the leader election problem has to be adapted to the mobile ad hoc environment. Thus, we define the leader election problem in MANETs as the problem of guaranteeing that *"every connected component of the mobile ad hoc network will eventually have exactly one leader"*.

In a previous work [3], we proposed a leader election algorithm which guaranties that the leader will be the process that has the smallest ID. But, in many situations, it may be desirable to elect a leader with some system-related characteristic as mentioned in [4]. For example, in a mobile ad hoc network it might be desirable to elect the node with maximum remaining battery life or computation capabilities to other nodes, as the leader. Therefore, the elected leader should be the node which has the highest priority value from among all nodes within that connected component, where the priority value of a node is a performance–related characteristic. Thus, the requirements for leader election algorithm becomes: *"Given a network of mobile nodes each with a priority value, after a finite number of topological changes, every connected component will eventually select a unique leader, which is the node of highest priority value   from among the nodes in that component"*.

The solution proposed in this paper to solve election problem in mobile ad hoc networks is based on the Ω failures detector [5]. The concept of unreliable failure detector was introduced by Chandra and Toueg as a mechanism that provides (possibly incorrect) information about process failures [6]. Each process has access to a local failure detector module. The output of the failure detector module of Ω at a process p is a single process, say q. We say that p trusts q to be up at time t. Ω ensures that eventually all correct processes trusts the same process and that this process is correct. The contribution of this paper is to use the Ω failure detector to solve election problem in mobile ad hoc networks. Otherwise, we will implement omega in the context of mobile ad hoc network. To elect a unique leader, the algorithm requires mobile nodes to communicate only with their neighbors.

The rest of this paper is organized as follows: the next section focuses on some leader election protocols developed for mobile ad hoc networks; Section 3 describes the system model; the leader election algorithm for mobile ad hoc networks is depicted in Section 4; Section 5 presents proofs of correctness; and Section 6 concludes this paper.

2   Related Works

Leader election is an extensively studied problem for wired and wireless networks. In the context of mobile ad hoc networks, the algorithms presented in [7], which are classified as Non-Compulsory and Compulsory protocols, are unrealistic as they require nodes to meet and exchange information in order to elect a leader. The algorithms presented in [8], [9] and [10] are based on a routing algorithm called TORA [11] wherein nodes adjust a locally maintained variable, called the height, to point to the leader, in a decrementing manner over a Directed Acyclic Graph (DAG). The work in [10] improves on the idea of [9] by devising an algorithm that is self-stabilizing with relatively fast convergence. The algorithm can tolerate multiple concurrent topological changes. By introducing the time-interval-based computation concept, the algorithm ensures that a network partition can within a finite time converge to a legitimate state even if topological changes occur during the convergence time. Vasudevan, Kurose and Towsley presented in [4] another leader election algorithm based on the classical termination-detection algorithm for diffusing computations by Dijkstra and Scholten [12]. This algorithm always requires each and every node to maintain information about its dynamic neighbourhood. The leader sends periodic heartbeat messages to other nodes. The absence of these messages at a node for some predefined time out indicates a departure from the leader and triggers a diffusing computation at that node to elect a new leader. The diffusing computation consists of constructing a spanning tree with the node that started off the diffusing computation as the root. The root then informs all the reachable nodes about the identity of the elected leader. Different diffusing computations can be executed concurrently. A total order on these diffusions is defined to determine the diffusing computation of the highest priority. A node participates in only one diffusing computation at a time. It stops its participation in diffusing computations of lower priorities in favor of the highest one. The algorithm in [13] presents a consensus–based leader election algorithm. The algorithm elects a local extrema as leader. Moreover, this algorithm can be tuned to the global extrema of the network visiting all nodes instead of majority of those. The algorithm in [3] is well-suited for use in mobile ad hoc networks. It is efficient in number of exchanged messages and requires processes to communicate with only a subset of their current neighbors. But the election in this algorithm is based on the identifiers of the processes. In this paper, we present an algorithm that chooses as leader the process with the highest priority value.

3   System Model

We consider a distributed system composed of a finite set of $n > 1$ processes $\Pi = \{p1,..., pn\}$, that communicate only by sending and receiving messages over a wireless network. The network affected by topological changes is modeled as a dynamically changing, not necessarily connected, undirected graph. Node (process) mobility may result in arbitrary topology changes including network partitioning and merging. Furthermore, nodes can crash arbitrarily at any time and can recover from crash–failure again at any time.

Our model considers various types of links, all of which satisfy the following property:

- Integrity: Process q receives a message m from process p at most once, and only if p previously sent m to q.

- Fair lossy: if p sends an infinitely many messages to q and q is correct, then q receives infinitely many messages from p.
- Eventual timely link: The link from p to q is eventual timely if there is a time t and a bound d such that each message sent by p to q at any time t' is received by q by time t' +d.

3.1   Specification of Ω

The concept of unreliable failure detector was introduced by Chandra and Toueg as a mechanism that provides (possibly incorrect) information about process failures [6]. Each process has access to a local failure detector module. Each local module monitors a subset of the processes in the system, and maintains a list of those that it currently suspects to have crashed. Note that at any given time the failure detector modules at two different processes may have different lists of suspects.

One failure detector of particular interest is Ω [5]. At every process p, and at each time t, the output of the failure detector module of Ω at a process p is a single process, say q. We say that p trusts q to be up at time t. Ω ensures that eventually all correct processes trusts the same process and that this process is correct. Thus, a failure detector Ω can be seen as an algorithm for electing a leader: the process trusted by all correct processes is *elected*.

The contribution of this paper is to use the Ω failure detector to solve election problem in mobile ad hoc networks. So, each correct process p of our system must have a local variable leaderp that holds the identifier of a single process. Eventually, all correct processes of the same component should retain the identifier of a single correct process. Specifically, we need the following property:

For every component C, there is a correct process l in C and a time t after which for each process p in C, leaderp = l.

If at time t, leaderp contains the same process l for all alive processes p, then we say that l is leader at time t. Note that a process p never knows if leaderp is really the leader at time t, or not. A process only knows that eventually leader p is leader.

4   Leader Election Algorithm

In our leader election algorithm, each process starts the execution by electing itself and then informs its neighbors by sending a message including its leader identifier and its priority value. A competition will take place between the different leaders. The winner will be the process that has the highest priority value.

Fig.1 shows the proposed algorithm to solve the election problem in mobile ad hoc networks. Each process starts execution of the algorithm by electing itself as a leader then starts its timer (a variable that is automatically incremented at each clock tick). The timer allows the process to detect the departure of the leader. During its execution, it checks if it is still the leader (Task 0). If so, it sends a message (ALIVE, p, priorityp) to all its immediate neighbors every δ time. Each process p, receiving a message (ALIVE, q, pri) tests whether q is higher priority than its leader. If so, p updates the identifier and the priority value of its leader and then sends (ALIVE, q, pri) to all its immediate neighbors. We can note that sending this message to the issuer is useless.

Our algorithm is well-suited for use in mobile ad hoc networks. It is highly adaptive to arbitrary and concurrent topological changes induced by node mobility, network partitioning and merging components. For example, if the leader breaks down, then after a bounded time, each process detecting the leader departure elects itself as leader and sends its identifier with its priority. If this failure causes partitioning of the component in two other components, each component will have a unique leader. Moreover, if a process other than the leader breaks down and causes the partitioning of the component, then nothing will change in the component that contains the leader, but the other component must elect a leader. This is guaranteed by the use of the timer. The nodes of the second component will detect the departure of their leader and will react as mentioned above.

Furthermore, if we are two components A and B in the ad hoc network, each component has a single leader. We assume that the priority value of A's leader is higher than B's one. Following the mobility of nodes, the two components may merge to build a single component. After merging, messages of each component can reach the other. Thus, the nodes of the component B update their leader (lines 9-14). Finally, the new component has a single leader which has the highest priority value.

```
        Code for each process p:
        Init:
(01)        leaderp ← p;
(02)        priority_leader ← priority_p;
(03)        timeoutp ← δ;
(04)        Set timerp to timeoutp;
(05)        Start tasks 0 and task1;


        Task 0:
(06)    loop forever
(07)        if [leaderp = p] then
(08)            send (Alive, leaderp, priority_leader) to all immediate neighbors every δ time;


        Task 1:
(09)    upon reception of message (ALIVE, q, pri)   from r do
(10)        if (priorit_yleader < pri)   or [(priorit_yleader = pri) and   (q ≤    leader)] then
(11)            leaderp ← q;
(12)            priority_leader ← pri;
(13)            send (Alive, q, pri) to all immediate neighbours except r;
(14)             reset timerp to timeoutp;
(15)    upon expiration of timer do
(16)            leaderp ← p;
(17)            priority_leader ← priority_p;
(18)                timeoutp ← timeoutp + 1;
```

Fig. 1. Ω-based Leader election algorithm

Our algorithm ensures that eventually each connected component of the topology graph has exactly one leader which has the highest priority value from among all nodes within that connected component. But this algorithm is not communication-efficient. To minimize the number of exchanged messages, we propose that each process p that receives (ALIVE, q, pri) such as q is higher priority, forwards this message to a subset of its immediate neighbors using heuristics.

5   Correctness

We assume that T is the moment when the topology is static, ie, we suppose we have a finite number of topology changes. We also assume that P_{max} is the process that has the highest priority value in its component. The following theorems establish the correctness of the leader election algorithm proposed above.

Lemma 1. *There is a time after which Pmax permanently satisfies that leader$_{Pmax}$ = Pmax and sends a message (Alive, Pmax, priority$_{pmax}$) every δ time.*

Proof:

Lemma 1 means that after time t> T, process Pmax will not receive any message (Alive, i, priority$_i$) such as (priority$_i$ > priority$_{pmax}$) or ([priority$_{Pmax}$ = priority$_i$] and [i < Pmax]). Therefore, it will not execute the lines (9-14) of the algorithm, and the property leader$_{Pmax}$ = Pmax is always satisfied at every time t> T. To see that it is satisfied, we distinguish the following cases:

Case 1: There was no process i in the Pmax's component such as (priority$_i$ > priority$_{pmax}$) or ([priority$_{Pmax}$ = priority$_i$] and [i < Pmax]). In this case, lines (9-14) of Task 1 had never been executed by the process Pmax. Leader$_{Pmax}$ = Pmax is always satisfied and will always be satisfied at every time t> T.

Case 2: There was at least one process i in the component such that (priority$_i$ > priority$_{pmax}$) or ([priority$_{Pmax}$ = priority$_i$] and [i < Pmax]) which sent (Alive, i, priority$_i$) by executing line 8 of the algorithm. In this case, leader$_{Pmax}$ = k has been satisfied after execution of Line 11. Then, after a finite number of topology changes, the process i (and definitely all processes that are higher priority than Pmax) left the component or crashed. Therefore, Pmax becomes the process that has the highest priority value in its component. So, after a time t> T, line 14 will not be executed, the timer will not be restarted and it will finally expired (line 15) and leader$_{Pmax}$ = Pmax will be satisfied (line 16).

Finally, according to task 0, and as leader$_{Pmax}$ = Pmax, Pmax sends permanently (Alive, Pmax, priority$_{pmax}$) every δ time.

Lemma 2. *There is a time after which every message (Alive, p, priority$_p$) with p ≠ Pmax disappears from the system.*

Proof:

- The links are eventually timely: any sent message is delivered at most $T + \Delta$.
- Note that initially, each process begins by electing itself as leader. i.e., leaderp = p (line 1). As long as it remains leader, it sends (Alive, p, $priority_p$) (line 8). Also note that each process p on receipt of each message (Alive, q, $priority_q$), makes leaderp = q if q is higher priority than p (lines 9-12).

At a time t⊳ T, Pmax is the process that has the highest priority value in its component and it periodically sends the message (Alive, Pmax, $priority_{pmax}$) (Lemma 1). Each process p ≠ Pmax, upon receipt of (Alive, Pmax, $priority_{pmax}$), makes leaderp = Pmax (line 11) and sends (Alive, Pmax, $priority_{pmax}$) to all its neighbours as shown on line 13 of the algorithm.

After time t⊳ T, timerp is sufficiently large that the process p can receive the message (Alive, Pmax, $priority_{pmax}$) before its expiration. The timer will not be expired as Pmax periodically sends the message (Alive, Pmax, $priority_{pmax}$), and p will never execute the line 18 of the algorithm (the message (Alive, p, $priority_p$) will never be sent).

Finally, every message (Alive, p, $priority_p$) with p ≠ Pmax was disappeared from the system.

Theorem. *There is a time after which each process p in the same component have leaderₚₘₐₓ = Pmax, where Pmax is the process that has the highest priority value in that component.*

$leader_{Pmax} = Pmax$

Proof:

Lemma 1 shows that there is a moment after which the process Pmax maintains leaderₚₘₐₓ = Pmax (ie it is the leader of its component) and periodically sends the message (Alive, Pmax, $priority_{pmax}$) to notify the other processes in its component that it is the leader. Lemma 2 shows that no other message will circulate into the component. So the only message that is circulating is the message (Alive, Pmax, $priority_{pmax}$) and all processes of the component have Pmax as a leader.

So, the algorithm ensures that:

For each component C in ad hoc network, there is a correct process ℓ in C and a moment after which, for every process p in C, leaderₚ = ℓ.

6   Conclusion

In this paper, we have proposed a leader election algorithm that is well-suited for use in mobile ad hoc networks in the sense that it can tolerate arbitrary and concurrent topological changes induced by node mobility, network partitioning and merging components. We have also proved that our algorithm ensures that eventually each connected component of the topology graph has exactly one leader which has the highest priority value from among the nodes in that component.

As mentioned above, this proposed algorithm is not communication-efficient. We are currently working on how we can modify this algorithm to make it communication-efficient without any compromise with impulsive behaviors of ad hoc networks.

The algorithm presented in this paper assumes that links are Fair lossy. It would be useful to modify the algorithm to deal with lossy links.

Another area to investigate could be the application of the proposed leader election algorithm in other problems in MANETS such as group communication and data aggregation problems.

References

1. Chettibi, S., Chikhi, S.: Adaptivity condition as the extended Reinforcement Learning for MANETs. Journal of Networking Technology, 122–129 (2011)
2. Sharma, R.K., Sharma, P.: Data Divergence with Consistency Based Replication in MANETs. Journal of Networking Technology, 157–164 (2010)
3. Melit, L., Badache, N.: An Energy Efficient Leader Election Algorithm for Mobile Ad Hoc Networks. In: Proceeding of the 10th International Symposium on Programming and Systems, pp. 54–59 (2011)
4. Vasudevan, S., Kurose, J., Towsley, D.: Design and Analysis of a Leader Election Algorithm for Mobile Ad Hoc Networks. In: Proceedings of the 12th IEEE International Conference on Network Protocols, pp. 350–360 (2004)
5. Chandra, T.D., Hadzilacos, V., Toueg, S.: The Weakest Failure Detector for Solving Consensus. Journal of the ACM 43(4), 685–722 (1996)
6. Chandra, T.D., Toueg, S.: Unreliable failure detectors for reliable distributed systems. Journal of ACM, 225–267 (1996)
7. Hatzis, K.-P., Pentaris, G.-P., Spirakis, P.-G., Tampakas, V.-T., Tan, R.B.: Fundamental control algorithms in mobile networks. In: Proceeding of the 11th Annual ACM Symposium on Parallel Algorithms and Architectures, pp. 251–260 (1999)
8. Malpani, N., Welch, J., Vaidya, N.: Leader election Algorithms for Mobile Ad Hoc Networks. In: Proceedings of 4th International Workshop on Discrete Algorithms and Methods for Mobile Computing and Communications, pp. 93–103 (2000)
9. Velayutham, A., Chaudhuri, S.: Analysis of a leader election algorithm for mobile ad hoc networks. Technical report. Iowa State University (2003)
10. Derhab, A., Badache, N.: A self-stabilizing leader election algorithm in highly dynamic ad hoc mobile networks. IEEE Transactions on Parallel and Distributed Systems 19(7), 926–939 (2008)
11. Park, V.D., Corson, M.S.: A highly adaptive distributed routing algorithm for mobile wireless networks. In: 16th IEEE INFOCOM, pp. 1405–1413 (1997)
12. Dijkstra, E.W., Scholten, C.S.: Termination detection for diffusing computations. Information Processing Letters, 1–4 (1980)
13. Masum, S.M., Ali, A.A., Bhuiyan, M.T.I.: Asynchronous leader election in mobile ad hoc networks. In: Proceedings of the 20th International Conference on Advanced Information Networking and Applications, pp. 827–831 (2006)

Cartography Gathering Driven by the OLSR Protocol

Mohamed Belhassen and Abdelfettah Belghith

HANA Research Group, University of Manouba, Tunisia
mohamed.belhassen@hanalab.org, abdelfattah.belghith@ensi.rnu.tn
http://www.hanalab.org

Abstract. Nowadays, the location awareness becomes a ubiquitous requirement for several computing applications. The utilization of such knowledge in mobile ad hoc networks is primarily limited by the scarcity of their resources. In this paper, we propose two cartography gathering schemes (OLSR-SCGS and OLSR-ACGS) that make use of the seminal OLSR signaling in order to endue nodes participating in the MANET with location awareness. The first proposed scheme (OLSR-SCGS) is inspired from the operation of OLSR during the process of routing table calculation. The simplicity of this scheme makes it subject to several limitations that we avoid in the second scheme (OLSR-ACGS). In this latter scheme, the nodes become able to identify the freshest position among the available ones thanks to a dedicated time stamping approach. Conducted simulations show the effectiveness of the two proposed approaches. Nevertheless, simulations portray the superiority of the second proposed scheme (OLSR-ACGS) regarding the first one (OLSR-SCGS) when the network dynamics increases. Through simulations, we show that the validity of the collected cartography is impacted by several factors such as the tolerated distance parameter, the frequencies of OLSR control messages and the network extent.

Keywords: OLSR, Cartography Gathering, MANET, Location Awareness.

1   Introduction

In recent years, the ubiquitousness of mobile equipments endued with localization capabilities has revolutionized both our everyday lives and the functioning of the underlying networks. In [1] authors study the impact of location-awareness on the social coordination performed between users when one of them needs to meet up with the other. Thanks to location awareness, the users make more informed decisions before initiating or canceling a rendezvous. Indeed, these techniques make the user more conscious about the virtual co-presence of their partners. Location-based advertising represent another potential application where the customer is solicited to visit a nearby shop [2]. The localization techniques impact not only our lives but also the functioning of the underlying networks. For

R. Benlamri (Ed.): NDT 2012, Part I, CCIS 293, pp. 491–505, 2012.

instance, these techniques could be used to enhance the security of wireless networks [2]. In such case, a malicious terminal could be prevented from accessing the local network if it is detected to be outside the expected network area. Another application of the location awareness consists in enhancing the efficiency of the routing function in the context of mobile ad hoc networks (MANETs). In fact, in these networks, the routing presents a difficult task. On the one hand, the ceaselessly evolving topology requires frequent updates of the link state information. On the other hand, the routing function has to keep its overhead as low as possible in order to save the valuable network resources. Therefore, the nodes have to utilize judiciously any available information without increasing the routing overhead. Recently, the researchers propose several positions based routing approaches where the routing decision is driven by the location information instead of link state ones. These schemes show a great robustness towards the increase of the network dynamics. Indeed, in [4], the conducted simulations show that location based routing is likely to be more suitable for vehicular ad-hoc networks than topology based mechanisms. In some protocols, such as [5], it is sufficient to know the position of the destination as well as those of the neighbors to make appropriate routing decision. When the greedy forwarding fails in finding a neighbor closer than it to the destination, the right hand rule is invoked in order to avoid the local maximum. In [6], the network cartography is utilized to self regulate the routing period of DSDV protocol. The ultimate goal of this protocol consists in reducing the routing overhead while keeping a good routing pertinence. Although its success in finding a tradeoff between these antagonistic goals, its deployment in real mobile ad hoc networks requires an adequate synchronization framework. This latter is necessary in order to communicate the number of current routing period, its time origin and its duration to nodes newly joining the MANET. At the contrary of this latter protocol, the ASARP [7] protocol operates asynchronously; the thing that makes it more suitable for practical use. The key concept of ASARP consists in adjusting the routing period size of each node according its own local dynamics. That way, the routing overhead is proportional to the node speed. Furthermore, during the routing process, the position awareness is utilized to enhance the stability of selected routes. For instance, in P-OLSR [8], the author proposes a simple neighbor prediction scheme that ensures the reachability of selected gateways and MPRs (Multi-Point Relays). According the P-OLSR protocol, each node in the network becomes able to assess, at any time, if a given neighbor is reachable or not. This is done thanks to a joint knowledge of the positions of its neighbors, their velocities and their transmission ranges. Therefore, once a neighbor is assessed to be out of range, it is prevented from being used as MPR or a gateway. In our previously proposed CE-OLSR protocol [9], we make use of the network cartography in order to enhance the efficiency of the routing function. In one hand, CE-OLSR increases the accuracy of the built network topology towards the reality. Indeed, in the other hand, the stability of selected routes is sustained thanks to a dedicated stable routing scheme. In [3]the authors propose to enhance the reliability of the decision of greedy routing by taking into account the velocity and the remaining power of forwarding nodes. Actually, the high speed of nodes as well as their low remained battery powers are seen as main causes of packet loss. Further location based schemes could be found in the literature such as [10,11,12], etc.

Although the usefulness of the network cartography, its utilization in MANETs still limited by the scarcity of their resources. Therefore, in this paper, we propose two schemes which utilize the seminal OLSR signaling in order to gather the locations of the nodes. In our previous works [9,13] our attention is solely focused on the enhancement of the routing function by utilizing the network cartography in several ways. However, a deep evaluation of the proposed cartography gathering schemes is needed to assess the adequation of these schemes when applied in various application domains.

The remainder of the paper is organized as follow. The section 2 is devoted to detail the functioning of the two proposed cartography gathering schemes. In section 3, we perform a deep evaluation of the proposed schemes. Finally, in section 4, we conclude the paper.

2   Network Cartography Gathering Using OLSR

2.1   Embedding the Cartographic Information into OLSR Control Messages

As we previously discussed, the network cartography is useful in several ways. For that reason, an efficient cartography gathering scheme is necessary to bring such knowledge to every node in the network. The simplest and obvious way to enable this feature consists in broadcasting periodically the node position in the entire network using new dedicated control messages. However, in the context of mobile ad hoc networks, resources are limited and need to be saved. In fact, each additional message will consume further valuable network resources; the thing that reduces the available bandwidth for data packets. Thence, we propose to make use of the seminal routing control messages (HELLO and TC) of OLSR in order to disseminate the cartographic information. These messages are used primarily, in OLSR, to discover the network topology. The HELLO messages are used to track the near neighborhood topological changes; while TC messages broadcast a covering sub-topology in the entire network. Both Hello and TC messages are patched in order to include the cartographic information. In the case of HELLO messages, we include the position of the sender as well as the position of neighboring nodes. That way, each node obtains the cartographic information of its 2-hop neighborhood by the means of HELLO messages. For distant nodes, the cartographic information is disseminated through TC messages. In fact, each MPR node has to include at least the positions of its MPR selectors in order to guarantee a full view about the network cartography

2.2   OLSR-SCGS: OLSR Simple Cartography Gathering Scheme

At the reception of a control message, the node has to extract the joined cartographic information and stores them in the seminal OLSR repositories. For that purpose, we extend the OLSR repositories structures (1-hop Neighbor Tuple, 2-hop Neighbor Tuple and Topology Tuple) by adding, for each of them, two new attributes (*x_coordinate* and *y_coordinate*) that store the coordinates of the corresponding node. When a given node receives a HELLO message, the position of the sender is stored in the 1-hop Neighbor Set; while the position of the published neighbors is held in the 2-hop Neighbor Set. If the corresponding link tuple already exists, it is updated with the new cartographic information. Similarly, the cartographic information contained in the TC messages are extracted then stored in the *Topology Set*. If the node receives a TC from a MPR with the same Advertized Sequence Number (Sequence Number of the TC), simply, it updates the positions of the corresponding published nodes. Up to now, what we have done consists in disseminating the cartographic information in the entire ad hoc network using the same OLSR signaling mechanism in terms of number of generated messages. For simplicity, we have chosen to store the collected cartographic information inside the basic OLSR repositories. These repositories (*1-hop Neighbor Set*, *2-hop Neighbor Set* and *Topology Set*) are primarily designed to store link state information about the network connectivity. Although the existence of some redundancy between the three sets, it does not affect the overall functioning of OLSR. In fact, OLSR prioritizes the use of the information extracted from HELLO messages regarding that extracted from TC messages. This is can be argued by the fact that this information is more likely to be fresher than that contained in the Topology Set. Recall that the periodicity of TC messages is much greater than that of HELLO ones. The redundancy is much more emphasized when considering the cartographic information. Indeed, the redundancy is not only between the 3 aforementioned sets but also inside the sets themselves (*2-hop Neighbor Set* and the *Topology Set*). For instance, a 2-hop neighbor may be published by more than one 1-hop neighbor. Moreover, a given node in the network is published by all its MPR nodes. In such a case, we cannot discriminate the freshest position of a given node among the available ones. In order to face this problem, we need to fix a rule permitting to decide which cartographic information we have to retain for each node in the network. In the mind to remain consistent with the seminal OLSR operation, we willingly decide to use the same scheme used by OLSR when constructing the routing table. That way, the cartographic information of a given destination (node) is extracted from the tuple (1-hop Neighbor Tuple, 2-hop Neighbor Tuple or Topology Tuple) corresponding to the link (last one in the path) used to reach this destination. In other words, the position of a given 1-hop neighbor (respectively 2-hop neighbor) will be extracted from the *1-hop Neighbor Set* (respectively *2-hop Neighbor Set*). Furthermore, the positions of farther nodes will be extracted from the *Topology Set*. This first proposed scheme for cartography gathering is called as the OLSR Simple Cartography Gathering Scheme (OLSR-SCGS).

2.3 OLSR-ACGS: OLSR Advanced Cartography Gathering Scheme

Although being simple and respecting the functioning of OLSR, the OLSR-SCGS does not guarantee the identification of the most recent cartographic information of a given node over the collected ones. For instance, in Fig. 1, since the nodes B and C are direct neighbors of the node A (at time=t1), this latter uses the corresponding positions that are contained in the 1-hop Neighbor Set. When the node C leaves the range of the node A (at time=t2), this latter continue using an old cartographic information of the node C that is known from the 1-hop Neighbor Set (until the expiration of the corresponding tuple) even though the new position (of the node C) is received from the node B. Fig. 2 portrays another case where the OLSR-SCGS scheme fails in identifying the appropriate cartographic information. In this figure, the node D is initially (time=t1) a 2-Hop neighbor of A which is reachable through both B and C. In such case, the node A may use whether the position known trough B or that known from C. Due to its mobility, the node D leaves the range of the node C (time=t2). Since the link sate information collected by the node A remain valid for a given period (until the expiration of this 2-hop Neighbor tuple), this node may continue using the cartographic information (of the node D) sent by the node C. It is obvious that the retained position is older than that announced by B given that this latter receives the subsequent update through the HELLO sent by the node D. For destination farther than 2 hops, the positions are extracted from the Topology Set. Since the position of each node in the network is announced by all its MPR nodes, it is clear that the OLSR-SCGS scheme is unable to guarantee the retaining of the most accurate position from the known ones. Indeed, in this scheme, the retained position of a given destination node is extracted from the topology tuple corresponding to the link used to reach it.

The main reason affecting the performance of the OLSR-SCGS scheme consists in the inability to discriminate the freshest cartographic information from the collected ones for each node in the network. Wherefore, we need to conceive a more sophisticated scheme which overcomes this limitation of the OLSR-SCGS scheme. In the second proposed cartography gathering scheme, that we name OLSR Advanced Cartography Gathering Scheme (OLSR-ACGS), each cartographic information is timestamped by the originator node using the associated HELLO Sequence Number (which is incremented with each generated HELLO message). That way, the freshness assessment between different cartographic information about a given node becomes possible whatever the source from which it is extracted. The OLSR-ACGS works as the following. When receiving a HELLO message, the node has to extract the corresponding sequence number. This latter is then stored in the corresponding 1-Hop Neighbor Tuple. After that, Before publishing a link, whatever in a HELLO or TC message, the node joins to it (the link) the cartographic information (of the neighbor) and the associated HELLO sequence number (timestamping it). At the reception of the control message (TC or HELLO), the node stores the cartographic information of each published link and its associated HELLO sequence number in the corresponding tuple (2-hop Neighbor Tuple or Topology Tuple). Therefore, the OLSR repositories (1-Hop Neighbor Set, 2-Hop Neighbor Set and Topology Set) tuples have to be extended by a new field (HELLO Sequence Number) that will retain the sequence number of the HELLO message from which the cartographic information is extracted. According the functioning of OLSR, a HELLO message contains the cartographic information of each known neighbor whatever it is symmetric or not. Being the fact that OLSR ignores the link information about asymmetric 2-Hop Neighbors, we need to retain the corresponding cartographic information in a new dedicated structure that we name *Asymmetric 2-Hop Neighbor Set*. Considering such information will speed up the responsiveness toward cartographical changes of incoming 2-hop neighbors.

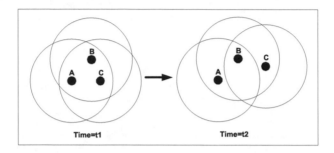

Fig. 1. A situation where the OLSR-SCGS fail to identify the freshest position of the node C

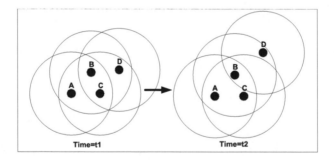

Fig. 2. A situation where the OLSR-SCGS fail to identify the freshest position of the node D

In OLSR-ACGS scheme, when the node need to get the current collected cartography, it has to run through all the OLSR repositories (1-Hop Neighbor Set, 2-Hop Neighbor Set and Topology Set) in addition to the Asymmetric 2-Hop Neighbors Set while keeping, for each node, the cartographic information having the greatest sequence number. That way, we ensure that the node (making the calculation) retains, for each node in the network, the newest known cartographic information.

3   Comparison of OLSR-SCGS and OLSR-ACGS

3.1   Validity of the Cartography

In this work, we conceived 2 schemes permitting the gathering of the network cartography. The ultimate goal of these two schemes consists in enduing the nodes participating in the MANET by awareness about the current positions of the different nodes in the network. The ceaseless motion of the nodes makes it difficult to retain up-to-date information about the network cartography. In fact, the mobility makes the collected cartography stale rapidly. Thence, each application using the network cartography in a mobile network has to deal with a certain amount of inaccuracy of the collected cartography. That is, it must tolerate some inaccuracy with the actual positions of the nodes. We name the upper bound of this tolerated inaccuracy the Tolerance Distance. Thence, the collected cartographic information about a node is said to be valid if the distance separating it from the real position is less or equal to the Tolerance Distance parameter. Note that the real position of a given node is not known by other nodes in the network. However, we allow the statistic collector node to access to the real positions retained by the simulator in order to assess the validity of its collected cartography towards the reality.

The metric called the *Validity of the Cartography* of a given node is the percentage of nodes participating in the MANET for which the current node (making the calculation) has valid cartographic information (i.e. the distance between the collected position and the actual position is less or equal to the Tolerance Distance).

3.2   Simulation Set Up

The two proposed schemes are implemented using the OMNET++ simulator (version 4.1). In the conducted simulations, we consider the following simulation parameters. The simulated network covers an area of 1000 m by 1000 m. It contains 100 mobile nodes which are randomly positioned. Among these nodes, 2 of them are willingly fixed (one on the middle of the network and the other at the corner of the network) in order to be used as statistic collectors. The remaining 98 mobile nodes follow the Random Way Point mobility model (Update Interval= 0.001 s, Wait Time=0 s) with constant speed. The transmission range is fixed to 250 m. The network capacity is set to 11 Mbps. The TC Redundancy parameter is set to 0. That is, MPRs nodes publish, in their generated TC messages, only the links with their MPR selectors. The OLSR jitter is randomly chosen between 0 s and 0.5 s. Each simulation is run for a simulation time equal to 300 s. The first period (100 s) corresponding to the transient regime is ignored. Within the remaining simulation time (200 s) we take an observation point each 0.5 s. The calculation of the validity of the cartography metric is performed at each observation point for every one of the two statistic collector nodes. The subsequent curves represent the average over these observation points.

3.3   Simulation Results

As we previously stated, each application using the network cartography has to tolerate some inaccuracy of the collected nodes positions (bounded by the Tolerance Distance parameter). This obligation comes from both the ceaseless network dynamics and the unavoidable waiting time required before receiving subsequent positions updates. That is why we should perform a deep study of the different parameters that impact the validity of the network cartography.

In the first simulation set, we study the effect of the Tolerance Distance parameter on the validity of the collected cartography in both OLSR-SCGS and OLSR-ACGS schemes for different nodes speeds. The following simulations results are related to the statistics collector node placed at the corner of the network. Fig. 3 and Fig. 4 portray the validity of the cartography of OLSR-SCGS and OLSR-ACGS schemes respectively when the TC period is set to 8 s and the HELLO one is set to 2 s. These two figures show the superiority of the OLSR-ACGS compared to OLSR-SCGS for different nodes speeds. For instance, for a high speed of 20 m/s, the validity of the cartography of the OLSR-ACGS scheme is greater than 60% and that of OLSR-SCGS is less than 17%. For both these two schemes, the more the Tolerance Distance is greater, the more the validity of the cartography metric is well. However, the increase of the Tolerance Distance affects the accuracy of the perceived cartography against the actual network state. For that reason, this parameter should be judiciously tuned according the network dynamics. Indeed, for a low speed of 2 m/s, a Tolerance Distance equal to 10 m is sufficient to obtain a high validity of the cartography that exceeds 93%. For a higher nodes speed of 5 m/s, the statistics collector node has to tolerate 25 m of inaccuracy in order to keep a good value of the validity of the cartography (89%). When the nodes speed increases greater than 10 m/s, the statistics collector node should tolerate 50 m of inaccuracy in order to keep satisfactory results in terms of cartography validity.

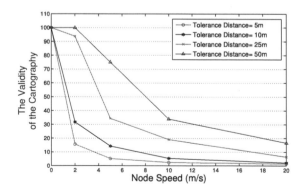

Fig. 3. The validity of the cartography in OLSR-SCGS for different values of Tolerance Distance parameter

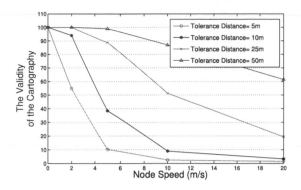

Fig. 4. The validity of the cartography in OLSR-ACGS for different values of Tolerance Distance parameter

Now we turn to assess the effect of the OLSR control messages (TC and HELLO) periodicities on the validity of the collected network cartography. Fig. 5, Fig. 6 and Fig. 7 show the validity of the network cartography collected by the statistics collector node placed at the network corner for a Tolerance Distance equal to 50 m and different periodicities of TC (TC= 5 s, 8 s and 15 s) and HELLO (HELLO= 2 s, 3 s) messages. These figures show that the OLSR-ACGS substantially outperforms the OLSR-SCGS for the different configurations of TC and HELLO messages. In addition, we note that both TC and HELLO periodicities have noticeable effect on the validity of the network cartography. Indeed, the more the HELLO (respectively the TC) period is low the more the validity of the cartography is higher. The best performance is obtained for TC equal to 5 s and Hello equal to 2 s. In such a case, the validity of the cartography is around 98% for a speed of 10 m/s. For a very high speed of 20 m/s, the validity of the network cartography drops to approximately 72%. This fall may be explained by the fact that for distant nodes, the time required to receive the new positions updates is greater than that required to exceed the

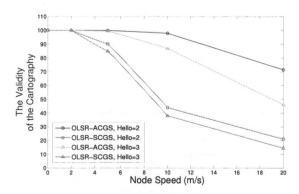

Fig. 5. The validity of the cartography for different HELLO periodicities as a function of nodes speeds (statistics collector node at the network corner): TC=5 s

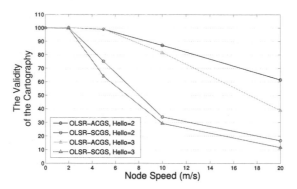

Fig. 6. The validity of the cartography for different HELLO periodicities as a function of nodes speeds (statistics collector node at the network corner): TC=8 s

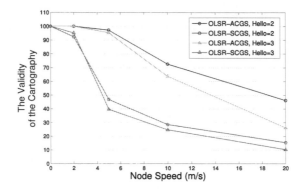

Fig. 7. The validity of the cartography for different HELLO periodicities as a function of nodes speeds (statistics collector node at the network corner): TC=15 s

tolerated distance. In fact, the forwarding of TC messages is delayed at each hop by a random waiting time ($OLSR_{jitter} \in [0, 0.5]s$); Recall that these curves correspond to the statistics collector node placed at the corner of the network. Although the usefulness of this jitter in the functioning of OLSR, it has a non avoidable negative impact on the collected cartography.

For Completeness purpose, we need to assess the performance of these two schemes for a statistics collector node placed at the center of the network (Fig. 8, Fig. 9 and Fig. 10). We note that for a central node, the performance of the two schemes is increased significantly for different configurations while keeping the superiority of OLSR-ACGS compared to OLSR-SCGS. This behavior is explained by the fact that for a central node, the majority of the network nodes are within its 2-hop neighborhood. That way, their positions updates are received more frequently through the HELLO messages. This is further confirmed by the fact that the variation of the TC periodicity has a little effect on the performance

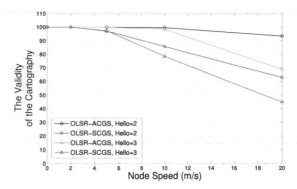

Fig. 8. The validity of the cartography for different HELLO periodicities as a function of nodes speeds (statistics collector node at the center of the network): TC=5 s

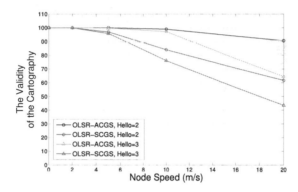

Fig. 9. The validity of the cartography for different HELLO periodicities as a function of nodes speeds (statistics collector node at the center of the network): TC=8 s

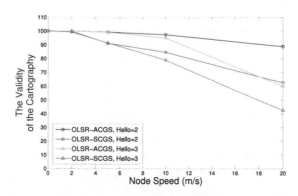

Fig. 10. The validity of the cartography for different HELLO periodicities as a function of nodes speeds (statistics collector node at the center of the network): TC=15 s

of the two schemes. For instance, for a high speed of 20 m/s and HELLO= 2 s, the performance of OLSR-ACGS scheme is surrounding the 90% for different values of TC periodicities (TC= 5 s, 8 s, 15 s). Similarly, the performance of OLSR-SCGS is approximately equal to 62% for different configurations of TC.

The previous simulations show that the performance of the two schemes (OLSR-SCGS and OLSR-ACGS) differs according to the position of the statistics collector node regarding the remaining nodes participating in the MANET. This returns to the fact that the positions of the near neighborhood ($\leq$ 2 hops) are obtained from the HELLO messages that are more frequent than TC ones (used to discover the position of farther nodes). In addition, at each hop, the forwarding of the OLSR control messages is delayed randomly ($OLSR_{jitter} \in [0, 0.5]s$) in order to decrease the probability of collisions. In the subsequent simulations set, we study the impact of the farness from the statistics collector node on the validity of the cartography. For that purpose, we divided, virtually, the network area into different regions as seen in Fig. 11. Thereafter, the validity of the cartography is computed for each of these regions separately for the different nodes speeds (Fig. 12, Fig. 13 and Fig. 14) while setting the Tolerance Distance parameter to 50 m, TC period to 5 s and HELLO period to 2 s. For a low speed of 2 m/s the two conceived schemes work impeccably. Indeed, the validity of the cartography reaches 100% for all regions. For a higher speed of 5 m/s (Fig. 12),

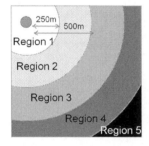

Fig. 11. Division of the network into different regions according the farness from the statistics colletor node

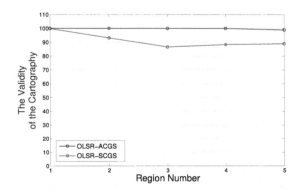

Fig. 12. The cartography validity as a function of region number: Speed= 5m/s

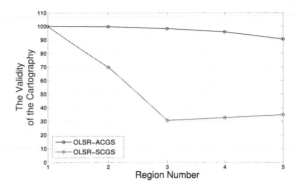

Fig. 13. The cartography validity as a function of region number: Speed= 10m/s

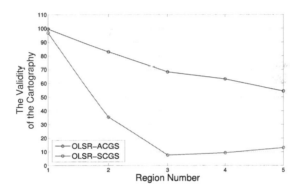

Fig. 14. The cartography validity as a function of region number: Speed=20 m/s

the OLSR-SCGS performance is affected for regions farther than 250 m; while the OLSR-ACGS keeps a high performance of 100% for almost all regions. For a further higher speed of 10 m/s (see Fig. 13), the accuracy of the cartography collected using OLSR-SCGS drops severely for distant regions (around 30% for regions farther than 500 m) while that of OLSR-ACGS maintains a perfect accuracy for the three first regions then it drops slightly for farther regions. For a high speed of 20 m/s, the performance of both schemes is affected as one move away from the statistics collector node. Even though, the OLSR-ACGS keeps its superiority regarding OLSR-SCGS. Fig. 13 and Fig. 14 highlight clearly the fish eye property of OLSR based protocols. Indeed, the collected cartography remains within the tolerated distance for all nodes belonging to the 1st region. Then, as long as the nodes move away as much as the validity of the collected cartography drops. The slight increase of the validity of the cartography obtained through the OLSR-SCGS for distant nodes (region 4 and 5) may be explained by the fact that for nodes belonging to these regions the number of MPRs is less than that of nodes belonging to region 3 (since they are at the network border). That way, the probability of selecting a topology tuple containing the freshest position gets higher.

3.4   Conclusion

In this paper, we proposed two schemes permitting the gathering of the network cartography (OLSR-SCGS and OLSR-ACGS). These two schemes utilize the seminal control messages (HELLO and TC) of OLSR in order to disseminate the nodes positions in the whole network. Although being suitable for low mobility MANETs, the performance of the first proposed scheme (OLSR-SCGS) is severely affected by the increase of the nodes mobility. In fact, this simple cartography gathering scheme is unable to identify the freshest position (of a given node) among the collected ones. In order to face this problem, in the second scheme (OLSR-ACGS), we proposed to timestamp the cartographic information using the sequence number of the associated HELLO. That way, each node in the network becomes able to identify the freshest known position of a given node. Conducted simulations show that OLSR-ACGS scheme is more suitable than OLSR-SCGS to MANETs with high dynamics. In addition, the performance of these two schemes is highly linked to the periodicity of OLSR control messages and the farness of the nodes. Indeed, the performance of the two schemes is better for short periodicity of TC and Hello messages. Moreover, the more the nodes are far the more the validity of the collected cartography decreases.

References

1. Dearman, D., Hawkey, K., Inkpen, K.M.: Rendezvousing With Location Aware Devices: Enhancing Social Coordination. Interact. Comput. 17, 542–566 (2005)
2. Kupper, A.: Location-Based Services: Fundamentals and Operation. Wiley, New York (2005)
3. Abdoos, M., Faez, K., Sabaei, M.: Position Based Routing Protocol With More Reliability. In: Mobile Ad Hoc Network, First Asian Himalayas International Conference on Internet, AH-ICI 2009, November 3-5, pp. 1–4 (2009)
4. Uler, H.F., Hartenstein, H., Mauve, M., Asemann, M.K., Vollmer, D.: Location-Based Routing for Vehicular Ad-Hoc Networks (2002)
5. Karp, B., Kung, H.T.: GPSR: Greedy Perimeter Stateless Routing for Wireless Networks. In: Proceedings of ACM/IEEE International Conference on Mobile Computing and Networking, MobiCom 2000 (August 2000)
6. Belghith, A., Abid, M.A.: Dynamically Self Adjustable Proactive Routing Protocols for Mobile Ad Hoc Networks. In: The 34th IEEE Conference on Local Computer Networks, LCN 2009, Zürich, Switzerland, October 20-23 (2009)
7. Abid, M.A., Belghith, A.: Asynchronous Locally Self Adjusted Routing Protocol for Mobile Multi hop Ad Hoc Networks. In: The 8th ACS/IEEE International Conference ACS/IEEE AICCSA 2010, Hammamet, Tunisia, May 16-19 (2010)
8. Sharma, S.: P-OLSR: Position-Based Optimized Link State Routing for Mobile Ad Hoc Networks. In: IEEE 34th Conference on Local Computer Networks (LCN 2009), Zurich, Switzerland (2009)
9. Belhassen, M., Belghith, A., Abid, M.A.: Performance Evaluation of a Cartography Enhanced OLSR for Mobile Multi-Hop Ad Hoc Networks. In: The 7th IEEE Conference on Wireless Advanced (WiAD 2011), London, UK, June 20-22 (2011)
10. Chawla, M., Goel, N., Kalaichelvan, K., Nayak, A., Stojmenovic, I.: Beaconless Position-Based Routing With Guaranteed Delivery for Wireless Ad Hoc and Sensor Networks. Acta Autom. Sin. 32(6), 847–855 (2006)

11. Zaruba, G.V., Chaluvadi, V.K., Suleman, A.M.: LABAR: Location Area Based Ad Hoc Routing for GPS-Scarce Wide-Area Ad Hoc Networks. In: Proc. of the First IEEE International Conference on Pervasive Computing and Communications (PerCom 2003), March 23-26, pp. 509–513 (2003)
12. Li, X.Y., Moaveninejad, K., Song, W.Z.: Robust Position-Based Routing for Wireless Ad Hoc Networks. Ad Hoc Networks 3(5), 546–559 (2005)
13. Belghith, A., Belhassen, M.: CE-OLSR: a Cartography and Stability Enhanced OLSR for Dynamic MANETs. Transactions on Internet and Information Systems, KSII 6(1), 290–306 (2012)

Distributed Self-organized Trust Management for Mobile Ad Hoc Networks

Mehran Misaghi[1], Eduardo da Silva[2,3], and Luiz Carlos P. Albini[3]

[1] MEP – Research Department – Educational Society of Santa Catarina
[2] Department of Informatics – Catarinense Federal Institute – Araquari
[3] NR2 – Department of Informatics – Federal University of Paraná
mehran@sociesc.org.br, {eduardos,albini}@inf.ufpr.br

Abstract. Trust is a concept from the Social Sciences and can be defined as how much a node is willing to take the risk of trusting another one. The correct evaluation of the trust is crucial for several security mechanisms for Mobile Ad Hoc Networks (MANETs). However, the implementation of an effective trust evaluation scheme is very difficult in such networks, due to their dynamic characteristics. This work presents a trust evaluation scheme for MANETs based on a self-organized virtual trust network. To estimate the trustworthiness of other nodes, nodes form trust chains based on behavior evidences maintained within the trust network. Nodes periodically exchange their trust networks with the neighbors, providing an efficient method to disseminate trust information across the network. The scheme is fully distributed and self-organized, not requiring any trusted third party. Simulation results show that the scheme is very efficient on gathering evidences to build the trust networks. It also shows that the scheme has a very small communication and memory overhead. Besides, it is the first trust evaluation scheme evaluated under bad mouthing and newcomers attacks and it maintains its effectiveness in such scenarios.

Keywords: Trust Management. Security. Self-organization. MANETs.

1 Introduction

Though plenty of research has been done in the recent years aiming to make Mobile Ad Hoc Networks (MANETs) more secure, security continues being one of the most challenging issues for such networks [31]. MANETs are highly vulnerable to security threats due to wireless communication and dynamic topology. The wireless communication channel allows adversaries to easily perform attacks, while the dynamic topology requires that all security mechanisms must be distributed. All these characteristics difficult the implementation of security applications for MANETs [33].

Cryptography is the main technique used to ensure data communication security. However, cryptography does not provide information about the reliability of the nodes [18]. Besides, many cryptographic mechanisms, such as key management [8, 19], rely on some degree of pre-established trust between nodes. However, trust in any kind of open networks is very difficult to be valued and have received a lot of attention from the security community [4].

R. Benlamri (Ed.): NDT 2012, Part I, CCIS 293, pp. 506–518, 2012.

Trust is a concept from the social sciences [17] and can be defined as the trustworthiness of a *trustor*, or how much it is willing to take the risk of trust, in a *trustee* [7]. In this context, trust management can be defined as a mechanism to allow nodes, without any previous interactions, to establish connections with a pre-defined level of trust among themselves [3]. Examples of using trust management include support in decisions as intrusion detection [1], authentication [12], access control [20], and isolation of misbehaving nodes for effective routing [21].

In MANETs, trust can be used in routing strategies, distributed storage, location management, and key management or establishment. The use of trust evaluation techniques to mitigate security threats is very relevant in open networks [2]. Several trust evaluation schemes have been proposed to MANETs in order to support and maintain trust evidences of nodes. In [15], it is proposed the Ant-Based Evidence Distribution (ABED), based on the swarm intelligence, which is claimed to be highly distributed and adaptive to nodes mobility. In ABED, nodes interact with each other through agents ("ants"), which are able to identify an optimal path to accumulate trust evidence. However, such a scheme was not evaluated under any type of attack.

In [28], a trust evidence evaluation scheme is proposed, modeled as a path problem in a direct graph. This scheme considers a source node as a trusted entity to support the infrastructure, violating the decentralized characteristics of MANETs. Further, trust and confidence values are binary represented rather than continuous-valued.

A concept of self-organizing trust-based Physical-Logical Domains for grouping nodes and support for distributed control in the network is presented in [30]. It introduces a security architecture based on trust-domain which uses trust to establish keys between nodes and to establish secure distributed control in MANETs. Nodes use trust information to form groups and to establish pair-wise key in the groups. Even though authors describe trust formalization and trust evaluation, the scheme was not evaluated under attacks, and it is suitable just for establishing group keys.

A distributed reputation evaluation which claims to prevent malicious nodes from entering the trusted community was proposed in [5]. However, no specific attack model was addressed. In [34], a trust calculation algorithm was proposed, to evaluate trust based on a trust certificate graph. However, the use of trust certificates implies in digital signatures verification within a trusted node or entity.

Trust evaluation schemes have also been used to support other applications in MANETs, such as authentication and packet routing. In [9], for example, it is proposed a trust evaluation scheme to support secure authentication for MANETs. It assumes that nodes form groups with primary and backup certificate authority servers inside. Trust values of nodes are augmented from their previous trust values using a Markov chain trust model. Then, the node with the highest trust value in the group is selected as the certificate authority server, and the node with the second highest trust value is selected as the backup server. However, the scheme creates a centralized certificate authority, which is not desirable in MANETs.

In [14], is presented SORI, which uses cooperation incentive based on reputation, stimulating packet forwarding and disciplining selfish nodes through punishments. In SORI, the reputation of a node is calculated using objective metrics, such as effectiveness in packet forwarding. However, it considers that the reputation of a node is only useful to physical neighbors of such node. This characteristic makes the implementation of SORI to support other applications very difficult. Other schemes that use reputation and trust estimation to enforce packet routing can be found in the literature [6, 10, 22]. However, none of them were evaluated under attacks and are limited only to support routing strategies.

In [29] is presented a trust model which claims to be resistant to slander attacks, a variance of the bad mouthing ones. Such a scheme provides nodes with a mechanism to build a trust relationship with their neighbors. However, the scheme just allow the nodes to evaluate the trustworthiness of direct neighbor. Thus, the solution is not suitable for applications that require trust information of nodes out of the radio range. In [25] is presented a trust evaluation scheme which considers malicious attacks. However, such a scheme is designed just to secure routing operations and detect malicious nodes acting in the routing strategies.

Even though trust evaluation schemes are essential for several security services, the most of schemes for MANETs either did not consider or were evaluated under mis-behavior attacks. Besides, the use of a non-secure trust evaluation scheme can harm the entire secure solution of the system. Further, the few schemes that considers the presence of malicious nodes are limited to one network operation, such as routing.

This work presents a trust evaluation scheme for MANETs to support any application in a dynamic and autonomic way, and resistant to misbehavior attacks. In the proposed scheme, each node creates in a self-organized way a virtual layer to support and provide trust information. The virtual layer, called trust network, contains all trust information that a node has about other nodes. Such information, or evidences, are gathered via direct interaction or via recommendation, considering the system security policies. The trustworthiness of a node is always locally computed, without any message exchange, based on the trust network of the node.

The proposed scheme was evaluated in scenarios under two kinds of attacks: bad mouthing and newcomer (or Sybil) attacks. Bad mouthing attacks consist of malicious nodes providing dishonest trust evidences to defame good nodes or enhance trust values of bad ones [11]. Newcomer attacks consist of a malicious node registering a new identity and assigning high trust values to it. If the trust evaluation scheme suffers from the newcomer attack, a malicious node might remove its bad history by registering itself with a new identity [27]. In all scenarios, attacks start after nodes build their trust graphs.

Simulations performed in Network Simulator (NS-2) confirm that the proposed scheme is robust and efficient. Results show that trust evidences are quickly disseminated through the network and nodes are able to effectively estimate the trustworthiness of other nodes. Also, it is possible to notice that the scheme is resistant to false accusation attacks, in which malicious nodes try to jeopardize other nodes.

The rest of the paper is organized as follows: Section 2 presents the used notation and the system model considered by the scheme; Section 3 details the operation of the proposed scheme and its procedures; Section 4 contains the evaluation of the proposed scheme; finally, Section 5 contains the conclusion and future work.

2   Notation and System Model

This section presents the notation and the system model which is used through the rest of this paper. First, Table 1 summarizes the notation used in the rest of the paper.

Table 1. Notation

Notation	Description
n_i	identity of node i
N	system nodes set
$TV_{(n_x, n_v)}$	trust value from a trustor n_x to a trustee n_v
$TC^x_{(n_x, n_v)}$	trust chain x from node n_x to node n_v
$a\|b$	information a concatenated with information b
G_{tr}	trust network graph
G^x_{tr}	trust network of node n_x
$|Z|$	size of a given set Z
$n_a \rightarrow n_b$	node n_a trusts node n_b
ΔT_{ex}	interval of information exchanges
TIM	Trust Information Message
α	threshold of trust exchanges
β	threshold of trust evaluations
$\cong$	approximately

Due to the unique characteristics of MANETs, some concepts and features of trust should be carefully defined [13, 26]:

D1 *trust is not necessarily transitive*: if node n_a trusts node n_b, and node n_b trusts node n_c, it is not really true that node n_a trusts node n_c, but it must be considered.

D2 *trust is asymmetric*: the fact that node n_a trusts node n_b does not necessarily means that node n_b also trusts node n_a.

D3 *trust is subjective*: as trust is inherently a personal opinion, two nodes can often evaluate trustworthiness about another node differently.

D4 *trust is context-dependent*: node n_a may trust in node n_b to provide a route service but it does not trust in node n_b to provide another service.

D5 *trust evaluation should be fully distributed*: trust management schemes must not rely on a trusted third party to determine the trustworthiness of nodes.

D6 *trust management should consider non-cooperative nodes*: resource-restricted environments, like MANETs, are composed by nodes which can present selfish behavior.

D7 *trust value must be continuous*: the level of trust in a node must be measured by a continuous real value.

D8 *trust is dynamic*: as the trust value represents a personal opinion, nodes can change its evaluation about other nodes.

Based on these concepts, a new trust management scheme is proposed. The scheme focuses on self-organized mobile ad hoc network consisting of a set of n nodes identified by $n_1, n_2, ..., n_n$. Without losing generality, such nodes are considered to have similar functionalities, contributing to network operations and maintenance.

The proposed scheme can be visualized as an overlay trust network independent from the physical one. The *trust network* can be represented by a direct graph $G_{tr} = (V_{tr}, E_{tr})$, in which the vertices V_{tr} are the nodes and edges E_{tr} represent the trust relationship between them. All trust information stored in the graph is related with a context, and cannot be evaluated out of its context. For simplicity, this paper considers only one context at a time. However, it is trivial to represent additional context information on trust network graphs.

3   Protocol

This section describes the operations of the proposed trust management scheme. Initially, it is presented how nodes create their own trust network graphs and how they can update such graphs, gathering evidences from other nodes. Then, it is described how nodes evaluate trust values of other nodes, and how they can integrate the information from different nodes.

3.1   Building Trust Network Graphs

When joining the system, each node creates its own trust network graph $G_{tr}^i = (V_{tr}, E_{tr})$ in a self-organized way. Initially, nodes have knowledge only about nodes with which they have direct trust relations, and only such data are stored in the trust network.

Periodically (ΔT_{ex})), nodes exchange trust evidences stored in their trust network graphs with their neighbors. Thus, trust values will quickly travel through the network following an epidemic behavior [16, 23, 32]. Without lack of generality, it is assumed that all nodes have the same ΔT_{ex}.

Trust information exchange happens as follows:

- In ΔT_{ex} intervals, each node n_x creates a Trust Information Message, denoted by $TIM = [G_{tr}^x \| n_x \| timestamp]$. This message contains all trust evidences stored in its trust network graph, its identity, and a timestamp.
- Upon receiving a TIM message, node n_v evaluates the relevance of the received evidences. Node n_v calculates the trustworthiness of node n_x ($TV_{(n_v, n_x)}$) and decides whether it accepts or not such evidences as trusted data, based on its policy managements rules. Note that, each node has a threshold value, α, in which it accepts trust evidences iff. $TV_{(n_v, n_x)} \geq \alpha$.
- If n_v accepts the trust evidences, it incorporates the received information on its trust network graph.

3.2   Trust Evaluation

To evaluate its trust on node n_u, node n_x must either have a direct connection with node n_u in G_{tr}^x or it finds at least one trust chain (TC) from n_x to n_u in G_{tr}^x. Trust chains represent a transitive trust from n_x to n_u. The trust network graph G_{tr}^x is depicted in Fig. 1. Note that node n_x can find several different trust chains between itself and n_u in G_{tr}^x, each chain is denoted as $TC_{(n_x, n_u)}^i$.

If n_x has a direct trust with n_u, so only this value will be considered in the trust evaluation. Considering the example of Fig. 1, it is possible to notice that n_x has a direct trust relationship with n_q, and it has 80% of confidence in services provided by n_q. However, in this example n_x does not have a direct trust relationship with n_u. Hence, it will try to find a trust path in G_{tr}^x, estimating the trustworthiness of each chain, and calculating a weighted mean for each one.

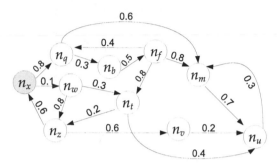

Fig. 1. Example of trust chain G_{tr}^x from node n_x

Upon finding a chain, node n_x must compute its trust. Consider n_1 to n_m the m intermediary nodes in the ith trust chain, denoted as $TC_{(n_x,n_u)}^i$, eq. 1 estimates the trustworthiness of $TC_{(n_x,n_u)}^i$:

$$TC_{(n_x,n_u)}^i = TV_{(n_x,n_1)} \times \prod_{j=1}^{m-1} TV_{(n_j,n_{j+1})} \times TV_{(n_m,n_u)} \tag{1}$$

Returning to fig. 1, there are several chains between n_x e n_u, for example:

1. chain $(n_x \to n_q \to n_m \to n_u)$, trust chain value $TC_{(n_x,n_u)}^1 = 0.8 \times 0.6 \times 0.7 = 0.336$;
2. chain $(n_x \to n_q \to n_b \to n_f \to n_m \to n_u)$, trust chain value $TC_{(n_x,n_u)}^2 = 0.8 \times 0.3 \times 0.5 \times 0.8 \times 0.7 = 0.067$.

Furthermore, nodes can use a threshold value for each edge of the trust chain (β value). If at least one edge of the trust chain has a trust value below this threshold, the node discards this chain before even compute the trust chain value. For example, if node n_x consider $\beta > 0.4$, it would discard chain 2 of the above example, as it has an edge with trust value equals to 0.3.

After calculating the trust value for all chains, the trust value $TV_{(n_x,n_u)}$ can be calculated applying a weighted mean, as follows (eq. 2):

$$TV_{(n_x,n_u)} = \frac{\sum_{i=1}^{k} (TC_{(n_x,n_u)}^i \times 1/|TC_{(n_x,n_u)}^i|)}{\sum_{i=1}^{k} \frac{1}{|TC_{(n_x,n_u)}^i|}} \tag{2}$$

The weighted mean reduces the impact of transitivity in trust chains. In fact, the greater the chain, the less reliable it is. Thus, this method aims to privilege small chains, following a social perspective.

4   Evaluation

The Network Simulator(NS) version 2.34 was used to evaluate the performance and effectiveness of the proposed trust management scheme. Simulations were made considering both honest and malicious nodes. Malicious nodes alter trust values of other nodes unpredictably and arbitrarily aiming to jeopardize the system.

In the simulations, 100 nodes use the IEEE 802.11 with distributed coordination function (DCF) as the medium access control protocol. The radio propagation follows the two-ray ground propagation model and the communication range is 120m. Nodes move on an area of 1000m x 1000m, following the random waypoint model with a maximal speed of 20 m/s, and pause time of 20s. The total time of simulations is 2000s and results are averages of 35 simulations with 95% confidence interval.

During network formation, each node randomly generates trust values for the nodes it trusts. Initial trusts relations follow a power-law distribution, in which only few nodes have many trust relationships (at most 15). The power-law distribution correctly approximates the trust operation in dynamic networks, as P2P and MANETs [24]. Then, trust values are set randomly following a normal distribution of continuous values from 0 to 1. The exchange information interval ΔT_{ex} is set to 10 seconds.

The proposed scheme was evaluated under three aspects: (i) the communication cost; (ii) the average calculated trust in trust graphs and the percentage of nodes which are considered reliable in scenarios without attackers; (iii) the average calculated trust in trust graphs and the percentage of nodes which are considered reliable in scenarios under bad mouthing and newcomer attacks.

4.1   Communication Cost

The communication overhead is extremely small. The proposed scheme uses only one hop messages to update trust network graphs, while it does not use any messages to build trust chains, i.e. it does not need any message to estimate the trust of another node. Note that it is even possible to piggyback update messages within other control messages. Thus, the communication cost of the proposed scheme depends exclusively on update message

Moreover, it is possible to increase ΔT_{ex} to reduce its communication cost. This function can be useful to postpone the battery exhaustion of a node. However, the time to disseminate trust evidences depends directly on ΔT_{ex}, a higher ΔT_{ex} implies on a higher delay to disseminate evidences.

The memory overhead is also small. Nodes must maintain only the virtual overlay graph. On the other side the computational overhead to maintain the scheme updated might be significant. Nodes must compute trust values for every TIM message received. If the node decides to accept a TIM message, it must recompute the entire virtual overlay graph considering such information. Consequently, the computational overhead depends directly on Tex and on the number of neighbors each node has.

4.2 Scenarios without Attackers

Considering scenarios without attackers, the proposed scheme was evaluated varying the threshold for information exchanges (α) and threshold for trust chains values (β). It is expected that in scenarios with more rigorous threshold values, nodes will be able to obtain information about a smaller set of nodes and, consequently, to estimate the trustworthiness of fewer nodes.

Fig. 2(a) shows the average calculated trust in trust graphs. In scenarios with $\alpha \cong 0.1$ and $\beta \cong 0.1$, the average trust value is also approximately to 0.1 due to node accepting recommendations from nodes with small trust value. In this case, trust chains can be formed using unreliable nodes.

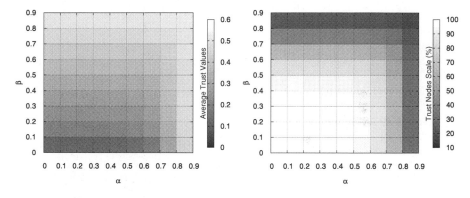

(a) Estimated trust values without attackers   (b) Reliable nodes without attackers

Fig. 2. Scenarios without attackers

On the other hand, in scenarios with $\alpha \cong 0.9$ and $\beta \cong 0.9$, the average trust value is approximately 0.6. It is possible to observe that β value has a higher impact on the results. With a small α and $\beta = 0.5$, the average of calculated trust values is higher than 0.4. It is important to point out that the objective of the scheme is not to increase the trustworthiness of nodes, but to estimate it.

Fig. 2(b) shows the percentage of nodes which are considered reliable by each node according to α and β values. This result is directly related with the ones presented in Fig. 2(a). In scenarios with both $\alpha < 0.5$ and $\beta < 0.5$, the percentage of nodes which are considered reliable is almost 100%. If $\alpha \cong 0.9$ or $\beta \cong 0.9$, the percentage of trust nodes is around 30%. If $\alpha = 0.9$ and $\beta = 0.9$, this percentage is close to 10%.

Table 2 shows the average time (in seconds) necessary to propagate a trust information through the network and the average size of the trust graphs, both considering the threshold for information exchanges (α). Note that the time to disseminate trust information is smaller with $\alpha = 0.0$ or $\alpha = 0.9$ and it is higher with $\alpha = 0.4$ and $\alpha = 0.5$. It occurs because with $\alpha = 0.0$ nodes accept trust evidences from any other node. Thus, data will be exchanged very quickly. At the other extreme, if $\alpha = 0.9$, nodes accept trust evidences only from very close friends. In this case, even if it does not have many

Table 2. Time to disseminate trust evidences and percentage of nodes in trust graphs

α	Time (sec.)	Nodes (%)
0.0	198.51	100.00%
0.1	713.54	99.99%
0.2	801.49	99.96%
0.3	885.14	99.92%
0.4	936.97	99.35%
0.5	926.96	96.94%
0.6	878.08	92.57%
0.7	768.51	78.98%
0.8	598.22	50.37%
0.9	281.08	17.34%

evidences stored locally, it will not accept information from other nodes. Also, increasing the value of α, less information is exchanged and the trust graphs are smaller, i.e. fewer nodes are stored in trust graphs.

4.3   Scenarios Considering Attackers

The proposed scheme was also evaluated in scenarios under two kinds of attacks: bad mouthing and newcomer (or Sybil) attacks. Bad mouthing attacks consist of malicious nodes providing dishonest trust evidences to defame good nodes or enhance trust values of bad ones [11]. Newcomer attacks consist of a malicious node registering a new identity and assigning high trust values to it. If the trust management suffers from the newcomer attack, a malicious node can remove its bad history by registering itself with a new identity [27]. In all scenarios, attacks start after nodes build their trust graphs.

First, the scheme was evaluated under bad mouthing attacks. In such attacks, malicious nodes change the value of other nodes to 1.0. It was also considered that malicious nodes can perform an attack in collusion, in which several attackers choose the same node to change the trust value.

Fig. 3 shows the impact of bad mouthing attacks in the proposed scheme. Note that in scenarios with small α and β the percentage of affected nodes is close to 0, as all

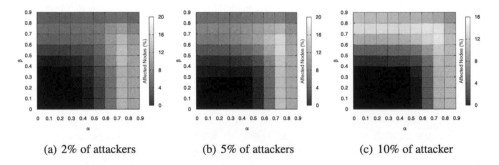

(a) 2% of attackers   (b) 5% of attackers   (c) 10% of attacker

Fig. 3. Scenarios under bad mouthing attack

nodes already trust on almost all nodes. Results also show that the worst case occurs with $\alpha \cong 0.7$ and $\beta \cong 0.7$ and 10% of attackers (Fig. 3(c)). In this case, the percentage of compromised nodes are only 15%.

Table 3 shows how much the system is affected in scenarios with attackers, evaluating the variation of trust values calculated by nodes. Such an evaluation considers just scenarios with $\alpha = 0.0$, i.e scenarios in which nodes exchange trust evidences with all other nodes. Note that under 5% of attackers and $\beta = 0.9$, the variation of trust values is 0.3277. Also, in scenarios with 10% of attackers and $\beta < 0.6$, the variation is always below 0.2.

Table 3. Trust variation in scenarios under attack

β	Attackers		
	2%	**5%**	**10%**
0.0	0.0055	0.0116	0.0158
0.1	0.0271	0.0503	0.0671
0.2	0.0365	0.0655	0.0868
0.3	0.0432	0.0803	0.1045
0.4	0.0561	0.0987	0.1290
0.5	0.0884	0.1355	0.1700
0.6	0.1619	0.2081	0.2390
0.7	0.3258	0.3403	0.3574
0.8	0.4300	0.4403	0.4339
0.9	0.2829	0.3277	0.3377

Finally, the proposed scheme was evaluated under newcomers attack. In such attacks, after the system initialization and construction of trust graphs, malicious nodes create a new identity and assign a high trust value to it. This attacks was also evaluated considering that malicious nodes act in collusion.

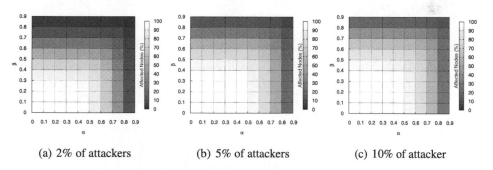

(a) 2% of attackers   (b) 5% of attackers   (c) 10% of attacker

Fig. 4. Scenarios under newcomer attack

Fig. 4 shows that the smaller α and β are, the more nodes will be affected by newcomers attack. In scenarios with $\alpha < 0.5$ and $\beta < 0.5$, almost 100% of the nodes are affected. On the other hand, increasing the values of α and β decreases the impact of the attack. In scenarios with 5% of attackers (Fig. 4(b)) and $\alpha \cong 0.8$ and $\beta \cong 0.8$, about 50% of nodes are compromised. With $\alpha = 0.9$ and $\beta = 0.9$ and 10% of attackers (Fig. 4(c)), less than 10% of nodes are affected, showing that the proposed scheme is still valid even in the presence of several attackers.

5   Conclusions

Cryptography has been the main technique employed to provide security in MANETs. Besides, several cryptographic mechanisms rely on pre-established trust relations between nodes. However, trust is very difficult to be valued in MANETs. Several trust management schemes have been proposed [5, 6, 9, 10, 14, 15, 22, 25, 34], but none of them were evaluated in scenarios under misbehavior attacks. Attacks such as bad mouthing or newcomer, if performed successfully against the trust management system, can compromise the entire security of the system. Moreover:

- No specific attack model was addressed nor evaluated on [5, 6, 10, 22].
- Some schemes are limited only to support routing strategies [6, 10, 22].
- Support for other applications is very difficult in [14].

This work presents a new trust management scheme in which nodes create a virtual trust network. Such trust network contains trust information about other nodes, gathered via direct observations or via recommendations. Then, each node estimates the trustworthiness of other nodes which it does not have previous interaction building trust from the information stored in the trust network.

Simulation results show that the proposed scheme is very efficient on gathering evidences to build the trust networks. Moreover, though the scheme has not been described to prevent attacks, it was evaluated under bad mouthing and newcomer attacks. The evaluations show that the scheme is able to resist up to 10% of attackers, if it is configured to take rigorous decisions. Future work includes the evaluation of the scheme under other kinds of attacks, such as on/off and conflicting behavior ones.

References

1. Albers, P., Camp, O., Percher, J.M., Jouga, B., Mé, L., Puttini, R.S.: Security in ad hoc networks: a general intrusion detection architecture enhancing trust based approaches. In: Proceedings of the 1st International Workshop on Wireless Information Systems (WIS 2002), pp. 1–12. ICEIS Press (April 2002)
2. Beth, T., Borcherding, M., Klein, B.: Valuation of trust in open networks. In: Gollmann, D. (ed.) ESORICS 1994. LNCS, vol. 875, pp. 3–18. Springer, Heidelberg (1994)
3. Blaze, M., Feigenbaum, J., Keromytis, A.D.: The role of trust management in distributed systems security. In: Ryan, M. (ed.) Secure Internet Programming. LNCS, vol. 1603, pp. 185–210. Springer, Heidelberg (1999)
4. Blaze, M., Feigenbaum, J., Lacy, J.: Decentralized trust management. In: Proceedings of the 1996 IEEE Symposium on Security and Privacy (SP 1996), p. 164. IEEE Computer Society (1996)

5. Boukerche, A., Ren, Y.: A security management scheme using a novel computational reputation model for wireless and mobile ad hoc networks. In: Proceedings of the 5th ACM Symposium on Performance Evaluation of Wireless Ad Hoc, Sensor, and Ubiquitous Networks (PE-WASUN 2008), pp. 88–95. ACM Press, New York (2008)
6. Buchegger, S., Le Boudec, J.Y.: Performance analysis of the CONFIDANT protocol. In: Proceedings of the 3rd ACM International Symposium on Mobile ad Hoc Networking & Computing (MobiHoc 2002), pp. 226–236. ACM, New York (2002)
7. Buskens, V.: Social Networks and Trust. Kluwer Academic Publishers, Dordrecht (2002)
8. Čapkun, S., Buttyán, L., Hubaux, J.P.: Self-organized public-key management for mobile ad hoc networks. IEEE Transactions on Mobile Computing 2(1), 52–64 (2003)
9. Chang, B.J., Kuo, S.L., Liang, Y.H., Wang, D.Y.: Markov chain-based trust model for analyzing trust value in distributed multicasting mobile ad hoc networks 59, 1846–1863 (2009)
10. Dai, H., Jia, Z., Qin, Z.: Trust evaluation and dynamic routing decision based on fuzzy theory for manets. JSW – Journal of Software 4(10), 1091–1101 (2009)
11. Dellarocas, C.: Mechanisms for coping with unfair ratings and discriminatory behavior in online reputation reporting systems. In: Proceedings of the 21st International Conference on Information Systems (ICIS 2000), pp. 520–525. Association for Information Systems, Atlanta (2000)
12. Ghosh, T., Pissinou, N., Makki, K.: Towards designing a trusted routing solution in mobile ad hoc networks. Mobile Networks and Applications 10(6), 985–995 (2005)
13. Golbeck, J.: Computing with trust: Definition, properties, and algorithms. In: Proceedings of the 1st International Conference on Security and Privacy in Communications Networks and the Workshops (SecureComm 2006), pp. 1–7. IEEE Press (August 2006)
14. He, Q., Wu, D., Khosla, P.: SORI: A secure and objective reputation-based incentive scheme for ad-hoc networks. In: Proceedings of the 2004 IEEE Wireless Communications and Networking Conference (WCNC 2004), pp. 825–830. IEEE Computer Society (2004)
15. Jiang, T., Baras, J.S.: Ant-based adaptive trust evidence distribution in manet. In: Proceedings of the 24th International Conference on Distributed Computing Systems Workshops (ICDCSW 2004), pp. 588–593. IEEE Computer Society (2004)
16. Khelil, A., Becker, C., Tian, J., Rothermel, K.: An epidemic model for information diffusion in manets. In: Proceedings of the 5th ACM International Workshop on Modeling Analysis and Simulation of Wireless and Mobile Systems (MSWiM 2002), pp. 54–60. ACM, New York (2002)
17. Lewis, J.D., Weigert, A.: Trust as a social reality. Social Forces 63(4), 967–985 (1985)
18. Li, X., Slay, J., Yu, S.: Evaluating trust in mobile ad hoc networks. In: Proceedings of the 2005 Workshop of International Conference on Computational Intelligence and Security, CIS 2005. Springer (2005)
19. Lima, M.N., Pujolle, G., Silva, E., Santos, A.L., Albini, L.C.P.: Survivable keying for wireless ad hoc networks. In: Proceedings of the 2009 IFIP/IEEE International Symposium on Integrated Network Management (IM 2009), pp. 606–613. IEEE Communications Society (June 2009)
20. Luo, H., Kong, J., Zerfos, P., Lu, S., Zhang, L.: Ursa: ubiquitous and robust access control for mobile ad hoc networks. IEEE/ACM Transaction on Networking (TON) 12(6), 1049–1063 (2004)
21. Marti, S., Giuli, T.J., Lai, K., Baker, M.: Mitigating routing misbehavior in mobile ad hoc networks. In: Proceedings of the 6th Annual International Conference on Mobile Computing and Networking (MobiCom 2000), pp. 255–265. ACM (2000)
22. Michiardi, P., Molva, R.: Core: a collaborative reputation mechanism to enforce node cooperation in mobile ad hoc networks. In: Proceedings of the IFIP TC6/TC11 6th Joint Working Conference on Communications and Multimedia Security, pp. 107–121. Kluwer, B.V., Deventer (2002)

23. Mickens, J.W., Noble, B.D.: Modeling epidemic spreading in mobile environments. In: Proceedings of the 4th ACM Workshop on Wireless Security (WiSe 2005), pp. 77–86. ACM, New York (2005)
24. Ripeanu, M., Foster, I., Iamnitchi, A.: Mapping the gnutella network: Properties of large-scale peer-to-peer systems and implications for system. IEEE Internet Computing Journal 6 (2002)
25. Sun, Y.L., Han, Z., Yu, W., Liu, K.J.R.: A trust evaluation framework in distributed networks: Vulnerability analysis and defense against attacks. In: Proceedings of the 25th IEEE International Conference on Computer Communications (INFOCOM 2006), pp. 1–13. IEEE Communications Society (2006)
26. Sun, Y.L., Yu, W., Han, Z., Liu, K.J.R.: Information theoretic framework of trust modeling and evaluation for ad hoc networks. IEEE Journal on Selected Areas in Communications 24(2), 305–317 (2006)
27. Sun, Z., Han, Y.L., Liu, K.J.R.: Defense of trust management vulnerabilities in distributed networks. IEEE Communications Magazine, 112–119 (2008)
28. Theodorakopoulos, G., Baras, J.S.: On trust models and trust evaluation metrics for ad hoc networks. IEEE Journal on Selected Areas in Communications 24(2), 318–328 (2006)
29. Velloso, P.B., Laufer, R.P., Duarte, O.C., Pujolle, G.: A trust model robust to slander attacks in ad hoc networks. In: Proceedings of 17th International Conference on Computer Communications and Networks (ICCCN 2008), pp. 1–6. IEEE Communications Society (2008)
30. Virendra, M., Jadliwala, M., Ch, M., Upadhyaya, S.: Quantifying trust in mobile ad-hoc networks. In: Proceedings of the IEEE International Conference on Integration of Knowledge Intensive Multi-Agent Systems (KIMAS 2005), pp. 65–71. IEEE Computer Society (2005)
31. Wu, B., Chen, J., Wu, J., Cardei, M.: A survey on attacks and countermeasures in mobile ad hoc networks, ch. 12, pp. 103–136. Springer, New York (2006)
32. Zhang, X., Neglia, G., Kurose, J., Towsley, D.: Performance modeling of epidemic routing. Computer Networks 51(10), 2867–2891 (2007)
33. Zhou, L., Haas, Z.J.: Securing ad hoc networks. IEEE Network 13(6), 24–30 (1999)
34. Zuo, Y., Hu, W.C., O'Keefe, T.: Trust computing for social networking. In: Proceedings of the 6th International Conference on Information Technology: New Generations (ITNG 2009), pp. 1534–1539. IEEE Computer Society, Washington, DC (2009)

Distributed Sensor Relay System for Near Real Time Observation, Control and Data Management on a Scientific Research Ship

Barry Tao, Jon Campbell, and Gwyn Griffiths

National Oceanography Centre Southampton, Southampton, UK
{bt,joc,gxg}@noc.ac.uk

Abstract. Adding intelligence to deployed instruments in an oceanographic environment of restricted bandwidth helps to improve service quality and enables autonomous observation and data management. Delay tolerance and remote access often pose challenges to providing near real time observation. We have experimented with a distributed hybrid web enabled sensor system and conducted its deployment in a scientific oceanographic cruise. The purpose of the experiment was to study the feasibility and performance of narrow-band network relay communication in an oceanographic environment to assist near real time observation and sensor control. The restriction of resources, in particular the unreliable Internet satellite connection and lack of bandwidth prevent a centralized real-time system from working properly. Bandwidth tests were conducted and a delay tolerant networked relay has been introduced by de-coupling the functions to make it like a distributed system. Multiple nodes are setup across the ship, cloud Internet, and laboratory ashore to form a loosely coupled and balanced networked system. The system also aims to form a foundation platform for integrating higher level services to support oceanographic observation, data management with interoperability, such as OGC SWE services and IEEE 1451 smart sensor standards.

Keywords: oceanography, sensor web enablement, data management, interoperability.

1 Introduction and Related Work

JC62 was a scientific cruise (24 July - 29 August, 2011) on the UK research ship *James Cook* to carry out scientific study and service a data buoy at the Porcupine Abyssal Plain (PAP) site in the North Atlantic off the Irish continental margin. Apart from scientific survey and operations, we got on board the cruise's first leg (24 July – 2 Aug) to conduct a web enabled sensors experiment in the ship environment. The purpose of the experiment was to investigate context where scientific oceanography instruments are deployed and to enable a near real time 2-way sensor communication in a low bandwidth, intermittent VSAT ship board internet connection. The experiment was designed with the following objectives in mind.

- Data acquisition with RS232 interface for measurements and sensor metadata
- Instrument control, platform control, communications tools
- Using Web technologies for oceanographic data and metadata management
- Higher level services to enable interoperability with unified interfaces

R. Benlamri (Ed.): NDT 2012, Part I, CCIS 293, pp. 519–535, 2012.

With an aim to make our system scalable and in line with existing standards, we have looked into some large scale integrations.

In UK, there is an operational UK air-sea carbon flux observation capability with the aim to measure basic parameters such as carbon dioxide (CO_2) and temperature at ocean surface from selected UK research ships. This is called CARBON-OPS. By monitoring surface ocean pCO_2 and measuring the exchange of CO_2 between the ocean and atmosphere, CARBON-OPS hopes to help provide early warning of changes in the oceans' capacity to absorb CO_2 and the consequences for climate change. The service collects data and send near real time to a dry land laboratory. Similarly, Integrated Marine Observing System (IMOS) [12] is a distributed set of equipment and data-information services which collectively contribute to observational data requirement of marine climate research around Australia. IMIOS uses OPeNDAP to archive sensor metadata in a standard manner. It includes data collection from ARGO floats, ships of opportunity, ocean gliders, AUVs, etc. Data is presented as layers on top of various GIS base maps. Real time data collection is proposed in EIF023 project [13] to automate and collect real-time publication of data from research vessels RVSS and RVAA. Observations includes sea surface, the water column and the sea-bed and immediate atmosphere. The project aims to provide a mechanism for managers in different vessels to work together with common data publication standards, which helps alignment of observations from these vessels so that data being received from the two vessels can then be integrated easily.

ExView [8] is a software tool that keeps track of the location of oceanographic vehicles. The NOAA Pacific Marine Environmental Laboratory maintains a fleet of research vessels in both the Pacific and Atlantic Oceans. Shipboard computers send out emails at regular interval, which are then processed at a data center to update a centralized database. A process is carried out at regular intervals to check any new information in the database in order to regenerate diagrams displayed on the website. Using ArcIMS, the web site provides graphical plots illustrating the current location of various ships in the NOAA fleet and the latest detailed weather and ocean conditions received from each ship [4]. This approach is similar to that of the Ferrybox project [5].

Often subsystems are designed and integrated together to meet different requirements at different levels while still providing interoperability at each level and harmonization across of the subsystems. At a lower level, there is effort to integrate intelligence into the sensor itself in order to provide smart sensors [19]. Most oceanographic sensors or actuators use rs232 serial communication for data and control management. Sensor manufacturers need to provide various drivers that interface the low level RS232 communication with high level programs that run in a PC to which the sensors are connected in order to control the sensors and manipulate measurement outputs. National Instruments has been working on a suite of IEEE1451 smart sensor standards [6] that are designed to provide a common set of interfaces where transducers are connected via wired or wireless means. Among the few implementations is the TinyTIM™ (Tiny Transducer Interface Module) designed by Smart Sensor System [1]. It provides the radio and wireless protocol as well as other resources through a 37-pin interface. It has a built-in transducer electronic data sheet (TEDS) memory that allows datasheets to be stored and accessed from the NCAP sever. At a higher level, relayed measurement data can be collected at various data nodes (gateway) and feed into more heterogeneous Sensor Network to support near real time data analysis using domain algorithm.

A general review and schematic approach using heterogeneous sensor network to enable future Environmental Science has been described in [3].

2   Work Flow and System Design

For design and testing purpose, we began with a few sensors (from Sea-Bird Electronics and Aanderaa Data Instruments) in a laboratory environment to simulate the experiment and evaluate their bandwidth consumption. The sensors were connected to a PC through RS232. Sensor metadata and observation measurements were read from the RS232 connection and saved in XML files at a defined interval. Whenever there was an Internet connection, the xml files were then synchronized to the web using cloud storage where they were transformed and injected to a master database.

We have demonstrated that oceanographic observation and control can be managed through deploying functions and components in different nodes across the observation site (ship in this experiment), cloud and the laboratory ashore. We adopt a bottom-up paradigm and a distributed relayed workflow, where light weight data acquisition systems are deployed between ship node and cloud node to transmit data from sensors, control and measurement while more resource-demanding tasks (e.g. data management and interoperability applications) are deployed on less restricted cloud and laboratory nodes to handle higher level post-processing application and services.

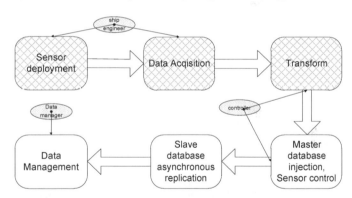

Fig. 1. Relayed workflow for web enabled sensor experiment

Cloud storage and computation is introduced to the system to improve resource load balance and optimization. The introduction of additional nodes in between the ship and laboratory nodes also allows us not to violate existing firewall security policies on the ship and in the laboratory, as all the external network requests originate from within the firewall of both sites, therefore saving the need of special arrangement of opening ports in firewalls. Multiple nodes can be deployed in the cloud to introduce redundancy and offer balance-load distributed services for scalability. As shown in Figure 1 (shade denotes on-ship operations), asynchronous database replication is used for data communication between the cloud database and the database ashore, the latter of which acts as a slave, i.e., replicating the master node regularly whenever there is an new data. Once the data arrives on shore, further manipulation and computational intensive work can be carried out without incurring expensive satellite Internet bandwidth. The aim of the system is to allow scalable multi-use of the near real-time observations, such as data analysis, semantics metadata management and their web distribution in a balanced manner. A more comprehensive illustration diagram is shown in Figure 2.

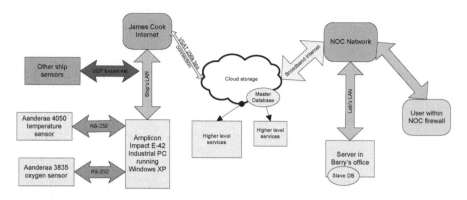

Fig. 2. JC 062 Web-enabled Sensors Experiment

3   Evaluation of the Bandwidth Consumption

To make sure that the bandwidth cost of these web connected sensors is within a reasonable range allowed by the ship's limited bandwidth, we have carried out a bandwidth experiment. The sensors connected through their RS232 interfaces output xml files during the data acquisition process. These xml files are then transformed in a predefined interval into SQL in order to inject measurement and sensor meta-data to the master database. An asynchronous replication process is set up between master and slave databases, which is the only operation that uses the ship's Internet bandwidth.

Table 1. XML output of the sensor's measurement

```
<?xml version="1.0" encoding="UTF-8"?>
<Device ID="unique number" Manufacturer="Aanderaa Data Instruments" ProdNo="4050" SerialNo="90" Descr="Web Sensor
Test" DeviceType="Sensor" SessionID="2010-11-12T13:10:18Z">
    <Time>2010-11-15T15:52:52Z</Time>
    <Status>0:OK</Status>
    <SiteInfo>
        <GeoPosition />
        <VerticalPosition>0.0</VerticalPosition>
    </SiteInfo>
    <Data RecordNumber="17932" Time="2010-11-15T15:52:52Z" SessionID="2010-11-12T13:10:18Z">
        <SensorData ID="4050-90" Descr="Temperature 4050 s/n90" ProdName="Temperature Sensor" ProdNo="4050"
SerialNo="90">
            <Status>OK</Status>
            <Parameters>
                <Point ID="0" Descr="Temperature" Unit="Deg.C" Format="%.4f" RangeMin="-5"
RangeMax="40">21.3515</Point>
            </Parameters>
        </SensorData>
    </Data>
</Device>
```

Both the Aanderaa and Seabird temperature sensors were configured to output a new value every 15 seconds, therefore the sensor data acquisition generated 8 files (samples) per minute that contain metadata and measurements as shown in Table 1. This operation generates 480 sample files per hour.

We have used a Linux network traffic monitor called bmon to evaluate bandwidth consumption of the master node doing asynchronous replication. Data replications are scheduled at regular interval. In this experiment, we set it to hourly, which incurs a bandwidth consumption spike in the order of 100KB per second for about 30 seconds, while idle consumption (for the rest of the hour) is only in the order of 0.1 KB per second when master node listens for the asynchronous replication attempts from the slave node to keep alive. The hourly monitoring of the bandwidth consumption is approximately 4.8MB (RX 1.7MB, TX 3.1MB) per hour. This translates very approximately as around 10KB per sample, although we need to do further experiments to discover how much of this is a fixed overhead.

A general estimate of the experiments revealed that the deployment would use well under 1MB per hour for both upload and download when active. The operation can be scheduled to become active at pre-defined times, therefore further load balance the bandwidth usage. It works with an unreliable network; processes can be resumed automatically once the connection is available. The test of the bandwidth enabled us to set for ship node with a bandwidth cap which is reasonably higher than the bandwidth requirement so that backlog can be cleared after the Internet connection resumes. This cap is used in the Dropbox cloud service (set at approximately download 2kB/s, upload 0.5kB/s) to minimize usage as much as it is sufficient for the communication purpose.

4   Deployment on the Ship

During the first leg of the 10 day cruise from Falmouth, UK to the PAP site southwest of Ireland, the VSAT satellite link lost Internet connection several times a day, particularly during the first few days due to the blocking of the satellite dish by other objects on the bridge top on certain ship's headings. Measurement data accumulated in the ship node, so did the new instructions at the cloud node. The backlog cleared within a short period of time once the Internet connection resumed.

The system allows automatic detection of sensor swapping for the same model of sensors, a local interface at the ship node, and a mechanism / web interface for remote configuration.

Two types of data sources have been used in the experiment, namely direct sensor data via RS232 interfaces and legacy ship-board sensors data being broadcast using UDP within the ship's internal network. Aanderaa temperature and conductivity sensors have been connected through RS232 at a ship node computer. LabWindows was used to program scripts that communicate with the RS232 sensors for measurement and control data. Java programs were used to intercept UDP broadcasts, in particular APPLANIX (Ship's attitude), SURFMET (surface meteorology) and EA600 (seabed depth) sentences. Selected data were sampled and transferred to a Linux cloud node off-ship using asynchronous file synchronization. We have chosen Dropbox to take advantage of its ability for cross-platform deployment, bandwidth management and cloud based computation. Once the data is in the cloud where bandwidth is no longer a problem, data is archived in a database, and interfaced to the Web, where control commands can be also sent. In addition, further data relay happens through database replication to a node back in the laboratory (NOC), where a data manager can inspect, quality control and further process the received data.

The ship node is also connected to the internal network to listen to UDP broadcasting messages (see appendix) that existing ship sensors produce, including GPS fixes. An NTP server GPS clock is fitted on the ship to allow on-board computers to synchronise their time to the ships GPS system for accurate data time stamping. A section of these data is given in Table 2.

Table 2. Fragments of data acquired via UDP broadcasting from legacy on-board sensors

```
jc-logger1.cook.local: $PRTSA,JCMES,31/07/11,15:48:51.168,apln1,
0,000,009,+00.90,+00.00,000.00,40755.658920,N,48,50.70159,W,
016,30.52252,+00.420,01,02,00.000,00.000,00.000,00.000,00.000,
$PRTSA,JCMES,31/07/11,15:53:51.171,apln1, 0,000,009,+00.90,+00.00,
000.00,40755.662392,N,48,50.74974,W,016,30.61902,+00.700,01,02,
00.000,00.000,00.000,00.000,00.000,
$PRTSA,JCMES,31/07/11,15:54:03.304,EA6_1, 0,15814.290000,
4820.200000,2635.720000
```

Basic CTD parameters (Conductivity, Temperature and Depth), GPS fixes and echo sounder data are picked up from this broadcast in order to associate with our measurement data for quality assurance and geo-tagging purpose. While sensors represented in the UDP messages cannot be controlled, the two RS232 sensors can be controlled by changing their parameters from the cloud node.

RS-232 Connection Interface

A key part of the web-enabled sensors experiment carried out during the JC062 cruise was a computer program written in C using the National Instruments LabWindows CVI development environment running under Windows XP. This program (called web_sensor_232.c) acts as the link between RS-232 enabled sensors and a computer network.

For this experiment two sensors from Aanderaa Data Instruments (AADI) were used; a model 4050 temperature sensor and a model 3919 conductivity sensor. These were chosen partly because they store metadata (calibration coefficients and the like) that can be retrieved, and partly because they were available from another project. Another feature of these sensors that was exploited in this experiment is that every data message they output contains the sensor model and serial numbers. This makes it easy to detect when a sensor is replaced.

Since the experiment aimed to evaluate web enabled sensors and their high level web communication and data management, rather than focusing at collecting scientific data, the sensors were operated in air rather than seawater.

The program could be tailored to work with virtually any sensor with an RS-232 interface that outputs less than 50 data values no faster than once per second. The program requires a configuration file that defines the locations to be used for different files, the COM ports to which the sensors are attached and the xml templates for each sensor type. The principal input is the data coming from the sensors via the COM ports. The program also checks for the arrival of a command file, which is the mechanism used for passing commands from a web interface to the sensor.

Figure 3 shows the main structure of the program. A software timer is used to repeatedly check for new messages from the sensors or the arrival of a new command file. A user interface panel shows the most recent data values from the sensors, the time since the last sensor message was received and plots some of the data values on a scrolling chart. The panel also has buttons to allow the user to request new metadata from the sensors. The principal output is the xml files that are generated after each sensor message is received. Separate xml files containing sensor metadata are generated upon request or after a sensor configuration is changed. Examples of both types of xml file can be found at the end of this section. When a command file is detected, a reply message is generated (as a file) to report the outcome of the command.

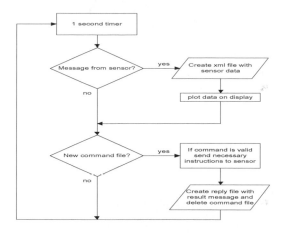

Fig. 3. Basic program structure for web_sensor_232.c

The templates used for the xml files were loosely based on templates used by AADI for their Seaguard instruments. The xml format was chosen as it presents the sensor data in a largely self-describing format (Figure 3), although this comes at the price of significantly larger files.

The program inserts a 'Session ID', which is the program start time, a data record and a data time stamp. The xml templates used also include placeholders for latitude and longitude but lack of time prevented this feature from being implemented for this experiment.

Command files are received from the cloud whenever they are issued and there is a connection. The program checks that the command file contents are valid and that the specified sensor exists before generating a suitable command sequence to send to the sensor through the RS232 interface. The program always creates a reply message file, starting with the original command message followed by an outcome message, e.g.

Interval, 3919, 136, 30, 2011-08-01T09:34:52Z - Model 3919 sernum 136 interval set to 30 seconds at 2011-08-01T12:47:50Z

During the cruise the program demonstrated the following functionality:-

- Convert Aanderaa sensor data messages into xml files according to a predefined template.
- Retrieve stored metadata from two types of Aanderaa sensor and insert into xml file.
- Parse remotely generated command files and generate appropriate response message files.
- Change an Aanderaa sensor sample interval setting in response to a remote command.
- Automatically detect when a sensor is changed.

The only aim that was not accomplished was the extraction of GPS position data from UDP messages and integrating it to the xml file. However, position data is picked up through a separate Java process and transmitted to and stored in the cloud node to enable geo-reference of the observational data.

It will be necessary to write software interface modules for each type of sensor to handle the actual RS-232 communications between server and sensor. The program was written in Lab Windows CVI, though for portability it should probably be written in Java. These modules need a common 'command set' to interface with the next level up, so that this interface is 'standard'. The IEEE1451 standard springs to mind for this, but it is unclear how widely this is likely to be used for oceanographic applications.

5   Data Storage Services and Control in the Cloud

Cloud computing is a concept for distributed storage, software, and computing using the Internet that does not require end-user's knowledge of the physical location and configuration of the system. Cloud technology is used to synchronize data files between the ship node and the cloud node. As bandwidth restriction is dramatically reduced once the data is in the cloud, it provides a good platform for more heavy-duty higher-level applications. We used Dropbox service, which can be run on multiple platforms to automatically and securely synchronize files by Amazon's Simple Storage Service (S3) in multiple data centres located across the U.S. To decouple the system and put some of the components off the ship, a distributed database system is set up as well in a cloud node as a master database, that relays data through a-synchronisation to a slave node deployed in the shore laboratory. The cloud node is responsible for synchronising files from the ship node, transcribing measurements xml files received in the cloud data storage into the database and coordinating sensor control instructions among the multiple nodes. Figure 4 shows the functional components in the system. Ideally, based on this system structure, we would like to plug-in higher level functionalities at this cloud node to provide standard interfaces for data interoperability as described in our previous work [17].

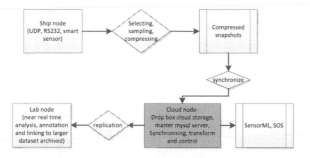

Fig. 4. Cloud node within the system

A MySQL database is designed to store data of observation and control, as shown the schema diagram of Figure 5.

The database server is set to master mode, with asynchronous replication with another MySQL server in the shore laboratory so that data are replicated in the slave by executing the same sql commands that are committed in the master node. The motivation behind this mechanism is many fold, including:

Scalability – this helps improve load balancing and security as writing only takes place in the master node where special arrangements can be made to improve security and performance. Read may take place on the slave nodes, whose number can be easily increased to accommodate demand.

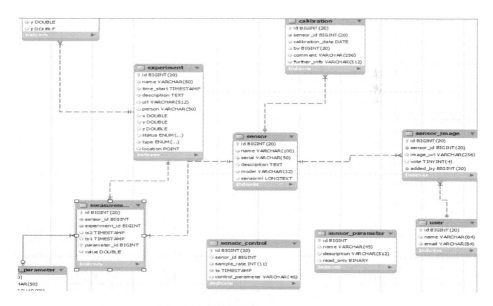

Fig. 5. Database schematic diagram

Long Distance Data Distribution – Data can be distributed to different sites, where a separate copy of the live data can be accessed for difference data analysis purposes without requiring site users to access the master node (Figure 6) and potentially affect processes running on it. In our case, we have a data manager working at the center's laboratory to monitor and quality-control the incoming observational data.

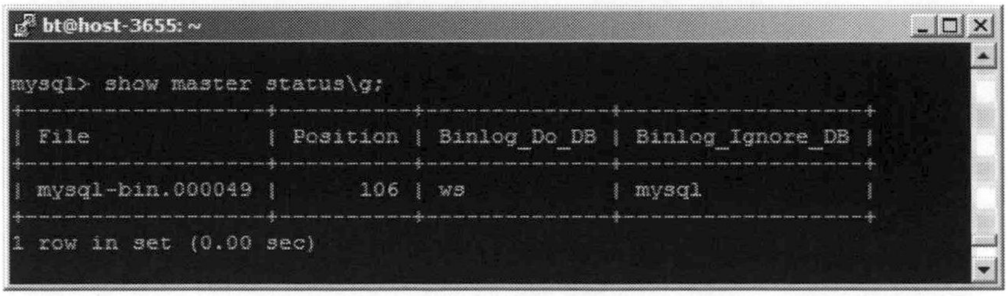

Fig. 6. Master database replication status

Database code reads measurements from the sensors and stores it in the database. It can also request metadata from each sensor and this is also stored in the database. The observations can be accessed via the web through a standard interface.

Sensor Control

Currently the "sample rate" control parameter has been used in the experiment to change interval of measurement for sensors connected through RS232 in the ship node computer.

A simple set of commands (or instructions) were defined, having 5 comma-separated fields containing:-

1. The command type, e.g. "Interval" to modify the sensor's sampling interval
2. The sensor model number
3. The sensor serial number
4. The command parameter value, in this example the new sample interval in seconds
5. The time the command was generated, e.g. Interval, 3919, 136, 30, 2011-08-01T09:34:52Z

The sensor commands will be relayed to the ship node eventually through file synchronisation. Once executed at the ship node, their result status will be sent back to the cloud node for archive. A simple user interface as shown in Figure 7 has been used to excute these commands.

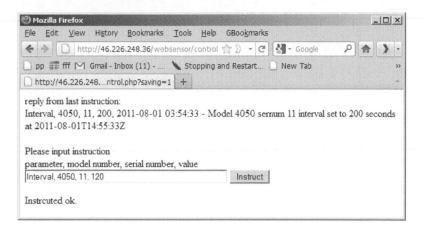

Fig. 7. Sensor instruction remote web interface

6   Services at Lab Node and Data Management

A slave MySQL server is set up in the shore laboratory to replicate whatever data is received in the cloud. Replication enables data from one MySQL database server (the master) to be replicated to one or more MySQL database servers (the slaves, status shown in Figure 8).

Replication is asynchronous - slaves need not be connected permanently to receive updates from the master. This means that updates can occur over long-distance connections and even over temporary or intermittent connections.

```
bt@cog: ~                                                    _ □ X
mysql> show slave status\G;
*************************** 1. row ***************************
               Slave_IO_State: Waiting for master to send event
                  Master_Host: 46.226.248.36
                  Master_User: repl
                  Master_Port: 3306
                Connect_Retry: 60
              Master_Log_File: mysql-bin.000049
          Read_Master_Log_Pos: 106
               Relay_Log_File: cog-relay-bin.001060
                Relay_Log_Pos: 251
        Relay_Master_Log_File: mysql-bin.000049
             Slave_IO_Running: Yes
            Slave_SQL_Running: Yes
              Replicate_Do_DB:
```

Fig. 8. Slave database replication status

A data manager in the laboratory was assigned during the cruise to check on this and to ensure data quality and carry out necessary data management tasks. An overview of the all the measurement readings is generated by the data manager as shown in Figure 9.

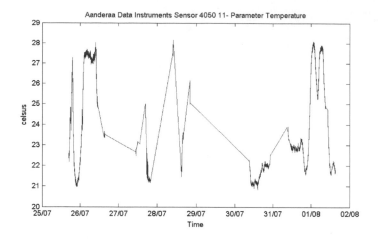

Fig. 9. Measurements activity of the Anderaa data instrument sensor

Due to technical problems at the deployment stage, measurements and web communications were not in normal operation until the last few days. This can be clearly noticed in

Figure 9 and can be further zoomed-in as shown in Figure 10.

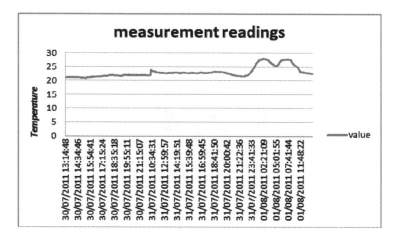

Fig. 10. Zoomed-in sensor measurement for a shorter period

Two timestamps are used to record the actual measurement time (from the RS232 interface of the sensors) and the time of the measurement data reaching the cloud node and archive in the database. By analyzing the difference between these two timestamps, we can find out how near real time this web enabled sensors experiment performed on the James Cook.

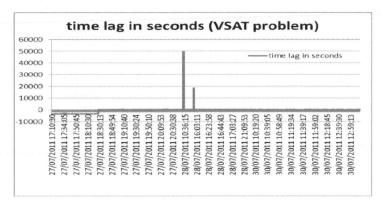

Fig. 11. Time-lags showing VSAT connection problems

As can be noticed in the graphs, there were several times of long delays due to the VSAT satellite connection problems (Figure 11) and some smaller delays (Figure 12), the average relay time for the near real time web enabled sensor measurement to reach the cloud database was within a minute.

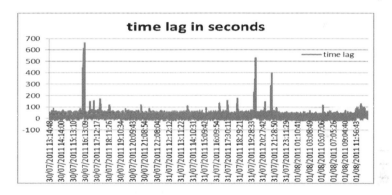

Fig. 12. Near-real-time delay between in-situ measurement and reaching database in the cloud

The experiment demonstrated that instruments can be controlled remotely through a web interface, and observational data and metadata can be distributed to the cloud and multiple nodes in near real time for data archive and analysis purposes. With more overhead but improved interoperability, higher level services can then be deployed there without being constrained by the ship node.

7   IEE1451 and OGC SWE Standards

We have investigated standards that facilitate interoperability, in particular IEEE1451 and OGC SWE. The Sensor Web Enablement (SWE) initiative of the Open Geospatial Consortium (OGC) aims to develop standards to improve interoperability of sensors and their measurements so that they can be managed more easily [14]. As interoperability is achieved at the lower level to provide the possibility of Plug&Play,

the smart sensor interface can be helpful for sensor deployment, networking and maintenance, making the engineer's life easier. However, enabling direct public access to this interface is often not suitable in practice due to the following reasons

1. Scalability and Bandwidth

Sensors and instruments are often deployed in a restricted environment where Internet bandwidth is narrow. In some sensor networks, for the reason of energy-saving and cost reduction, only the gateway sensor node possesses limited Internet bandwidth while the rest simply relay using even lower power communication protocols such as Bluetooth or Zigbee. The relatively light-weight smart sensor protocols are compatible to this design and allow limited but real-time access to sensor's metadata and measurement data. Their nature prevents them from driving more powerful data assimilation, analysis and general public access. Often these applications incur high bandwidth usage and scalability but may require less real-time access to the sensors.

2. Security

The use of SWE standards provide a separated layer of high level functionalities above the more direct sensor access/networking layer supported by smart sensor standards such as IEEE1451 family. As the two layers of standards are designed to facilitate different types of roles, the security implications are different.

3. Data integrity and harmonization

Often sensors have metadata such as manufacturer related data and calibration records. The IEEE 1451 standard allows data to be encoded within the sensor a manner that facilitates its Plug&Play. Furthermore, some of the data such as instrument identification, platform condition and calibration information can be passed to the higher level SWE where it can be used for checking and automated quality control of the observation.

4. Lack of higher level interoperability for Web enablement the IEEE1451 smart sensor standards are designed to facilitate sensor system integration at the deployment level without emphasizing the scalability requirement of measurement data to be reused at the web level, and the interoperability at this level to facilitate 3rd party data mashing.

This can be summarised in Table 3.

Table 3. comparison of the standards

	IEEE1451 standard family	OGC SWE (SOS, etc)	Integration & Harmonisation
Level (close to the physical sensor deployed)	Low	High	Flexible yet consistent
Bandwidth requirement	low	High	Balanced. Supports more sophisticated data analysis without incurring unnecessary bandwidth cost at the low level.
Security requirement	High, restricted	flexible	Satisfied
Data integrity	Tight, original source of the metadata	Loose and rich	Consistent across the layer yet can be extended upward
Interoperability	yes	yes	
Communication and protocol	Low energy, network, internet, TCP/IP	Web, XML, HTTP	Consistent
Scalability	Usually within a small area or a physical platform	Nodes can be both virtual and real. can be distributed in the cloud	Complementary

To this end, OGC SWE (Sensor Web Enablement) provides more promising standards at a higher level. The standard specifies interoperable interfaces and metadata encodings that enable web connecting higher level sensor and measurement data. The specifications can be categorized into the following classes.

1. Observations and Measurements (O&M)
2. Sensor Model Language (Sensor)
3. Transducer Model Language (TransducerML or TML)
4. Sensor Observation Service (SOS)
5. Sensor Planning Service (SPS)
6. Sensor Alert Service (SAS)
7. Web Notification Service (WNS)

At present, there are several implementations including SANY Sensor Anywhere [15] and 52North [16]. Both of them aim to conform their implementation to the OGC SWE specification.

There are many initiatives to integrate these standards. In [10] [11], a service oriented architecture is proposed to harmonize these two standards in order to provide a unified interface for web enabled sensor systems.

We have worked within the context of the ESONET project to conduct the IEEE1451 smart sensor experiments. At a more generic level, there is an attempt to provide virtual sensing platforms where the focus is a mash-able data platform to enable Internet of Things. As a pilot in this direction, Pachube is "a data service that enables you to connect, tag and share real time sensor data from objects, devices, buildings and environment around the world." [7] Instead of focusing on the sensor itself and its deployment and operations, the data platform provides RESTful Web services that allow third party sensor operators to feed their measurement to a system that helps to build a global system of Internet of Things. Open data standards such as EEML, JSON, XML and CVS are used in Pachube to ensure easy data reuse and interoperability based on what new business model, novel data discovery, mash-up, analysis and visualization can be made.

8   Conclusion

From the investigation and experiments, we have learned that relatively abundant internal network and computer resources exist on the research ship *James Cook* albeit restrictive external Internet. There are large amounts of data, both engineering and scientific, collected on the ship and some of them are broadcast within the ship's internal network through UDP messages using predefined formats (see appendix) so that any computer within the ship's network will be able to have read-only access to these data in real time. However, it is neither possible nor necessary to transmit all of them off-ship in real time. Web enabled sensors are possible as long as only light weight tasks are allocated to the ship node, particularly those demanding less bandwidth. We have designed and deployed a system that enables near real time 2-way sensor communication in a low bandwidth, intermittent VSAT Internet connection in an oceanographic environment. This is by sampling only part of the measurements for transmission. The distributed system works with unreliable and restricted narrow-band Internet connections by integrating functional components of RS232 communication, UDP broadcasting, cloud computation, database management and replication of sensor data (measurement and metadata) from a research vessel at sea. The system will be able to tolerate temporal Internet disconnections with trade-off of increased delay and bandwidth usage for clearing up backlogs. We have monitored these events in the experiment conducted at sea and the results are acceptable. The system also allows automatic detection of swapping sensors of the same model. Lab Windows has been used to program data acquisition functionality through accessing sensors' RS232 port and to output measurements and metadata in XML format at the ship node. Data are then relayed to the cloud and eventually to the lab node for observation and control management.

We have also analyzed the delay of data transmission caused by satellite connection problem and illustrated how the system copes with this problem by a-synchronized data relay and backlog clearing in order to provide near real time observation in restrained environment.

Based on this system structure, higher-level functionalities can be plugged-in at the cloud node to provide standard interfaces for data interoperability. To this end, we have used the Semantic Web technologies [18] to manage ontology based oceanographic metadata. It is our hope to set its integration into the system as a future work. We have also done some work previously on IEEE1451 smart sensor interface and OGC SWE. We have compared in this paper the IEEE1451 and OGC SWE standards, which we plan to deploy on the ship node and cloud node respectively to facilitate interoperability.

Acknowledgement. This is part of the defined tasks in Ocean2025 work package 8.3, namely to research and develop suitable methods to use in the oceanography context for multi-use of ocean data. Great appreciation goes to the James Cook crews, in particular Leighton Rolley (Ship IT), and Maureen Pagnani (BODC [9]) for providing ship-side technical support and monitoring receiving observation data stream at lab node during the deployment of the experiment.

References

1. Smart sensor System, http://www.smartsensorsystems.com
2. JC62 Cruise Blog, http://noc.ac.uk/news/porcupine-abyssal-plain-rrs-james-cook-cruise-062-%E2%80%93-28-july-2011
3. Hart, J.K., Martinez, K.: Environmental Sensor Networks: a revolution in the earth system science? Earth-Science Reviews 78(3-4), 177–191 (2006)
4. Near Real-Time Mapping of Ship Locations and Sensor, http://shiptracker.noaa.gov/shiptracker.html
5. The Ferrybox project, http://www.noc.soton.ac.uk/ops/ferrybox_index.php
6. Lee, K.: IEEE 1451: A Standard in Support of Smart Transducer Networking. In: IEEE Instrumentation and Measurement Technology Conference, Baltimore, MD USA, May 1-4 (2000)
7. http://www.pachube.com

8. Maffei, A.R., Lerner, S., Lynch, J., Newhall, A., Fall, K., Sellers, C., Glenn, S.: ExView: A Real-time Collaboration Environment for Multi-ship Experiments. In: OCEANS. Woods Hole Oceanogr. Instn., Woods Hole (2007)
9. British Oceanographic Data Centre, http://www.bodc.ac.uk
10. Song, E.Y., Lee, K.: Integration of IEEE 1451 Smart Transducers and OGC-SWE Using STWS. In: SAS 2009 – IEEE Sensors Applications Symposium, New Orleans, LA, USA, February 17-19 (2009)
11. Song, E.Y., Lee, K.: Service-oriented Sensor Data Interoperability for IEEE 1451 Smart Transducers. In: I2MTC 2009 - International Instrumentation and Measurement, Technology Conference, Singapore, May 5-7 (2009)
12. http://www.imos.org.au/
13. http://imos.org.au/rtunderway.html
14. Botts, M., Percivall, G., Reed, C., Davidson, J.: OGC® Sensor Web Enablement: Overview and High Level Architecture. In: Nittel, S., Labrinidis, A., Stefanidis, A. (eds.) GSN 2006. LNCS, vol. 4540, pp. 175–190. Springer, Heidelberg (2008)
15. Sensor Anywhere, http://www.sany-ip.eu
16. 52 North, http://52north.org/
17. Tao, F(B.), Campbell, J., Pagnani, M., Griffiths, G.: Collaborative Ocean Resource Interoperability: Multi-use of Ocean Data on the Semantic Web. In: Aroyo, L., Traverso, P., Ciravegna, F., Cimiano, P., Heath, T., Hyvönen, E., Mizoguchi, R., Oren, E., Sabou, M., Simperl, E. (eds.) ESWC 2009. LNCS, vol. 5554, pp. 753–767. Springer, Heidelberg (2009)
18. Toma, D.M., O'Reilly, T., del Rio, J., Headley, K., Manuel, A., Bröring, A., Edgington, D.: Smart Sensors for Interoperable Smart Ocean Environment, SARTI, Technical University of Catalonia, daniel.mihai.toma@upc.edu, MBARI, oreilly@mbari.org IEEE Conference, 3 52°North - Initiative for Geospatial (2011)
19. O'Reilly, T., et al.: Instrument interface standards for interoperable ocean sensor networks. In: MTS/IEEE OCEANS 2009 Balancing Technology with Future Needs, pp. 1–10. IEEE Press, Bremen (2009)

Energy Efficiency Mechanisms Using Mobile Node in Wireless Sensor Networks

Teddy Mantoro[1], Media A. Ayu[1], Haroon Shoukat Ali[1], Wendi Usino[2], and Mohammed M. Kadhum[3]

[1] Integ Lab, Kulliyyah of Information and Communication Technology
International Islamic University Malaysia
Jalan Gombak, 53100, Kuala Lumpur, Malaysia
[2] Faculty of Information Technology
University of Budi Luhur, 12260, Jakarta, Indonesia
[3] InterNetWorks Research Group, School of Computing
UUM College of Arts and Sciences, Universiti Utara Malaysia, 06010 UUM Sintok,
Kedah Darul Aman, Malaysia

Abstract. A traditional network consists of gateway sensors which transmit data to the base stations. These nodes are considered bottlenecks in multihop-networks as they transmit their data as well as data from other nodes and hence they deplete faster in energy. One way to optimize energy efficiency in a WSN is to deploy a mobile base station which could collect data without a need for gateway nodes, and hence the multihop bottleneck would be minimized. We compare these two variations of WSN, one consisting of the multihop approach with gateway nodes, and we propose the other network structure, whereby a mobile base station collects data individually from each node using double Fermat's spiral model.

Keywords: energy efficiency, mobile base station, 3-level WSN structure, spiral pattern, pattern routing.

1 Introduction

Wireless sensor networks, due to their manner of operation, act as a bridge to the physical world. They have captured the attention and imagination of many researchers, leading to a broad spectrum of ideas, ranging from environmental protection and military applications.

A wireless sensor network is made up of spatially distributed sensors which are deployed on a wide range of area, and these sensors are used to monitor physical or environmental conditions such as temperature, pollution, pressure and motion. Sensor networks are keys in gathering information needed by smart environments. Each node in a sensor network is equipped with a radio transceiver, a small microcontroller and an energy source, mostly a battery. One of the most distinguished components of wireless sensors networks are the base stations. They have increased computational energy and communication resources. They act as gateways between sensor nodes and the end user.

R. Benlamri (Ed.): NDT 2012, Part I, CCIS 293, pp. 536–550, 2012.

One of the core challenges in wireless sensor networks is the wise management of energy [1, 2]. Since the nodes are deployed without a support infrastructure, they only have finite energy reserves from a battery and manual energy replenishment is nearly impossible. The efficient management of energy is a critical issue in wireless sensor networks. There are many causes which lead to depletion of wireless sensor batteries which ultimately leads to network failure. Firstly, there is packet collision, leading to retransmission of corrupted packets which leads to additional energy consumption. Idle listening is another issue, as the nodes are always on and ready to receive any packet, thus the receiver and radio transmitter are always on. Thirdly there is a problem of overhearing, in which the nodes pick up data which is intended for other nodes. The fourth, and the most common cause of all, is multihopping, in which the nodes which are closer to the base station get depleted faster as they do the additional task of forwarding packets from other nodes in addition to theirs.

The bottleneck problem is an effect of multihopping [3]. An alternate solution to this is employing a mobile base station to the network. This can really balance the energy consumption and increase the efficiency of the network. This paper proposes a system where we deploy a robot as a base station into the network. The benefit of this is that we can have it move on a predetermined path and it will collect data from the various nodes scattered around the network. Its job will be that of a data gatherer. The network configuration proposed by us has the option of deploying multiple base stations as well, as we believe that will be a solution for the slow movement of the base station. The path of the moving base station is determined in such a way that all the nodes in the network can transmit data to it by determining the shortest distance between each node and the base station when it crosses the points on the path.

We will be evaluating activity of a multihopping network structure by varying the size of the network in terms of number of nodes. The evaluation criteria will be the energy of each node and the distance of the nodes from each other, which will determine the energy used to transfer. Then we will evaluate the same on the proposed network structure, that with the mobile base station and without gateway nodes. Comparisons will be made on the data transmission throughput obtained at end of each round under different setups and the amount of energy usage per round. The objective is to efficient and produces greater throughput.

The remainder of the paper is organized as follows. In section 2, we explore related works in this area. This is followed by section 3, where the methodology of the two structures is discussed, and the algorithms used to simulate and test results are formulated. Section 4 gives a view of the mathematical concepts used in the performance evaluation in the two cases. Section 5 conducts simulation analyses on the multihopping structure, and section 6 does the same for the proposed structure with mobile base station. This is followed by section 7 which presents energy and throughput based comparison between the two network structures. Section 8 concludes the paper.

2   Related Work

Several researchers working closely with the issue of energy efficiency have considered employing a mobile sink approach in different ways with different strategies
while others propose strategies of solving problems within the multihopping structures.

Sarma et al. in their paper devise a communication protocol for different network
topologies. The two main types of networks under their consideration are those with
mobile base stations (BSs) and those with mobile nodes as well as BSs. They argue
that the overall topology of the network is dynamic due to the sudden death of the
nodes and availability of nodes. They propose a framework for the routing problem
for the WSNs called Sensor system for Hierarchical Information gathering through
Virtual triangular Areas (SHIVA) [2]. Akkaya and Younis address the issue of energy
depletion in gateway nodes by presenting approaches to move the location of the gateway (sink) for optimized communication energy and timeliness. One of the proposed solutions is to move the gateway to an area where the volume of real-time data
is high, and thus balance the traffic load among the nodes in that area. The basic issues like when and where the gateway should be relocated and how the traffic would
be managed during its movement are also tackled [4].

Gandham et al. present an integer linear programming model to determine locations of multiple sinks in the network where new mobile base stations could be deployed to deal with the energy depletion due to gateway nodes, in addition to a flow
based routing protocol. The locations of the base stations would be periodically
changed [5]. Vass and Vidacs also propose strategies to position the mobile base stations in order to prolong sensor network lifetime. The use the strategies of minimizing
the maximum transmission energy and minimizing the consumed energy and use
these to determine convenient locations for the mobile BS [6]. Xing et al. propose the
formation and deployment of rendezvous nodes in each node cluster in a network,
whose function would be to aggregate the data from the sub-cluster of nodes and
communicate with the base stations. This solves the problem of a slow moving base
station around the network [7]. Jerew and Liang propose a similar solution whereby,
an entire network is divided into clusters of nodes and the base stations visit these
clusters to collect data. So that the base stations don't have to visit each and every
node, each cluster of nodes is appointed a cluster head, which is chosen based on
traffic and distance evaluations [8].

The energy provisioning problem for two-tier WSN has been studied [9], this approach proposed two level of WSN, i.e. relay nodes which content of aggregation and
forwarding nodes. In this paper we extend this approach by proposing 3-level of WSN
structure.

3   Mathematical Model for Energy Consumption

The mathematical concepts used in this section is the model used for energy
consumption in nodes. We use the mathematical model that we proposed in [10]. In
generally nodes are placed arbitrarily in space for the 3-level WSN structure and
the radial propagation WSN structure. In the radial propagation WSN structure, the

Fermat's spiral or parabolic spiral follows are used and the equation is $r = \pm\theta^{1/2}$ where θ is the angle; r is the radius or distance from the center in polar coordinates. The general Fermat's spiral follows $r^2 = c\ 2\theta$. Fermat's spiral traverses equal annuli in equal turns. Vogel, H. in 1979 [11] proposed the full model as follows:

$$r = c\sqrt{n}, \ \theta = n \times 137.508^0$$

where n is the index number of the cycle and c is a constant scaling factor. The angle 137.508° is the golden angle which is approximated by ratios of Fibonacci numbers [12, 13].

This study used the the radial propagation WSN structure modeling energy consumption of nodes as proposed in [10] and combine with Fermat's spiral path for two moving robot in reducing the energy consumptions. If nodes are placed arbitrarily in space and maximum transmission distance of a node and the number of energy levels are d and n, transmission distances r, for each level i can be written as

$$r_{i+1}^2 - r_i^2 = \frac{2}{3}\left(r_i^2 - \frac{r_{i-1}^3}{r_i} \right), r_n = d \tag{1}$$

where $r_0 = 0$ and $i = 1,2,\cdots,n-1$.

A node consumes energy E_i to transmit a signal to distance $r(r_{i-1} < r \leq r_i, i = 1,2,\cdots,n)$. Let $r_0 = 0$, $v_0 = 0$ and $v_i = \frac{4}{3}\pi r_i^3$, then v_i is the sphere that is covered by energy level i and $v_i - v_{i-1}$ is the volume that a signal with the energy level i can reach but energy level $i-1$ does not. Now let E_{mean} can be written as follows.

$$E_{mean} = \frac{3}{4\pi d^3} \sum_{i=1}^{n} kr_i^2\left(v_i - v_{i-1}\right) \tag{2}$$

$$= \frac{3}{4\pi d^3} \sum_{i=1}^{n} kr_i^2\left(\frac{4}{3}\pi r_i^3 - \frac{4}{3}\pi r_{i-1}^2\right) \tag{3}$$

$$= \frac{k}{d^3} \sum_{i=1}^{n} r_i^2\left(r_i^3 - r_{i-1}^3\right) \tag{4}$$

$$= \frac{k}{d^3}\left\{r_1^2\left(r_1^3 - r_0^3\right) + r_2^2\left(r_2^3 - r_1^3\right) + \cdots + r_n^2\left(r_n^3 - r_{n-1}^3\right)\right\} \tag{5}$$

Because $v_1, v_2, \cdots, v_n$ are linearly independent, we can take partial derivation of E_{mean} for each v_i to acquire $v_1, v_2, \cdots, v_n$ that minimize E_{mean}.

$$\frac{\partial E_{mean}}{\partial v_n} = \frac{k}{d^3}\left(5r_i^4 - 2r_{\cdot}r_{i-1}^3 - 3r_{i+1}^2 r_1^2\right), i = 1, 2, \cdots, n-1$$

$$\frac{\partial E_{mean}}{\partial v_n} = 0, \left(\therefore v_n = \frac{4}{3}\pi d^3\right) \tag{6}$$

The solution of above equation that make $\dfrac{\partial E_{mean}}{\partial v_i} = 0$ is as following:

$$0 = \frac{k}{d^3}\left(5r_i^4 - 2r_{\cdot}r_{i-1}^3 - 3r_{i+1}^2 r_1^2\right) \tag{7}$$

$$= \frac{k}{d^3}r_i\left\{2(r_i - r_{i-1}) - 3r_i\left(r_{i+1}^2 - r_i^2\right)\right\} \tag{8}$$

Since $r_i \neq 0$, it can be written as

$$r_{i+1}^2 - r_i^2 = \frac{2}{3}\left(r_i^2 - \frac{r_{i-1}^3}{r_i}\right) \tag{9}$$

Therefore propagation distances r_i for each level i that minimize energy consumption can be written as

$$r_{i+1}^2 - r_i^2 = \frac{2}{3}\left(r_i^2 - \frac{r_{i-1}^3}{r_i}\right), r_n = d \tag{10}$$

where $r_i = 0$ and $i = 1, 2, \cdots, n-1$.

4   The Algorithms of the 3-Level WSN Structure and the Radial Propagation WSN Structure

The aim of the study is to present an avid comparison between two distinct configurations of wireless sensor networks. One is the traditional multihopping sensor network, where we have gateway nodes which perform the extra work of forwarding the data from other nodes, and thus deplete their energy quicker. The other is the proposed network, where the concept of gateway nodes is excluded. Instead a mobile base station moving on a fixed path is employed which moves along its predetermined path and collects data from the nodes individually. In both of these configurations, the distance between node and the distance between the node and the BS play a major role in determining whether data transfer takes place or not.

4.1   The 3-Level WSN Structure

For evaluating and simulating the multihop network, we considered an approach which divides this network into 3 levels. The 3rd level will consist of nodes which are furthest away from the base station. They transmit their data to the 2nd level nodes, which act like an interface between level 3 and level 1. They partially perform the function of relay nodes and transmit their data and data from level 3, to level 1, which are the original relay nodes which transmit all the data to the base station. The algorithm for simulating this network and its operations in MATLAB, is given below.

```
// 3-level structure, calculating throughput and energy with distance
```

Input:
Coordinate (x1, y1): sensors position level 1
Coordinate (x2, y2): sensors position level 2
Coordinate (x3, y3): sensors position level 3
Energy e: energy available for a sensor

Output:
Total energy consumed in one run, E
Total bits transferred in one run, B'
Data Throughput

n1 = number of nodes on level 1;
n2 = number of nodes on level 2;
n3 = number of nodes on level 3;
en1 = energy for each node on level 1;
en2 = energy for each node on level 2;
en3 = energy for each node on level 3;
flags for level 1, f1 = 1;
flags for level 1, f2 = 1;
flags for level 1, f3 = 3;

initiate counter = 0;
initiate energy = 0;

```
//level 1
for i=1:n1 do
    counter+1;
    energy+1;
    energy at node -1;
    if energy at node = 0 then
        flag = 0
    end
end
```

```
//level 2
for i=1:n2 do
    for j=1:n1 do
        calculate the propagation distance nodes of levels 1 and 2;
        place them in array;
    end
end

for t=1:n1 do
    arrange nodes base on their distance;
    check flags of level 1 for transferability of data, and if yes, transfer;
    calculate the energy consumption after transferring data
    count if any die node
    calculate the throughput if any active node after transfer data
end

//level 3
repeat above level 2 procedure for level 3;
```

4.2   The Radial Propagation WSN Structure

For the proposed network, we have the network of nodes scattered around a field. We devise a spiral path for the mobile base station to follow. We devise paths for 2 mobile base stations to travel at same time. The nodes around the network on the other hand, calculate distances of points of the path where the BSs will pass, and find the closest path, and when the base station arrives at these points the data transmission takes place. The algorithm for this is given below.

```
//spiral structure, calculating throughput and energy along with distance in consid-
    eration, each node
//transmits 1 bit of data, and consumes energy proportional to distance between it
    and the base station

Input:
Coordinate (x, y): sensors positions
Energy e: energy available for a sensor
N is the total number of nodes in the network

Output:
Total energy consumed in one run, E
Total bits transferred in one run, B'
Data Throughput
```

Initiate x1 = 0, x2 = 100, y1 = 0, y2 = 100;
Find central location, x0 = (x1+x2)/2, y0 = (y1+y2)/2;

```
for i=1:N do
    find d, distance of points from the central location
    loop through points, locate closest node to the central location
end
coordinates (u,v), assign nearest point.
plot the data;

for i=1:6000 do
    plot spiral (path of the BS);
end

for j=1:100 do
    if x(j) is in the specified range then
        for k=1:n1 //n1 is the number of spiral plot points
            if xz(k) is in the range then
                d, calculate the propagation distance of spiral points from all nodes;
                find the minimum distance;
            end
        end
        save shortest distance in an array;
    end
end

//repeat the above procedure for the rest of data ranges along the entire grid

data = N; //total expected data
D = 0; E = 0;

for p=1:N do
    calculate en,
    calculate energy value based on number of hops according to the distance;
if energy at node > en then
        energy at node – en;
        calculate D+1;
        E+en;
    end
end
D = total data transferred;
E = total energy consumed;

Throughput = D/data;
```

5   Simulation Analysis of the 3-Level WSN Structure

In our experiments, we first conducted evaluation on the multihop structure of the wireless sensor networks. In these simulations random points were generated on a 100 x 100 grid and then divided into 3 regions, each indicating the 3 levels as per our definition of the structure of the network. Once the algorithm is run, it will find distances between nodes of each level, and transfer the data towards the nodes of shortest distance, provided energy is present. We conducted tests on different network sizes of 60 nodes, 120 nodes, 200 nodes, 300 nodes and 450 nodes respectively. The simulations of these networks are presented in Figures 1-5 below.

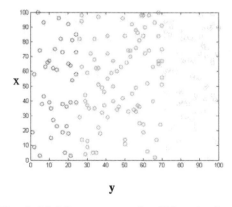

Fig. 1. Multihop structure for 60 nodes in100 x 100 grid

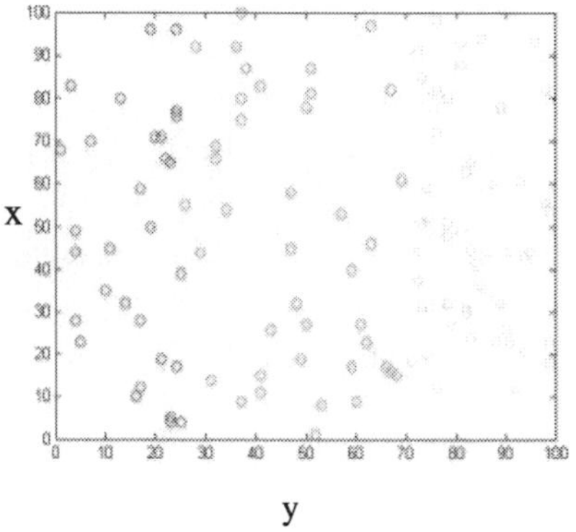

Fig. 2. Multihop structure for 120 nodes in 100 x 100 grid

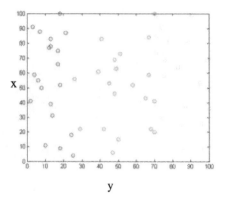

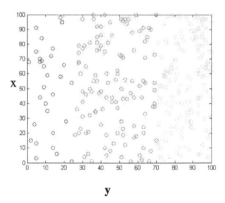

Fig. 3. Multihop structure for 200 nodes in 100 x 100 grid

Fig. 4. Multihop structure for 300 nodes 100 x 100 grid

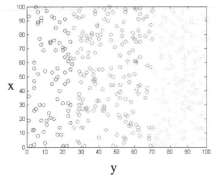

X

y

Fig. 5. Multihop structure for 450 nodes 100 x 100 grid

6 Simulation Analysis of the Radial Propagation WSN Structure

For our proposed solution, we are concentrating on reducing the energy wastage caused by the multihopping case of the relay nodes. The proposed network structure was simulated on a similar 100x100 grid, where the nodes were randomly generated and deployed all around the grid. Note that these are the same random nodes used for the 1st analysis, since we are comparing the results; the data has to be the same. The nodes were given the same random energy values. The network initially looks like the Figures 6 and 7.

Then, a central location was determined for the network structure and a point nearest to the central location was found out, so as to act as the starting points for the path of the base station.

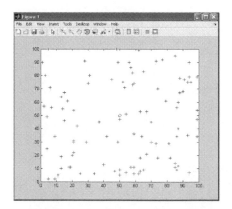
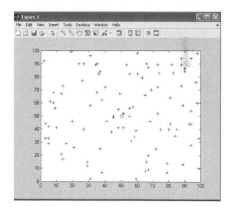

Fig. 6. Initiation state of the network   **Fig. 7.** Determined cluster head of the network

This is the followed by plotting the spiral paths of the base stations. As mentioned, the network does not have relay nodes, and so every node transmits its own data to the nearest point on the path of the base station, when the base station is travelling on that point. This was when we were attempting to save energy and maximize data transmission. In order to cover a wider area of nodes, we deploy 2 mobile base stations at a time. They move simultaneously. These experiments were conducted using the same 5 previous network sizes. The depictions are as shown in Figure 8-12.

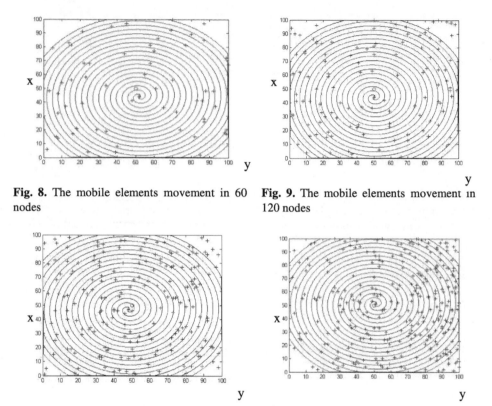

Fig. 8. The mobile elements movement in 60 nodes

Fig. 9. The mobile elements movement in 120 nodes

Fig. 10. The mobile elements movement in 200 nodes

Fig. 11. The mobile elements movement in 300 nodes

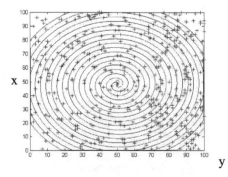

Fig. 12. The mobile elements movement in 450 nodes

7 Experimental Results

After conducting the necessary simulations, the results of each simulation were compared against each other, to determine the favorable outcome, and thus to give us an indication that the proposed solution is a better solution and is successful.

The outcomes of the 5 tests on the multihop simulations are given below.

Table 1. Multihop simulation outcomes for 5 different sizes of networks

No. of Nodes	Throughput %	Energy (J)
60	40	38
120	40	79
200	28	118
300	16.7	130
450	23.8	220

The resulting graph showing variations is shown in the figure below.

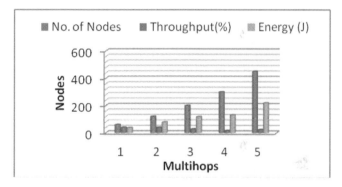

Fig. 13. Throughputs and energy consumptions for 5 different sizes of multihop networks

From the figure, we can notice that as the size of the network increases, the energy consumed increases in small amounts, but the throughput does not show a formidable increase over network size, and tends to decrease eventually.

The results of analysis on the proposed spiral path BS structure are shown in the figure below.

Table 2. Spiral path BS simulation outcomes for 5 different sizes of networks

No. of Nodes	Throughput %	Energy (J)
60	85	74
120	81.7	135
200	88.5	238
300	88.3	373
450	91.1	573

The graph showing variations over network size is given below.

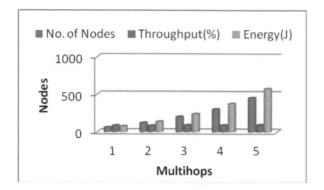

Fig. 14. Throughputs and energy consumptions for 5 different sizes of spiral path BS networks

As can be seen from figure, this method is very efficient in terms of data transmission throughput. The throughput in all the experiment runs is more than 80% and stays pretty consistent and tends to slightly increase as network size increases. The energy used up is used efficiently as can be seen.

A graph comparing the throughputs of both the methods under consideration is given below.

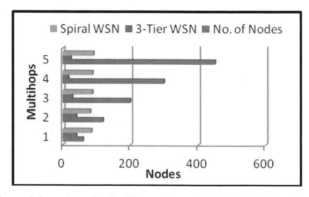

Fig. 15. Comparison of throughput for 5 different sizes of spiral path BS and multihop (3-tier) networks

The graph above compares the throughputs of the 2 WSN structures that we have compared. Both the WSNs are deployed with the same number of points each with the same energy values. As can be clearly seen from the graph, the spiral WSN, or in other words, the radial propagation WSN, excels in throughput all through. There is a certain level of consistency in throughput no matter how different the size of the network is. Whereas in the other network, the throughput is pretty less, and is not consistent, and it appears to be decreasing as the size of the network grows. Thus, the proposed WSN structure can be considered as one of the solutions to the energy efficiency problems in WSNs, as this method makes efficient use of the available energy and produces high throughput.

8 Conclusion

In this paper we attempted to find a solution to the multihop type of wireless sensor networks. There is a high need of energy in multihop wireless sensor networks, for catering to the energy needs of the gateway nodes, and thus, there is always an issue of energy efficiency in these networks.

We proposed an alternative solution to this problem. The proposed network contained the nodes scattered around the network, but the base station is a mobile base station moving along a fixed path, and thus the nodes, instead of transferring the data to each other, they transfer the data directly to the moving base stations and avoid the energy wastage and data dropping caused by the gateway nodes problem. The network also can deploy multiple base stations, further aiding in energy efficiency.

Our experimental results proved that the proposed method fared much better in terms of energy efficiency and produced very high data transmission throughputs all through.

For future work, it is proposed to include more measurement metrics into the equations and calculations to better determine the energy efficiency and thus to explore the solution further. Some of these metrics include:

- Transmission radius of the poles
- The implementation of cluster heads in the structure
- Time of transmitting data
- The implementation of mobile nodes along with mobile base station
- Further controlling base station mobility to allow deviation from the path

References

1. Chang, J., Tassiulas, L.: Maximum Lifetime Routing in Wireless Sensor Networks. IEEE/ACM Transactions on Networking 12(4) (2004)
2. Sarma, H.K.R., Kar, A., Mall, R.: Energy Efficient Communication Protocol for Mobile Wireless Sensor Network System. International Journal of Computer Science and Network Security 9(2) (2009)
3. Somasundara, A., Ramamoorthy, A., Srivastava, M.: Mobile Element Scheduling with Dynamic Deadlines. IEEE Transactions on Mobile Computing 6(4) (2007)
4. Akkaya, K., Younis, M., Bangad, M.: Sink Repositioning for Enhanced Performance in Wireless Sensor Networks. Elsevier Computer Networks Journal 49(4), 512–534 (2005)
5. Gandham, S.R., Daw, M., Prakash, R., Venkatesan, S.: Energy Efficient Schemes for Wireless Sensor Networks with Multiple Mobile Base Stations. In: Proceeding of IEEE GLOBECOM, San Francisco, CA, pp. 377–381 (2003)
6. Vass, D., Vidacs, A.: Positioning Mobile Base Station to Prolong Wireless Sensor Network Lifetime. In: Proc. of ACM Conference on Emerging Network Experiment and Technology, Toulouse, France, pp. 300–301 (2005)

7. Xing, G., Wang, T., Jia, W., Li, M.: Rendezvous Design Algorithms for Wireless Sensor Networks with a Mobile Base Station. In: Proceedings of MobiHoc 2008 (2008)

8. Jerew, O., Liang, W.: Prolonging Network Lifetime Through the Use of Mobile Base Station in Wireless Sensor Networks. In: Proceedings of MoMM 2009, Paris (2009)

9. Hou, Y.T., Shi, Y., Sherali, H.D., Midkiff, S.F.: Prolonging Sensor Network Lifetime with Energy Provisioning and Relay Node Placement. In: IEEE Communications Society Conference on Sensor and Ad Hoc Communications and Networks, pp. 295–304 (2005)

10. Mantoro, T., Usino, W., Ali, H.S., Ayu, M.A.: Energy Efficiency Mechanism Using Mobile-Based Fermat's Spiral in WSN. In: The 11th WSEAS International Conference on Applied Computer Science (ACS 2011), Penang, Malaysia (2011)

11. Fredman, M.L., Tarjan, R.E.: Fibonacci heaps and their uses in the improved network optimization algorithms. J. ACM 34, 596–615 (1987)

12. Vogel, H.: A better way to construct the sunflower head. Mathematical Biosciences 44(44), 179–189 (1979)

13. Prusinkiewicz, P., Lindenmayer, A.: The Algorithmic Beauty of Plants, pp. 101–107. Springer (1990)

Hovering Information Based VANET Applications

Muhammad Shoaib and Wang-Cheol Song[*]

Department of Computer Engineering
Jeju National University 690-756 Jeju South Korea
muhammad.shoaib@live.com, philo@jejunu.ac.kr

Abstract. In this paper, we propose using Hovering Information in vehicular applications to enhance their ability to deal with the dynamics of environment. In particular, we have designed and developed architecture for vehicular applications that employs Hovering Information, and described how hovering information can be utilized in decision-making module made using fuzzy logic. The system based on Hovering Information takes advantages of both hovering and local information published by other nodes and collected from local sensors respectively. The use of Hovering Information allows obtaining dynamically updated information from surrounding nodes during travel and allows information sharing within an ad-hoc network without network infrastructure. Finally, a simulation of decision-making module based on fuzzy logic that uses hovering information as an input of fuzzy controller, has been presented to demonstrate importance of hovering information in real time applications.

Keywords: hovering information, VANET, vehicular applications, real time information in VANET.

1   Introduction and Background

During last few years, Inter-Vehicle Communication (IVC) has emerged as one of the promising fields of research, where advances in Wireless and Mobile Ad-Hoc Networks have been applied to real-life problems and led to a great market potential [4][5]. Applying MANET solutions to inter vehicular communication and content distribution has received a lot of attention in network communities. Meanwhile, many researchers are trying to use these technologies to get benefits by investigating transport layer protocols for VANET environments [10]. However, work in the domain of application architecture in VANET environment still needs to be delved in order to shift the benefits to the real users.

Processes for automation of vehicle operations require data for different parameters. These values are of three types, The first type of data can be obtained using on board sensors e.g. road condition, out-side temperature, and current vehicle speed. The second type of data can be obtained from on-road sensors e.g., maximum speed on a specific road segment. The third type of data needs to be calculated [4]. The

---

[*] Corresponding author.

R. Benlamri (Ed.): NDT 2012, Part I, CCIS 293, pp. 551–564, 2012.
© Springer-Verlag Berlin Heidelberg 2012

calculation of data uses values obtained from on-board sensors and information of other vehicles as well e.g. calculated density of a road or calculated average speed for a specific time on a particular segment of road, which requires hello information from other vehicles to acquire number of vehicles and speed of other vehicles moving on that road segment respectively. This information is not supposed to be stored on the large basis, but requires periodic calculation because of dynamic condition of traffic on roads.

One key limitation of existing Vehicular Applications [4][5][6] is lack of inter vehicle communications. The majority of applications developed for vehicular environments, such as emergency brake messages, traffic jam warnings, lane change warnings, and finally yet importantly, position based routing, use context information. These applications collect context information from either on-board sensors or from context databases. Context Databases are based on the client/server model, where all subscribed vehicles submit their data to a centralized server periodically. Applications subscribe to those servers to collect and submit data. Therefore; these applications have to rely on infrastructure-based services to obtain and use information.

A number of decentralized traffic information systems have been proposed to reduce the maintenance costs of the centralized server approach [9][13]. These systems have banked on traffic condition data collected and shared somewhere by vehicles themselves. However, limitations of these systems are that they do not address information sharing and storage. Thus, information is broadcasted to all vehicles, and vehicles have to store it somewhere because broadcasted information does not have information about its validity (time period and location). Because As there is no common way of information sharing among vehicular applications, this issue of information sharing becomes more difficult if different vehicles run different applications where each application has its own policy for information sharing and storage. Heterogeneous policies of information sharing and storage increase chances of not receiving important information in time. Loss of important information affects the performance and results of systems, and odds of getting wrong warnings and alarms become very high.

Hovering Information enables sharing of information in a specific geographical area that is kept alive or stored for only that particular topographical content [1][2]. A piece of hovering information is generated by some application running on a specific node and is valid for a specific geographical area called hovering area. Each node within hovering area stores and broadcasts the hovering information periodically within its own domain where nodes in hovering area may be connected to each other through ad-hoc connectivity. Part of hovering information is omitted when nodes leave out of hovering area.

In our this work we introduce hovering information as an approach to share information between vehicles moving in a same geographical area and being connected with each other in the ad-hoc network. Why we take this ad hoc networking approach is to keep information in a geographical area without infrastructure networks. Our proposed architecture combines locally collected sensor data and hovering information, and create an integrated source of data for decision making in vehicular applications. We have defined some part of hovering information as a hovering information message that can be represented in XML – a well-known language for information representation – to enhance its interoperability among different applications.

The advantages to use Hovering Information in VANET applications are as follows; Firstly it provides a mechanism to share, store and manage information in VANET environment to overcome the limitations of decentralized vehicular applications. Secondly, it provides an agreed-upon means of describing and sharing road condition, weather status, current traffic information and vehicles statistics such as speed, acceleration and directions. Thirdly, making such information available greatly may increase the interoperability between VANET applications, by enabling both humans and machines to search for and reason upon them.

To fulfill our objectives we have proposed hovering information based architecture for vehicular decision-making applications. The proposed architecture considers hovering information as a source of information for decision-making. We also have briefly described how hovering information message can be stored using XML – the most commonly used language for sharing information in network. Most important contribution of this work is development of architecture for hovering information module and describing its functionalities that will leads towards future research in hovering information based application.

The rest of paper is organized as follows; section 2 explains role of hovering information in vehicular applications. Furthermore, It also explains overall architecture of a vehicular application that uses hovering information in conjunction with local data. Section 3 explains architecture of Hovering Information Module of the system in depth. Section 4 explains usage of hovering information in real applications. Finally, section 5 concludes the paper.

2   Overall Architecture

To describe and demonstrate role of hovering information in vehicular applications we take a scenario of hilly track Highway where 40-70 vehicles per minutes pass on the road. We assume that all vehicles are equipped with GPS, speed measurement sensors and wireless network interface for communications. Overall, all vehicles are part of ad-hoc networks and can communicate each other in such a way that a network application can be installed on these vehicles. Figure 1 shows a wireless ad-hoc network of vehicles running on the road. A network layer protocol is installed on all vehicles for broadcasting, multicasting and geo-casting. Sensors to monitor vehicle status is installed in vehicles for real-time data collection. The sensors' data are transferred to computing systems installed on those vehicles such as a control system.

Since data are collected using local sensors, thus it can only be used for the local applications. However, this meaningful data is for not only local usage but it could be as much useful for the other applications running on other neighboring vehicles moving on the road.

In this architecture depicted in figure 2, the primary components of the methodology gather sensor data, receive and geo-cast hovering information messages and make decisions. These modules work in conjunction with one another, based on the principle of data sharing. Decision making module cannot make any decision without local sensor data of other vehicles, gathered from local sensor database and hovering database. Data in sensor and hovering databases are inserted by sensor data manger and hovering information after receiving data from sensors and other vehicles respectively.

The proposed architecture integrates locally collected data from on-board sensors, Hovering information, and sensor data from neighbor vehicles together. The Sensor Data Handling Application collects environmental data using on-board sensors, pre-processes to convert it into standardized format and then stores the formatted data in local sensor data repository. This paper does not address pre-processing and standardization methods of sensor data because describing these techniques is not in scope of this paper.. The Information Management Module is local data driven system being implemented with a request-response engine. It acts as a bridge between Decision Making unit, Sensor Data and Hovering Information module (HIM). The Decision Making unit is an interactive module, which uses a hypothesis driven intelligent inference engine to aid the user in analyzing the current traffic situation on road in order to take suitable actions. The storage of knowledge is facilitated by the distributed knowledge bases consists of hovering information database and sensor database, which are used by hovering information managers and information management modules. In this methodology, the Information Management Module acts to determine the type of information requested by Decision Making Module. As the part of the Hovering Information Unit, Information Hovering module contains the building blocks that provide the framework for publishing, receiving and storing Hovering information. It further requests the Hovering information from Hovering Information modules of other vehicles moving on road..Each vehicle in the network broadcasts its sensor data in the form of hovering information in the network periodically for a specific location that becomes Hovering area for that broadcasted information. The data is obtained from sensor database and geo-casted using hovering information manager and is received by HIM which also keeps looking for hover information..

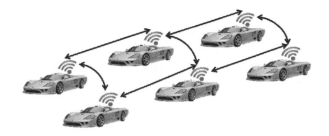

Fig. 1a. A view of VANET environment

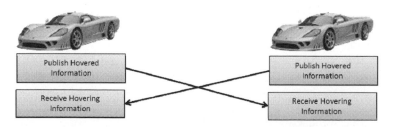

Fig. 1b. Two vehicles are sharing hovering information

3   Hovering Information Manger

Hovering Information Manager (HIM) is a software program for the front-end devices that provides an interface between the vehicles for sharing local information. It is installed on the front-end device with a two-way real-time data exchange channel and works on ad-hoc networks. Responsibilities of HIM includes

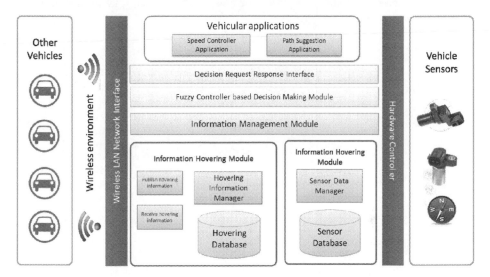

Fig. 2. Overall architecture of a vehicular application that uses Hovering information

1. Automatically geo-casting local information – speed, direction of moving, and current location – to HIM installed on other vehicles periodically,
2. Automatically receiving information from HIMs installed on other vehicles connected through ad-hoc network,
3. Preserving and geo-casting hovering information – density road situation and traffic conditions on road
4. Deleting old and un-necessary information from hovering database
5. Manually requesting HIMs of other vehicles for piece of information

A piece of hovering information is written in XML and is a composition of two parts 1) information header and 2) information body. The header is defined in XML and it contains sender's information, dispatched time, message life, hhovering area, message modification condition, message forwarded strategy, where sender information contains current location of vehicle, moving speed and direction, and vehicle engine no. Moving speed and direction is used to estimate the location of the vehicle before sending response in case of an initiated request. All hovering messages are dispatched using UDP so they do not have any acknowledgement of reception, which eventually saves bandwidth that annihilates the chances of network conjunctions. Message body can be defined either in XML or plan text that is enclosed in body tag of message. Figure 3b and figure 3c show textual and XML based sample message body of hovering information message respectably.

Representing hovering information messages using XML standard structures information and add semantics to message, while using one XML schema enhance their inter application compatibility.

A piece of hovering information can be classify into three categories, 1) request, 2) response, 3) information message. An HIM Request message consists of normal message header, with extension of request tag in header. The request tag contains total number of responses required and deadline time for responding to request. The response message's header contains

```
1   <?xml version 1.0 ?>
2   <hovered-information>
3       <header>
4           <message-type>
5           </message-type>
6           <sender>
7               <engine-no>GTA420</engine-no>
8               <current-location>
9               <Location>
10                  <longitude>N</longitude>
11                  <latitude>E</latitude>
12                  <radiusInMeters></radiusInMeter>
13              </Location>
14          </sender>
15          <hovering-area>
16              <longitude>N</longitude>
17              <latitude>E</latitude>
18              <radiusInMeters></radiusInMeter>
19          </hovering-area>
20          <time-to-live>200s</time-to-live>
21          <forward-policy>0-hop</forward-policy>
22          </header>
23      <body>
24      ....................................
25      </body>
26  </hovered-information>
```

Fig. 3a. A sample of hovering information message

```
1   Time recorded: 132110364
2   Speed-at-point: 35.858
3   speed-measurement: kmph
4
5   Position East: -0.156812667846679
6   Position North: 51.5138705487239
7
8   Moving Direction: N 25 Degree
```

Fig. 3b. Textual body of Hovering Information Message

```
11  <vehicle-data>
12      <time-recorded> 132110364 </time-recorded>
13      <speed>
14          <unit>kmph</unit>
15          <value>35.858</value>
16      </speed>
17      <position>
18          <east>-0.156812667846679</east>
19          <north>51.5138705487239</north>
20      </position>
21      <moving-direction>
22          <direction>North</direction>
23          <angle>28</angle>
24          <angle-unit>Degree</angle-unit>
25      <moving-direction>
26  </vehicle-data>
```

Fig. 3c. XML based body of Hovering Information message

Each message is either sent to specific user or geo-casted. If it is sent to specific user, it is delivered to recipient node only. In this type of message header tag contains a sub-tag <receiver>. However usually message is geo-casted that is delivered to each node in the hovering area.

As shown in Fig. 4, the architecture of Hovering Information Module (HIM) in vehicular application includes four parts: 1) Hovering listener with hovering message parser, 2) hovering publisher with hovering message builder 3) HIM controller for collecting and publishing Hovering information for surrounding vehicles and other hovering sources and 4) Hovering database that stores received hovering information.

3.1   Hovering Listener and Message Parser:

Hovering Message is an XML based textual message, which can be classified as, information, warning, notification, request and response of a request. Hovering information is being spread in a hovering area by different nodes using geo-casting continuously. These pieces of information need to be collected, stored and forwarded to other nodes. We implemented hovering listener in java as a java thread using UDP client that keep listening continuously on a specific port. The task of the hovering listener is to continuously look for the Hovering piece of information in surroundings. While listener receive any piece of hovering information it forwards to message parser that parse its XML into data structure and forward to HIM controller.

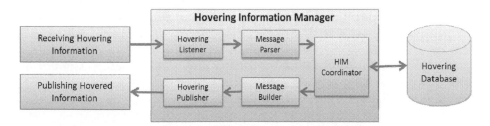

Fig. 4. Detailed architecture of Hovering Information Module

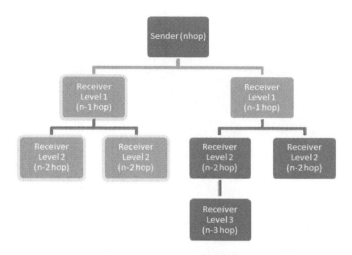

Fig. 5. policy of forwarding hovering message

3.2   HIM Controller

For each packet received to HIM controller (HIMC) it checks either the piece of information received is valid at current time t or has been already obsoleted using time-to-live property of information message. Outdated packets are discarded while other messages are further examined for their message type. Responses are forwarded to their requested modules from where they are initiated e.g. Information Management Module. Another task of HIMC is storing and forwarding hovering messages. As we explicated, each message has its own storing and forwarding policy. After forwarding the message and checking its validity, HIMC stores message in hovering database. Next task of HIMC is to keep monitoring hovering database periodically for messages that need to be geo-cast further. Each message has its Boolean status code that tells either the message should be further geo-casted or not. When first time a message is received that has value n-hop in forwarded policy that means this message can be geo-casted by hierarchy of n nodes as described in figure 5. In figure 5, depicts a case where source node geo-casts a message with n-hop forwarding policy that is received by receivers at level 1 before further processing receivers decrease the forwarding policy by one hop that becomes n-1 hop. When level one nodes geocast the message, it is received by receivers at level 2 and they reduce the forwarding policy again by one hop and it becomes n-2 hop. Similarly, when the same message is geocasted by nodes at level two and is received by nodes at level three, its value is further decreased by one and it becomes n-3 hop.

Last responsibility of HIMC is to delete outdated records from hovering database to keep database update and make memory available for new message. A message is classify as out-dated if sum of its time to live and sent time is less then current time.

Here by time we mean UNIX timestamp. For this job it keeps looking the hovering database periodically and determines the outdated message using time-to-live and initiated date properties of the message. If message is known as outdated, it is deleted from database.

3.3   Hovering Publisher and Message Formatter:

Request to publish Hovering Message is generated by HIMC controller that keeps looking for up-published alive information. As it realizes un-published alive packet, packet is forwarded to message formatter that embed the XML based HI header an generates an XML based hovering information message. Finally XML generated message is returned back to Hovering publisher that broadcast / geocast the packet as defined in message header. Hovering publisher has been implemented using UDP server that broadcast the piece of information for all nodes in network on a specific port.

4   Simulation of Hovering Information for Decision Making

This section presents practicality of hovering information for decision making in VANET environment. The system consists of 5 to 10 vehicles connected to each other via ad-hoc network,. Each vehicle has GPS receiver, speed measurement sensor and small-embedded computer. Embedded computer can control the speed of the vehicle and restrain it from accessing a certain limit. Our aim is to find that maximum speed limit suitable on the highway on which vehicles are moving on. The rationale for simplifying our example is to make an easier understandability of architecture.

When a vehicle enters in a defined road-segment, its wireless network card automatically connects it to existing ad-hoc network. Each vehicle in network geocasts its speed and current direction for other vehicle in the form of hovering information message. We call this message a hovering information message because 1) it is geocasted for a specific location, 2) it is valid only for certain time when the vehicle is present on road and 3) it is updated by the source vehicle periodically. All vehicles in network receive geocasted speed data of other vehicles using hovering information receiver – a component of HIM. Decision-making module keeps asking for updated speed form HIMC. As, HIMC receives updated message it forwards it to Decision making module. Outdated hovering information messages contain speed of older vehicles are deleted periodically to keep the database up-to-date for efficient determination of speed

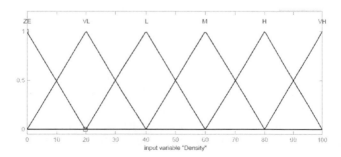

Fig. 6a. Input Membership function

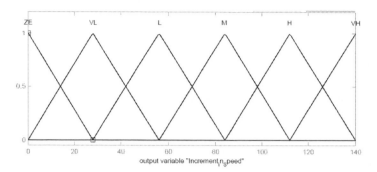

Fig. 6b. Output Membership Function

```
RULE 2 : IF density IS VH THEN speed IS ZE;
RULE 3 : IF density IS H THEN speed IS ZE;
RULE 4 : IF density IS M THEN speed IS VL;
RULE 5 : IF density IS L THEN speed IS M;
RULE 6 : IF density IS VL THEN speed IS H;
RULE 1 : IF density IS ZE THEN speed IS H;
```

Fig. 6c. Rules for Fuzzy Controller

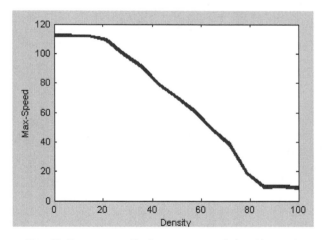

Fig. 6d. Fuzzy controller input, output relationship graph

We have designed fuzzy controller to determine the maximum appropriate speed. Fuzzy controller takes road density as input and provides maximum suitable speed as output. As shown in the figure 6a density is determined on basis of vehicle running per minute on a defined road-segment. To determine number of vehicles moving on a particular road segment, we use hovering information message that vehicles geocast periodically. The density of a particular road segment is calculated after each minute and it reflects the number of vehicles pass through that specific road segment in that minute.

Figure 6a and 6b show the membership for input and output values respectively where figure 6c shows the rules for fuzzy controller. Fuzzy controller applies Center of Gravity to calculate output from given output. Figure 6d shows the input-output relationship graph.

5   Experiments and Results

Our system has a quite few parameters, but we present results for a limited subset of parameter values that can provide new insights. For the rest of the results, we will vary the number of nodes N = {20, 40, 60, 80, 100 ...... 200}, the placement of the node as random, the movement of nodes using random walk of NS2. Other parameters are kept unchanged and chosen as follows. The transmission radius of all nodes is set to R = 180 meters and the packet size of a message that is needed to be transferred as 2KB and storage capacity for each node was 128KB. However, our work and results can be easily extended to the case of dynamic and adaptive radius, dynamic size of packets. The N nodes are randomly deployed within a square of area S 4 X 4 Km. The speed of nodes was incremental starting from 10 km/h to 40 km/h. The result was compared with the client server architecture for accessing information and blind forwarding and selective forwarding of data within the network. We measure the results as following matrix.

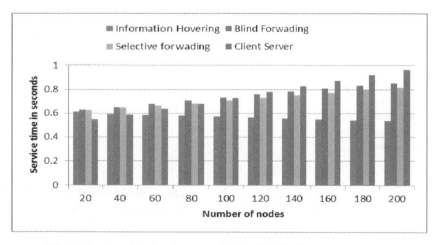

Fig. 7a. Service time for the transmission of 24KB data on the network

Figure 7a shows the time needed to get the data of 24KB in the system as the answer of the query. We computed this metric in terms of units of time. In general, a short service time is desirable.

In Fig. 7b we examine the number of messages exchanged to share the information. Our results shows that client server architecture transferred the minimum number of messages however its query answering time is increase because of minimum packet exchange as shows in figure 7a. It is because every query is answered by the servers and no local query answering was permitted.

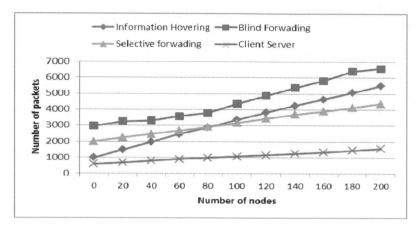

Fig. 7b. Number of packets transfmited on the network during the time of 300 sec simulation

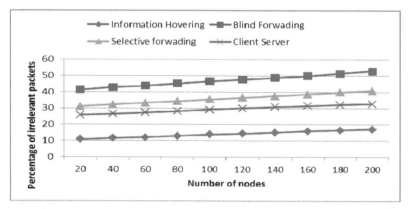

Fig. 7c. Percentage of irrelevent packets transfmited on the network during the time of 300 sec simulation

Finally figure 7c shows the irrelevant packets transmitted to the vehicles. An irrelevant message is message that contains information about the vehicle far away from 720m. Achieving a low number of emitted/useless chunks is essential to save energy and bandwidth resources. Yet, these two metrics are meaningful only under hovering information and client server. Actually, in blind forwarding and selective forwarding, these metrics provide no new insights at all and their values are known in advance. For instance, under the scenario where there is no hovering area defined, every node forward messages to other nodes. In addition, every node receives additional messages from each neighbor. Since there is no concept of message replicas in both techniques the query and answers needs to be travel to large distance over the network every time.

6   Conclusion

This paper reports research of hovering information in vehicular applications. For all vehicles lying within a network, hovering information can be used to gather data from surrounding nodes within network. Although, intelligent vehicular applications are not new in vehicular research, however, these applications either use data from local sensors or take data from internet. The use of hovering information in vehicular applications shows how real-world data is used in decision-making and/intelligent applications. This paper introduces how hovering information can be represented in XML. It also explains how hovering information can be used in vehicular applications. To prove our concept we first provided architecture for publishing hovering information in vehicular network on application layer. We used fuzzy logic to demonstrate a scenario of using hovering information in vehicular applications.

Acknowledgements. This research was supported by Basic Science Research Program through the National Research Foundation of Korea (NRF) funded by the Ministry of Education, Science and Technology (2011-0012329).

References

1. Villalba, A., Masood, A.: Towards Hovering Information. In: Havinga, P., Lijding, M., Meratnia, N., Wegdam, M. (eds.) EUROSSC 2006. LNCS, vol. 4272, pp. 250–254. Springer, Heidelberg (2006)
2. Castro, A.A.V., Serugendo, G.D.M., Konstantas, D.: Hovering Information - Self-Organising Information that Finds its Own Storage. In: IEEE International Conference on Sensor Networks Ubiquitous and Trustworthy Computing, pp. 193–200 (2008)
3. Martens, J., Bareth, U.: A Declarative Approach to a User-centric Markup Language for Location-based Services. In: 6th International Conference on Mobile Technology, Application & Systems. ACM Press, New York (2009), doi:10.1145/1710035.1710073
4. Luo, J., Gu, X., Zhao, T., Yan, W.: MI-VANET: A New Mobile Infrastructure Based VANET Architecture for Urban Environment. In: 2010 IEEE Vehicular Technology Conference Fall (VTC 2010-Fall), pp. 1–5 (2010)
5. Minhas, U.F., Zhang, J., Tran, T., Cohen, R.: Intelligent Agents in Mobile Vehicular Ad-Hoc Networks: Leveraging Trust Modeling Based on Direct Experience with Incentives for Honesty. In: 2010 IEEE/WIC/ACM International Conference on Web Intelligence and Intelligent Agent Technology, pp. 243–247 (2010)
6. Liaskos, C., Papadimitriou, G.I., Pitsillides, A.: Balancing Wireless Data Broadcasting and Information Hovering for Efficient Information Dissemination. IEEE Transactions on Broadcasting (2011), doi:10.1109/TBC.2011.2163449
7. Khaled, Y., Tsukada, M., Santa, J., Ernst, T.: On the Design of Efficient Vehicular Applications. In: IEEE 69th Vehicular Technology Conference, pp. 1–5 (2009)
8. Merlin, C.J., Heinzelman, W.B.: A study of safety applications in vehicular networks. In: IEEE International Conference on Mobile Adhoc and Sensor Systems Conference, pp. 102–109 (2005)
9. Kellerer, W.: (Auto) Mobile Communication in a Heterogeneous and Converged World. IEEE Personal Communications 8(6), 41–47 (2001)

10. Ohta, T., Ogasawara, K., Kakuda, Y.: End-to-End Transfer Rate Adjustment Mechanism for VANE. In: Third International Conference on Dependability (DEPEND), pp. 1–6 (2010)
11. Kulovits, H., Stogerer, C., Kastner, W.: System architecture for variable message signs. In: 10th IEEE Conference on Emerging Technologies and Factory Automation, pp. 902–909 (2005)
12. Gerlach, M.: Trust for Vehicular Applications. In: Eighth International Symposium on Autonomous Decentralized Systems (ISADS 2007), pp. 295–305 (2007)
13. Tsao, S.L., Cheng, C.M.: Design and Evaluation of a Two-Tier Peer-to-Peer Traffic Information System. In: Automotive Networking and Applications (2011)
14. Zafeiropoulos, A., Konstantinou, N., Arkoulis, S.: A Semantic-based Architecture for Sensor Data Fusion. In: The Second International Conference on Mobile Ubiquitous Computing, Systems, Services and Technologies, pp. 116–121 (2008)
15. Zafeiropoulos, A., Konstantinou, N., Arkoulis, S.: A Semantic-based Architecture for Sensor Data Fusion. In: The Second International Conference on Mobile Ubiquitous Computing, Systems, Services and Technologies, pp. 116–121 (2008)
16. Gurgen, L., Labbe, C., Olive, V., Roncancio, C.: A Scalable Architecture for Heterogeneous Sensor Management. In: Proceedings of the 16th International Workshop on Database and Expert Systems Applications (DEXA 2005), pp. 1108–1112 (2005)

Improving the Lifetime of Wireless Sensor Networks Based on Routing Power Factors

Abdullah Said Alkalbani, Teddy Mantoro, and Abu Osman Md Tap

Department of Computer Science, Kulliyyah (Faculty) of Information & Communication
Technology
International Islamic University Malaysia, Kuala Lumpur, Malaysia
abdullah.said@student.iium.edu.my, teddy@iium.edu.my,
abuosman@kict.iium.edu.my

Abstract. In this paper the power efficiency of Wireless Sensor Networks (WSNs) Power is studied. Power consumption is the main challenge during the routing of data. The objective of this study is to address three routing parameters that affect the network life time such as initial power of the nodes, the residual power in the nodes and routing period. Simulations of the effects of these parameters are presented in different network sizes. Contribution on how to improve network lifetime through consideration of power consumption factors during routing is added.

Keywords: WSNs, Power Efficiency, Power Consumption, Routing factor.

1   Introduction

Within the last decade, Sensor Networks and related technologies and applications have gained considerable momentum. This is due to the fact that the technology is maturing and moving out of the purely research driven environment into commercial interests. A number of factors have contributed to this effect: better chip technology allows for increased platform sophistication, higher integration, as well as lower power consumption and cost. Additionally, advances in low power radio technologies have created better wireless protocols and implementations suited for the Sensor Network market. This has led to more reliable operation which enabled credible pilot deployments in the commercial space.

WSNs are a main part of the networking infrastructure for pervasive computing. Pervasive computing and ubiquitous computing are terms nowadays used interchangeably, although they had different meanings in their early stages. Pervasive computing mean immersive computing whereas ubiquitous computing described techniques for embedded and invisible computing. With the development of the two computing paradigms, people gradually use the two terms interchangeably to mean both and combined aspects of the future trend of computing technologies. Pervasive computing has been forecasted by Mark Weiser in 1990's as the computing paradigm for the 21st century [1, 2, 3].

R. Benlamri (Ed.): NDT 2012, Part I, CCIS 293, pp. 565–576, 2012.

Pervasive computing is a model of information processing that augments computers with sensing capabilities and distributes them into the environment. Many pervasive computing applications are reactive in nature, in that they perform actions in response to events (i.e. changes in state of the environment) [4]. However, these applications are typically interested in high-level complex events, in contrast to the low-level primitive events produced by sensors. However, these applications are typically interested in high-level complex events, in contrast to the low-level primitive events produced by sensors. Supporting complex event detection in pervasive computing environments is a challenging problem. Sensors may have limited processing, storage, and communication capabilities. In addition, battery powered sensing devices have limited energy resources. Since they are embedded in the environment, recharging may be difficult or impossible. The energy consumption of each sensor node is dominated by the cost of transmitting and receiving messages. To prolong the lifetime of the system, it is vital that these energy resources are used efficiently [5], [6], [6].

Energy-constrained sensor networks have been deployed widely for monitoring and surveillance purposes. Data gathering in such networks is often a prevalent operation. Since sensors have significant power constraints because battery life is limited, energy efficient methods must be employed for data gathering to improve network lifetime. In this paper we select the routing parameters that effect sensors power consumption during routing. Simulation displays the effect of these parameters on the network life time. Using appropriate consideration for these parameters in routing protocol maximizes network life.

The rest of the paper is organized as follows: In Section 2, the related work in this area is given. Section 3 shows our model for improving WSN life time. In Section 4, extensive experiments by simulation are conducted to evaluate the effects of power consumption factors during routing. The conclusion is given in Section 5.

2   Related Work

One important issue when designing wireless sensor network is the routing protocol that makes the best use of the severely limited resource presented by WSN, especially the energy limitation [8]; because of that efficient routing protocols are required to address power efficiency of the wireless sensor network. Shortest routing path is not always the best path from node to base station. A number of studies have explored the issue of energy aware, lifetime-maximizing routing approaches for wireless sensor networks [9], [10], [11], [12].The problem of these protocols that find optimal paths and then consume the energy of the nodes along those paths, leaving the network with a wide disparity in the energy levels of the nodes, and eventually disconnected the subnets [13].

In [14] an optimal energy efficient routing strategy proposed. In which nonlinear min–max programming problem with convex product form is applied. Geographical forwarding schemes are proposed to improve network lifetime by considering the residual energy of neighboring nodes in deciding next-hop while preserving the localized, scalable and nearly stateless property of geographical routing [15]. An online heuristic model, in which each message is routed without knowledge of future route requests, is proposed to maximize network lifetime [16]. Also much work has been done during recent years to increase the lifetime of the WSN from researchers [17], [18], [19], [20].

3   Routing Factors Model for Improving the Lifetime of WSN

We need to consider other factors such as initial power of the nodes i.e. the emphases placed on the initial energy of the nodes in making routing decision. Another important factor is the residual power in the nodes i.e. the emphases placed on the residual energy of the nodes in making routing decision. The third factor is routing period which is the amount of time between packet-routing decision updates. So to do this we need to choose balanced routing schema of messages through sensors considering these factors.

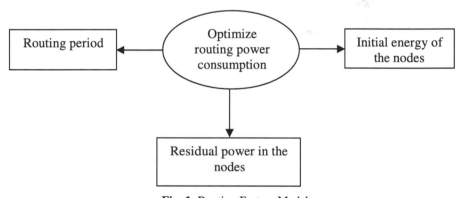

Fig. 1. Routing Factors Model

Figure 1 shows the factors that must be considered during the implementation of the routing protocol. In the next step we are going to simulate different WSN sizes considering these factors individually and together.

4   Simulation and Results

In this section, we evaluate the WSN performance of the proposed approach through simulations. The simulation was applied for several networks sizes with different routing factors. We compared the results of our approach when the three factors namely the initial power, residual power and routing period to the ones of did not consider the proposed factors in their simulations.

4.1   Simulation Tool

The Wireless sensor network simulator version 1.1 used to simulate routing. This simulator has the ability to run successive simulations on a network and report the mean network lifetime across 1,000 trials. The network routing parameters can be changed to allow testing of different network sizes and configurations.

The network may be deployed based on a wide range of parameters such as network size (number of nodes or sensors), communication distance, energy costs for transmitting and receiving data packets, etc. The network can then be used to simulate the detection of vectors traveling across the sensor network field. In this simulation, when a vector trips the sensor of a network node, the node generates a data packet and sends it to a downstream network node. The packets are routed appropriately until they reach a sensor within the area. Each node also simulates an energy store, which is depleted by sending receiving packets, and by detecting vectors. Since the nodes have limited energy, they will eventually power down and drop out of the communications network, causing network failure.

In this research, simulation applied for four different network sizes. These networks contain 35, 169, 212 and 410 sensors respectively. The three proposed factors initial power; residual power and routing period are used as parameters for simulation. These parameters tested individually and at the end all the factors considered together. In the following sections, the simulation results and evaluation for proposed factors will be presented.

4.2   Simulation Using Initial Energy of the Nodes

In this simulation we tested the effects of considering initial energy level for nodes when the routing path created. Table 1 show the comparison of the simulation results with and without considering the initial energy of the nodes during routing.

Table 1. Simulation results with considering/ without considering the initial energy of the nodes

# of sensors	The emphases placed on the initial energy	# of received packets	Mean lifetime test (Average steps)
35	Y	259	566
35	N	99	555
169	Y	441	412
169	N	211	395
212	Y	772	409
212	N	493	381
410	Y	1402	379
410	N	1231	385

Figures 3 and 4 indicates that initial energy factor have small effect on the network life time improvement whereas its effects more in increasing number of received packets during network life.

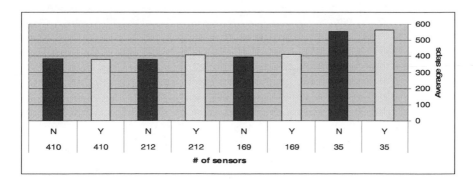

Fig. 2. Comparison of network lifetime with considering/ without considering the initial energy of the nodes for different network sizes

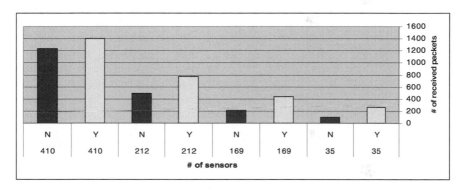

Fig. 3. Comparison of number of received packets with considering/ without considering the initial energy of the nodes for different network sizes

Figure 3 plots the comparison between number of received packets with and without considering the initial energy of the nodes for different network sizes. We can observe that the increase in the number of packets received is approximately 14% for large networks. Such increase could significantly improve the WSN performance.

4.3   Simulation Using the Residual Power in the Nodes

From simulation that considering residual power in the nodes during routing shows that in small WSNs this factor increases the network life time and the number of packets received.

Table 2. Simulation results with considering/ without considering residual power in the nodes

# of sensors	The emphases placed on the Residual power	# of received packets	Mean lifetime test (Average steps)
35	Y	215	821
35	N	92	518
169	Y	707	491
169	N	593	472
212	Y	1032	740
212	N	958	662
410	Y	1409	532
410	N	1256	496

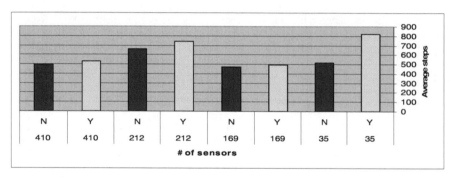

Fig. 4. Comparison of network lifetime with considering/ without considering the residual power of the nodes for different network sizes

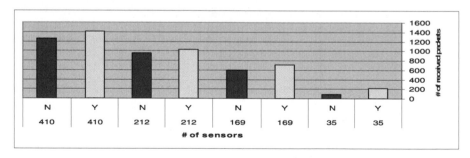

Fig. 5. Comparison of number of received packets with considering/ without considering the residual power of the nodes for different network sizes

Figure 4 displays the comparison between mean network lifetime with and without considering the residual power of the nodes for different network sizes. We can find that the increase in the network lifetime is approximately 37 % for small networks. In addition, Figure 5 plots the comparison between number of received packets with and without considering the residual power of the nodes for different network sizes. We can infer that by considering the residual power of nodes during routing the increases are approximately 58 %, 17 % and 11% for small, medium and large networks respectively.

4.4   Simulation Using the Routing Period

Simulation shows that considering routing period individually without regard to other factors will not improve the network life time. For small network this will decrease its life time. For large networks this factor can increase the number of packets received.

Table 3. Simulation results with considering/ without considering routing period

# of sensors	Routing Period	# of received packets	Mean life-time test (Average steps)
35	High	203	501
35	Low	154	647
169	High	588	432
169	Low	442	391
212	High	681	398
212	Low	924	390
410	High	1621	374
410	Low	1018	363

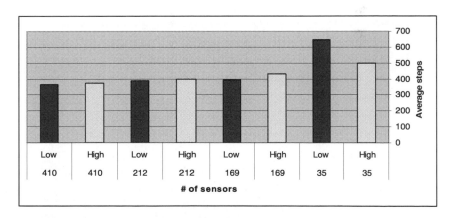

Fig. 6. Comparison of network lifetime with considering/ without considering the routing period for different network sizes

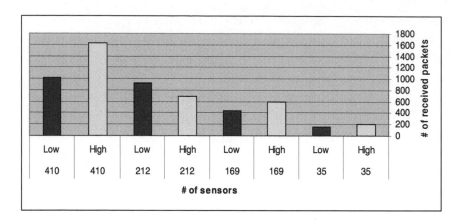

Fig. 7. Comparison of number of received packets with considering/ without considering the routing period for different network sizes

We can find from Figure 7 the increase in the number of received packets during network life is approximately 24 % for small networks and 38% for large networks.

4.5   Simulation Considering Initial Power, Residual Power and Routing Period

Simulation results indicates that considering the three factors (initial power, residual power and routing period) together during routing will effect widely on performance of the network. The life time will be increased and the data packets also. As shown in Figures 8 and 9 it's clear that for large WSNs the number of packets can be duplicated and the network life time is better three times if we considered these factors.

Table 4. Simulation results with considering/ without considering initial power, residual power and routing period

# of sensors	Considering all factors	# of received packets	Mean lifetime test (Average steps)
35	Y	222	849
35	N	192	581
169	Y	660	949
169	N	539	404
212	Y	963	968
212	N	766	388
410	Y	2211	1097
410	N	1196	363

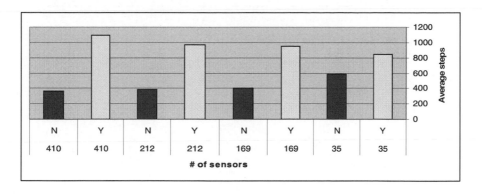

Fig. 8. Comparison of network lifetime with considering/ without considering initial power, residual power and routing period for different network sizes

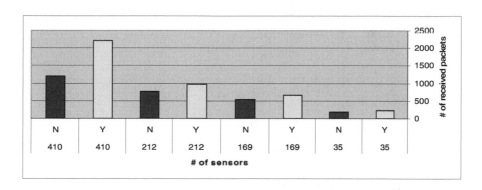

Fig. 9. Comparison of number of received packets with considering/ without considering initial power, residual power and routing period different network sizes

Table 5. Improvement percentage in the number of received packets and Mean lifetime fro different network sizes

Network size	Improvement percentage in # of received packets	Improvement percentage in Mean lifetime
35 nodes	15%	32%
169 nodes	18%	57%
212 nodes	20%	60%
410 nodes	46%	67%

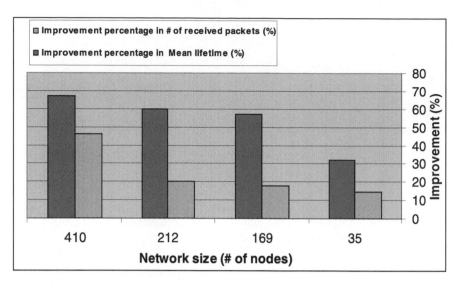

Fig. 10. Improvement percentage in the number of received packets and Mean lifetime fro different network sizes

Table 5 and Figure 10 show the approximate improvement percentage in the number of packets and the mean lifetime for different WSN sizes in case for combined consideration of power factors. We can observe that improvement percentage directly proportion with network size

Simulation results have shown the effects of power factors on the performance and mean lifetime of the WSNs. From this we can contribute the following:

a)   Considering initial power factor individually improves the number of received packets during network life.

b)   For the small WSNs the residual power in the nodes must be considered in the routing method.

c)   For the large WSNs, considering all the three factors (initial power, residual power and routing period) will improve the network life time and increase the number of the packets can be received by the sink nodes.

5   Conclusions

It is well known that, efficient and optimize use of energy is critical issue for network lifetime. The goal of the proposed approach in this research is to reduce energy consumption. We first presented generic power consumption factors model for data gathering in WSNs. Three factors that mainly effect on the network life time addressed. These factors are simulated individually and together. We can contribute that considering residual power in the nodes individually can improve the small networks life time whereas considering all the proposed factors increase the performances of the all WSN networks especially large networks. As future work, we will optimize WSN routing protocol with consideration power factors stated in this research. This would lead to better results ensuring the prolongation of the lifetime of the WSN and improve the number of the packets can be routed during this lifetime.

References

1. Alchaita, M., Nasri, K., Nakcha, M.: Adaptive Server Availability Protocol for Multihop Wireless Networks. Journal of E-Technology 1(1), 8–21 (2010)
2. Mumtaz, S., Tu, L.T., Sadeghi, R., Gameiro, A.: Performance Evaluation of Fixed and Mobile Relay in WiMAX System. Journal of Digital Information Management 8(3), 190–195 (2010)
3. Zheng, Y., Cao, J., Chan, A., Chan, K.: Sensors and Wireless Sensor Networks for Pervasive Computing Applications. Journal of Ubiquitous Computing and Intelligence (2007)
4. Mantoro, T.: Distributed Support for Intelligent Environments, PhD thesis, The Australian National University, ACT 0200, Australia (2006)
5. Okeefee, D.: Distributed Complex Event Detection for Pervasive Computing (2010)
6. Nasser, N., Chen, Y.: SEEM: Secure and energy- efficient multipath routing protocol for wireless sensor networks. Computer Communications 30(11-12) (2007)
7. Srinath, R., Reddy, A., Srinivasan, R.: AC: Cluster Based Secure Routing Protocol for WSN. In: Third IEEE International Conference on Networking and Services, ICNS (2007)
8. Ming, Y., Wong, W.S.: An energy-efficient multipath routing protocol for wireless sensor networks. International Journal of Communication Systems 20, 747–766 (2006)
9. Akyildiz, I.F.: Wireless sensor networks: a survey. Computer Networks 38, 393–422 (2002)
10. Al-Karaki, N., Kamal, A.E.: Routing Techniques in Wireless Sensor Networks: a survey. IEEE Wireless Commnications (2004)
11. Frey, H., Stojmenovic, I.: Geographic and Energy-Aware Routing in Sensor Networks. In: Handbook of Sensor Networks: Algorithms and Architectures, 552 pages. Wiley (2005) ISBN 978-0-471-68472-5
12. Krishnamachari, B.: Networking Wireless Sensors, 214 pages. Cambridge University Press (2005) ISBN 0521838479
13. Bhuyan, B., Sarma, H., Sarma, N., Kar, A., Mall, R.: Quality of Service (QoS) Provisions in Wireless Sensor Networks and Related Challenges. Wireless Sensor Network 2, 861–868 (2010)
14. Shiou, C., Lin, Y., Cheng, H., Wen, Y.: Optimal energy-efficient routing for wireless sensor networks. In: Proceedings of the 19th International Conference on Advanced Information Networking and Applications, vol. 1, pp. 325–330 (2005)
15. Lim, T.L., Mohan, G.: Energy aware geographical routing and topology control to improve network lifetime in wireless sensor networks. In: Proceedings of the Second International Conference on Broadband Networks, vol. 2, pp. 771–773 (2005)
16. Park, J., Sahni, S.: An online heuristic for maximum lifetime routing in wireless sensor networks. IEEE Transactions on Computers 55(8), 1048–1056 (2006)
17. Chang, J.H., Tassiulas, L.: Routing for maximizing system lifetime in wireless ad-hoc networks. In: Proceedings of 37th Annual Allerton Conference on Communication, Control, and Computing (1999)

18. Chang, J.H., Tassiulas, L.: Energy conserving routing in wireless ad-hoc networks. In: IEEE INFOCOM (2000)
19. Das, A.K., Marks, R.J., El-Sharkawi, M., Arabshahi, P., Gray, A.: Mdlt: A polynomial time optimal algorithm for maximization of time-to-first-failure in energy constrained wireless broadcast networks. In: Proceedings of IEEE GLOBECOM (2003)
20. Das, A.K., El-Sharkawi, M., Marks, R.J., Arabshahi, P., Gray, A.: Maximization of time-to-first-failure for multicasting in wireless networks: Optimal solution. In: Proceedings of MILCOM (2004)

Redirect Link Failure Protocol Based on Dynamic Source Routing for MANET

Naseer Ali Husieen, Osman Ghazali, Suhaidi Hassan,
and Mohammed M. Kadhum

InterNetWorks Research Laboratory,
School of Computing,
Universiti Utara Malaysia,
Malaysia
naseerali@internetworks.my, {osman,suhaidi,kadhum}@uum.edu.my
http://www.internetworks.my

Abstract. Ad hoc networks are characterized by multi-hop wireless connectivity. Due to frequent topology changes in wireless ad hoc networks, designing an efficient and dynamic routing protocol is a very challenging task,and it has been an active area of research. This work is part of ongoing research on the link failure problem caused by the node's mobility in Dynamic Source Routing (DSR) protocol. In this paper, we propose an extension of DSR protocol called Redirect Link Failure Protocol (DSR-RLFP) in order to solve link failure and avoid propagation route error message back to the source upon link failure in a different way from the existing solution. RLFP protocol contains two models namely, Link Failure Prediction Model and Link Failure Solution Model. The main benefit of RLFP is to reduce the frequent route discovery process after link failure happened, which leads to save network resources.

Keywords: MANET, routing protocol, RLFP, DSR protocol.

1 Introduction

The most difficult and important issue in the developing of mobile ad hoc network is routing protocols because the efficiency of the network, and the internet depends on the performance of routing algorithms. Therefore, finding efficient routing protocol is not an easy task. The primary goal of using routing protocols in ad hoc networks is to discover and establish routes between two pairs of nodes to send the data packets between the source and destination. Several routing protocols for ad hoc wireless networks have been developed to establish a connection short or fast routes. Routing protocols can be divided into two categories: Proactive routing and Reactive routing. In case of the proactive routing approach, the route is always available before sending data packets from the source to the destination. Every node keeps updating and maintains complete routing information of the network. For the proactive approach, power and bandwidth consumption is increased due to the exchange of routing table

R. Benlamri (Ed.): NDT 2012, Part I, CCIS 293, pp. 577–591, 2012.
© Springer-Verlag Berlin Heidelberg 2012

among nodes after each change in the node's position. In this aspect, it takes a place even if the network is in the standby mode, which means there is no data transmission in the network. The most common proactive protocols are namely, Destination Sequenced Distance Vector (DSDV), Optimized Link State Routing (OLSR), and Wireless Routing Protocol (WRP). While in case of Reactive routing approach, the route is established only when data packet is needed to be delivered to the destination. Reactive routing takes a different approach for routing than table driven protocols such as DYMO, TORA, AODV, and DSR. The routes to the destination are discovered only when actually needed. Reactive routing protocols are based on Distance-Vector concept (DV), which can significantly decrease routing overhead and power consumption, because reactive routing does not need to keep searching and maintain the routes on which there is no data traffic to send as stated in [2]. According to the authors in [2-7] have evaluated the comparison of proactive and reactive with multi-hop routing protocols namely DSDV, TORA, DSR, ABR, and AODV. Through their simulation results, they have observed that reactive routing protocols outperform proactive routing protocols in terms of a packet delivery ratio, routing overhead, energy efficiency and stability. Therefore, this paper focuses on reactive protocols especially on DSR protocol regarding the link failure problem between two mobile nodes.

2   Dynamic Source Routing (DSR)

DSR protocol is designed in an ad hoc network to allow being totally self-organizing and self-configuring without the need for any existing network infrastructure or administration [1]. DSR has two main mechanisms, namely Route Discovery and Route Maintenance Process. In the route discovery process, two packets will be generated, which are called Route Request Packet (RREQ) and Route Reply Packet (RREP), in the route maintenance, Route Error Packet (RERR) will be generated. These mechanisms work together to allow nodes to discover and maintain a route to the destination. DSR protocol does not use any periodic routing message, link status sensing, and neighbour detection packets. In addition, DSR protocol is completely on demand routing protocol used for multi-hop wireless network.

2.1   Link Failure in DSR Protocol

The most weakness of mobile ad hoc network is the lost connectivity between the source and the destination during data transmission, because of the time elapsed between link failure discovery, and alternative path connection can be high. In reactive routing protocols, frequent broadcasting route request to the destination node is costly in terms of delay and waste network resources. In DSR protocol, a source node could broadcast route request packet to the entire network in order to obtain the routing information to a particular destination, this route request packet specifies the desired destination in its header. When the nodes receive the route request packet, this packet attaches itself to the routing header of request packet and keeps on broadcasting this packet. Hence, when the desired destination received this packet, a route from source to the destination is formed in the packets routing header. In this respect, the new formed of routing information will be carried in RREP packet that transmitted from the destination to the source. In addition, all data packets are transmitted with the complete path in their routing header through intermediate nodes.

2.2   Handling Link Failure in DSR Protocol

Most of the routing protocols for mobile ad hoc networks have a route maintenance mechanism, which can handle the link failure or link errors. There are several factors that can cause link failure, including node mobility, environment conditions, lack of energy power, and hard medium contention. A route maintenance play an important role in ad hoc networks by reducing or eliminating the broken link in order to avoids disruption in the services that the network can offer. Route maintenance is a mechanism by which the initiator node can detects and discover a link failure as it can send a packet to the target node in order to fix and find a new route to maintain and to keep the transmission of the data packets. Maltz et al. [1] proposed a new technique for recovering the link failure called "packet salvaging", which can salvage the packets during the link failure. Packet salvaging technique is generated by intermediate nodes only, which uses its own route cache information to forward a packet to its desired destination. However, when no alternative route in the route cache of the intermediate nodes is existed to forward the incoming packets, the packet salvaging technique will not work and the data packet will be dropped. In this case, intermediate node sends back a Route Error Packet (RRER) to the source node. The source node removes all the unnecessary routes from the route cache and re-initiates a route discovery process. Fig.1 illustrates how the DSR protocol handles the link failure between two mobile nodes. Fig.1 shows link failure between the Current Node (CN) and Moving Node (MN) due to node mobility or any other reason. According to Johnson et al. [1], the current node which detects the link failure will try to find an alternative route from its route cache in order to forward the data packet to the destination node D, if there is no an alternative route in the route cache of Current Node (CN) to forward the incoming packet to the desired destination D, the packet salvaging mechanism will not work and the data packet will be dropped as well as the current node will propagate a Route Error packet (RERR) to the source node S. when a source node receives a RRER packet, it will remove all the routes that contains errors from its route cache. If there is no more routes remain in the route cache to that desired destination, then a new RREQ packet is broadcasting in order to discover and establish new routes to the desired destination. The new RREQ packet is generated assuming that a route to the destination node is still required to deliver the rest of the data packets.

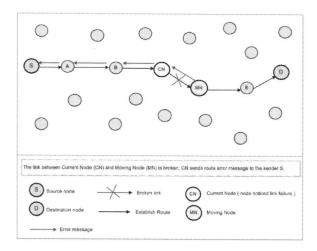

Fig. 1. Standard Link Failure in DSR Protocol

3   Related Work

On mobile ad hoc wireless networks, the route failure has a significant negative impact on the packet delivery ratio to the destination. The common drawbacks and main consequences of route failures are packet dropping, end-to-end delay, and minimum throughput. These result in overall network inefficiencies. In addition, the interval time for link break detection, the time for a route error message propagate back to the source node, and construction time of the alternative path can be high. Therefore, many link predication studies have been proposed, recently, which focus on improving route repair in advance. In N. Alsharabi et al. [8] proposed Packet Received Time (PRT) to predict the link status between two nodes to prevent the link failure in the active route. PRT uses power measurement of the received packets to predict the changes in the network. This mechanism has a weakness as many other mechanisms that sending unnecessary warning messages propagating back to the sender node, which leads to increase the number of route discovery process again increases the traffic in the network. A. Rhim et al. [9] proposed Link Expiration Time (LET) prediction with DSR protocol to predict the link before disconnected in order to reduce packet loss due to link failures. LET algorithm is based on the three predictions algorithms namely Global Position System (GPS), Radio Propagation Model, and Signal Strength (SS). Instead of waiting for link breakage, LET algorithm started by predict the link is about to be broken with the next node. Proactive route maintenance was applied in LET algorithm in order to avoid link breakage that can reduce packets drop. However, GPS has some issues; such as the cost of the device associated with their use, and they might not work well because of fading. In addition, LET algorithm needs synchronization between the internal clocks of nodes. In Song Oliver et al. [10] proposed Backup Source Routing (BSR-DSR). BSR is another extension of DSR protocol is based on route reliability. Through their observation, they concluded that BSR has a longer delay than DSR protocol, because of BSR is based on the backup approach that may take a longer path backup than DSR. In addition, BSR leads to increase the traffic congestion at high-traffic load. Hyun et al. [11] proposed a new Local Repair Scheme where the source node recovers the route breakage caused by shifting of a node with an aid of the adjacent nodes instead of re-routing the whole path. When the link connectivity failure between two nodes, the mobile node needs to keep contact with two intermediate adjacent nodes of the disconnected node. To achieve the goal of route repair, a scheme that adopts a promiscuous mode is applied in order to save the time for searching the nearest node and decrease the overhead. However, continuous process of promiscuous mode to obtain the routing information for each node, it can results in extreme energy overhead of the whole the network and decrease the efficiency of the protocol. M. Aissani et al. [12] proposed GSM which is an extension of DSR protocol in order to enhance the link failure by using two optimization techniques called generalized salvaging mechanism and cache update of the intermediate nodes with source route discovered during the route request propagation. However, the salvaging mechanism works only if there is alternative route in the upstream node's cache, otherwise the data packets will be dropped. Susmit et al. [13] proposed Repaired Backup Approach (RB-DSR) to enhance the link failure in DSR protocol by adds backup approach (second best route) to the existing DSR algorithm. However, there is a weakness by using backup approach in RB-DSR scheme. The backup route might fail during the data transmission, while the source node is still using primary route, and the source node would remain unaware of that failure. In this respect, if the primary route fails due to node mobility or other reason and the source node switches immediately to the backup route, then the source node discovers that the backup route has been breakdown already. In addition, if the source node tries to search for another route with high quality in order to be second best route. In case if the source node cannot find this route, it results in long route discovery process, which can cause long delay. M. Hussein [14] proposed an extension of DSR protocol called NRRA in order to enhance the link failure in DSR protocol. However, the main drawback of NRRA is that an unnecessary warning message is sent back to the source node after certain period of time, which leads to increase the routing overhead, increase the size of additional packets, and the complexity of routing protocol. MLR [15], MRFT [16], and IM-DSR [17] protocols proposed based on the local recovery and multipath routing approach in order to improve the performance of DSR protocol. However, the main drawback of these protocols is the local route recovery use routing information collected in the last route discovery process, which becomes invalid routes promptly in high mobility networks. Nonetheless, since they did not think about any avoidance of a reverse route propagation back to the source node upon a link failure, the approach will not be different much from the standard DSR link failure mechanism.

4   Redirect Link Failure Protocol (RLFP)

RLFP is proposed to prevent completely link failure caused by node mobility and to eliminate the route regenerating by the source upon link failure on the way to the destination by utilizing link signal strength on active route and redirect the data packets from the current node (node noticed link failure) into a new path. The main objective of using signal strength as one of the prediction methods is to predict the link between two mobile nodes before a breakdown. After the current node receives signal information from the next hop indicate that the link is soon broken, the current node constructs a new route and re-forward the data packet smoothly without any loss to the destination. In this way, RLFP protocol avoids sending route error message (RRER) back to the source node, which is results to minimize the delay, reduce the overhead, and save network resources.

4.1   Link State Prediction Algorithm

This phase involves with a prediction algorithm in order to avoid a link failure in advance by using signal strength based method. As stated in [18-21], this method predicts the link breakage based on received signal strength from the upstream node. In this respect, each and every signal power is registered then compared with a predefined threshold value. If the received signal strength is less than the threshold value, then it considers that this link will be broken soon, as demonstrates in Fig.2, when the link between the Current Node (CN) and Moving Node (MN) is going to break down soon. The concept that uses received signal strength to predict link failure has been proposed in cellular networks to perform handover as mentioned [22]. At first, we assume that the sender power level is constant. Received signal power samples are measured from packets received from the sender. From this information, it is possible to compute the rate of changes for a particular neighbour's signal power level. Because the signal power threshold for the wireless network interface is fixed, the time when the power level drops below the acceptable value can be computed. It uses computation of relative movements between two mobile nodes and assumes that the nodes move with constant speeds and directions. The parameters speeds, directions, positions (location) are important to calculate the distance between two nodes and link connection expiration time. Normally, these parameters provided by GPS as stated in [18]; so if the GPS is not available, the distance of nodes can be obtained by measuring the received signal powers. In the distance method, the received signal power solely depends on its distance to the transmitter. In this method as mentioned above assumes that the speed, direction, and transmission range are constant. Therefore, the speeds and directions for node A and node B does not change from t_0 & t_3, where t_0 is the start point. It can calculate the distance d from A to B at time t. However, from this simple calculation, it can predict the distance d when the mobile node A and B is going to be disconnected as stated in [24 and 25]. Thus, the speeds (v_A, v_B), and directions (θ, l and m)

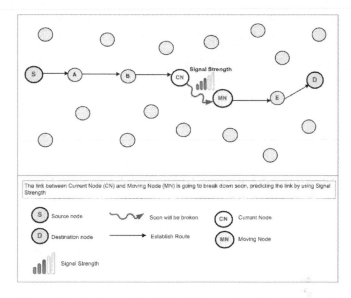

Fig. 2. Prediction of the Link Failure using Signal Strength

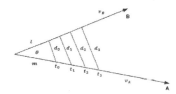

Fig. 3. Distance Prediction Method

for A can be computed as illustrated in Fig. 3. So the distance between A and B is: $d = \sqrt{(l + v_A t)^2 + (m + v_B t)^2 - 2cos\theta(l + v_A t)(m + v_B t)}$

$$= \sqrt{at^2 + bt + c} \tag{1}$$

where: $a = v_A^2 + v_B^2 - 2v_A v_B cos\theta$
$b = 2lv_A + 2mv_B - 2lv_B cos\theta - 2mv_A cos\theta$
$c = l^2 + m^2 2lm cos\theta$ Alternatively if known the values of d_0, d_1 and d_2 at time

$t_0, t_1, and\ t_2$, but unknown speed and direction then it can predict the distance d_3 only at time t_3 through this equation:

$$d_3 = \sqrt{lt_3^2 + mt + n} \tag{2}$$

Where: $l = \dfrac{(d_1^2 t_2 - d_2^2 t_1) - d_0^2(t_2 - t_1)}{t_1 t_2(t_1 - t_2)}$ $m = \dfrac{(d_1^2 t_2^2 - d_2^2 t_1^2) - d_0^2(t_2^2 - t_1^2)}{t_1 t_2(t_1 - t_2)}$, $n = d_0^2$

From this simple calculation, we can predict the time t when the mobile node A and B are going to be disconnected. Thus, this method is solely depends on the distance between nodes. The time prediction method, having knowledge of the distance d, it can predict the time t when the node. A and node B is going to be disconnected. In addition, it can be also calculated the remaining time that the link will stay connected with known transmission range r. For example, A and B are within the transmission range r at (x_A, y_A) and (x_B, y_B) move with speed v_A, v_B at direction θ_A, θ_B, where θ_A, θ_B, are in the range of (0 to 2π), respectively. So the Link Expiration Time (LET) is:

$$LET = \frac{-(ab+cd) + \sqrt{(a^2+c^2)r^2 - (ad-bc)^2}}{(a^2+c^2)} \tag{3}$$

Where: $a = v_A cos\theta_A - v_B cos\theta_A, b = X_A - X_B, c = v_A sin\theta_A - v_B sin\theta_B, d = y_A - y_B$ Even though these two methods for distance prediction method and time prediction method are identical same and can be derived from each other for their equations, the time method prediction can be much easier than the distance prediction method if the distance d is known. But most likely the distance between two mobile nodes is unknown due to the MANET topology may change frequently and hosts move randomly with unpredictable speed. Finally, Signal Propagation Models is used in our prediction algorithm in order to predict the propagation characteristics such as received signal power of each packet. These models can be "Free Space Model" and "Two Ray Ground Reflection Model." The Free Space Mode is considered a single line-of-sight path, and it is the most popular model of radio propagation to compute the received signal powers at near distance as stated in [16] and its equation is as follows:

$$P_r(d) = \frac{P_t G_t G_r}{L} * \frac{\lambda^2}{(4\pi)^2 d^2} \tag{4}$$

Where P_t is transmitted signal power, G_t is the antenna gain of the transmitter, G_r is the antenna gain of the receiver, L is system loss, λ is the wavelength, and d^2 is opposite proportional to the received signal power by receiver side where the square is the distance to the node that sent the signal. The Two Ray Ground Reflection Model is more useful in terms of long distance propagation signal in addition this model not considers only single line-of-sight path. The formula for the Two Ray Ground Reflection Model is as follows: [19].

$$P_r(d) = \frac{P_t G_t G_r}{L} * \frac{h_t^2 h_r^2}{d^4} \tag{5}$$

4.2   Link Failure Solution Model

Link Failure Solution model is proposed in order to solve link failure after the current node predicts the link to the next hop is going to break down soon.

To achieve this goal, this paper is proposed a useful mechanism to prevent the link failure in advance and create a new path locally (where the link failure takes place). In this point of view, we proposed two models called Discovery Model (DM)" and "Construct New Route Model (CNRM). These two models are proposed to predict the signal strength in order to find out a link status before it becomes invisible and establishes a new path to the destination node to redirect the current link into a new route with a strong link communication and less number of hops, respectively. In addition, Comparison Algorithm also proposed in order to integrate the models. The link failure solution model's architecture is shown in Figure 4.

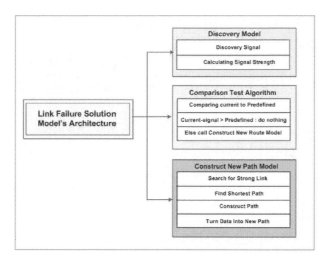

Fig. 4. Link Failure Solution Model's Architecture

Discovery Model. The discovery model contains two sub-models, Discovery signal and Calculating signal strength.

Discovery Signal. This study utilizes the link state prediction method through the signal strength by using mathematical equations to estimate when two mobile nodes are going to disconnect each other. Thus, the main task of this function is to collect the current link signal status which will be used the prediction of the link failure.

Calculating Signal Strength. The task of this model is to calculate the signal strength by create table, which depends on the discovery signal model. Thus, the Calculating Signal Strength picks up the signals from that table and measures the status of the signal power, and this status will be used to find out the circumstance of the current connection whether it will be broken soon or not.

Comparison Test Algorithm. The comparison Test Algorithm also called decision maker of the models. The Comparison Test Algorithm compares the current signal statues to the signal power predefined C_{sgl} to $P_{defined}$ and test the condition $C_{sgl} < P_{defined}$. It gives an order to all actions on the Models to be interconnected and interlinked each other in order to unify the functions of the models.

Construct New Route Model. Construct new route model contains four sub-functions, Search Strong Link, Find Shortest Path, Construct Path, and Turn data into new route.

Search for Strong Link

The main function of this model is to determine the strong link after the current node noticed that the link going to break down soon. The current node utilizes IEEE 802.11 of wireless standards for beacon frames, which sends every 100 ms and through the beacon mechanism, we will be able to get the nodes information for every 100 ms and in this respect, we are only interesting the signal status. However, this action will be taken if the current link signal status is less than the predefined signal power. If this requirement is fulfilled, the current node monitors all available signals among neighbour nodes of the current node (the node that noticed the link will failure soon) to find out a node that has a stronger signal according to the current connection signal strength by create an array for each node to keep the signal information, this array called signal-status array. This array holds three packets for signal strength and their reception time. This is done by Lagrange Interpolation method, which has the following general definition: $L_j(x) := \Pi_{0 \leq f \leq k, f \neq j} \left(\dfrac{x - x_f}{x_j - x_f}\right) = \left(\dfrac{x - x_0}{x_j - x_0}\right)...\left(\dfrac{x - x_{j-1}}{x_j - x_{j-1}}\right)\left(\dfrac{x - x_{j+1}}{x_j - x_{j+1}}\right)...$

$$P = \left(\dfrac{(t - t_1) * (t - t_2)}{(t_0 - t_1) * (t_0 - t_2)} * P_0\right) + \left(\dfrac{(t - t_0) * (t - t_2)}{(t_1 - t_0) * (t_1 - t_2)} * P_1\right) +$$

$$\left(\dfrac{(t - t_0) * (t - t_1)}{(t_2 - t_0) * (t_2 - t_1)} * P_2\right) \tag{6}$$

The strength powers and time intervals are p_0, p_1, p_2, t_0, t_1 and t_2, respectively.

Find Shortest Path Function

The main drawback with source routing approach is that in large network, DSR protocol does not perform well, because as the number of intermediate nodes increases in each route, the size of the packet header increased as well, which leads to incur an extra overhead carried in each header of the data packet. This extra overhead is occurred not only when the packet is initiated, but also originated in each time the packet when it forward to the next hop. However, this extra routing overhead result in the decrease the bandwidth available during the data transmission, increases the latency, and consumes extra battery power in the network. This routing overhead is directly proportional to the path length. Therefore, based on the drawbacks mentioned about the source routing approach, this study focuses to find a shortest path from the current node (node noticed the link failure) to the destination in order to redirect the link failure into a new route. This paper is combining the Shortest Path Function with Strong Signal Function in order to ensure the selected path from the current node to the destination node is the best route not simply selected, which means less interference in the network, higher throughput, high bandwidth, and lower latency. After the current node noticed the link to next hop going to break down soon, it sends one hop neighbour packet called Local Conditions Request Packet (LCRP) to the adjacent neighbour nodes, which is carry the three requirements: search for strong link, route to the destination, and find the shortest path to the destination. Each adjacent neighbour node to the current node will check whether it has these three requirements or not. The flow chart of finding shortest path function shows in Figure 5. Figures 6 and 7 shows how the current node

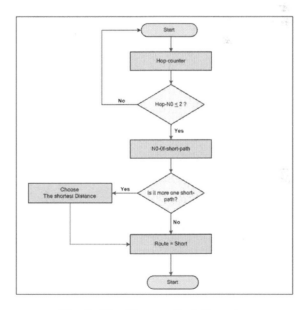

Fig. 5. The Shortest Path Function

redirects the link failure into a new route based on the three requirements. In Fig.6, it shows how the Current Node (CN) reacts after receives signal information status from the next hop which is Moving Node (MN), indicate that the link between them is going to fail soon. In this case a CN node circulates LCRP packet to its adjacent neighbour nodes except the CN node is receiving from (it does not circulate to upstream node), in order to find out if there is a node that

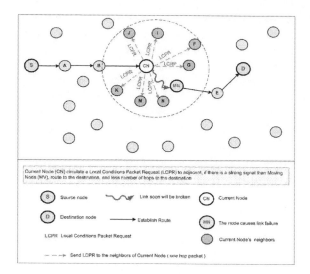

Fig. 6. Current Node (CN) Circulates Request to Adjacent Nodes

has a stronger signal than the current active link, route to the destination, and the number of hops in each route is less than or equal 2 hops to the destination in order to construct the new path and forward the data packets to the desired destination. The CN node will not forward the data packets until one of the adjacent nodes fulfilled the three conditions together. In Fig.7, it shows that the

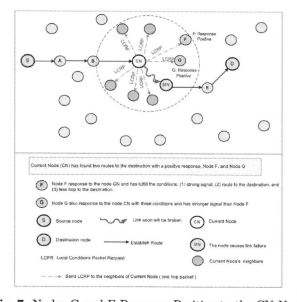

Fig. 7. Nodes G and F Response Positive to the CN Node

current node receives a two positive reply packet from its adjacent nodes, which is node F and node G, it means these two nodes has fulfilled three conditions, and the current node has to choose one of them in order to redirect the link and construct a new route. In case, if the number of hops in each route is equal in both nodes, the current node considers the one has shorter distance to the next hop, in this scenario, node G indicates a stronger signal than a node F. If the distance between the positive node and the current node is far, it means that the signal strength is low, which results in low bandwidth and low throughput. Therefore, based on this aspect in this scenario, the CN node selects the node G to redirect the link into a new direction and forward the data packets to the destination node.

Construct Path

When the above three conditions are fulfilled, the Construct Path function will create a new path (new direction) and re-forward the data packets into the new path which is < S-A-B-CN-G-D > as shown in Fig.8, it shows how the data packets transfer through new route to the destination.

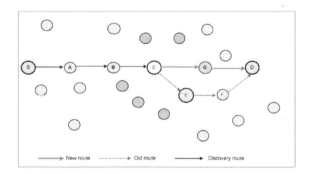

Fig. 8. Redirect the Data Packet through a New Route

5   Conclusions

This paper is proposed an extension to the Dynamic Source Routing (DSR), namely Redirect Link Failure Protocol (RLFP) to avoid complete link failure from the current node (node noticed the link failure) to the destination. RLFP-DSR protocol could function as an alternative solution for the overall wireless link failure enhancement. In the future work, we are going to implement RLFP protocol in order to validate the models by an experiment test using Network Simulator (NS-2) and evaluate the models performance as well. In addition, we are going to analyze the RLFP protocol outcome of the result and compare with DSR protocol by using different metrics.

References

1. Johnson, D.B., Maltz, D.A.: Dynamic Source Routing in Ad Hoc Wireless Networks. In: Imielinski, T., Korth, H. (eds.) Mobile Computing, pp. 153–181. Kluwer Academic Publishers, Heidelberg (1996)
2. Royer, E.M., Toh, C.: A Review of Current Routing Protocols for Ad Hoc Mobile Wireless Networks. IEEE Personal Communications, 46–55 (1999)
3. Broch, J., Maltz, D.A., Johnson, D.B., Hu, Y.C., Jetcheva, J.: A Performance Comparison of Multi-Hop Wireless Ad Hoc Network Routing Protocols. In: MobiCom, pp. 85–97. IEEE Press, New York (1998)
4. Lee, S.J., Gerla, M., Toh, C.K.: A Simulation Study of Table-Driven and On-Demand Routing Protocols for Mobile Ad Hoc Networks. IEEE Network 13, 48–54 (1999)
5. Das, S.R., Perkins, C.E., Royer, E.M.: Performance Comparison of Two On-demand Routing Protocols for Ad Hoc Networks. In: INFOCOM, pp. 3–12. IEEE Press, New York (2000)
6. Das, S.R., Castaneda, R., Yan, J., Sengupta, R.: Comparative Performance Evaluation of Routing Protocols for Mobile, Ad hoc Networks. In: 7th International Conference on Computer Communications and Networks (IC3N), pp. 153–161. IEEE Press (1998)
7. Royer, E.M., Toh, C.K.: A Review of Current Routing Protocols for Ad Hoc Mobile Wireless Networks. IEEE Personal Communication 6, 46–55 (1999)
8. Sharabi, N., Lin, Y.P., Rajeh, W.: Avoid Link Breakage in On-Demand Ad-hoc Network Using Packet Received Time Prediction. In: 19th European Conference on Modeling and Simulation, ECMS, pp. 802–807 (2005)
9. Rhim, A., Dziong, Z.: Routing Based on Link Expiration Time for MANET Performance Improvement. In: IEEE 9th Malaysia International Communications Conference (MICC), pp. 555–560. IEEE Press (2009)
10. Guo, S., Yang, O., Shu, Y.: Improving Source Routing Reliability in Mobile Ad Hoc Networks. IEEE Transaction on Parallel and Distributed Systems 16, 362–373 (2005)
11. Sung, D.-H., Youn, J.-S., Lee, J.-H., Kang, C.-H.: A Local Repair Scheme with Adaptive Promiscuous Mode in Mobile Ad Hoc Networks. In: Jia, X., Wu, J., He, Y. (eds.) MSN 2005. LNCS, vol. 3794, pp. 351–361. Springer, Heidelberg (2005)
12. Aissani, Senouci, M.R., Demigna, W., Mellouk, A.: Optimizations and Performance Study of the Dynamic Source Routing Protocol. In: Third International Conference Networking and Service, ICNS, p. 107 (2007)
13. Susmit, M., Saha, S., Sahnawaj, S., Kumar, B., Bhunia, C.: Pre-emptive Dynamic Source Routing: A Repaired Backup Approach and Stability Based DSR with Multiple Routes. Journal of Computing and Information Technology - CIT 16 2, 91–99 (2008)
14. Mamoun, H.: A New Reliable Routing Algorithm for MANET. International Journal of Research and Reviews in Computer Science (IJRRCS) 2(3), 638–642 (2011)
15. Khazaei, M., Berangi, R.: A Multi-path Routing Protocol with Fault Tolerance in Mobile Ad Hoc Networks. In: Proceedings of 14th IEEE International CSI, Tehran, Iran (October 2009)
16. Esmaeili1, E., Akhlaghi, P., Dehghan, M., Fathi, M.: A New Multi-Path Routing Algorithm with Local Recovery Capability in Mobile Ad hoc Networks. In: 5th International Symposium on Communication Systems, Networks and Digital Signal Processing (CSNDSP 2006), Patras, Greece, pp. 106–110 (2006)

17. Khazaei, M.: Improvement Dynamic Source Routing Protocol by Localization for Ad hoc Networks. International Journal of Computer Science and Information Security (IJCSIS) 8(6), 1–6 (2010)
18. Jardosh, A.P., Royer, E.M.B., Almeroth, K.C., Suri, S.: Real World Environment Models for Mobile Network Evaluation. IEEE on Selected Areas in Communications 23, 622–632 (2005)
19. Manoj, B.S., Murthy, C.S.R.: On the Use of Out-of-Band Signalling in Ad Hoc Wireless Networks. Elsevier Computer Communications 26, 1405–1414 (2003)
20. Klemm, F., Ye, Z., Krishnamurthy, S.V., Tripathi, S.K.: Improving TCP Performance in Ad-hoc Networks using Signal Strength based Link Management. J. Ad-hoc Networks 3, 175–191 (2005)
21. Chang, R.S., Leu, S.J.: Long-lived Path Routing with Received Signal Strength for Ad-hoc Networks. In: 1st International Symposium on Wireless Pervasive Computing, pp. 1–6. IEEE Press (2006)
22. Kaplan, E.D.: Understanding the GPS: Principles and Applications. Artech House, Boston (1996)
23. Su, S.J., Gerla, M.: Wireless Ad Hoc Multicast Routing with Mobility Prediction. ACM J. Mobile Networks and Applications 6(4), 351–360 (2001)
24. Dajing, H., Shengming, J., Jianqiang, R.: A Link Availability Prediction Model for Wireless Ad Hoc Networks. In: International Workshop on Wireless Networks and Mobile Computing, pp. D7–D11. IEEE Press (2000)
25. Rappaport, T.S.: Wireless Communications: Principles and Practice. Prentice Hall, Upper Saddle River (2002)

Resource-Aware Distributed Clustering
of Drifting Sensor Data Streams

Marwan Hassani and Thomas Seidl

Data Management and Data Exploration Group
RWTH Aachen University, Germany
{hassani,seidl}@cs.rwth-aachen.de
http://dme.rwth-aachen.de

Abstract. Collecting data from sensor nodes is the ultimate goal of Wireless Sensor Networks. This is performed by transmitting the sensed measurements to some data collecting station. In sensor nodes, radio communication is the dominating consumer of the energy resources which are usually limited. Summarizing the sensed data internally on sensor nodes and sending only the summaries will considerably save energy. Clustering is an established data mining technique for grouping objects based on similarity. For sensor networks, k-center clustering aims at grouping sensor measurements in k groups, each contains similar measurements. In this paper we propose a novel resource-aware k-center clustering algorithm called: *SenClu*. Our algorithm immediately detects new trends in the drifting sensor data stream and follows them. *SenClu* powerfully uses a light-weighted decaying technique that gives lower influence to old data. As sensor data are usually noisy, our algorithm is also outlier-aware. In thorough experiments on drifting synthetic and real world data sets, we show that *SenClu* outperforms two state-of-the-art algorithms by producing higher clustering quality and following trends in the stream, while consuming nearly the same amount of energy.

1 Introduction

Nowadays, sensor networks are deployed in tens of applications from everyday scenarios. Particularly in Wireless Sensor Networks (WSNs), these applications start from home scenarios like the smart homes to environmental applications and monitoring tasks in the health sector [12], but does not end with military applications. In all of these applications, monitoring is the dominating task of WSNs. Collecting useful data from remote sensor nodes is the ultimate goal of researchers and domain people who want to monitor some parameters using the WSN. The collection of all of the sensed data from all of the nodes within the network directly when they are sensed results usually in a perfect information gain about the monitored phenomena. However, not all of the sensed data are *always* interesting "enough" to be sent directly to the gathering station. The resulted excessive energy consumption when sending all sensed data to the gathering station encourages us to consider the previous sentence.

R. Benlamri (Ed.): NDT 2012, Part I, CCIS 293, pp. 592–607, 2012.
© Springer-Verlag Berlin Heidelberg 2012

Wireless sensor nodes are spread in many scenarios over mountains or deserts or under the sea, where a continuous energy supply is impossible. In such cases, nodes are powered by batteries with a limited capacity. Moreover, the cost of changing the battery is in most of the cases bigger than getting a completely new sensor node deployed again. Sensor nodes consume energy while sensing, performing internal computations and during the communication of data with other nodes or with the central station. The radio part is the dominating energy consumer. Thus, minimizing the communication times of sensor nodes is mainly targeted when optimizing the energy consumption of a sensor network.

By summarizing the sensed data internally on each sensor node, and then sending only the summaries of these data, one can considerably reduce the updating frequency between the sensor node and the data collecting station. Apparently, this will compromise the information quality of the collected data. To obtain the maximum out of this trade off, some aggregation techniques should be carefully used that both the information gain and the resources usage time are maximized. In data mining, clustering is a task for summarizing data such that similar objects are grouped together while dissimilar ones are separated. In the special case of sensor networks, clustering of the streaming data aims at the summarization of similar sensor measurements. By detecting k representative measurements in k-center clustering for instance, one ensures good clustering quality if each representative is assigned to only very similar measurements. In addition to the clustering quality which constitutes the final information gain, one aims at an efficient cluster computation.

1.1 Challenges and Contribution

When designing an energy aware in-sensor-network clustering algorithm that considers drifting data with outliers, the following challenges appear:

- **Up-to-date Incremental Clustering:** The algorithm must incrementally cluster the stream data points to detect evolving clusters over the time, while forgetting outdated data.
- **Single Passing, Storage Awareness:** Due to the limited processing and storage resources in the sensor node, the clustering algorithm must perform only a single pass over the incoming data stream and storage must be independent on n the size of input stream.
- **Minimal Communication:** As the energy consumption of transceiving data between the nodes is usually too big compared to the computation cost inside the node, the size of data being sent from the sensor nodes to the base station must be minimized.
- **High Clustering Quality:** The algorithm must show a good approximation to the optimal clustering by reducing the clustering radius as much as possible.
- **Outlier Awareness:** The algorithm should not be sensitive to outliers, nevertheless, it must be able to detect trends in the input stream.

Apparently, not only the two parts of the last aspect are contradicting each other. The third aspect is met when additional in-the-node computations are done to reduce the size of the data to be sent to other node or to the base station, which opposes the second aspect. On the other hand the fulfillment of the third and fourth aspect contradicts again achieving the second one, high-quality incremental clustering needs to store summaries of old points and needs additional processing.

When considering the *k-center* clustering (will be explained later in Section 2.1), many attempts in the literature tried to fulfill the last two aspects, only limited work [4], [6], [9] has considered the first and the third ones. The EDISKCO algorithm [10] was the first algorithm designed to consider the last four aspects together. In spite of its powerful performance and efficient usage of energy, EDISKCO [10] did not mainly address the first aspect.

In this paper, we propose a novel energy efficient k-center clustering approach: *SenClu* that incrementally groups the data locally on each sensor node and computes its k representatives. The algorithm gives more importance to newly received data for a faster adaptation to the evolving trends in the stream and more information gain of recent data on the collecting station. SenClu improves the clustering quality by using a novel light-weighted decaying technique to give less importance to old sensed values. It uses also a smart merging technique for the decayed clusters. The clusters with the least weight represent decaying data are smartly treated in SenClu as outliers. This gives a space for grouping the new emerging clusters, and thus following the current trend in the input streams. We sustain the powerful features of EDISKCO [10] but show that SenClu produces considerably better clustering results than EDISKCO [10] and another state-of-the art competing algorithm, while consuming nearly the same amount of energy.

The remainder of this paper is organized as follows: Section 2 reviews previous work related to our clustering and communicating problem. In Section 3 we pass through some preliminaries. Section 4 describes our proposed SenClu algorithm in detail. And finally Section 5 presents the experimental results. And finally we concludes the paper in Section 6.

2   Related Work

We will list some previous work done in two strongly related areas: approaches for sensor data clustering (particularly k-center clustering) and energy and data aware routing approaches for sensor networks.

2.1   Stream and K-Center Clustering Algorithms

DenStream [1] was the first stream clustering algorithm which used the weighing method to give recent data more influence by weighing the objects down according to their age. This work was followed by many other algorithms which used similar techniques (e.g. [5]). Although some of them were storage aware, these techniques were designed to perform the decaying method using enough processing and energy resources. Our algorithm in contrast applies a novel decaying and merging techniques that is light-weighted enough to be implemented on the limited resources of sensor nodes.

In the k-center clustering problem of a group of points P, we are asked to find k points from P and the smallest radius R such that if disks with a radius of R were placed on those centers then every point from P is covered [9]. The quality of the k-center clustering algorithms is measured using the approximation to the optimal clustering. Many clustering solutions have been presented for the k-center problem.

Offline Approaches assume that all of the n input points are stored in the memory. The "Furthest Point Algorithm" [8] and the "Parametric Pruning" [14] gave a 2-approximation to the optimal clustering by making $O(kn)$ distance computations. It is *NP*-hard to find a $(2 - \epsilon)$-approximation to the optimal clustering of the k-center problem for any $\epsilon > 0$ [7].

Online Approaches were developed to cope up with streaming input, the "Doubling Algorithm" [2] is a single pass streaming algorithm which guarantees an 8-factor approximation to the optimal clustering and uses $O(k)$ space. Cormode et. al [6] has formulated the "Parallel Guessing Algorithm" resulting with a $(2 + \epsilon)$-approximation to the optimal clustering. This algorithm uses the first points in the input stream to make Δ guesses of R as $(1+\frac{\epsilon}{2}), (1+\frac{\epsilon}{2})^2, (1+\frac{\epsilon}{2})^3, \ldots$ and then scans in parallel this part of the input stream using the different guesses. For each guess, it stops when it returns k centers of this input stream using its radius. This will end up by storing $O(\frac{k}{\epsilon} \log \Delta)$ points, where Δ is the maximum number of guesses of the clustering radius that can be done. The smallest guess is then first used for clustering input data. Whenever a new point that is not covered by the recent clustering arrives, the current guess is announced as invalid, and another bigger guessing must be selected. The algorithm is very sensitive to the first k centers selected from received points and some of them might even be outliers, which reduces the clustering quality by using a big guess. The storage is dependent on Δ which can be in reality a big value for the limited storage of sensor nodes. In addition, the parallel nature of the algorithm does suite the limited processing ability of sensor nodes even for small values of Δ.

Distributed Approaches where distributed *sites* are considered, each is maintaining a k-center clustering algorithm on his local input stream. The idea was originally raised in [6]. Here we have m remote sites applying the parallel guessing algorithm or an *online* furthest point algorithm on its local data. The site send its k-centers to a central site called *coordinator* which in turn applies another k-center clustering algorithm on the $k \times m$ centers. They proved that if the k-center clustering algorithm on the site side gives an α-approximation and the one on the coordinator site gives a β-approximation then the resulting k-center clustering algorithm offers a $(\alpha + \beta)$ approximation to the optimal clustering of the whole input data. A similar idea for a light weighted processing was used in [10] where sensor nodes are considered.

K-Center Clustering with Outliers was first presented by Charikar et. al [3] in an offline algorithm with a 3-approximation which drops z outliers. Mc-Cutchen et. al [15] presented an algorithm which gives a $(4 + \epsilon)$-approximation using $O(\frac{kz}{\epsilon})$ memory space. The algorithm reads the input in batches of size (kz), stores them, drops all *non-outliers* and then applies an offline k-center clustering algorithm with outliers on them. EDISKCO [10] online drops z far and non-dense outliers by achieving $(2 + \epsilon)$-approximation. In contrast, our algorithm: SenClu considers aged clusters with the least weights as outliers.

2.2 Energy-and-Data-Aware Routing Approaches in Wireless Sensor Networks

After collecting their measurements from the physical environment and processing them, sensor nodes have to send these data to one or more base stations. By having the base station(s) within the radio range of each sensor node, the naive single-hop communication between each node and the base station is possible but not energy-efficient and not reliable because of possible resulting interferences. Figure 1 (Left) illustrates one solution to this problem. Low-Energy Adaptive

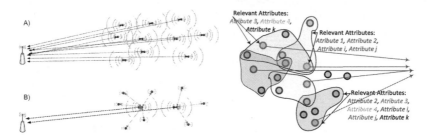

Fig. 1. Left: An example of a routing protocol: A) All sensor nodes use a big sending power to send their data to the base station. B) Sensor nodes use lower sending power to send data locally to a local node which aggregates and sends them to the base station. **Right:** AN example how ECLUN [11] performs the grouping of nodes and the selection of representatives additionally according to similarity w.r.t. some attributes.

Clustering (LEACH) protocol [13] dynamically groups sensor nodes in a small number of clusters. The randomly chosen representatives (cluster heads) locally fuse data from their neighboring and transmit it to the base station, which results of a factor of 8 improvement compared to direct transmissions. In the Hybrid Energy-Efficient Distributed HEED Clustering Approach [16] the cluster head selection is mainly based on residual energy and the neighbor proximity of each node. In ECLUN [11], a smarter representative selection process is performed not only by considering spatial similarities, but also similarities over some dimensions of measured data. This considerably increases the stability of the clusters and the representatives within the network, which results in an additional saving of the energy (cf. Fig 1 (Right)). Similar to EDISKCO [10], our algorithm uses a networking protocol that extends the lifetime of the wireless sensor network. The protocol efficiently groups local sensor nodes that locally send their data to a one of them called coordinator which in turn aggregates these data and sends it to the far base station. The coordinator is iteratively changed depending upon the residual energy which is accurately estimated by our algorithm.

3   Preliminaries

3.1   The K-Center Problem

Given a set P of n points $P = \{p_1, \ldots, p_n\}$, a distance function $d(p_a, p_b) \geq 0$ satisfying the triangle inequality and an integer $k < n$, the k-center set is $C \subseteq P$ such that $|C| = k$.

The k-center problem is to find a k-center set C that minimizes the maximum distance of each point $p \in P$ to its nearest center in C; i.e., the set which minimizes the quantity $max_{p \in P} min_{c \in C} d(p, c)$. The well-known k-median clustering problem is the the minsum variant of this problem where we seek to minimize $\sum_{p \in P} min_{c \in C} d(p, c)$ [9].

3.2   Incremental K-Center Clustering Problem

Let $S = \{c_1, c_2, \ldots, c_k, R\}$ be a *current* solution of a k-center clustering algorithm **A** applied on n input points that are arriving to the algorithm one by one in a sequence of updates, where: c_i; $i = 1 \ldots k$ are the centers and R is the radius of all of the clusters. **A** is an incremental clustering algorithm if it can always maintain a valid solution over the flow of stream. In other words, whenever a new point arrives to the algorithm it should either be assigned to one of the clusters indicating the validity of current clustering, or it does not fit in any of the current clusters then the current S must be changed into another solution S' such that this new point is assigned to some cluster in the new solution S'. S' can differ from S by the centers, radius or by both of them.

3.3   Weighted K-Center Clustering

A weighted k-center clustering algorithm **A** uses the following structure to save information about a clustering $\mathcal{C}$: $\{c_1, w_1, t_{u1}, c_2, w_2, t_{u2} \ldots, c_k, w_k, t_{uk}, R\}$. Where w_i is the weight of cluster i, c_i is its center and t_{ui} is the last time when the cluster i was updated by a point from the stream input. Let t_{now} be the current time, then the weight of cluster i is calculated as follows:

1. $[w_i = 2^{-\lambda \cdot (t_{now} - t_{ui})}]$ if the cluster i was not updated by the current stream input point (at time t_{now}).
2. $[w_i = 2^{-\lambda \cdot (t_{now} - t_{ui})} + 1]$ if the cluster i was updated by the current stream input point (at time t_{now}).

Where $1 \leq \lambda \leq 0$ represents the decaying factor. Larger values of λ result in a faster decaying of old members of the current cluster, while smaller values represent more contribution of old members in the calculation of the weight of the current cluster.

3.4   The Distributed Clustering

In distributed clustering we track each sensor node data locally, process it and then combine the results in a central node or a *coordinator*. The target is to minimize the communication and share the resources. We define the **distributed clustering problem.** Let $1, 2, \ldots, d$ be distributed sites, each site i applies a clustering algorithm A_i on its stream input of data X_i and produces a solution S_i. It is required to perform a global clustering of all X_i; $i = 1 \ldots d$ input streams distributed over the sites. One efficient solution to do that is to have a central site which collects the union $\bigcup_{i=1}^{d} S_i$ and answers the querying or monitoring requests of the whole input streams. It is also possible that a further clustering algorithm B at the coordinator to be applied on $\bigcup_{i=1}^{d} S_i$. In the distributed k-center clustering problem, we will consider in this paper, the solution of A_i at each site i is $S_i = \{c_{i1}, c_{i2}, \ldots, c_{ik}, R_i\}$, and on the coordinator side, we perform another k-center clustering algorithm over the whole k centers coming from the whole d sites, i.e., $\bigcup_{i=1}^{d} \{c_{i1}, c_{i2}, \ldots, c_{ik}\}$. When applying incremental clustering algorithms, continuous updates with the new solutions must be sent from the sites to the coordinator. Figure 2 illustrates an example where the coordinator applies another k-center clustering over the $k \times d$ centers sent from the sites.

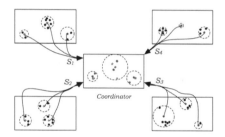

Fig. 2. An example of a distributed k-center clustering for $k = 3$ clusters of data coming from $d = 4$ sites, the coordinator applies another k-center clustering over the $k \times d$ centers sent from the sites

3.5   The Problem of Weighted K-Center Clustering with Outliers

Sensor data are usually noisy. If a clustering algorithm is not outlier-aware the results will become extremely sensitive to the noise. This sensitivity has two effects: (a) On the clustering quality which appears in Figure 2 for example in site 3 where the cluster on the left has a bigger clustering radius (worse clustering quality) because of not considering one point too far from the center as an outlier. And (b) On the energy consumption in the distributed model since outliers cause current solutions to be invalid and result in additional updates with the coordinator. Formally in the weighted **k-center clustering problem with outliers** we group m out of the n input points into the k clusters by dropping maximally $z = n - m$ points. The decision of labeling those z or less points as *outliers* is done according to their small weights compared to other clusters. Noisy data form less dense clusters that receive updates less frequently, the weight of such clusters will soon decrease.

4 The SenClu Algorithm

In this section we present SenClu. Each local sensor node receives its input stream through its sensors, produces a weighted k-center clustering solution to it by considering the existence of outliers and sends this solution to the coordinator. The coordinator performs another clustering algorithm to the solutions coming from the sites. A server part of the algorithm manages iteratively assigning coordinators and receiving data from them. Therefore, similar to EDISKCO [10], the input streams are processed at each node locally, and a global clustering of all sensors data is performed globally in the coordinator. SenClu uses for a

---

Algorithm 1. *insert(h,p)*

In *A heap h of current clusters and an input point p from the stream*

Out *0:if OK, j: if p is a new cluster in position j or*
  err:if there is no place to add new cluster p

1. **for** $j = 1$ to *size(h)* **do**
2.   **if** $d(p, c_j.center) \leq R$ **then**
3.   *//decay all clusters then and increase the weight of j by one using maintain(h)*
4.   *maintain(h)*;
5.   **return** 0;
6.   **end if**
7. **end for**
8. **if** *size(h)* $< (k + z)$ **then** /* *there is still a place in the heap to insert p* */
9. $c_j.center = p$;
10. $c_j.weight = 1$;
11.   *maintain(h)*;
12.   **return** j
13. **if** $c_{k+z}.weight \leq w_{min}$ **then** /* *there is an old cluster replace it* */
14.   *delete(h, k + z)*;
15.   *//maintain the weights using maintain(h)*
16.   *maintain(h)*;
17.   **return** (the insertion position)
18. **return** err /* *we have to recluster* */

---

heap structure h for storing maximally $k + z$ weighted clusters. Each member c_j; $j = 1 \ldots (k + z)$ in this heap represents a cluster, where: $c_j.center$ represents the center of this cluster, $c_j.weight$: the weight and $c_j.up\_time$: the last time when c_j was updated. The members in this heap are arranged in a descending oder according to $c_j.weight$. The top k members represent the clusters, while the rest which could be maximally z represent the outlier clusters. Arranging the clusters according to the weights needs to be done only once after each reclustering. Once the members are arranged, only the updated cluster needs to be rearranged such that it is in the correct place of the list. All non-updated clusters decay with the same factor together. We define the following functions on h:

- **maintain(h)**: applied after each reclustering or birth of a new cluster such that for all $1 \leq j, q \leq k + z$ we have $q > j$ only if $c_q.weight \geq c_j.weight$. Whenever a point is inserted in a cluster, *maintain(h)* simply performs a decaying step for all clusters weight: $c_i.weight = 2^{-\lambda} \times c_i.weight$ for all $1 \leq i \leq k + z$, and then in the next step increases only the weight of the cluster where the input point was inserted by 1. The decaying step will leave the order of the heap correct, after the increasing step, one scan step is needed to insert the updated cluster in its correct place in the arranged list. The previous step is performed to avoid the complicated mathematics associated with calculating: $w_i = 2^{-\lambda \cdot (t_{now} - t_{ui})} + 1$ in general, which most sensor node processors can not afford.
- **size(h)**: returns the number of the members in h which can be any value between 0 and $k + z$.
- **get(h,j)**: returns the member j from the heap.
- **delete(h,j)**: deletes the member j from the heap and directly maintains the heap.
- **insert(h,p)**: inserts an input point p from the stream in h, (see Algorithm 1). It scans the members of h beginning with the high-weighted ones. When a cluster is found where p is not further than R from its center, all the cluster are aged by $2^{-\lambda}$, and only the found cluster's weight is incremented by 1, and p is forgotten. If p was further than R from all available cluster centers and there were less than $k+z$ members in h, then a new cluster is established with p is its center. Otherwise check if the least weighted cluster $k + z$ has less weight than w_{min} (the minimum weight), if yes, delete it and insert the new point in a new cluster and return its position. Otherwise, an error is returned for not having a place to add p.

4.1   On the Node Local Side

Each node i receives an input stream $X(i)$ and runs the SenCluNode algorithm (see Algorithm 2) and sends updates to the coordinator with k center outlier-and-weight-aware clustering representation of $X(i)$ in addition to the corresponding radius R_i. Please mind that during the initialization phase (not shown in Algorithm 2 for readability), the node increases the radius without sending updates to the coordinator until n input points are received. Then the running phase of SenCluNode starts. SenCluNode is explained in details in Algorithm 2.

4.2   On the Coordinator Side

The coordinator side algorithm is explained in SenCluCoordinator (cf. Algorithm 3). Lines 15-20 explains the communication messages between the server

---

Algorithm 2. SenCluNode($X_i, k, z, \lambda, w_{min}, \epsilon$)

In *An input stream X_i, num of clusters k, num of outlier clusters z, decaying factor λ, minimum weight w_{min} and step size ϵ*

Out *update the coordinator with the new opened clusters' centers and radii*

   1. $X_i(t) \rightarrow p, c_1.center = p, c_1.weight = 1, R = R_{min}$
   2. **while** there is input stream $X_i(t)$ **do**
   3. $X_i(t) \rightarrow p$
   4. $fit = insert(p, h)$
   5.   **if** $next\_coordinator$ signal from server **then** //*current node becomes coordinator*
   6.   Save current local centers in C_{local} // *in order not to lose its local solutions*
   7.   Switch to *SenCluCoordinator*
   8.   **end if**
   9.   **if** $fit \neq err$ **and** $0 < fit \leq k$ **then**
 10.   Send the new center $get(h, fit)$ with a *new_center* signal to the coordinator.
 11.   **end if**
 12.   **if** $fit == err$ **then** // *we need to recluster by increasing the radius*
 13.   Send $radius\_increase$ request to coordinator
 14.   **while** there is no reply from coordinator **do**
 15.   Buffer incoming input points from X_i
 16.   **end while**
 17. $R \leftarrow max\{R(1 + \frac{\epsilon}{2}), R_{global}\}$ // *get the biggest possible next R*
 18.   **while** $j < size(h)$ **do** // *search for overlapping clusters and merge them*
 19. $q = j + 1;$
 20.   **while** $q < size(h)$ **do**
 21.   search for the closest j and q to each other;
 22.   increase the weight of the higher-weighted of them by 1;
 23.   delete the lower-weighted one;
 24. $q + +;$
 25.   **end while**
 26. $j + +;$
 27.   **end while**
 28. $maintain(h);$
 29.   Keep only the the clusters whose weight is at least w_{min} in h;
 30.   Run this algorithm on buffered points;
 31. $C_i = \{c_1.center, c_2.center, \ldots, c_{\hat{k}}.center\};$ // *get the heaviest $\hat{k} \leq k$*
 32.   Send C_i, R_i as an update to the coordinator;
 33.   **end if** // *end of the reclustering phase*
 34. **end while**

---

and the coordinator for managing the selection of the next coordinator according to the residual energy that each node still possesses. The coordinator keeps a special space for saving summary about the energy consumption of each node i. The total number of centers that were sent from a node i and the total number of *radius_increase* requests sent from a node i during this phase are saved under $numCenters_i$ and $numRequests_i$ respectively. These are important for the server to calculate the total energy consumption of each node including the coordinator during this phase. The server sends from time to time

---

Algorithm 3. SenCluCoordinator($C_i, R_i, c_{ij}.center$)

In *solutions C_i, R_i, new opened cluster centers, cluster_increase requests from node i*
Out *send ack and R_{global} to nodes, maintain C_{global}, R_{global} and*
    send them to next coordinator

---

1. **if** this is **not** the first coordinator **then**
2.   Receive C_{global}, R_{global} from last coordinator; // *undertake the solutions*
3. **end if**
4. Broadcast *I_am_coordinator* signal to all nodes;
5. $C_{global} \leftarrow FurthestPoint(C_{global}, C_{local})$; // *as in [8]*
6. **if** *radius_increase$_i$* **do** // *received: radius_increase request from node i*
7.   Send to node i an *ack* with R_{global};
8.   Receive C_i, R_i from node i; // *new solution from i w.r.t. the new value of R*
9. $C_{global} \leftarrow FurthestPoint(C_{global}, C_i)$; // *update C_{global} with the new solution*
10. $R_{global} \leftarrow max\{R_{global}, R_i\}$; // *update R_{global} with the new solution*
11. **end if**
12. **if** *new_center$_i$* **do**// *coordinator received: new centers on node i*
13. $C_{global} \leftarrow FurthestPoint(C_{global}, \{c_{ij}.center\})$
14. **end if**
15. **if** *consumption_update* received from server **then**
16.   Send $\{numCenters_i, numRequests_i\}$ for all $i = 1 \dots m$
      nodes during this phase to server
17. **end if**
18. **if** *chg_coordinator* received from server **then**
19.   Send C_{global}, R_{global} to next coordinator
20.   Switch to *SenCluNode* using R_{global}
21. **end if**

---

consumption_update requests to the coordinator which in turn replies to them. The server uses an energy model similar to the one in [10]. According to the residual energy of each node and the coordinator, the server makes a decision of changing the current coordinator by sending *chg_coordinator* message to it, with the *id* of the next coordinator.

5 Experiments

We have evaluated the performance of SenClu using extensive experiments on both synthetic and real data. As competitors, we have chosen two state-of-the-art algorithms: EDISKCO [10] and Global-PG [6] (we refer to it as PG in the experiments). Both competitors represent single-pass distributed k-center clustering algorithm on the node sides which also applies the furthest point algorithm on the coordinator side. In order to have fair results, we have implemented our suggested node-coordinator-server model also on the Global-PG. We have implemented simulations of the three algorithms in Java. We have chosen one synthetic dataset and two real world datasets, we give here a small description of each.

Synthetic data set: RandomWalk (RW)[1]. A synthetic data set based on the random walk model. The increments between two consecutive values are independent and identically distributed. Each increment: t_{i+1} is produced by randomly adding or subtracting from t_i a uniformly random value from the interval [1,10] . We generated 19 different data sets each for one node, each contains 42,000 measures. Subsequently, to produce a natural outliers effect, we replaced randomly selected values (4.5% of the dataset size) with noise values, uniformly at random in the interval $[min, max]$ of the dataset.

Real Dataset: I9 Sensor Dataset[1]. We have collected a real data from a sensor network. We deployed 19 TelosB motes in our department area. All motes were programmed to collect temperature samples each 30 seconds and send them directly to a sink connected to a computer. The data was collected for more than 14 days between the 10th and the 23rd of April 2009 and forming 40,589 measures of each node. The minimum difference between raw measures is 1. The nodes were not always able to communicate perfectly with the sink due to collisions or loss of signal, this appeared in 2.9% of the total data. Instead of each measure that did not reach the sink, we introduced a noise data. In a different way of adding outliers to that of RW, a uniformly at random value from the interval $[0.1 \times (max - min), 0.25 \times (max - min)]$ was selected and then uniformly at a random either added to max or deducted from min, the resulting value was inserted instead of the lost measure.

Real Dataset: Physiological Sensor Dataset. This data was presented in ICML 2004 as a challenge for information extraction from streaming sensor data. The training data set consists of approximately 10,000 hours of this data containing: userID, gender, sessionID, sessionTime, annotation, characteristic 1, characteristic and sensor[1..9]. We have extracted the first 24,000 readings of sensor2 by userID. We have chosen the data of 12 different userIDs with the same gender, each representing a node. We did not add outliers to this dataset as they naturally exist in such datasets.

We have used the following three criteria to evaluate SenClu w.r.t. EDISKCO and the PG algorithm:

Silhouette Coefficient: We use this measure to evaluate the clustering quality on the nodes side. It reflects how appropriate is the mapping of data objects to clusters. It subtracts the average distance of objects to their representative from the average distance of objects to their second closest cluster and then divides the results over the bigger average. When calculating the average of these values for all objects in all clusters, the final value will range from -1 to +1. Where -1 will reflect the worst clustering and +1 a perfect one. For the streaming case, we have used a sliding window over the stream input and then performed the calculation of the Silhouette coefficient at the end of each window for all the objects within it.

---

[1] dataset is available under
http://dme.rwth-aachen.de/SenClu

Global Clustering Radius: Another measure to reflect the clustering quality, this time on the coordinator side. In k-center clustering, better clustering uses smaller radius to cover all of the input points.

Energy Consumption: Evaluated through the average energy consumption of the one sensor node in the network in Joule based on the detailed cost model suggested in [10] and the datasheets of TelosB mote, TI MSP430 microcontroller and the CC2420 radio chip in addition to the TinyOS 2.0.2 operating system installed on the motes.

5.1   Experimental Setup and Results

For all experiments, we selected the parameters for SenClu and EDISKCO for all datasets as: $k = 15$, $z = \frac{k}{4} = 4$, $\epsilon = 0.5$. For SenClu only we selected: $w_{min} = 0.5$, and λ as: (0.005 in RW dataset) and (0.018 in I9 Sensor Dataset) and (0.01 in Phyosiological Dataset). For EDISKCO only: the number of the most dense clusters to be sent to the coordinator after each cluster increase: $l = \frac{k}{4} = 4$, the maximum allowed number of input points after which the node can send a solution to the coordinator: $n = 100$, and the maximum allowed number of outliers in total: $o = 10\%n$. For the Global-PG we have selected the number of points collected at the beginning to perform the parallel guessing equals to our $n = 400$ and also $\epsilon = 0.5$. We performed the evaluations on a 3.00 Ghz core Duo, 4 GB RAM machine. For all algorithms we set the initial radius as $R_{min}(P) = min_{p,q \in P, p \neq q} d(p, q)$ for each dataset P separately. Figure 3(a) shows that SenClu achieves consid-

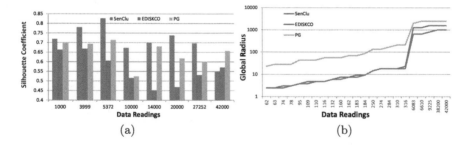

(a)   (b)

Fig. 3. The clustering quality using the Random Walk Synthetic Dataset over different parts of the input stream data. (a) Silhouette Coefficient, (b) R_{global}.

erably higher Silhouette coefficient values than both EDISKCO and PG over almost all of the data stream of the RW dataset. This high clustering quality of SenClu is due to its novel weighing technique that allow new emerging trends to influence the clustering result, and thus grouped in the correct cluster. Also on the clustering performed on the coordinator side, Figure 3(b) shows that SenClu has always smaller global radius than EDISKCO which constitutes a better clustering. PG has considerably worse performance than SenClu and

EDISKCO on the coordinator side (mind the logarithmic scaling in Figure 3(a)). Also in Figure 4(a) we can see that SenClu has a better clustering performance on the node side than both competitors over the whole data measurements of the I9 Sensor Dataset. Figure 4(b) shows again that the decaying nature and the smart merging technique that SenClu has, result in a smaller radius on the coordinator side and thus better overall clustering results than both PG and EDISKCO. Figure 5(a) shows on another real dataset (Physiological Sensor Dataset) that SenClu always has a better clustering q uality than both competitors on the node side. Because PG is more sensitive to noise than SenClu and EDISKCO, it is performing considerably worse than others on this relatively noisy dataset. Figure 5(b) is showing that on the node side, SenClu is having most of the time the same global radius as EDISKCO. Only for a short time, SenClu is having a bigger radius than EDISKCO. Table 1 shows that SenClu consumes a bit more energy on average than both EDISKCO and PG when applied on RW dataset. This can be explained by the random nature of the Random Walk dataset that results in different new trends in the data, that SenClu tries to follow. This results in multiple updates to the coordinator of new created clusters. This is not the case for EDISKCO and PG where a very lazy update of newly emerging clusters saves some energy while extremely affects the clustering quality (cf. Figures 3(a) and 3(b)). This effect does not appear when using natural real datasets. We can see from Table 1 that on I9 Sensor Dataset, SenClu consumes

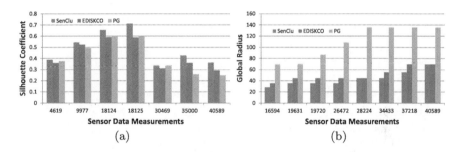

Fig. 4. The clustering quality using the I9 Real Sensor Dataset over different parts of the input measurements. (a) Silhouette Coefficient, (b) R_{global}.

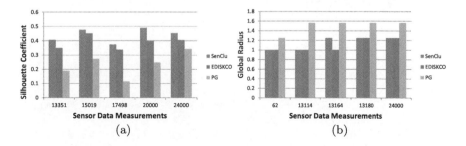

Fig. 5. The clustering quality using the Real Physiological Sensor Dataset over different parts of the input stream data. (a) Silhouette Coefficient, (b) R_{global}.

Table 1. Average energy consumption in Joule of a single node in the network by the end of each dataset when using SenClu, EDISKCO and PG

Dataset	Size	Nodes	SenClu	EDISKCO	PG
RW	42000	19	29805.7	**29776.4**	29792.11
i9-Sensor	40589	19	28770.2	**28768.38**	28792.5
Physio	24000	12	**17074.3**	17074.4	17078.9

less than two Joules more than EDISKCO, and absorbs considerably less energy than PG. When using the Physiological Sensor Dataset, SenClu consumes less energy than both competitors.

6   Conclusions and Future Work

In this work we present our novel energy efficient weighted k-center clustering solution. We presented our algorithm: *SenClu* as a single-pass algorithm that immediately detects new trends in the drifting sensor data stream and follows them. The light-weighted decaying technique which we used to enhance the clustering quality, gives lower influence to old data. As sensor data are usually noisy, *SenClu* is also outlier-aware. In thorough experiments on drifting synthetic and real world data sets, we showed that *SenClu* outperforms two state-of-the-art algorithms by producing higher clustering quality and following trends in the stream, while consuming nearly the same amount of energy.

In future work, we aim at a further improvement of the clustering quality. One possible way for that is the usage of a new data structure and a dedicated distance function for the weighted k-center clustering in the distributed case. Additionally, we would like to discuss the possibility of tracking clusters which are available in some subspace of the data. Some existing techniques already try to achieve that on static data. But it will be definitely interesting to check the possibility of including the streaming case.

Acknowledgments. This research was funded in part by the cluster of excellence on Ultra-high speed Mobile Information and Communication (UMIC) of the DFG (German Research Foundation grant EXC 89).

References

1. Cao, F., Ester, M., Qian, W., Zhou, A.: Density-based clustering over an evolving data stream with noise. In: SDM, pp. 326–337 (2006)
2. Charikar, M., Chekuri, C., Feder, T., Motwani, R.: Incremental clustering and dynamic information retrieval. In: Proc. ACM STOC, pp. 626–635 (1997)
3. Charikar, M., Khuller, S., Mount, D.M., Narasimhan, G.: Algorithms for facility location problems with outliers. In: Proc. SODA, pp. 642–651 (2001)
4. Charikar, M., O'Callaghan, L., Panigrahy, R.: Better streaming algorithms for clustering problems. In: Proc. ACM STOC, pp. 30–39 (2003)

5. Chen, Y., Tu, L.: Density-based clustering for real-time stream data. In: KDD, pp. 133–142 (2007)
6. Cormode, G., Muthukrishnan, S., Zhuang, W.: Conquering the divide: Continuous clustering of distributed data streams. In: Proc. IEEE ICDE, pp. 1036–1045 (2007)
7. Feder, T., Greene, D.: Optimal algorithms for approximate clustering. In: Proc. ACM STOC, pp. 434–444 (1988)
8. Gonzalez, T.F.: Clustering to minimize the maximum intercluster distance. Theoretical Computer Science 38(2-3), 293–306 (1985)
9. Guha, S.: Tight results for clustering and summarizing data streams. In: Proc. ICDT, pp. 268–275 (2009)
10. Hassani, M., Müller, E., Seidl, T.: EDISKCO: energy efficient distributed in-sensor-network k-center clustering with outliers. In: Proc. SensorKDD 2009, pp. 39–48 (2009)
11. Hassani, M., Müller, E., Spaus, P., Faqolli, A., Palpanas, T., Seidl, T.: Self-organizing energy aware clustering of nodes in sensor networks using relevant attributes. In: Proc. SensorKDD 2010, pp. 87–96 (2010)
12. Hassani, M., Seidl, T.: Towards a mobile health context prediction: Sequential pattern mining in multiple streams. In: Proc. of IEEE MDM 2011, vol. 2, pp. 55–57 (2011)
13. Heinzelman, W.R., Chandrakasan, A., Balakrishnan, H.: Energy-efficient communication protocol for wireless microsensor networks. In: Proc. HICSS (2000)
14. Hochbaum, D., Shmoys, D.B.: A best possible approximation algorithm for the k-centre problem. Math. of Operations Research 10, 180–184 (1985)
15. Matthew McCutchen, R., Khuller, S.: Streaming Algorithms for k-Center Clustering with Outliers and with Anonymity. In: Goel, A., Jansen, K., Rolim, J.D.P., Rubinfeld, R. (eds.) APPROX and RANDOM 2008. LNCS, vol. 5171, pp. 165–178. Springer, Heidelberg (2008)
16. Fahmy, S., Younis, O.: Heed: A hybrid, energy-efficient, distributed clustering approach for ad hoc sensor networks. IEEE Transactions on Mobile Computing 3(4), 366–379 (2004)

Robust Wireless Sensor Networks with Compressed Sensing Theory

Mohammadreza Balouchestani, Kaamran Raahemifar, and Sridhar Krishnan

Department of Electrical and Computer Engineering
Ryerson University, Toronto, Canada
{mbalouch,kraahemi,krishnan}@ee.ryerson.ca

Abstract. Wireless Sensor Networks (WSNs) consist of a large number of Wireless Nodes (WNs) each with sensing, processing, communication and power supply units to monitor the real-world environment information. The WSNs are responsible to sense, collect, process and transmit information such as pressure, temperature, position, flow, vibration, force, humidity, pollutants and biomedical signals like heart-rate and blood pressure. The ideal WSNs are networked to consume very limited power and are capable of fast data acquisition. The problems associated with WSNs are limited processing capability, low storage capacity, limited energy and global traffic. Also, WSNs have a finite life dependent upon initial power supply capacity and duty cycle. The WSNs are usually driven by a battery. Therefore, the primary limiting factor for the lifetime of a WN is the power supply. That is why; each WN must be designed to manage its local power supply of energy in order to maximize total network lifetime [5]. The life expectancy of a WSN for a given battery capacity can be enhanced by minimizing power consumption during the operation of the network. The CS theory solves the aforementioned problem by reducing the sampling rate throughout the network. A combination of CS theory to WSNs is the optimal solution for achieving the networks with low-sampling rate and low-power consumption. Our simulation results show that sampling rate can reduce to 30% and power consumption to 40% without sacrificing performances by employing the CS theory to WSNs. This paper presents a novel sampling approach using compressive sensing methods to WSNs. First, an overview of compressed sensing is presented. Second, CS in WSNs is investigated. Third, the simulation results on the sampling rate in WSNs are shown.

Index Terms: Wireless Sensor Network, Sampling-rate, Power consumption, Sparse signals, Compressed sensing.

1   Introduction

Wireless Sensor Networks (WSNs) consist of a large number of Wireless Nodes (WNs) each with sensing, processing, communication, and power supply units to

R. Benlamri (Ed.): NDT 2012, Part I, CCIS 293, pp. 608–619, 2012.
© Springer-Verlag Berlin Heidelberg 2012

monitor and control the information of real environments. As a communication system, in the WSNs, sources are WNs, which measure some quantity; the channel is the space between the WNs and receiver which is another WN or Base Station (BS). The WSNs are now used in a variety of fields such as health monitoring in designing Electronic Health (EH), transportation automation in designing Traffic Control System (TCS), industrial control monitoring in designing Web Controlling System (ISC), business and residential areas in designing Energy Management System (EMS), and military for providing Electronic War Systems (EWS). The WSNs suffer of some problems like limited processing capability, low storage capacity, limited energy, and high sampling rate. The compressive sensing that also known as compressed sensing is a revolutionary idea proposed recently to achieve much lower sampling rate for sparse signals such as biomedical signals, WSN's signals, and signals of Wireless Body Area Networks(WBAN's) [5]. By compressing data, the data size is reduced, and less bandwidth is required to transmit data: therefore, less power is required to process the data. The CS helps in data gathering and transferring and can change the traditional theorem and technology in wireless networks, which may lead to some other improvements in capacity, delay, size, and energy management [4]. This theory says a small number of random linear measurements of compressible signals contain enough information for reconstruction, processing, and communication [8]. To extend WSNs to many areas including: health monitoring, home automation, control monitoring, military, transportation automation, and energy management, a combination of the CS theory to WSNs is the best solution for designing autonomous networks with low sampling-rate, low-power, self-organizing and self-maintenance[6]. The aim of this paper is to investigate how CS theory can be employed in WSNs to design a robust network with low-sampling rate and low-power consumption. The structure of this paper is organized as follows: Section 2 presents a background about the CS theory. Section 3 investigates the CS theory to WSNs. Section 4 the simulation result on sampling-rate and power consumption in WSNs is shown. Finally, the conclusion is drawn in Section 5.

2   Overview of Compressed Sensing Theory

The CS theory is emerging for such WSNs by compressing, the date size reduced, and fewer bandwidth is required to transmit data and therefore less power is required to process data[9]. This theory says a small number of random linear measurements of compressible signals contain enough information to recover the original signal [10]. This idea attracts many talented researchers on areas like Information Communication Technology (ICT), Random Variables (RVs), Optimization Procedures (OPs) and Mathematical Statistics (MSs) [8]. A basic block diagram of the CS scheme is provided in Figure 1.

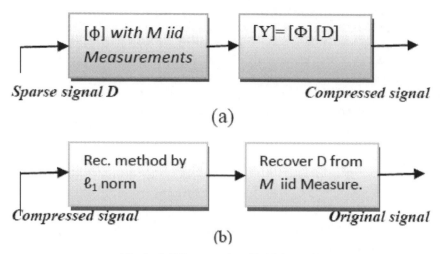

Fig. 1. a) CSin transmitter b) CS in receiver

The CS theory exploits that many natural signals such as WSNs's signals are sparse or compressible in sense that they have concise representations when expressed in the proper basis[1]. With CS theory,WSNs can achieve a higher transmission rate, a lower time delay, and high probability of success of data transmission. In this section, we first, discuss the CS theorem. Second, the reconstruction method to recover the original signal in the receiver side is investigated.

2.1   Basic Theorem

Regarding the Nyquist theory, each signal must be sampled at least twice its bandwidth in order to be represented without error. Our goal in the CS theory as a new sampling scheme is to reduce load of sampling rate. The CS theory says many signals are sparse or in the practice near sparse and can represent by small number of random measurements [11]. Any compressible signal D in $\mathbb{R}^N$ can be expressed in terms of a basis of $N \times 1$ vectors $\{\psi_i\}$ such that $1 \leq i \leq N$. Forming the $N \times N$ basis matrix $\Psi = [\psi_1, \psi_2, \ldots, \psi_N]$ by stacking the vector $\{\psi_i\}$ as columns, the compressible signal D including K non-zero and $(N-K)$ zero coefficients can be represented like[12]:

$$D = \sum_{i=1}^{N} S_i \psi_i \quad \text{or} \quad [D]_{N \times 1} = [\Psi]_{N \times N} [S]_{N \times 1} \tag{1}$$

Where S is the $N \times 1$ column vector of weighting coefficients $S_i = <D, \psi_i> = \psi_i^T D$. Therefore any compressible signals D can be represented of an orthogonal basis of $N \times 1$ vector $\{\psi_i\}$. On the other hand, any compressible signal has a small number of large coefficients and a lot of number of small coefficients [13]. That is why any compressible or sparse signal has K nonzero coefficients and $(N-K)$ zero coefficients with $K \ll N$. In fact, the CS theory offers a stable measurements metrics with M

independent and identically distributed (i.i.d) elements of the compressed signals such as $K \leq M \ll N$. Therefore the compressed signal $\mathbb{Y}$ is found like:

$$[\mathbb{Y}]_{M \times 1} = [\phi]_{M \times N}[D]_{N \times 1} \tag{2}$$

By substituting (2) in (1) we have [13]:

$$[\phi]_{M \times N}[\Psi]_{N \times N}[S]_{N \times 1} = [\Theta]_{M \times N}[S]_{N \times 1} \tag{3}$$

Thus CS scenario has two steps. First, offers a stable measurement matrix that ensures that the salient information in any compressible signal is not damaged by the dimensionality reduction from $D \in \mathbb{R}^N$ down to $\mathbb{Y} \in \mathbb{R}^M$. In the second step, the CS theory offers a reconstruction algorithm under certain condition and enough accuracy to recover original signal D from compressed signal. Fortunately, the $[\phi]_{M \times N}$ matrix has the following interesting properties:

▶ The $[\phi]_{M \times N}$ matrix is incoherent with the orthogonal basis with high probability and enough accuracy

▶ The $[\Theta]_{M \times N} = [\phi]_{M \times N}[\Psi]_{N \times N}$ matrix is also i.i.d Gaussian for every possible Ψ

▶ The $[\Theta]_{M \times N} = [\phi]_{M \times N}[\Psi]_{N \times N}$ matrix has the RIP with high probability if (the number of random measurements) M verifies the following equation:

$$M \geq cK \log (N/M) \tag{4}$$

where c is a small constant. As the result, CS theory focus on few number of linear combination of all points of the signal instead of huge number of samples to find compressed signal with matrix ϕ. Selecting the measurement ψ_j into $M \times 1$ vectors $\mathbb{Y}$ and the measurement vector ϕ_j^T to rows into an $M \times N$ matrix ϕ we can write:

$$\begin{pmatrix} \psi_1 \\ \psi_M \end{pmatrix} = \begin{pmatrix} \phi_{11} & \cdots & \\ \vdots & \ddots & \vdots \\ & \cdots & \phi_{M \times N} \end{pmatrix} \begin{pmatrix} d_1 \\ d_N \end{pmatrix} \tag{5}$$

2.2   Reconstruction Scheme

The compressed sensing theory provides the guarantee that a compressible signal can be fully describe by only M random measurements. Consequently, we can recover the original signal D from the compressed signal with only M random measurements with high probability and enough accuracy. Our goal is to find the signal's sparse coefficient vector S in the translated null space. Therefore, the reconstruction method needs only M random measurements of random matrices ϕ, Ψ to recover the original signal [1].

We define the ℓ_p norm of the vectors s as $(\|s\|_p)^p = \sum_{i=1}^{N} |s|^p$. When $p=0$ we obtain the ℓ_0 "norm" that counts the number of non-zero coefficients in S; hence a

K-sparse vector has ℓ_0 norm K. The main procedure to solve inverse problem in ℓ_2 norms is by least squares that shows ℓ_2 minimizations will almost never find the data vector D, and also solving ℓ_0 is numerically unstable method. That is why; the ℓ_0 and ℓ_2 minimizations are not convenient to recover original signal from the compressed signal but fortunately we can exactly reconstruct the original signal by ℓ_1 norm with high probability and enough accuracy [3]. To summarize, the CS theory offers a reconstruction mechanism to recover original signal D from the compressed signal Y with high probability and enough accuracy with only M random linear measurements [22]. Therefore, we can expect to recover the original signal D with high probability from just $M \geq cKlog(N/M) \ll N$ random Gaussian measurements. We also thank to the properties of the i.i.d Gaussian distribution to make Gaussian measurements ϕ which are universal to generate $\Theta = \phi \, \Psi$ which has the RIP with high probability.

3 WSNs with CS Theory

This section presents the basic theory of WSNs, and then we investigate how compressed sensing could improve the limiting characteristics such as power and delay in wireless nodes. The WSNs consist of important units such as sensing unit (SU), power supply unit (PS), communication and controlling unit (CC). The important concept of WSNs is based on a simple equation like:

$$PS+SU+CC= \textit{Thousands of potential applications} \qquad (6)$$

In this part, we want to investigate how to employ the CS theory in WSNs, which mostly involve data of a large number of WNs. Typically; in WSNs we have the following properties:

▶ There are a total of N sources randomly located in a filed
▶ We denote K as the number of event that active sources generate to be measured
▶ K is a random number and is much smaller than N
▶ We denote $[D]_{N\times 1}$ as the event vector
▶ Each component of $[D]_{N\times 1}$ has a binary value
▶ Obviously $[D]_{N\times 1}$ is a sparse vector since $k \ll N$
▶ There are M active monitoring wireless sensors trying to capture K events
▶ The number of events K, the number of wireless sensors M and total of sources N has the following relation: $(K \leq M \ll N)$

Also in WSNs we have:

▶ Very limited number of active wireless sensors compared with total of wireless sensors
▶ Very limited number of events compared to the number of sources
▶ Thus, the events are relatively sparse compared to the number of sources

Therefore, we can say data vectors in WSNs are sparse vectors and consequently CS theory can employ to WSNs [3]. A WSN with N sources, each node acquiring a sample Di. The final goal is to collect Data vector $D = [D_1, D_2....., D_N]$. D has an M-Sparse in a proper basis like:

$$\Psi = [\Psi_1, \Psi_2...\Psi_N] \tag{7}$$

CS suggests that, under certain condition, instead of collecting D we can collect compressed vector $Y=\Phi D$, where $\Phi= \{\Phi_{ji}\}$ is $K \times N$ sensing Matrix whose entries are i.i.d random variables. In non-CS WSNs with N nodes a node is receiving $N-1$ packets and send out N packets $(N-1)$ received packets plus its data) each packet corresponding to data sample from a node and the BS needs to receive all N samples[21]. In WSNs with CS theory the BS needs only to receive M $(M \approx K)$ packets. Obviously, in order to use CS, each node needs to know the value of Compressed Ratio $(CR=N/K)$ that is constant and known and value of N. The node i computes $K=N/CR$ and generate K values Φ_{ji} $(1 \leq j \leq k)$ and create a vector like:

$$D_i [\Phi_{1i}, \Phi_{2i}, ..., ,\Phi_{ki}] \tag{8}$$

where D_i is its own data. Typically, node i will wait to receive from all its downstream neighbors. Each received packet carries its *index from 1 to K* so that it can *be added to the data already waiting in i with the same index* (either locally produced or received from a neighbor). Then node i will send exactly K-*Packets* corresponding to the aggregated column vectors. Finally, compressed vector Y is generated like:

$$\begin{pmatrix} Y_1 \\ \vdots \\ Y_M \end{pmatrix} = \begin{pmatrix} \Phi_{11} & \cdots & \Phi_{1N} \\ \vdots & \vdots & \vdots \\ \Phi_{M1} & \cdots & \Phi_{MN} \end{pmatrix} \begin{pmatrix} D_1 \\ \vdots \\ D_N \end{pmatrix} \tag{9}$$

Now the different between CS and non-CS operation becomes clear: CS operation requires each node send exactly M packets irrespective of what it has receive and each node needs to know CR and N and then computes value of $(M \approx K)$. The received vector in Base Station (BS) can be Witten as:

$$[Y]_{M \times 1} = [\Phi]_{M \times N} [D]_{N \times 1} + \varepsilon_{M \times 1} \tag{10}$$

where $[Y]_{M \times 1}$ is compressed data vector that is received by BS and $\varepsilon_{M \times 1}$ is the thermal noise vector whose components are independent and has zero mean and unit variance. Consequently, the received vectors in BS are an condensed representation of the sparse events.

3.1   Two Important Questions

The first question is that, whether or not the information of K-*Sparse* signal is damaged by the dimensionally reduction from N bits of information to M bits of information [20]. Surprisingly the information is not damaged because of the D vector of date is the sparse vector. If D is not sparse enough, as long as $M \leq N$, the signal is damaged since there are fewer equations than unknowns. The next question is how to develop a reconstruction algorithm to recover data vector from the compressed data vector Y under the certain condition and high probability [19]. We can recover data vector D, by solving a convex optimization via ℓ1 norm. Our model shows in Figure 2. That is why; the compressed data can be generated from only M bits of information instead of N bits of information such as $M \approx K << N$ which K is the number of the events in WSNs [18]. Regarding the explanation above, we can apply the CS theory to WSNs as a new sampling method to reduce sampling rate and power consumption.

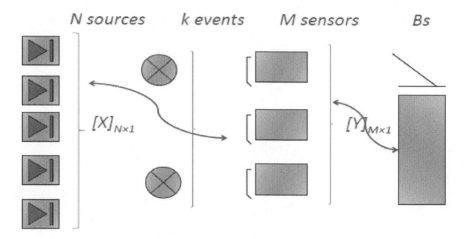

Fig. 2. Sparse data vectors in WSNs

4   Simulation Results

Our simulation shows that the sampling rate in WSNs can reduce to 30% and power consumption to 40% without sacrificing performance and with further decreasing the sampling rate and power consumption, the performance is gradually reduced until 12% sampling rate and 15% power consumption. In this section, we fist, the simulation results on sampling-rate present. Second, the simulation results about power consumption are investigated.

4.1   Simulation Results on Sampling-Rate

To simulate sampling-rate, we have gotten some assumption to simulate sampling rate [2]. The important assumption is:

- $N=100$ (Total number of sources randomly located within 500m-by-500m area)
- M as the number of wireless nodes is also randomly located within this area
- Sampling Rate $(SR) = M/N$
- K as the number of random events which is a random and small number
- The propagation loss factor is very small
- The transmitted power is normalized to 1
- PDF of random variable is Gaussian
- $\varepsilon_{M \times 1}$ as the thermal noise is very small and can be discard

Our result shows, we can reduce sampling rate in SSWSNs until 30% without any problem in detection [4]. The following results are extracted:

- If sampling rate is higher than 30%, the detection probability is almost 100%
- The performance gradually reduces as the sampling rate reduces and as K (the number of events) increase
- $CR=N/K$ is increased when K is decreased

By increasing the number of events the accuracy of detection events decreased. Table 1 shows our simulation on sampling rate with different values for K.

Table 1. Sampling rate reduction for different values of K

Number of events	SR(Non-CS network)	SR(CS-based network)	Detection Probability
K ≤ 10	100%	25%	100%
10 < K ≤ 25	100%	30%	100%
K > 25	100%	35%	100%

Figure 3 shows our simulation on sampling rate with Gaussian distribution and different values for K=5, K=10, K=50. In the non-CS scenario a wireless node is receiving $N-1$ packets (each packet corresponding to a data sample from a wireless node) and will send out N packets (the $N-1$ received packets plus its own data sample); the base station, in particular, will need to receive all the N packets. Now the difference between CS and non-CS operation becomes clear: CS operation requires each node in WSNs to send exactly K packets irrespective of what it has received. In non-CS networks each wireless node needs send N packets with $K<<N$. In the CS scenario by compressing, the data size is reduced and fewer bandwidths is required to transmit data and therefore, less power is required to process and transmit data[15].   Table 2 compares our simulation results with non-CS network [7].

Table 2. Simulation results for non-CS network and CS network

Number of events	Sampling rate reduction	Detection probability
K ≤ 10	Until 25%	100%
10 < K ≤ 25	Until 30%	100%
K > 25	Until 35%	100%

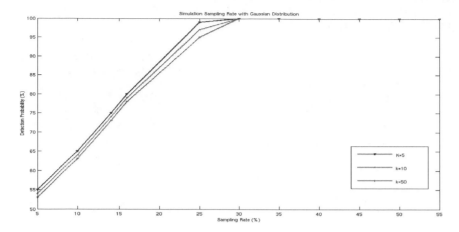

Fig. 3. Sampling rate for K=5, K=10, K=50 with Gaussian distribution

4.2   Simulation Results on Power Consumption

An important key of any WSN is to minimize the power consumed by the units of WN such as PS, CU, and SU. That is why; power consumption can be divided into three domains: sensing, processing, and communication units. The power available in the WN is often restricted. It makes power optimization more complicated in WSNs. By applying the CS to WSNs the sleep time increases by decreasing the number of bits in communication and processing units. After increasing the sleep time, the power consumption should be minimized to extend the life of each WN.   Our simulation results that show compressed sensing theory as a new sampling method in WSNs are beneficial in reducing the total of power consumption [6]. The simulation results are produced using the simulator developed C^{++} and MATLAB. In this simulation we use some assumption including [14]:

- Number of WNs are 100
- WNs are uniformly distributed in the area about 2000×2000 m
- The power supply of each WN has a 15 Jules for CU, PU and SU
- The effective rate for communication unit of each WN is 200m
- The simulation time is 825 seconds
- Power consumption for communication unit in sending mode is 550 mw and in receiving mode is 25 mw
- Each WN consume 9 milliamps in active mode and 5 μA in sleep mode
- Bandwidth for WSN is 1.5 $Mb/_s$
- Each WN has enough time for sending its data to BS
- Simulation packet size 1500
- Simulation interval is 150
- Network topology is star
- The data of WNs are driven form a uniform distribution between 1 and 200
- compressed sensing has *N=100* and *M=10*

Figure 4 shows the power consumption in term of Compressed Ratio (CR) in small scale of WSNs with 100 wireless nodes [16].

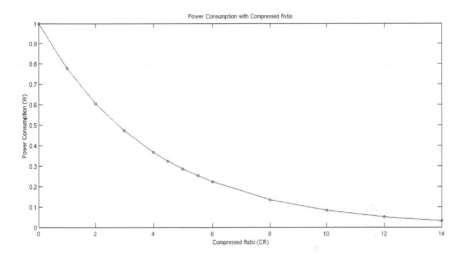

Fig. 4. Simulation of power consumption

The results of simulation are shown in Table 3 and compared in WSN with CS and without CS theory.

Table 3. Results of power consumption

Parameter	Without CS with	N=100	With CS with M=10	
Power cons. in CU	600	mw	110	mw
Power cons. in SU	200	mw	90	mw
Power cons. in PU	180	mw	80	mw

5   Conclusion

In this research proposal, we have investigated the benefit of applying the CS theory to data collection in the WSNs. We first described how to employ the CS theory to WSNs for achieving low sampling-rate and power consumption. Second, we formulated the requirements to apply the CS theory in WSNs. We also employed the CS theory to the WSNs to design low sampling-rate and power consumption network in order to design robust networks with low power consumption. From the simulation results, we investigated that sampling-rate in WSNs can reduce to 30% and power consumption to 40% without sacrificing performances.

6   Further Works

We have investigated how to employ the CS theory in WSNs. It will be part of our future work to provide a general scheme of the CS to any WSNs. We are also going to develop the CS theory to reduce power consumption to provide low-power WSNs with more than 100 WNs. We also want to apply the CS theory to reduce sampling-rate in large scale WSNs with more than 100 WNs.

References

[1] Balouchestani, M., Raahemifar, K., Krishnan, S.: Increasing the reliability of wireless sensor network with a new testing approach based on compressed sensing theory. In: Wireless and Optical Communications Networks (WOCN), 2011 IEEE International Conference on Wireless Sensor Networks, pp. 1–4 (May 2011)

[2] Aeron, S., Saligrama, V., Zhao, M.: Information Theoretic Bounds for Compressed Sensing. IEEE Transactions on Information Theory 56, 5111–5130 (2010)

[3] Balouchestani, M., Raahemifar, K., Krishnan, S.: Power Management of Wireless Sensor Networks with Compressed Sensing Theory. In: 16th IEEE International Conference on Networks and Optical Communications and 6th Conference on Optical Cabling and Infrastructure (OC&I 2011), pp. 122–125. Northumbria University, Newcastle upon Tyne (2011)

[4] Zhuang, X., Wang, H., Dai, Z.: Wireless sensor networks based on compressed sensing. In: 2010 3rd IEEE International Conference on Computer Science and Information Technology (ICCSIT), pp. 90–92 (2010)

[5] Beutel, J., Dyer, M., Lim, R., Plessl, C., Wohrle, M., Yucel, M., Thiele, L.: Automated wireless sensor network testing. In: Fourth International Conference on Networked Sensing Systems, INSS 2007, pp. 303–303 (2007)

[6] Choi, K., Wang, J., Zhu, L., Suh, T.S., Boyd, S., Xing, L.: Compressed sensing based cone-beam computed tomography reconstruction with a first-order method. Med. Phys. 37, 5113–5125 (2010)

[7] Balouchestani, M., Raahemifar, K., Krishnan, S.: Low-Power wireless Sensor Networks with Compressed Sensing theory. In: Fly-By-Wireless (FBW 2011), Montreal, Quebec, pp. 1–4. IEEE Xplore (July 2011)

[8] Chang, C.H., Ji, J.: Compressed sensing MRI with multichannel data using multicore processors. Magn. Reson. Med. 64, 1135–1139 (2010)

[9] Doneva, M., Bornert, P., Eggers, H., Stehning, C., Senegas, J., Mertins, A.: Compressed sensing reconstruction for magnetic resonance parameter mapping. Magn. Reson. Med. 64, 1114–1120 (2010)

[10] Donoho, D.L.: Compressed sensing. IEEE Transactions on Information Theory 52, 1289–1306 (2006)

[11] Haupt, J., Bajwa, W.U., Rabbat, M., Nowak, R.: Compressed Sensing for Networked Data. IEEE Signal Processing Magazine 25, 92–101 (2008)

[12] Luo, J., Xiang, L., Rosenberg, C.: Does compressed sensing improve the throughput of wireless sensor networks? In: 2010 IEEE International Conference on Communications (ICC), pp. 1–6 (2010)

[13] Wang, H., Miao, Y., Zhou, K., Yu, Y., Bao, S., He, Q., Dai, Y., Xuan, S.Y., Tarabishy, B., Ye, Y., Hu, J.: Feasibility of high temporal resolution breast DCE-MRI using compressed sensing theory. Med. Phys. 37, 4971–4981 (2010)

[14] Al-Karaki, J.N., Kamal, A.E.: Routing techniques in wireless sensor networks: a survey. IEEE Wireless Communications 11, 6–28 (2004)

[15] Capella, J.V., Bonastre, A., Ors, R., Peris, M.: A Wireless Sensor Network approach for distributed in-line chemical analysis of water. Talanta 80, 1789–1798 (2010)

[16] Balouchestani, M., Raahemifar, K., Krishnan, S.: Compressed Sensing in Wireless Sensor Networks: Surway. Canadian Journal on Multimedia and Wireless Networks 2(1), 1–4 (2011)

[17] Meng, J., Li, H., Han, Z.: Sparse event detection in wireless sensor networks using compressive sensing. In: 43rd Annual Conference on Information Sciences and Systems, CISS 2009, pp. 181–185 (2009)

[18] Keong, H.C., Yuce, M.R.: Analysis of a multi-access scheme and asynchronous transmit-only UWB for wireless body area networks. In: Conf. Proc. IEEE Eng. Med. Biol. Soc., vol. 2009, pp. 6906–6909 (2009)

[19] Ko, J., Gao, T., Rothman, R., Terzis, A.: Wireless sensing systems in clinical environments: improving the efficiency of the patient monitoring process. IEEE Eng. Med. Biol. Mag. 29, 103–109 (2010)

[20] Balouchestani, M., Raahemifar, K., Krishnan, S.: Concepts for Designing Low-Power Wireless Sensor Networks with Compressed Sensing Theory. In: 2011 International Conference on Communication and Broadband Networking (ICCBN 2011), Kuala Lumpur, Malaysia, pp. 47–51 (June 2011)

[21] Halder, A., Bhattacharya, S., Chatterjee, A.: System-Level Specification Testing of Wireless Transceivers. IEEE Transactions on Very Large Scale Integration (VLSI) Systems 16, 263–276 (2008)

[22] Chou, C.T., Rana, R., Hu, W.: Energy efficient information collection in wireless sensor networks using adaptive compressive sensing. In: IEEE 34th Conference on Local Computer Networks, LCN 2009, pp. 443–450 (2009)

RTIC: Reputation and Trust Evaluation Based on Fuzzy LogIC System for Secure Routing in Mobile Ad Hoc Networks

Abdesselem Beghriche and Azeddine Bilami

LaSTIC laboratory, Computer Sciences Department, UHL Batna
05 Avenue Shahid Boukhlouf, 05000 Batna, Algeri
abdesselem_beghriche@hotmail.com, abilami@yahoo.fr

Abstract. Ad hoc networks are vulnerable to many types of attacks. Their success will undoubtedly depend on the trust they bring to their users. To enhance the security of MANETs, it is important to rate the trustworthiness of other nodes without central authorities to build up a trust environment. This paper expands on relevant fuzzy logic concepts to propose an approach to establish quantifiable trust levels between the nodes of Ad hoc networks. The proposed solution defines additional operators to fuzzy logic in order to find an end to end route which is free of malicious nodes with collaborative effort from the neighbors. In our scheme (RTIC) the path with more trusted decision value is selected as a secure route from source to destination. In order to prove the applicability of the proposed solution, we demonstrate the performance of our model through NS-2 Simulations.

Keywords: Ad hoc networks, Security, Routing, Trust, Trust model, Trust management, Fuzzy logic, Reputation and Recommendation.

1   Introduction

Ad hoc networks are wireless networks without fixed infrastructure. Nodes must collaborate to organize the exchange of control information and allow the routing of traffic. The networks must have the ability to self-configure, without human intervention. As defined group MANET (Mobile Ad hoc NETwork) of the IETF (Internet Engineering Task Force) [4], a mobile Ad hoc networks, is an autonomous system of mobile nodes connected by wireless links whose union forms an arbitrary graph.

MANET network has specific requirements in terms of security, because of its peculiarities: unreliable wireless media (links) used for communication between hosts, constantly changing network topologies and memberships, limited bandwidth, battery, lifetime, and computation power of nodes, etc. These characteristics make Ad hoc mobile networks capable of operating in difficult conditions, but also vulnerable to various security issues, such as encryption key management, certificate distribution, management of trust between nodes, cooperation, etc. Therefore, new protocols specific for this type of network have been proposed and developed.

R. Benlamri (Ed.): NDT 2012, Part I, CCIS 293, pp. 620–634, 2012.

Most of the protocols and applications for Ad hoc networks consider the perfect cooperation among all nodes. In general, it is assumed that all nodes behave according to the application and protocol specifications previously defined for the network. Nevertheless, this assumption may be false, due to resource restrictions or malicious behavior. Consequently, the nodes may not behave as expected causing the network to not work properly. The assumption that nodes behave correctly can lead to unforeseen pitfalls, such as low network efficiency, high resource consumption, and a higher vulnerability to attacks. Therefore, a mechanism that allows a node to infer the trustworthiness of other nodes is necessary.

Although several secure routing protocols [11] have been proposed to defend against predefined attacks, they are vulnerable to new and dynamically changing attacks. Often the vulnerability results from the fact that the design of secure routing protocols does not take the trustworthiness of nodes into account. This has led to the development of several trust models [11], in which mobile nodes capture evidence of trustworthiness of other nodes to quantify and represent their behavior, and then to establish trust relationships with them. Trust models vary in their properties and also from the way they make trust enhanced decisions based on those established relationships and specified policies.

Providing a trust level to each node is not only useful when nodes misbehave, but also when nodes exchange information [3]. According to the paradigm of autonomic networks, a node should be capable of self-configuring, self-managing, and self-learning by means of collecting local information and exchanging information with its neighbors. Thus, it is important to communicate only with trustworthy neighbors, since communicating with misbehaving nodes can compromise the autonomy of network.

However, these trust systems may suffer from slander and collusion attacks [3]. A slander attack consists of sending false recommendations to injure the reputation of other nodes. Moreover, malicious nodes can work together to improve the effectiveness of the attack for instance, nodes could lie about a misbehaving node to try to cover its real nature. These attacks can reduce or even ruin the performance of a distributed trust system.

The focus of this paper is to develop a framework that defines trust metrics and develop models of trust propagation in Ad hoc networks. In this framework a new approach that is based on fuzzy logic concepts to optimize the evaluation of trust between nodes is introduced. Fuzzy logic provides a simple way to arrive at a definite conclusion based upon vague, ambiguous, or imprecise input information. Different factors and parameters should be identified and combined in order to determine if a node is acting maliciously. Incorporating trust in Ad hoc routing protocols and thereby mimicking human behavior can facilitate the detection of nodes that misuse the trust placed in them.

To achieve this, the remainder of this paper is organized as follows. After this introduction, the second section describes and comments on related work that has been done in the field of trust model and reputation. The background about trust relationship, fuzzy logic, and system design requirements in this work is described in section three. Section four presents our trust model and describes intuitive properties that any scheme under this framework should have. Finally, before concluding, we discuss and comment in section five, the simulation results of the proposed solution.

2   Related Works

Establishing security associations based on distributed trust models among nodes is an important consideration while designing a secure routing solution in MANETs [1]. Not much work has been done to develop a trust model to build up, distribute and manage trust levels among the Ad hoc nodes. Some of the proposed schemes talk about the general requirements of trust establishment [1]. Some of the algorithms think about the direct and recommendation trust to come up with trust computations [6]. We can classify all the works that have been done in trusted routing, in three categories: "Systems credentials", "Reputation systems" and "Trust from a social network". In this section, we will overview some proposed protocols that have been given to designing trusted routing protocols.

2.1 Systems Credentials (Certificates-Based)

This framework is based on the establishment of one or more security policies and a system of certificates: nodes use the certificate verification to establish a relationship of trust with other nodes [2]. The main purpose of such systems is to enable access control. Therefore, their concept of trust management is limited to the policy rules defined by each application [5]. In this framework, there are several models such as:

Hierarchical Trust Model and "Web of Trust" Model. In this context, trust is generally managed via a public key infrastructure (PKI) of some sort. Existing PKI schemes utilize either hierarchical trust model or "web of trust" [8]. In the hierarchical model, a root certificate authority (CA) issues certificates to delegated CAs or end users. The CAs in turn issue certificates to end users or to other CAs. In the "web of trust" model [8], there is no distinction between a CA and an end user. End users are responsible for certificate management. End user tasks include: issuing and revocation of certificates, and vouching for the credibility of other users. This model offers more flexibility than the hierarchical trust model and seemingly ideal for application in decentralized environments especially Ad hoc networks [9]. But, these trust models therefore, may not be suitable for applications where high degrees of accountability and security are required [9].

Distributed Public Key Model. The Distributed Public-Key Model [20] makes use of threshold cryptography to distribute the private key of the Certification Authority over a number of servers. An $(n, t+1)$ scheme allows any $(t+1)$ servers out of total of n servers to combine their partial keys to create the complete secret key. Similarly, it requires that at least $(t+1)$ servers must be compromised to acquire the secret key. The scheme is quite robust but has a number of factors that limit its application to pure Ad hoc networks [20]. Primarily it requires an extensive pre-configuration of servers and a distributed central authority, secondly the $(t+1)$ servers may not be accessible to any node desiring authentication and lastly asymmetric cryptographic operations are known to drain precious node batteries.

2.2 Reputation Systems

In this context, the reputation can be seen as the hope brought in achieving a goal fictitious. The reputation system of MANET is very important, because it is able to avoid misbehavior of nodes. A number of reputation mechanisms have been suggested and studied. A comprehensive survey and more detailed overview of reputation systems for mobile Ad hoc networks can be found in [10]. Such systems provide a mechanism for which a node requesting a resource, can assess the confidence he brings to the supplier to provide it, and each node establishes trust relationships with other nodes and assigns trust values to its relations [16]. The value assigned to the trust relationship is based on a combination between the overall reputation of the node and the evaluation of perception of the node, that is to say based on his own experience. CONFIDANT [10], CORE [18], PGP [8], XREP, NICE, DCRC/CORC [14], Beta [15] and Eigen-trust [17] are examples of such systems.

2.3 Trust from a Social Network

Finally, in this context, the social network underlying conditions under trust management. Social relations are used to calculate the values of reputation and recommendation from each node. Such systems analyze the social network that represents the relations existing in each community in order to draw conclusions about levels of trust to be given to other nodes, they are based on mechanisms of reputation, credibility, honesty and also process recommendations. Here are some models:

The Resurrecting Duckling Model. The proposed Ross Anderson and Frank Stajano [19] aims to create a relationship of master-slave type between two communicating entities. In this model, the entities in a network have a master-slave relationship. The master entity is the mother duck and the slave entity is the duckling. The relationship among nodes is a tree-like trust relationship. An entity controls all the entities in its sub-tree. Breaking the relation between two entities causes the relationships in the entire sub-tree to break. This model is appropriate for devices that can't perform public-key cryptography. However, the model requires an out-of-band secret channel to deliver the secret key, which might not be feasible in some networks, such as Ad hoc networks [19].

Distributed Trust Model. Abdul-Rahman and Hailes [7] proposed and developed a distributed recommendation based trust model. They propose *"conditional transitivity of trust"*, which hypothesizes that trust is transitive under some conditions. The model's motivation comes from human society, where human beings get to know each other via direct interaction and through a grapevine of relationships. The same is true in distributed systems. In a large distributed system, every entity can't obtain first-hand information about all other entities. As an option, entities can rely on second-hand information or recommendations. However, because recommendations have uncertainty or risk, entities need to know how to cope with second-hand information.

Nuglet. In [13], Buttyan and Hubaux present two important issues targeted specifically at the Ad hoc networking environment: first, end-users must be given some incentive to contribute in the network operation (especially to relay packets belonging to other nodes), second, end users must be discouraged from overloading the network. The solution consists of a virtual currency call Nuglet used in every transaction.

3   Context for Our Approach

3.1 Trust Relationship

In our work we define trust as the value that reflects the behavior history that a node has about a specific neighbor. This information is used as an expectation of its neighbor future behavior. Therefore, similar to the concept of human trust, the computation of the trust level of a given neighbor is based on previous experiences and also on the opinion of other neighbors.

In MANETs, trust is represented and realized by the trust relationships interacted with each other. The node to be assessed for trustworthiness will be called "*trusted node*" and the node assessing the trusted node's trustworthiness will be called "*trusting node*". Nodes which share information about their past experiences with the requesting node are called "*recommending nodes*".

Trust relationships are determined by the rules to evaluate the evidence with a quantitative way, generated by the previous behaviors of a node. The contact between the trusting node and the trusted node is formed by the three means: as shown in fig.1:

(a) Direct personal contact or interaction with one another (Direct trust).
(b) Recommendations based trust (Indirect trust).
(c) Contact through reviewing the history records.

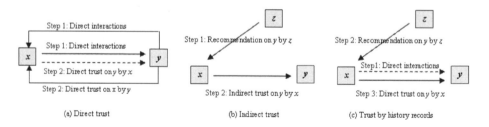

(a) Direct trust   (b) Indirect trust   (c) Trust by history records

Fig. 1. Various schemes for trust relationship

3.2 Fuzzy Logic for Trust

Trust plays an important role in the cooperation and interaction between real world entities. It is well established that fuzzy logic is suitable to quantify trust among entities that comprise a network or a group. One of the advantages of using fuzzy logic to quantify trust between nodes in Ad hoc networks is its ability to quantify imprecise data or uncertainty in measuring the security index of Ad hoc nodes [22].

A fuzzy system is typified by the *inference system* that includes the system rule base, input membership functions that fuzzify the input variables and the output variable de-fuzzification process.

For every element x in the set of X, there is a mapping, $x \rightarrow \mu(x)$ in which $\mu(x) \in [0, 1]$. The set $\Delta = \{(x, \mu(x))\}$ is defined a fuzzy set for trust in MANETs. $\mu(x)$ is defined as the membership function for every x in Δ. A membership function defines the degree to which a fuzzy variable is a member of a set. Full membership is represented by 1 and no membership by 0.

Fuzzy set theory defines fuzzy operators on fuzzy sets. The problem in applying this is that the appropriate fuzzy operator may not be known. For this reason, Fuzzy logic usually uses "IF/THEN" rules, or constructs that are equivalent, such as fuzzy associative matrices. Rules are usually expressed in the form: *"IF variable IS set THEN action"*.

3.3 System Design Requirements

We suggest three important design criteria to address in any MANETs trust model:

- The trust model should be without infrastructure. Because the network routing infrastructure is formed in an Ad hoc fashion.
- The trust model should be robust. That is, it can be robust to all kinds of unfriendly attacks and the network itself should not be susceptible to attacks by unfriendly nodes.
- The trust model should have minimal control overhead in accordance with computation, storage, and complexity.

4 Proposed Model

Trust is a natural fuzzy concept, which poses a fuzzy constraint on the trusted routing decision making, so the different nodes might provide diverse routings about the same nodes, i.e., different nodes would have the different and even opposite trust evaluations toward a same node. Based on fuzzy model, each node can calculate the trust value for its neighbors and maintain in its neighbor trust table. As the trusted routing process is also fuzzy, RTIC is proposed to make the trusted routing decision in MANET.

4.1 RTIC Mechanism

In this part, the scheme for choosing the most secure path in MANET is proposed, and also the evaluation mechanism of trust and the fuzzy logic routing decision is introduced. Fig. 2 shows the trusted decision model that based on trust and reputation (RTIC mechanism). Our model will make a logical decision, which may not be the most excellent but a safe selection among the nodes in Ad hoc network.

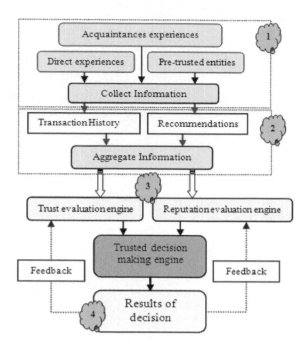

Fig. 2. RTIC mechanism

Description of the Proposed Mechanism. The steps of RTIC mechanism are detailed below:

1. A gathering information function (collect information) should receive a collection of experiences and a collection of pre trusted entities as parameters. The experiences could be represented as reputation values, or as a collection of positive and negative previous transactions.
2. Aggregating all the received information properly and somehow computing a score for every node in the network. That is, it would receive either a collection of recommendations about which entity is more trustworthy, or a collection of weighted transactions (or maybe both).
3. This function would be to use the mechanism of fuzzy logic in order to provide a local or global (or perhaps both) the values of all parameters of some or all entities in the network.

   - Trust evaluation engine: It is an implementing result with a trust model. By evaluating the parameters on trust, the engine receives the trust values and sends them to trusted decision engine.
   - Reputation evaluation engine: It is used to evaluate the reputation value of nodes based on the parameters on reputation by using some evaluating methods [13]. Then it also sends them to trusted decision engine.

4. It is the core subject in this mechanism. This process is divided into several associated phases and there have been several designed feasible plans in each phase. The objective of the trusted decision is to select the most suitable solutions to get the best overall effect of the whole decision process.

Trust Evaluation. We define the trust level evaluation from node *"a"* about node *"b"* as a sum of its own trust and the contribution of other nodes, in the same way as defined by [5]. The fundamental equation is:

$$X_a(b) = (1 - \xi) Y_a(b) + \xi Z_a(b) \tag{1}$$

Where: $\{0 \leq \xi \leq 1, 0 \leq Y_a(b) \leq 1, 0 \leq Z_a(b) \leq 1\}$, $Y_a(b)$ represents the trust node a has on node b based only on its own observations and $Z_a(b)$, is the aggregate value of the recommendations from all other neighbors. The variable ξ, is a parameter in that allows nodes to choose the most relevant factor. In our model, the value of $Y_a(b)$ is given by:

$$Y_a(b) = \lambda E_a(b) + (1 - \lambda) X_a(b) \tag{2}$$

Where: $\{0 \leq \lambda \leq 1\}$, $E_a(b)$ represents the value obtained by the judgment of neighbor actions, and the variable $X_a(b)$ gives the last trust level value stored in the Trust Table. The variable λ allows different weights for the factors of the equation, selecting which factor is the more relevant at a given moment.

Reputation Evaluation. It is assumed that the reputation of every node is between 0 and 1 in an MANET. The lower reputation indicates that the node is low reliable, and vice versa. The reputation of a node is refreshed after forwarding packets. The reputation in our model can be obtained by the following equation [12]:

$$R_i = \frac{\sum_{j \in S} W_j T_{ji}}{\sum_{j \in S} W_j} \tag{3}$$

Where: R_i is the global reputation of node i, S is the set of nodes with whom node i has conducted transactions, T_{ji} is the local trust score of node i rated by node j, and W_j is the aggregation weight of T_{ji}. The global aggregation process runs multiple iterations until each R_i converges to a stable global reputation rating for node i.

Fuzzy Logic Controller. In the present section, we design our fuzzy inference system that allows a resource owner to infer the trusted decision of a requester in an Ad hoc fashion. There are two main players in our system, a resource owner and a requester. We assume that the requester may be malicious and submitting false information to the resource owner in order to gain access. We do not assume any prior trust relationships between the resource owner and the requester, i.e., they may not know each other.

Our fuzzy system for computing trusted decision takes into account of two input variables, trust value and reputation value. The absolute value of each of these parameters can take a large range at different points on the network. We have considered the normalized values for each parameter. Now, 'crisp' normalized values are being converted into fuzzy variables.

For this, four fuzzy sets have been defined for trust variable and three fuzzy sets were defined for reputation variable as shown fig. 3. The normalized value of each parameter is mapped into the fine sets. Each value will have some grade of membership function for each set. The memberships that have been defined for each of the fuzzy set for any particular input variable are triangular in shape.

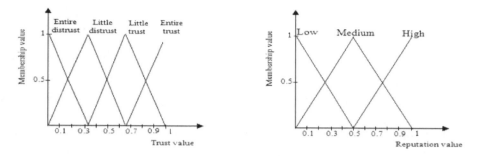

Fig. 3. Membership functions for the input variables

Trusted Decision Evaluation. The output variable that represents the trusted decision factor of a node is defined as trusted decision value. This variable has six fuzzy sets represented by the membership function and are shown in fig. 4.

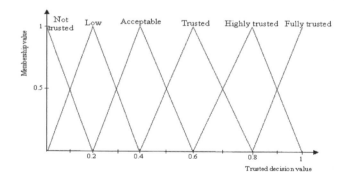

Fig. 4. Membership function for the output variable

The result of the fuzzy logic inference is the value of a linguistic variable. The conversion of such a linguistic result to a real value which represents the trusted decision level of a node is called defuzzification. Therefore, the input for the defuzzification process is a fuzzy set and the output is a single number. The aggregate of a fuzzy set encompasses a range of output values, and so must be defuzzified in order to resolve a single trusted decision level for the node. The de-fuzzification step is to compute a crisp output by combining inference results using a fuzzy centroid algorithm, as specified in equation 4:

$$f(x) = \frac{\sum_{i=1}^{n} C_i * P_i}{\sum_{i=1}^{n} P_i} \tag{4}$$

Where C_i denotes the center point of f_i's membership function, P_i denotes the firing strength of a fuzzy variable f_i and n is the number of input fuzzy variables. We give the formula for computing the firing degree P_i of a fuzzy variable f_i using Root-Sum-Square method in Equation 5:

$$P_i = \sqrt{\sum_{i}^{n} \sum_{j}^{k} d_{ij}^{2}} \tag{5}$$

To illustrate how fuzzy rules can be defined for our attributes, we give the 10 rules of our system as follows:

Rule 1: If (Trust is entire distrust) and (Reputation is anything) then (Trusted decision is not trusted).

Rule 2: If (Trust is little distrust) and (Reputation is low) then (Trusted decision is not trusted).

Rule 3: If (Trust is little distrust) and (Reputation is medium) then (Trusted decision low).

Rule 4: If (Trust is little distrust) and (Reputation is high) then (Trusted decision is acceptable).

Rule 5: If (Trust is little trust) and (Reputation is low) then (Trusted decision is acceptable).

Rule 6: If (Trust is little trust) and (Reputation is medium) then (Trusted decision is trusted).

Rule 7: If (Trust is little trust) and (Reputation is high) then (Trusted decision is highly trusted).

Rule 8: If (Trust is entire trust) and (Reputation is low) then (Trusted decision is trusted).

Rule 9: If (Trust is entire trust) and (Reputation is medium) then (Trusted decision is highly trusted).

Rule 10: If (Trust is entire trust) and (Reputation is high) then (Trusted decision is fully trusted).

5   Performance Evaluation

Simulation is used to validate the proposals made in this paper. We study how the number of nodes participating in the network operation increases when fuzzy logic based approach is used. We have used the NS-2 simulator for analyzing our approach. Various network scenarios are analyzed to prove the accuracy of the model and its characteristics. The fixed parameters for the simulation are shown in Table 1.

Table 1. Simulation Parameters

Parameter	Value
MAC	802.11
Placement	Uniform
Movement	Random Waypoint
Number of nodes	100
Area	2000*1000 m^2
Speed	20 m/s
Radio range	250 m
Sending capacity	2 Mbps
Simulation time	1000s
Pause time	10 m/s
Packet size	512 B
Application	CBR
Maximum malicious nodes	15% (15 nodes)
Type of attack	Coordinated attack

In this model the nodes move with a constant speed, and then they pause for some time and move again in a random direction. The MAC layer protocol simulates the IEEE 802.11 Distributed Coordination Function (DCF). The network topology is generated using the "setdest" utility of NS-2.

The performance evaluation is an average of 10 different simulations for each studied case. When the simulation starts, packets sent by the source node takes their path to the destination node. For this we will follow the steps in the following procedure:

- A source node starts to flood RREQ packets to its neighboring nodes until they arrive at their destination node. Each RREQ consists of Id-sourced, Id-destination, trust value and reputation value of nodes along the path.
- If the intermediate node N receives a RREQ packet and it is not the destination, then the information of node N is added to the RREQ packet which is appended to packet fields. After that node N re-forward the packet to all the neighboring nodes of itself.
- If node N receives a RREQ packet and node N is the destination, it waits a period of time. There fore, the destination node may receive many different RREQ packets from the source. Then it calculates the value of trusted decision value for each path from source to the destination using the information in each RREQ packet. Finally, destination node sends a route reply (RREP) packet along the path which has a maximum trusted value.

In the simulation, RTIC mechanism should be used as a routing protocol to ensure a reliable and secure routing. To get the different level of the performance, various numbers of the malicious nodes are set to run the simulations. In the experiments, it is assumed that the malicious nodes percentage is 5% (5 malicious nodes, some nodes may be out of the communication range), 10% and 15% respectively. After the implementation of our protocol, the simulation results have been compared with AODV and S-AODV protocols [23], from the aspects of Data Packet Drop Ratio, End to End Delay and Throughput.

Data Packet drop ratio. The data packet drop ratio indicates the data transmission performance of the MANET routing protocols. The basic character of the malicious nodes is to take the attack by dropping packets deliberately or forcedly when they are overloaded.

End to End Delay. Average end to end delay is the delay experienced by the success-fully delivered packets in reaching their destinations. This is a good metric for com-paring protocols and denotes how efficient the underlying routing algorithm, because delay primarily depends on trustworthiness of path chosen.

Throughput. One of metrics is the result of the total throughput of a network with n nodes [21]. That is, the data forwarded to the correct destination for each node *i* is denoted as follow:

$$Throughput = \frac{\sum_{i=1}^{n} Packet_{Received}}{\sum_{i=1}^{n} Packets_{Oriented}} \qquad (6)$$

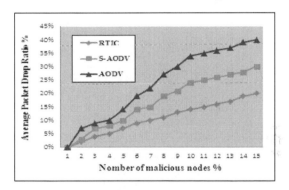

Fig. 5. Packet drop ratio with various malicious nodes

Fig. 5 shows the experiment results of the packets drop ratio under RTIC, AODV and S-AODV respectively. It can be found that RTIC protocol maintains a lower drop ratio and the curve fluctuates smoother than others. This is mainly because the tradi-tional AODV protocol only considers the hop count as the source for routing selec-tion, and S-AODV chooses the optimal secure route. While RTIC has used the trusted decision making process, this can eliminate malicious nodes' influence and mitigate the attack caused by packet drop. Take the cases with 5% malicious nodes as an ex-ample, the packet drop ratio of RTIC is 9%, S-AODV is 10% and AODV 14%. When the malicious nodes increase from 10% to 15%, the packets dropped by RTIC increase only 5% while S-AODV increase 10%. The results also have shown that RTIC is more trustworthy than S-AODV and AODV.

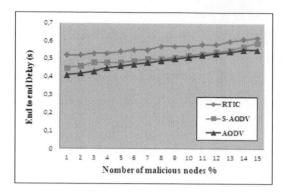

Fig. 6. End to End Delay in the different protocols

The end to end latency of RTIC turns to be averagely 8% longer than AODV and S-AODV, and because S-AODV has avoided the decision making process, its delay is less than RTIC. While the calculation in RTIC is more complex than that in AODV and S-AODV, so its delay is longer generally. Fig.6 shows the result.

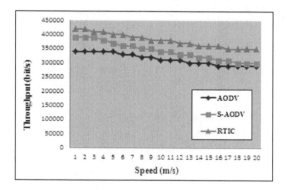

Fig. 7. Throughput at different speed

In Fig.7, the simulation result shows that throughput of these three protocols reduces when the speeds increase. When the speed of the mobile node increased, the routing path was more unreliable. The reason is that there were more chances for routes to break when the speed of the mobile node was faster. Thus, the number of rebroadcasts increased. Since RTIC has chosen more reliable route than AODV and S-AODV, we can see that it has performed better at all speeds.

Fig. 8 shows the average end to end delay. It is clear here that AODV and S-AODV have less delay than RTIC. Higher delay in the proposed method is obtained because of the wasted time spent while searching a route with a longer lifetime; the packets still stay in the buffer until a valid route is found. This will increase the average delay whereas AODV chooses the shortest path as a valid path.

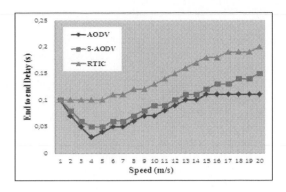

Fig. 8. End to end Delay at different speed

6   Conclusion

Evaluating trust levels between nodes of Ad hoc networks poses a big challenge due to the lack of infrastructure in such networks. To overcome this limitation, a new approach based on fuzzy logic concepts is proposed to facilitate the trusted decision between nodes of Ad hoc networks. In this paper, we have proposed a secure routing mechanism for Ad hoc networks, where a secure end-to-end path is found free of malicious nodes. We determine two parameters: trust value and reputation value that are used for finding a secure route from source to destination in an Ad hoc network. During route discovery, every node records its trust value and reputation value in RREQ packet .In the destination, based on trusted decision value, is decided which route is selected. The path with more trusted value is candidates to route data packets from source to destination. The performance of this scheduler is studied using NS2 and evaluated in terms of quantitative measures such as data packet drop ratio, average end-to-end delay and throughput. Simulation shows that the approach is efficient, promising and applicable in Ad hoc networks.

References

1. Ghosh, T., Pissinou, N., Makki, K.: Towards Designing a Trusted Routing Solution in Mobile Ad Hoc Networks. Mobile Networks and Applications 10, 985–995 (2005)
2. Luo, H., Lu, S.: Ubiquitous and Robust Access Control for Mobile Ad Hoc Networks. IEEE/ACM Transactions on Networking 1, 1049–1063 (2004)
3. Velloso, P.B., Laufer, R.P., Duarte, O.C., Pujolle, G.: A Trust Model Robust to Slander Attacks in Ad Hoc Networks. In: 8th IFIP IEEE International Conference on Mobile and Wireless Communication Networks, MWCN 2006, Santiago (2006)
4. Hubaux, J.P., Buttyan, L., Capkun, S.: The Quest for security in mobile Ad hoc Networks. In: Proceedings of ACM Symposium on Mobile Ad Hoc Networking and Computing, MOBIHOC, Long Beach (2001)

5. Velloso, P.B., Laufer, R.P., Duarte, O.C., Pujolle, G.: Trust Management in Mobile Ad Hoc Networks Using a Scalable Maturity Based Model. IEEE Transactions on Network and Service Management 7(3) (2010)
6. Li, J., Li, R., Kato, J.: Future trust management framework for mobile Ad hoc networks. IEEE Communications Mag. 46(4), 108–114 (2008)
7. Abdul-Rahman, Hailes, S.: A distributed trust model. In: Proceedings of 1997 New Security Paradigms Workshop, pp. 48–60. ACM Press (1998)
8. Zimmermann, P.: The Official PGP User's Guide. MIT Press (1995)
9. Hubaux, J.P., Buttyan, L., Capkun, S.: Self-organized public-key management for mobile Ad hoc networks. IEEE Transactions on Mobile Computing 2(1) (2003)
10. Buchegger, S., Le Boudec, J.V.: Self-Policing Mobile Ad hoc Networks by Reputation Systems. IEEE Communications, 101–107 (2005)
11. Deng, H., Li, W., Agrawal, D.P.: Routing security in wireless Ad hoc networks. IEEE Communications (2002)
12. Song, S., Hwang, K., Zhou, R., Kwong-Kwok, Y.: Trusted P2P Transactions with Fuzzy Reputation Aggregation, 1089-7801. IEEE Computer Society (2005)
13. Buttyan, L., Hubaux, J.P.: Nuglets: a virtual currency to stimulate cooperation in self-organized Ad hoc networks. Technical Report, DSC/2001/001, Swiss Federal Institute of Technology, Lausanne (2001)
14. Gupta, P., Judge, P., Aniniar, M.H.: A reputation system for peer-to-peer networks. In: Papadopoulos, C., Almeroth, K.C. (eds.) NOSSDAV, pp. 144–152. ACM (2003)
15. Ismail, S., Josang, A.: The beta reputation system. In: Proceedings of the 15th Bled Conference on Electronic Commerce (2002)
16. Zacharia, G., Maes, P.: Trust management through reputation mechanisms. Applied Artificial Intelligence 14(9), 881–907 (2000)
17. Kamvar, S.D., Schlosser, M.T., Garcia-Molina, H.: The Eigen-trust algorithm for reputation management in p2p networks (2007)
18. Michiardi, P., Molva, R.: CORE: A Collaborative Reputation Mechanism to Enforce Node Cooperation in Mobile Ad Hoc Networks. In: 6th IFIP Conf. Sec., Slovenia (2002)
19. Stajano, F., Anderson, R.J.: The Resurrecting Duckling: Security Issues for Ad hoc Wireless Networks. In: Malcolm, J.A., Christianson, B., Crispo, B., Roe, M. (eds.) Security Protocols 1999. LNCS, vol. 1796, pp. 172–194. Springer, Heidelberg (2000)
20. Marti, S., Giuli, T., Lai, K., Baker, M.: Mitigating routing misbehavior in mobile Ad hoc networks. In: Proceedings of the Sixth International Conference on Mobile Computing and Networking, Boston (2000)
21. Rishiwal, V., Kush, A., Verma, S.: Backbone nodes based Stable routing for mobile Ad hoc network. UBICC Journal 2(3), 34–39 (2007)
22. Srinivasan, A., Teitelbaum, J., Liang, H., Wu, J., Cardei, M.: Reputation and Trust-Based Systems for Ad hoc and Sensor Networks. In: Boukerche, A. (ed.) Algorithms and Protocols for Wireless Ad hoc and Sensor Networks. Wiley & Sons (2007)
23. AbdulRahman, A., Zuriati, A.Z.: Performance Comparison of AODV, DSDV and I-DSDV Routing Protocols in Mobile Ad Hoc Networks. European Journal of Scientific Research 31(4), 566–576 (2009)

Sink Mobile for Efficient Data Dissemination
in Wireless Sensor Networks

M. Guerroumi, Nadjib Badache, and S. Moussaoui

USTHB, Electronic and Computing Science Department,
Algiers, Algeria
mguerroumi@usthb.dz, Nbadache@wissal.dz,
moussaoui_samira@yahoo.fr

Abstract. Among the challenges posed by the problem of data dissemination in wireless sensor networks one that has recently received considerable attention concerns the minimization of the node energy consumption for increasing the overall network lifetime. The sensor devices are battery powered thus energy is the most precious resource of a wireless sensor network since periodically replacing the battery of the nodes in large scale deployments is infeasible. Disseminate the collected data peer to peer to a static control point consumes significant amounts of energy especially for the sensor nodes around to the static sink. In this paper, we present new sink mobility-based data dissemination protocol to minimize energy consumption. We define new sink mobility scheme in which sensor sink periodically moves towards any destination based on the data dissemination frequency calculated during the last period.. The simulation result shows that the proposal protocol permits to reduce the energy consumption and prolong the network life.

Keywords: wireless sensor networks, data dissemination, energy efficiency, mobile sink.

1 Introduction

A wireless sensor network is a multi-hop wireless network composed of a large number of sensor nodes. A sensor node is generally battery power with relatively small memory, restricted computation capability, and short wireless communication range. Furthermore, wireless sensor networks have the advantages of fault tolerance, easy deployment and accurate sensing, which can be applied in many fields, such as battlefield surveillance, environment monitoring, industrial sensing and diagnostics, critical infrastructure protection and biological detection [23].

Sensor nodes independently sense the environment and collaborate to achieve data sensing and dissemination. Several algorithms and protocols have been proposed in the last few years to achieve more efficient and reliable data dissemination in wireless sensor network. Simply, a flooding is the most reliable scheme to forward data from sensors to a sink without any extra cost for topology maintenance or route discovery, it is very simple and easy to implement. However, flooding may suffer from significant redundancy with too many duplicated messages and consumes more energy.

R. Benlamri (Ed.): NDT 2012, Part I, CCIS 293, pp. 635–645, 2012.

Data dissemination is a process by which the sensing data will be transmitted form the source sensor node to the sink. It consists to determine the optimal path on which the information will be disseminated. The characteristics of the networks of sensors, like the significant density and the limited energy require specific data dissemination protocol. In this paper, we extend our protocol Data Dissemination and Power Management (DDPM) [17] by introducing mobility of the sink to more optimizing energy consumption.

The remaining parts of this paper are organized in the following way. Section 2 reviews a set of related data dissemination protocol and summarizes some recent works. Section 3 presents the parameters and the assumptions of our environment. Section 4 presents our proposal and gives the necessary description of the different concepts used in our design. Performance analysis and simulation results are presented in Section 5. Section 6 concludes this paper.

2   Related Works

Several data dissemination protocols for sensor networks have been proposed in the literature to address the data communication problem in these networks. Protocol LEACH proposed in [2] is one of the first approaches of the hierarchical data dissemination sensors networks. LEACH has been considered as an effective protocol in energy consumption this protocol can extend the lifetime of the network [2], compared with the other protocols. Moreover, this protocol organizes the sensor nodes in clusters form, the elected cluster heads collect the data from its sensor nodes, aggregate and transmit them directly to the sink node, these cluster heads changed and elected periodically. TEEN is a protocol of data dissemination based on the clustering technique proposed by Anjeshwar & Al [4]. TEEN uses the same strategy as LEACH to create the clusters node, but adopts a different approach during the data transmission phase. In this phase, TEEN uses two parameters called hardware threshold and software threshold to determine the need of collected data transmission. PEGAGIS [13] is another data dissemination protocol designed for sensor networks which improves the previous LEACH. In this protocol, a sensor node communicates only with the closest neighbors, it should wait its turn to transmit its data to the sink node.

CODE [1] is a protocol based on a virtual grid structure, where each cell of the grid contains a node called coordinator playing the role of an intermediate node. Only these nodes coordinators take part in the process of data dissemination. This protocol is principally inspired from some previous works like GAF [6], [7].

Other protocol SPIN [3] considers the end-to-end communications in sensor networks. It supposes that two sensor nodes can communicate between them without any interference with other nodes. This protocol supposes also that the energy consumption does not constitute a constraint, and the data are never lost.

In the directed diffusion protocol [15], data are inherently dispersed with the physical object and retrieved via queries transferred to the object through the network. It also envisions that the querying and monitoring the physical space may rely on multicast mechanisms. Protocol PDDD [5] tries to surmount the disadvantage of the multicast mechanisms used in the directed diffusion protocol. It eliminates the gradient algorithm of directed diffusion and exploits the information of neighbor nodes.

According to user importance, SAFE [12] considers service differentiation between data sinks, allowing each data sink itself to specify the desired data update rate. This aspect entails multiple level provision of data freshness.

Other protocol MMSPEED [11] presents an evolution in the protocols oriented quality of service. MMSPEED offers several transmissions speed and establishes more than one route form the source node to the destination. Therefore, each offered speed defines a level of temporal QoS and each additional route helps to improve the quality of traffic. These two mechanisms respectively make it possible to respect the degree of criticality of each application, to transmit the data within the required times and to avoid the problems frequently encountered like the congestion and packets loss.

Several approaches exploiting mobile sinks for efficient data collection in wireless sensor networks have been proposed [14], [18], [19]. To optimize energy consumption, authors in [18] propose mechanism to provide sinks mobility, in this mechanism, sinks can move into their perimeter in optimal way in order to maximize the lifetime of a sensor network through load balancing. This mechanism provides uniform energy consumption on one hop between sink neighboring nodes, for multi-hop communications with long path, energy consumption still high because the sinks are located on the perimeter of the sensor network. In [19], authors introduce sink mobility through multi-hops. The mobile sink reconstructs the data dissemination paths from all source nodes by updating the topology change according to its movement using global update. TTDD [14] considers sink mobility, by constructing grid networks for each data source and selecting a grid node as the communication portal of mobile data sinks. The mobile sink renews its location to the dissemination node for moving within a cell and reselects a new nearest dissemination node via a local flooding for moving between cells. In [20], a mobile sink moves linearly through a linear path and collects sensing data. Before the data gathering, the mobile sink floods a route construction packet while moving along the linear dissemination path and sensor nodes send their data to the nodes close to this dissemination path. In [22], the authors consider random mobility with destinations. This protocol is similar to the data dissemination approach based on predefined path mobility. It allows source nodes to forward their data on the next movement path of a mobile sink. However, a mobile sink in this protocol does not move along predefined path, but randomly toward the destination. Others data dissemination and energy schemes have proposed in [8], [10].

3   System Model and Assumptions

We consider a large scale sensor network with a large number of sensor nodes scattered randomly. Each node acts as either a source to sense information from the environment or a router to forward data through the sensor field to the interest users. In this paper, we consider only the detected events occurred in the sensor network, the end users receive frequently and randomly the new detected events. Therefore, sensor nodes should be preconfigured to send a notification if the new event verifies some parameters, example if the temperature exceeds or decreases under predefined degree. In this environment we assume that:

- Each sensor node should be aware of its own geographic location using location services such as GPS [16], or other techniques such as triangulation [21].
- After having been deployed, sensor nodes remain stationary at their initial locations and only sink that can mobile.
- The sensor nodes are stationary, homogeneous and each sensor node has constrained battery energy.
- Sensor nodes communicate with sinks via a multiple hops path.

4   Mobile Sink Data Dissemination Protocol (MSDDP)

As given in [17], the proposed protocol is based on a structure of indexed virtual grid the same used in [1], where each cell represents a cluster that contains a selected head. The selected head collects the data from all the nodes of its group, aggregates and transmits them to the basic station using the multi hop communication.

The proposed solution starts with an initialization phase, during which, the virtual grid will be constructed and a header will be selected for each group. Thus, the process of data dissemination will start in the second phase.

During the second phase, the head of the group receives the data collected by the nodes of its group, then, it transmits them to the interested sinks hop by hop, the next hop is defined by the indices of next cell in the grid.

During the dissemination phase, each head of group executes the necessary data aggregation to decrease the number of transmission packets. When the head receives data from one of its members, it will ignore all the same ones received in the next **T** second, where **T** is the necessary time for transmission of data between the two farthest nodes in the group. According to the blow Figure1:

$$R^2 = r^2 + r^2 => R = r\sqrt{2} \text{ so } \mathbf{T} = r\sqrt{2}/v \qquad (1)$$

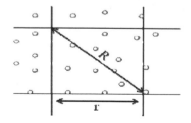

Fig. 1. Grid cell (cluster)

Where: v is radio speed and r is cell size.

This operation permits to reduce the number of the transmitted packets. Moreover, when an event is observed by several nodes, only one message will be transmitted to the sink and the other messages will be ignored.

4.1   Cluster Head Management

Cluster head disseminates sensing data from the source sensor node to the sink witch consume more energy. Thus, to determinate the cluster head we use the same energy scheme given in [17] which based on the below formula:

$$New\_threshold = Old\_threshold-(Old\_threshold/k) \qquad (2)$$

K is positive integer.

Threshold_max is the initial threshold, and tthreshold_min is the lowest sufficient energy that permits the cluster head to advertise its energy exhaustion in order to select another one.

Initially the energy available of the selected cluster head should be more than the threshold_max, after certain time, the energy of the head will be decreased and when becomes   inferior   to   the   threshold_min.   the   head   sends   a   message   of Select_newHeaderr(Old_threshold) in order to select new head. The nodes which have a residual energy higher than the threshold sent by the head will replay by sending their energy available (Ack_newLeader(Residual_ Energie).

The sensor node which has the highest residual energy available will be selected as new cluster head. In the worst case, where no sensor node replies on the selected new header message, which means that all the sensor nodes have residual energy less than the specified threshold (Old_threshold). In this case, the head defines new threshold using the above formula and select new cluster head according to it.

However, if the residual energy of the current cluster head is less than or equal to the threshold_min , it sends a Death_Leader(Old_threshold) message to advertise its energy exhaustion, and the nodes will cooperate between them with the same manner to choose a new cluster head the node which has the highest residual energy.

4.2   Sink Mobility Scheme

Exploiting mobility of the sink could be considered as an interesting concept to enhance the network lifetime by avoiding excessive relaying overhead at nodes close to the static sinks. Our sink mobility model bases on three main points: 1) at what time the sink has to move, 2) in which manner the sink will move and 3) towards which destination.

In our protocol, the sink mobility occurs periodically. In each period MTP (Mobility Time Period) sink calculates its new destination and moves towards it randomly. The new destination is defined by the cell ID or the cell coordinates based on the data dissemination frequency. As shows in the table 2 below, the sink maintains in its cache the number of data dissemination by cell ID. The data dissemination frequency is number of data dissemination received during the previous period PM. The new destination of sink is the cell that has the highest data dissemination frequency. The sink initializes data dissemination frequency after calculates its destination by each period. To inform the sensor nodes by the new destination, the mobile sink sends its new positions over the network.

Table 1. Data dissemination frequency

Cluster ID	Data dissemination frequency
[2,1]	10
[1,1]	3
[2,3]	0
[0,1]	1
[2,1]	10

5   Performance Evaluation

This section is reserved to discuss the performance evaluation results of our proposal protocol. The evaluation has been carried out by simulation using Glomosim simulator [16]. To simulate the sensing data, the sensor nodes are randomly chosen to detect and send new sensing event during the simulation time. The sensing process follows the model of POISSON where 60 seconds value fixed as an interval average of this model. This interval has been varied between 1 second and 60 seconds in order to simulate the network load and the energy consumption in case of many detected event occurred. In this simulation, energy consumption, response time or latency from the source node which detect the event to the sink node and traffic parameter have been evaluated according to different metrics. Moreover, the proposal protocol has been compared with Leach and Code using the same environment's parameters in the same simulator.

To move between the actual and the new calculated position, the mobile sink follows random waypoint mobility model. It moves randomly in the direction of the destination in a speed uniformly chosen between MOBILITY-MIN-SPEED and MOBILITY-MAX-SPEED (meter/sec). After it reaches its destination, the sink node stays there for mobility time period (MTP).

The blow table 1 shows the parameters of our environment. The default dimension of the network is 1000x1000m2. And, in order to test the scalability, the number of nodes can reach 250 on a site of 5000x5000m2.

Table 2. Configuration parameter

Parameter	Default value	Variation interval
Number of nodes	100	100 - 700
Initial energy available(KW)	100	
Threshold_max(KW)	3	60
Threshold_min (KW)	1	
Bandwidth(Mbps)	2	
New event detection period (S)	60	1 - 60
MTP (S)	60	
Speed Min(M/S)	0	
Speed Max(M/S)	1	
Simulation time duration(M)	15	

Energy consumption represents the average of energy consumption by a sensor node. It is calculated using following formula:

$$\text{Energy\_consumption} = \text{NbMsg\_Sent}*\text{Eng\_TX} + \text{NbMsg\_recevied}*\text{Eng\_RX} + \text{tandby\_energy\_ consumption} \tag{3}$$

NbMsg_Sent: number of sent messages.
NbMsg_recevied: Number of received messages.
Eng_TX: Energy of an emitted packet.
Eng_RX: Energy of a packet received.
Standby_energy_consumption: Energy consumption during the standby mode

The response time is the needed average duration to disseminate the sensing data from the source to the sink node. The average time is calculated as below:

$$\text{TpsAcc} = \sum \text{Resp\_time} / I, I \in [1, N] \tag{4}$$

$$\text{Resp\_time} = \text{Sent\_time} - \text{Received\_time} \tag{5}$$

Sent_time: The time of the sending data.
Received_time: The receiving data time by the sink node.
Resp_time: The needed time for successful delivered data.
N is the number of successful delivered data.

The Figure2 below represents the evolution of energy consumption according to the density of sensor nodes. It permits also to evaluate the impact of scalability on energy consumption.

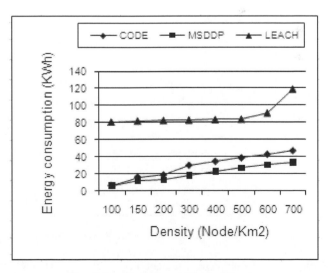

Fig. 2. Energy consumption and density

For LEACH the energy consumption is very high comparing with two others protocols. It remains stable for density of 100 and 500 nodes/Km2, and then increases when the density reaches 600 and 700 nodes/Km2. This is explained by the dynamic creation group's procedure which needs to send high number of control messages. Concerning protocol CODE and our proposal, the energy consumption increases in parallel with the density. This is caused by the flooding technique used by some nodes in network to communicate their co-ordinates.

Comparing these protocols, CODE is more effective than LEACH, because the last one consumes more energy for the creation and the re-creation of the dynamic groups, whereas CODE uses a static virtual grid. However, more our protocol appeared more effective than CODE, because the initialization and transferred request phases used in CODE have been eliminated.

The below figure (Fig.3) shows the evolution of energy consumption according to the detection event frequency.

For the three protocols, the energy consumption is not very affected by the number of detected event, which means that the most energy consumption provided from the protocol design. Energy consumption increases slowly with the sensing data increasing. In our protocol, sensor sink can move towards the cluster node that provides more data, thus optimize energy and latency also. Moreover, using dynamic energy threshold to select cluster head improves load balancing and prolong sensor node's life time.

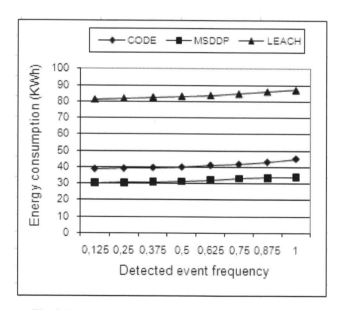

Fig. 3. Energy consumption and detected event frequency

The bow figure (Fig. 4) represents the evolution of the response time according to the density of sensor nodes. The response time for LEACH protocol is unstable. This permits to say that the density does not have a direct influence on the response time and this instability is related to the protocol design.

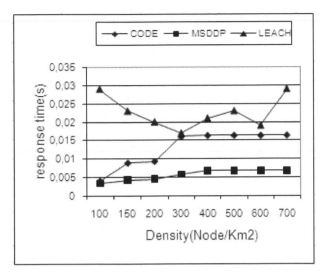

Fig. 4. Response time and density

Concerning the two other protocols, the response time increases slowly in the beginning and becomes stable. The highest response time is usually corresponds to LEACH protocol, this last uses the concept of period transmission which impacts data dissemination process. Our protocol appears more effective than CODE and gives the best response time.

In the below Figure5, we evaluate the behavior of the response time according to the detected event frequency. When the detection frequency increases the network overhead decreases also, therefore the response time or the latency will be increased. Consequently, the real time application will be influenced.

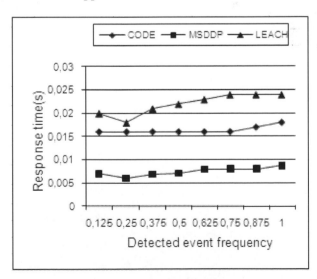

Fig. 5. Response time and detected event frequency

During this experience we notice that the protocol Leach gives the highest response time which increases in parallel with the detected event frequency. In the other hand, the response time in Code is not more influenced and remains stable until the value 0,75 request/second where the response time starts to increase. Moreover, the best response time is that given by our protocol, where it remains low and not influenced by network density. In MSDDP, sink moves periodically towards the sensor nodes that provide more data dissemination and thus, improves energy consumption both for source sensor node and the other nodes participated in data dissemination process.

6   Conclusion

In this paper we saw that the particular nature of the sensor networks, such as the limited lifetime of the sensors in consequence of their limited size, the multiplicity of the components and their performances require a specific mode of communication and represents considerable constraints.

According to the studied related works we noticed that each protocol has advantages and disadvantages, this study allowed us to understand the mechanism of data dissemination wireless sensor networks, which helped us to propose a new solution that considers the requirements of the sensor networks. In this solution, we took into account mainly the advantages and the disadvantages of the two protocols CODES and LEACH.

The proposal protocol is based on a virtual grid structure, where each cell in the grid contains a head responsible on the dissemination and the aggregation of the sensed data. This head is selected periodically according to the dynamic power threshold. In this paper we considered only the detected events and the sensed data are disseminated from the source sensor node to the sink. The user's requests are not considered in this work and will be the object of our future paper. In this paper we have also considered the mobility of the sink. In our model sink moves periodically and randomly towards a specified destination that has chosen based on data dissemination frequency

References

1. Xuan, H.L., Lee, S.: A Coordination-Based Data Dissemination Protocol for Wireless Sensor Networks. In: Proceedings of the Sensor Networks and Information Processing Conference, pp. 13–18 (December 2004)
2. Heinzelman, W., Chandrakasan, A., Balakrishnan, H.: Energy-effcient Communication Protocol for Wireless Microsensor Networks. In: Proceedings of the 33rd Hawaii International Conference on System Sciences, HICSS 2000 (January 2000)
3. Heinzelman, W.R., Kulik, J., Balakrishnan, H.: Adaptive protocols for information dissemination in wireless sensor networks. In: Proceedings of the ACM MobiCom 1999, Seattle, Washington, pp. 174–185 (1999)
4. Manjeshwar, D.P., Agrawal, A.: TEEN: a routing protocol for enhanced efficiency in wireless sensor networks. In: International Proceedings of 15th Parallel and Distributed Processing Symposium, pp. 2009–2015 (2001)

5. Lee, M.-G., Lee, S.: Data Dissemination for Wireless Sensor Networks. In: Proceedings of the 10th IEEE International Symposium on Object and Component-Oriented Real-Time Distributed Computing, pp. 172–180. IEEE (2007)
6. Akkaya, K., Younis, M.: An Energy-Aware QoS Routing Protocol for Wireless Sensor Networks. In: The Proceedings of the IEEE Workshop on Mobile and Wireless Networks (MWN 2003), Providence, Rhode Island (May 2003)
7. Xu, Y., Heidemann, J., Estrin, D.: Geographyinformed Energy Conservation for Ad Hoc Routing, Rome, Italy (2001)
8. Tinabo, R.: A Mechanism for Selecting Appropriate Data Mining Techniques. Journal of Intelligent Computing 2(1), 35–41 (2011)
9. Bulusu, N., Heidemann, J., Estrin, D.: Gps-less low cost outdoor localization for very small devices. IEEE Personal Communications Magazine 7(5), 28–34 (2000)
10. Xie, M., Zhang, G.: The Design and Challenges of Online Reprogramming System for Wireless Sensor Networks. Journal of Digital Information Management 9(6), 255–260 (2011)
11. Felemban, E., Lee, C., Ekici, E.: MMSPEED: Multipath Multi-SPEED Protocol for QoS Guarantee of Reliability and Timeliness in Wireless Sensor Networks. IEEE Transactions on Mobile Computing 5(6), 738–754 (2006)
12. Kim, S., Sang, H., Stankovic, A., Choi, Y.: Data Dissemination over Wireless Sensor Networks. IEEE Communications Letters 8(9), 561–563 (2004)
13. Lindsey, S., Raghavendra, C.: Pegasis: Power-efficient gathering in sensor information systems. Proc. of the IEEE, 924–935 (2002)
14. Luo, H., Ye, F., Cheng, J., Lu, S., Zhang, L.: A TwoTier Data Dissemination Model for Large scale Wireless Sensor Networks. In: Proc. ACM MOBICOM (September 2002)
15. Intanagonwiwat, C., Govindan, R., Estrin, D., Heidemann, J., Silva, F.: Directed diffusion for wireless sensor networking. IEEE/ACM Transactions on Networking 11(1), 2–16 (2003)
16. Bagrodia, R., Zeng, X., Gerla, M.: GloMoSim - A Library for Parallel Simulation of Large-scale Wireless Networks. Computer Science Departement, University of California at Los Angles (1999)
17. Guerroumi, M., Badache, N., Moussaoui, S.: Data Dissemination and Power Management in Wireless Sensor Networks. In: Abraham, A., Mauri, J.L., Buford, J.F., Suzuki, J., Thampi, S.M. (eds.) ACC 2011, Part IV. CCIS, vol. 193, pp. 593–607. Springer, Heidelberg (2011)
18. Gandham, S., Dawande, M., Prakash, R., Venkatesan, S.: Energy efficient schemes for wireless sensor networks with multiple mobile base stations. In: Proc. IEEE GLOBECOM (December 2003)
19. Luo, J., Panchard, J., Piorkowski, M., Grossglauser, M., Hubaux, J.: MobiRoute: Routing toward a Mobile Sink for Improving Lifetime in Sensor Netowrks. In: Proc. IEEE/ACM DCOSS (June 2006)
20. Kansal, A., Somasundara, A., Jea, D., Srivastava, M., Estrin, D.: Intelligent fluid infrastructure for embedded networks. In: Proc. ACM MobiSys (June 2004)
21. Bulusu, N., Heidemann, J., Estrin, D.: Gps-less low cost outdoor localization for very small devices. IEEE Pers. Commun. Mag. 7(5), 28–34 (2000)
22. Lee, E., Park, S., Yu, F., Kim, S.: Exploiting Mobility for Efficient Data Dissemination in Wireless Sensor Networks. Journal of Communications and Networks 11(4) (August 2009)
23. Akyildiz, I.F., Su, W., Sankarasubramaniam, Y., Cayirci, E.: Wireless Sensor Networks: A Survey. Journal of Computer Networks 38, 393–422 (2002)

Author Index